AF803568

LAWYERS ON TRIAL

LAWYERS ON TRIAL

UNDERSTANDING ETHICAL MISCONDUCT

RICHARD L. ABEL

OXFORD
UNIVERSITY PRESS

OXFORD
UNIVERSITY PRESS

Oxford University Press, Inc., publishes works that further Oxford University's objective of excellence in research, scholarship, and education.

Oxford New York
Auckland Cape Town Dar es Salaam Hong Kong Karachi Kuala Lumpur Madrid Melbourne
Mexico City Nairobi New Delhi Shanghai Taipei Toronto

With offices in
Argentina Austria Brazil Chile Czech Republic France Greece Guatemala Hungary Italy
Japan Poland Portugal Singapore South Korea Switzerland Thailand Turkey Ukraine
Vietnam

Copyright © 2011 by Oxford University Press, Inc.

Published by Oxford University Press, Inc.
198 Madison Avenue, New York, New York 10016

Oxford is a registered trademark of Oxford University Press
Oxford University Press is a registered trademark of Oxford University Press, Inc.

All rights reserved. No part of this publication may be reproduced, stored in a retrieval system, or transmitted, in any form or by any means, electronic, mechanical, photocopying, recording, or otherwise, without the prior permission of Oxford University Press, Inc.

Library of Congress Cataloging-in-Publication Data
Abel, Richard L.
Lawyers on trial : understanding ethical misconduct / by Richard L. Abel.
p. cm.
Includes bibliographical references and index.
ISBN 978–0–19–976037–4 (hardback : alk. paper)
1. Lawyers–California–Discipline. 2. Legal ethics–California.
3. California. Medical Injury Compensation Reform Act of 1975.
4. Practice of law–California. I. Title.
KFC76.5.A2A72 2010
174'.309794–dc22 2010028284

1 2 3 4 5 6 7 8 9

Printed in the United States of America on acid-free paper

Note to Readers
This publication is designed to provide accurate and authoritative information in regard to the subject matter covered. It is based upon sources believed to be accurate and reliable and is intended to be current as of the time it was written. It is sold with the understanding that the publisher is not engaged in rendering legal, accounting, or other professional services. If legal advice or other expert assistance is required, the services of a competent professional person should be sought. Also, to confirm that the information has not been affected or changed by recent developments, traditional legal research techniques should be used, including checking primary sources where appropriate.

(Based on the Declaration of Principles jointly adopted by a Committee of the American Bar Association and a Committee of Publishers and Associations.)

You may order this or any other Oxford University Press publication by visiting the Oxford University Press website at www.oup.com

CONTENTS

Preface vii

Chapter 1. The Politics of Self-Regulation 1

Chapter 2. Cops Chasing Ambulances 67

Chapter 3. Medical Injuries Compensation Reform Act: Unconstitutional Until Proven Otherwise 121

Chapter 4. Playing Games with Sega 227

Chapter 5. Reaching for the Brass Ring 269

Chapter 6. Serving Two Masters 327

Chapter 7. Championing the "Defenseless" and "Oppressed," Protecting "Widows and Children" 375

Chapter 8. Making Regulation Work 443

Tables 477
References 485
Index 495

PREFACE

This book continues my exploration of how lawyers betray trust, which I began in *Lawyers in the Dock.*[1] I opened the previous book by arguing that trust is the foundation of social life.[2] All human beings are dependent on others: at the very least as children, in order to reproduce, and in illness and old age. Dependence increases as societies grow and differentiate (with all the advantages those changes bring). Interaction is possible only if people can trust that others will fulfill role expectations; at the same time, it is more difficult to trust strangers. Trust is a social glue, a structural concomitant of the division of labor. Because readers of the earlier book saw ambiguities in my conceptualization of trust,[3] I want to stress that I am concerned with *behavior*, not mental states or motivations. One party to an interaction need not believe that the other is a good person, only that the other will act predictably.

Law is one vital manifestation of the division of labor. Clients must trust lawyers: not just to be loyal (the fiduciary obligation) but also to be competent, diligent, and bill fairly. Opposing counsel and courts (and other fora) must trust lawyers to be truthful about facts and law and obey court orders.[4] Ethical rules seek to specify these obligations, a task complicated by the fact that they may conflict. Legal scholars devote their energies to refining, clarifying, qualifying, and reconciling ethical rules. My goal is different. I want to understand *how* and *why* lawyers betray trust, the circumstances of and reasons for lawyers' violation of the legitimate expectations of clients, adversaries, opposing counsel, and fora.

Disciplinary proceedings document lawyer misconduct in great, often excruciating, detail. I have focused on New York (my previous book) and California (the present one) for several reasons. Those are the two largest jurisdictions in the United States; together they contain one out of every four American lawyers, more than the legal profession of any other nation. Their discipline records are public. I have additional reasons for choosing California. Unlike other states (including New York), California's State Bar Court produces extensive accounts of what the lawyers did, which informed my selection of cases. And I taught professional responsibility at UCLA for 35 years. I fully acknowledge the biases inherent in relying on these records. The content of ethical rules and the behavior of complainants (overwhelmingly clients) and prosecutors (the Office of Trial Counsel)

1. Abel (2008).

2. Id. chapter 1: "Trust and Betrayal."

3. E.g., Paterson (2008).

4. Others have analyzed lawyer behavior in terms of trust: Burt (1980–81); Brien (1998); Arts et al. (2001).

profoundly influence *which* betrayals of trust become reported cases. I hope others will be moved to offset these biases by looking at the full range of lawyer misconduct, not just the subset that is sanctioned to examine the full range of lawyer misconduct.[5]

I chose my six cases by reading all of the slightly more than 200 cases decided by the State Bar Court between 1990 (shortly after it was founded) and 2002 (when I began this research). As I read, I constructed categories, whose identity emerged and changed in the process.[6] Over the last two decades, the State Bar has classified complaints in eight categories (see Table 3, page 480). I excluded two of the most common: misappropriation (which fluctuated between 8 and 21 percent) because the behavior is straightforward and could be greatly reduced through regular audits of client trust accounts and bank reporting requirements; and failure to perform (which fluctuated between 34 and 43 percent) because three of my six New York cases dealt with that subject. I also excluded crime, for which discipline is just an appendage of a more powerful social control mechanism,[7] and violations of the disciplinary process, which were largely an adjunct of convictions for other substantive offenses. I ended up choosing cases from the remaining categories: duties to clients (fluctuating between 14 and 20 percent) (Chapters 2, 4, 5 and 6), fees (5–15%) (Chapter 3), and interference with justice (5–12%) (Chapter 7). Although I do not claim that complaints are fully representative of lawyer misconduct (which would be impossible to determine, given our ignorance of the "dark figure" of uncorrected behavior), I believe each of the categories represents an importance instance of lawyers' breach of trust.

Complaints also targeted certain kinds of practitioners. A few substantive areas are greatly overrepresented: personal injury (22%) and workers compensation (19%), family law (21%), criminal law (8%), bankruptcy (5%), probate (4%), and real estate (3%).[8] The lawyers in the present book practiced personal injury law (chapters 2, 3, and 7), criminal law (chapter 6), real estate (chapter 5), and corporate law (chapter 4).[9] Solo and small firm lawyers have long complained of being unjustly targeted for discipline.[10] They were more overrepresented in my

5. See Mercer et al. (1996) for a proposal to do so by asking practitioners in Ontario, Canada, about ethical dilemmas they encountered.

6. My method resembles that of Cressey (1953: chap. 1).

7. I excluded two cases of mental illness for the same reason.

8. Office of the Chief Trial Counsel to Discipline Evaluation Committee, "Correlation of firm size and practice area with complaints received and action taken" (7.1.94) (data for 1.1–5.31.94).

9. The others were house counsel for a corporation and a general litigator.

10. Carlin (1966); Handler (1967); see Abel (2008: 54–55). A Canadian study found no difference between solo and large firm lawyers in their attachment to professional ideals.

earlier book (five solo or small firm, one boutique firm, one of counsel to mid-sized firm); this one includes four solo and small firm practitioners, three in larger (very successful) personal injury firms, one house counsel and one entrepreneur.[11] Two empirical studies have concluded that any overrepresentation is caused by (client) complaints, not prosecutorial bias.[12] About nine out of ten complaints deal with private practitioners.[13] We know that certain categories, such as prosecutors, are almost entirely absent from the disciplinary process.[14] Large firm lawyers, as I argued in my earlier book, require separate treatment because of the complexity of their cases.[15] Given the correlation between law school attended and practice setting,[16] lawyers from lower status law schools are also overrepresented among those disciplined. But only three of my New York lawyers graduated from lower status schools, and the others were alumni of NYU (2), Michigan, and Harvard. And my California lawyers graduated from the entire range: San Fernando Valley (2), Southwestern, Loyola, South Carolina, USC, George Washington, and Harvard. Finally, women are absent from both books; but they were only 5 percent of the more than 200 lawyers tried by the State Bar Court.

Wallace & Kay (2008).

11. On the distinctive challenges of solo practitioners (who constitute a stunning 84% of New York State lawyers), see Commission to Examine Solo and Small Firm Practice (2006).

12. OCTC to DEC, supra note 8.

Firm size	% of lawyers about whom calls received	% of lawyers against whom action taken
Solo	69	55
2–5 lawyers	23	29
6+ lawyers	8	16

State Bar of California (2001b)

Firm size	% of lawyers for whom investigations opened	% of lawyers disciplined
Solo	68	78
2–10 lawyers	26	19
11+ lawyers	5	2

13. State Bar of California (2001b: attachment 8).

14. Zacharias & Green (2009a). Chapter 6 involves misconduct by a prosecutor who was admitted only in Arizona.

15. E.g., abusive tax shelters, Lynnley Browning, "7 Indicted on Charges of Selling Tax Shelters," New York Times B1 (6.10.09). Consider the book devoted to the aftermath of Kaye, Scholer, Practising Law Institute (1992).

16. Heinz & Laumann (1982).

Once I chose my categories, I still had to select cases within them. With the benefit of the detailed narratives in the State Bar Court opinions, I picked cases I thought would capture and engage the readers' attention. Although these tend to be extreme examples even within the domain of deviance, eminent scientists have demonstrated their utility. William Harvey, the great seventeenth-century English physician who discovered the circulation of the blood, wrote in 1657:

> Nature is nowhere accustomed more openly to display her secret mysteries than in cases where she shows tracings of her workings apart from the beaten paths; nor is there any better way to advance the proper practice of medicine than to give our minds to the discovery of the usual law of nature, by careful investigation of cases of rarer forms of disease.[17]

Three centuries later, Sigmund Freud made the same argument: "Pathology has always done us the service of making discernible by isolation and exaggeration considerations that would remain concealed in a normal state."[18]

I have presented these stories in narrative form[19] with detailed descriptions that are intended to make the characters come alive. My goal is pedagogic as well as scientific: I want these to be read as cautionary tales by lawyers, law students, and the general public. My hope is that some readers will feel compelled to say to themselves, "That could have been me."

* * * * *

I am grateful to many people and institutions for invaluable help in writing this book. The UCLA Academic Senate and UCLA Law School Dean's Fund supported summer research. The UCLA Law Library (as always) promptly supplied everything I wanted, including bibliographic guidance. Four UCLA Law students assisted my research: Sundari Wind (2004), Michael Campion (2005), Nathaniel Bach (2006), and Daniel Cha (2008). Robert and Julianne Fellmeth of the Center for Public Interest Law, University of San Diego School of Law, provided copies of Robert's indispensable reports as Bar Monitor. Professor William Gallagher of Golden Gate University School of Law gave me a copy of his essential Ph.D. dissertation.

Presiding Judge Ronald Stovitz gave me permission to read the complete disciplinary files of the six cases that follow. Scott Drexel, who has served in several senior roles at the California State Bar, helped me gain access to them, and Chuck Nettles in the Los Angeles office actually organized file retrieval.

I wrote all the disciplined California lawyers I studied, offering to send them draft chapters and giving them an opportunity to write a response for inclusion

17. Letter to John Vlackveld, quoted in "Chapter & Verse," *Harvard Magazine* 18 (May-June 2010).

18. In his essay "Feminity," in *New Introductory Lectures on Psychoanalysis* (1965), quoted in "Chapter & Verse," *Harvard Magazine* 24 (March-April 2010).

19. Amsterdam & Bruner (2000).

in the book. For *Lawyers in the Dock,* I made a similar offer to the disciplined New York lawyers whose stories I addressed; two of them took advantage of my offer. Of the lawyers whose stories appear in this book, Robert Scapa and Michael Brown (Chapter 2) and Robert Crane and Brian Depew (Chapter 4) read their chapters; only Depew made suggestions (which I have incorporated). Barry Tarlow, who played an entirely admirable role in Chapter 6, generously devoted substantial time to correcting errors and helping me understand the complex facts. He also sent me a good deal of supplemental material. Nicholas Damer (Chapter 7) sent me ten single-spaced pages of e-mail comments (which I have used in the chapter), but chose not to respond in print. I am grateful to all of them for their willingness to revisit what must have been very unhappy experiences. R. Browne Greene (Chapter 3), Ernest Lee Brazil (Chapter 5), and James Twitty (Chapter 6) did not respond. David Harney (Chapter 3) died before I began the book.

1. THE POLITICS OF SELF-REGULATION

Self-governance and self-regulation are defining characteristics of all professions.[1] The British Royal Commission on Legal Services began its list of the "five main features of a profession" with "a governing body" that "represents a profession and . . . has powers of control and discipline over its members."[2] The preamble to the American Bar Association (ABA) Model Rules of Professional Conduct acknowledged why professions claim such authority: "To the extent that lawyers meet the obligations of their professional calling, the occasion for government regulation is obviated."[3] But these core powers are ambivalently asserted, expediently exercised, and constantly contested. This chapter traces the institutional history of lawyer discipline in California in order to show how the system's capacities and limitations influence the way it constructs lawyer deviance.

I. BECOMING SELF-REGULATING

Until 1927, bar associations were local, weak, ephemeral, and found in only 18 of the state's 58 counties. A contemporary observer called them "little more than social clubs." In 1916, the chairman of the Los Angeles Bar Association publicity committee deplored that all it offered members was a "little protection through the Grievance Committee."[4] In San Francisco, local grievance committees made disciplinary recommendations to the city association (the strongest in the state), but the respondent's friends often were able to block action; even after conviction only the District Attorney or Superior Court could seek penalties. Four statewide organizations arose and fell before World War I, enrolling only a tiny fraction of all lawyers, partly because rural practitioners resented urban dominance. One member remarked ruefully, "we are laughed at in the interior," where lawyers "not only do not join, but they ridicule us."[5]

1. Parsons (1968); Carr-Saunders & Wilson (1933).

2. Royal Commission on Legal Services (1979: vol. 1, pp. 28, 30).

3. American Bar Association (1981: 1–2).

4. Robinson (1959: 159).

5. 28 Los Angeles Bar Association Bulletin 9 (10.52); John A. Wright, *How to Get Good Judges* 38, 40 (1892); Charles S. Wheeler, After-Dinner Proceedings of the Bar Association of San Francisco (May 20, 1910); 1 California Bar Association Proceedings 30 (1910); 8 California Bar Association Proceedings 192 (1917); A.Y. Wood (1926), "State Bar Organizations in California," in Historical and Contemporary Review of the Bench and Bar of California 41 (1926). I rely heavily on Gilb (1956: 4, 33–34, 38–39, 102–03).

Inspired by a 1912 visit to Ontario, Canada, whose lawyers had to join a "unified" self-governing bar, Herbert Harley, secretary of the American Judicature Society, drafted a model State Bar Act, published in 1918 and endorsed by the ABA Conference of Delegates two years later. North Dakota created the first such bar in 1921, followed by Alabama in 1923, and New Mexico and Idaho in 1925. California was next, but the effort took a decade. In 1917, the legislature reacted to worsening judicial backlogs and corruption scandals (ranging from judges in police courts to those in the state Supreme Court) by threatening to take over the entire judiciary, which finally prompted lawyers to take collective action. One urged his colleagues to "take a leaf out of the book of the labor union movement and establish a quasi principle of closed shop." At the (voluntary) California State Bar Association meeting that year, the president of the San Francisco Bar Association proposed that all such groups be granted subpoena power and the authority to discipline because they were "practically impotent in the investigation of charges." Bills to accomplish this died in the legislature in 1919 and 1921. Between 1922 and 1924, the California State Bar Association appointed a Special Committee on the "Self-Governing Bar," adopted the subsequent report of the committee's findings, and persuaded twenty local bar associations to concur. A bill to create a unified bar was passed by the legislature (unanimously in the Senate, and by 65–11 in the Assembly) and was endorsed by the entire California Supreme Court as well as national notables like Charles Evans Hughes and Elihu Root. Nevertheless, Governor Richardson refused to sign it because he wanted to appoint the governing board. But others also had reservations: rural lawyers feared urban dominance and resented paying for discipline, which they saw as a uniquely urban problem; others worried that discipline would target those who challenged powerful interests.[6]

The California State Bar Association persisted, empowering rural lawyers by giving each congressional district a delegate and enlisting the support of competing occupations: realtors, title insurance and trust companies, and banks. Although a new bill was opposed by the influential chairman of the State Senate Judiciary Committee, who wondered why only lawyers should be self-governing, it passed in the Senate (25–14) and the Assembly (61–15) and was signed by Governor Young, flanked by Joseph J. Webb, chairman of the Campaign

6. Herbert Harley, *Redeeming of the Profession*, 2 J. Am. Jud. Soc'y 105 (1918); 20 J. Am Jud. Soc'y 202 (1937); Dayton David McKean, The Integrated Bar 30–51 (Boston: Houghton Mifflin Co. 1963); The Recorder 12 (Sept. 21, 1917); The Recorder 1 (Jan. 11, 1919); 8 California Bar Association Proceedings 201 (1917); 9 California Bar Association Proceedings (1918); Wood (1926: 69–70); California Assembly Journal 2161 (1919); Gilb (1956: 37, 39–40, 53, 55–57, 61–63).

Committee for the State Bar Bill, who became president of the new State Bar (SB) of California. The voluntary California State Bar Association was dissolved.[7]

In its early decades, the State Bar was more interested in restricting entry and suppressing competition than in disciplining its members.[8] (Indeed, a referendum that repealed a 1921 bill prohibiting the unauthorized practice of law was one reason lawyers embraced the unified bar.) A month after the State Bar adopted the nation's first Rules of Professional Conduct, President Webb appointed a committee to investigate ambulance chasing, focusing on Los Angeles. Two years later, SB President Beardsley warned that the ambulance chaser was "apt to be an outlaw generally. Subornation of perjury, blackmail, forgery embezzlement and general disregard of the interests of the individual client are frequent companions . . .." Violators "offend against the profession as a whole by obstructing the natural course of professional employment so as to prevent it from being spread out normally among the members of the bar . . .." The State Bar also created committees to deal with trust and title companies, claims adjusters, and unlawful practice generally; their contributions to the 1930 annual meeting occupied twenty-six of the thirty-five pages devoted to committee reports. Discussion was "intense," sometimes "vehement." One newspaper "said the applause at times would have done credit to a group of 'college rooters.'" A lawyer expressed confidence that "society will, when informed," never "consent to the destruction of the profession and practice of law by unlicensed persons." The following year, the State Bar appointed a new Committee on Suppression of Soliciting Legal Business, which submitted a fourteen-page report to the annual meeting; and the *State Bar Journal* endorsed two Assembly bills to outlaw lay solicitation. Although the State Bar passively responded to client grievances, its proactive investigations of advertising and solicitation accounted for about five percent of cases heard. Two committees on ambulance chasing in San Francisco and Los Angeles submitted eleven pages of statistics documenting the magnitude of the problem in 1934. That year, the Los Angeles City Council criminalized the practice, and a Los Angeles Special Local Administrative Committee (LAC) of the State Bar prosecuted twenty-six cappers under it, winning convictions of all but one.[9]

---

7. Wood (1926: 70–71); *State Bar Organization Assured,* 1 SBJ 157 (1927); *State Bar Bill Signed,* 1 SBJ 179 (1927); *The First Step Toward Organization,* 1 SBJ 227, 236 (1927); Gilb (1956: 45, 69, 71–74); SB 9 (Nelson & Weller), Chap 34, Stats. of 1927.

8. Robinson (1959: Chapter 10).

9. 2 SBJ 203–05 (1928); Joseph J. Webb, *A Message from the President,* 2 SBJ 206–07 (1928); *The Story of the Pasadena Convention,* 3 SBJ 75, 82 (1928); *The Work of the Board of Governors,* 3 SBJ 175 (1928); *Report of Committee on Ambulance Chasing,* 4 SBJ 28–30 (1929); Charles A. Beardsley, *A Message from the President,* 4 SBJ 154–55, 224 (1930); *The Unlawful Practice of Law,* 4 SBJ 234 (1930); *Report of the Adjusters Committee,* 4 SBJ 240 (1930); 5 SBJ 11–36 (1930); Frank G. Tyrell, *Unlawful Practice—Convention Action,* 5 SBJ 410–11 (1930); Ewell D. Moore, *The Trust Companies and the Bar Associations,* 6 SBJ 58, 85 (1931);

Although ambulance chasing was the most visible competitive threat, and the most easily demonized, there were many others. The State Bar began agitating against nonlawyers practicing in the (lay) justices' courts in 1930 and succeeded in ousting lay advocates three years later; but a similar campaign against lay representation before administrative agencies failed. A lawyer complained in 1931 that "the illegal practice of law in Los Angeles County alone . . . costs the attorneys over six million dollars annually in loss of fees." A year later, another lawyer urged his colleagues not to "raise the standards of our profession upon the fallen bodies of our fellows. A decent chance will make a decent lawyer. Clean up encroachment and lawyers will 'clean up' themselves—and gladly!" The State Bar Board of Governors (BoG or the Board) "strongly disapproved" of radio stations that broadcast advice by judges in response to "tales of human misery." A special LAC concluded that patent attorneys should not be allowed to call themselves attorneys or solicit business. The State Bar vigorously resisted proposals to transfer the growing number of automobile accident claims to a commission, before which lawyers would be unnecessary (as had become the practice with workplace injuries).[10]

Vernon S. Gray, *The Practice of the Law,* 6 SBJ 105 (1931); Philbrick McCoy, *The Unlawful Practice of the Law,* 6 SBJ 111 (1931); Wallace E. Hyde, *Is There No Common Ground?* 6 SBJ 130 (1931); Oscar J. Seiler, *Suppression of Soliciting of Legal Business,* 6 SBJ 153 (1931); *Committee on Suppression of Soliciting of Legal Business,* 6 (Pt. II) SBJ 18–32 (1931); *More Proposed Measures Affecting Practice of Law,* 6 SBJ 69–70 (1931); Leonard B. Slosson, *A Message from the President,* 6 SBJ 166–67 (1931); E.V. Knauf, *Ambulance Chasing and Related Evils,* 7 SBJ 22 (1932); *Report Concerning Work of Special Committee on Ambulance Chasing for San Francisco,* 9 SBJ 225 (1934); Marion P. Betty, *"Ambulance Chasing" Ordinance,* 9 SBJ 165 (1934); *Report of Special Committee on Ambulance Chasing for Los Angeles County,* 9 SBJ 238 (1934); John E. Biby, *Ambulance Chasers,* 10 SBJ 42–43 (1935); 10 SBJ 295 (1935); T.P. Wittschen, *A Message from the President,* 10 SBJ 299–300 (1935); John E. Biby, *Chasing Ambulance Chasers,* 11 SBJ 97 (1936); Gilb, 1956: 43–44, 104–06. A defense of ambulance chasing, James F. Brennan, *The Bugaboo "Ambulance Chasing,"* 6 SBJ 37 (1931), provoked furious replies: Bartley C. Crum, *Clean Up the Legal Profession,* 6 SBJ 54 (1931); Fred L. Berry, *The Bugaboo "Ambulance Chasing,"* 6 SBJ 66 (1931); John W. Hart, *Ambulance Chasing,* 6 SBJ 79 (1931); David B. Maxwell, *Science of Law, or Law as a Business,* 6 SBJ 148 (1931). Brennan retorted: *Concerning Soliciting Professional Employment,* 6 SBJ 97 (1931).

10. Arthur P. Hayne, *The Right of Unlicensed Persons to Practice in the Justices' Courts,* 4 SBJ 208 (1930); George Allan Smith, *Compensation for Automobile Accident Injuries,* 6 SBJ 19 (1931); James C. Nichols, *What Is a Complete Policy for the Bar to Adopt in Personal Injury Cases?* 6 SBJ 21 (1931); A.G. Bailey, *No More Commissions,* 6 SBJ 94 (1931); *Problems of the Claims Adjuster,* 6 SBJ 151 (1931); *More Proposed Measures Affecting Practice of Law,* 6 SBJ 69 (1931); Alfred L. Bartlett, *The President's Message,* 11 SBJ 267–69 (1936); John W. Hart, *Are Patent Attorneys Practicing Law?* 13(2) SBJ 18 (Feb. 1938); Gray v. Justice's Court of Williams Judicial Township, 18 Cal. App. 2d 420 (1937); 21 SBJ 167 (1946); Gilb (1956: 221–22).

But the greatest challenge was corporate competitors. As early as 1926, the Attorney General responded to local bar association complaints by successfully prosecuting a corporation for practicing law. The State Bar Board of Governors declared, in 1930, that "the most important problem before the bar . . . is the activities of the banks, title and trust companies." Candidates for the BoG campaigned on this issue, complaining that "Control of your State Bar is now vested in banks, trust companies, casualty insurance companies and other business groups . . .." The preferred solution was a treaty dividing markets with competing trade associations. In 1932, the State Bar negotiated an agreement limiting automobile clubs to representing members only in small claims. When the State Bar sued banks for the unauthorized practice of law in 1933, two of the state's largest banks sought legislation allowing laypersons to give free legal advice; they were joined by the California Bankers Association, California Real Estate Association, Retail Merchants Credit Association, California Land Title Association, and Life Underwriters Association. The State Bar negotiated a treaty in which banks and trust companies agreed not to draft wills, appear in court except through an attorney, or advertise legal services. A 1936 State Bar treaty allowing the California Land Title Association to fill in blanks or retype forms outraged the Napa, Sonoma, and San Joaquin county bars, which had concluded far more restrictive local agreements. Seven years after the Los Angeles Superior Court affirmed the right of realtors to fill in blanks, the State Bar persuaded the State Real Estate Commissioner to remove certain legal forms from the real estate handbook. In 1939, the State Bar secured legislation requiring collection agencies to use attorneys; thirteen years later, it reached a further agreement with the California Association of Collectors and the Associated Credit Bureaus of California. Although a 1944 treaty between the American Bar Association and the American Institute of Accountants surrendered much of the tax field to the latter, a California court ruled, in 1954, that an accountant who did legal research for a client was engaging in unauthorized practice; and when the U.S. Tax Court was established in 1947, the State Bar sought to limit practice to lawyers.[11]

If lawyers were united by efforts to curb external competition, they were much more ambivalent about disciplining themselves. The Legal Ethics section report

11. People v. Calif. Protective Corp., 76 Cal. App. 354 (1926); People v. Sipper, 61 Cal. App. 2d 544 (1936); California Statutes 2753 (1939); *The Work of the Board of Governors*, 4 SBJ 167, 170 (1930); Hubert C. Wyckoff, *Trust Companies and Lawyers*, 7 SBJ 54 (1932); 9 SBJ 85, 88, 142 (1934); 10 SBJ 139 (1935); *Agreement Between The State Bar of California and the California Land Title Association*, 11 SBJ 190 (1936); *The Treaty with the Title Companies; Correspondence*, 11 SBJ 223, 229 (1936); A.G. Bailey, *Unlawful Practice by Collection Agencies*, 13(6–7) SBJ 48 (6–7.38); 13(8 Pt. II) SBJ 117 (8.38); 14(8) SBJ 75 (8.39); 15(8) SBJ 80 (8.40); 16(8) SBJ 181 (6.41); 18 SBJ 467 (1943); 19 SBJ 289 (1944); 25 SBJ 21 (1950); 22 SBJ 476 (1947); Gilb (1956: 234–35, 239–42); *Bar Periscope*, 54 CSBJ 532–33 (1979). All these treaties were revoked in 1979, after the U.S. Department of Justice questioned whether they violated anti-trust laws.

to the State Bar's first annual meeting in 1927 blamed "the unfavorable comment received by the legal profession" on the fact that "the public is altogether lacking knowledge of just what they may reasonably expect." The section proposed to remedy this with "a carefully written series of articles . . . setting forth in simple language the ideals and principles of the profession," while reassuring lawyers that the State Bar's policy was "to keep 'hands off' in all matters of grievance where there is a local Bar Association" and noting that, although the State Bar had handled eight complaints, "in none of these cases was any prosecution undertaken or hearing held . . .." President Webb appointed a Committee on Legal Ethics to answer members' questions, which dealt primarily with advertising and ambulance chasing; but it was abolished after two years because it was "inadvisable to advise lawyers in advance upon questions that might later form the basis of disciplinary action." His successor reiterated that "the Board is ever zealous of protecting the interests of the attorney in all disciplinary matters." A year later, a State Bar Governor reported the "very gratifying" "experience" that "complaints are fewer and more than a majority of these are trivial." "Every member of the Board is impressed with the fact that in suspension and disbarment cases the accused has his life's work at stake . . .." The Board found "that over 80 percent of the complaints were without any merit at all" and prompted by "a lack of understanding on the part of the client as to just what are the duties of a lawyer." The fourth SB president reiterated this statistic and sought to dispel "the altogether . . . erroneous impression . . . that The State Bar's principal occupation to date has been to investigate its members for their alleged delinquencies, great and small, and to suspend or disbar as many as possible." On the contrary, the Board had adopted a process "by which complaints against members may be quickly investigated and tried, with a minimum of publicity to the accused attorney if the facts are found not sufficient to warrant discipline." A month later, the president was "glad to say that there has been a pronounced falling off recently in the number of disciplinary cases coming before the board." At the end of the first decade, the SB president attributed the steady decline in punishment to "the fact that any lawyer who might be inclined to forget his oath and his professional obligations realizes that he cannot get away with it and also the fact that the type of men and women admitted to the bar in the last several years has much higher standards than formerly."[12]

As this defensiveness showed, members strongly resented discipline. One wrote the *San Francisco Recorder*. "[W]e are zealously raising the standards of our

12. *The Coronado Convention Program,* 2 SBJ 228–30 (1928); *The Work of the Board of Governors,* 3 SBJ 94–95 (1928); Frank James, *The Board of Governors' Page,* 3 SBJ 208–09 (1929); *Questions in Legal Ethics Answered,* 3 SBJ 11, 54–57 (1928); *Report of Committee on Legal Ethics,* 3 SBJ 30–32 (1929); Leonard B. Slosson, *A Message from the President,* 5 SBJ 404–05 (1930); Leonard B. Slosson, *A Message from the President,* 6 SBJ 10 (1931); Phillips & McCoy (1952: 90).

profession upon the fallen bodies of our fellow lawyers and unwittingly building a barrier of distrust between our profession and the public. Return to reason. Stop the witch-burning; leave off the inquisition." A State Bar president felt compelled to devote his monthly message to a four-page defense of the disciplinary record. His successor deplored that

> the public thought that all the crime, all the dishonesty, all the fraud, all the delays in the administration of justice, all drought, all floods, all wind storms, all the overproduction, all the lack of proper distribution, were due to the delinquencies of lawyers.

But after declaring that "no other class of citizens is making such diligent efforts to weed out those who are unworthy to be trusted," he conceded that "the surface of discipline in this State has been scarcely scratched" and placed responsibility "at your door and mine."

> I venture to say that there is not a man in this room who has not, at some time in his career, become possessed of facts which, if they had been brought to the attention of the proper authorities, would have resulted in the discipline, perhaps the disbarment, of some lawyer.

But they had done nothing. "It is [also] the duty of the judge, when the misconduct of attorneys is brought to his attention, to report with the record to The State Bar. But how many times is it done?" The Board successfully opposed members' efforts to fend off discipline: a one-year statute of limitations, a requirement that grievances be verified (exposing complainants to prosecution for perjury), a ban on publicity until the Supreme Court acted, even a proposal that all discipline be subject to referendum and all governors subject to recall. The *State Bar Journal* resisted these "step[s] backward" to "the old ineffective procedure under which but 27 attorneys were disciplined in [the] 78 years" before the State Bar was established, compared with the 53 disbarred or suspended in the *three* years since then. But the new regime was hardly punitive: in its first twenty years, the Board heard an average of one hundred complaints annually, dismissing half for lack of jurisdiction or because they charged "minor negligence or discourtesy or ignorance of the law . . . or that fees are too large." By the 1950s, California was disbarring just a few each year—sometimes none.[13]

---

13. AB 423 (1931); Leonard B. Slosson, *A Message from the President,* 6 SBJ 62 (1931); *Legislation Sought by or Affecting The State Bar,* 6 SBJ 48, 50–52 (1931); Charles A. Beardsley, *Investigation and Discipline Without a Verified Complaint,* 6 SBJ 183 (1931); Charles A. Beardsley, *The Disciplinary Procedure of The State Bar,* 6 SBJ 241 (1931); In re Herron, 81 Cal. Dec. 549 (1931); Hubert C. Wyckoff, *State Bar Policies,* 7 SBJ 160 (1932); M. Mitchell Bourquin, *State Bar Policies: A Reply to Hubert C. Wyckoff,* 7 SBJ 186 (1932); Guy R. Crump, *Message from the President,* 7 SBJ 274 (1932); Norman A. Bailie, *The President Speaks,* 9 SBJ

For its first half century, State Bar discipline relied entirely on volunteers: 178 members of the 35 LACs, which investigated complaints, decided whether to issue a notice to show cause (NTSC), and then held a formal hearing (closed to the public). The BoG could accept the LAC disciplinary recommendation or hear the case *de novo*. From the outset, discipline occupied a distressingly large proportion of the Board's time; for instance, the entire two-day July 1928 meeting. The Supreme Court heard every case *de novo*; as of 1956, it had *never* increased the penalty and frequently reduced it. (In the first ten years, it reduced the penalty in 23 percent of the 119 cases it reviewed and dismissed the proceedings in another 8 percent.) The view of one justice that only intentional misconduct should be punished demoralized the entire process, according to contemporaneous observers. The *State Bar Journal* published monthly (anonymous) reports of State Bar convictions and recommended punishments, as well as the names and penalties of those punished by the Supreme Court (without identifying the offenses). The State Bar suspended all disciplinary proceedings for months after the Supreme Court required verified complaints, causing a "decided falling off" of discipline for a year. To strengthen the appearance that justice was being done, the president, in 1933, urged that smaller counties create two LACs, one for investigation, accusation, and prosecution; the other to hear trials. Although he rejected the charge that "a group of ambulance-chasing lawyers has contrived to get control of the Board of Governors and has thus made disciplinary action impossible," he warned that "subversive elements of the bar are organized and keep up a campaign to thwart the activities of the organization. They would scuttle the ship if they could."[14]

The threat was not just internal. James F. Brennan (who had defended ambulance chasing) became chair of the assembly committee to investigate "the present status, conditions and mode of operation of the State Bar of California." Together with William B. Hornblower (a fellow Assemblymember who had earlier introduced a bill to divert all State Bar dues to the State Treasury), the committee asked the State Bar in February 1935 to conduct a plebiscite on the question: "Do you favor repeal of The State Bar Act?" The State Bar disparaged the initiative as a misguided expression of lawyer discontent with discipline and admissions. But it made the mistake of asking, "[W]hat better way can be suggested for the handling of these important and sometimes intricate problems that is more democratic than a self-governing Bar?" Brennan retorted: "[I]f the

301 (1934); Phillips & McCoy (1952: 95, 101); Blaustein & Porter (1954: 254–55); Turrentine (1935); Gilb (1956: 80–83, 101, 104, 110).

14. Joseph J. Webb, *A Message from the President*, 2 SBJ 142–43 (1928); *The Work of the Board of Governors*, 3 SBJ 1 (1928); *The Story of the Del Monte Convention*, 6 SBJ 267 (1931); *Disciplinary Proceedings Suspended*, 5 SBJ 335–40 (1930); Hubert C. Wyckoff, *A Message from the President*, 8 SBJ 242–43 (1933); *A Message from the President*, 8 SBJ 292–93 (1933); Phillips & McCoy (1952: 98, 100–04); Gilb (1956: 108–09); CAG (1977c).

Bar is to be self-governing, its members should be allowed to express themselves through a plebiscite . . ..” The results strongly vindicated the State Bar; but a quarter of those voting favored repeal, and 42 percent did not vote.[15]

Although the State Bar concentrated on issues closely related to the legal profession, it inevitably became involved in politics. Soon after its founding, the State Bar retained a lobbyist in the state capital of Sacramento, who not only advocated on its behalf but also examined *every* bill. In 1934, it created a Conference of Bar Association Delegates (the Conference), representing local (and later specialist) organizations, which reviewed legislation proposed by State Bar committees before it was presented in Sacramento. But the Conference cautiously avoided controversial issues such as foreign affairs, national politics, adultery, animal control, even adapting tort law to the growing number of automobile accidents. During the McCarthy era, the Board resisted the demands to expel communists voiced by the House Committee on Un-American Activities; the ABA Special Committee on Communist Tactics, Strategy and Objectives; and even the State Bar's own Rules Committee. The September 1966, Conference of Delegates held a “lively debate” about whether the State Bar should take positions on anything other than “procedural law.” While acknowledging that this boundary was “often blurred,” the president insisted that it excluded abortion and the death penalty, although “it can be argued that capital punishment is merely a step in the administration of criminal justice.” Even the automobile guest statute was out of bounds because “the State Bar should not advocate the repeal of legislation that has been enacted as a matter of public policy—particularly when the repeal would result in a financial benefit to one segment of the bar . . ..” He added that, until the U.S. Supreme Court clarified its opaque decision about the activities permitted the unified Wisconsin bar,[16] the Conference should limit itself to the administration of justice, judicial reform, and procedure. The next president agreed that the Conference should not address “questions of moral, social, or political policy.” The Board of Governors was “gravely concerned” that the very number of bills proposed might “wear out our welcome in our State Capitol.”[17]

---

15. *Legislation Sought by or Affecting The State Bar,* 6 SBJ 48, 50–52 (1931); *The State Bar Plebiscite,* 10 SBJ 57, 83 (1935).

16. Lathrop v. Donohue, 367 U.S. 820 (1961).

17. *Report of the Committee on Rules of Professional Conduct to the Board of Governors,* 29 SBJ 349 (1954), 30 SBJ 348 (1955); William P. Gray, *President's Message,* 38 SBJ 162 (1963); *Report of Committee on Communist Lawyers to Board of Governors,* 38 SBJ 172 (1963); A. Stevens Halsted, Jr., *Message of the President: Role of the State Bar in Social Reform: Procedural: Not Substantive,* 42 SBJ 321 (1967); Daniel A. Weber, *A Dissent: The Role of the State Bar,* 42 SBJ 849 (1967); John M. Cranston, *Scope of State Bar Legislative Activity,* 42 SBJ 858 (1967); J. Thomas Crowe, *Message from the President: The Question of Purview,* 44 SBJ 769 (1969); Gilb (1956: 142–50).

The State Bar was particularly vulnerable because the 1927 Act required the legislature to approve State Bar dues. These rose from $5 (for active members) in 1927 to $20 in 1963. But when the Bar sought an increase to $50, members of both judiciary committees authorized only $35, expressing "their very strong view that the State Bar should intensify its activities in respect to the enforcement of discipline and in the field of unauthorized practice of law." Returning to an Extraordinary Session in 1964, the State Bar argued that it needed "a full staff of capable investigators" because clients did not complain about ambulance chasing; furthermore, lawyers paid substantially lower dues than doctors, and expenditures on both discipline and unauthorized practice of law had doubled between 1960 and 1964. It won the $50 ceiling.[18]

The State Bar consistently demonstrated its reluctance to regulate. Although its first president had noted, as early as 1928, that "a large percentage of the serious charges made against attorneys grow out of the use of funds coming into their possession and their inability to pay their clients when demand is made for same," it was not until 1956 that the Rules of Professional Conduct (RPC) mandated lawyers to deposit all client funds into a separate trust account. A few years later, the Board approved a unanimous Rules Committee recommendation that "no Rule of Professional Conduct constituting negligence as a basis for discipline be adopted." In 1961, a former president urged the Bar to create a clients' security fund for the "moral" reason that "when a lawyer betrays . . . trust by stealing a client's money, all lawyers are to a degree responsible . . .." Such a plan would also "improve the profession's public relations" and avoid the threat of legislation mandating individual malpractice insurance. But opponents argued successfully that such a plan would "be an official recognition of the fact that the legal profession is the one profession in this country whose members are so corrupt that it must assess itself to indemnify the public." It would "publicize the dishonesty of lawyers" and "unjustifiably encourage and increase charges of dishonesty against members of the bar" as well as "actions for malpractice based upon claims of simple negligence." The estimated $5 charge "would succeed only in getting a proverbial foot in the door."

Although the 1957 SB president praised the Bar's "commendable" record in "disciplining the small number of its members who are complained against," on the basis of a "thorough study of our disciplinary system," the Board approved adding two more staff lawyers to the two already devoted to discipline, freeing the latter "to 'ride circuit' among the disciplinary committees in the nonmetropolitan areas and assist them in a more expeditious handling of their cases." Another indication of the limits of volunteerism was the fact that the Board was spending "close to half" its time on disciplinary matters in 1959, a week

18. *The First Step Toward Organization,* 1 SBJ 227, 236 (1927); Samuel H. Wagener, *President's Message,* 39 SBJ 7 (1964); SB 7, Chap 29, First Extraordinary Session of 1964.

every month by 1965. It responded in several ways: promulgating "Guides to Disciplinary Procedure," delegating hearings to two Disciplinary Review Boards (DRBs, soon merged into a single fifteen-person board), and assigning primary responsibility for discipline to the general counsel (assisted by five new attorneys). Although the State Bar defended itself against Governor Reagan's criticism of its disciplinary record (which was echoed in the press), it doubled bar dues to finance more activity.[19]

II. THE RISE OF CONSUMERISM

These reforms were unlikely to satisfy the rising tide of criticism, reflected in the ABA's creation in 1968 of a special committee, chaired by retired Supreme Court Justice Tom C. Clark, to investigate lawyer discipline nationwide. Its 1970 report began by decrying:

> a scandalous situation that requires the immediate attention of the profession. With few exceptions, the prevailing attitude of lawyers toward disciplinary enforcement ranges from apathy to outright hostility. Disciplinary action is practically nonexistent in many jurisdictions; practices and procedures are antiquated; many disciplinary agencies have little power to take effective steps against malefactors.[20]

The committee found disbarred attorneys practicing in other jurisdictions and routinely securing reinstatement in their own; tax evaders and convicted felons continuing to practice and lawyers covering up their peers' unethical and criminal conduct, especially in smaller communities. It identified thirty-six problems, including inadequate funding; decentralization; delay; reliance on volunteers; dependence on complaints by clients (who were discouraged from making them); poor recordkeeping; lack of lesser penalties for minor offenses; inadequate procedures for the resignation of attorneys who had charges pending or were incapacitated; no mechanism for reciprocal discipline in other states; no procedure for interim suspension; excessive secrecy; no protection for clients abandoned by counsel; no compulsory accounting and auditing of client trust funds;

---

19. 2 SBJ 203–07 (1928); 31 SBJ 293 (1956); Graham L. Sterling, *Report of President for 1958–1959,* 34 SBJ 808, 811–12 (1959); Burnham Emersen, *President's Message: The Supreme Court and the State Bar,* 34 SBJ 893, 897 (1959); Graham L. Sterling, Sr., *The Argument for a Clients' Security Fund,* 36 SBJ 957 (1961); Galen McKnight, *The Argument Against Clients' Security Fund,* 36 SBJ 963 (1961); August F. Mack, Jr., *Annual Report of the Board of Governors,* 40 SBJ 659, 661–64 (1965); John H. Finger, *President's Message: Disciplinary Procedure Updated and Streamlined,* 43 SBJ 9 (1968); ABA Special Committee (1970: 35); Business & Professions Code (BPC) §6086.5; Gallagher (1993: 92).

20. ABA Special Committee (1970: 1).

and no mandatory malpractice insurance, client security funds (CSFs), or fee dispute arbitration.[21]

Based on the Clark Report's occasional praise for the California State Bar, President Plant boasted that it "utilizes most of the disciplinary procedures recommended." The report's criticism "that 'at the root of the problem (of self-policing) is the widespread disinclination of individual lawyers and bar associations to take action against fellow attorneys,' is not true in California." The State Bar relied on 600 volunteer lawyers, and 15 attorney and 21 clerical employees; "recordkeeping procedures are being revised and updated, and a determination has been made to initiate the use of professional staff examiners in place of volunteer examiners, at least on a trial basis." The president recognized that, "in the public view our effort to deal with misconduct of attorneys . . . is the major task facing the organized bar" and warned that "unsatisfactory performance" could threaten the "precious right of self-discipline," as had happened in Michigan with the addition of public members. He urged lawyers to report misconduct, even though this was "not the recommended way of becoming the most popular fellow at the cocktail hour preceding the local bar association's annual dinner meeting."[22]

The Clark Report was just the first salvo in a continuous cycle of criticism, defense, and piecemeal reform. In 1970, the DRB rejected an examiner's proposal that it give reasons for dismissing charges, because "it may not be possible to get a majority of the [DRB] to agree on the reasons for dismissal." But the Board of Governors did recommend that the LAC hearing any given case be different from the one that investigated it. The following year, President Robinson opposed a bill (supported by the Attorney General) making incompetence a basis for discipline. "[T]he Supreme Court has stated in these situations that no discipline is warranted." In response to "justifiable" criticism of "delay and inefficiency," the State Bar had made "major improvements in our disciplinary procedures" and would "be able to intensify our efforts" if the dues increase were approved. The "State Bar's activities and results in this field have been major and second to no association in the nation." "[O]ne of the most important changes in policy" was the Supreme Court's decision to issue press releases about disciplinary decisions. Over the next few years, the Bar would replace volunteer examiners with employees. "We have now developed a modern system of record keeping so that we can keep track of all of our cases and know which ones are delinquent and why, and compare our progress with prior periods."[23]

---

21. *Id.* 19, 24, 30, 46, 48, 60, 71, 74, 77, 86, 92, 97, 101, 110, 116, 122, 138, 147, 150, 156, 167, 172, 186.

22. *Id.* 35–36, 122; Forrest A. Plant, *President's Message: The Disciplinary Problem: A Call for Individual Dedication,* 46 SBJ 130 (1971).

23. Disciplinary Board, *1970 Annual Report to Board of Governors,* 46 SBJ 538, 540–41 (1971); David K. Robinson, *President's Message: Leadership Exercised by the Organized Bar,*

Noting that delay had been a "continuing" problem and was becoming "serious," the next president, Leonard Janofsky, warned: "If we fail to meet this challenge, the administration of this exceedingly important responsibility may be assumed by some other public body." A SB special committee recommended that parties should be able to stipulate for a single hearing officer, only one continuance should be granted without good cause, and a staff examiner should be able to file an NTSC without a preliminary hearing in commingling cases and refer complaints lacking probable cause to client relations committees. His successor, Seth Hufstedler, blamed Watergate for the fact that "the State Bar probably receives more questions from lawyers, the press and the public about our disciplinary system than any other subject." Having served three years on the Board and several more on LACs, he believed that "the system is quite good" and the results "acceptable to the public, the bench and the bar" as shown by the fact that, in three recent years, the DRB had followed LAC recommendations in 162 out of 300 matters and the Supreme Court had followed the DRB in 76 out of 93 cases. Noting that 83 percent of the last 42 lawyers disciplined were solo practitioners and all but one belonged to firms of fewer than six lawyers, he urged "periodic supervision and review of financial records." Because proceedings were "still too slow," taking "years not months," the BoG had approved "a new, imaginative proposal" to combine the formal LAC hearing and DRB review. Since "by far, the largest share of complaints we receive is about lawyers who have failed to perform in a pleasing and satisfactory manner," he suggested a "non-disciplinary complaint committee—a 'friend of the client,'" to deal with neglect. To reduce excessive secrecy, "we should now consider whether or not a [NTSC] should be made public when it is issued." For the fourth successive year after the Clark Report, the SB president urged lawyers to anticipate complaints about neglect and delay by sending clients "a copy of every paper and letter you file," returning phone calls, and "keep[ing] your client informed about the progress of his matter, without waiting to be asked." His vice president urged local bars to create fee arbitration panels with lay participation and engage in an "aggressive campaign" to persuade lawyers to submit to them. "[W]hen our level of enforcement of the rules of professional responsibility fail [*sic*] to adequately protect those for whom they were designed, we must necessarily expect that the task of disciplinary enforcement and administration will be taken from us, as has happened in other states." The 1979 SB president again pronounced that California's disciplinary system was "widely regarded as the nation's best" and "the Bar here was moving further out front as the national leader . . .." He urged earlier publicity of proceedings, random trust account audits, conciliation of non-disciplinary complaints, and mandatory continuing education in legal ethics and law office management.[24]

---

46 SBJ 570 (1971); David K. Robinson, *Annual Report of the Board of Governors,* 47 CSBJ 501, 512 (1972).

24. Leonard S. Janofsky, *President's Message: Reducing Delays in Lawyer Discipline,* 48 CSBJ 8 (1973); Seth M. Hufstedler, *President's Message: Another Look at Discipline,* 49 CSBJ

The pressure for reform was not just talk. The California Supreme Court ruled in 1971 that the statute of limitations for legal malpractice ran from the date the client should reasonably have discovered it. Five years later, the SB president proposed that the Bar negotiate a malpractice insurance policy for all members, effectively making it mandatory. After malpractice insurance premiums increased as much as 400 percent between 1976 and 1977, and the number of insurers dropped from six to three, the president promised a lawyers' mutual insurance companyas soon as three thousand members subscribed.[25] The client security fund, first proposed by a SB president in 1961, was finally established in 1972.[26] California responded to the ABA's 1969 Code of Professional Responsibility by revising its own rules in 1973, prohibiting illegal or clearly excessive fees, requiring lawyers to maintain records of client funds, and exposing to discipline those who willfully or habitually performed legal services for which they lacked the skills or knowledge or failed to use reasonable diligence.[27] In 1975, the *California State Bar Journal* finally began reporting the misconduct underlying Supreme Court disciplinary decisions.[28] The BoG embraced mandatory fee arbitration in 1977.[29]

In 1976, the Bar implemented "a comprehensive change in the procedure . . . which completely revolutionizes the concept and administration of the trial and review phases of the disciplinary panel." It replaced the LACs and DRB with a new Disciplinary Board composed of 40 lawyers and 7 laypeople, assisted by another 80 lawyers and 3 lay pro tem referees. Parties could stipulate to a single hearing officer and request review, which was merely advisory. Three years later, the Bar delegated all disciplinary authority to the State Bar Court (SBC), divided into investigation (260 referees), hearing (315 referees), and review (12 lawyers and 3 laypersons sitting *en banc*).

---

224 (1974); Brent M. Abel, *President's Message: Are You Subject to Complaint?* 50 CSBJ 6 (1975); Brent M. Abel, *President's Message: Following the Rules,* 50 CSBJ 70 (1975). Hufstedler's identification of the most frequent bases for discipline was confirmed four years later. Richard Blum, *A Perspective on the Bar,* 53 CSBJ 98 (1978); Charles H. Clifford, *President's Message,* 54 CSBJ 490 (1979).

25. Neel v. Magana, Olney, Cathcart & Gelfand, 6 Cal. 3d 176 (1971); Ralph J. Gampell, *President's Message: Malpractice Insurance: Equal Burden for All?* 51 CSBJ 575 (1976); Ronald E. Mallen, *Panacea or Pandora's Box? A Statute of Limitations for Lawyers,* 52 CSBJ 22 (1977); David J. Levy, *President's Message,* 54 CSBJ 366–67 (1978).

26. David K. Robinson, *Annual Report of the Board of Governors,* 47 CSBJ 501, 508 (1972).

27. Leonard S. Janofsky, *President's Message: After 45 Years—New Rules of Professional Conduct,* 48 CSBJ 224 (1973).

28. *Disciplinary Board Proceedings,* 50 CSBJ 279 (1975).

29. Ferdinand F. Fernandez, *The Pending Proposal for Mandatory Fee Arbitration,* 52 CSBJ 520 (1977).

The chair of the State Bar's Committee on Discipline rejected the criticism "that the disciplinary process is a backscratching, self-protecting exercise." The Bar was reducing delay by using staff examiners, setting fixed time limits, and holding hearings on evenings and weekends. It was increasing uniformity by training referees and publishing a "Summary of Discipline Imposed." Review became binding rather than advisory. The chair was "absolutely convinced" that using volunteer "lawyer-peers with a mix of public members provides benefits which far outweigh any other procedure." Critics who glibly compared the approximately 5,000 complaints with just 200 NTSCs and 75 serious penalties were playing a "truly superficial" "numbers game." Lawyers

> are probably monitored more closely and by more people than persons who are engaged in any other type of activity . . . many complaints arise that are totally lacking in merit . . .. When the result is not in accord with [clients'] optimistic expectations, they often attribute the loss not to the merits but to either their own attorney or opposing counsel, and are quick to translate that into a charge of violating the Rules of Professional Conduct.

The disciplinary process was "not a procedure for testing or reviewing competence . . . a wholly separate subject." Because "every member of the bar has been through a rigorous screening process" and had reached "25 years of age or older, without serious instances of misconduct . . . it is to be expected that deliberate violations of moral or ethical standards would be unusual." When the Director of the California Office of Administrative Hearings called "the use of volunteer lawyers from the community . . . a defect" and its "secret nature" the "worst indictment against the Bar's disciplinary process," a lawyer responded that "the entire system of justice under which we operate involves a trial by peers," and the process was far from secret: "[O]ne newspaper in Los Angeles County rejoices in publishing each and every transgression." (He meant the *Los Angeles Daily Journal*, which was read only by lawyers.) The lawyer dismissed administrative agencies as "usually composed of hearing officers who can't make it in the private sector." Nevertheless, reports by Bar committees in 1979 (Sproul/Steiner) and 1982 (Hanst) "reluctant[ly]" recommended "consideration of permanent staff as State Bar Court referees." In 1981, SB President Robert D. Raven again claimed that "the ABA's model system [proposed by the Clark report] was the California discipline system," which was "nationally recognized as 'outstanding'—an example for other states to follow." Sentiments like these help to explain why the BoG rejected a 1981 proposal to open disciplinary proceedings to the public (all 13 lawyer members voting against, all 6 public members voting for) and opposed mandatory continuing education in 1983 and written fee agreements in 1984.[30]

---

30. E. Dean Price, *President's Message: The Hewes Plan and Disciplinary Procedures,* 51 CSBJ 175 (1976); Peter J. Hughes, *President's Message,* 54 CSBJ 6 (1979); Herbert W. Nobriga, *Letter to the Editor,* 54 CSBJ 215 (1979); Clifford R. Anderson, Jr., *Letter to the*

External critics remained unsatisfied. The cover sheet of a 1976 report by the California Auditor General—featuring a fat man in a wig and robe clutching an equally bloated money bag and sticking out his tongue—was captioned "incredulous membership fee increase." Noting that two years earlier, the Auditor General had found that the Bar had "not yet fully developed workload standards upon which to make a satisfactory analysis of projected staffing needs," the chair of the Joint Legislative Audit Committee derided the request for a 32 percent increase in dues on the ground that the Bar would have a $250,000 surplus even without the augmentation. When the Bar resisted what it called "deficit financing," the Auditor General reiterated that proposed expenditures could not be "verified without . . . an allocation of expenses among departments." Subsequent Auditor General reports urged the Bar to make full use of existing facilities before constructing new ones, replace lawyer employees with laypersons, increase *California State Bar Journal* advertising revenues, and budget for several years. It also criticized the Bar's continued reliance on volunteers to prosecute two-thirds of disciplinary cases, despite the 1970 Clark report's recommendation to make ending this practice "a first priority" and the BoG's 1972 resolution to do so as soon as possible.[31]

Journalistic exposés were another prod for change. In 1981, the *Los Angeles Daily Journal*—read by virtually every local lawyer—published the results of a six-month investigation, which reached "the unavoidable conclusion that California lawyers seldom are held accountable for their misdeeds." Lawyers rarely reported misconduct; less than one complaint in five was investigated; few of those investigated were disciplined; most of those disciplined were just reprimanded; and nothing was done about incompetence.[32]

But the Bar remained impervious to criticism and slow to recognize the chronic and worsening delay in the disciplinary process. Lily Barry (who had joined the State Bar as a staff lawyer in 1966) became chief trial counsel (CTC) in 1976, the year the Bar replaced LACs with the DB and began using staff attorneys to prosecute cases. More comfortable managing a small law office than a large bureaucracy, Barry let backlogs accumulate and then made staff work overtime to clear them. She believed "the backlog shouldn't determine your long-range staffing"

Editor, 54 CSBJ 420 (1979); Gert K. Hirschberg, *The New State Bar Court,* 54 CSBJ 438 (1979); Robert D. Raven, *President's Message,* 56 CSBJ 268–29 (1981) (also published in San Diego Union, 5.24.81); *Bulletin Board,* 1(2) California Lawyer 67 (10.81); *Bulletin Board,* 3(7) California Lawyer 49 (7.83); *Bulletin Board,* 4(4) California Lawyer 49 (4.84); *Bulletin Board,* 5(12) California Lawyer 67 (12.85); Coyle (1984: Appendix 5).

31. CAG (1976; 1977a; 1977b; 1977c).

32. Jon Standefer, *Is the Legal Profession Guilty of Failing to Police Itself?* LADJ 5 (May 15, 1981); *State Meting Out Fewer—and Lighter—Penalties,* LADJ 6 (May 18, 1981); *Attorney Incompetence Presents Difficult Problem,* LADJ (May 19, 1981); *State Bar Resisting Discipline Changes,* LADJ 8 (May 29, 1981); Gallagher (1993: 95).

and refrained from seeking more funds because the Board would "laugh at you" and cut even her modest budget. Barry resigned under pressure in February 1983. A few months after taking over, Susan Mahoney-St. Clair discovered 6,000 uncatalogued complaints, some ten years old. Although she requested $1.1 million to clear them, the Board appropriated only $100,000. By October, however, the Board made backlog reduction the highest priority, resolving to eliminate it within two years. Philip Schafer, who had won election to the Board in 1982 on a promise to reform discipline and become head of the Committee on Adjudication and Discipline, appointed a Subcommittee on Expediting the Discipline Process, chaired by Robert E. Coyle.[33]

The subcommittee's 1984 report found "systemic" inefficiencies: Contested cases averaged forty months; even cases with stipulated facts could take two years to conclude. At the ABA's February meeting, Chief Justice Warren Burger had called for comprehensive examination of disciplinary mechanisms, warning that "State legislatures may move independently if our profession does not act." Coyle agreed this was not "unduly alarmist." U.S. Senator Bob Packwood had recently introduced a "consumer protection" bill to transfer all attorney discipline to the Federal Trade Commission (FTC), which had sent "voluntary" questionnaires to state disciplinary bodies in 1978 and 1981. Some Ninth Circuit Court of Appeal judges had proposed a separate disciplinary system for lawyers appearing before them. The subcommittee found 4,392 complaints under investigation, 2,300 of which had been pending more than six months; more than 200 NTSCs had been waiting three months for charges—some much longer. But "the statistics only indicate delay. They are almost useless for anything else and are deceptive." It was "particularly disturbing" that the same criticism had been made ten years earlier "because of the vast amount of money spent on computer resources in the intervening years." Predicting that California's 80,000 attorneys would increase in number by four percent a year while the annual number of complaints per lawyer (then one in ten) would grow even faster "because of the larger number of underemployed attorneys and more stringent rules governing attorney competence," the subcommittee recommended that the "temporary" backlog team created by the BoG be made permanent. It further advised that the Office of Trial Counsel (OTC) should be empowered to issue a NTSC without returning to the investigative referee and to impose admonitions without trial. Simple cases should be heard by a single referee; more complicated ones by a compensated referee (although the subcommittee resisted eliminating volunteers).[34]

Asked by the Coyle subcommittee to evaluate the prosecutorial function, Mark C. Kroeker (a Los Angeles Police Department commander) reported in

33. *Bulletin Board,* 3(10) CALIFORNIA LAWYER 50 (10.83); Robert Egelko, *State Bar Discipline Under Fire,* 6(6) CALIFORNIA LAWYER 55 (6.86); Gallagher (1993: 96–97).

34. *Shorthand,* 56 CSBJ 173 (1981); Coyle (1984: 1, 18–19, 28–29).

June 1985 that investigators should handle no more than between 35 and 40 cases; the actual caseload of "100 or more is completely unrealistic." Investigation and prosecution should be separated. Less serious cases, "which are obviously not going to result in disciplinary dispositions," should be mediated by paralegals empowered to draft admonitions and warnings. A "massive effort will be needed to catch up" with the backlog, but "*the establishment of numerical closure goals or the ratio of cases per investigator is highly speculative.*"[35]

The BoG responded by allowing OTC lawyers to issue NTSCs, constituting two referee pools (a few paid to conduct long or complex cases and many volunteers for fee arbitrations), creating a master calendar in order to complete trials in a continuous hearing, separating the Office of Investigations (OI) from the OTC, constructing a career ladder to retain investigators, and instituting mandatory settlement conferences in eleven counties (accounting for 85 percent of complaints). It expected these changes to halve the 40 months from complaint to decision.[36]

The taxpayer revolt that produced Proposition 13 in 1978 also affected the Bar's dues requests. The legislature granted a $5 increase that year conditioned on a day-long hearing by the Senate and Assembly Judiciary Committees, which resulted in a $10 *decrease* the following year. The legislature rejected the Bar's proposal to index dues for inflation and membership growth. Another SB bill to raise the dues floor permanently, for the first time since 1976, was amended at the last minute to impose a one-year $5 decrease. Only on the last day of the 1982 legislative session did the SB obtain a substantial increase (to $90 and $160).

In 1978, State Senator Robert Wilson also introduced a bill to reduce dues to a flat $50, limit Bar activities to admissions and discipline, assign discipline to administrative hearing officers reviewed by panels of four laypersons and a lawyer, and eliminate the Conference and all SB committees. The voluntary associations also wanted the Conference to have more power and less state control. At its annual meeting in Monterey, the Conference of Bar Presidents created a study group, which reaffirmed support for the integrated bar. But concerned about a recent U.S. Supreme Court decision limiting the right of unions to use mandatory dues for political advocacy,[37] it proposed to transfer all lobbying (other than for bar dues) to the Conference of Delegates, which would be made more representative and financed voluntarily. Seeking to avoid guilt by

35. Kroeker (1985) (emphasis in original).

36. *Bulletin Board,* 4(8) CALIFORNIA LAWYER 49 (8.84); *1983–84 The State Bar of California Annual Report,* 4(12) CALIFORNIA LAWYER 77–78 (12.84); Gallagher (1993: 100–01).

37. Abood v. Detroit Bd. of Education, 431 U.S. 209 (1977).

association, the Bar authorized the Conference of Delegates to lobby without seeking BoG approval.[38]

III. THE PERILS OF POLITICAL ENGAGEMENT

This cycle of complacency, external criticism, and piecemeal reform might have continued indefinitely but for a political explosion. The Conference of Delegates took positions on increasingly contentious issues, convincing the BoG in 1976 to support the decriminalization of prostitution. SB President Shallenberger "became convinced that it was within our purview because so much time and money is taken up in the judicial system processing prostitution cases." But Board members objected to Conference stances on abortion, affirmative action,[39] and the Equal Rights Amendment. In 1980, the assembly's Judiciary Committee held a hearing entitled the "Use of Mandatory State Bar Dues." Two years later, the BoG urged that private clubs be subjected to federal anti-discrimination laws if a "substantial portion" of their revenue came from business sources, and it opposed two law-and-order measures: a constitutional amendment introduced by state Senator Robert B. Presley (D-Riverside) to deny bail to defendants charged with capital crimes and other violent felonies, and the just enacted Victims' Bill of Rights proposition.[40] In August 1984, Pete Wilson, then a candidate for U.S. Senator, threatened a recall campaign against any California Supreme Court Justice who voted to invalidate the proposition.

This prompted a strong response from SB President-Elect Anthony Murray, who was echoed by the Bar Associations of San Francisco and Los Angeles, among others. Murray used his inaugural speech to the September SB annual meeting to defend the Court's independence.

> We must make it clear that the only legitimate basis for refusing to retain or recalling a justice is a showing of incapacity or misconduct in office. We must make it clear that judges cannot be removed because the politicians disagree with their judicial philosophies or with specific decisions.

---

38. David J. Levy, *President's Message,* 54 CSBJ 138 (1979); Bert Z. Tigerman, *Letter to the Editor,* 54 CSBJ 286 (1979); Jack Stutman, *President's Message,* 54 CSBJ 210 (1979); *Shorthand,* 54 CSBJ 528 (1979); Mary A. Eikel, *Where Is the State Bar Going?* 55 CSBJ 154 (1980); Mary A. Eikel, *The Monterey Committee Report,* 55 CSBJ 380–81 (1980); *Shorthand,* 54 CSBJ 462 (1979); *Sacramento Scene,* 54 CSBJ 531 (1979); *Bar World,* 55 CSBJ 265 (1980); *Bar World,* 56 CSBJ 168 (1981); *Bulletin Board,* 2(2) California Lawyer 44 (Feb 1982).

39. In response to Bakke v. Regents of the University of California, 438 U.S. 265 (1978).

40. Presley, who played a pivotal role in subsequent events, was a World War II veteran who spent twenty-four years in the Riverside County Sheriff's Department, twelve as undersheriff, focused on the plight of domestic violence victims.

Denouncing the proposition as a "dangerous measure," which "pretends to deal with the deep complexities of crime by throwing slogans at the problems," Murray called on the Bar to defend courts from

> the idiotic cries of the self-appointed vigilantes; the committee on law and order; the court watchers; the self-seeking prosecutors and lawyers who want to be judges; *and every unscrupulous politician who thinks there is something in it for him if he gets in line to kick the courts, which he sees as inert and defenseless.* [emphasis added]

While not naming Wilson, he attacked "a candidate for national office, himself a lawyer, who threatens a recall of our chief justice if the Supreme Court dares to overturn Proposition 8." At the same meeting, the Conference endorsed propositions for handgun control and a bilateral nuclear weapons freeze, urged that Martin Luther King, Jr.'s birthday be made a national holiday, and echoed Murray's criticism of Wilson. The BoG unanimously adopted a resolution strongly supporting the independence of the judiciary.[41]

A group of fifty-five lawyers, led by Eddie T. Keller (a sixteen-year veteran of the Attorney General's office, angered by opposition to the death penalty), protested that "it was totally improper for the state bar to have become embroiled in an issue which is so obviously political," which "disenfranchises those in the membership who disagree." The Conference executive committee chair replied that the resolution "was fully debated," "no speaker sought to defend the conduct," and "the vote was the expression of a substantial majority of the delegates." This provoked a *California Lawyer* article declaring "the rock-hard fact . . . that the state bar has long involved itself in ideological pursuits" and demanding that it be "split[] in two." President Murray retorted that "if we believe that our profession must preserve its dedication to public service, we should retain our unified bar with its commitment to the interests of the public." The following year, the Conference called for abolishing the death penalty (on a show of hands because the voice vote was too close to call) and opposed retention elections for California Supreme Court justices. Even before then, however, Keller and co-worker Raymond Brosterhous contacted the conservative Pacific Legal Foundation, which sued on behalf of them and nineteen others (including Assemblymember Patrick J. Nolan) to enjoin the State Bar from taking political positions and using

---

41. 53 CSBJ 190–91 (1978); Garvin F. Shallenberger, *President's Message,* 53 CSBJ 214 (1978); Claude D. Morgan, *Letter to the Editor,* 54 CSBJ 363 (1979); Joseph Carr, *Letter to the Editor,* 54 CSBJ 420 (1979); Kenneth Hopp, *Letter to the Editor,* 54 CSBJ 493 (1979); Michael V. McIntire, *Letter to the Editor,* 54 CSBJ 493 (1979); *Bulletin Board,* 2(5) California Lawyer 43–44 (May 1982); *Bulletin Board,* 2(7) California Lawyer 89 (7–8.82); *Bulletin Board,* 2(9) California Lawyer 67 (Oct. 1982); *Annual Meeting Wrap,* 2(11) California Lawyer 28 (Dec. 1982); *Bulletin Board,* 2(1) California Lawyer 64 (Dec. 1982).

dues to do so. On May 24, 1984, the trial court granted the State Bar summary judgment, finding that, as a governmental agency, it had not acted improperly.[42]

In March 1985, while the *Keller* plaintiffs were appealing, the *San Francisco Examiner* published a six-part series entitled "The Brotherhood," which resembled the *Los Angeles Daily Journal* exposé four years earlier but was now on the front page of a major newspaper. It quickly grabbed readers' attention.

> There are convicted criminals practicing law in California. They include lawyers who have lied, cheated and stolen. A bagman in a bribery scheme is allowed to practice law. So is an attorney who burglarized a client's market. So are a drug smuggler, an embezzler and a stock swindler. So is a lawyer who impersonated a cop. So is an attorney who did dirty tricks for the White House, and another who tried to raise campaign funds for President Nixon by selling an ambassadorship. After punishments ranging from a wrist slap to a few years on the sidelines, all were judged to be fit attorneys.

Although the SB had received nine thousand complaints the previous year, it investigated only two out of five and held formal hearings for just 6 percent, disbarring 11 lawyers while suspending five times as many for failing to pay bar dues than for ethical transgressions, in a process that was too slow and secretive.[43]

Once again the Bar insisted everything was fine. Former President Kenneth Jost called California's disciplinary system the "envy" of other states; current President Burke M. Critchfield insisted it was the "most effective" regulatory system "of any bar or other professional group in the country." The *Examiner*'s findings characterized only "an extremely small percentage of California lawyers." And though Critchfield warned local bar leaders that "the number of complaints we are receiving each year exceeds the resources we have available to carry out this important function," he assured them that "a great many reforms have been implemented, and more are proposed to make the discipline program faster [and] more efficient." At its June meeting, the Board diverted money from other functions to let the OTC hire more staff. At the end of his term, Critchfield welcomed the "intense public and legislative scrutiny" as "healthy attention," which had simply "sped the bar along" in "the very areas the bar itself already had targeted for reform." But other insiders were more skeptical. David Clare,

---

42. Keller v. State Bar, Superior Court of Sacramento County, No. 307168 (Cechettini, J.); Edward L. Lascher, *Dismantle the Unified Bar,* 3(5) CALIFORNIA LAWYER 12 (May 1983); Anthony Murray, *The Unified Bar Serves the Public Interest,* 3(5) CALIFORNIA LAWYER 13 (May 1983); *Conference Calls for End to Capital Punishment,* 4(12) CALIFORNIA LAWYER 21 (12.84); James Evans, *Behind the Keller Case,* 10(5) CALIFORNIA LAWYER 35 (May 1990).

43. K. Connie Kang and James A. Finefrock, *The Brotherhood: Justice for Lawyers,* SAN FRANCISCO EXAMINER (3.24–29.85). Journalistic exposés also prompted reform of discipline in West Virginia, Washington State, and Oregon. Collins (1992).

who had resigned as assistant chief trial counsel after thirteen years with the SB, declared: "With one or two exceptions, I never knew a member of the Board of Governors who had the least interest in discipline." And Harriet Katz, a public member of the Board from 1976 to 1981, recalled that when she raised the bar's consumer protection responsibilities at a meeting, "a mild-mannered lawyer stood up and slammed his fist on the table and said, 'The State Bar is not a consumer protection agency.'"[44]

The *Examiner* series had many ramifications. A month after it appeared, Senator Presley created a task force to explore the problem and propose solutions. In September, a majority of the committee recommended transferring discipline to an independent agency responsible to the Supreme Court, a proposal the *Sacramento Bee* felt "deserves serious consideration." The entire task force recommended a random audit of client trust accounts; standardized written fee agreements; itemized bills; arbitration of fee disputes; less delay in discipline; expansion of the client security fund beyond dishonesty; mandatory malpractice insurance; a prohibition on lawyers conditioning the settlement of malpractice claims on clients agreeing not to file disciplinary complaints; a public majority on the Board of Governors; the exclusion of trivial matters (such as marijuana possession) from discipline and its extension to "the most common client grievances: overcharging, incompetence, negligence;" reduction of investigative caseloads; heightened penalties; the discipline of more elite lawyers; reporting of ethical violations by lawyers and judges; and the authority to place lawyers on inactive status early in an investigation.[45]

The *Examiner* series also reignited smoldering legislative resentment toward the dues bill, which Senator Dan Boatwright had introduced on February 13. At a Senate Judiciary Committee hearing on the bill, Presley demanded that the Bar first clear up the disciplinary backlog. The Senate passed a bill requiring the Bar to use any additional fees exclusively for discipline, report to the legislature on disciplinary reforms, reduce its backlog by 80 percent by the end of 1987, and establish goals for promptly handling future cases. But the bill did not reach the Assembly until Friday, September 13, the final day of the 1985 session. At the last minute, Republican minority leader Patrick Nolan (a *Keller* plaintiff), invoked a

---

44. Kenneth Jost, *The Public's Stake in Lawyer Discipline,* LADJ 2 (Apr. 8, 1985); Burke M. Critchfield, *The Bar Is Improving a Good System's Shortcomings,* LADJ 4 (Apr. 10, 1985); Karen Ringuette, *Cleaning Up the Act,* 5 California Lawyer 12 (1985); *Bulletin Board,* 5(7) California Lawyer 71 (May 1985); *Bulletin Board,* 5(9) California Lawyer 60 (Sept. 1985); Burke M. Critchfield, *Looking Back,* in *The State Bar of California Annual Report 1984–1985,* 5(12) California Lawyer 67, 69 (Dec. 1985); Robert Egelko, *State Bar Discipline Under Fire,* 6(6) California Lawyer 55 (June 1986).

45. *Recommendations of Senator Presley's Task Force on Bar Discipline, Following Meeting in San Francisco,* (Sept. 18, 1985), in California Assembly (1985: App. A); Philip Carrizosa, *Task Force Urges Stripping State Bar of Discipline Cases,* LADJ 1 (9.19.85); *Editorial,* Sacramento Bee (10.85), reprinted in LADJ 1 (Oct. 7, 1985).

recently enacted procedural rule requiring that legislators receive conference committee reports a day before voting. Although the Senate had voted that day (after its secretary found the rule to be no obstacle), the chief clerk of the Assembly disagreed. Although a legislative counsel agreed with the Senate secretary, Speaker Willie Brown temporized (perhaps because, the previous spring, the Board had opposed his bill to require malpractice insurance). At 5:30 A.M, he ruled that it was a new legislative day, allowing the assembly to vote, but Nolan successfully objected that the legislature had been required to adjourn by the previous midnight unless two-thirds of both houses overrode this. The bill died.[46]

On September 30, the Assembly Subcommittee on the Administration of Justice, chaired by Lloyd G. Connelly, held a joint hearing of the assembly and Senate judiciary committees immediately after the SB annual conference in San Diego. Orville A. Armstrong, outgoing chair of the Committee on Admissions and Discipline (CAD), criticized the *Examiner* for focusing on seventy "exceptional cases" out of "tens of thousands." "[R]adical changes" had created a "new State Bar discipline system," which would "cure the backlog very quickly." Armstrong's successor, Joe S. Gray, proposed to alleviate investigators' intolerable burden of 130 cases by "calling on a resource that's available only to the State Bar . . . the large number of volunteers." Susan Mahony-St. Clair, Chief Trial Counsel, boasted that "an investigation in the past that may take six months . . . has been able to be completed in five to seven working days." SB President David M. Heilbron had "said yesterday before perhaps a thousand people that we are committed to solving this problem . . . this is not an idle promise. It's a commitment."[47]

But legislators were skeptical. Assemblymember Richard Robinson (not a lawyer) had chaired three previous Bar dues conference committees, which had been "hung up until the very waning hours" by questions about discipline. He criticized the SB's heavy dependence on volunteers "where a lot of . . . the 'old boy syndrome' operates." Lawyer friends told him that LACs often refused to find moral turpitude because "you're talking about somebody's ability to make a living." Senator Bill Lockyer (judiciary committee chair and a lawyer) asked for something "that would be confidence inducing" because he did not see the "small discrete changes" as a "new discipline system." Robinson got Gray to agree that "an attorney who files excessive paper" or engages in "other types of fee running-up procedures is just as much guilty of stealing a client's money as the attorney who converts a client's trust funds." Connolly noted that a few days earlier, the *Examiner* had criticized the Bar for failing to distribute a report (pre-

---

46. California Assembly (1985: Exhibits J and K); Gallagher (1993: 110–14). On BoG opposition to Brown's malpractice bill, AB 2087, *see* James E. Towery, *Malpractice insurance should be mandatory*, 5(7) CALIFORNIA LAWYER 16 (5.85).

47. California Assembly (1985: 2–10, 12–14).

pared at Heilbron's request), which found that it took an average of 488 days from the filing of a complaint to the filing of formal charges. Claiming not to know that lawyers conditioned the settlement of malpractice claims on clients agreeing not to file grievances, Gray said he "would consider that grounds for discipline . . . and expect a push for disbarment."[48]

Heilbron offered multiple arguments against transferring disciplinary authority. These included that the state constitution lodged it in the judiciary, creating separation of powers issues; "[W]e're geared up to fix [the backlog], and nobody else is;" the Bar's "500 volunteers" made its disciplinary process cheaper; and many observers were properly skeptical about the Department of Consumer Affairs; a lawyer could not "freely" "represent people against the state . . . if that lawyer has to be afraid that . . . the state can punish him."[49]

Presley task force members were unpersuaded. Stanford Law School Professor Deborah Rhode testified that "the consistent conclusion of all this scholarship is that . . . professional sanctions and regulations generally ought not to rest with the bar itself." But her inability to identify a successful regulatory agency moved Lockyer to dismiss the possibility of devising something "independent of politics" as "little more than slogans." Boalt Hall Professor Stephen Bundy agreed with Rhode that self-regulation was "simply a matter of conflict of interest," confirmed by the "history of poor performance." Although Bar Governor Philip Schafer had established the Coyle Commission, he opposed divestment of disciplinary power. "We are not a brotherhood . . . a Cosa Nostra that's devoted to trying to cover up and protect our brethren."

> Every single complaint is investigated. . . . It may be a review saying: " . . . because you don't like the suit your lawyers [*sic*] wears it's not a disciplinary matter." Some of them reach that level of absurdity.

Philip Martin, who had prosecuted disciplinary cases for three years and now represented legal malpractice plaintiffs, supported divestment. The lawsuit he had had to bring to force the State Bar to grant due process rights to client security fund claimants showed the "kind of stuck-in-the-mud type bureaucracy that is operating."[50] Three weeks earlier, the Bar had directed the OTC to close all complaints filed in 1983, which "may not be good faith compliance with what the legislature had in mind." Public Bar Governor Richard Annotico also wanted discipline transferred to an agency composed of a lay majority and lawyers who were appointed rather than elected.[51]

---

48. *Id.* 16, 19–21, 23–26, 28, 30.

49. *Id.* 33–36.

50. Saleeby v. State Bar, 39 Cal. 3d 547 (1985).

51. California Assembly (1985: 37–43, 47–66, 77). Annotico graduated from law school but acquired his wealth from real estate. David O. Weber, *"Still in Good Standing": The Crisis in Attorney Discipline,* ABAJ 58, 60–61 (November 1987).

In October, the SB sought authority to collect dues from the Supreme Court, but it deferred to objections from Governor Deukmejian and legislators. In response to a plea for voluntary dues, 54 percent of active members and 90 percent of inactive had paid by February 25, 1986, when the Governor finally signed a dues bill. This legislation required the Auditor General to survey lawyers' views on discipline. Although the State Bar was forbidden to communicate with members, presidents of thirty-three voluntary bar associations endorsed the integrated bar. This time, half the 90,000 members responded. Although only a small plurality thought the Bar was doing "an adequate job of disciplining attorneys" (45 to 38 percent), four out of five still felt it was "the appropriate organization to receive and investigate complaints." Lawyers split almost evenly (49 to 48 percent) over whether the Bar should be able to advocate on topics other than technical law revision, court reform, and issues directly related to the legal profession. If it did, 69 percent wanted dues to be voluntary; and only 44 percent thought they should support the Conference of Delegates. By the time these results were reported, a divided Court of Appeal had reversed *Keller*, holding that the SB had failed to sustain its burden of proof to justify Murray's speech and the BoG might be personally liable for violating the petitioners' rights.[52]

IV. PROFESSIONALIZING DISCIPLINE

In January 1986, Senator Presley introduced two bills. SB 1543 would entrust disciplinary hearings to administrative law judges supervised by a fifteen-member commission with a lay majority, all of whose members would be appointed (4 by the Governor, 6 by the Legislature, 4 by the State Bar, and one by the Chief Justice); SB 1569 made lesser changes but required lawyers to disclose fees and provide written agreements if fees exceeded $1,000 and report three or more malpractice claims filed within a year, as well as some judicial sanctions. In addition, the State Bar could audit trust funds and had to process complaints within six months and report to the legislature annually. A supportive *Sacramento Bee*

> deplored the general pattern of laxity that plagues the State Bar's disciplinary proceedings. The bar is slow to act against lawyers who steal from clients, lie to them, misuse drugs and commit felonies. When it does act, it is far less likely than disciplinary authorities in other states to hand out serious punisment

52. *Bar Watch: Lawyers back the bar,* 6(5) California Lawyer 11 (5.86); *Bar Watch: Local bars support State Bar,* 6(7) California Lawyer 11 (7.86); *Bar Watch: State Bar plebiscite results,* 6(7) California Lawyer 12–13 (July 1986); Gallagher (1993: 115); Keller v. State Bar, Court of Appeal, Third Dist., Civ. No. 24124 (May 1986).

such as disbarment and suspension. The State Bar...has failed in its duty to protect the public from misbehaving lawyers.[53]

Although the *Los Angeles Herald* had no doubt that "the State Bar's disciplinary system is not working properly" and is "besieged by some 6,000 backlogged cases, as well as complaints that the discipline it delivers is often absurdly lenient for the violations," it opposed the bills because the Bar had "already acted to reform itself."[54] When the BoG opposed the first bill 18–1 (with only Annotico dissenting) and it seemed doomed to fail, Presley proposed an independent director for the Bar's disciplinary system. When the Bar successfully blocked this as well, he settled for a monitor. President Heilbron declared victory. Although Attorney General John Van de Kamp initially envisaged a retired judge as monitor, in January 1987, he picked Robert Fellmeth, a former Nader's Raider turned law professor, who directed the University of San Diego Law School's Center for Public Interest Law.[55] The Long Beach *Press-Telegram* lauded Fellmeth's "impressive consumer advocacy credentials" and hoped lawyers would "feel constrained to take extra care in dealing with clients' money and legal rights."[56]

Just when the Bar was taking comfort from the fact that it remained under the protective wing of the judiciary, the Supreme Court harshly criticized the State Bar Court. Drastically reducing a lawyer's punishment from disbarment to a year's suspension, the Supreme Court said: "This record, like others we are receiving with increasing frequency, leaves material gaps in the analytic path from charges to proof to findings and conclusions to recommendations."[57] The SBC had failed to "relate individual facts to specific professional duties and rules." The Supreme Court found "important evidentiary deficiencies"; in several "significant" instances, "conduct not charged, or not proved, is found and relied upon as a basis for discipline." While upholding the penalty in a second case, the Supreme Court deplored that "the record is otherwise deficient with respect to both the findings and the conclusions reached therein."[58] It was "essential that the records offered in support of the disciplinary recommendations be adequate to permit [the Supreme Court] to act upon those recommendations."

Presley returned to the fray in February 1987, successfully seeking an Auditor General investigation of the Bar's record in disciplining lawyers who stole from client trust accounts.[59] But this was nothing compared with Fellmeth's first

53. *A New Court for Lawyers, Sacramento Bee,* reproduced in LADJ 4 (Mar. 6, 1986).

54. *A Second Chance, Los Angeles Herald,* reproduced in LADJ 4 (Mar. 20, 1986).

55. Gallagher (1993: 124–31).

56. *Monitoring the Bar,* reproduced in LADJ 4 (Feb. 5, 1987).

57. Maltaman v. State Bar, 43 Cal. 3d 924, 931 (1987).

58. Guzzetta v. State Bar, 43 Cal. 3d 962, 968 (1987).

59. Robert Fairbanks, *Sen. Presley Takes Aim at the California State Bar Once Again,* LADJ 4 (Apr. 9, 1987).

report that June.[60] The disciplinary system's toll-free number was not listed in any telephone directory. "Middle-level bar staff is candid about the reason": fear of increasing backlog. Even so, callers encountered a busy signal between 62 and 72 percent of the time. Seven out of eight local bars surveyed accepted complaints they had no power to resolve, referring them to "Client Relations Committees." Only 20 percent of complainants to whom forms were sent bothered to return them. In order to reduce the backlog, the Bar had revived the Volunteer Investigative Assistance Program, whose investigators usually lived and worked in the respondent's community. Of 38 volunteers in one program, only 13 attended the workshop; a large proportion of them did nothing; and most of those who did anything missed the deadline. Staff investigators had caseloads of 150 to 200 cases (although Kroeker had recommended no more than 35 to 40). They had to obtain special permission to conduct on site inquiries, photocopy, travel, or subpoena, could not identify the respondent to potential witnesses, and required approval by three members of CAD to interview other clients. They needed bank names and account numbers to subpoena records, information the Legal Services Trust Fund possessed but would not disclose. The Bar took attorney fingerprints at admission but would not use them in investigations. Although lawyers had to report criminal convictions and malpractice claims to the membership office, the office would not release such information to investigators. Investigations were routinely abated for pending criminal or civil actions and not always revived when those ended. Only five interim suspension motions had been filed in Los Angeles in the first half of 1987, and some investigators were unaware they had that power. The Bar had to "prove up" default cases, which could take a year, although members who failed to pay dues were placed on inactive status within weeks. OTC lawyers needed special permission to spend any money or take depositions (and hence took very few). Turnover among OTC lawyers was high, and 10 of the 13 who left in 1986 were not replaced. Salaries started at $2,000 a month and peaked just over $3,000, provoking lawyers to strike.[61]

As the backlog rose, the Bar began sending complaining witnesses (CWs) a form letter warning there would be a six-month delay before any response. The first real contact, 12 to 18 months later, often was just a request for more information. Failure to respond led to closure of the case, accounting for much of the backlog reduction. Another strategy was to classify an increasing proportion of phone calls as "inquiries." Of the 8,574 calls found to be complaints in 1986, 7,715 were closed for not sufficient facts (NSF). Although the Bar increased case closings from 580 in January 1987 to 1,096 in March, those producing NTSCs fell from 20 to 2 percent. CWs were not informed of admonitions or

60. Fellmeth (1987a; 1987b).

61. *See also, Bar Watch: Board of Governors: Three-week strike settled,* 6(7) CALIFORNIA LAWYER 9 (July 1996).

private reprimands. Because the Hearing Department still relied on 448 lawyers and 80 laypersons, "wide inconsistency exists among the rulings and standards applied by the many briefly-trained referees." Although the SBC boasted that disbarments and resignations with charges pending rose from 59 in 1985 to 107 in 1986, almost all the increase was attributable to the 69 resignations; per capita disbarment rates in other states were ten times higher.

When SB President Armstrong claimed that Fellmeth's report showed that disciplinary procedures just needed some "fine tuning," the *San Francisco Examiner* replied: "Wrong. They need a complete overhaul." "[T]ogether with the hiring of greater numbers of investigators, the use of administrative law judges would go a long way toward restoring public confidence in the bar and in practicing attorneys."[62] But at the end of his term, Armstrong continued to insist that lawyers had "the best professional disciplinary program in California."[63] He boasted that the Bar had anticipated by a year the legislatively mandated goal for reducing the backlog and gave "much credit" to the 450 volunteer lawyers, whom he hoped "will continue to be a part of the discipline system in the future." By the end of the year, California would be "a model system for other states." Fellmeth was more cautious: "If California doesn't have a model system within two years, then I haven't done my job. Or they haven't listened to me."[64]

Although Fellmeth's next semiannual report called the Bar's response "constructive," he still found that "fundamental" deficiencies rendered the disciplinary system "unacceptable."[65] Investigative caseloads were too heavy; complex cases required vertical prosecution. Both Fellmeth and Van de Kamp "strongly" endorsed professional judges in the Hearing and Review Departments; but the SBC dismissed "any suggestion that [referees] are or have been biased" as "unsupported by any empirical evidence." Although Fellmeth urged the Bar to seek a $50 dues surcharge for discipline, it sought only $25, because "upper staff" had engaged in "blockage of the grim facts concerning backlog, abeyance, and low staff morale." The Bar "should require all local bar associations to immediately transmit any complaint received about any attorney which might facially involve a breach of the Rules of Professional Conduct." The Bar should use and improve systems for notifying it of criminal convictions, malpractice claims, and contempt orders or sanctions. It should address incompetence, perhaps by limiting practice areas. The "highly funneled pattern" of terminating more than

62. *Cleanup Task for the Bar*, SAN FRANCISCO EXAMINER, reproduced in LADJ 5 (June 6, 1987).

63. Orville A. Armstrong, *Reflections, in The State Bar of California Annual Report 1986–1987*, 7(12) CALIFORNIA LAWYER 60–61 (Dec. 1987).

64. Weber (1987: 63).

65. Fellmeth (1987c: 1, 6).

95 percent of cases without a hearing had become even more "exaggerated" in the preceding six months.[66]

The Bar responded by seeking a dramatic dues increase to improve discipline (from $276 to $470, which the Legislature cut to $417).[67] President Anderlini declared that "it is the legal profession's responsibility to run a strong discipline system and that anything less will risk having the responsibility taken away but not the cost."[68] The *Los Angeles Daily News* agreed that increased dues should fund improved discipline: "At least this is a reform for which lawyers would pay. The public has paid enough."[69] While also supporting the increase, the *San Gabriel Valley Tribune* warned that the state would assume "complete control of the discipline process...if attorneys don't get their house in order."[70] The *Sacramento Bee* praised the Bar for taking a "first step toward laying the financial basis for some long-overdue reforms in the legal profession's notoriously inept system of self-discipline."[71] The

> bar's current enforcement efforts constitute a system that might as well have been designed to fail. Every conceivable barrier has been enacted to frustrate consumer complaints, prevent investigations into attorney wrongdoing and safeguard the license of lawyers who steal from their clients.

But the newspaper warned that "The Los Angeles and San Francisco bar associations and the state's major corporate law firms exercise a lot more political clout than the board of governors, and they've been able to block reforms proposed by the State Bar in the past." Quoting Anderlini's admission that the disciplinary system is "not one we can be proud of," the *Los Angeles Times* said that "some overdue changes have been undertaken since the Legislature scared the bar,"

---

66. *Id.* 12, 16, 18, 28, 30–34, 37–38, 47–51, 56, 60, 173, 175 and Exhibits I and XII.

67. Tom Dresslar, *Legislators Trim State Bar Dues, Discipline Bills,* LADJ 1 (May 18, 1988); Tom Dresslar, *Assembly Judiciary Panel Approves Bar Dues Bills,* LADJ 2 (May 19, 1988); Tom Dresslar, *Assembly Approves Landmark Attorney Discipline, Dues Bill,* LADJ 2 (June 6, 1988); Tom Dresslar, *State Legislators Return Today to Full Plate of Bills,* LADJ 1 (Aug. 1, 1988); *Tom Dresslar, Dispute Stalls Action on State Bar Two-Bill Dues Package,* LADJ 2 (Aug.4, 1988) (public members on BoG and power to appoint SBC judges); Tom Dresslar, *State Bar Discipline, Dues Bills Clear Senate Judiciary Panel,* LADJ 2 (Aug. 10, 1988); Tom Dresslar, *Senate Passes Bar Dues Hike, Companion Bill Stalls,* LADJ 2 (Aug. 19, 1988); Tom Dresslar, *Assembly Sends Bar Dues, Discipline Bills to Governor,* LADJ 2 (Aug 23, 1988).

68. Terry Anderlini, *President's Message,* 8(3) CALIFORNIA LAWYER 66 (Mar. 1988); *President's Message,* 8(4) CALIFORNIA LAWYER 75 (Apr. 1988); *Discipline, Fee Bills Advance,* 8(7) CALIFORNIA LAWYER 75 (July 1988); AB 4391.

69. *It's Broken, So Fix It,* LOS ANGELES DAILY NEWS, reproduced in LADJ 4 (Jan. 23, 1988).

70. *Cleaning House,* SAN GABRIEL VALLEY TRIBUNE, reproduced in LADJ 4 (Feb. 8, 1988).

71. *Self-Discipline,* SACRAMENTO BEE, reproduced in LADJ 4 (Feb. 19, 2009).

but "problems remain" (listing Fellmeth's criticisms).[72] It endorsed the professionalized State Bar Court and criticized "resistance to a dues increase" as "unbecoming to the profession." "California could learn to respect lawyers—if, this once, they demonstrate that they are willing to pay what it takes to police their own ranks."

Fellmeth's April 1988 report found little improvement. True, in its first eight months the Complainants' Grievance Panel (created by SB 1543 for clients dissatisfied by dismissal of their complaints) had completed 320 cases, ordering further investigation in 88 and recommending action in 10. But intake had cleared its backlog by classifying calls as inquiries rather than complaints, the ratio between which had increased from 1:1 to 4:1. And the bottleneck had simply moved downstream: nearly 2,000 cases had been in investigation more than six months (the legislative definition of backlog), more than half for at least a year, and 700 to 1,000 cases were awaiting NTSCs. The Supreme Court' Attorney General Select Committee on Internal Procedures (the Richardson Committee) had complicated institutional reform by recommending that the Court of Appeal review SBC decisions. Fellmeth preferred SB 1498 (supported by the Attorney General and State Bar staff), which would professionalize the SBC (and make many of the other changes he had urged).[73]

The auditor general's first annual report mandated by the 1986 legislation seconded Fellmeth's criticisms.[74] From 1984 to 1986, the State Bar met the six-month goal for resolving complaints in less than half the cases. Even though it obtained 46 new positions in 1986, "it still has been unable to meet its six-month goal because it also lacks an effective case management system." The SB had done no work for 180 consecutive days on 40 out of a random sample of 131 cases and none for almost 18 months on one of them. Although New York paid CSF claimants within two months of discipline, California took an average of 18 months. Between 1984 and 1987, disciplinary complaints took an average of 640 days to complete. President Anderlini responded that the report "looks at a limited number of cases" and "concerns history rather than the present." The problem was the number and complexity of the cases, and the scarcity and inexperience of staff.

Looking back on his year as president, Terry Anderlini called passage of SB 1543 "the most massive administrative reform of a state agency ever accomplished in California." As a result, "the California attorney discipline system will be the model for the nation." Senator Presley "hope[d] this all works, and I think it will. The bar now seems seriously concerned about reforming its discipline system." Although incoming President Colin Wied thought it "a little premature

72. *A Little Respect,* Los Angeles Times, reproduced in LADJ 4 (Apr. 6, 1993).

73. Fellmeth (1988a: 5–6, 21–23, 31–51, 53, 56, 72).

74. CAG (1988: s-1 to s-3, 10, 20–21, Table B-4); Letter from Terry Anderlini, State Bar President, to Auditor General Thomas W. Hayes (June 16, 1988), in *Id.*

to declare victory," it was "not too early for the board to return its attention to the bar's other responsibilities." Optimistically entitling his first president's message "Life after Discipline—1989," Wied congratulated California lawyers "for overwhelmingly supporting the change to (and cost of) a system that will protect the public from the few among us who discredit the profession."[75]

But as Wied began his (unopposed) presidential term, Fellmeth's next report found that the backlog was increasing at all stages and "greater than it has ever been in the bar's history."[76] He voiced new criticisms. A recent survey found that 28 percent of full-time private practitioners carried no malpractice insurance; of those who had gone bare, over half had done so since premiums began increasing dramatically in 1985. Although there were few unsatisfied awards, plaintiffs' lawyers discouraged claims against uninsured attorneys. Fellmeth urged that malpractice insurance be mandatory (a reform the State Bar had abandoned under pressure from large urban bars) and an unsatisfied judgment be a disciplinary offense leading to interim suspension until it was paid. Lawyers who were the object of malpractice claims were also more likely to face disciplinary complaints. But the State Bar had successfully defeated requirements that plaintiffs filing malpractice claims inform the disciplinary system, attorneys report the settlement of all civil judgments, and courts report serious contempt and non-discovery sanctions. The Bar opposed Fellmeth's proposal that disciplinary proceedings be public if there was a criminal investigation or charge, a high priority investigation, or multiple CWs. The current rejection letter, informing the CW that "the Supreme Court has ruled that the State Bar's decision must be in favor of the attorney" if there was no evidence beyond the CW's word, was "somewhat dishonest." Although the Board had rejected mandatory continuing legal education in 1983, it now was sponsoring legislation to require 36 hours every three years, at least eight hours of which were to concern legal ethics and practice management. Fellmeth also urged specialist certification through additional examinations. Although "at least 30% of meritorious disciplinary cases involve some form of chemical dependency," existing programs enrolled a "miniscule" number of lawyers. Despite "substantial evidence that overbilling is common," the requirement of a written agreement was enforceable only if the lawyer sought more than the fair value of services (i.e., a contingent fee). "[C]harging fees beyond those agreed to or consistent with time competently expended" should be "a very basic part of the disciplinary jurisdiction of the Bar." The client security fund had a 30 percent overhead and did not pay until discipline was final

75. *Beyond Discipline,* 8(7) CALIFORNIA LAWYER 76 (7.88); Colin Wied, *Life After Discipline—1989,* 8(10) CALIFORNIA LAWYER 100 (10.88); *Bar Has Fee Bill, Discipline Goals,* 8(11) CALIFORNIA LAWYER 99 (Nov. 1988).

76. Fellmeth (1988b: 1, 5, 13, 17–18, 35–36, 39, 45–46, 50–51, 60, 62–63, 67, 76, 95, 106–08, 110–11, 112–19, 132–34, 147–55, and Ex. I (David Long, *Malpractice Insurance Report,* Mar. 29, 1988)).

(which often took four to five years); and its backlog was approaching 2,000 claims. Fellmeth urged that it be better publicized, expanded to inadequate professional service, and authorized to grant default judgments up to $1,000 and recover them from the lawyer.

Gert K. Hirschberg (who had been a bar governor and presiding referee of the volunteer SBC, and represented two of the lawyers in the disciplinary cases described below) passionately defended the old system and attacked the new.[77] "On balance, I trust a lawyer more than a non-lawyer" client. The dues bill imposed "onerous conditions" to promote reforms that "demeaned lawyers." The "whole tenor" of Fellmeth's "demeaning" report was that "attorneys are crooks, clients are honorable, and we the lawyers of California must be watched on a twenty-four-hour basis with the precision of a national anti-nuclear defense system. I don't like the concept that attorneys should be treated like burglars." The elimination of volunteer referees was "devastating" and responsible for "the onslaught of disciplinary filings that we now have in technical and/or Mickey Mouse matters." The volunteer system was "speedier and more efficient." "I believe that only an attorney can evaluate an attorney." "[O]n balance we had the best system." Hirschberg offered examples of "recently enacted changes [that] should be repulsive to any lawyer": "failure to cooperate can be another basis of discipline;" "confidentiality disappears" after issuance of an NTSC; the hypocritical claim that "the function of discipline is protection of the public and not punishment." He ended apocalyptically: "If California lawyers continue to be passive, non-assertive and silent, then read my lips: The State Bar, as we now know it, is bound to die."

In February 1989, the California Supreme Court reversed the Court of Appeal decision in *Keller*.[78] Justice Broussard (writing for just three others) upheld the general authority of the State Bar, as a public corporation, to engage in lobbying and file amicus briefs to promote "the improvement of the administration of justice" but agreed it could not participate in electoral politics. Although Murray's speech crossed that line, the governors were not personally liable.

At the end of his term, Wied looked back on "a very good year" and called his annual report, "Discipline, A Done Deal."[79] But Fellmeth's next three reports continued to find "serious problems." The number of complaints opened for investigation had fallen from 7,542 in 1987 to 4,376 in 1988, while the number of communications to the SB had increased from 8,000 to 14,000. The toll-free number still was not adequately listed in telephone directories. Self-reporting of malpractice claims, sanctions, criminal convictions, fraud judgments, and discipline in other jurisdictions was a farce. But Fellmeth praised the use of letters of

---

77. Gert K. Hirschberg, *The State Bar Has Wimped Out on Discipline*, LADJ 6 (Mar. 17, 1989).

78. Keller v. State Bar, 47 Cal. 3d 1152 (1989).

79. Colin Wied, *President's Report*, 9(9) California Lawyer 103 (Sept. 1989).

warning (instead of admonitions) and agreements in lieu of discipline (ALD), a form of diversion for substance abuse. OI was issuing nearly twice as many Statements of the Case (SOCs). The dues increase had allowed the Bar to increase disciplinary personnel from 381 to 494.[80] Investigator workload fell from 180 to between 40 and 50 and the OI backlog from 4,000 to fewer than 700. Formal discipline in 1988 was twice the previous seven-year average. That 60 to 75 percent of respondents had other pending complaints suggested that a "hard core" of 1,000 to 2,000 lawyers were responsible for "an extraordinary proportion" of consumer complaints.[81] The Bar responded by creating a "Repeaters' Task Force," which "identified just over 50 attorneys responsible for 570 currently open matters." By January 1990, the OI had further reduced its backlog to 352 "in the face of an extraordinary increase in the number of new cases filed by a more active public" and without "dumping" cases. Cases classified as complaints and those submitted for formal discipline both had tripled. Median case age had declined to eight months, its lowest level in ten years. The twenty-nine interim suspensions were several times the previous number. Whereas only 10 percent of investigated cases used to lead to discipline, 20 percent now led to informal and 30 to 40 percent to formal discipline.[82]

In February 1990, SB President Alan I. Rothenberg held a press conference in the state Capitol to present the Bar's first annual report on "a reformed, revitalized and rebuilt system that I believe will set new standards in professional discipline" and "serve as a model for all professions and businesses in this country." He praised members for having "footed the bill—more than $100 million over the past three years—to improve their discipline system." Senator Presley agreed that "we're now doing a reasonably good job." Assemblymember Nolan concurred that "the bar has put in place an effective system."[83] But not all lawyers were convinced.[84] A San Francisco lawyer waged an unsuccessful BoG campaign based on dissatisfaction with increased dues, which was not "worth the output." "We are not going to appreciably affect the discipline problem . . . by simply adding 50 disbarments a year." A lawyer who had quit the OTC found "the emphasis on numbers . . . very distressing." Another defector said the OI "were more concerned with moving numbers than with properly preparing cases to prosecute at trial." Fellmeth conceded that "in the frenzy to reduce the backlog, there very likely were cases that weren't adequately investigated." But defense

80. Fellmeth (1989a: 1, 13–14, 20, 24–25, 44–45, 49, 59–61).

81. Fellmeth (1989b: 2, 13–17, 19, 51, 67).

82. Fellmeth (1990a: 1–3, 7, 19, 22, 27–28, 57, 61–6, 66–69, 72–73, 75–76).

83. State Bar of California (1990b: 3, 5, 15, 20); *Rothenberg, Legislators Praise California Lawyers for Revitalization of Discipline System,* 10(4) CALIFORNIA LAWYER 65 (Apr. 1990).

84. Michael J. Hall and Clyde Leland, *The State Bar Court One Year Later: Is it working and is it worth the cost?* 10(12) CALIFORNIA LAWYER 30 (Dec. 1990).

lawyers praised the SBC for consistency and striking "a good balance between sterner discipline and fairness."

In June 1990, the U.S. Supreme Court unanimously reversed *Keller*.[85] Justice Rehnquist began by listing some of the issues on which the Conference had taken numerous political positions to which the plaintiffs had objected. These included mandatory polygraph tests for government employees; armor-piercing handgun ammunition; standing to sue for air pollution; the display of drug paraphernalia for sale to minors; individualized education programs for special needs students; gift-tax exemptions for the costs of education and medical care; life imprisonment without parole for minors tried as adults and convicted of murder; voter approval for low rent housing; guest worker programs; the constitutionality of a victim's bill of rights; a nuclear weapons freeze; and limitations on federal court jurisdiction over abortion, school prayer, and school busing. The Court followed its 1997 decision limiting the use of dues from nonunion public employees in agency shops to support political and ideological causes unrelated to collective bargaining,[86] finding that the State Bar was much more like a trade union than a government agency. Although the line between permitted comment on regulation of the legal profession and "activities having political or ideological coloration which are not reasonably related to the advancement of such goals" was "not always easy to discern," gun control and a nuclear weapons freeze were "clear[ly]" at the "extreme ends of the spectrum."

President Rothenberg spun the decision as "a ringing affirmation of the constitutionality of the unified bar and its important relation in the administration of justice." "Since the vast majority of all State Bar funds are in fact dedicated and used for" permissible purposes, "in my view this decision will not affect the bulk of our activity." The president of the conservative Pacific Legal Foundation (PLF), which represented the plaintiffs, agreed that "bifurcation was never discussed . . .." And a member of the PLF board of trustees declared: "It would be terrible if the bar were dismantled because of the suit."[87]

Gert Hirschberg used the first anniversary of the reforms to declare that "The New State Bar Court Has Become a Monster."[88] "The new system is a catastrophe and the good lawyers of California have been irreparably damaged." "The immediate past leadership of the State Bar has greatly—very greatly—increased our Bar dues to satisfy the insatiable appetite of the new disciplinary system." He described "a recent case in which my client committed the unforgivably serious,

85. Keller v. State Bar, 491 U.S. 1 (1990).

86. Abood v. Detroit Board of Education, 431 U.S. 209 (1977).

87. *The Keller Decision: U.S. Supreme Court Upholds Concept of Unified Bar,* 10(8) California Lawyer 67 (Aug. 1990); James Evans, *Behind the Keller Case,* 10(5) California Lawyer 35 (May 1990).

88. Gert K. Hirschberg, *The New State Bar Court Has Become a Monster,* LADJ 7 (Oct. 24, 1990).

heinous offense of not returning one or two phone calls." "[T]he matter was eventually dismissed because it turns out that the complaining witness was even more irresponsible than he claimed the respondent attorney to be." "A certain number of investigators, armed with the power of subpoenaing trust accounts, not only use their power indiscriminately, but wield their authority as a threat to the attorneys they contact." "Much attorney misconduct was created by the U.S. Supreme Court when it legitimized lawyer advertising."

Fellmeth's last three reports between September 1990 and September 1991 were generally positive. Client calls were leveling off. Warning letters had removed hundreds of cases from OI, and settlement conferences before and after NTSCs resolved 60 to 65 percent of cases. The Bar was using information on NSF checks and criminal charges and random trust account audits to reduce attorney theft.[89] But the bottlenecks had shifted from OI to the charging stage. And "the vast majority of consumer complaints directed to us now concern the delays and unresponsiveness of the Complainants Grievance Panel." A 1990 letter to all judges from Chief Justice George produced three or four calls a week about attorney misconduct. The entire process had speeded up: seven to nine months from NTSC to decision and another 219 days to the end of an appeal. Fellmeth called the Supreme Court's decision to make Review Department rulings final a "vote of confidence manifested beyond rhetorical support."[90] His final report noted that even though the toll-free number still was not listed in most directories, it received 70,000 calls a year.[91] "Most important, the backlog is gone," and not through "summary closure of cases." But "the elimination of the OI backlog created a backlog in OT as a 'bubble' of cases has moved through the system over the past four years. The State Bar Court is now receiving the full brunt of this bubble," an expected 1,800 cases in 1991, forcing it to depend on pro tem judges. The magnitude of the change reflected the "inadequacy of the Bar's discipline system in January 1987."

But the real test was the "impact on the profession," which remained seriously deficient in the two areas most critical to regulatory purpose: "the personal dishonesty and incompetency [*sic*] of large numbers of licensees . . .." "The measures undertaken by the Bar over the past four years to address the incompetence problem have been well-intentioned but are grossly inadequate . . .. The failure of the Bar to establish overall standards of personal honesty is similarly stark." Fellmeth had fundamental doubts about self-regulation: "Political reality makes it difficult for the Bar's governors or its electorate . . . to burden themselves substantially for the benefit of a larger population or purpose." His own survey of client complaints identified the most common (in descending order): untruthfulness, abandonment, keeping unearned money, not returning calls,

89. Fellmeth (1990b: 2, 4–5, 7, 23, 29–30, 53–55, 71, 95).

90. Fellmeth (1991a: 21–22, 25–26, 31–33, 35, 48, 62, 68–75, 78–80, 98).

91. Fellmeth (1991b: 21–22, 28–31, 41–42, 45, 47, 52–53, 56, 61, 63, 67, 69, 94, 119).

failing to investigate, and overcharging. Listening to the toll-free number for two days had been a "deeply troubling" experience. Several callers had "spent half a day looking" for the number, and half still encountered a busy signal. Because so many did not return complaint forms, "the bar should consider capturing oral complaints into its pattern detection system." The State Bar

> must understand that the disrepute of what should be a proud profession is not the product of media bias, and is not curable through public relations campaigns . . . it is the cumulative impact of thousands upon thousands of these experiences, endured and then shared by word of mouth.

Perhaps regretting some of his earlier praise, Fellmeth told the *Los Angeles Times* that "the State Bar is prone to excessive spates of self-congratulation." It was

> regrettably likely to focus on the deserved acknowledgment of progress to dampen the equally important need for further reform. In point of fact, in terms of bottom-line performance by attorneys, we are still in a state of crisis.

Indeed, SB President John M. Seitman declared that Fellmeth "has now confirmed that the State Bar's turnaround has been truly unique, and that we today have the finest attorney discipline system in the nation." Not all his constituents agreed. One called the disciplinary system "a behemoth that consumes 75 percent of the bar's annual budget" and quoted an even angrier colleague, who denounced the SB as a home for "self-regarding power-mongering, duplicitous punks with ethical standards far beneath those of the lawyers they regularly pillory."[92]

Establishment figures also were critical, if in more measured tones. The ABA Commission on Evaluation of Disciplinary Enforcement (created in February 1989 and chaired by Robert B. McKay until his death in 1990) submitted a draft report in 1991, which was adopted by the ABA House of Delegates the following year.[93] Although it found "revolutionary changes" since the Clark Report twenty years earlier, "times . . . have changed." "The existing system . . . is narrowly focused on violations of professional ethics" and did not address "complaints that the lawyer's service was overpriced or unreasonably slow" or "incompetence or negligence except where the conduct was egregious or repeated" or situations in which "the lawyer promised services that were not performed or billed for services that were not authorized." "Some jurisdictions dismiss up to ninety percent

---

92. Philip Hager, *State Bar Steps Up Disciplining of Lawyers,* Los Angeles Times A25 (Sept. 21, 1991); Michael J. Hall, *Gotcha! The care and feeding of the state's disciplinary watchdog,* 12(8) California Lawyer 44 (Aug. 1992).

93. ABA Commission on Evaluation of Disciplinary Enforcement (1992: xi–xx, 14, 33, 43, 48–50, 75).

of all complaints," many of which "state legitimate grounds for client dissatisfaction." "Complainants should be permitted a reasonable opportunity to rebut" the respondent's defense and be "notified in writing when the complaint has been dismissed" with "a concise recitation of the specific facts and reasoning upon which the decision to dismiss was made." "The disciplinary system also does nothing to improve the inadequate legal or office management skills that cause many of these complaints." "Every year, millions of dollars of clients' money are stolen by a relatively few lawyers. Yet, most disciplinary systems lack authority to take basic preventive measures such as auditing trust account records or monitoring trust account overdrafts." Unless these deficiencies were remedied, "the public may remove the authority of the judiciary to regulate lawyers." Because "control of the lawyer discipline system by elected officials of bar associations . . . creates an appearance of conflicts of interest and of impropriety," "the state high court should control the disciplinary process *exclusively*."

SB President Vogel called the report an endorsement of California's disciplinary system. "Virtually all of the recommendations contained in the report already have been implemented . . .." Indeed, when New Jersey commissioned a comparison with California, the latter looked far better. It investigated a higher proportion of its lawyers (6.6 versus 2.2 percent), imposed discipline on more (0.5 versus 0.1 percent), and concluded the vast majority of simple cases in less time (16 months versus 666 days).[94]

But these figures also could justify criticism of both states. And in December 1993, SB President Margaret M. Morrow appointed the Discipline Evaluation Committee (DEC) chaired by Judge Arthur Alarcon (who had recently taken senior status on the Ninth Circuit) to report on the system's cost effectiveness and fairness in order "to ensure consumer protection and fair process for attorneys." Its August 1994 report found that the Bar's response to the crisis exposed by the *Examiner* was "A Success Story—The Backlog Eliminated—The Delay Reduced."[95] Nevertheless, it suggested numerous changes. Because the Complainants Grievance Panel "raises false expectations" but "recommended discipline in only one percent of cases," it should be replaced with random audits of rejected complaints by the Office of Consumer Advocate. The State Bar should "respond in writing to all written complaints and provide complainant a chance to rebut the respondent's story before the case is closed." Disagreeing with Fellmeth, the DEC supported a pilot SB program "to turn over certain discipline related matters to the local bars." It also recommended reversing Kroeker by placing investigators under OTC supervision (although "total verticalization" was not possible). Moreover, attendance at Ethics School should be part of all

94. *State Bar's Discipline System Mirrors Most Recommendations in ABA Commission Report*, 11(7) CALIFORNIA LAWYER 92 (July 1991); Gillers (1993: 26–27, 32–33).

95. State Bar of California Discipline Evaluation Committee (1994: 16, 24–36, 38–44, 47–48, 50–68); California Legislative Analyst's Office (1991).

formal discipline since only 9 percent of its graduates were recidivists, compared with 62 percent of all respondents. Summary and permanent disbarment should be expanded. The system should also investigate billing fraud and publish the names of firms whose attorneys were disciplined.

Making "reducing the cost of the discipline system . . . a priority" because of the lawyers' "widespread perception" that it "is too high," the report proposed reducing Bar dues from $578 to $450 in 1995 and $399 in 1996. The "first place to look for overstaffing" was "in the supervisory and management ranks," which supervised only 2.7 employees, compared with 7 in other courts. SBC judges also had too many legal and lay assistants. Travel costs were too high, perhaps because at least one employee commuted from San Francisco to Los Angeles at State Bar expense. In a "classic example of Parkinson's Law, the SBC has engaged in practices to make its work expand to occupy the ample time available for its completion." Caseloads were "significantly lower" than in federal and state trial courts despite the fact that SBC judges "specialize in one area of the law." The number of judges should be reduced from six to four and the seventh position not filled. Because of their low caseload, hearing judges "spend one-half of their time writing scholarly twenty-page opinions in every case before them, including default matters." They should limit opinions to the 11 percent of cases appealed and dispense with evidentiary hearings in the 20 percent of cases in which the respondent defaulted (since defaulters should lose their right to appeal). Judges should play an active role in settlement to achieve the higher rates found in other courts. The Review Department's low caseload—approximately forty a year—did not justify three judges and their support staff. (A 1991 review by the Legislative Analyst's Office had reached the same conclusion.) The department should not review the entire record *de novo*. Having published more than a hundred opinions, it should publish more only if the case established, altered, modified, or clarified a rule, resolved an apparent legal conflict, made a significant contribution to the legal literature, or involved legal or factual issues of special public interest.

An angry State Bar began its rebuttal by noting that "none of the committee Members . . . ever observed a SBC proceeding."[96] The SBC had underspent its budget by several hundred thousand dollars every year since 1990, reducing staff from 80 to 74 while processing 2.5 times as many cases. The "radical surgery" proposed would "cripple" the SBC to save lawyers only about two dollars a year. A recent 81 percent increase in pending investigations would soon cause "a major spike in court filings." Estimates of judicial workload should take account of the fact that one judge was a layperson, while the presiding judge spent half her time on administration. Hearing judges had increased their average dispositions

96. State Bar of California, State Bar Court (1994: 2–25, 29–30, 37); memorandum from Scott Drexel, Chief Court Counsel (Feb. 9, 1994) in *Id.*

from 100 in 1990 to 190 in 1994, and their settlement rates rose from 17 to 51 percent. Disciplinary cases were more complicated than other civil matters. The SBC maintained that written opinions were legally required; almost half were less than fifteen pages. The publication of Review Department decisions had a prophylactic effect on lawyer behavior, increased public confidence, and encouraged settlement. The Supreme Court required *de novo* review. The judges unanimously believed "it would be impossible for the SBC competently to perform its mandated functions with only four hearing judges statewide." The recommendation that a single manager execute policies set by the Board of Governors was "contrary to the dictates of the key 1988 reforms ensuring separation of powers," as well as the "ABA McKay Commission's recommendations for reducing the role of elected bar officials." The response concluded that the "recommended reductions to the SBC [are] both misguided and dangerous to the continued effectiveness and credibility of the California attorney disciplinary system."

Nevertheless, the Bar made some changes. The Office of Intake "formalized use of directional letters as a viable alternative to discipline," "developed a pilot program to refer matters to [alternative dispute resolution or] ADR programs operated by local bar associations," and expanded other diversion alternatives: ethics and client trust accounting schools, attorney substance abuse programs, a law office management assistance program, ADR camp, civility programs, and agreements in lieu of discipline. The Bar eliminated the OI, subordinating investigators to Office of Chief Trial Counsel (OCTC) attorneys. The Complainants' Grievance Panel was phased out and replaced with a volunteer Discipline Audit Panel reporting to the OCTC.[97] Declaring that "the time has come for the bar to steer away from a numbers-based system which focuses on the speed of completing cases rather than on the severity of disciplinary offenses," Judy Johnson (the new CTC) created "strike teams" focused on insurance fraud, probate abuses, the unauthorized practice of law, uncertified lawyer referral services, worker's compensation abuses, billing and bankruptcy fraud, and capping at major disasters (earthquakes, fires, plane, rail, and bus accidents). Legislation expanded the definition of involuntary inactive status, authorized nolo pleas, and prohibited lawyers from conditioning settlement of malpractice claims on clients withdrawing disciplinary complaints.[98]

In addition to these contradictory pressures for more effective discipline at lower cost, eleven discipline defense lawyers (most of them former SB prosecutors)

---

97. CTC Judy Johnson supported this change, arguing that the DGP cost about $1 million a year and only led to discipline in 1–2 percent of cases, mostly a warning or directional letter.

98. State Bar of California (1995: 1–2, 4, 9; 1996: 3, 21; 1997: 3–5, 12–15); *Bar's chief prosecutor signals new approach to attorney discipline,* CBJ 1 (Jan. 1995).

wrote the president and BoG charging "highly questionable" prosecutorial conduct.[99] They objected to "the withholding of evidence which should have been made available through discovery and also to the withholding of exculpatory evidence favorable to the accused, possible tampering with witnesses, [and] the improper leaking of confidential information to third parties." During the recent disciplinary proceeding against palimony progenitor Marvin Mitchelson, a "deeply disturbed" Judge Langhauser recommended dismissal because of prosecutorial overcharging and failure to comply with discovery requests, the first time that had ever happened. Declaring that the OTC "shoot with a shotgun...-they're not officers of the court. They're just interested in winning," Ted Cohen (one of the letter's signatories) urged the BoG to appoint a special prosecutor. SB President John Seitman called this unnecessary. "We just went through about three years of a discipline monitor. Generally, he made a lot of very laudatory comments about the system." At the end of 1992, four defense lawyers appeared at the SB's annual hearing on discipline to press their case.[100]

Others had personal reasons to resent the disciplinary system. In March 1993, Assembly Speaker Willie Brown, Jr., introduced AB 1544 to increase knowingly filing a false complaint from a misdemeanor to a felony and extend the statute of limitations from one year (which made it almost impossible to charge) to three.[101] Brown, who unsuccessfully advocated this before, had been investigated twice, and though no charges were filed the allegations became public. Defense lawyer Ellen Tabachnick (who had helped draft the bill) said it "will cause people filing vindictive complaints to think twice." The bill also would preclude future charges following a decision not to charge (absent new evidence), deny the Bar costs, and make it liable for defense costs if prosecutors failed to secure a penalty more severe than what the respondent had accepted, exclude doctors from complaining about unpaid medical liens, mandate settlement conferences before the filing of charges, and require the OTC to produce exculpatory evidence. Fellmeth warned that these changes would "debilitate the discipline system severely and are irresponsible." "You have a consumer already terrified and who has to stand up against someone who is familiar with the legal system. And the first thing you tell them is, '[I]f what you're saying here is proved wrong, you're going to jail.'" "Prosecutors may have a very good reason for seeking disbarment. This may deter them from doing so." The *San Diego Union-Tribune* editorialized against this Lawyer Protection Act, which would "nullify many of the improvements the

99. William Vogeler, *State Bar Asked To Investigate Discipline Staff,* LADJ 1 (Aug. 26, 1992). The signatories were Ted Cohen, David Clare, Diane L. Karpman, Ken Kocourek, Tom Low, Arthur Margolis, Susan Margolis, R. Gerald Markle, Ellen A. Pansky, Michael J. Rochford, and Erica Tabachnick.

100. Jean Guccione, *Lawyers Join Consumers in Attack On Discipline System, Profession,* LADJ 1 (Dec. 3, 1992).

101. Tom Dressler, *Bill by Brown Would Modify Bar Discipline,* LADJ 1 (Mar. 9, 1993).

reforms have produced."[102] The perjury threat "would have a chilling effect on many clients . . .." The newspaper blamed the bill on "howls of protest from a few lawyers" angered by the 300 and 500 percent increases in disbarments and suspensions. But at the Italian American Lawyers Association, Willie Brown implicitly threatened to block the dues bill (which he was carrying) if the Bar did not accept his discipline bill.[103] A few days later, just before the Senate Judiciary Committee was to take up the latter, Brown defended the perjury threat: "those who criticize it are really bordering on being the lynch mob . . . of a particular group."[104]

It was not just celebrities who attacked the system. Richard Gayer, a gay rights sole practitioner, filed a federal civil rights action alleging that State Bar discipline discriminated against sole practitioners and its use of newspaper stories in investigations violated the First Amendment.[105] The bar was investigating reports that Gayer entered a San Francisco apartment through a window during a 1989 probate dispute between an executor and the decedent's former roommate. Gayer was ordered to pay the defendant in the probate case over $5,000. "My main motivation for filing the lawsuit is the clipping service. I think it is outrageous. They must get enough complaints as it is." "When somebody writes a letter, they go out and find the allegations . . . why go digging? They had to do a lot of research to even find the case." "There has to be an ulterior motive. Maybe it's as simple as having something for their bloated bureaucracy to do."

If the popular press generally called for more discipline, professional journals sometimes sided with disciplined lawyers. A series of five lead articles in the *Los Angeles Daily Journal* quoted a complaint by an "outspoken consumer advocate" that SB prosecutors "go after the easy fish," which was seconded by former CTC Lily Barry: "the bar goes too far with minor discipline. They see their mission as being out to get the lawyers."[106] Defense lawyers who had signed the letter above agreed: "a great deal of resources [are] being spent on low-level cases" (Ellen A. Pansky); "investigators . . . don't know the law they are supposed to enforce" and were "heavy-handed" (David A. Clare); "you have got some Dirty Harrys there" (Arthur L. Margolis); and "important and complicated cases get pushed to the back of the file cabinet while the number-crunchers push easier cases that generate better statistics" (Jerome Fishkin). Roberta M. Yang, director of trials, acknowledged that trust account violations "are our bread and butter" and investigators

---

102. *Kill the "Lawyer Protection Act,"* San Diego-Union Tribune, reproduced in LADJ 6 (Apr. 23. 1993)

103. Susan McRae, *Brown to State Bar: I'm Ready for Battle,* LADJ 2 (Aug. 20, 1993).

104. *Speaker Assails State Bar on Discipline,* LADJ 3 (Aug. 25, 1993).

105. Michael J. Hall and Jessica Guynn, *S.F. Lawyer Alleges Bias in Bar Discipline,* LADJ 3 (June 4, 1993). Gayer v. State Bar, N.D.Ca C93-2085.

106. Jean Guccione and Michael J. Hall, *Is Too Much Evidence Given to Minor Violations?* LADJ 1 (July 12, 1994). The first article on July 11 dealt with intake.

got frozen turkeys for clearing their caseloads at the end of the year. But though complaints had increased greatly, charges were still close to their 1989 level because the system was at capacity, and about half of them settled.

The third article questioned the system's cost, repeating criticisms that the three Review Department judges wrote just forty opinions a year and hearing judge opinions did not become case law.[107] Judge David S. Ewsley replied: "If I could say, "Guilty," and check a box, I would do it," but it would lead to more appeals. The court spent had spent $214,851 on temporary judges in 1992 (at $350 per day) and budgeted $72,756 for 1994. A third of their decisions were appealed, compared with 11 percent of those by the six full-time judges. Defense lawyer Theodore Cohen commented: "You would think your death penalty cases—which is what disbarment is equivalent to in this system—would be handled by State Bar Court judges." Full evidentiary hearings were held for the one in five respondents who defaulted but could still appeal. Defense lawyers who had severely criticized prosecutors lavished praise on the SBC: "almost perfect compared to the old system" (Ellen Pansky); "an oasis in the discipline system. Even when we lose, we feel we have been heard" (Arthur Margolis). But prosecutors felt that the court, which dismissed more than a quarter of the cases heard in 1993, was "too lenient" toward lawyers and generally hostile to the OTC. In response to these criticisms, Presiding Judge Lise A. Pearlman decided that the other two Review Department judges would begin working just 60 percent of the time.

Soon after the Supreme Court proposed that each SBC judge would compete with two others for reappointment, SBC Presiding Judge Lise Pearlman and four of the eight others were not reappointed, to the surprise and dismay of prosecutors, defense counsel, and former judges. Although some attributed the action to criticisms of excessive lenience, Pearlman said the Applicant Evaluation and Nomination Committee had been interested only in her relations with the BoG. One committee member had asked, "why I should be recommended for reappointment if I couldn't 'get along' with the board." Pearlman had resisted the DEC proposal to strip her of control over staff, which "has severe implications for the independence of the court." Several months earlier, Towery (CAD chair and president-elect) had criticized Pearlman for failing to offer a staff reduction plan in response to the DEC report. A DEC member criticized her testimony as "a defense of the status quo." Pearlman called the remark "regrettable," complaining that her court had been "left out of the loop recently." Eight months after being removed, Pearlman said she initially had been "highly praised by bar leaders for establishing the court's credibility as an independent entity," but in the last two years, "Bar leaders began giving administrative orders to court staff,

---

107. Jean Guccione and Michael J. Hall, *State Bar Court Lavish, Wasteful, Critics Claim*, LADJ 1 (July 13, 1994).

bypassing me and the State Bar Court Executive Committee. . . ." She was "vilified by new board members for defending the very same degree of independence with which the court had started." California was "moving in the opposite direction" from the 1991 ABA committee recommendations.[108]

V. BACKLASH

When Willie Brown introduced a bill in 1992 to abolish the State Bar, President John Seitman persuaded him to withdraw it by agreeing to establish a Commission on the Future of the Legal Profession (a majority of whose thirty members would be appointed by his successor and the rest by Governor Pete Wilson and legislative leaders). Its 1995 report recommended shifting control of the SBC (14–6) but not the entire discipline system (10–11) to the Supreme Court (even though Chief Justice Lucas resisted); it favored keeping the unified bar with its current functions (13–8), including admissions and discipline (17–2), and opposed a voluntary bar to handle all other functions (12–6). A contemporaneous poll of 500 lawyers found that large majorities believed that the bar should remain mandatory (74 percent) and continue to discipline (76 percent) and license lawyers (79 percent). The BoG responded by affirming the status quo over the dissent of two public members, one of whom (Wendy Borcherdt) objected: "we seem to err on the side of the tainted attorney . . . .I urge you to consider public protection and not always protecting your own."[109]

But politicians continued to use the Bar as a whipping boy. Contemporaneously with the commission report, state Senator Quentin L. Kopp (I-San Francisco) introduced SB 60 to reduce bar dues by $100 and require the Bar to conduct yet another plebiscite on its mandatory status. SB President Don Fischbach protested that the reduction would cripple Bar programs. Dues had not been increased since 1991; even the DEC report recommended only a $79 cut over two years. The Bar had responded to that report by cutting expenditures by $700,000, and a budget review ordered by Fischbach had saved another 5 percent, avoiding a fee increase. A month later Willie Brown. introduced AB 1435 to freeze dues

---

108. Michael J. Hall, *S.F. Bar Votes to Oppose Discipline Plan,* LADJ 3 (Jan. 13. 1995); Nancy McCarthy, *Tensions rise in discipline overhaul,* CBJ 4 (Mar. 1995); *Bar committee votes to slash 13 positions from the State Bar Court,* CBJ 1 (May 1995); Nancy McCarthy, *Presiding judge, 4 others bounced from bar court,* CBJ 1 (Aug. 1995); Nancy McCarthy, *Five new judges prepare to join bar court; job cuts seen by end of year,* CBJ 1 (Sept. 1995); Lise A. Pearlman, *Declare Independence,* 16 CALIFORNIA LAWYER 27 (Apr. 1996). Pearlman had been the subject of a glowing profile at the time of her appointment. Michael J. Hall, *Profile: Lise Pearlman,* LADJ 1 (June 26, 1989).

109. *Lucas: 'No' to bar court control,* CBJ 5 (1.95); Patricia Phillips, "Commission charts future of bar," CBJ 11 (Jan 1995); *Board votes to keep bar mandatory,* CBJ 1 (Sept. 1995); Nancy McCarthy, *Where does the bar go from here?* CBJ 1 (July 19.96).

for two years, and state Senator Nicholas Petris (D-Oakland) introduced SB 596 to limit the Bar's power to admissions and discipline. After Brown's bill easily passed the assembly, Kopp dropped his dues cut but retained the plebiscite and added an annual budget audit. Fischbach objected that the Bar had been audited 71 times since 1986 at a cost of $3 million. Although "we're not afraid of an audit," the plebiscite needed "to let attorneys know they will continue to be regulated and they'll have to pay for that regulation." President-elect James Towery saw no "groundswell of requests from our rank-and-file that the State Bar go through an extraordinary effort." But Governor Wilson signed Kopp's bill. Although the State Bar did not directly urge a *no* vote, it organized a volunteer Committee to Save the Unified Bar, operating through county committees, which was opposed by Attorneys for a Voluntary Bar. Although Towery initially proposed to reduce bar dues $20 (for the first time ever), he soon withdrew this pledge.[110]

Although the California District Attorneys Association had originally backed Kopp's bill to abolish the State Bar, it remained neutral on the plebiscite. Towery asked a meeting of 200 district attorneys (DAs) whether "we want to give up control of our profession . . . ethical standards, discipline and budget and transfer it to some unnamed state agency?" Peter Keane, a former Bar Governor who now led the Lawyers Committee for a Yes Vote, responded that "the State Bar is a sham, a shell game, one large fraud. It exists for the perpetuation of the officers at the top who run an enormous fiefdom." He claimed that $139 of dues went to administration, "$19 more than you would pay to belong to the New Jersey bar." If discipline were transferred to the state "the public would see an entity at arm's length from the bar association and we'd have a much better reputation." Because of limitations imposed in the wake of *Keller*, "we do not have a statewide association to advocate for us as a profession." When a DA called the State Bar irrelevant, Towery boasted that it had "successfully resisted legislative proposals for recertification by [*sic*—read "of"] lawyers, random audits of lawyers' bank accounts, and expanded roles for unsupervised paralegals." The California Judges Association urged a *no* vote. Governor Wilson leaned toward a *yes* vote, accusing trial lawyers of frivolous strike suits and applauding *Keller*'s limitation on advocacy. But he conceded that "the disciplinary side is a serious problem." "I would

110. *Fischbach says proposal to slash dues would devastate bar programs*, CBJ 1 (Feb. 1995); *Speaker Brown introduces measure to freeze bar dues at $478*, CBJ 1 (Mar. 1995); *Key bills affecting the state bar and lawyers advance in Sacramento*, CBJ 1 (June 1995); *Bar President-elect James Towery opposes plebiscite on State Bar*, CBJ 1 (Aug. 1995); Nancy McCarthy, *Forces mobilize to decide bar's fate*, CBJ 17 (Dec. 1995); James Towery, *Ask the President: Towery works toward dues decrease*, CBJ 5 (Dec. 1995); *Opinion: Budget: Courage or folly?* CBJ 8 (Jan. 1996).

like to see something that is effective but doesn't require the creation of a new state agency."[111]

The Bar was defended by more than 70 local and specialty organizations, the California Public Defenders Association, the 17 Section Chairs, and the Conference of Delegates. Towery insisted that "legislative control of our profession . . . is not a scare tactic." Keane asserted that "the sole reason for the comparatively high cost of dues in California is wanton inefficiency and gross mismanagement of State Bar finances by its unchecked bureaucracy." The DEC had "found a pattern of waste, overspending, lack of economy of scale and staff indifference to the abuses which were so appalling that . . . these problems could only be forced to be redressed by measures such as an immediate reduction of $100 in every lawyer's dues." The State Bar was "a timid, bloodless entity which is constantly looking over its shoulder in terror at the legislature." Patricia Phillips warned that *yes* vote supporters included minority members of the Futures Commission (which she had chaired), who wanted "a bar exam for every lawyer every five years," random audits of law office accounts, and mandatory malpractice insurance and pro bono. But Peter Appleton (past Beverly Hills Bar Association president, former Los Angeles County Bar Association trustee, and a member of the Conference of Delegates executive committee) urged a *yes* vote. The BoG "do not represent lawyers and they do not take positions on behalf of lawyers." "Lack of financial accountability is a primary reason why we have the most expensive bar dues in the country," caused by "our 'Cadillac' discipline system. Why must we pay for the hotline the bar continues to urge clients to use against lawyers," a "legislatively driven and law professor-designed discipline system" that "last year generated 128,063 calls."[112]

Three days before the ballots went out, the legislatively mandated audit praised the discipline system for making changes that increased its "efficiency, effectiveness and reliability" but believed the Bar could reduce dues by recovering costs from disciplined attorneys and charging for voluntary programs. Towery said "no fair reading of this report can support abolishing the bar,"

111. *Board backs'96 budget, appoints new NJE chair,* CBJ 28 (Jan. 1996); Nancy McCarthy, *Towery, Keane debate bar's future,* CBJ 17 (Feb. 1996); Nancy McCarthy, *Disciplining errant lawyers is the bar's biggest task,* CBJ 1 (Mar. 1996); "CJA supports bar," CBJ 6 (Mar. 1996); James Towery, *Ask the President: The plebiscite: Why should I care?* CBJ 7 (Mar. 1996); Dean Kinley, *The Governor reflects on law and the legal profession,* CBJ 1 (Apr. 1996).

112. *Update: Towery, Keane tapped to write arguments for/against SB 60,* CBJ 1 (Apr. 1996); James Towery, *Ask the President: Scare tactics, or real loss of control?* CBJ 12 (Apr. 1996); Peter G. Keane, *Longtime bar opponent says it's time for lawyers to make history by closing down the mandatory bar,* CBJ 16 (Apr. 1996); Patricia Phillips, *Veteran bar proponent says abolition would lead to lawyers having no hand in governing themselves,* CBJ 17 (Apr. 1996); Colin W. Wied, *Opinion: Sever the ties that bind,* CBJ 13 (May 1996); Peter M. Appleton, *For lawyers in California, the time is here to decide between the status quo or taking risks to do better,* CBJ 14 (May 1996).

adding that one hundred bar groups recommended a *no* vote. When close to half of members who returned ballots voted *no*, Towery claimed "decisive support for an independent profession," and President-elect Thomas Stolpman said it had "validate[d] the legal profession." Kopp retorted that "the State Bar had better seize the opportunity to improve its performance" and threatened a bill to reduce dues $40 the following year. "I think that the State Bar now knows that at least 35 percent is dissatisfied and would like an end to forced conscription." Keane was even more belligerent: "The results show 70 percent of lawyers either voted against the bar or felt it was so out of it it wasn't worth the powder to blow it up." "This was just a dress rehearsal. If the bar thinks it was the final scene, they're kidding themselves."[113]

Senator Bill Lockyer, who had voted *no*, felt that compliance with *Keller* had softened legislative criticism of the Bar: "It doesn't seem as intensely partisan as it used to be." But he spoke too soon. When President Stolpman defended a $900,000 lobbying contract with Mel Assagai, Vice President Peter Kaye (a public member appointed by Wilson) wondered out loud "if the State Bar is too important an organization to be left in the hands of lawyers." He called the contract "lobbygate . . . conceived in darkness, nurtured in secret, authorized behind closed doors and executed without discussion or disclosure." A $75,000 bonus for successfully negotiating a multiyear dues bill was excised when it was revealed. Wendy Borcherdt (another Wilson appointee) said her fourth year on the Board was "not . . . a happy experience." "From the beginning it was clear that the bar's business was to be run by a small clique of lawyer members" with "disastrous" results.[114]

State Senator John Burton (D-San Francisco) introduced SB 1145 to authorize dues for two years. But before it could be voted, the State Bar supported AB 250, which state Senator Sheila Kuehl (D-Santa Monica) had introduced to raise the medical malpractice nonpecuniary damage cap. The Association for California Tort Reform, which opposed AB 250, asked legislators to reduce dues from $458 to $160 and said the group was "looking at the broader issue of the politicization of the bar." The State Bar responded that

> the original balance struck in 1975 by MICRA had, by 1997, become skewed. The vast majority of the lawyer board members who voted in support of AB 250 represent business interests or public entities. The Board viewed AB 250

113. Nancy McCarthy, *Update: Kopp says he wrote new bill mostly to dispel "untruths,"* CBJ 1 (June 1996); Nancy McCarthy, *Lawyers vote 2 to 1 to keep California's State Bar unified,* CBJ 1 (July 1996); Nancy McCarthy, *Where does the bar go from here?* CBJ 1 (July 1996).

114. *Lockyer supports unified bar, says criticism is diminished,* CBJ 2 (Jan. 1997); Thomas G. Stolpman, *The Bar's president says the new contract will save money as well as retain the skills of its veteran lobbyist,* CBJ 10 (Mar. 1997); Peter F. Kaye, *A leading critic says the contract was negotiated in secret, presented as a fait accompli without a vote,* CBJ 11 (Mar. 1997); Wendy Borcherdt, *Anxious for an unhappy year to end,* CBJ 8 (May 1997).

only as a modest step to restore the balance in certain egregious cases, rather than a statement endorsing the expansion or repeal of MICRA.

When Burton limited the dues bill to one year just before the vote, it passed by the bare minimum (21–13). Assemblymember William Morrow (R-Oceanside), vice-chair of the Judiciary Committee, then proposed a $25 reduction. Three Wilson-appointed Governors (Kaye, Borcherdt, and Jo Ellen Allen) testified in favor of the reduction and claimed that at least two other governors agreed. Allen questioned "whether the Bar exercises its authority to influence the legislature in a prudent manner," citing its position on medical malpractice damage caps, funding for "the highly controversial Legal Services Corporation," and the decision to appeal a Court of Appeal judgment holding mandatory continuing legal education (MCLE) unconstitutional. "As long as membership in the State Bar is mandatory and fees are extracted forcibly, the Board is obligated to avoid as much as possible taking positions which are likely to divide attorneys . . .." But after the Judiciary Committee defeated the reduction (7–7) and passed the one-year dues bill (10–4), the Assembly concurred in September. Morrow and two other legislators had also sued the State Bar in June for violating *Keller*, complaining about State Bar support for four bills (including the medical malpractice damages cap and a gay rights bill). Judge Garland E. Burrell, Jr., dismissed the action in September, holding that the plaintiffs failed to show "they have been forced to make or support politically expressive acts of the State Bar." (The Ninth Circuit affirmed 3–0 two years later.)[115]

Governor Wilson told Wendy Borcherdt he was thinking of vetoing the dues bill. Lunching with her daughter in England several days later, he said "Tell your mom, I'll veto again unless there are some significant changes." California Supreme Court Chief Justice George, Associate Justice Chin, the California Judicial Council, and SB President Marc Adelman (a San Diegan like Wilson) urged the Governor not to do so. But Wilson vetoed the bill on October 11, a day before the deadline. Although he attacked the lobbying contract and supported the $25 dues reduction, he really seemed to be reacting to the dismissal of Morrow's lawsuit. "Last year, a substantial minority of bar members voted to abolish the mandatory bar in favor of a voluntary model embraced in 10 other states." That vote exposed "what might be charitably characterized as an almost chronic disharmony." Some members "believe that the bar cannot function effectively as both a regulatory and disciplinary agency as well as a trade organization." Recent lawsuits "illustrate the long held belief of some members that the bar is partisan . . .." Although "less favored members were vindicated" by

115. Nancy McCarthy, *Burton agrees to amend fee bill to one year, setting dues at $458*, CBJ 1 (June 1997); *$458 fee bill goes to Assembly floor*, CBJ 6 (Aug. 1997); Joe Ellen Allen, *Losers don't forfeit right to dissent*, CBJ 8 (Aug. 1997); Kathleen O. Beitiks, *Federal judge dismisses lawsuit challenging State Bar activities*, CBJ 1 (Oct. 1997).

Keller, the bar had responded "by conducting business as usual while offering a miniscule rebate to those opposed."[116] "[I]n recent months, as disgruntled members have leveled charges that the bar is bloated, arrogant, oblivious, and unresponsive, the bar has promptly done its best to verify each indictment." He cited the $900,000 lobbying contract, which "initially included an illegal $75,000 bonus," and the hiring of a new executive officer for $200,000 plus perks (much more than Wilson was paid). Both the state auditor and the DEC had "found a significant glut in the bar's budget and called for a substantial reduction" in its dues, which were "more than twice the average of the other 49 states." "None of this appears to be of any consequence to the bar, but then the bar's own small army of staff attorneys pays no bar dues at all."

Wilson accused "delegates" at the annual State Bar conference in his San Diego hometown (actually the separate Conference of Delegates) of adopting resolutions "in favor of legalizing same-sex marriages; to prohibit discrimination against transvestites and transsexuals; to reduce penalties for drug dealers; to reduce penalties for repeat child molesters; to thwart the will of voters relative to affirmative action at state law schools."

> The bar has drifted . . . and become lost, its ultimate mission obscured. It is now part magazine publisher, part real estate investor, part travel agent, and part social critic, commingling its responsibilities and revenues in a manner which creates an almost constant appearance of impropriety. It is time for the bar to get back to basics: admissions, discipline, and education standards. I would look with favor upon a bill that required bar members to pay only for functions which were, in fact, a mandatory part of a responsible, cost-efficient regulatory process...to scrupulously heed Thomas Jefferson's admonition that "to compel a man to furnish contributions of money for the propagation of opinions which he disbelieves, is sinful and tyrannical."

The *San Francisco Examiner*, which had exposed lax discipline a decade earlier, now came to the defense of a Bar that "was all but disbarred by a furious attorney," a "lame-duck Republican," who "happens to be the Governor."

> In effect, the state's legal eagles were told to bow to whatever rules are dictated by whoever happens to be Governor. It raises a pertinent question: Why should politicians have this power? . . . lawyers, like members of other professional associations and labor organizations, should be allowed to govern themselves without fear of budgetary swings.

Wilson had timed his response so "as to block for at least three months any attempt at compromise." This "punitive action could have a devastating effect on the orderly conduct of the State Bar's most important functions," including discipline. (Indeed, CTC Judy Johnson warned that "the system will come to a grinding

---

116. Never more than a few dollars.

halt. We're going to have to dump all but the most serious cases and only try the equivalent of homicide.") Across the bay, the *Oakland Tribune* called Wilson's "spiteful veto" "irresponsib[le]." "[S]ince [the plebiscite] failed, it appears the Governor now wants to find another way to kill" the State Bar. "To eliminate a pesky fly that's annoying him, he used a bulldozer." The Bar insisted that its role was "to seek improvements in the administration of justice, and occasionally the issues are political." President Adelman asked Borcherdt and others to seek a compromise with Wilson, but Towery "shudder[ed] to think what the compromise will be." Peter Keane triumphantly declared the Bar dead: "Only a nostalgia for the past or blind intransigence on the part of advocates of a unified bar keeps this organization propped up." Even defenders wondered if it had a future. Former president Fischbach had "to admit the chances" for bifurcation "are much stronger than I ever believed possible before." John McGuckin, Jr., (a former Bar Governor and presidential candidate) thought "we need to face up to the fact that the governor and a significant number of legislators feel the bar has to shed some voluntary functions." But the San Diego County Bar Association president urged members to pay their dues voluntarily; Pillsbury Madison & Sutro became the first large firm to do so. By mid December, 76 firms and corporate law departments and 52 nonprofits and public agencies had followed suit. (When the Bar later offered refunds or credits for voluntary donations, very few lawyers took advantage.)[117]

Senator Kopp introduced SB 1371 on the first legislative day of 1998 to abolish the State Bar and transfer admissions, discipline, minimal MCLE, and the CSF to the Supreme Court. "Let's eliminate lawsuits over that amount of annual dues allocable to political and ideological expenditures, end the 'closed shop' and release California's lawyers from conscription." Nine days later, Assemblymember Robert Hertzberg (D-Van Nuys) introduced AB 1669 as urgency legislation to divide the Bar into mandatory and voluntary units, set dues at $419 for 1998 and $399 for 1999, require bidding on all contracts over $50,000 and an annual independent audit, prohibit the Bar from spending dues on lobbying for legislation unrelated to the profession itself, the regulation of lawyers, or the improvement of legal services; and prohibit funding for the Conference of Delegates or the eighteen practice sections. The purpose of the voluntary bar was "to insure responsibility over advocacy." He was under pressure to cut dues further because "there's no constituency out there who wants to

117. Kathleen O. Beitiks, *Wilson vetoes fee bill; bar moves to secure funding,* CBJ 1 (Nov. 1997); Nancy McCarthy, *The question looms again: Will California's bar remain unified? Ibid.*; Kathleen O. Beitiks, *Bar will assess $77 fee, ask members to pay the remainder voluntarily, Ibid.*; *Bulldozing a Pesky Fly,* Oakland Tribune (Nov. 11, 1997), reprinted in SBJ 8 (Dec. 97); San Francisco Examiner (Oct. 16, 1997); *77 Law Firms, Corporate Legal Departments Pledge to Pay Voluntary Dues,* CBJ 1 (Jan. 1998); *Generosity of members adds up to donation of $11 million,* CBJ 1 (5.00).

support lawyers." There also were "problems with Republicans on IOLTA [Interest on Lawyers' Trust Accounts]." The governor's office was saying "Let's have lawyers regulated and look like other professions." The BoG split on AB 1669 (10–4 with 4 abstentions). Based on "reading countless letters from members" and "talking to attorneys and consumers statewide," Adelman had found "very few complaints focused on the workings of the discipline system." The emphasis was on the bar's political positions and the dues level.[118]

Morrow introduced a third bill, AB 1798, to cut dues to $317 ($272 in 1999) and limit expenditures to admissions and discipline. The Bar would no longer be able to certify lawyer referral services, mandate CLE, operate the CSF, evaluate judicial nominees, or use IOLTA to fund legal services. He praised Wilson's "bold step"; "there is too much opportunity for abuse when the State Bar takes political positions on matters its members oppose." The BoG would be subject to the Brown Act (mandating open meetings) and could take positions only after polling the entire membership. Hertzberg was willing to compromise on everything but IOLTA. President Adelman predicted optimistically that if Morrow "starts to take away things that serve the public, I think he'll start to lose allies." The Bar's chief financial officer said it would have to close its doors in May. The Bar's executive director warned that "we couldn't run the discipline system on [$272] in'88, so certainly we can't run it today on less."[119]

Hertzberg dropped his bill's urgency status (which would let it pass by a simple majority but not take effect until 1999) and gained the support of the *Los Angeles Times*, *San Francisco Chronicle*, and *San Jose Mercury News*. Morrow tried (unsuccessfully) to amend Hertzberg's bill to "plug a giant loophole that allows the State Bar to lobby." The CSF created "a whole new class of victims by penalizing all good lawyers." MCLE was a "joke that should be done away with." The Bar was "howling" at dues cuts "like the boy who cried wolf." Although the Bar negotiated with the Association for California Tort Reform about lobbying activities, Hertzberg balked: "they wanted . . . far too much." But the Joint Legislative Audit Committee approved Kopp's request for an audit of the Bar's admissions operations, which he claimed had generated a $2.2 million reserve.[120]

---

118. Kathleen O. Beitikis, *Bills vie to restructure bar,* CBJ 1 (Feb. 1998); Hertzberg, *The option is, "Fix it, or lose it,"* CBJ 1 (Feb. 1998); Marc Adelman, *Rebuilding the State Bar,* CBJ 8 (Feb. 1998); Sen. Quentin Kopp, *Time to end conscription,* CBJ 9 (Feb. 1998).

119. Kathleen O. Beitiks, *Bar battles against time,* CBJ 1 (Mar. 1998); Nancy McCarthy, *Whittling away ultimately may harm public,* CBJ 1 (Mar. 1998); Assemblymember Bill Morrow, *Time for meaningful change,* CBJ 8 (Mar. 1998).

120. Nancy McCarthy, *Bill inches to lawmakers,* CBJ 1 (Apr. 1998); Nancy McCarthy, *Kopp wins audit of admissions,* CBJ 1 (Apr. 1998); *Serving the Public Interest,* Los Angeles Times (Mar. 2, 1998); *Getting Closer to the cliff's edge,* San Jose Mercury News (Mar. 26, 1998); *The State Bar and its leaders deserve another chance,* San Francisco Chronicle (Mar. 25. 1998).

Without the dues bill, the Bar was authorized to collect only $27 for discipline. In April, it laid off nearly 500 employees and rejected any new cases. Left with only three or four of its 65 investigators, the Bar halted all investigations. CTC Judy Johnson warned complainants to "expect years of delay." She would prioritize those of the 1,400 pending matters most likely to lead to suspension or disbarment. All monitoring of the thousand probationers would cease. "It's like the sheriff will have left town on a Saturday night when he knows the cowboys are coming in." Although the SBC had set 121 cases for trial between April 1 and June 26, director Scott Drexel said the other 600 pending cases would be delayed because he had to cut his staff from 52 to 7; the 8 judges agreed to share the salary of 3 positions. The Bar's executive director warned that failing to authorize dues would "bankrupt the organization and force it to rebuild the discipline system all over again from scratch." The Senate Judiciary Committee approved Hertzberg's bill and rejected Kopp's. Adelman complained that "every good faith effort we've made to restructure has been met with stony silence or with intemperate comments about the bar and attorneys." Morrow gloated: "When you have them by the family jewels, their hearts and minds will follow." In order to get Republican support, Hertzberg accepted amendments requiring user fees for some programs, reducing lawyer contributions to the CSF, transferring funding for the Commission on Judicial Nominees Evaluation to the state, and suspending MCLE while it was reviewed.[121]

The *San Francisco Examiner* urged compromise. The "months-long impasse over bar funding could victimize the public by inviting rogue lawyers to see how much they can get away with." The Bar was

> partly responsible for the mess. It has given ammunition to its enemies with a long record of arrogance toward critics and questionable use of dues money for lobbying and liberal-leaning political advocacy with which many members disagree.

Dues had been "twice the average in the other 49 states." But

> the important thing is to retain and improve whatever protections the non-lawyering public can get against professional misconduct, and put the serious offenders out of business. Wilson's grievances about lawyers who have not supported him are trivial compared to the people's stake in the outcome.

---

121. Nancy McCarthy, *Revised bar bill awaits action,* CBJ 1 (June 1998); Marc Adelman, *Avoiding a bigger problem ahead,* CBJ 7 (June 1998).

The *Los Angeles Times* asked Wilson "to be specific and constructive about solutions to a crisis he created."[122]

By the end of June, the Bar had shut most of its operations, retaining only 200 employees. Adelman denounced this as "politics," which "has nothing to do with the administration of justice." Even the concession of an entirely appointed Board (7 by the Supreme Court, 6 by the Governor, and 2 each by the Assembly and Senate) failed to win sufficient support. Adelman had vainly sought to meet Wilson during nearly 30 visits to Sacramento. The day before the June 26 layoffs, the governor's spokesman said he would not negotiate the issue in public. Hertzberg now introduced AB 1374 as an interim measure authorizing $100 dues exclusively for discipline. On June 22, Adelman wrote the Supreme Court a nineteen-page letter asking it to authorize $287 in dues. Although the court declined to act, it

> recognize[d] the importance of the core functions relating to the admission and discipline of attorneys carried out by the State Bar and encourage[d] the other two branches of government and the State Bar to resolve this matter as quickly as possible in light of the interest of the public and the potential impact on the operations of the court of the Bar's inability to carry out its disciplinary functions.

Although Chief Justice George offered his good offices, only the Bar accepted. The discipline system staff dropped from 283 to 20, who concentrated on trials, freezing all but 50 of the 700 pending cases. Written complaints (which was all the Bar would accept) fell to half the usual level.[123]

Accusing Wilson of "indulging a long-festering political grudge," whose "main victims" were "people reporting what they believe is lawyerly malpractice or theft," the *San Francisco Examiner* urged both sides to "make a deal . . . without delay." But the *San Diego Union Tribune* blamed the Bar alone and condemned its "audacious bid to circumvent the legislative process" by appealing to the Supreme Court. Wilson had "ample justification" for his complaint "that the bar was using its hefty dues for a variety of political purposes rather than for its central mission of enforcing ethical rules and disciplining wayward members." The $295 he proposed was "enough to maintain the bar's exemplary disciplinary system."[124]

---

122. *Raising the bar,* San Francisco Examiner (5.18.98); *Californians poorly served by the stalemate,* Los Angeles Times (May 29, 1998).

123. Marc Adelman, *The last few gasps of a dues bill,* CBJ 8 (10.98); Nancy McCarthy, *Bar operations pared to barest essentials,* CBJ 1 (July 1998); Nancy McCarthy, *200 remain to navigate "The Ark," Ibid.*

124. *Time to end the grudge,* San Francisco Examiner (June 28, 1998); *Both the Governor and bar must compromise,* San Diego Union Tribune (June 25, 1998).

The antagonists just moved further apart. Adelman complained that "posturing by many in Sacramento left virtually no chance of a resolution."

> All one hears from Sacramento is that the bar isn't willing to reform. That we are trying to circumvent the governor's wishes. That the shutdown of the attorney discipline system was not motivated by a lack of funds but set in motion for political purposes and effect. That despite the impasse in the legislature, our request to the Supreme Court for relief was nothing more than a "slap in the face of the legislative process."

There were even accusations that Hertzberg's interim bill "was introduced at the insistence of bar leaders in order to circumvent the governor's proposal and resist impending reforms." Two months after the shutdown "the number of calls and correspondence concerning lawyer discipline" reaching Adelman's office was "increasing with each passing day." The California Republican Party chairman responded by accusing the Bar of "arrogance." It had "stolen interest from client trust accounts." MCLE was "replete with politically correct courses." It was "arrogant . . . to claim that the entire amount of non-mandatory dues spent for political activities was only $1." It "arrogantly abused the JNE . . . procedures when the governor's nominee to the Supreme Court was not sufficiently liberal." Its "numerous fiscal abuses" included paying "State Bar officials more than the Governor and than the judges." The two state gubernatorial candidates also weighed in. Republican Dan Lungren said the Bar "should concentrate on serving as the guarantor of the quality and integrity of the legal profession." Other activities had become "unacceptably politicized." Democrat Gray Davis noted the 2:1 vote to retain the unified bar two years earlier. "Allowing the executive branch or the legislative branch to appoint a majority of the Board of Governors would effectively transform the bar into an arm" of those branches. Although the Bar must serve "its appointed purposes rather than becoming primarily a lobbying organization," Wilson's veto was "a heinous act."[125]

On September 28, Wilson asked Chief Justice George to take over discipline to "protect the public while giving the legislature time to consider the issues of governance, the scope of legitimate functions, and the membership fee level of the State Bar." He also warned the Bar that "it would be a serious mistake" to ask the court "to take the unprecedented step of imposing a membership fee that the legislature had declined to enact, thereby intruding on the legislative process and raising serious separation of powers questions." But two days later, the Bar did just that. At its annual conference (October 1–4), the Chief Justice said "the crisis

125. Marc Adelman, *Exhausting every conceivable effort,* CBJ 12 (July 1998); Marc Adelman, *A sad time for public protection,* CBJ 7 (Aug. 1998); Michael J. Schroeder, *At the mercy of the rebels it created,* CBJ 8 (Sept. 1998); Nancy McCarthy, *In the race for governor . . . Lungren, Davis look at the bar, the legal profession and laws,* CBJ 1 (Sept. 1998).

in bar discipline has had a detrimental impact on the protection of the public." Two weeks later, the court agreed to hear the petition, taking the unusual step of soliciting public input. The same day, the *Los Angeles Times* urged the court to recreate the "vigilant and highly regarded" disciplinary system, blaming Wilson for having "precipitated the crisis" and then having "foiled legislative efforts to fix the problem until it was too late." On November 2, Davis was elected Governor, and the Democrats gained five seats in the assembly and two in the Senate (but not a two-thirds majority in either house). By the time of the November 9 hearing, the court had received 50 written submissions. In oral argument, SB President Ray Marshall described a "crisis situation": a backlog of 7,000 complaints, with 500 more arriving every two months. Dan Kolkey argued for Governor Wilson that levying a fee would "undo" his veto and interfere with a "legislative creation." But Chief Justice George noted that "the legislature hasn't acted and that's why we're here, isn't it." He was "troubled" by the governor's suggestion that his court take over discipline and "question[ed]" how it would pay the $41 million annual cost.[126]

The court decided in less than a month, rejecting Wilson's separation of powers argument, as well as the suggestion "that there is no real need for a disciplinary system, and . . . attorney misconduct should be dealt with exclusively through criminal complaints and civil lawsuits brought by injured clients." Many ethical violations would not interest a plaintiff's attorney or criminal prosecutor. "More generally, the objective of the discipline system is not punishment of the attorney, but protection of the public." "[E]very other licensed profession in the state of which we are aware is regulated by a board that has the power to suspend or revoke the license of an errant practitioner—and practitioners pay a fee for licensure." "An unregulated profession soon may lose its right to call itself a profession." The courts would suffer because doubts would grow about "the integrity of the profession and the legal system." The court was grateful that the SBC had relieved it of a significant burden of deciding disciplinary cases (40 a year until SBC judgments were granted finality in 1991). The court unanimously ordered dues of $173, $1.56 of which was dedicated to a special master, Judge Elwood Lui.

> Our action today is intended to respond to an unprecedented emergency threatening the protection of the public, the integrity of the legal profession, and the interests of the courts. In short, the administration of justice is at risk. . . . California has had ample reason during the past 10 years to take pride in an attorney discipline system that has been recognized as one of our

126. Nancy McCarthy, *Supreme Court to hear petition on discipline,* CBJ 1 (Nov. 1998); *No bar, no discipline,* Los Angeles Times (Oct. 14, 1998); Nancy McCarthy, *Election results give bar backers new hope,* CBJ 1 (Nov. 1998); Nancy McCarthy, *Supreme Court weighs discipline fate,* CBJ 1 (Nov. 1998).

nation's finest. We anticipate that in the near future, it will again return to normal operation with appropriate funding as determined by the legislature and the governor.[127]

The Bar's executive director warned that restarting the disciplinary system would be slow because it had to "restore our human resources department" and "engage in an intensive effort of recruiting and training dozens and dozens of new people with no experience whatsoever." The Bar sent members a $173 bill on December 31. The hotline reopened on March 1, 1999, for four hours a day (reaching eight hours only in 2004). The OTC would be 25 percent smaller and exclusively address cases presenting great risk to clients or likely to result in at least a year's suspension and those involving criminal convictions, failure to perform legal services, misrepresentation to the court, or unconscionable fees. The SBC cut its staff from 52 to 37. Presiding Judge Obrien felt "the court now is relatively stable" but worried that "there are some aspects of our fundamental role that are very fragile, and the political machinations that have gone on have really exploited that fragility."[128]

Senator Adam B. Schiff (immediate past chair of the Judiciary Committee) introduced SB 144 on January 5 (co-sponsored by Robert Hertzberg). Schiff wanted "more clarity in terms of the functions of the bar and a greater level of confidence that dues are being spent on appropriate functions," but he was "not willing to sacrifice the consumer protection functions" or the "democratic features of the bar." The bill retained the Conference and sections but did not fund them out of the mandatory dues (which increased the deduction for lobbying to five dollars and offered hardship reductions for low-income lawyers). There were limitations on bar lobbying. (The following year, the BoG required two-thirds votes, first whether the subject matter of lobbying fell within the *Keller* guidelines and then whether to take the position; it also required sections, committees, and the Conference to disclaim that they represented the Bar.) Bar contracts over $50,000 had to comply with the public contracts code. Attorneys had to cooperate with investigations. MCLE was extended to retired judges but cut from 36 hours to 25, while law practice management was eliminated and ethics reduced to four hours. A companion bill (SB 143) replaced the only lay Review Department judge with a lawyer and empowered the Governor, Senate Rules Committee chair, and Assembly speaker each to appoint one of the five hearing judges.

---

127. In re Attorney Discipline System, 19 Cal. 4th 582, 606, 608, 610–14, 623–34 (1998).

128. Nancy McCarthy, *Supreme Court orders $173 fee,* CBJ 1 (1.99); Nancy McCarthy, *Marshall sets eye on new fee bill,* CBJ 1 (Jan 1999); *Complaint hotline also up and running,* CBJ 1 (Mar. 1999); Nancy McCarthy, *Bar starts to rebuild discipline,* CBJ 1 (Mar. 1999); Nancy McCarthy, *Bar court trimmed by $1 million,* CBJ 1 (Apr. 1999); Nancy McCarthy, *Opening a new front in discipline,* CBJ 1 (May 1999); Nancy McCarthy, *State Bar Court bounces back,* CBJ 1 (Feb. 2001); State Bar of California (2005: 3).

(Three SBC judges unsuccessfully challenged this on separation of powers grounds.)[129] The bill also limited the Review Department to a review of the record. (In later cases, the Supreme Court struck this down in order to "relieve [itself] of the burden of intense scrutiny of all disciplinary recommendations" and held that the Review Department's plenary review with a right to petition the Supreme Court satisfied due process.)[130] When Governor Davis signed both bills on September 7, SB President Andrew J. Guildford celebrated this "great day for the bar" but warned it "to be careful not to repeat the mistakes of the past." (The political threat seemed to recede. The Legislature authorized dues of $395 in 2001 by large votes: 63–7 in the Assembly and 23–12 in the Senate; large margins also passed the 2002 dues bill—the first extending over two years—and the 2004 dues bill.)[131]

The month Davis signed the 2000 dues bill, the Bar won another victory. Lew Warden, who had lost his license in 1993 for refusing to satisfy MCLE, had convinced a Court of Appeal in 1997 that the program violated equal protection by exempting retired judges, full-time law professors, legislators, elected state officers, and federal and state attorneys. The Supreme Court now rejected the challenge 5–2.[132] About half of all lawyers took advantage of the two-year hiatus not to register for courses. President Guilford called MCLE "probably a good thing" but added that "we need to . . . make it painless." Although a survey found that 60 percent of respondents wanted to cut MCLE hours down from 25, the BoG refused and voted 13–1 to keep an hour each for substance abuse and bias elimination. The new SB President Karen Nobumoto (the first African-American in this post) commented: "Two hours in three years? If we can't take the heat on that, we don't belong in this job."[133]

---

129. Obrien v. Jones, 23 Cal. 4th 40 (2000).

130. In re Rose, 22 Cal. 4th 430 (2000).

131. Ray Marshall, *From the President: It's time to move on,* CBJ 9 (Jan. 1999); Nancy McCarthy, *Fee bill fate back to Sacramento,* CBJ 1 (Feb. 1999); Matt St. George, *Funding the conference,* CBJ 9 (Mar. 1999); *Board tentatively approves budget based on dues of $384,* CBJ 34 (Apr. 1999); Nancy McCarthy, *Schiff bill would set dues at $395 per year,* CBJ 1 (May 1999); Raymond C. Marshall, *From the President: An update on the bar's progress,* CBJ 7 (July 1999); Raymond C. Marshall, *From the President: A long struggle finally pays off,* CBJ 9 (Sept. 1999); Nancy McCarthy, *Governor signs $395 fee bill, ending 2-year political battle,* CBJ 1 (Oct. 1999); *Board mandates two-thirds vote twice, in backing any legislation,* CBJ 1 (Jan. 2000); Nancy McCarthy, *Supreme Court rejects bar court suit,* CBJ 1 (July 2000); *Gov. Davis signs 2001 bar fee bill,* CBJ 3 (Aug. 2000); Nancy McCarthy, *High court reaffirms its ultimate control over discipline cases,* CBJ 1 (Apr. 2000); *Bar court judge appointments process to be reviewed,* CBJ 4 (Apr. 2000); *Davis signs diversion bill, nixes more access money,* CBJ 3 (Sept. 2001); *State Bar fee bill moves through the legislature,* CBJ (Aug. 2003).

132. Warden v. State Bar, 62 Cal. Rptr. 2d 32 (1st Dist. Ct. of App. 1997), rev'd, 21 Cal. 4th 628 (1999).

133. A second challenge to MCLE as "compulsory governmental propaganda" was rejected in 1996, affirmed in 2000. Nancy McCarthy, *MCLE: A little, a lot, or none at all,* CBJ

But the Bar lost yet another challenge to its political activity. In 1992, two years after *Keller*, Raymond Brosterhous (Keller's colleague and co-plaintiff, again represented by the Pacific Legal Foundation) challenged the Bar's lobbying, its programs on minority relations and women lawyers, Volunteers in Parole, and the Conference of Delegates. In August 1999, the trial judge found that the Bar had improperly spent dues on political and ideological activities in 1991 and set trial for the amount of the refund (which would go only to the named plaintiffs). When the Court of Appeal upheld the first decision in April 2000, the Bar decided against a further appeal because the ten-dollar refund was so trivial, settling the plaintiffs' lawyers' $2.35 million fee claim for $900,000.[134]

The Conference of Delegates struggled to survive without Bar dues. Only 25,000 members voluntarily checked off three dollars on their 2000 dues bill, raising less than a third of its $240,000 target. Lacking staff, the Conference was virtually unable to lobby. In 1999, to avoid further alienating the legislature, the Conference had confined itself to technical issues: attorneys fees, unemployment insurance, discovery practices, and arbitration. The Bar had refused to let it urge the Governor to declare a moratorium on the death penalty. President Nobumoto appointed a commission to resolve the relationship between the two.

> The Conference has a justifiable desire to continue its long tradition of helping shape and analyze legislation in our state. The bar has a justifiable desire not to be dragged continually into political hot water for positions the conference takes and which the bar does not choose to endorse.

On the commission's recommendation, the BoG authorized the Conference to reorganize as a separate nonprofit; the Bar would continue to provide services (for pay), help the Conference collect donations from members, and meet consecutively in the same venue. The Conference executive committee chair was pleased that "our purview rules will be free of *Keller*." Fewer members donated

---

1 (June 1999); Nancy McCarthy, *Supreme Court upholds bar's MCLE program in its entirety*, CBJ 1 (Oct. 1999); *Reprieved for one year, but lawyers still must comply*, CBJ 1 (Oct. 1999); Nancy McCarthy, *Appeals judges appear unswayed by new challenge to MCLE program*, CBJ 1 (Feb. 20.00); Nancy McCarthy, *Challenge to MCLE program turned back one more time*, CBJ 1 (3.00); Sharon Lerman, *MCLE commission calls for better quality, more hours*, CBJ 1 (June 2001).

134. Nancy McCarthy, *Bar's use of dues money scrutinized again in courtroom*, CBJ 1 (June 1999); *Agreement to avert damage phase, speed bar appeal*, CBJ 3 (May 2000); *Judge grants $10 refund, refuses future preclusion*, CBJ 3 (Sept. 2000); Nancy McCarthy, *State Bar drops its appeal of dues case after 10-year fight*, CBJ 1 (Feb. 2001); *Bar hit with $2.35 million fee demand in lawyer dues case*, CBJ 7 (Apr. 2001); Nancy McCarthy, *State Bar and PLF spar over $2 million for Brosterhous fee*, CBJ 1 (Aug. 2001); *State Bar settles Brosterhouse case for $900,000*, CBJ 1 (Sept. 20.01).

in the next two years (14,800 and17, 109), but the ten-dollar check-off generated greater resources.[135]

Both sides praised the appointment of Judge Lui as Special Master. Even though he found that the investigations backlog was down to 2,000 (partly because new complaints were half the pre-closure level), he urged the Bar to set priorities and refer less serious complaints to local bar ADR, allowing it to close approximately 1,200 cases. Before filing charges the Bar offered respondents Early Neutral Evaluations (ENEs), about a third of which produced settlement. The SBC had cut its budget from $5.3 million to less than $3 million and its staff positions from 52 to 37, of which it planned to fill only 29. Even with the revival of many abated cases, the hearing department caseload was only about half its former level. To increase efficiency, Lui urged standardized pleading, easier default, and an expedited procedure for less serious cases, entailing limited sanctions and less discovery and hearing time. Noting that "the climb to full strength will be long and slow," the *Los Angeles Times* said that "the bar's travails and its slow return present an object lesson for Gov. Davis and his successors: It's easy to tear down a valuable institution but very hard to rebuild it."[136]

The confrontation over dues led to several external reviews of the disciplinary system. The ABA urged the Bar to focus resources on "alternatives" to discipline, especially for "single instances of minor neglect or minor incompetence," whose "summary dismissal . . . is one of the chief sources of public dissatisfaction with disciplinary systems." But most of the report recommended greater severity. For more than 30 years, it had been ABA policy that lawyers who withdrew from practice while under investigation should be treated as disbarred. Similarly, the 35 to 40 percent of lawyers who defaulted should not receive the existing "low level discipline," but be suspended and required to petition for reinstatement. Prosecutors should use subpoenas "to compel recalcitrant respondents to provide information," rather than waiting for the ENE or letting respondents use that to delay. No hearing should be required to place lawyers on involuntary inactive enrolment, nor should the bar have to consider "whether the lawyer's clients or the public are likely to suffer greater injury from the denial of the petition than the lawyer is likely to suffer if it is granted." "The interests of clients and the

---

135. Nancy McCarthy, *Targeted by Wilson, conference struggles to get back on feet,* CBJ 1 (Apr. 2000); Nancy McCarthy, *Bar rebuffs conference death penalty move,* CBJ 1 (May 2001); *Presidential panel will review role of bar's conference,* CBJ 1 (Oct. 2001); Nancy McCarthy, *Whither the Conference of Delegates?* CBJ 1 (May 2002); Karen Nobumoto, *New era of Bar-Conference cooperation,* CBJ 8 (May 2002); Nancy McCarthy, *Conference of Delegates and State Bar are likely to divorce,* CBJ 1 (May 2002); Nancy McCarthy, *Bar board OKs separation from conference,* CBJ 1 (June 2002); Karen Nobumoto and Stephen Marsh, *A beneficial split for both parties,* CBJ (June 2002);

136. *Lui selection hailed by friend and foe,* CBJ 1 (Jan. 1999); Lui (1999a; 1999b; 1999c; 2000); *Easy to destroy, hard to rebuild,* Los Angeles Times (Feb. 23, 2000); *see also,* State Bar of California (2001a).

public in cases like these are paramount." Respondents should pay the cost of reinstatement proceedings, as they did of discipline. The legislature should repeal the law making a knowingly false and malicious report to the Bar a misdemeanor and grant complainants absolute immunity.

Noting that "as a result of the 1998 shutdown of the system, the OCTC lost approximately 700 years of collective experience," and the "bulk" of the 14 lawyers in Los Angeles "have 18 months or less experience," the ABA feared that the current system lacked sufficient "stability" to "assure public confidence in the competency and integrity of the bar." It urged transfer of the OCTC and SBC to the Supreme Court, which would either administer them itself or delegate responsibility to an appointed commission and would promulgate "a rule designating the disciplinary budget as a protected fund consisting of a court imposed regulatory fee collected by the bar at the same time as it collects its dues."[137]

The state auditor praised the Bar for having "reduced costs and improved the effectiveness of its disciplinary process by developing a priority system." Dues were reasonable and used "to support only the State Bar's mandated functions." But the Bar failed to recover the costs of discipline and client security fund payments from the lawyers responsible; indeed, the proportion of disciplinary costs collected fell from 39 percent in 1995 to 29 percent in 2000. (Far lower proportions were collected from lawyers who were disbarred or resigned, or to recoup CSF payments.) Although the Bar expected to reduce its disciplinary backlog to 600 by the end of 2001, it closed more complaints in intake in 2000 than in 1995, and the percentage of cases closed without discipline in intake and enforcement also rose. Declaring that "these numbers tell it all," SB President Jim Herman declared: "The bar is doing a great job as stewards of the members' dues and as protectors of the public interest."[138]

VI. THE CHRONIC CONTRADICTIONS OF SELF-REGULATION

Although the Bar's separation from the Conference seems to have averted further external challenges to self-regulation, chronic controversies continue to expose basic internal tensions. A study of whether discipline unfairly targeted solo and small firm practitioners (mandated by the companion bill to the 1999 dues authorization) found that prosecutions merely reflected the overrepresentation of those lawyers as complaint targets.[139] Malpractice insurance was another

137. ABA, 2001: 9, 15–16, 19–22, 24–26, 30–31, 33–34, 36–38, 4–45, 51.

138. California State Auditor (2001; 2003: 18–21; 2005); Nancy McCarthy, *Audit affirms bar's use of member dues,* CBJ 1 (May 2003).

139. Business & Professions Code § 6095.1, SB 143, Chap. 221, Stats of 2001; State Bar (2001b). In fact, solo practitioners were 23 percent of attorneys, 54 percent of inquiries, 68 percent of investigations, and 78 percent of prosecutions, whereas those in larger firms

festering problem. In 1992, Senator Presley introduced a bill requiring that clients be told whether lawyers were insured. Over the opposition of the Los Angeles County Bar Association, the legislature imposed such a requirement in cases where fees were contingent or exceeded $1,000.[140] On behalf of the California Trial Lawyers Association, Willie Brown promptly made an unsuccessful attempt to repeal it, arguing, "If you're going to do it for lawyers, do it for everybody."[141] After the expiration of the disclosure law in 2000, a survey found that one in five California lawyers went bare. When nine underwriters quit within nine months, premiums rose rapidly in 2002, from $8,000 to $30,000 for intellectual property and patent attorneys.

In 2004, the ABA approved a model rule requiring lawyers to tell state licensing authorities whether they had insurance. In response, SB President John Van de Kamp appointed an Insurance Disclosure Task Force in 2005, chaired by former President Towery, which proposed, in early 2006, that lawyers make such disclosure both to the Bar (for posting on its website) and in writing to new and existing clients (fifteen states had such a requirement and seven were considering it). Nearly 80 percent of the more than 100 responses to a request for public comment were opposed, including the Conference of Delegates. Solo and small firm lawyers complained they could not afford insurance. One lawyer called the proposal "nothing less than an open invitation to a dissatisfied client to cut losses by suing the non-insured attorney in the hope of a quick cash settlement." (States adopting the requirement actually found no significant change in the number of malpractice claims or the cost of insurance.) By contrast, the ethics, professional liability, and mandatory fee arbitration committee chairs supported the proposal. The task force eliminated the obligations to notify existing clients or obtain a signed acknowledgment of the notification from new clients and again sought public comment. John Dutton, a bar governor representing a rural northern California district, many of whose lawyers practiced alone or in small firms, warned that "we're alienating thousands of California lawyers." When the BoG split 7–7, President Sheldon Sloan cast the deciding negative vote because he opposed posting the information on-line.

Towery refused to admit defeat: "strong client protection is in the interest of the bar. It is one of our raisons d'être . . .. Clients ought to be empowered with information." Dutton retorted that the Bar did not know how many malpractice judgments went unsatisfied because lawyers were uninsured. Former Bar

---

were 42, 11, 5, and 2. Some of the difference was attributable to the content of client complaints: 23 percent concerned failure to communicate and 18 percent failure to perform, delay, or abandonment.

140. Arleen Jacobius, *LACBA Opposes Pair of Discipline Proposals*, LADJ 2 (Apr. 10, 1992).

141. *Speaker Assails State Bar on Discipline*, LADJ 3 (Aug. 25, 1993).

Governor JoAnn Grace called the proposal "bull pucky."[142] Ed Pohl (former chair of the Law Practice, Management & Technology Section) asked: "Why don't you give [the uninsured lawyers] a yellow armband?" But Jim Penrod (a Bar Governor and Morgan, Lewis & Bockius partner who handled malpractice and insurance cases) said 90 percent of clients "think they ought to know if their attorney carries malpractice insurance." SB President Jeff Bleich, who had voted for the proposal, argued that "the public will feel better protected and better served if we have disclosure."

At its next meeting, the BoG voted 10–9 to endorse disclosure in principle but accepted an amendment by Richard Frankel (San Ramon) mandating it only when the rules already required the lawyer to provide the client with a written retainer (fees that were contingent or over one thousand dollars but not if the client had retained the lawyer in similar matters). When Bleich objected, the BoG sent the proposal to its Committee on Regulation, Admissions and Discipline. Dutton continued to contend that disclosure was impractical if non-clients casually sought advice. "We get those calls on a regular basis," three to five a week. Penrod replied that, "any time you give anyone legal advice and someone relies on it, you have an attorney-client relationship." The committee voted 4–3 for a rule drafted by Dutton, requiring disclosure if it was reasonably foreseeable that the work would take more than four hours, unless it was an emergency or the client previously had been told the lawyer was uninsured. State Bar staff called the four-hour requirement arbitrary and the qualifier ambiguous. John Peterson (Fresno) proposed online disclosure as a more effective alternative than "requiring a lawyer to communicate with a client." Dutton strongly objected, warning that angry members would urge legislators to block bar dues. "I can't think of any proposal that will more severely shoot this bar in the foot." The committee rejected Peterson's proposal 4–3. In May 2008, despite continuing opposition by the Law Practice Management and Technology Section and the Committee on Professional Responsibility and Competence, the Board finally voted 16–4 for disclosure in writing before beginning representation that would take four hours. Peterson condemned this as "an unnecessary irritant to the attorney-client relationship." Dutton called the rule (which he had drafted) "oppressive;" lawyers should only be required to disclose if they had lost a case because of a mistake or been sued for malpractice. By this time, 23 states had adopted disclosure requirements (although 18 only in the annual bar registration).[143]

---

142. A euphemism for *bullshit.*

143. Nancy McCarthy, *Malpractice premiums skyrocket,* CBJ 1 (July 2002); *Possible disclosure rule for uninsured lawyers,* CBJ (Jan. 2006); Diane Curtis, *Malpractice insurance disclosure circulated for public comment,* CBJ (July 2006); Nancy McCarthy, *Broad opposition to insurance disclosure,* CBJ (June 2007); Nancy McCarthy, *Bar board will tackle malpractice insurance disclosure again,* CBJ (Nov. 07); Nancy McCarthy, *Board ducks malpractice disclosure,*

Lawyers also objected to the severity and form of sanctions. In 2000, defense counsel sought to have technical recordkeeping errors in client trust accounts diverted from the disciplinary process. Although the Discipline Committee, Conference of Delegates, and former and present SB presidents agreed, the Bar Ethics Committee was opposed. So were senior staff lawyers, who noted the Bar got some 4,000 NSF notices from the banks each year.[144] In 2001, the Bar created a drug court in response to the fact that nearly a third of the thousand lawyers on probation at any time were substance abusers. But prosecutors had become concerned about the inappropriateness of some of the approximately 15 percent of cases diverted to the Alternative Discipline Program (ADP), established in June 2007 for alcohol, drug, and mental health problems. CTC Scott Drexel proposed limiting diversion to lawyers whose offenses did not warrant disbarment, were reasonably likely to succeed in the program, and did not seek to participate "as a means of delaying the ultimate disposition of the proceeding or avoiding disbarment." Twenty-one other states limited their diversion programs to minor misconduct not involving misappropriation or significant client harm. Drexel sought other changes: every diverted attorney should be considered for inactive enrollment; lawyers facing serious charges would be able to resign only after admitting or pleading no-contest to charges; lawyers seeking diversion would have to offer stronger evidence of the connection between misconduct and substance abuse or mental health; and the OTC could appeal to the Review Department. The Supreme Court shared many of his concerns, but defense counsel resisted.[145]

Drexel also proposed to place disciplinary charges on the State Bar website as soon as an NTSC was filed. The only other ways to obtain such information were to pay fifty cents a page and wait several weeks or make an appointment to visit the SBC in San Francisco or Los Angeles. Drexel noted that only 10 percent of complaints resulted in charges, more than 90 percent of those charged in 2006 through 2007 were found culpable, and some of the others enrolled in ADP or received informal sanctions. Few were acquitted of all charges: none in 2006, one in 2007, and two in 2008. Most public comment on the proposal was negative, including unanimous votes by the Los Angeles County and Beverly Hills Bar Associations. "It's going to snare up the innocent along with the guilty." David Carr (president of the Association of Discipline Defense Counsel) claimed

---

CBJ (Dec. 2007); *Board committee approves another version of insurance disclosure rule,* CBJ (Jan. 2008); *Finally, board approves an insurance disclosure rule,* CBJ (June 08); State Bar of California (2007: 25).

144. Nancy McCarthy, *Proposal for diversion class sparks debate,* CBJ 1 (Oct. 2000).

145. Nancy McCarthy, *State Bar will open nation's only drug court for lawyers,* CBJ 1 (July 2001); Nancy McCarthy, *50 sign up for State Bar's new diversion program,* CBJ 1 (July 2002); Nancy McCarthy, *Prosecutors want tighter rules for diversion programs,* CBJ (June 2007); Nancy McCarthy, *Prosecutors want tighter rules for discipline diversion program,* CBJ (Jan 2008); *Board tightens disciplinary resignation rules,* CBJ (Apr. 2008).

that the OTC frequently overcharged, and there was "something about" the Internet "that lets people accept what they read" uncritically. Defense counsel Diane Karpman said posting would violate the "presumption of innocence" and be "profoundly destructive" to the lawyers. One Governor called the proposal "an unnecessary blow." "Is what we are doing helping the profession or hurting the profession? . . . What we are doing here is to highlight issues, highlight charges." But the Board adopted the proposal 18–4 (all six public members voting in favor), although it would apply only to new charges.[146]

In 1992, seventeen years after being disbarred, Ronald Silverton was readmitted on his fourth petition. When he committed additional misconduct two years later, the SBC recommended suspension, but the Supreme Court disbarred him a second time in 2004 and asked the Bar to act on a 1996 proposal for permanent disbarment. Each year about a hundred lawyers were disbarred, another hundred resigned with charges pending, and 15 to 20 sought reinstatement, about half of whom succeeded. Between 1990 and 2005, nearly three-fourths of reinstated lawyers were the subject of grievances; six were disbarred again, and another 6 to 12 resigned. The Committee on Regulation, Admissions and Discipline narrowly approved (3–2) proposals to require disbarred lawyers to wait seven years rather than five before petitioning for reinstatement; compel anyone seeking reinstatement to pass the attorney bar examination; and make disbarment permanent for stealing client funds, committing crimes of public malfeasance, engaging in unauthorized practice of law while disbarred, or engaging in "conduct so egregious that the member should be permanently disbarred." Although comment was evenly split, every nonlawyer favored permanent disbarment. Defense lawyer Joann Robbins objected that most disciplined attorneys are "good people who do bad things" in a crisis. SB President James Heitung was opposed, because of his "personal experience with the idea of getting close to second degree murder" when he severely injured someone while driving drunk. Had the victim died, "I would never have had the opportunity to come back here." Nevertheless, the Board approved the last two proposals while refusing to extend the time to petition for reinstatement.[147]

The divisions exposed above did not emerge when the Bar adopted a civility code. President Sheldon Sloan (who had opposed mandating disclosure of malpractice insurance) made civility the focus of his year in office. But though the task force chair emphasized that the guidelines were aspirational, Joann Robbins warned that they "will inevitably be considered standards that will lead to disciplinary sanctions." In response, they were revised to state specifically that

146. *Misconduct charges may be posted online,* CBJ (June 08); Nancy McCarthy, *Lawyer misconduct charges will go online,* CBJ (Aug. 08); Mike McKee, *California Bar OKs Posting Discipline Charges Online,* MINORITY LAW JOURNAL (July 14, 2008).

147. Nancy McCarthy, *Permanent disbarment moves forward,* CBJ (Apr. 06); Nancy McCarthy, *Board OKs permanent disbarment,* CBJ (Sept. 2006).

they are "not mandatory rules of professional conduct, nor rules of practice, nor standards of care" and cannot be used in disciplinary proceedings.[148]

VII. THE PROFESSIONAL IS POLITICAL

The lesson of this sorry story is inescapable. Professional self-regulation is always an arena of political contestation, both within the legal profession and between it and outsiders, who include clients, competitors, politicians, and the media. The professional project is born of self-interest, which was and continues to motivate it long after the core of professionalism has been firmly secured. The State Bar dedicated its first four decades to controlling entry (educational requirements, law school accreditation, bar examinations, and character and fitness tests) and limiting competition, first from outsiders (unauthorized practice, market division treaties) and then among lawyers (bans on advertising and solicitation, minimum fee schedules). Although Terrence Halliday entitled his superb study of the Chicago Bar Association "Beyond Monopoly," lawyers have never transcended monopoly; they have simply convinced others to take it for granted.[149] Limitations on monopoly power were imposed on this strongly resistant profession by outside forces, primarily the U.S. Department of Justice and the U.S. Supreme Court, responding to the consumer movement of the 1960s. The profession still seeks to limit competition by adjusting the difficulty of the bar examination, restricting entry by lawyers from other states and countries, and regulating the institutional structures within which lawyers may practice (such as restricting partnerships with other professionals and non-lawyer equity interests in law firms).

Nascent bar associations faced a classic collective action problem: how to persuade lawyers to participate (join, pay dues, vote, attend meetings, and serve on committees) rather than free ride.[150] Most state bars remained voluntary, accepting free riders as the price of political autonomy. California opted for the unified bar's compulsory membership, perhaps because voluntary associations were weakened by the state's size and diversity, evidenced by rural lawyers' fear of urban dominance. But this choice had its own price, which often has been very high (partly because of the historical quirk that the state legislature must approve State Bar dues). Resistance by *any* dissenter severely constrains the political positions compulsory organizations can take. University public interest groups funded by student fees offer vivid illustrations. For its first few decades, the State Bar pursued policies that united lawyers (the professional project described above),

148. *Guidelines for lawyer civility move forward,* CBJ (May 07); *Board adopts civility code,* CBJ (Aug. 2007).

149. Halliday (1987).

150. Schneyer (1983).

leaving more controversial topics to the voluntary Conference of Delegates. But perhaps because this was California, the Conference took positions on highly volatile issues—the death penalty, law and order, affirmative action, prostitution, abortion, nuclear disarmament—subjects well outside what Halliday describes as the core of lawyers' moral authority.[151] Inevitably, the Conference became a lightning rod for attacks. And because most of the same actors met immediately after and in the same venue as the State Bar, the two were readily conflated.

Even though a high proportion of state legislators were lawyers, they tended to be suspicious of the State Bar (perhaps because many had graduated from lower status, sometimes unaccredited, law schools and practiced alone or in small firms). Some legislators may have cynically calculated that lawyer-bashing was good populist politics. But others had particular axes to grind. Robert Presley (from the Riverside Sheriff's Department) and Patrick Nolan were law and order champions. Willie Brown was angry about the State Bar's opposition to his mandatory malpractice insurance bill—and perhaps about its treatment of the grievance against him. (Brown was one of the many prominent disciplinary targets who testified on behalf of David Harney, as described in Chapter 3, "Medical Injuries Compensation Reform Act: Unconstitutional Until Proven Otherwise.") Most critically, Pete Wilson had been personally vilified by SB President Anthony Murray (for threatening California Supreme Court Justices who voted against the death penalty) during Wilson's successful U.S. Senate campaign; this may partly explain Wilson's veto of the SB dues bill thirteen years later. For all these reasons, the State Bar was under constant attack from the moment of its founding: repeated plebiscites (all which resulted in member endorsements, to the dismay of critics), endless external audits and reviews, numerous lawsuits challenging its authority to take political positions, and two shutdowns when the legislature or governor blocked the annual dues bill.

Self-regulation poses its own difficulties. The State Bar had to convince external critics (dissatisfied clients and hostile legislators) that it was more effective than an independent regulatory agency. At the same time, it had to persuade members that it was less stringent and less expensive than an independent agency, whose creation was a real threat.[152] (Some lawyers opposed the mere existence of a disciplinary system as an admission that lawyers might misbehave.) Talking out of both sides of its mouth, the Bar rarely convinced either audience.[153] This is a classic dilemma, whether phrased in Latin (*quis custodiet custodes*) or English (setting the fox to guard the henhouse). For analogies, think

151. Halliday (1987: chap.2).

152. The Illinois bar voluntarily relinquished regulation to the state in the 1980s. Powell (1986).

153. Lloyd Fallers (1965) described this difficult intermediate position in the context of British colonial rule in Uganda.

about how the police or military handle misconduct, politicians deal with corruption, corporations set executive compensation, or the Roman Catholic Church covered up sexual abuse by priests. The Bar told the public that most complaints were unfounded, the dissatisfactions inevitably engendered by an adversary system in which one party's victory is the other's defeat. It warned that reform would only encourage more frivolous grievances. The Bar told its members that refusal to pay dues or accept cosmetic reforms would lead to direct regulation. Bar leaders spun every criticism as praise. They boasted about making "radical" reforms that conceded the inadequacy of the unreformed system, rather like answering the question, "[W]hen did you stop beating your wife?" They claimed perfection—or at least superiority to every other state's bar and every other California profession—and expressed frustration when critics kept asking for more. But the observers could (and did) object that the same criticisms were made decade after decade—the Clark Report, the *Los Angeles Daily Journal* and *San Francisco Examiner* exposés, Fellmeth's detailed semi-annual reports—yet nothing changed.

The Bar constantly dragged its feet about creating and operating an effective regulatory system. It required lawyers to maintain client funds in a trust account only in 1956. It created the Client Security Fund only in 1972. It refused to require lawyers to carry malpractice insurance or even tell clients they did not have it. The Bar mandated the arbitration of fee disputes only in 1972. It successfully resisted making neglect—the single most common complaint—a ground for discipline. It opposed professionalizing the investigation, prosecution, and adjudication of client grievances as long as possible (even though the California Supreme Court was highly critical of decisions by volunteer referees). Its explanations for the extraordinarily few client "inquiries" that resulted in punishment failed to satisfy outsiders. It allowed backlogs and delays to reach intolerable levels; and when the public outcry became too vociferous, it focused all its energy on reducing those numbers without regard to the behavior underlying client grievances.

Because the contradictions of self-governance and self-regulation are structural, they are unlikely to be resolved. They generate endless debates over publicity and secrecy, alleged bias, lenience and severity, and recidivism, while failing to address the fundamental problems of lawyer behavior. For all those reasons, adjudicated cases represent only one window into the many ways in which lawyers betray trust. Nevertheless, I hope the following chapters show that the analysis of disciplinary cases is an essential first step in mapping what is still a largely unknown terrain.

2. COPS CHASING AMBULANCES

Once lawyers have successfully organized to act collectively, one of their first concerns is to suppress ambulance chasing. The prohibition on solicitation enacted in the early twentieth century has survived constitutional challenge.[1] California prohibits lawyers from soliciting business,[2] sharing legal fees with non-lawyers (who may solicit), or paying for referrals.[3] Despite repeated exposés and crackdowns,[4] however, many lawyers continue to violate the rules in their search for business. Decisions of the State Bar Court (SBC) Review Department reveal their modus operandi.

Bruce E. Nelson worked for Licker, Rothstein and Delchop in Los Angeles while in law school and for two years after graduation.[5] Like most firms representing car accident victims, Licker got clients "almost exclusively" through tow truck drivers, insurance agents, and other runners and cappers, paying about $500 per case. Thomas Carr, a law clerk for the firm, said he knew many insurance agents who could refer cases and proposed to split the profits with Nelson. For four months, Nelson remained at Licker while Carr set up practice elsewhere as an "administrator," got and interviewed clients, signed retainers, obtained medical records, negotiated settlements, and managed the trust account. His wife acted as his secretary and receptionist. Learning of this, Licker terminated Nelson, whose new practice flourished. Some cases came from Chamino, who had "administered" another firm but left after a conflict. When Nelson rejected a case for "bad liability" and "nominal" damages, Carr warned that Chamino had to agree. Although Nelson secured Chamino's consent, he became uneasy and moved to Sacramento, telling Carr to find another attorney. After Carr chose Samuel Tolbert (who had an adjacent office but had been admitted only sixteen months), Nelson told his 50 to 60 clients that Tolbert was "highly experienced and competent." Soon thereafter, the Carrs removed all the files (returning them a few weeks later). Carr also took between $40,000 and $50,000 from the client trust account and refused to repay it. Carr and Tolbert persisted in the misconduct, but Nelson made restitution for misappropriated client trust funds.

---

1. Compare Bates v. State Bar of Arizona, 433 U.S. 350 (1977) with Ohralik v. Ohio State Bar Ass'n, 436 U.S. 447 (1978) and Florida Bar v. Went For It, 515 U.S. 618 (1995).

2. California Rules of Professional Conduct (RPC) Rule 1-400 (formerly Rule 2-101).

3. Rule 1-320 (formerly Rule 3-102).

4. *E.g.*, Ward (1974).

5. Matter of Nelson, 1 Cal. State Bar Ct. Rptr. 178 (1990) (six months suspension, two years probation).

Francis E. Jones III had practiced insurance defense in several firms, including a large one in downtown Los Angeles.[6] Having lived in Taiwan for two years, he was fluent in Mandarin and connected to the Chinese-American community. Ye K. Lok, an insurance agent, suggested that Jones remain in his insurance defense firm while Lok set up a practice in Alhambra as "administrator," bringing in clients and splitting the profits. Jones signed articles of incorporation and gave them to Lok, who designated himself as president and chief executive officer (CEO). Jones authorized Lok to interview prospective clients, file claims with insurers, and negotiate settlements (subject to Jones's approval). Over the next two years, Lok handled hundreds of cases, many obtained from cappers; Jones visited the office (to which he had no key) only 10 to 15 times, meeting 10 to 15 clients, whom he believed were the entire clientele. There was no trust account. Then Jones terminated the arrangement, taking the 15 to 20 cases Lok said remained and telling Lok not to accept new ones. Although Lok removed Jones's name from the building directory (as instructed), he kept the office. Jones did not object, even though he knew Lok was not working for any other lawyer. Six months later, Lok's employee told Jones that Lok was still accepting cases in the lawyer's name. The next day Jones went to the office, seized all the files and documents bearing his name, and learned for the first time that Lok had forged his signature to open another bank account, into which he had deposited 400 insurance settlement checks totaling more than $2,150,000. (Jones evaluated those settlements as being at least as good as his own.) A few days later, Jones called the police. Lok was convicted of forgery. Jones spent $57,000 to settle medical liens.

Lawrence Bragg operated a high-volume personal injury practice in Hacienda Heights (east of Los Angeles) for three decades.[7] In 1992, Bruce Hickman approached him, claiming experience as an insurance adjuster, and offered to improve Bragg's advertising and management of prelitigation matters. They agreed that, for ten months, Bragg would move all prelitigation files to Hickman's Ontario office, pay Hickman's office expenses and salary out of the fees, and give Hickman 25 percent of the profit on transferred cases and half on clients he signed up. All new client calls were sent to Hickman, who interviewed prospects, prepared retainers (using Bragg's signature stamp), and did the investigations. Bragg's name was displayed in Hickman's Ontario office and on the signage and telephone messages in Hickman's other offices. Bragg rarely visited the Ontario office and provided little supervision for the 30 to 50 cases Hickman settled each month. Bragg paid Hickman about $350,000 under the agreement. Following a controversy, Hickman removed many files from the office and was arrested.

---

6. Matter of Jones, 2 Cal. State Bar Ct. Rptr. 411 (1993) (two years suspension, three years probation).

7. Matter of Bragg, 3 Cal. State Bar Ct. Rptr. 615 (1997) (one year suspension, two years probation).

Seven years after being admitted, Corey Steele hired Jim Gray as a clerk in his personal injury practice.[8] With Steele's acquiescence, Grey took over the office, conducting initial interviews, obtaining medical records, sending demand letters, negotiating settlements, signing for trust and general bank accounts, and doing the office's bookkeeping. Over Steele's protestations, Gray even represented himself as a partner. Steele spent only 15 to 20 hours a week in the office and did not know 85 percent of the clients—or how many there were. When Gray asked for payment on commission, Steele objected that it was illegal but agreed to pay a percentage of the gross. When Gray admitted embezzling at least $25,000 and sought to resign, Steel persuaded him to remain; but he quit when Steele left for a planned vacation two days later. When Steele threatened to report him, Gray went to the Los Angeles District Attorney first (and was convicted of grand theft).

After Robert Crowell and his sons Nathan and Sidney were injured in a car accident, Steven Kroff called their unlisted home number (which he got from the accident report) and asked Nathan to call back.[9] Because Nathan was only three, Robert's wife did so. When Kroff returned the call, Robert asked why they needed a lawyer. Kroff claimed to have been referred by a mutual friend whom he refused to identify, invoking attorney-client privilege. When Crowell disputed this and acknowledged being an attorney, Kroff declared: "Well, then, you can represent yourself," and hung up. In the disciplinary proceeding, Kroff insisted someone had urged him to phone Crowell but admitted making similar approaches to three other injury victims: a paralegal, a personal injury law firm employee, and a Boalt Hall law student! The day after yet another solicited client discharged Kroff, he wrote an insurance company claiming to represent her.

In June 1994, Marc A. Duxbury received a phone call from Dr. Hudgins, a chiropractor, who suggested he meet with Antonio Barajas of South Bay Marketing (SBM), a "guy with cases to sell."[10] "Barajas" was actually Tony Torres, an undercover state police officer with a wire, who offered to sell Duxbury cases for $500, including the police report, third-party insurance information, intake interview, photos, witness interviews, and property damage estimates. Duxbury said on tape:

> I'm gonna be frank with you . . . in the past I've had [an] arrangement [like] this with somebody and they were throwing cases that were kinda dogs, you know, they weren't real good cases. They were questionable liability and slip and fall. He was giving clients the idea that his cases were worth, you know [unintelligible] and that's how he was getting his clients and I didn't know it. I got no problem with that but to make it legitimate and legal and through the State Bar correct,

8. Matter of Steele, 3 Cal. State Bar Ct. Rptr. 708 (1997) (also commingled; disbarred).

9. Matter of Kroff, 3 Cal. State Bar Ct. Rptr. 838 (1998) (three years suspension, five years probation).

10. Matter of Duxbury, 4 Cal. State Bar Ct. Rptr. 61 (1999) (six months suspension, two years probation).

I've got to pay for some sort of a service. And what I'm paying for is the investigative service. I understand that. I like the way you guys set it up.

Duxbury got two cases from SBM. He paid $1,000 for the first (which had two plaintiffs), not charging this purported "investigation" expense to the clients. When he could not locate them, he hired a private investigator who discovered that they had given bogus Social Security numbers and addresses and SBM was just a mail drop. Duxbury refused to pay the $1,000 fee for the second case, complaining that he was not given the investigation results.

These cases suggest that solicitation is widespread and open. Lawyers learn it from mentors and peers, as well as the cappers themselves (who often use ethnic identity to attract minority clients). Many cappers initiate and dominate the scheme, doing everything except litigate. Lawyers seek to disguise cappers as independent contractors and "investigators," in order to preserve deniability. The arrangement is highly profitable to both sides. The following case reveals an unusually inventive method for connecting automobile injury victims with lawyers and doctors.

I. THE CAPPERS' MODUS OPERANDI

From late 1987 to September 1988, Joseph Gumban, a former San Francisco Police Department (SFPD) officer, and Robert Buchanan bought automobile accident reports from SFPD officers Betty Brown and John Arsanis, paying each about $3,000.[11] (Brown and Arsanis were later convicted and fired.) Buchanan and Gumban signed up victims, sent them to medical clinics (earning kickbacks of between $250 and $300 per case), and then sold them to lawyers: 50 to 60 to the partnership of Robert B. Scapa and Michael S. Brown for cash payments of up to $1,000 a case and 25 to 30 to John R. Pollitt for about $10,000 in cash.[12] Buchanan scrupulously recorded the names of 250 to 300 clients, noting when they were contacted and when he was paid by the medical clinic and attorney. Scapa and Brown admitted paying Gumban and Buchanan about $5,600 for other services. Pollitt claimed to have warned Gumban (his office manager) against solicitation, but his real focus was on avoiding discipline. Pollitt's retainer agreement required the client to "declare under penalty of perjury that my decision to retain the law firm of John R. Pollitt is not a result of . . . any solicitation made." When Brown learned that Gumban and Buchanan were buying police reports and soliciting clients, he warned they could get in trouble but kept buying their cases, requiring clients to sign a declaration like Pollitt's, that the decision to retain the firm "was not the result of any solicitation made by the LAW OFFICES

11. Notice to Show Cause (11.2.89) in Cases 88-O-12498 and 12499.

12. Pollitt's case, 88-O-11844, was originally joined with those against Scapa and Brown but later severed.

OF SCAPA & BROWN . . ..” The firm also asserted excessive fee liens when capped clients tried to fire them. The State Bar charged Scapa and Brown with solicitation, sharing fees with non-lawyers, failing to supervise Buchanan and Gumban, neglecting clients, and extorting unconscionable fees from those who sought to discharge them. The respondents' pretrial statement described Gumban and Buchanan as “independent contractors” retained “to do investigative work.”[13] Respondents had “thoroughly explained the ethics of case referral and believed at all times that Buchanan and Gumban were adhering to the guidelines they had set forth.” Any capping was “without their knowledge or acquiescence;” once they learned of it “they promptly took steps to prevent such activity from occurring.”

After the district attorney granted Buchanan immunity, Gumban unsuccessfully sought it, too. The respondents and their lawyer, Daniel Drapiewski, vigorously resisted State Bar discovery. Drapiewski claimed to have learned of the charges from a reporter contacted by the Office of Trial Counsel (OTC), which “gives some indication as to the motive behind this entire investigation.” OTC counsel Donald Steedman denounced this as “false.” Drapiewski objected to the State Bar obtaining releases from the respondents' clients to see their papers, denouncing this aspect of the investigation as a “witch hunt.” Steedman sought sanctions for violation of the discovery orders. After hearing examiner Alan K. Goldhammer ordered the respondents to answer interrogatories and produce documents, Drapiewski served interrogatories on the State Bar, asking for information about their contacts with witnesses, which the Bar refused to answer, citing attorney-client privilege. The respondents rejected the State Bar's offer of three years suspension.

When the hearing began, Goldhammer criticized the respondents for not complying with production orders. Drapiewski claimed the State Bar had not shown probable cause, prompting Steedman to make an offer of proof: Michael Milner had been romantically involved with the firm's office manager, Joanne Lopez (whose daughter, Arlene Gamit, also worked there). When the relationship ended, Milner refused the firm's request to do something improper and instead gave the State Bar the firm's business card identifying Gumban as “personal injury investigator and field representative.”[14] Steedman criticized the respondents' “hyper-technical reading” of the production order, which forced the State Bar “to drag these records, kicking and screaming” from the respondents to get them to state in deposition: “Well, yes, we do have other checks and we've given them to our attorneys, but the attorneys aren't turning them over to the State Bar.” Drapiewski found it “offensive” to have Steedman “taint the record” by suggesting that he and his clients were “involved in a scheme to manipulate the court system and to defraud him.” Steedman accused Drapiewski of doing at Gumban's deposition what he had failed to do at Buchanan's: “wait[ing]

13. Filed April 9, 1990.
14. State Bar Exhibit 46.

until the witness was . . . alone and attempt[ing] to advise the witness of his rights . . . until Mr. Gumban stopped testifying" and invoked the Fifth Amendment.

A. Gumban

When the hearing resumed two days later, and after the Superior Court granted Gumban immunity, Drapiewski wanted to repeat the warning that it was limited (which earlier had scared the capper into clamming up), claiming Gumban "was enticed into his testimony by misleading misrepresentations from the prosecutors," whose "outrageous" conduct should exclude Gumban's testimony and the OTC's use of his deposition. Steedman responded that Drapiewski should not be allowed to do "a long-winded objection intended to intimidate this witness." But though Goldhammer declared that the Superior Court order "confirms immunity with regard to capping," Gumban still resisted "because of the irregularity as far as granting of the immunity . . . I would rather risk to be charged with contempt . . . ."

He finally testified that he worked for the SFPD from 1985 to 1987 and knew Betty Brown. When Goldhammer twice overruled Drapiewski's objection to Steedman asking why Gumban left, Gumban objected, "[D]o I have a right to question the prosecution, also? . . . Because it seems unfair . . . what does my background have to do with my relationship with Scapa & Brown?" After Goldhammer declared Gumban a hostile witness, he said he told the partners he left the SFPD for "the same reason that I told them why I left the Philippines . . .. Because they're unfair." He had not disclosed his firing because "there was no need to elaborate." He had gone to work for Scapa & Brown because they were "a reputable law firm" and "I heard that they're widely used by Filipinos in their claim against insurance companies that are slow in paying." When he claimed not to remember how he learned of them, Steedman asked if it was from Jesse Reyes.

GUMBAN: The question is leading, and it's highly improper.

GOLDHAMMER: . . . I've ruled that you're a hostile witness.

GUMBAN: . . . [S]o I can be hostile now, right? . . .

GOLDHAMMER: Well, hostile is a legal—

GUMBAN: I understand the word "hostile," Your Honor.

Asked about capping, he said

> the partners orientated me to the procedures as to what the type of work I should be doing and what are the cautions that I have to exercise by way of avoiding illegal practices of capping and soliciting . . . my duty was to investigate cases and so I did. . . . the word gets around that the AAA [American Automobile Association],[15] who owns this particular building, by the way,

15. As an automobile insurer, the AAA's local branch, the California State Automobile Association (CSAA), had a reputation in the plaintiffs' bar for unreasonably denying liability and refusing to pay those injured by its insureds.

> where the State Bar Association sits, is conducting an investigation of all cases that may be exorbitant to the claim . . . a lot of attorneys, including Scapa and Brown . . . are leery about the situation . . . [O]ne of his employees may be . . . soliciting . . . . They said they don't want any practice of this sort in the office, because . . . it's obvious. They don't want to be disbarred.

He had told "only one" partner he could obtain cases through SFPD contacts.

> I didn't specifically and exclusively say that all my contacts would be coming from the Police Department . . .. I'm a popular man . . .. In fact, I'm running for office in Daly City as a councilman, and I think I'm going to win. And I get all my cases from the general public out there. I just happen to be a police officer, you know, an ex-police officer.

He had told both partners he "could help bring in cases to the law firm" through "a marketing concept where I can expose myself in the general public to come across people that needs representation." Only "a very small percentage" would come from the SFPD. Because his wife worked at a hospital, "I'm exposed to a lot of patients . . . that need an attorney . . . in the same token that if you work for the attorney, you can get the same cases, too, if you meet somebody in the hospital. What's wrong with that?" He never said that whenever, "she takes the blood that she will . . . find out whether he needs legal representation . . .."

During the eight months he worked for the firm, he bought police reports legally for $5 to $6 apiece, first claiming not to know who staffed the accident report counter but then admitting he might have mentioned Betty Brown to Buchanan. Although he denied knowing whether he had bought those reports before clients signed retainers, his testimony continued as follows:

GUMBAN: [I]f someone had come to me and said, "I got into an accident. . . . I need an attorney," before an attorney would accept it, the first thing they'd say [was] . . . "is there a police report?" and so what I'd do is, prior to taking them to an attorney, I would get the permission of the person . . . to give me the case number . . . and we'd go over there and pick up the police report. What's irregular about that?

STEEDMAN: And in some case, you got the police reports without having been contacted by the client; is that correct?

GUMBAN: On occasions—let's put it this way, okay? I would be driving on the freeway. I'd stop at an accident. I'd talk to the people, and I said, "What happened? Are you hurt? Do you have an attorney?" And he says, "No," and I says, "Well, I think I can get you an attorney." And he'd have the case number. And then I'd go to the PD [police department] and get a copy of the police report. It's a matter of public record. And then I'd go to the attorney's office, and I said, "Look. I have this case. Would you like to accept it?" . . . I'd tell them, "Look. This was referred to me by a friend," although I did, in fact, stop and . . . talk to the person. But, the attorney doesn't have to know this. I'd have to lie sometimes to make some money.

STEEDMAN: . . . [Y]ou never bought a police report without having first spoken to the client?

GUMBAN: . . . There were some instances where some police reports may be floating . . . on a few occasions, I did, in fact, call some clients who were not represented by any attorney out of the police report. But, those police reports were obtained, I think, legally over the counter. . . . [H]owever Robert Buchanan purchased it, whether he—and I'm not suggested he's doing this—from a police report number—it's so easy to do it, you know. You get a case number from 1.00.83 and you work your way up consecutively . . . and there's 3,000 accidents that occurs in . . . San Francisco today.

He admitted giving the firm some clients he contacted after buying the police report but denounced as "stupid" the question of how many he had solicited. After being reminded that he had waived the Fifth Amendment, he invoked "equal protection of the law." While admitting that "a very small percentage of the cases that I had referred" to the firm "are solicited over the phone," he insisted the "attorney doesn't know this . . .."

Asked if he got "a share of attorney's fees," Gumban said:

> There was discussion about bonus at the end of the year, after . . . evaluation of performance of any investigator. . . . That could still be construed through this percentage . . . of a specific case, it could be lumped all the pieces together . . . there's a bonus on the number of cases that stays in the books . . . every attorney pays a bonus to a secretary . . . .

Warned not to be defensive, Gumban complained: "It's not so easy, sir, to be answering all the questions here. I wish I can ask questions, too." As an investigator, he was paid $25 to $50 a case plus expenses. He conceded the bonus would be based "partly" on the number of cases but added "it was too early" to fix those arrangements when he was hired. When he raised the question—because "I'm unemployed now. I need some help"—they had to "look at the books and see . . . how many of the cases that I have investigated turn out to be good . . .." But the firm ultimately said, "[T]hey're losing money . . .. There's no bonus."

The hearing recessed for ten minutes, but Goldhammer broke for lunch when Gumban did not return and admonished him for this when they resumed. Gumban testified that he told the partners, "I met the client on the street. I lied about it to them." He claimed there had been "repetitive" warnings against solicitation because the lawyers "don't want to get involved in any of that." He sometimes had clients sign retainers before meeting a lawyer because "it just happens on occasions when no one's there to have the client sign the documents." "I have this fancy about being an attorney . . .. I'd like to sometimes volunteer doing things like that . . . I'm not being paid to do." He was taking the LSAT in few days in order to apply to law school. Asked if he had told anyone else in the office how he got cases, Gumban was evasive, finally saying "I don't think I'd be that stupid . . . if I know I was doing something . . . irregular . . . ." He denied calling clients from police reports before partnering with Buchanan although he had acknowledged doing so at his deposition. In colloquy with Goldhammer, Drapiewski twice called Gumban his client before correcting himself. Gumban admitted that, the day before, Drapiewski had "cautioned me for talking too much."

Drapiewski began cross-examination by moving to strike Gumban's testimony. He then tried to show that Gumban was an independent contractor, with no fixed salary or hours. At his first meeting, the respondents told him "not to solicit prospective clients" and gave him a "policy memorandum that identified the do's and don't's" of his work, quoting Business & Professions Code (BPC) Section 6152 in full and declaring[16]

> [T]he policy of these OFFICES, and any of it's [sic] agents, or employees, to be strictly bound by the express terms . . . . Therefore, do not contact any party regarding employment unless that party has first expressed an interest in discussing the matter or retaining us to represent them.

The firm "strictly prohibits the payment of money . . . for the direct acquisition of cases." The "investigator" was "to make it clear that it is illegal to offer or pay any form of compensation for the procuring of cases." Because the firm "will be able to obtain much better settlements then [*sic*] those lawyers who offer such inducements . . . their net recovery . . . will be higher." The investigator agreed "to follow the outlined Policies and [understood] that any violation of them will be grounds for instant termination of my contract of employment." Gumban "fabricated stories about how I had gotten the client . . . because, as you can see, if I had told them the truth about how I got—," but Steedman interrupted that this was narrative. "Some [medical] clinics had paid [for] some referrals," which Gumban admitted were "kickbacks." But he never informed the lawyers. Asked on redirect why he had risked his job by soliciting cases if he was not being paid for them, Gumban said he would "have more cases to investigate and that puts more money in my pocket." He gave a convoluted answer to Goldhammer's question about how he was paid: "Whoever the attorney that might be present at the time that I introduced the client to . . . how much I'm going to get paid is after the client has been met by the attorney . . . how much is involved in the process of investigating the case."

While this proceeding was maturing, complaints were filed on behalf of three former clients, accusing the firm of improperly withholding medical payments

16. "Policy Memorandum of the Law Offices of Scapa and Brown," Respondents' Exhibit B.

received from insurance companies and ignoring the successor attorney's requests. Although Drapiewski eventually promised that the funds would be "disbursed consistent with the law firm's trust obligations," the State Bar added these charges.

The State Bar's trial brief alleged that the partners solicited clients from February to September 1988, stopping only when Buchanan could not explain to Brown how he got a police report with the officer's original handwriting. Steedman alleged that, despite the warnings and suspicions, Brown bought cases from both cappers for large cash payments and $2,757 in checks, keeping no receipts or records. "[P]ayment by case" and "cases assigned in accordance with who brought the case into the office . . . encouraged Buchanan and Gumban to solicit clients." Although Scapa claimed the firm had given the cappers a list of 500 doctors, they referred almost everyone to Mission Family Medical Clinic. Buchanan would testify he "was paid based on the value of the particular case involved." If the case "was worthless, Buchanan received no compensation for his work. The amount of the payment had nothing to do with the amount of work performed." Scapa "promised Buchanan additional funds if cases settled for large figures."

The respondents replied that they operated "a Los Angeles based law office with a substantial, volume personal injury clientele," serving "primarily the Latin and Asian communities."

> Using computerized calendaring, filing, logging, correspondence, and pleadings systems, the firm was able to substantially reduce the time and cost of opening, working, and closing files. By training non-attorneys to perform tasks ordinarily assigned to lawyers, the firm further reduced its overhead. By aggressive self-promotion through direct mailings, television, print advertising, personal appearances, social and business networking, the law firm attracted a volume of business that made small cases attractive and profitable.
>
> The success of Scapa and Brown was the success of its clients. Claimants who would not otherwise know of their rights had those rights identified for them. . . . In years past, uneducated, unsophisticated accident victims did not receive any recovery for modest, soft tissue injuries. Through the efforts of Scapa and Brown and other law firms like it, such people learned that their claims were compensable, learned that the system indexed their claims for general damages to their special damages, and learned to take full advantage of their insurance, medical, and legal rights.

The firm blamed the prosecution on "Trial Counsel's primal, visceral reaction to professional marketing and volume practice," rather than "twelve or so incidents of alleged solicitation." Although

> nominally this is a case about the misuse of a few police reports . . . intrinsically it is [about] Scapa and Brown's ability to succeed in a volume practice and the threat this poses to the insurance industry that stands behind this

> State Bar prosecution. . . . Two years and the time of a dozen attorneys, paralegals, and investigators have gone into the interview of scores of witnesses, review of hundreds of files, and the subpoena of thousands of papers. The inquiry has resulted in investigation pacts with criminal prosecutors and the insurance industry. . . . [T]here has never been a State Bar investigation (not even the Watergate investigation) that has taken such time, money, and energy. . . . [T]he message is that Trial Counsel does not yet accept the opening of the profession as the courts and the public are demanding.

The respondents were being pilloried for "innovations." "An attorney can pay a 'referral fee' to a lay person just as he/she would to an attorney so long as it is not based upon a 'promise, agreement, or understanding.'" They defended satellite offices: "[T]he economics of their practice require substantial work by non-attorneys from offices in the communities that are served." "[M]odern thinking" maintained "that in routine cases there is no necessity that the attorney ever interview the client. Modest claims can be handled from start to finish with the attorney's participation limited to the review of documentation at critical stages in the operation."

> Traditional thinking suggests that an attorney should sit behind her desk and wait for clients to come to her. Modern practitioners cannot afford to be so passive. They must hustle clients in the same way that other business men and women hustle customers. Mr. Scapa and Mr. Brown . . . surround themselves with employees whose background, language skills, and the like make these employees the social bridges between the minority world of the clients and the legal profession.

In the summer of 1987, they decided to expand by opening a northern California branch to serve their 15 to 25 existing clients and seek new ones. They chose San Bruno for its proximity to the airport and large Latino and Asian communities. "They hired staff from the minority communities they hoped to serve." While "not absentee businessmen," they "relied upon a completely new group of employees in a location that was hundreds of miles from their home base." They admitted lacking "satisfactory control over staff and cases in northern California."

Gumban and Buchanan would testify they created a partnership for "the illegal solicitation of law clients" before contacting the firm. During the six months of the "plot," they "had access to virtually every police report generated" and developed "a referral system through which they would receive fees from the medical providers, auto tow operators, and auto repair shops their claimants use." They "needed attorneys who might be easily duped into innocent participation" and "did volume work," so that "the cases that came in through the solicitation plot would be lost in the shuffle of cases which came through legitimate sources." They also "needed to place the cases in more than one outlet." They began interviewing attorneys in early 1988. One could "reasonably conclude" that they made the same pitch "to numerous other Bay Area attorneys over a period of months" and referred more cases to other attorneys, including Pollitt & Pollitt, and Buchholtz and Canter. The respondents were ignorant of "THE GUMBAN/ BUCHANAN PLOT." The cappers "sold their services as investigators . . . in order to conceal their illicit activities" and "did all of those things that were expected of investigators including witness interviews, site drawings, document recovery, etc." In a volume practice, "each small file does not get the attention that a large file would get . . .." Because "Asian and Latin communities 'network' along clan and village lines in a way that is totally alien to mainstream America . . . a single patron will be the conduit through which an extended group of neighbors and family members receive professional services." Even if respondents had analyzed the cappers' referrals, "their reaction would [have been] nothing more than . . . pleasant surprise . . .."

When the hearing resumed, Drapiewski moved to dismiss for insufficiency of the notice to show cause (NTSC), which Steedman called an oral, out-of-time "surprise motion," and moved to limit evidence of solicitation to the police reports. Goldhammer denied both. Steedman opened by arguing that this was "a very high-priced law firm . . . not a cut-rate law firm designed for minority groups." Respondents had testified that they opened the San Francisco office because "their clients in Los Angeles were drying up," not "because they had a successful Los Angeles office." Although respondents claimed lack of control over northern California staff, the cappers attended the office when the partners were there "because those were the days [the cappers] could discuss their cases" and "get paid." The cappers did not rely on a "network along clan and village lines" because the solicited clients were "a cross-section of the community . . . essentially, a random sampling of the best police reports that would come into San Francisco . . .."

B. Buchanan

After Buchanan was sworn, Drapiewski moved that the immunity grant was insufficient. Steedman admitted that the San Francisco District Attorney (DA) had only informally promised it but objected that Buchanan had already given a long police statement and deposition and criticized this "intimidation of the witnesses" and "surprise motion." Goldhammer said only Buchanan could invoke the Fifth Amendment. Doron Weinberg (who had become Brown's lawyer) urged Goldhammer to warn Buchanan he had no immunity. Drapiewski added that because Starr Babcock (the original trial counsel) had "directly, expressly, and unmistakably" told Buchanan he "was Mr. Buchanan's attorney," it was "improper" to have Buchanan testify "with that history of misconduct." Goldhammer advised Buchanan that "although those representations by the deputy District Attorney are honored by the District Attorney's office . . . they don't have to be."

Buchanan testified that he had graduated from the University of San Francisco in 1957 and attended law school for a year before working in sales. Gumban's wife and his own were friends from the same Philippine village. In December 1986, Gumban asked Buchanan to join him "essentially, soliciting clients" for three law firms.

> [I]nitially, Gumban apparently was able to get reports across the counter because he had been a policeman and had a good relationship down there with the counter people. And then later, he made a contact with a police officer and for money he purchased the police reports.

Buchanan met Arsanis and Betty Brown and saw her give Gumban reports. After getting them free for three to four months, Buchanan started paying $750 per week in cash "in the general area of the Hall of Justice." The two police officers divided the money equally. For about ten weeks, Buchanan got 40 to 60 reports a week, selected by the police. "I reviewed them and then I'd call what I believed to be likely prospects for attorney services." He told those prospects, "I was with a law firm, without identifying the law firm . . . and if they seemed receptive, I would go and see them." If the victims "were so inclined" he had them sign retainers containing the disclaimer:

> I hereby declare under penalty of perjury that my decision to retain the law offices of Scapa & Brown does not result in [sic] any promises, offer, monetary or otherwise, and was not the result of any solicitation made by the law offices of Scapa & Brown or any of their employees, agents, representatives or assignees, or by any person whatsoever.

After Gumban introduced him to the respondents in January 1988, he stopped selling cases to the Pollitt firm, which he did not like. The respondents never asked him to do investigative work on cases other than those he solicited. Gumban told Michael Brown that Buchanan would be working with him "getting the cases." Brown repeated three or four times, "that I was not supposed to solicit and that I would get into trouble and our relationship would be terminated." "Gumban and I had a falling out. I felt he wasn't living up to his end of making the payments . . . for the police reports." Buchanan "stopped doing it for . . . maybe a week . . . and then I reactivated my relationship with the two police people" for another two or three months. He thought Brown knew

> we were purchasing the reports from the police department. . . . Gumban would just run off at the mouth endlessly as to . . . how we did everything. . . . Michael Brown was . . . very strong in his statements that our relationship would come to an end if I continued my methods of operation, but he was never specific on anything . . . he must have been aware of the fact that I was soliciting and getting police reports.

About two-thirds of the way through the relationship Buchanan had "one very clear" conversation in which Brown said he should stop what he was doing, but Buchanan kept selling the firm cases, ceasing only when Sgt. Bacca came to his house to investigate the purchase of police reports. Even after that, however, Buchanan met with the firm and "was paid for several cases that . . . were essentially completed." He sold it 30 to 40 cases, for up to a $1,000 each (in cash except for one or two checks), making about $1,000 a week (after paying for the reports). Although there had been a "discussion" about "a possibility" of further payment for a "good settlement," he never got any. He referred about half the cases to Mission Family Medical Center (for $250 each) and half to Pacific Heights Clinic (for $300), both of which paid after patients "completed a number of treatments," usually five or six. Although "we were told not to spend time in the office," which "was not to be considered our office," he went there twice a week, when the partners were present, "to negotiate the best deal we could get for the case" and "turn in the cases and collect any money." The cappers had the use of a desk, phone, and room but preferred to work from home.

Buchanan authenticated a notebook in his handwriting recording "the date of the accident, the time that they signed up with me, the [SFPD] case number, the money that was paid to me, what clinic they attended, and the number of times they visited the clinic, and the property damage."[17] The entries, which began in June 1988 and referred only to the respondents, recorded nineteen payments (three for $1,000; nine for $800, two for $600; and one each for $500, $400, and $200). "[F]or fractures, generally I'd receive more money." Many of the recorded cases produced no payments. The column headed "final" was "for the ultimate disposition of the case to see if I was entitled to any more money or if . . . the insurance claim was not recognized or whatever contingency could have arisen." "The great majority" of these cases came from police reports, with only "two, three, possibly four" from other sources. During voir dire, Weinberg asked Buchanan about his notebook and was told, "Gumban started me on this and he set it up, and eventually, I synthesized it so it was somewhat better." Goldhammer admitted it as past recollection recorded. Steedman introduced an $800 check by Rosalyn Brown to American Ladder (Buchanan's legitimate business), which Buchanan described as "payment on a case."[18] (Drapiewski objected but was reminded that it was *his* exhibit.)

C. Seronio

Constance Seronio testified that five or six weeks after her husband Robert's April 1, 1988, car accident, there was a message on her answering machine: "My name is Bert Gabriel. I understand you had an accident. Please contact me," at a phone number that was provided. When she called, he said, "he'd like to come over and talk to us because he was referred to us by my ex-brother-in-law," who confirmed this. Gabriel, "a tall Filipino man . . . pulled up in front of home in a

17. State Bar Exhibit 1A.
18. State Bar Exhibit 3.

big Mercedes sedan . . . very well-dressed . . . a lot of fine jewelry," and "said he was representing Attorneys Scapa and Brown." Although her husband had "not really" suffered any injuries and was "only a bit sore here and there," Gabriel had him sign a retainer and referred him to the Mission Family Medical Clinic. The OTC submitted the retainer and a business card identifying Gabriel at "Law Offices of SCAPA, BROWN & ASSOCIATES," giving their address and phone number (with his home phone written in).[19] On June 3, Robert told the firm he had retained Madison J. Marcus and asked that his file be transferred.[20] Constance testified that she "called Gabriel several times getting nowhere." He refused to contact the CSAA about property damage, saying "that's not in your contract," although that was all they needed "because my husband wasn't injured to the point where he would have needed any kind of compensation for medical expenses." Gabriel canceled two appointments with the lawyers because they were in Southern California. The firm did no work on her husband's case "as far as I'm concerned." Marcus wrote the firm on June 24, requesting the file and an itemization of time and costs.[21] Although he never got the latter, Brown sent the file with a letter asserting "equitable liens for both services rendered and costs advanced." Brown also wrote CSAA asserting a lien and threatening to seek compensatory and punitive damages if it was ignored. Steedman noted that the file "consisted of one document, specifically, an assertion of the lien."

CSAA settled on April 10, 1989, for $1,800, payable to Seronio and Marcus. Virginia Espinoza (Brown's secretary) wrote Marcus on July 11 that her firm "was on the settlement draft." Marcus denied this, agreeing with Steedman that the only document in the file was the lien assertion. When Weinberg asked for the complete file, Marcus said it was privileged. Weinberg insisted there was "considerably more," seeking to show that the firm wrote four letters (to insurers, medical care providers, and Seronio). When Steedman objected to the "personal attack" on Marcus, Weinberg assailed "the intrusion by the State Bar into the relationship between Scapa and Brown and their clients . . . which prevented Scapa and Brown from getting recompensed to the extent they were entitled . . .."

D. Behrmann

After a night in the emergency room following her April 7, 1988 accident, Michelle Behrmann got home about noon, still medicated and in shock. She had just enough time to phone the SFPD for the police report and learn she could not get it for seven working days before she got a call from "Jacqueline or Joaquin" (Joanne Lopez), who "said that she had my police report and that she had some recommendations for attorneys, Scapa and Brown" and could help find a doctor. Because Behrmann wanted to see the report, "I told her to

19. State Bar Exhibits 26 and 24.

20. State Bar Exhibit 25.

21. State Bar Exhibit 27.

come down." The 30- to 35-year-old Asian American woman arrived within an hour. Behrmann agreed to talk about attorneys and doctors, "but I didn't want to make no promises being that I was under medication, and I wasn't quite all there," from having bashed her head. Lopez said "No problem. No problem. You can always . . . cancel at any time" by giving written notice within seventy-two hours. Behrmann signed the retainer,[22] and Lopez recommended a chiropractic clinic (which could have been Mission). But because "it seemed funny," and Behrmann was not "comfortable," she called a friend, who recommended Larry Murray (a lawyer). Behrmann called him at 3 P.M. and saw him later that day. He advised her to revoke the retainer orally and confirm that in writing. The next day she talked to the firm's receptionist.

> First, I asked for Jacqueline, and she said—she didn't know who I was talking about, okay? And then I said, "Well, is one of the attorneys there?" And she asked me who this person was, too, and I . . . didn't know. And then I told her that I was going to cancel, okay? I no longer needed them, and she stated that she would send me a form.

On April 18, she got a letter from Arline Gamit, asking for a copy of her automobile insurance policy and other papers. She returned it two days later, writing on the back: "Scapa and Brown. I would like you to know that I got my own attorney. Thank you for your consideration anyway." But she could not get her car repaired because on July 6, Scapa and Brown asserted a lien on her insurance company payment. She talked to a firm secretary, who promised to have someone call back, but no one did. The second time she called, the secretary said she could not speak with the lawyers, who were in Los Angeles, but someone would call. No one did. She made eight to ten calls to the San Bruno office, and at least five to Los Angeles, where Virginia Espinoza "was very rude," saying she could not find the file, which was locked up downstairs. Repairs were delayed for two months. On October 4, Espinoza sent Murray a $1,145.02 "itemization" of services, including $200 for an initial interview that had never occurred, $100 for the telephone call in which Behrmann terminated the retainer, and another $300 for reading Murray's substitution letter and writing the clinics.

When Behrmann insisted she had been solicited, Weinberg introduced the form she signed on April 8, declaring "under penalty of perjury that my decision to retain the LAW OFFICES OF SCAPA AND BROWN was not the result of . . . any solicitation . . .." Ridiculing the idea that Behrmann "was so out of it that it was an imposition on her . . . for anyone to have her sign a retainer agreement," Weinberg argued that either "she wasn't in such bad shape," or "Mr. Murray is equally culpable." She denied waiting to fire the firm for two weeks or that it had

22. State Bar Exhibit 17.

worked on her case during that period. Weinberg suggested that the lawyers refused to talk to her because it would have been improper after she fired them.

Murray testified that he wrote Scapa & Brown on June 18 that Behrmann "indicated to me that she had terminated any relationship with your office as of April 25, 1988." If the firm asserted a lien, it should itemize its time and send the lien and all correspondence. On July 6, Brown sent Murray the file and asserted the lien. He also asserted it against her two insurers (CSAA and the Fireman's Fund), threatening punitive damages if it were disregarded. On July 13, Murray's associate again requested an itemized bill, now maintaining that Behrmann had terminated the firm's services the day after retaining it. David Bailey of CSAA wrote Murray on August 17, repeating their phone conversation five days earlier that he could not pay Behrmann's repair bills because of the lien by Scapa & Brown, who would not respond to him. Murray wrote Brown again on August 28, noting his repeated requests for an itemization, without which he could not settle with Behrmann's insurers and get her car repaired. Since she terminated the retainer within a day, "your hours and total lien amount cannot be that great." He repeated that on September 5, finally producing an itemization on October 4. Murray responded a week later that there was no initial interview with a lawyer (for which they had charged $200), and he objected to the claim of an hour to prepare three letters, another for two phone calls, and a third for "two standardized letters requesting medical records." A phone call lasting no more than a minute or two was billed at half an hour. He asked for a "reasonable bill" and Brown's comment on the validity of his contingency fee contract, since BPC Section 6147 required that it be signed by the attorney, and again requested the file.

On October 25, Brown offered to negotiate a lower lien and wrote again on January 16, asking for a response. Murray remembered calling Brown and citing a recent case that made an unsigned retainer voidable. When Murray challenged the time accounts, Brown called the bill "fair" but offered to "arbitrate it, present it to the court, or take the difference and put the difference in the [pro-plaintiff] Prop. 103 campaign." "[T]empers flared, [and] hostile words were exchanged," during the conversation. Brown's contemporaneous notes indicated *he* had called; Murray was a "real ass," who had offered $100; Brown countered with $750; Murray, "said I was out of my mind—I hung up on him."

E. Tashiro

Three days after Kenneth Tashiro broke his wrist in a February 17, 1988, motorcycle accident, Gumban called to say the firm was "interested in representing me and at least talking to me about that," and asked "if they could come by my house." Since "the officer who took the accident report . . . told me that my accident report would be on file in five days," Tashiro asked how they had found him, but "it was kind of just sort of brushed over." Gumban and Buchanan visited him the next day, dressed in suits, and gave him a Scapa & Brown business card with their home phone numbers on the back.[23]

> Initially, I thought they were attorneys, when they first came to my door. They had briefcases and such. . . . They thought it was a good idea that I see a chiropractor, and I believe they had the name of a chiropractic that they wanted me to visit . . . . I told them that I had my own . . . . They told me that it was a fairly major law firm . . . they had an office in Los Angeles but they also had a smaller office on the Peninsula.

Tashiro consulted Ilson Woo New on March 2 and signed a retainer two days later.[24] On March 17, New phoned the firm and told Arline Gamit that Tashiro "had been solicited by some people from their office" and "may have signed an agreement" but "didn't know if it was an agreement."[25] He asked for a copy. Although Gamit said Tashiro had called the firm, he denied it. He had been "shocked" when they called before he could get the police report and "couldn't understand how they got his telephone number." New drafted a latter about this to Scapa on March 21[26] and phoned Virginia Espinosa twice on March 22, but she returned neither call. He sent the letter on March 23 and finally spoke to Scapa on March 25. New observed that the date of Scapa's letter to Tashiro had been changed from March 25 to March 19 "to make the letter appear that it had gone out before I had talked to that office." Scapa was "very cordial," even "saccharine and syrupy," insisting "our office doesn't do things like that" and "Mr. Tashiro is all yours." Scapa did not want anything because he had invested "very little time" and was "very apologetic" about the solicitation, saying "I'd really like to know how aggressive they were, because we don't want our people to do things like that . . .." On May 16, Brown finally answered New's two-month-old letter, enclosing the file but reasserting a lien for fees and costs.[27] New answered on June 6 that this was a "substantial surprise" and urged Brown to discuss it with Scapa.[28] Scapa wrote back on June 28 that the firm was not asserting any lien.[29]

F. Sandles

Buchanan phoned Janice Sandles soon after her April 27, 1988, accident, representing that he worked for Scapa & Brown and had the police report "because he was also a consultant to the SFPD." He brought it when he visited, making an appointment at and accompanying her to Mission Family Health Clinic. He convinced her

23. State Bar Exhibit 55.
24. State Bar Exhibit 27.
25. State Bar Exhibit 28.
26. State Bar Exhibit 29.
27. State Bar Exhibit 31.
28. State Bar Exhibit 33.
29. State Bar Exhibit 34.

"this was the best law firm in the State of California." Because the other car was insured by AAA, he explained, she "would be in a conflict of interest with AAA" and not the uninsured driver. She could avoid this "by letting Scapa and Brown represent me." She signed a retainer on May 7.[30] A week later Buchanan drove her to the office to meet Brown, who described Buchanan as his "agent" and "representative." She said she did not want to sue AAA, but just "get my car back together, my body back together, see if Ms. Kooch or whoever had insurance." When she asked how Buchanan got the accident report so quickly, given that the police had told her it would take five to ten days and she had an unlisted number, Brown said Buchanan "was a representative for the police department," which made her "comfortable" and "secure." Brown explained that because he would be commuting between his southern and northern California offices, "Robert [Buchanan] would be the person that I would talk to most of the time."

Sandles was "clear" she could withdraw from the retainer "without fees or anything." Because her car needed repairs and AAA refused to authorize them or talk to her, she tried to reach Brown, who was always out and did not return calls. When she finally went to the office and insisted on seeing him, he told her to take the car to Don's Auto Body shop. He even offered to advance the money when she said she could not afford it, but she wanted AAA to pay. She asked if Ann Kooch had insurance, but the firm had not checked. Brown eventually called and said Kooch was irrelevant because she had not been driving the car. Sandles kept phoning the firm, but Brown was never in. She finally reached Scapa and told him "I was trying to find Mr. Robert Buchanan," whose number had been disconnected. Scapa said Buchanan "no longer worked for them, and he had no way of telling me where I could find him." When she tried to terminate the retainer, "they told me that I could not get out of the contract; that they were going to settle with AAA . . .."

Drapiewski tried to show that the State Bar had persuaded her to complain about solicitation. Her Informal Complaint alleged:[31]

> Mr. Michael Brown have not and will not release me from a contract that I signed against the people that hit me in the rear end of my car. According to Attorney Robert Buchanan and Brown no money was to be exchanged if the parties that is envolved [sic] had no insurance. Scaple [sic] & Brown have refused to return my phone calls now for months. Please find out for me where is Mr. Robert Buchanan he have just disappeared.

The second page alleged that Buchanan contacted her, claiming to work for "Scape [*sic*] & Brown," and "signed the retainer for Michael Brown." Sandles said she wrote both the same day. Drapiewski argued she had no "legitimate grievance" and had been manipulated by the Bar. The firm was just waiting for her

---

30. State Bar Exhibit 42.
31. Respondent's Exhibit E (March 13, 1989).

medical condition to stabilize; once that happened in December, they promptly sent a demand letter to AAA (authorizing the insurer to discuss the case with Sandles but insisting that "any settlement negotiations should be discussed with our office").[32] Although Drapiewski tried to show the firm had filed her case, Steedman said Sandles was complaining about its failure to return phone calls, and Goldhammer agreed that "a client is entitled to be unhappy with their attorneys over reasons that are important to the client, regardless of whether the attorneys were or were not doing, from a strictly legal standpoint, correct work."

Weinberg then moved to exclude Sandles's testimony, based on an offer to prove she was unhappy with AAA's failure to pay property damage, not with the firm. When she realized she would get only $15,000 because the driver was uninsured, she got upset and demanded to talk to AAA directly. On January 20, AAA refused to do so without the firm's consent, which it gave three days later. Determined to explore a pre-existing condition, however, AAA insisted she sign medical authorizations and waivers, which she refused to do. She complained to the State Bar in March 1989 that the firm was not calling her back. "Part of the reason . . . is because she was calling every day for them to take care of a problem which was of her creation." After that complaint, the State Bar asked about solicitation, which is "why there is a second, separate document attached which starts all over again."

The respondents' lawyers derided Sandles, who was "somewhat incredible," "just spewing forth ad lib," "can't tell a consistent story," and had "an extraordinary lapse" of memory. "[W]e can get her to say just about anything we or the Court wants." But Goldhammer cautioned them that "I'm the one here hearing the evidence, folks." In response to his question, Sandles insisted she had asked about Buchanan because he "had certified papers or something that said he worked for the PD," and Brown "admitted" that. "I felt that Mr. Robert Buchanan worked for the PD and Scapa and Brown." When she and her girlfriend met Buchanan in Wendy's, he said, "he could sign either one" of the lawyers' names. When he initialed changes in the retainer "RB," "my girlfriend and I asked Robert Buchanan if he had the right to sign Michael's name . . . and this is when he showed us this paper that he was a representative of them and he was authorized by them to sign their name . . . "

G. Cohen

When Alan Lee Cohen (an OTC attorney until September 1989) came home from work in March 1988, three days after being injured in an accident, his wife said she had received a call from "an attorney, or on behalf of an attorney" and was "quite surprised" because they had not discussed consulting anyone. When Cohen returned the call that evening, Buchanan "made it clear that he was working

---

32. Respondent's Exhibit F.

for the law firm of Scapa and Brown," which was interested in representing Cohen—whom Buchanan called "the plaintiff, although no action had been filed." Buchanan said he had gotten the information, including the names of all the drivers, from Bay Area Referral Service. Although Buchanan was "very complimentary" about Cohen's wife, "trying to butter me up," Cohen rebuffed Buchanan's offer to come to his home and instead went to the firm's office with Laura Triantafyllos, a State Bar investigator impersonating Cohen's wife. They talked in "what I assumed was Mr. Buchanan's office," where there was "part of a police report," which Cohen saw for the first time. Buchanan told Cohen that Scapa would represent him because Brown was about to get married; and he indicated "that one of the attorneys had already reviewed my case and thought it was a good case." Buchanan asked about Cohen's medical treatment and "advised me that the law firm had doctors and chiropractors who they worked with that I could go see if I wanted to." "There were a number of other . . . police reports or correspondence that were sort of stacked up . . . on his desk." Cohen noted the names of clients and doctors. Buchanan tried to get Cohen to sign various forms and "let me read them, but he wouldn't let me leave the office with them." Buchanan said Cohen could not see an attorney until he signed.

Writing up these events a week later, Cohen noted that in their first phone call Buchanan had said the attorneys thought it "a highly winnable situation."[33] The law firm would advance the cost of his medical care, vehicle repair, rental car, and lost wages. Buchanan boasted "his office had just signed up the 'plaintiffs' in a five-car chain reaction which had occurred the preceding night at 11:45 P.M. near the airport." At the meeting two days later, Buchanan said Cohen could expect to get some money in six or seven months. Buchanan "was very interested in my medical treatment, and suggested several physicians . . .." He also implied that Cohen could change or cancel the retainer at any time, saying "Hey, we don't want unhappy clients!"

On cross-examination, Drapiewski accused Cohen of visiting the firm "under a pretext" and making "misrepresentations"; and he charged the State Bar with "setting up a sting" and behaving "in improper ways." It had been "illegal" for Triantafyllos (actually Cohen's wife) to listen to the phone conversation and take notes. Cohen admitted seeing documents on Buchanan's desk but denied touching them. A "number of police reports" were "fanned out" in "plain view." "I sort of assumed that Mr. Buchanan was showing me these to try to get me to believe that, yes, we have a lot of clients."

H. Expert Witnesses

Arne Werchick had practiced plaintiffs personal injury law for 25 years and been California Trial Lawyers Association president in 1980. In voir dire, Weinberg

33. State Bar Exhibit 30.

sought to show that Werchick had built his practice on his father's reputation, arguing that "it was standard practice in that period to pay referral fees to lawyers who sent cases." But though Werchick admitted giving "somebody a turkey at Christmas," he never made payments "on a case-by-case basis." "[B]efore a retainer agreement is entered into between a lawyer and a client, there should be some communication between the lawyer and the client." The lawyer had a duty "to make sure that the client understood the terms" and could not delegate this task to "paralegals or secretaries or investigators." "[I]t starts to stretch coincidence if you get 10 or 20 going to the same doctor . . . that's probably contrary to the interest of the clients . . .." Cash payments to an investigator "don't just represent a legitimate fee for a legitimate service." He would suspect he was "paying for something other than the $6 it would cost to get a police report." He also would begin to wonder if an independent contractor working for other firms began to produce "a flow of cases." Ilson New's letter would be another "good cause for suspicion." Werchick criticized the solicitation disclaimer: "I cannot imagine a legitimate motive myself in asking a client to say he was not induced to come to your firm."

> I think that capping is one of the most highly anti-competitive things that can happen in the legal profession . . . the theory under which the profession has had to . . . accept advertising . . . is that . . . making the public aware of a wider variety of legal resources . . . will contain the cost . . . . Capping . . . is exactly the opposite. . . . [I]t is using improper resources to get that client into a law firm, irrespective of whether that law firm is the best or most able to handle the client's problem in the best way. . . . [I]t is a particularly obnoxious, deplorable, and unacceptable thing when capping is done in order to get clients to agree to the highest, most expensive type of legal services . . . . The client has been disserved. The public has been disserved. And the profession has been embarrassed.

The firm's $200 an hour fee was "a top hourly fee" for experienced personal injury attorneys in litigation. It was "very unusual," even "unconscionable," "to specify that the lawyer gets $600 even if the lawyer hasn't done any work . . .." Although liquidated damages probably were unenforceable, it "can be really intimidating to the client to say . . . 'You better think about it, because you can't discharge me without owing me $600.'" The contingent fee seemed to be based on gross recovery, which was inappropriate here and uncommon. That was "a pretty important thing when you're talking about a three or four or five thousand dollar claim where there might be five hundred dollars or a thousand dollars in costs . . .." He was "very disturbed" that the retainer "slipped in" a contingent fee of 40 percent when suit is filed—"the maximum types of fees used in the last five or ten years"—and applied it to uninsured motor vehicle coverage and medical payment coverage, which "are paid on a no-fault basis." This was "very unfair" unless the lawyer "has a very good reason" and "explains it to the client."

Although Drapiewski called it "a violation of these clients' due process to have to listen to Mr. Werchick make a speech," Werchick continued: "[Y]ou don't bill $200 an hour because a paralegal got a call from a client saying, 'I'm going to change lawyers.'" Fewer than half of lawyers who were replaced would say, "darn it, on top of everything else, I'm going to record every minute I spent, even the time I had to write to the insurance company to say I'm not in the case anymore and charge for it." "Responsible and respectable" law firms did not threaten loss insurers with punitive damages for disregarding their liens. This was without precedent, and "the only effect . . . is to interfere with the client's opportunity to get bills paid promptly . . .." Werchick ridiculed the respondents' claim to be one of the few firms representing "uneducated, unsophisticated accident victims" with "modest soft-tissue injuries." There were many such firms and thousands of hungry recent law graduates, "I don't think I ever had difficulty providing such a client with several names . . .." Forty percent was "the highest contingent fee" and "commonly only invoked in cases of extreme complexity and high risk," such as malpractice or products liability, "where counsel who is advancing costs may risk the loss of 30 or 50 or more thousand dollars . . .." Automobile cases were "low risk," especially if screened for liability.

On cross-examination, Werchick conceded that some lawyers charged 40 percent but never at "the filing of the complaint," an event that was "entirely in the lawyer's control." Doing so was "bad for the profession." It cost his firm just a dollar to open a file. Although it was proper to advise the client to "go to a doctor for a checkup even though the client has no apparent injuries," Werchick was reluctant to propose a specific doctor, instead offering three or four names if the client did not know a suitable specialist. The "reasonable response" of a lawyer who suspects a case has been capped "is to ask the client, 'How did you happen to come to this office?'"—not to have the investigator "get a second piece of paper that says the case wasn't capped." Many injury victims are uneducated and "sign things because they're told to sign them." He did not charge for helping a client claim against a first-party insurer. He made a

> very important distinction between a referral fee where an agreement is made or understood to be paid for the bringing of a case as opposed to a post hoc, after the fact expression of gratitude to people who maybe sent you cases that you didn't take or didn't do anything at all for . . . or that you lost . . . [I]t's like advertising . . . .
>
> What I think the overwhelming majority of personal injury lawyers would do, if they walked into an office of a Monday morning and there were five new files sitting on the desk and the lawyer had never heard of those clients before and the lawyer either had paid or was paying cash to a certain investigator for bringing in each of those five files, that would immediately call for some action on the part of the attorney . . . .

Weinberg relied in cross-examination on an unpublished "study" by former State Bar President David Casey, Jr., purporting to show that contingent fees were 33 to 40 percent of gross and were applied to medical payments. Weinberg claimed it cost $165 to file a complaint in San Francisco. Clinics like Jacoby & Meyers and

Hyatt Legal Services used paralegals to screen cases and sign up clients. Drapiewski made another offer of proof:

> If an attorney routinely files a personal injury case, the attorney may have a routine done where it takes him five minutes, ten minutes, a half hour to do that work, but he will charge the client . . . for an hour's time, two hours' time, or three hours' time, based upon an analysis that says the attorney's development of a routine is something which he can pass onto the client.

When the hearing resumed, Drapiewski moved to strike Cohen's testimony and dismiss the entire proceeding because of his improper conduct. Weinberg assailed Cohen's "junior birdman investigation," his "extreme" and "grave misconduct . . . a conscious invasion of attorney-client information." The State Bar "for five months allowed a condition to continue . . .." Prompt action "would have prevented any of these further complaining witnesses . . . many of them were fished out by the bar . . .." Goldhammer dismissed the motion with prejudice. Drapiewski then moved to strike Sandles's testimony because the State Bar had contacted seven clients who had not complained, an "intolerable" "interference with that professional relationship." Goldhammer also denied this motion.

I. Other Solicited Clients

Many other clients testified about solicitation. Buchanan phoned Hazel N. Taylor after her accident, came to her home with the police report, had her sign a retainer, and directed her to Mission Family Medical Clinic.[34] He phoned Hermelinda Zaparolli after her accident and said, "he worked for a lawyer's office." Asked how he knew her name, address, and grandchildren's names, he said he had gotten the accident report (which she could not obtain) because "they have people that work with them in the police department and that they gave them lists of people that have had accidents." He asked "How's Robert doing? How's Richard doing . . . How is Reuben doing?" "[I]t really struck me as funny that he would know their names . . .." She was reluctant to say if she had been hurt "because I didn't know who he was." It was her complaint to the SFPD records room that someone was selling police reports that provoked the police investigation. The morning after an accident involving Aida Taula's father (who spoke Samoy but little English), he and his daughter were phoned by Gumban, who "said he was a representative from Scapa and Brown." Gumban and Buchanan came that day and had Aida's father sign some documents. Thereafter, each time she tried to talk to the lawyers, Virginia Espinoza said they were unavailable and someone would get back to her; but no one did. After her May 1988 accident, Janet Thomas was called by Buchanan, who came to see her car, brought a police report, and gave her the firm's business card. He had her sign

34. State Bar Exhibit 40.

a retainer and sent her to Mission Family Medical Clinic. No one from the firm contacted her for another six months, and Buchanan "never returned my phone calls." After Mary Caston's March 1988 accident, Buchanan phoned and "presented himself as an attorney or assistant . . .." When he visited a few days later, she told him she was not really interested. "I've had lawyers before and . . . I just didn't want to go through . . . having a case and all that kind of stuff." But because Buchanan insisted, "you really should do something about it," she signed the retainer and solicitation disclaimer.[35] A week later she called Scapa, who "convinced me that he could handle my case and . . . [it] would be worthwhile for me to go on," persuading her to switch from Kaiser to Mission Family Medical Clinic.

Buchanan called two or three days after Alex Lavita's March 11 accident and said, "if I were to agree to have this law firm represent me that my medical expenses would be taken care of and any lost wages and so forth . . .." Although Lavita had not sought treatment because "I wasn't sure if I had any injuries," he "figured, well, I should just take advantage of being treated." At Buchanan's recommendation, Lavita visited Mission Family Medical Clinic 10 or 11 times over the next two weeks. Buchanan arranged for him to meet Scapa, who said "three weeks of treatment would receive a certain amount of funding . . . and less than that would not receive as much . . .." "The doctor at the clinic, Mr. Lackey, wanted me to come once a day for these treatments." Scapa called Lavita two or three days after he stopped treatment and "told me that . . . Dr. Lackey . . . had informed him that I was no longer going in for treatments." When Scapa asked why, Lavita said "I wasn't injured and I didn't see any point in going to the clinic." Scapa replied, "you still may be injured, and if you don't go for a certain amount of treatments, we don't have as big of a case, and I won't be able to represent you." But Lavita was determined to stop. Later, he got a "termination," "a discarding of the case altogether, saying that they were no longer going to represent me." After dealing directly with AAA (which insured the other driver), and saying he wanted only medical costs and lost wages, Lavita got a $500 check. The AAA adjuster said, "she had problems with this firm." "CSAA was investigating claims that were filed through the law firm of Scapa and Brown."

Gumban phoned Mary C. Haskins on March 5, three days after the bus in which she had been riding was struck by a minivan. She replied when he called her a second time at work. Gumban and Buchanan came to her house. "They were paralegals and they went out and they talked to people that had been in accidents, and they went back and carried the information back to Scapa and Brown." Buchanan wanted to take a picture of the bruise on her left hip. Asked if she should deal with them, a friend replied: "Well, you need a lawyer.

35. State Bar Exhibit 19.

Why not?" Thinking, "they must be honest people," she signed the retainer.[36] When she said she could not get therapy until May because Kaiser was overbooked, they used her phone and "called Family Mission Clinic and set an appointment up for me that same afternoon." She went there daily for about six weeks. She did not meet Scapa until he observed the defendant's deposition two years later. On cross-examination, Drapiewski tried to elicit that Brown had agreed to a one-third contingent fee, but Steedman objected that he had done this *after* disciplinary charges were filed. The judge warned that if the defense explored later events, so could the OTC.

J. The Cappers Again

Joseph Arsanis worked for the SFPD from 1971 until January 1989, earning numerous citations. He supervised the record room from late 1987 until he was fired after being convicted of the behavior described above. In February 1988, Betty Brown, who had been giving Gumban accident reports for six months, introduced him to Arsanis, describing Gumban as "a current police officer that was moonlighting . . . by picking up copies of accident reports that victims were injured and were good litigation cases that he would try and sign them up for the law firm that he worked for." Arsanis joined Brown in sending Gumban these reports through April 1988. "Gumban based his payment on how well the case worked." Arsanis gave each capper five or six reports several times a week. When Buchanan worked by himself (April through August), Arsansis gave him 10 to 15 reports once or twice a week: "the good litigation cases," in which "the innocent victim was injured and the party at fault was insured . . .." There was "a little friction" because the cops "didn't think [Gumban] was being honest in his amount of people that he was able to sign up" (a suspicion Buchanan shared), and "payment was erratic." Arsanis "just didn't feel good about it, and I just stopped" for about three weeks. Then "Buchanan became involved and contacted Betty Brown and said that he would come and pick up copies of the reports and payment would . . . be on time . . .."

> Joe Gumban would pay Officer Brown according to the clients that he was able to sign up. And this would vary from a hundred dollars a week to two hundred to nothing for two or three weeks. . . . when Buchanan worked by himself, he paid us . . . $500 a week regardless as to the amount of clients he was able to enlist.

Arsanis pocketed half of the $6,000.

He overheard Buchanan making phone calls from his house "using the copies of the reports that Betty or myself had given him . . . stating that 'you were

36. State Bar Exhibit 21 (Mar. 11, 1988).

injured and that you are going to need representation, and if you don't have an attorney, we'd like to provide one.'" Arsanis once accompanied Buchanan to solicit a client. "Buchanan wanted me to act as . . . [though] I was involved, so I carried the camera. He had me take a couple of photos of the injured party's helmet and motorcycle." After signing up the client, "Buchanan, I, and the client went to a medical building." The sale of reports ended with the arrests of Buchanan and Betty Brown in August or September.

Buchanan laid the foundation for introducing his spiral notebooks. They began with the medical clinics to which he had referred clients and then listed the names and addresses he had gotten from police reports, dates the clients signed up, and whether the firm had paid him. "Charge back" meant he might have to return the money. "No treatment" cases were dropped. Buchanan was paid by Mission Family Medical Clinic for referrals and sometimes shared Gumban's kickbacks from St. Paul Clinic. He usually phoned clients two days after the accident. When Weinberg objected to the notebooks as hearsay because some of the contents represented what Gumban had told Buchanan, Goldhammer replied that "the purpose of this court is not to play games with the evidence, but to find out what it shows." Nevertheless, he excluded the notebooks because the only real dispute was not "the fact of the cappings" but "whether they pertain to Michael Brown and Robert Scapa, and this notebook doesn't further that."

During cross-examination by Drapiewski, Buchanan said Gumban proposed the solicitation scheme in 1987, a year after they met, and introduced him to Michael Brown. Buchanan did investigative work: talking to clients and witnesses, taking photos, checking insurance, diagramming accident scenes, driving clients to doctors and garages, and obtaining police reports. He met the lawyers weekly to report and get paid. Brown said solicitation was illegal and Buchanan would be fired, which he believed. They had one conversation about solicitation at the beginning of their relationship and another in August or September. When Brown discharged him, the lawyer said nothing about solicitation or police reports. Buchanan "absolutely" agreed that he tried to hide his solicitation from the lawyers, one reason for working from home. Returning money was an obligation he imposed on himself. At this point, Goldhammer reversed himself and admitted the notebooks.

On redirect, Buchanan said the weekly discussions with the lawyers included the "value of the cases," which depended on "how much work that was involved . . . whether or not there was insurance . . . the greater the severity of the injury . . . ." "I'd receive five hundred initially and if the case was settled favorably . . . there might be an additional five hundred." He was always paid in cash, never gave a receipt, and estimated the total at $25,000 to $30,000. He explained the solicitation disclaimer to clients, emphasizing "that there was no promises or offer—monetary or otherwise" and "minimiz[ing] the solicitation aspect of it."

K. Legal Arguments

On October 19, 1990, Goldhammer asked both sides to brief six questions:

1. Could he consider unconscionable fee contracts?
2. Was a solicited retainer illegal, and did that depend on the lawyer's knowledge of the solicitation?
3. Or its illegality?
4. Could the assertion of a grossly excessive attorneys fee lien constitute charging an unconscionable fee?
5. Was the State Bar's failure to caution an attorney about continuing violations relevant to culpability?
6. Could the State Bar Court consider how State Bar investigators obtained evidence?

In response, the State Bar brief argued that charging $200 an hour for three hours regardless of the work done was unconscionable and a lien was a fee.[37] BPC Section 6154 declared void any contract secured "through the services of a runner." Buchanan was not entrapped; he invited Cohen into his office, where the lawyer could look at evidence in plain view. The claims of State Bar wrongdoing were "frivolous in the extreme." The State Bar was not prohibited from contacting clients.

The respondents' brief renewed the motions to exclude Cohen's evidence and dismiss the charges.[38] The State Bar "did nothing to deactivate Buchanan and Gumban" for months. To implicate the respondents, it "bought the testimony" of the cappers. Immunity offers were an "artifice" "without precedent" and "unacceptable conduct." Such "false" promises rendered the cappers' testimony "the product of a deliberate and continuous ruse." It was "probably improper" to interview uncomplaining past clients and "certainly improper to interview present clients." The Cohen/Triantafyllos visit to the firm was "an unlawful invasion of privacy, an illegal entrapment, and an unlawful search." Press coverage of this investigation beginning February 1989 showed that "apparently the State Bar was interested in publicizing the efforts of its 'insurance task force'" and had collaborated with CSAA. This proceeding should be dismissed for "cummulative [*sic*] misconduct."

The respondents submitted a separate memorandum of law challenging the unconscionability charge.[39] Werchick was not an expert. The NTSC had not included unconscionability. Since the fee of a discharged attorney would be deducted from that of the successor, "it cannot operate to increase the cost of the case to the client." "[I]t was successor counsel and not Respondents who violated their legal and ethical obligations . . . by ignoring Respondents' liens . . .."

37. State Bar Examiner's brief (Mar. 14, 1991).

38. Respondents' brief (Mar. 14, 1991).

39. Respondents' Memorandum of Law re: Count Five of the NTSC (Mar. 14, 1991).

"Respondents should be credited for their restraint in forebearing [*sic*] from proceeding against either attorney, let alone either client . . .."

When the hearing had to be postponed because Drapiewski's mother was dying, Goldhammer urged the parties, especially the OTC, to settle. The hearing had to be postponed again because Scapa had torn his Achilles tendon playing basketball. Although the judge wanted him to participate by phone, Weinberg objected that "given the kind of quasi-criminal nature of these proceedings," Scapa "has an absolute right to be personally present." Goldhammer again urged settlement. Although the liens were part of the fee contract, he felt they were irrelevant since discharged attorneys could recover only under quantum meruit. "The attempt to collect the three-hour minimum fee might be unconscionable," but the State Bar Court should not "use disciplinary proceedings as a way of telling the Bar how it ought to handle attorney/client contracts." He was more interested in solicitation. Cohen's actions were not a "search" and certainly not "outrageous conduct."

L. Respondents' Testimony

The hearing resumed with Brown's testimony. He was admitted in 1982 and immediately associated with Scapa (a childhood friend), taking primary responsibility for firm management and pre-litigation matters (he had never completed a jury trial). In 1985, he became an equal partner with Scapa and they opened a second office in Downey because "our practice was on the west side of Los Angeles, which has a tremendous amount of competition . . .." A year later, they decided to open an office in the Bay Area, where Brown bought a home. "Our plan was to make ourselves available for all segments of society throughout the state." Emulating Jacoby & Meyers and Hyatt Legal Services, they wanted "to see how far you can go" through advertising. Criminal law was "drying up." "Family law was becoming more expensive to practice, and it's a highly competitive field." Neither of them had a "substantial" client base. "In order to stay competitive, we broadened our client base. To do that, we had to branch out geographically and to promote ourselves through marketing and advertising . . .." By the time they were charged, their practice was 75 to 80 percent personal injury.

They opened the Bay Area office in 1987. Brown used Bert Gabriel (the real estate agent who negotiated their lease) as a "gofer," "running errands, helping set up the office, move furniture." He called Gabriel an independent contractor, but there was no contract and no hourly fee. Brown claimed to be surprised that Gabriel handed out business cards identifying him with the "Law Offices of SCAPA, BROWN & ASSOCIATES" and denied authorizing it.[40] Gabriel had referred two or three cases but was not paid for this. Confronted with checks to Gabriel for $1,800 and $957, Brown called them payments for real estate brokerage, but Steedman maintained they would have been made out to Gabriel's

40. State Bar Exhibit 24.

employer, Century 21. Brown also paid Gabriel up to $1,250 in cash, for which he kept no records, although the firm deducted it as a business expense. Brown initially denied Gabriel ever used the office, but later admitted "he used the phones. He used the copying machine, drank my coffee, ate my food." "I considered it being hospitable" because "he did me a favor" and "seemed to be somewhat down on his luck."

> [T]he subject of, "I had referred some clients to you," also came up when he's asking me for money to compensate him for the work that he was authorized to do. . . . I did not compensate him specifically for referring a client to me, but on the other hand, I was glad and appreciative for the recommendation.

Brown was evasive about his relations with Manolet Umali (who failed to answer a State Bar subpoena). He admitted employing Umali from February to July 1988, when he left for unknown reasons, and signing the articles of incorporation for Umali's American Legal Referral Services on July 15, 1988.

Scapa introduced Brown to Gumban and Buchanan, who were "to help out in signing up of clients and obtaining certain evidence necessary for the files." They did not need a private investigator's license "because they weren't really investigators. They were doing an in-house job of gathering information . . . they went to accident scenes and photographed the area," transported clients, and "helped them with many of the problems that generally arise when somebody is the victim of an accident." Brown went over the non-solicitation policy (which he had drafted) at their first meeting, not because of "problems with solicitation" in Los Angeles but because "it contained issues that were important to address and our practice was becoming busier and busier. And I tried to exercise as much supervision and control over the office as I could . . .." He described the client disclaimer of solicitation as "a generic form I've copied from other law firms" but could not identify any firms using it.[41] He denied noticing that the cappers were sending Mission Family Medical Clinic most of their cases or knowing about the kickbacks. He sought no references from either capper. He knew Gumban had been a policeman but did not ask why he had left the force. He paid them "based upon the quality of the work that they did and the quantity of the work that they did . . .." The going rate "was anywhere from a hundred to a hundred and fifty to sign somebody up . . .." Gumban's "wife was a nurse and she had obvious access to people that would need our services." "I don't believe that I anticipated anyone making direct contact with someone they didn't know, but I assume that through conversations our name would come up." He agreed that "the second way that Mr. Gumban might refer cases . . . would be through his contacts . . . as a former police officer" but denied knowing that these were in the

41. He probably copied it from Pollitt (who used almost identical language) but was reluctant to acknowledge this since Pollitt had already been suspended for six months.

record room. He hired Gumban because he was "well connected in the Philippine community" but denied noticing that "very few of these people had Philippine surnames." He did not ask how the cappers got cases because "I understood it to be . . . through their wives and through their family and friends and their social contacts."

The cappers referred about 30 cases and worked on 40 to 50 over a period of 6 to 8 months. Brown estimated he had paid them $5,000 to $10,000, half in cash. "I did not charge the client back for 95 percent of what" they did. To show that payment did not depend on case quality, he claimed to have paid for "garbage" cases but could cite no examples.

> Initially if they had somebody they wanted to refer to the office, they would call me up or call my partner up and discuss the nature of the case and see whether or not we were interested and then we would let them go and sign it up. Over time, when it became apparent that they were signing cases up the way we wanted them to be signed up . . . they didn't have to check with us first.

The one to three cases he got from each weekly when he visited San Bruno "didn't mean that much to me" out of the 20 to 30 on his desk. "I was pleasantly surprised to have the business, but it did not ring any bells." Capper referrals represented less than a third of the total. "Probably everybody in my office at one time or another has referred business to us . . .."

Although Scapa had talked to Kenneth Tashiro the day before attending Brown's wedding, the lawyers did not discuss the matter before Brown left for his Australian honeymoon on March 27. Scapa told Tashiro in June (on the basis of further correspondence with New) that Brown had erroneously sent out a lien notice. Both lawyers were "surprised" by New's June 6 letter. Although Brown denied concluding that solicitation had occurred, "if you take the two documents together, that's the inference." Scapa said he had asked New about allegations against the cappers and had "gotten no response" but had said he "would contact Mr. Buchanan and Gumban and try to get the story." Scapa had not pursued the solicitation issue for three months because "New was concerned about attorneys fees" and "getting the file." Brown also did not pursue this.

> We just did not go into that kind of detail on it. I was absolutely inundated with work. This document on one of possibly hundreds of files came to my attention. It was having to do with something that my partner was working on. I inquired, and the conversation probably lasted 15 seconds. He said he would take care of it, check it out.

Scapa later said Gumban and Buchanan "had assured him that they were referred from one of their friends." Brown continued to pay them cash for cases, never asking about their origin.

At some point, Brown saw what seemed to be an "original" or "official document." But it turned out to be "innocuous . . . just a police report . . . somebody had gone over the writing on the photocopy . . .." In his deposition, however, he said that after New's complaints about solicitation and "a similar type of complaint from another attorney" he started thinking, "you know, next time I see these guys, I'm going to start looking a little closer." Then Buchanan showed him a police report. "And I suddenly noticed that . . . portions of it were in ink in the same handwriting as the actual police report . . . a light went off in my head . . . that this is an original police report or was obtained directly from the Police Department, and . . . I exclaimed, 'you know where did you get this?'" But since the deposition, he now testified, he had concluded that "the police report itself was innocuous."

Brown abandoned the solicitation disclaimer "on the advice of counsel . . . subsequent to the Bar's actions." He also stopped asserting liens on property damage or car rental reimbursement, admitting he had simply copied another lawyer's form; but he still believed he was entitled to them. He had never researched liability for punitive damages for failure to protect a lien and could cite no supporting case. He claimed an hour of attorney time for dispatching three "standardized letters" because "an attorney had to write them in the first place." He maintained "it's okay to charge $200 an hour for work by non-attorneys" but did not know how much he charged for it. He could not explain a $50 charge for leaving a phone message. He charged a client $100 for "file review" after being substituted out because "it was work that was necessary." Asked why he claimed half an hour to review a file containing only the police report, he said, "this is merely an itemization of time and expense . . . not a bill. This is not meant to be a very specific itemization." Noting that the cover letter said, "Please forward your check in the total amount to this office," Steedman asked if this "communicates something other than a bill for eleven hundred and forty-five oh two?" Brown replied: "Mr. Murray knew exactly what this was, which was an overture towards settlement." He responded to Murray's objection by saying he would "consider a settlement offer" but added: "my review of the file and the itemized bill again indicates its reasonableness."[42] Although he did not recall reviewing the file, "generally speaking, I tried to tell the truth in my letters." But he admitted signing a letter dated when he was in Tahiti. He agreed to arbitrate the fee dispute.

Robert Scapa testified that he was admitted in 1977 and worked for other lawyers, in partnership and alone, before joining Brown in 1985. He was in charge of litigation; promotion was "more Mike's responsibility." They had 10 to 20 clients in the Bay Area when they opened that office. "We advertised. We also participated in political and social groups specially tailored to the minority community.

42. State Bar Exhibit 17.

And that turned out, along with family referrals . . . to be a foundation for our clientele." Some of the Bay Area groups were related to those in Southern California, like the Filipino American Council of Los Angeles. "We would sponsor beauty pageants and things of that nature to go along with some of their holidays in the Philippines." The new office was getting 15 to 20 cases a month by January. Asked how they managed that in just four months, Scapa said, "we started a pretty aggressive advertising campaign." He met Gumban at a Filipino Christmas or New Year's Eve party. "He was doing investigative services for several other law offices in the area," and "indicated that he had been in the police department and either was retired or disabled . . .." "You got to consider that . . . we were in our somewhat incubation . . . just starting to grow. So we were trying to hire the best people that we could and could afford to hire at the time." Gumban "seemed a nice, kind of jovial guy" if "sometimes a little crazy," so "why not give the guy a try." The reason for the client solicitation disclaimer was "two-fold. One is to protect us, and the second is to clue the client that if there is any impropriety . . .." In his deposition, Scapa had explained that "we didn't have the financing to hire the best, highest caliber people that existed." But now he said, "I didn't think that I had bad people working for me," even if they were "definitely not" the "cream of the crop." In their initial discussions, Gumban "intimated" he "had substantial contacts in the community from his years as a police officer, as well as in the Filipino community," through Buchanan's wife as well as his own. When Steedman noted that most clients were not Filipino, Scapa replied "I've never gone through an objective survey of the surnames." "Generally, if I sent them out on a call, it would be a client that had called in from advertising . . .." But often Gumban "would call me up and say, 'listen . . . I've . . . met someone who was involved in a motorcycle versus auto accident . . . .' I'd say I was interested." At one of their first meetings "we talked about how important it was that clients . . . get the best type of [medical] treatment . . . I could give Mr. Gumban a list of doctors . . .." Compensation "was a pretty loose arrangement," $100 to $150 for initial intake. They had discussed bonuses: "We attempt to award . . . our employees and our independent contractors if they do . . . good work for us." But he did not proportion pay to liability or damages.

When Ilson New called on March 25, "he did not say, 'my client has been capped.'" Scapa did not read New's March letter until June.

> [I]nadvertently . . . between Mike getting back [from his honeymoon] and taking care of all the business and my running around like a chicken with my head cut off running the operation, Mike sent out a lien letter on this file.

When he got the June 6 letter, he talked to the cappers. Gumban "indicated that the case was a legitimate referral . . . either from his wife or a friend of his wife's . . .." "I was satisfied with their explanation. And to be honest with you, I interpreted my conversation with Mr. New as being one really of sour grapes." None of the clients he interviewed "directly or indirectly ever indicated any concern about how they had been contacted or that they were capped . . . ." When Brown confronted Buchanan about an original police report, "Mr. Buchanan clammed up. Mike saw no point in . . . further pursuing the matter." After firing Buchanan, Scapa did not review the files for evidence of solicitation: "we had no way of doing that."

> There was never anything, nothing whatsoever that could have clued me to the fact that these guys were out hustling people as a result of getting these police reports from the police department. It just—it wasn't there. There was no way I could have known . . . .

Questioned by Drapiewski, Scapa emphasized the (non-liability) cases he had resolved without fee and the fees he had reduced. The firm dropped Alex Lavita when it learned he only wanted property damage "and the next thing . . . I heard . . . is that he was . . . paid a $500 bribe by CSAA to settle his case and file a complaint against us." Scapa insisted that in Southern California, "the standard in the industry is 33.3 for handling the soft-tissue personal injury cases, and when a complaint is filed it is 40 percent;" it was "customary" to "charge on gross recovery." Whereas "Werchick handles low-volume, high-profit cases," Scapa's firm handled "higher volume, lower impact" cases.

> [I]n order to make them at all economically feasible . . . an attorney cannot do all perhaps the traditional things that Mr. Werchick envisions . . . .I can't go out and interview every client.

Behrmann's successor attorney was the only one who demanded "an itemization of the time and work that we did." "That is not the trade and practice . . . in this community."

Scapa defended what he charged for printing a form.

> Every day in this state in every law office, attorneys put the effort into creating the form work. That all goes into a ball of overhead. . . . [if] you want a limited partnership agreement from a major law firm, it's all on the word processor. . . . It's not uncommon for attorneys to charge . . . from a thousand to five thousand dollars for that type of work, even though it may take them a half an hour. It may take them no time.

He also defended his use of Mission Family Medical Clinic. "I never had really any complaints of any clients . . .. It was not a dump . . . it was what I think most of our clients were accustomed to going." The clinic provided medical care "on a lien basis." "Dr. Lackey is Filipino and speaks Tagalog."

Scapa objected that "CSAA has embarked on a campaign of doing whatever is necessary . . . to thwart out victims from getting their claims prosecuted." Spending "easily double" the value of a case on experts had "somewhat worked" to deter "a great deal of plaintiffs' counsel from taking simple soft-tissue cases." In at least a dozen of his 40 to 50 uninsured motorist arbitrations with CSAA, "this investigation has been brought up . . . to distort the facts . . . and my ability to prosecute my clients' claims." CSAA had complained to a state agency that the firm's "conduct was improper because they were Los Angeles-based attorneys." But Goldhammer did not "think much of the line of questioning," which was not "relevant or material."

Asked why he did not learn about solicitation before September, Scapa replied that the Northern California office was "a whole new baby." They had no "check and balance system for keeping track of the source of our clientele." The cappers' cases would fall into "the pool of other cases and become camouflaged." "[W]e had illusions of grandeur. Maybe we wanted to hopefully dot . . . the map with offices of Scapa and Brown." Because of his wedding, Brown was "useless probably two to four weeks before . . . and about four to six weeks thereafter." Scapa "had to run almost three offices by myself, in addition to handling the non-litigation work and an extremely busy calendar." Since the charges were filed the firm "tried to make changes," shutting the Downey office and hiring "more" and "better personnel."

> Gumban and Buchanan duped us. They were able to camouflage where these cases were coming from. It's not that we didn't ask. We did ask periodically. . . . when that very explicit letter came on June 6th with details to me of the first time of this solicitation and this contacting of Mr. Tashiro by Mr. Gumban or Mr. Buchanan, I was satisfied with the explanation that was given to me by Mr. Gumban and Mr. Buchanan . . . no one else ever told us. State Bar, they knew about this on March 22nd 1988, never called us in. . . . The Police Department never did. . . . CSAA never mentioned anything about it. District Attorney never mentioned anything about it.

On redirect, Scapa admitted that the firm began advertising only *after* receiving the NTSC, targeted just Filipinos, and did not know what they were spending or whether it was producing clients. Steedman asked why, if Gumban had duped them, Scapa had called him the day before he was to testify. Scapa admitted that in his "periodic discussions" about "where these clients came from," he talked about "kickbacks" but denied using the words "capping" or "soliciting."

Weinberg objected to Goldhammer's questions because the burden of proof "rests with the State Bar." Goldhammer agreed not to question if Weinberg insisted but said he sought "a clear understanding of what happens" and might comment "on whose responsibility . . . it was to have blocked the information." The respondents withdrew the objection. Brown told Goldhammer the San Bruno had 150 to 200 cases in the first half of 1988, then lowered his estimate to 100 to 150, and then raised it to 200 to 250. Drapiewski offered newspaper articles to show "that the motive of the State Bar . . . was to promote the activities of its task force on fraud and not to do justice," but Goldhammer said this was not exculpatory.

M. Mitigation and Aggravation

After Goldhammer tentatively found culpability, the respondents offered mitigating evidence of satisfied clients, many of whom had received advances from the firm while their cases were pending. A lawyer who had made appearances for the firm since 1990 praised it. A lawyer before whom the respondents had arbitrated cases said they "represent their clients very well." Charles David "Chuck" Tarr testified that Scapa had been "shocked" by the allegations, since they "feel they've done nothing wrong because they weren't aware of what was going on . . . they're remorseful in the sense that this has caused a big problem for them . . .." On cross-examination, however, he acknowledged telling the firm to eliminate the claim on its letterhead that they were "of counsel" to his firm, which they had made without his consent. Presented with the facts in hypothetical form, Tarr conceded they were not "something that I would do"; but he had "a difficult time in saying that directly impeaches [their] integrity or honesty," given the *Bates* decision. He did not know the Supreme Court had upheld rules against solicitation. He had known Scapa for 17 or 18 years. "[Y]ou don't just dump somebody and change your opinion about their honesty and integrity based on allegations . . . lawyers know allegations are just that . . .."

Scapa testified in mitigation that

> [W]e wanted to try to put a niche in the market for handling small soft tissue personal injury cases with an eye towards earmarking the minority communities. I speak fluent Spanish. We wanted to go over to the Latino community, the Filipino community, some of the other minorities that we felt did not have direct access to lawyers . . . to make it economically feasible to handle these type of cases, we wanted to streamline some of the more traditional roles[43] that were played by lawyers and use non-lawyers to fill some of those roles . . . . We devised a lot of forms, the client interview sheets . . . so that there would be easy questions that would need to be filled out . . . whether it be by the client, a paralegal, an investigator . . . . These cases run an average attorney fee of anywhere from a thousand to three thousand dollars. You're talking about a case that really doesn't have a value . . . of more than ten, twelve thousand dollars. . . . probably 50 cents of each dollar at least goes to overhead . . . . So, in order to make it economically feasible, we felt that we had to assign certain roles that were traditionally done by lawyers to non-lawyers . . . where the client could get good legal service, a good result . . . .

In November 1989, Brown and Scapa met Tarr at the California Trial Lawyers Association convention in San Francisco.

> I walk into my seminar room and on each and every desk is a copy of *The Recorder* newspaper, and you can imagine the humiliation and embarrassment.

43. "Rules" in original.

> The paper's title was something to the effect like—in big, bold, black print, "Scapa, First Case Prosecuted by State Bar Fraud Task Unit". . . . What I categorically denied to Chuck was that we were engaged somehow in handling fraudulent cases . . . purchasing police reports . . . and using those to contact clients . . .. But I never said to Chuck that we didn't make mistakes, and for those mistakes, I am truly sorry.

On cross-examination, he blamed his failure to uncover the capping on poor supervision. The firm had since reduced its staff and "tried to use better personnel." Depending "on the results of this hearing and when we can finance or afford it, we're going to staff the San Jose office [which had replaced San Bruno] with a full-time lawyer." He now spent much more time in San Jose. "I review files till I can't keep my eyes open any further at night every night I'm up here." He had eliminated the non-solicitation declaration, deleted retainer provisions the State Bar "found objectionable," and made sure clients got a carbon copy of the retainer "then and there." The firm now had a computer network "to better respond to the client's questions about the status of their case." Although he had no system for monitoring the source of cases, "if it starts to appear that somebody's name comes up consistently, like Joe Gumban or Robert Buchanan, well, obviously, now a red light goes on." "We were negligent in hiring, obviously, Mr. Gumban and Mr. Buchanan." He had replaced them with Blue Knight Investigations (but could not remember either investigator's name), which referred no cases, and he no longer paid investigators based on case value. "I can assure you, 99 percent of all the cases that [Blue Knight] signs up, myself or Michael talks to those clients." Whenever a client he had not interviewed signed a retainer, "I call them." The firm had increased the use of contract attorneys and paid a contract lawyer "to complete that client's cases" even when the offer was only $1,000 to 1,500. "I don't walk away from my clients, because, all of a sudden, the case is just not economically feasible to pursue."

The OTC called Karen Elaine Kirby, a specialist in personal injury defense and fraudulent claims. She had opposed Scapa in five cases, and all the 20 other lawyers in her firm had at least one case with him. "[T]here have been circumstances where I felt that he has misrepresented himself to the Court and also . . . to me . . .." His clients "tend to be [seen by] the same person, Cecil Lackey," who uses "unlicensed personnel" to treat patients. Scapa had failed to respond to requests for depositions or rescheduled them on flimsy pretexts. He recently told her he did not have a Bay Area office, when he had one in San Jose. "I have not seen a case [with Scapa] that doesn't involve some aspect of fraud."

Commenting that "the last testimony didn't get anywhere," Goldhammer warned both sides against "a long, drawn out, extended examination and cross-examination on these peripheral things." Nevertheless, the State Bar called Linda Laura Voydeat, CSAA house counsel, who had opposed both respondents, whom she viewed "unfavorabl[y]." They used a single San Jose doctor regardless of the plaintiff's injury or residence. She had seen "evidence of capping" and patients who "did not receive the medical treatment they were billed for." Medical expenses were "excessive." One attorney told her that "if he put Scapa and Brown on a scale of one to ten with . . . one as a skuzz ball . . . they'd be a two." In cross-examination, Drapiewski asked what was wrong with capping.

> Before [1927] it was not illegal . . .. Is capping *malum prohibitum* or *malum in se*? . . . What's immoral about capping? . . . do you know anybody who feels it's immoral to solicit clients?

Although Goldhammer directed Drapiewski not to argue, Weinberg said that at the next hearing, he might challenge "the validity of the solicitation prohibitions." Goldhammer warned he was "not going to rule the statutes unconstitutional."

Thomas M Warden testified that he had known Scapa for 12 years and Brown for 7 or 8. In the close Encino legal community, "I've never heard anything to the negative aspect regarding any of their conduct," but he had never discussed their "business operations," which were a "private matter." Leonard David Black, who had leased space to Scapa and worked on a case with him, had "never heard anything bad about him." Black was a "traditionalist" but felt that "ever since this thing with Jacoby & Meyers and all this advertising . . . the lines are a little blurred as far as what attorneys may or may not do." "I don't do [solicitation], but is it wrong?" Although Scapa may have been guilty of "sloppy business practice . . . most of the time . . . he was in court." Richard Jacinto called Scapa "very competent." Failing to record cash payments to investigators was "not a good business practice" but only because you could not charge them to clients. Daniel Kaufmann, a retired judge who had arbitrated cases involving the respondents, found them "average" with respect "to the competency and professionalism that I expect from members of the Bar." Barry Weisz called Brown "a very competent attorney . . . of the highest moral character." "[W]e have advertising and things of that sort. So the line for me is fairly mushy." Weisz saw no "great distinction between a non-lawyer who is taking a fee to get a lawyer for an immigration client or a bankruptcy client to paying somebody who refers you to a personal injury client." He did not know capping was a crime; in any case, "a victimless crime is different." When the respondents' behavior was described hypothetically, he saw "no harm to the client, maybe it's a client who wouldn't have representation otherwise . . .." "I've never really believed that anyone can deliver a case . . . ." Melvin Belli was often "on the scene" of an air crash "before the embers die down . . . signing up cases left and right." Kickbacks would not change Weisz's "definition of whether there's harm . . . unless you can say to me that the medical care that these people were provided with was substandard . . .." The past president of the Reseda Chamber of Commerce expressed satisfaction with the work Scapa had done for her. Maria Alana Tuttle was a satisfied personal injury witness, but she had met Brown only once and never met Scapa. "[I]t wouldn't really bother me" to be solicited: "I would find it kind of helpful." Irv Edwards described Brown as "very caring and very professional in terms of my legal needs . . .."

Maria Rodriguez was a satisfied client. Dr. Jonathan Serebrin testified that Brown "felt the allegations were groundless and that he was angry that these allegations were being brought against him." Brown's "basic reaction is anger at others for bringing these charges rather than a feeling of regret for his inability to control what the people working for him did . . .."

In mitigation, Brown acknowledged having "inadequately" handled his responsibility for office management, drafting employment contracts, and hiring and firing Gumban and Buchanan. The firm still retained licensed investigators as independent contractors but stopped using one (Hummell) whose fees were too high: "four or five hundred dollars . . . to do a simple sign-up." "[W]e never take clients that are being brought in by investigators" and "only send an investigator out when we have already been contacted by the client." Although he "would still consider taking a case if an investigator brought it to my attention," he "would insist upon the handling of the client interview by myself or my partner in person . . .." On cross-examination, he increased his estimate of the number of clients Hummell had signed up from 3 to 4 to 4 to 5, then to no more than ten, and finally claimed not to know.

> [W]e're not talking about a whole lot of cases here. You know, my business since this Bar thing has happened has dropped off radically. . . . for a short period of time, we had an Hispanic paralegal in the San Jose office and a couple of those cases went to there. . . . [A]t the present time, 99 percent of . . . any prospective clients are brought into the office or we go out, personally, to meet them. The few occasions where we have sent investigators out to do a sign-up has been where we know . . . where the client came from.

They paid $150 to $200 for this.

Scapa belonged to the Los Angeles Trial Lawyers Association, the California Trial Lawyers Association, and the Association of Trial Lawyers of America. He had been quite active in the referenda about insurance reform and felt "there was still much that needed to be done" but "could not appear publicly on [behalf of trial lawyers] without risking the exposure of the State Bar's prosecution and lending credence to certain segments of society's claims that all trial lawyers involved with plaintiff's work are ambulance chasers." He was on the board of Rags for Riches, "which raises about a quarter of a million dollars a year for disadvantaged or abused children" and "on the advisory committee for the Valley community clinic which provides either low cost or no charge for both legal and medical services . . .."

N. Closing Arguments and Briefs

In closing, Steedman argued that the firm paid Buchanan and Gumban $30,000 to cap 76 clients and contended the respondents were still soliciting cases. Their own witness, Kevin Franzwa, testified that he was referred to the firm in November 1990 by Mike Moe, who "does gofer work for Scapa & Brown."

Drapiewski called this argument "offensive." Steedman had put together "a series of half-truths and sometimes outright fiction," playing "to the court's prejudices . . . that if somebody . . . does something in cash, they have an ulterior motive." It "doesn't matter what Arne Werchick has to . . . say about his practice . . . it doesn't matter what Mr. Steedman thinks a good lawyer should do. And with great deference to the court, it doesn't matter what the court thinks a good lawyer should do." Weinberg criticized the State Bar's "lack of proportion" in seeking a three-year suspension and proposed 45 days. The "truth tends to lie somewhere in between." "[Y]ou have to scratch the record to find any indication that these clients were in any way treated other than professionally and well." There was "extraordinary mitigation" in the "clients and lawyers who hold these men in the highest esteem." "[I]f the Court finds . . . that there was a failure to supervise . . . a satellite office which has now been brought into rein . . . the Court need not and should not impose any actual discipline."

The respondents' closing brief blamed Gumban and Buchanan for "the impetus for this whole operation," in which Scapa and Brown "got caught up . . . quite incidentally and innocently." The cappers "were not the best [employees] that money could buy, they were simply the best that Scapa and Brown could afford." The respondents were only guilty of "failure to supervise and failure to recognize an evil which was being perpetrated in their name." At worst, "they were willing to take the solicitation scraps left by others." They "instructed" employees and independent contractors "on professional responsibilities." "The strict prohibition was reinforced with a policy memorandum . . . to establish ethical guidelines for the office . . .." They "never learned" about the business cards or noticed the "thirty or so cases" among the hundreds, or the one or two in a stack of 20 or 30 on their desks. Payments differed "because investigation requirements vary from case to case." "[T]he attorney who solicits tends to be the marginal practitioner who cannot attract clients to his office without the assistance of runners and cappers," whereas the respondents were "very competent attorneys." Lawyers solicited "significant personal injury claims" not "clients whose claims are marginal at best." Lawyers had no reason to be interested in referral mechanisms "where there are many very small cases from many sources." "Clients were not aggressively importuned . . . nor was there an attempt to take advantage of their particular vulnerability." Clients were not harmed. Having failed to stop respondents' activities when they first learned about them, the Bar could not complain that these "extended over a significant time." "Indeed, it appears that Mr. Brown and Mr. Scapa were more harmed by the State Bar's failure to give them notice than were any of their clients." "The only arguable victims of the conduct were other attorneys who may have lost business that was directed to Mr. Brown and Mr. Scapa." Pollitt, who only got a six months suspension, received more cases from Gumban and Buchanan, who settled some without his approval and misappropriated client funds.

The OTC closing brief accused the respondents of a "sophisticated conspiracy" to get clients through "runners and cappers" while creating "circumstances of plausible deniability." Gumban and Buchanan referred only San Francisco cases, not those from the large Filipino community in San Mateo, where the office was located. They signed up clients without consulting respondents. Buchanan "investigated" only cases he solicited, was not paid for those not accepted, and returned payments for cases that were dropped. Payment varied with case value, and Brown discussed bonuses with both cappers. Although canceled checks showed legitimate purchases of police reports, each was dated after the case was accepted. The inflated lien claims could discourage successor counsel from accepting the cases. The clients testifying in mitigation, who had large claims and had been loaned money by respondents, were "obviously not representative of the small personal injury cases in which Respondents specialize." Steedman recommended five years suspension, three actual for Brown and two for Scapa.

Respondents' reply brief deplored the "invective," "bile, frustration, and antipathy," "systematic mischaracterization of the evidence," and "almost inexplicable antipathy" of an OTC driven by a "rambling obsession with Mr. Scapa, Mr. Brown, their counsel, and this arcane proscription of solicitation." Respondents were not "scum," "fly-by-night ambulance chasers," and do not deserve "ruinous suspensions." As "an officer of the court," Weinberg was prepared to represent that an attorney "employed by a large insurance defense firm that regularly works for CSAA" wanted to testify that he had "the highest regard" for the respondents but had been threatened with "severe professional consequences, including perhaps termination" if he did so.

II. THE HEARING AND REVIEW DEPARTMENT JUDGMENTS

Goldhammer filed his 77-page decision on March 30, 1992. He was "clearly convinced" the respondents knew that the cappers had solicited approximately 50 cases—a third to a fifth of the firm's caseload—over eight or nine months. The "substantial" amounts of money involved "tend to show respondents were involved as principals." The rate of pay "considerably exceeded" the "duties and abilities" of "go-fers." It was "implausible, especially if respondents were advertising for clients, that they wouldn't try to quantity [*sic*] how clients came to their law firm—unless they otherwise knew." That "untrained and inexperienced staff" made first contact with clients suggests they were "being used to solicit the clients . . . particularly when the supposed independent contractors have open access to offices, office phones and equipment." That they were paid only if the clients signed up was "consistent with their having been hired for the purpose of soliciting cases . . .." The rate of pay varied with "a subjective evaluation" of "the quality of the case." Paying cash to investigators was "highly suspicious" and "consistent with a desire not to have records of transactions." Buchanan suggested that Brown's warnings against solicitation "were given with an implicit wink." The forms clients signed were "designed to exculpate;" respondents probably would have rejected those who refused to sign. The respondents' claim not to have noticed the "coincidence" that so many clients used the same medical service was "incredible." Their disregard of Ilson New's disclosures helped persuade Goldhammer that they knew about the solicitation. Paying the cappers by the case without a fixed rate "constituted fee-splitting." Both conspiracy and concealment should affect punishment.

Goldhammer also found that respondents charged unconscionable fees. They had bargained for a contingent fee, not an "outrageously unfair," "fixed-service fee" of $600 if clients replaced them. The clients "were very unsophisticated one-time . . . users of legal services, and the clauses were never or inadequately explained." Respondents made impermissible threats to claim "funds they were not likely to be entitled to receive" for the "clearly oppressive" purpose of making it "more difficult to obtain successor counsel."

The offense, aggravated by the duration of capping and number of clients, "resulted in significant harm to clients, the administration of justice, and the public." Although respondents denied any difference between advertising and solicitation, a year after *Ohralik*, the California Supreme Court had declared, "it is the public and the profession which suffer the greater damage from solicitation practices."[44] Goldhammer agreed that the harm of ambulance chasing "to the public perception of attorneys as professionals should not be underestimated."

> The public perceives direct solicitation and corruption as going hand-in-hand, and that is exactly what occurred here. . . . medical kickbacks and bribes of public employees did occur here and[45] respondents were responsible for that harm . . . . The privacy of accident victims was invaded by the use of confidential accident reports the victims had filled out. There was also overreaching of clients . . . another danger of direct solicitation . . . is the encouragement of unnecessary litigation.. . . the very real economic harm to those attorneys who earn their livelihood in an honest and incorrupt fashion is also not to be underestimated.

He found "no significant improprieties" in the State Bar investigation. Although he gave respondents "credit for steps they have taken to prevent solicitation of clients by staff and for stopping their unconscionable fee practices," those "actions are not entitled to that much weight in the absence of any acknowledgement that respondents were involved in wrongdoing . . .." Because "direct solicitation of clients through runners and cappers is a pernicious practice that

44. Kitsis v. State Bar, 23 Cal. 3d 867 (1979).
45. "Are" in the original.

undermines legitimate plaintiff's personal injury practice," he recommended 30 months suspension stayed and 15 actual, with four years probation.

The respondents sought reconsideration of an opinion written "in the spirit of advocacy." Goldhammer had rejected their estimate of the number of solicited cases because he "presumes Respondents to be liars." He ignored the hostility of "Behrmann and Sandles who had obviously been inflamed against Respondents by the Bar." Werchick's testimony "was simply purchased by the Bar." Ilson New, Madison Marcus, and Lawrence Murray were all "disgruntled competitors who profited by refusing to pay Respondents anything for their services." The court used a "rough sense of its own 'outrage'" as the criterion of unconscionability. The size of the lien claims was "irrelevant" since successor counsel "could not possibly have been influenced by the attribution of a dollar amount." "[W]hat the Court has really done is to disguise its hostility to Respondents' alleged solicitation as an argument against unconscionable fees."

> When stripped of the abject misstatements of the record and hysterical exaggerations, it is clear that the entire issue [of unconscionable fees] reduces itself to one unfortunate breakdown in communications between a willful and difficult client [Behrmann], the overburdened administrative staff of her former attorney's office, and an opportunistic insurance company [CSAA] willing to use any excuse to take advantage of its own client.

Goldhammer denied the motion on May 22. It was "hopefully cathartic but more of a bombastic and misplaced appeal than a reasoned request." After rebutting several arguments, he concluded that the rest "appears as inaccurate, incorrect, illogical, or otherwise as badly flawed . . .." He declined to respond to "the inflammatory claims that the Decision was based on speculation and conjecture, or relied on inadmissible evidence."

Respondents sought review and asked to pay the transcript costs in six monthly installments, noting that they "have conservatively expended in excess of $500,000 in attorney fees, costs, time, energy and effort." Drapiewski wanted a $15,000 retainer for the review (Weinberg having dropped out). "[S]ince this matter became public, our reputation and, therefore, our business has declined substantially." Judge Pearlman responded with a notice of intent to dismiss unless the respondents paid for the transcript in full.

Having obtained a month's extension, Drapiewski filed a 101-page brief. No lawyer "should have to spend four years of his time and allocate much of his resources to an investigation and prosecution which was so haphazard." Failure to supervise exposed a firm to malpractice liability but had "no place in a State Bar proceeding." Goldhammer's analysis was just "an excuse to further deprecate and punish Mr. Brown and Mr. Scapa." There was no "blanket prohibition" against paying non-lawyers bonuses. The Court just indulged "its philosophical abhorrence of incentive programs." Its "hypersensitive" reaction to the "trifling" matter of Scapa's claim in a 1979 advertisement that he was of counsel to Tarr "makes one question its evidentiary evaluations elsewhere." Solicitation might offend "many traditional practitioners" as well as the Hearing Department, but "standing alone it is relatively innocent."

> [A]ttorneys who solicit are not necessarily evil. They do not see their aggressive pursuit of clients as wrongful. . . . An attorney who solicits puts himself into the marketplace in the same way that other business people do and they do so in the good faith belief that their conduct is appropriate.

The only "arguable victims" were lawyers who lost business to the respondents, an "insignificant harm" that "does not call for significant punishment." Respondents are "excellent lawyers" who "made an extraordinary showing of good character." "[A]t best [they were] innovative practitioners who market their legal skills creatively and aggressively and by doing so provide those services to a group of clients whose cases would otherwise be neglected." At worst, they overstepped "the bounds of the law in an area of constitutional uncertainty." The OTC "intended a witchhunt" using "casual, inflammatory language suggestive of endemic misconduct" and presenting "unrestricted evidence including suggestion, innuendo and inference."

> Trial Counsel began these proceedings years ago with great fanfare and the promise, with the help of the insurance industry, to rid California of insurance fraud. It applied enormous resources to the assignment. . . . The net sum of that effort was this simple prosecution for solicitation[,]

The 142-page OTC response reiterated its arguments. The advice to the cappers sought to "create artificial corroboration for the Respondents in the event that the capping was discovered" and to "remind the cappers that what they were doing was illegal and that they should take steps to avoid being caught." The cash payments were "non-verbal statements" that "the money was being paid under-the-table . . . no permanent records were being kept, and thus both parties could later deny that the payments had taken place" and they "were being made for illicit services." The scheme caused actual harm. The cappers

> (1) lied to clients concerning the source of the police reports, (2) refused to let the clients speak with Respondents, (3) sold the clients' cases to the law firm that the cappers decided was best, (4) caused the injured clients to be referred to a medical clinic in exchange for kickbacks, (5) failed to give clients copies of the documents they signed, (6) caused the clients to sign documents under penalty of perjury falsely stating that they had not been solicited, and (7) purchased police reports and thereby engaged in corrupt and unlawful acts with police officers.

Over the OTC's objection that the respondents just sought delay, the Review Department allowed them to file a reply brief. It attacked the NTSC's "sloppiness" and the prosecution's "vagueries" (*sic*). The OTC had organized "a pretext search of another attorney's office . . . without any judicial authority or intervention . . . lie[d] to that attorney's representatives, and . . . surreptitiously rifle[d] through that attorney's papers." The brief retried the entire case. The OTC had adopted a "maniacal approach towards this prosecution . . . lac[ing] its presentation to the Review Department with wild conjecture and statements of fact outside the record." It "obsesses" over the case because Scapa and Brown "had the audacity at the outset to suggest that these solicitation charges were not such major offenses against humanity and the State Bar that their lives and careers should be forever destroyed."

The Review Department upheld Goldhammer, approving his factual findings and rejecting the respondents' procedural objections and "most hollow claim" that solicitation was constitutionally protected speech.[46] Their "frivolous" complaint that the OTC failed to notify them promptly of its suspicions about solicitation or "deactivate" the cappers "completely misunderstands that respondents had a personal duty to obey the State Bar Act and Rules of Professional Conduct." The Department found respondents guilty of attempting to charge unconscionable fees, improperly dividing fees with non-lawyers and making payments to them, all of which warranted severe punishment because of the "broad disregard of fiduciary duties."

> From the very time their clients were solicited, respondents left it to non-lawyer contractors to explain their complex retainer agreement. These "gatekeeper" agents would not even allow prospective clients to study the agreement for a day or two before signing it nor would they allow prospective clients to speak to respondents about the contract until the clients bound themselves to it.

Although the retainer purported to be a contingent fee agreement revocable at will, it "committed most clients to a minimum of $600 of legal fees . . . regardless of whether any work was done . . .." Respondents asserted liens for this, supporting their claims "by charging exorbitant amounts for perfunctory services performed almost entirely by support staff" and "threatening insurers with punitive damage actions." Clients "were disserved by referral to the same medical clinic for identical types of repeated, serial physiotherapy treatment." "This record reveals just why the public continues to press attorneys to be subject to the same specific consumer protection duties as those who operate an ordinary business." Solicitation alone warranted a year's suspension; the other offenses, "which showed their manifest disregard of client interest," deserved another six months.

Judge Pearlman wrote a concurrence addressing respondents' claim of constitutional protection as "innovative practitioners" providing services "to a group of clients whose cases would otherwise be neglected." She catalogued the ways

46. Matter of Scapa and Brown, 2 Cal. State Bar Ct. Rptr. 635 (10.27.93) (Stovitz, J.)

in which those clients had been betrayed by the respondents, who "did not show that the persons so solicited would have been unable to find adequate counsel. . . ." "[I]f respondents were willing to pay a portion of the fee to illegal cappers, the same services . . . should theoretically have been available for less cost to the clients . . . most attorneys would incur no time or expense to recover medical pay insurance coverage and thus could be expected not to bargain for a share of such proceeds in the contingent fee agreement." Respondents' "lack of recognition of the seriousness" of their misconduct "and their attempt to characterize themselves as merely technical transgressors who were taken advantage of by unscrupulous independent contractors is itself cause for grave concern." "Respondents engaged in despicable 'marketing' practices that members of the public dread—generation[s] of 'gotcha' agreements designed as traps for the unwary." Their "legalistic attempt to shield themselves with deniability by the use of forms disseminated by the very same unsupervised cappers is the type of slick conduct that gives attorneys a bad name." Their conduct was "all the more pernicious because it is sanctimoniously characterized as intended to benefit persons who otherwise might not receive proper legal representation." Their misconduct "appears motivated solely by greed."

A week later, Werchick wrote Stovitz that he had meant to criticize respondents only for billing to recover medical payments, not for taking "a share of all parts of the clients' recovery, including uninsured motorists." Respondents moved for reconsideration, claiming they had never been charged with using an unconscionable fee contract and had been discouraged from rebutting Werchick's "often preposterous" testimony. Had they done so, the Review Department might "conclude, as have thousands of California practitioners, that there is nothing improper in these fee agreements. . . ." The respondents requested three weeks to conduct a "thorough review" of the twenty-six volumes of transcripts, which they had not done before "because of time and financial limitations." Granted the additional time, they again assailed Werchick's "ridiculous trial testimony." His "word on contingent fees, advertising practices, and community standards is not gospel." The Review Department denied reconsideration. Although the Supreme Court affirmed that decision, respondents asked it to reconsider and "take a hard look at the instant matter." They had "chosen to incur the expense and to risk further public humiliation because they believe that their situation presents important, novel issues of law relevant beyond their own State Bar predicament." Substantive law "should more accurately reflect community standards of practice." Respondents "were victims of a solicitation scheme in the same way that their clients were also victims." Respondents terminated "the misconduct of others" "immediately" after learning of it. The proceedings had "resulted in a gross miscarriage of justice." The court "should not adopt the absurdly naïve prejudices of Mr. Werchick." They defended their liens. "What petitioners did was to involve themselves in all aspects of their clients' recovery and did so in a way that made compensation for that work reasonable."

"After all, it was the originating attorney who had identified the legal claim, preserved evidence, and organized prompt medical intervention." "The retention itself is something for which the attorney should be paid. When an attorney is retained, he cannot perform services for others." "Opening a file in modern times is more costly than it has ever been." On July 22, 1994, more than four and a half years after the NTSC, the Supreme Court again affirmed the penalty and awarded the State Bar costs.[47] Scapa and Brown were reinstated in 1996 and still practice in the San Fernando Valley—but separately.[48]

III. DEFENDING SOLICITATION

The brazenness of all the participants suggests that they either believed their behavior was acceptable or were confident they would not be caught. Those beliefs may reflect the pervasiveness of ambulance chasing in both Los Angeles (where the respondents had practiced for years) and San Francisco (where they launched the scheme), as shown by the cases at the beginning of this chapter.[49] Brown described the $100 to $150 per client he paid the cappers as the going rate. He claimed to have copied the client disclaimer from another lawyer; the Pollitt firm also used it. Gumban initially sold cases to other firms, and Buchanan claimed to have gotten one client from the Bay Area Referral Service. Michelle Behrmann testified that she had been solicited by Joanne Lopez, a firm employee. Even before meeting Gumban, Brown was paying Bert Gabriel for cases. Brown claimed Gabriel was a "go-fer," to whom he gave money out of charity. But the firm was hardly a charitable endeavor, and it could not explain the substantial payments (which it took as a business expense) or Gabriel's business card (claiming an association with the firm). The firm also seems to have used Manolet Umali to solicit cases (presumably from Filipinos). When Scapa met Gumban, he was doing "investigative" work for other firms—a euphemism for capping.[50] Even in the disciplinary proceeding, the respondents maintained they could pay the cappers for referrals as long as there was no "promise, agreement or

---

47. Philip Carrizosa, *Pair Suspended for 'Capping' Scheme,* 107(140) Los Angeles Daily Journal 20 (7.22.94).

48. Both accepted my offer to read this chapter, but neither made comments.

49. See the history of self-regulation in Chapter 1; bar associations in other states were equally preoccupied with the problem in the first half of the twentieth century. *See also* Reichstein (1964; 1965); Ward (1974). Lay solicitation is also common in immigration law, *e.g.,* Matter of Valinoti, 4 Cal. State Bar Ct. Rptr. 498 (2002); Matter of Phillips, 4 Cal. State Bar Ct. Rptr. 315 (2001) (both PI and immigration).

50. Marc Duxbury, described at the beginning of this chapter, was pleased that "Antonio Barajas" (actually undercover State Police Officer Tony Torres) suggested disguising payment for cases as "investigative service." "I like the way you guys set it up." In fact, they set *him* up.

understanding" (though of course there was). They told the cappers not to pay for cases but disregarded their own payments to the cappers. Scapa's repudiation of Brown's lien against Tashiro suggests concern that Ilson New—a lawyer competitor—would complain about the firm's solicitation.

The cops who bought and sold the cases took few precautions against detection. Gumban literally chased ambulances, stopping at accident scenes to give victims the law firm's card. The cappers telephoned personal injury victims at work as well as home, persisting until they got a response. They knew the victims could not yet have the police reports and therefore would be surprised—and impressed—that the caller did. Buchanan bragged to one prospective client about having signed up another victim right after the accident. The cappers boasted about their police contacts to both the victims and respondents, representations Brown confirmed to at least one client. Gumban even referred to himself as a police officer before correcting that to ex-officer. He told one partner he could get cases from the police but attributed most of them to "a marketing concept where I can expose myself in the general public [an unfortunate malapropism] to come across people that needs representation." He claimed (unconvincingly) not to know who staffed the police reports counter but admitted he might have mentioned Betty Brown to Buchanan. Because Gumban's wife worked in a hospital, "I'm exposed to a lot of patients . . . that need an attorney." At least one client believed Buchanan *was* an attorney, a misapprehension he did not discourage, calling one victim "the plaintiff" and assuring him that he had a "highly winnable situation." (Unfortunately, this victim was an OTC lawyer!)[51] Buchanan signed retainers on the firm's behalf. Gumban enjoyed signing up clients who had not yet seen a lawyer, which made him feel like one himself. (After his capping was exposed, he still believed he could become a lawyer and even took the LSAT.) Gumban kept a written record of the cases he solicited; Buchanan improved this by adding information about kickbacks. The lawyers paid by the case, only if it succeeded, and according to its value. Buchanan hoped for bonuses, and his notebook entries anticipated the need to repay the lawyers if cases failed. The cappers, in turn, paid the police in proportion to case value (which they felt capable of estimating). That the firm paid the cappers enough to let them pay the police shows how lucrative the scheme was for all.

The cappers misrepresented to victims the size and speed of recoveries, encouraging those reluctant to litigate with promises that the firm would take care of medical expenses and car repair and rental (by providers who took a lien on the recovery). The cappers referred most victims to two clinics, which paid them kickbacks and performed unnecessary treatments, inflating the clinics' bills, clients' recoveries, and lawyers' contingent fees (the last doubly, since general damages

51. Just as Steven Kroff, described at the beginning of this chapter, solicited the cases of a lawyer, a paralegal, a personal injury law firm employee, and a law student!

are proportioned to specials). Scapa himself told Lavita his recovery would increase with the number of treatments. Dr. Lackey complained to Scapa when Lavita stopped treatment, since the clinic had not received full value for its kickback. Although most clients had great difficulty getting to see or talk to the lawyers (and some never did), Scapa promptly called Lavita, threatening to terminate representation and ultimately doing so when Lavita refused to continue the medically useless visits. Some clients felt no need for medical care until the cappers made it a condition of representation. The cappers (and other firm employees) misrepresented to potential clients that they could cancel retainers at any time. By withholding retainers from clients, however, the firm made it difficult for them to reconsider the terms, consult another attorney, or revoke. (Buchanan refused to let Cohen take a copy of the retainer out of the office and insisted he sign it before seeing a lawyer.) The firm tried to stop clients from rescinding and asserted a lien for $600 or more, partly to discourage cancellation. The firm sometimes delayed forwarding client files to successor counsel. The firm's *quantum meruit* claim bore little relation to services rendered, for which the firm had scanty documentation. The firm's lien also delayed insurance company payments (even no-fault) and car repairs. Brown's willingness to "negotiate" liens suggested he knew they were unreasonable and hoped successor lawyers would simply acquiesce.

The respondents' behavior throughout the disciplinary proceeding was consistent with the conduct that had provoked it. Although Pollitt admitted involvement in the same capping scheme, these respondents protested their innocence to the end. They mocked a client who complained of neglect. They boastfully claimed to be too competent to have to solicit but acknowledged needing clients for their new San Bruno office. They maintained that low-value soft-tissue cases were not worth soliciting; but their payments to the cappers showed that the cases were very profitable. Scapa could not explain his failure to ask why Gumban left the police department or to read Ilson New's March 23 letter until June (especially when New followed up with a phone call two days later). The respondents asserted a "good-faith" belief that solicitation was legal as long as they did not pay clients for cases. They continued to invoke the no-solicitation instructions and disclaimer even after Goldhammer found those were part of their cover-up. They claimed not to have noticed the capped cases, which were just a fraction of their much larger caseload; but they could not explain how they got the other cases. First, they attributed them to advertising but did not know how much they spent or how effective it was. Later they admitted doing no advertising until after the charges were filed and then targeting only Filipinos. They claimed that lawyers who handle a high volume of low-value cases pay little attention to source; but the need for volume makes such lawyers even more dependent on case-flow. Scapa then maintained that he periodically asked about case source and did so systematically after New's letter. The respondents offered unsatisfactory justifications for sending almost all clients to Mission Family Medical Clinic: it was "not a dump" bur rather the kind of place where "most of our clients were accustomed to going;" it provided medical care on a lien basis; the doctor was Filipino and spoke Tagalog (although most clients were not and did not). The respondents contradicted themselves. Brown said in his deposition that "a light went off" when he saw Buchanan with an original police report; but he testified in the disciplinary hearing that he concluded someone had just gone over the Xerox with a pen.

Some arguments failed the laugh test: payments to cappers varied with the investigative work done, not case value; *every* time lawyers used a form they could bill for the effort originally invested in its preparation; the State Bar could not contact uncomplaining clients;[52] doing so violated the attorney-client privilege (which belongs to clients, not attorneys); the OTC interfered with the firm's relations with clients and hence its ability to recover fees; improper assertion of a lien could hurt only successor counsel, not clients. Brown argued, implausibly, that the $100 to $150 he paid cappers to sign up clients represented the cost of opening a file. The respondents blamed the State Bar for not stopping their solicitation sooner (like a robber complaining that the cops failed to arrest him before he stole). They were hurt by this failure more than clients. Indeed, their "lives and careers" had been "forever destroyed." They also said the district attorney, police department, and CSAA should have complained to them. They accused the "maniacal" OTC of using the disciplinary proceeding to justify its massive expenditure on an insurance fraud investigation broader than the Watergate inquiry and of indulging in "wild conjecture and statements of fact."[53] The CSAA collaborated to stop the firm from representing soft-tissue victims. The respondents kept asserting procedural objections that had been decisively rejected: Cohen's conduct in Buchanan's office; the immunity offered the cappers; the State Bar's collaboration with CSAA; alleged press leaks. They moved for reconsideration by attacking Goldhammer.

The respondents were unrepentant. Tarr (with whom they had been associated) said, "they're remorseful in the sense that this has caused a big problem for them . . .." Brown expressed "remorse" only about the fact that the disciplinary charges kept him from lobbying for trial lawyers. The firm dropped the solicitation disclaimer on the advice of counsel—not because the lawyers were convinced it was wrong. Brown still believed he was entitled to a lien for his fees on insurance payments for property damage and car rental. The firm threatened punitive damages against those who failed to respect their lien, although they had never researched the legality of that claim and could cite no supporting authority. Brown defended charging $200 an hour for non-attorney labor, $50 for leaving a

52. There used to be numerous restrictions on the State Bar contacting non-complaining clients, *see* Chapter 1.

53. Although the respondents did not mention it, the Special Operations Unit of the Office of Investigations focused on solicitation in the wake of the Cerritos air crash. Fellmeth (1987a: 7).

telephone message, $100 for reviewing the file when substituted out. He characterized a letter requesting a check for the lien amount as an opening gambit in negotiations—and then renewed the claim. The respondents defended their liens: "After all, it was the originating attorney who identified the legal claim, preserved evidence and organized prompt medical intervention." But it was the *cappers* who had done all this, not the attorneys, and the "medical attention" was often unnecessary. The respondents justified the lien on the ground that the retainer prevented them from accepting other clients—but also claimed to operate a high-volume practice in which they constantly did just that. Even after the NTSC the firm continued to use investigators to sign up clients (they did not know how many). Some investigators charged more than $500, a suspiciously high amount. All the clients who testified to their satisfaction with their representation (irrelevant, since no neglect was charged) had been loaned money by the respondents. The disciplinary process simply made the respondents regret the time, money, and effort they expended in defending themselves and the effect on their practice. By using every conceivable device to delay sanctions, the respondents gained four to five more years of profitable practice before suspension.

The respondents compounded their offense with an elaborate cover-up, undermining their claim to have acted in good faith. *They* were "victims of a solicitation scheme in the same way that their clients were also victims" (the only time they admitted that clients had been hurt). They insisted that Gumban and Buchanan had initiated the whole scheme, choosing lawyers who could be "easily duped."[54] They thinly disguised the cappers as investigators, "independent contractors" rather than employees. They claimed to be surprised by the business cards naming the firm. The policy memorandum and oral exhortations against solicitation they gave the cappers and the non-solicitation disclaimer they made clients sign all sought to create deniability. The respondents explained the disclaimer disingenuously as intended "to clue the client[s]" (who already knew they had been solicited) but then acknowledged candidly that it served "to protect us."

Gumban loyally took the fall. He shared the firm's hostility toward CSAA. He had hidden his solicitation of cases because the firm made it clear they did not want to be implicated. (This ruse might have worked had Buchanan not testified for the State Bar, in part because he felt Gumban was failing to pay his share to the cops. Buchanan maintained that Brown knew the cappers were buying reports from the police.) Gumban had bought cases legally from the SFPD for $5 to $6 (but he also bought them illegally for much more). He had been paid only $25 to $50 a case plus expenses (but Buchanan's notebooks showed much

54. What one might call the Uriah Heep syndrome, after that clerk's dominance of solicitor Wickfield in Charles Dickens's *David Copperfield*, actually occurred in the cases of Bruce Nelson, Francis Jones, Lawrence Bragg, and Corey Steele at the beginning of this chapter. Even in this case, Gumban seems to have been capping for other firms before starting to work for Scapa & Brown.

higher payments). Although Gumban stopped at crash sites to offer legal representation, he told the firm that such cases had been referred by a friend. (He may have been a gregarious local pol, but how many friends did the firm think he had, especially outside the Filipino community?) He concealed the medical clinic kickbacks (because he did not want to share them). The firm talked to him the day before he testified (although it had fired him). When Goldhammer rejected Gumban's challenge to the adequacy of the immunity grant the capper became extremely evasive. Drapiewski twice called Gumban his client before correcting himself. He challenged the immunity granted both cappers, although he was not their lawyer (and Buchanan rebuffed his assistance). Gumban admitted that Drapiewski had warned him against saying too much.

The respondents offered three justifications for their actions. They sought to transform their behavior from solicitation into inadequate supervision, from ethical misconduct into negligence, for which they would only be liable to clients who sued for malpractice. Scapa initially blamed Brown, who was in charge of office management and prelitigation matters, but then seemed prepared to take the rap, insisting that Brown was preoccupied with his marriage and honeymoon for six to ten weeks. Scapa claimed to have overlooked New's complaint during this period because of the press of work. When the respondents opened the San Bruno office, "we didn't have the financing to hire the best, highest caliber people that existed." (But why hire Gumban, whom Scapa called "a little crazy," except for the capping opportunities promised by his police contacts?) The respondents presented themselves as innocent dupes of sophisticated crooks. But their claim that the cappers were independent contractors over whom they exercised little control was belied by the business cards, the meetings in which they touted the cappers' police connections to clients, the firm office from which the cappers worked, and the fact that the cappers regularly visited the firm when the lawyers were there.

Second, the respondents assumed the mantle of altruistic champions of access to justice. Like legal clinics (Jacoby & Meyers, Hyatt Legal Services), they cut costs by using forms and substituting lay employees for lawyers.[55] They were "modern practitioners," innovators who braved the resentment of hidebound traditionalists (like the OTC, Werchick, and, by implication, Goldhammer). "Modern thinking" and "economics" dictated that clients never see an attorney. The prosecution was motivated by insurance industry opposition to "the opening of the profession as the courts and public are demanding." The respondents were fulfilling the unmet legal needs of soft-tissue victims. The San Bruno satellite office reached out to new populations. (In fact, the expansion was motivated by rising competition in Los Angeles and insufficient demand for criminal and family law.) The respondents built "social bridges" to minorities—Filipinos,

---

55. Seron (1996); Van Hoy (1997).

Hispanics—whose access to law was structured by ethnic networks whose nodes were the cappers. The respondents educated those ignorant of their legal rights. Their inadequate supervision of the cappers was motivated by a noble desire to serve too many people. This was only a partial truth. The firm's claim of good-faith behavior was undermined by the cover-up. Non-lawyers and forms can cut costs, but every client needs an initial interview with a lawyer before deciding to sign a retainer. The claim of increased access was belied by clients who constantly complained of being unable to talk to the lawyers. Few of the San Bruno clients were Filipino. The high-volume practice was motivated more by money than access. The firm made soft-tissue injuries profitable by sending clients to clinics that accepted liens for performing unnecessary medical procedures, inflating both special and general damages and hence the contingent fee. It pressured clients who wanted only non-fault medical expenses (which they could get without a lawyer) and property damage (whose amount was rarely in question) to claim general damages for soft-tissue injuries. It was most difficult to reconcile the respondents' altruistic pretensions with the firm's resistance to being substituted out, its assertion of $600 liens regardless of services rendered, its routine overcharging, and its requirement of a retainer with a 40-percent contingent fee as soon as the complaint was filed.

Finally, the respondents sought to elide the U.S. Supreme Court's distinction between constitutionally protected advertising and unprotected solicitation, which California prohibited. Like any other businessmen, they simply sought to "hustle" customers. Their lawyer maintained that the respondents did "not see their aggressive pursuit of clients as wrongful." (It takes real chutzpah for lawyers to maintain that their belief that an act is lawful makes it so.) Brown could see no distinction between answering an injury victim's questions and offering unsought advice. The respondents observed that lawyers routinely paid each other referral fees; but that does not legalize fees to lay cappers. The respondents appeared not to understand that paying cappers for signing up clients was illegal. They saw nothing wrong with nurses referring patients to their capper husbands, who were paid for the cases. The respondents characterized solicitation as "relatively innocent," a victimless crime, *malum prohibitum* rather than *malum in se.* The cappers were not aggressive, and clients were not harmed and did not complain (but some were and did). Drapiewski went further, seeking to persuade first Goldhammer and then the Review Department to invalidate the law against solicitation. He asked the California Supreme Court to modify the ethical rules to reflect "community practice." But it was not clear the State Bar Court had the power to do so, and the Supreme Court was disinclined. Goldhammer clearly felt that the most significant harm from solicitation was to law-abiding competitors who lost the opportunity to represent solicited clients. But he also offered other reasons why the respondents' behavior was reprehensible: it eroded public respect for lawyers; it involved kickbacks to medical clinics and bribes to public employees; and some victims felt pressured to sue or make specific claims.

3. MEDICAL INJURIES COMPENSATION REFORM ACT
Unconstitutional Until Proven Otherwise

I. OVERCHARGING CLIENTS

Overcharging and neglect are the two most common client complaints. Lawyers must not "enter into an agreement for, charge, or collect an illegal or unconscionable fee."[1] In 1975, the California legislature enacted the Medical Injuries Compensation Reform Act (MICRA), which set limits on the contingent fees of plaintiffs' lawyers and required them to give clients a duplicate copy of the retainer.[2] Although that is the focus of this chapter, lawyers have been disciplined for other excessive fees.

After her nine-year-old daughter Cory was injured in a car accident, Bobbie Rufu negotiated a $7,500 settlement and then orally agreed to pay Gloria Brimberry $500 to review it and a quarter of any excess the lawyer recovered.[3] Bobbie later signed a retainer for a one-third fee, "subject to court approval if necessary," believing that this applied only to the amount over $7,500. Without authority, Brimberry signed Bobbie's name to the settlement, deposited the $7,500 in her client trust account, missed three hearings to confirm the settlement, and paid herself a $2,500 fee. The judge who finally reviewed the settlement found that Brimberry did not even earn the $500 fee because she failed to review the agreement or handle the settlement correctly. Nevertheless, Brimberry claimed $2,533.50 by adding the defendant's insurer's $2,634 (no-fault) medical care payment and seeking 25 percent of the total.

After Simi Akin-Olugbade was injured, she and Brimberry met a claims adjuster, who offered $50,000. Akin-Olugbade told Brimberry the next day she did not want representation, repeating this several days later and retaining Ola Moore to seek her file. Instead of responding to Moore's written request, Brimberry filed a declaration to confirm the settlement offer without informing either of them and failed to answer Moore's repeated request for the file.

Richard Turner and Walter Lias consulted Brimberry about a dispute concerning the remodeling of the Ninevah Baptist Church, on whose board they served. Although she warned that the legal alternatives might be futile, that Friday they gave her a $5,000 check on the church for her expenses and fees.

1. California Rules of Professional Conduct (RPC) Rule 4-200 (formerly Rule 2-107(A)).

2. Business & Professions Code (BPC) §§6146–47.

3. Matter of Brimberry, 3 Calif. State Bar Ct. Rptr. 390 (1995) (disbarred).

She said she would do nothing until they brought the corporate papers and seal on Monday. But reconsidering the same day, the men left her a message that they had decided against legal action, would not deliver the papers and seal, and wanted the $5,000 back. Turner left another message on Monday, asking her to stop all work. When she returned the call later that week and was asked how much they owed, she promised to send papers. Two weeks later, she sent a "Declaration of Richard Turner" but no accounting and declared the $5,000 nonrefundable. She failed to answer Turner's repeated phone calls, but met the board several times and promised to refund some or all of the money. When the church sued her in small claims court, she produced a statement of services (which she claimed to have sent months earlier), alleging she had worked thirty-two hours over the first weekend and another five hours later, and seeking an additional $500. Although the court decision was typical in that it split the difference, Brimberry never paid, and the disciplinary proceeding found she had earned only $300 for the initial two-hour meeting.

As *Cumis* counsel for The Dentists Insurance Company (TDIC), Jerome Berg represented four dentists in forty-one cases.[4] Based on an oral agreement for $150 an hour, TDIC paid him $357,024.86. An audit later found that he billed for work before doing it and claimed to have worked many days for twenty-four hours (some for more than 100 hours). Berg defended this "bulk billing" on the ground that his time records had been destroyed. His disorganized files showed little evidence of settlement conferences. Many of the forty-one cases contained identical documents, each billed separately. Berg continued billing after the legislature overturned *Cumis*, claiming the work had been performed before the statute's effective date. TDIC sued him, winning over $282,000.

In February 1998, at the suggestion of an Indian Wells neighbor, Stuart Smith consulted Joseph L. Shalant about a possible medical malpractice action for an intrathrecal injection of depo-medrol for lower back pain, paying him $5,000 for four to five months of research and agreeing to a contingency fee if Shalant took the case.[5] Without contacting Smith, Shalant sent a $10 million notice of claim against Drs. Robert W. Murphy and Donald Drew, and filed a complaint. Learning about this seven months later, Smith was uncomfortable about the close-knit community's reaction and again asked about the fee arrangement. Shalant affirmed it would be contingent and explained MICRA but never offered a written retainer. When Shalant expressed skepticism that the injection had caused arachnoiditis, Smith researched his medical condition for a month and

4. Matter of Berg, 3 Calif. State Bar Ct. Rptr. 725 (1997) (disbarred). At the time, *Cumis* counsel were paid by an insurer to represent an insured's divergent interest. San Diego Navy Fed'l Credit Union v. Cumis Ins. Soc'y, 162 Cal.App.3d 358 (4th Dist. 1984). TDIC denied coverage because patients sought punitive damages.

5. Matter of Shalant, 4 Calif. State Bar Ct. Rptr. 829 (2005) (four earlier disciplines; disbarred).

sent Shalant the results. Three days before Smith's deposition, Shalant again warned about the difficulty of proving causation, declared he had done much more than the $5,000 fee required, and expressed reluctance to continue on a contingency basis. The day before the deposition, Smith faxed Shalant, objecting to this last-minute change, questioned Shalant's readiness for the deposition, and asked that it be postponed. Someone in Shalant's office said this was impossible. Although Shalant represented Smith at the deposition, he said, during and after it, that he would continue only if Smith paid him a nonrefundable $25,000 (to be credited against the contingent fee if Smith prevailed) and $10,000 in costs. He rejected Smith's counteroffer and sent a Medical Malpractice-Modified Contingency Retainer Agreement. Without signing it, Smith sent Shalant a $25,000 check, which the lawyer deposited in his general account. When Smith called eighteen months later to ask about the trial date, Shalant put him on hold several times and shouted at him. Smith terminated the retainer, asked for the file, and demanded return of the $25,000 for violation of MICRA. Smith's new lawyer settled his malpractice claim for $500,000. After the State Bar (SB) charged Shalant with entering into an agreement for, charging and collecting an illegal and unconscionable fee, he demanded additional fees and costs from Smith and sought arbitration of his *quantum meruit* claim.

All these disputes concerned contingent fees in personal injury cases.[6] Some of the lawyers billed too much, did too little, changed the agreement in midstream, or refused to accept being fired. None of that is true of the cases below, in which the lawyers performed at the highest technical level. But all the cases illustrate the vulnerability of personal injury clients and the vital importance of lawyers respecting fee regulations.

II. THE MEDICAL INJURIES COMPENSATION REFORM ACT OF 1975

In fall 1972, the California Assembly established the Select Committee on Medical Malpractice, which held hearings and issued a preliminary report in June 1974 on dramatic increases in both claims and judgments.[7] On New Year's Day 1975, the Pacific Indemnity and Star Insurance Companies refused to renew the medical malpractice policies of 2,000 Southern California doctors, and Argonaut Insurance

6. *See also* Matter of Van Sickle, 4 Calif. State Bar Ct. Rptr. 980 (2006); Matter of Wells, 4 Calif. State Bar Ct. Rptr. 896 (2006) (employment discrimination); Matter of Silverton, 4 Calif. State Bar Ct. Rptr. 647 (2004) (taking all of the difference in a compromised medical bill in addition to a contingent fee).

7. California Assembly, Select Committee on Medical Malpractice, Preliminary Report (June 1974).

raised premiums 380 percent for 4,000 Northern California doctors.[8] Companies writing insurance in California reported that annual claims per 100 doctors had doubled in the last six years (from 11.8 to 25 in Northern California and 13.5 to 26 in Southern California). The *Los Angeles Times* reported in March 1975 that premiums could exceed $20,000.[9] Assemblymember Barry Keene, who chaired the Assembly's Health Committee, attributed these changes to the "legal rights explosion," the "increased proficiency of trial lawyers," and especially "a 'no-fault' mentality in society at large" and "the belief that insurance companies have an unlimited source of funds." In response to the New Year's Day shocks, the Assembly's Finance, Insurance and Commerce Committee proposed a bill requiring all liability insurers in the state to participate in a joint underwriting association whenever the insurance commissioner found insurance was unavailable; but though that might ensure availability, it did not lower premiums.[10]

The media and the public initially supported the doctors, who lobbied for a special session of the legislature. The Assembly Health Committee found that 46 cents of every premium dollar went to litigation costs and only 34 cents to the plaintiff.[11] Chairman Barry Keene felt that

> reason was on our side because the existing system absolutely dictated change. Even if it were not a medical disaster for the rural patient, the Medicaid patient, the acute care patient, the high risk patient, and the economically marginal patient, it was a consumer disaster in terms of the half-billion dollars per year spent on defense [*sic*] medicine in California, and a disaster for the lawyer's injured client . . . .

Keene concluded that there was "no source of additional funds for the system." His first proposal, Assembly Bill (AB) 926, would have extended limited no-fault compensation to "all injuries which were the unanticipated results of medical intervention or unreasonable omission."

While the bill was on its way to Governor Jerrold Brown, Northern California doctors went on strike on May 1, the same day he convened a special extraordinary session of the legislature and "called for equal sacrifices." His proclamation declared:

> The cost of medical malpractice insurance has risen to levels which many physicians and surgeons find intolerable. The inability of doctors to obtain such insurance at reasonable rates is endangering the health of the people of

8. Keene (1976). Insurance for the 27,000 physicians who had personal policies was negotiated by two groups, representing those practicing in the northern and southern halves of the state.

9. Fred Hiestand, *Health Care Loss a Bitter Pill for Public,* Los Angeles Times §6, p. 5 (March 2, 1975).

10. *When Doctors Went Out On Strike,* U.S. News & World Report 4 (May 26, 1975).

11. Keene (1976: 28).

this State and threatens the closing of many hospitals . . .. In my judgment, no lasting solution is possible without sacrifice and fundamental reform.

On May 19, after the no-fault bill was deemed "too radical," Keene substituted AB 1, which limited "attorney fees—some have gone well over a million dollars in California—to assure that the plaintiff receives the bulk of the money.[12] An "attorney should not be able to get a windfall if a severely-injured 'perfect client' walks into his office . . . it is unconscionable to make the attorney a partner in his client's pain and suffering." "Perhaps the most controversial tort law change was the limitation on 'pain and suffering.'" Keene confronted a "moral dilemma. Unless we took drastic steps we were denying patients access to reasonably-priced health care in California; yet if we did, in addition to curtailing a system that provides inordinate benefits to a few, we might run the risk of under-compensating some of those few."

"Since the bill demanded sacrifices from all parties, all parties were opposed to some segment of the bill." By "pitting the various concerned and powerful interest groups against one another . . . we had a better change [*sic*—"chance"] of getting something out. This is called the 'equal bite' theory behind AB 1." The Speaker sent it to the Judiciary Committee, nine of whose eleven members were lawyers. "We arranged early discussions with the Governor so that he would have no good political basis on which to veto the bill."

Keene complimented the California State Bar for acting "in a very conservative manner through the entire medical malpractice crisis," taking no position until its select committee reported. The California Trial Lawyers' Association, by contrast, "blame[d] the insurance crisis on the insurance companies . . . continually rais[ing] the issue of insurance rate 'rip-offs' to pay for tremendous losses in the stock market."[13] But the state Auditor General, investigating on behalf of the assembly, concluded "that malpractice insurance companies are on the verge of bankruptcy principally due to significant increases in medical malpractice claims in recent years" and that "rates demanded by insurance companies appear to be actuarially reasonable."[14] The "Trial Lawyers' Association was never willing to accept this verdict." The lawyer-dominated Judiciary Committee seemed unable "to completely

---

12. Of the forty-one states that were considering reforms of the medical malpractice scheme, eight others joined California in capping contingent fees or requiring that lawyers offer hourly fees. Grossman (1976).

13. In fact, Argonaut had lost $21 million on its investments in 1974 and saw the paper value of its bond and stock portfolio drop by nearly $90 million that year. Lindsey, *For Argonaut, Profits Proved Illusory*, New York Times 49 (6.8.75). Argonaut was owned by Teledyne, a "fast-moving acquisitive California conglomerate that plunged into the business expecting big profits and then decided to leave it as soon as possible when the profits failed to materialize."

14. In fact, the California Joint Legislative Audit Committee (1975: 1) found that no crisis existed.

divorce itself from its own professional bias" and "severely amended" the bill but "could not kill [it] outright because of the public outcry that would have developed."

> Perhaps one of the most significant political forces involved in the medical malpractice crisis was the ability of local doctors to arouse their patients and have those patients demand substantial reform. Members of both the California assembly and senate were literally swamped with thousands of letters from constituents demanding immediate reform.

While continuing to oppose quality control reforms, the California Medical Association (CMA) backed the bill, which contained all eight tort reforms it had sought. The legislature might have enacted even more stringent controls if the Judiciary Committee had not "so severely watered down the tort reforms," reducing the legislature's leverage with the doctors. There was concern that the doctors would strike again, which they could do "with merely a day's notice"; "such a strike would likely have had widespread support among the non-sick populace of California." "The State Bar undermined its own position by not accepting many of the suggestions proposed by its own committee on medical malpractice . . .." Although the CMA withdrew support because of the Judiciary Committee amendments, the bill passed the assembly 67–8. The senate's Insurance and Financial Institutions Committee, "which was much more responsive to the doctors' outcries and perspective," passed a "reinvigorated" bill. "We could not have hoped to bring about change had the measure been referred to a lawyer-dominated committee in both houses." In September, the assembly passed the measure, 60–19, after "an indescribably bitter controversy" of "several days," and Governor Brown signed the bill twelve days later. The preamble of the new law, known as the Keene Act, declared:

> There is a major health care crisis in the State of California attributable to skyrocketing malpractice premium costs and resulting in a potential breakdown of the health delivery system, severe hardships for the medically indigent, a denial of access for the economically marginal, and depletion of physicians such as to substantially worsen the quality of health care available to citizens of this state.[15]

III. BROWNE GREENE

A. Genesis of the Fee Dispute

In 1982, Judith Shepherd "claimed to have a headache."

> [S]he went to the Kaiser emergency room and complained of this, and she said that the Kaiser emergency doctors failed to examine her and told her to

15. 175 Cal. Stat. c. 1, at 4007.

> go home and have an aspirin. And a matter of a few days thereafter, she had a neurovascular accident, and she went into a comatose state and had to be taken to the ER at Kaiser. And they had diagnosed that she had had a subarachnoid hemorrhage. And thereafter, she developed a form of hemiplegia.[16]

On July 21, 1982, she and her husband Richard retained R. Browne Greene to file a medical malpractice claim against Kaiser, agreeing in writing to pay him 40 percent of recovery with or without litigation. The case settled in 1984 for $650,000. On July 5, the Shepherds wrote Greene that $153,350 of his fee violated Business & Professions Code (BPC) Section 6146 (the MICRA fee cap), which they denied waiving orally.

A State Bar Special Investigator wrote Greene on October 2, asking that he respond by October 16 whether the disputed sums had been placed in an "interest hearing [*sic*] trust account" and whether he had "failed to furnish [the Shepherds] with the photographs, charts, reports, and displays they have requested."[17] Greene's partner, Charles B. O'Reilly, replied on October 25, apologizing for the delay, which he attributed to Greene being on trial in two matters.[18] "[I]t was practically impossible to have submitted it any sooner."

> At the time that the Shepherds retained this firm, we advised them of the provisions of Business and Professions Code Section 6146 . . .. We informed them that the difficulty, costs and risks associated with the case rendered it unfeasible for the firm to represent them given the limit on fees posed by the Code Section . . .. [T]hey informed this firm that they desired to waive the Code Section . . .. They also . . . wanted a commitment that Mr. Browne Greene, Esq. . . . would personally try their action . . ..[T]he Shepherds then expressly waived the Code provision. . . . In light of the Shepherds' waiver, the numerous trial and appellate decisions invalidating provisions of the Keene Act and the standard of practice at that time, the firm believed there was nothing improper about the retainer agreement. . . . Mr. Greene obtained time off from a case he was trying in Ventura so that he could personally try the arbitration matter on behalf of the Shepherds. . . . As a result of Mr. Greene's efforts, Kaiser eventually offered a sum far in excess of the settlement amount recommended by the appropriate personnel conducting the arbitration . . .. [A]t the beginning of the hearing there was, practically speaking, no offer but as a result of Mr. Greene's efforts in presenting the Shepherds' case and cross-examining the defense witnesses, the Kaiser offer exceeded the evaluation placed on the case by all concerned. When this offer was communicated to the Shepherds, they were fully advised as to what the attorney's fees would be . . .. They completely agreed with the breakdown and advised Mr. Greene

16. Taken from Greene's direct testimony.
17. Respondent's Exhibit C.
18. State Bar Exhibit 16.

> to accept the offer . . . . [T]he Shepherds were advised that the firm had received a draft for the settlement amount . . . . [T]hey again agreed with the breakdown and made no mention of any complaint or dispute about the attorney's fees. Just prior to the Shepherds' meeting with Mr. Greene, their attorney, Mr. Needle, delivered a letter disputing the attorney's fees . . . . At . . . the meeting the Shepherds signed and approved the accounting, which contained the breakdown of attorney's fees and costs . . .. The firm did not at that time place the funds in dispute in an interest bearing trust account . . . [because] it was not made clear whether or not the Shepherds were going to genuinely contest any of the funds earned by this firm as attorney's fees.

The Office of Trial Counsel (OTC) filed a notice to show cause (NTSC) on June 5, 1987, charging Greene with violating BPC Sections 6068 and 6106 and Rules of Professional Conduct (RPC) Sections 2-107 and 8-101(A)(2). The case initially was assigned to Hearing Judge William Crosby, who knew Greene, then president of the California Trial Lawyers Association. Djinna Gochis was the examiner. The respondent was represented by his own firm: Greene, O'Reilly, Broillet, Paul, Simon, McMillan, Wheeler & Rosenberg. He answered, on July 22, that he had been retained by the Shepherds' attorney, Joshua Needle, "after they expressly agreed, on Mr. Needle's advice, to waive any rights or claims to the statutory fee provided by MICRA." In May 1984, a month before the case settled, Richard Shepherd and Joshua Needle "privately agreed to create a fee dispute with Respondent" and "to deny the earlier waiver of the MICRA fees and to divide the amount obtained from Respondent between them." "[T]he claimed dispute was not genuine but was fabricated by Richard Shepherd and his attorney, Joshua Needle, Esq." Greene had not put the disputed amount in a client trust account

> because Respondent was not aware, under the circumstances, that the amount should be placed in a trust account . . . . When the State Bar did not indicate that the amount should be placed in a trust account after they received the October 1984 letter . . . Respondent assumed he was correct . . .. The State Bar first advised Respondent that the amount should have been in a trust account approximately two years later . . ..

The hearing began on April 19, 1988; Greene was represented by Donald B. Caffray (of Long Beach) and Charles B. O'Reilly, of his own firm. Thomas P. Foye, a retired judge, replaced Crosby as referee. Richard testified that he met Greene on July 21, 1982, to discuss his wife Judith's medical malpractice claim against Kaiser. The meeting included Judith, their daughters Adela Kelin and Irene Shepherd, the Shepherds' lawyer Joshua Needle, and Ken Collins (an associate in Greene's firm and acquaintance of Needle). The written retainer made the Shepherds liable for costs and "to pay our attorneys a sum equal to 40% of any recovery in the event settlement is reached without litigation or in the event suit is filed."[19] "In the event no recovery is made, no charge will be made for services." Greene never mentioned BPC Section 6146. When the Shepherds asked if 40 percent was reasonable, Needle said it was. The case settled in June 1984, and Kaiser issued a $650,000 check to the Shepherds and Greene on June 13.[20] At the beginning of July, Richard endorsed the check after the firm's administrator, Francis Cholko, orally estimated the expenses at $23,000 to $24,000. On July 9, there was a meeting for disbursements, including both Shepherds, Needle, Greene, Andrew Ellis Rubin (another attorney present at Needle's request), and Cholko. Greene provided an accounting of actual disbursements, including $30,333.68 in costs and $260,000 as his fee. At Needle's suggestion, the accounting included a note initialed by the Shepherds and Greene that "$153,350.00 in dispute subject to negotiation/litigation."[21] This was "the difference between what he was taking and what we felt he was entitled to." That day the firm gave the Shepherds a check for $359,666.32.[22] On the back, they wrote that "endorsement of this check does not constitute a waiver of disputed attorneys fees ($153,350) nor, consequently, an acknowledgement that all funds have been received in this case." Greene

> was very indignant that we were questioning the statute. That we had filed and were expecting him to disburse the funds according to the statute. He yelled at Mr. Needle, he—I think he called him a leech, a shyster. He called me a liar, he called me a cheater, he called me a conspirator, and other names which I can't remember exactly.

On July 23, Shepherd wrote Greene:[23]

> The fiasco at your office on July 9, 1984 was distasteful to both my wife and myself. We felt that you were at your worst, unprofessional and rude. We felt that your conduct was unbecoming to your standing in your profession. Calling my attorney names was particularly childish.
>
> You accused me and my wife of planning all along to "cheat" you out of your fees. This is untrue. When I tried to tell you what happened, you interrupted and called me a liar. Your conduct was disgraceful. After the abuse that we suffered at the hands of your young associate, we expected better from you.
>
> We were shocked when we found out about your illegal contract but thought that you would obey the law. I believe that we all have to follow the law. And even though we signed an illegal contract, we were willing to pay you the legal amount

19. State Bar Exhibit 1.
20. State Bar Exhibit 2.
21. State Bar Exhibit 3.
22. State Bar Exhibit 4.
23. State Bar Exhibit 5.

> due as if you had written a contract which was legal, but you refused any suggestions and told us to "try and get it." You can be sure we shall do our best.
>
> Having now reviewed that "accounting" of yours, I see that I have paid for everything, and I want that everything. This includes all of the photos of my wife, the displays and the reports that we paid so dearly for. I also question some of the expenses I had deducted from the amount you gave us . . . .
>
> We shall take this dispute to any board or court that handles these types of illegal fee arrangements. We definitely will report your conduct to the Bar Association.
>
> We are sorry that our relationship with your office soured, but we are going to try to recover all the money that is legally ours. You can avoid all the unpleasantness by returning to me, at once, the amount that you have kept illegally.

Shepherd testified, "I was really numb from that meeting from Browne Greene. And I felt that I should write him and tell him that I intended to pursue it and that I was disappointed in him as an attorney and as a man." Shepherd got no response. He finally obtained the disputed $153,000 on January 9, 1987, after State Bar arbitration and lawsuits.

On cross-examination by Caffray, Richard said he had shown Needle the letter before sending it but got no suggestions. He had told Needle: "I thought that Browne Greene was just angry that day and would come to his senses . . . and realize that he had done something wrong and correct it. After all, he was a lawyer." Caffray asked: "You realized, of course, that you were seeking to not comply with the written contract that you—," but Gochis objected. Richard agreed they wanted the case handled exclusively by Greene, not others in the firm but denied telling him, "we agree to waive the statutory Keene bill or Business and Professions Code requirements so that you personally . . . would handle our medical malpractice case."

At Judith's stroke clinic, about May 10, 1984, Richard met Jay Rose, an attorney who handled medical malpractice cases, who asked what Richard was paying Greene.

> I said 40 percent. He said, "He can't charge you 40 percent." I said, "Yes, he can, because I signed a contract." And he said, "It's an illegal contract." I said, "Browne Greene wouldn't sign an illegal contract. He's too big an attorney for something like that." He said, "I am right and I will send you a copy of the code." And he knew it by number.

When Rose sent the code a few days later, Richard raised the issue with Needle, who promised to look into it. On June 1, when Greene said he had an offer, Richard again asked Needle about BPC Section 6146, but his lawyer had not researched its applicability. Over the following weekend, Greene called again to say they were going into a settlement conference, so Richard asked Needle a third time: "Did you check it out?" Needle said "Yes, and it does not pertain." On June 5, Richard went to Needle's Santa Monica office to sign a power of attorney so Needle could accept the offer, since Richard was leaving town. He brought BPC Section 6146.

> I said, "Show me why this does not pertain." [Needle] had maintained that it did not pertain to our case. He took that and discussed it with an associate in his office—or not an associate. They like share a suite of offices . . . Jack Dunne. Mr. Dunne came back and said "Yes, it pertained to the malpractice suit that we had had Browne Green represent us on." . . .

CAFFRAY: Did you have a discussion with Mr. Needle wherein . . . you said to him, "Don't say anything to Browne about raising the issue of us paying a lower fee until he has finished the case because he might not try as hard"? . . .

RICHARD: Yes . . . .

CAFFRAY: That occurred before you made the deal to get the money?

RICHARD: Yes. . . . [Needle] was in for a percentage . . . he referred me to Browne Greene . . . it was called a referral fee . . . .

Rubin (who attended the July 9 meeting at Needle's request), testified that Greene said

> that he had gotten them a really terrific settlement . . . that no other lawyer would have been able to do it, and that that is the reason they had come to him, because he was the best lawyer around for medical malpractice; that he would not have taken the case for the amount of money that MICRA would have limited it to . . . he had advised them at the time that they had signed the agreement that there was a limitation on fees, and that by signing the agreement they were waiving that . . .. [H]e considered that agreement . . . binding and MICRA non-binding.

The Shepherds did not agree they had waived MICRA. Needle suggested the disputed amount be put into a trust account, but "Mr. Greene said he didn't want to do that."

On cross-examination, Rubin said he attended the meeting at Needle's request for a $150 fee. "[T]he Shepherds were old friends" of Needle's family. "My impression from looking at Mrs. Shepherd was that she acted very much like somebody who had had a stroke." Needle had referred the case to Greene's firm because he knew someone there (presumably Collins). Needle had hand-delivered Greene a letter stating "that he had learned about MICRA; and that he felt that Mr. Greene's fee . . . was excessive . . . Mr. Greene had called him and had insulted him, had screamed at him over the telephone, had called him vile names . . .." Needle "wanted me there as an independent observer or as an attorney representing his interests, because . . . there was a fee-referral arrangement between Browne Greene's firm and Mr. Needle."

He wanted to have someone else there who was, number one, not emotionally involved in the case, number two, could listen to what happened, and number three, would represent him and he also said would try to keep him from flying off the handle because . . . . "[Greene] said such things to me that I really want somebody there to look at me and make certain I don't start screaming back at him if he screams at me again."

Needle testified he was unfamiliar with MICRA and Greene had said nothing about it at the July 1982 meeting. After Greene gave Richard the retainer, "we went outside . . . and Dick was a little upset because it was a flat 40 percent, rather than as he had heard, if something settles, it's a third and then it goes up to 40 percent at some later point. Mr. Shepherd was quite upset about that. And I reassured him." On July 5, 1984, Needle wrote the letter he hand-delivered to Greene the morning of the July 9 disbursement meeting.[24] It stated:

In discussing the settlement of this matter with friends in the personal injury field I was referred to Business & Professions Code Section 6146 . . . . I have come to the inescapable conclusion that the retainer agreement signed by the Shepherds was and is in violation of that Code section and must be brought into conformity with the law. Obviously this reduces the amount of attorney's fees to be paid to your office, and subsequently to myself as the referring attorney, but since we are under a duty to do what's in the best interest of our clients I see no alternative since the Code puts something in the neighborhood of $150,000.00 into the client's pocket over and above what is called for in the retainer contract. There is just no question about what is in their best interest.

He calculated the difference between the 40 percent fee ($260,000) and the Section 6146 fee ($106,650) as $153,350.

When distributing the funds to the Shepherds, I will assume that you will follow the dictates of the Code . . .. If for some reason you believe that your retainer overrides the Code—without any reference to or [*sic*—"any"] purported waiver thereof—then I will expect that you will set aside in a special interest-bearing trust-account the amount in dispute while the matter is litigated before either the State Bar mandated attorney-client fee dispute panel of the Los Angeles County Bar Association or the courts. In any event they are to receive the undisputed portion of their award ($390,000.00) per the schedule set earlier this week by your office administrator; any deviation from this would, as you well know, simply exacerbate their already severe problems beyond imagination.

If you reject this analysis please be aware that the Shepherds and I intend to pursue this matter; they are fully aware of the contents of this letter. If, for

24. State Bar Exhibit 6.

instance, you insist upon taking your contractual 40% and I receive 20% of that fee, i.e., $52,000.00, I will immediately refund to them everything over and above what I consider to my legally valid claim of $21,330.00; to wit: $30,670.00; this action would obviate any potential conflict that I might have so that I can continue to represent my clients as I see fit and proper.

Waiving attorney fees is not my idea of a good time either, Browne, but frankly my license is worth considerably more than $30,000.00 and I feel that one of my duties as an attorney is to follow and enforce the law as it applies to my clients's [*sic*] best interests.

Greene called right after receiving the letter. He

was exceptionally upset, very angry, yelled and screamed at me over the phone, how I was betraying trusts or not acting fairly and I had stabbed him in the back, trying to steal his fees . . . . I tried to explain just what I put in the letter . . . . I probably didn't get out much from my side. Mr. Greene was yelling quite vigorously.

At the meeting, Greene said,

we were trying to cheat him, that we had no right to cheat him out of his fees; that we had conspired against him; that I was a little slime. He called me several variations on a theme, from "bastard" to "little shit," I think he used "thief," "liar," all sorts of names.

The State Bar introduced Rose's May 8 letter to Shepherd, attaching Section 6146.[25] "I believe the code section, although complicated, will be understood by you. Please review it and compare it to your existing retainer." But "rather than expose Mr. Shepherd to any invective," Needle told Greene "I had heard about it through friends and colleagues who I discussed the settlement with." When he added the reservations during the accounting and check endorsement, Greene retorted "Well, give it your best shot," or "Get it if you can."

Needle wrote Greene again on July 26.[26]

Now that you have had time to reflect upon this matter and to consider the Supreme Court's [July 20] ruling in *American Bank*[27] . . . [I]t is my hope that

25. State Bar Exhibit 7.

26. State Bar Exhibit 8.

27. The first time the California Supreme Court heard a challenge to MICRA, it invalidated the periodic payment provision. American Bank & Trust Co. v. Community Hospital of Los Gatos-Saratoga, Inc., 33 Cal.3d 674, 190 Cal.Rptr. 371 (1983). Justice Mosk wrote the opinion for himself, Chief Justice Bird, and Justices Rattigan and Racanelli sitting by designation. Justice Kaus wrote the dissent for himself and Justice Broussard and pro tem Justice Feinberg. After Justice Grodin was appointed to the Supreme Court, it reheard the case and upheld the section, 36 Cal.3d 359, 683 P.2d 670, 204 Cal.Rptr. 671 (1984). Justice

> you will voluntarily disgorge the disputed legal fees that you have withheld and obviate the need for, in your words, a battle. The constitutional defense that you raised is no longer available to you, and to prolong this matter is truly in nobody's interest.

He also asked Greene for the Shepherds' records. If Greene did not send a "positive response" by mid-August, "you will leave me no alternative but to pursue this matter by all legitimate means." Answering this "erudite and interesting letter" on August 7, Greene said it was "beyond" him to understand how Needle could "interpret that opinion as ruling on the issue in this case," since it "deals only with another section of the act, to wit the periodic payment issue. The issue of attorney's fees is still before the Supreme Court in other cases . . . .[28] That "specific act, to with [*sic*] the MICRA Act in regards to attorney's fees, has been held to be unconstitutional as a deprivation of equal protection." Greene

> took this case only on the assurance that we would have an attorney's fee for myself as well as you would have a referral fee based upon the negotiation between the clients and myself demanding that I be the attorney from the beginning through the end of the case, to with [*sic*] a 40% attorney's fee. You were present when that was negotiated and know that I stated completely the fact that I would take this case only on that basis and if they demanded the MICRA Act be applied then they could go elsewhere.

The Shepherds and Needle "demanded that I handle this matter through the final conclusion of the Arbitration hearing . . . based upon what Dick Shepherd said was my great reputation as a trial attorney." Before the distribution the Shepherds were told of the 40 percent attorney's fee, "and no issue was raised whatsoever until the final day that the monies were disbursed at which time the final seeds of the set-up were shown by your letter which arrived shortly before the meeting with the Shepherds and my telephone call with you." He refused to send the Shepherds' documents and photos. "If they desire to pick up anything here . . . they can make arrangements with my secretary . . .."

The Shepherds sought State Bar arbitration of the disputed fee and were awarded $101,450 (plus interest from July 9) on December 27, 1984.[29] The Bar found that the contingent fee agreement was voidable and the Shepherds did not waive Section 6146. But Greene rejected binding arbitration, demanding trial *de novo*. Before the Shepherds answered, Needle wrote Greene again on February 26, 1985.[30] The *Roa v. Lodi Medical Group* decision "seemed to me to answer the

---

Kaus now wrote the majority opinion for himself and Justices Broussard, Grodin and Feinberg., while Chief Justice Bird and Justice Mosk both wrote dissents, joined by Justice Rattigan.

28. State Bar Exhibit 9.

29. State Bar Exhibit 11.

30. State Bar Exhibit 10 (not in evidence).

question completely, and this is a letter requesting that he drop the lawsuit and follow the law as upheld in the *Roa* decision."[31] Throughout the State Bar arbitration, Greene had

> argued that the entire MICRA act was unconstitutional and that 6146 in particular was unconstitutional, and also that there was an oral waiver on the part of the Shepherds. *Roa* answered all of those questions . . .. It sustained 6146 against all of the challenges.

The clients in *Roa* had asked for a waiver of MICRA in open court. "So even if there had been a waiver, it would be ineffective." Needle filed a petition on April 26 to correct and confirm the arbitration award. The Superior Court rendered judgment for the Shepherds on June 4 for $137,969.95 and 10 percent interest; the Court of Appeal confirmed on September 23, 1986, and the Supreme Court denied review in late 1987. Greene sued for breach of contract on February 1, 1985, lost, and appealed on August 5.[32] The Court of Appeal affirmed on April 29, 1986, noting that the Supreme Court had explicitly rejected waiver the previous year.[33] Greene issued the Shepherds a check for $157,462.99 dated December 24, 1986,[34] and there was a satisfaction of judgment on June 30, 1987.[35]

Cross-examined by O'Reilly, Needle agreed that sometime between mid May and early June 1984, Richard and he discussed "what do we do with this information [about Section 6146]? . . . Do we put it up to your firm at this point or do we wait . . . making sure the arbitration is done?" They realized "Mr. Greene would be upset if [Needle] advised him that you were going to now insist on MICRA." "My opinion was that it would be ridiculous to bring up this derisive [*sic*—'divisive'] subject at that point in time. It would in no way possibly help my clients." But he denied either waiting "because [Needle] and Mr. Shepherd knew that you had promised [Greene] that MICRA was going to be waived if he would personally handle the matter" or delaying delivery of the letter "until right before this disbursement" in order "to precipitate an angry reaction" by Greene.

The Shepherds "were exceptionally upset with how they felt they were being treated by Mr. Greene and asked me what . . . avenues of recourse existed." In addition to disputing the fee, Needle explained, they could complain to the State Bar. "I probably prepared the documents for their signature and they filed them." He drafted a contingent fee retainer for the fee dispute: a minimum of 20 percent, a third if litigated; and 40 percent if appealed. Richard "didn't like that and said 'all you are getting is 20 percent.' So he struck what I proposed . . .." Needle then referred the Shepherds' case against Greene to Mr. Clifford, taking a

---

31. Roa v. Lodi Medical Group, Inc., 37 Cal.3d 920 (1985).
32. State Bar Exhibit 12.
33. Waters v. Bourhis, 40 Cal.3d 424 (1985).
34. State Bar Exhibit 14.
35. State Bar Exhibit 13.

referral fee for doing so. "Mr. Shepherd and Mrs. Shepherd are friends of my family for many years. When I referred the medical malpractice case to your firm, they were concerned I get a referral fee. When I referred the other case, they also were concerned that I would get a referral fee. And they liked the fact that I get referral fees." Gochis successfully objected to O'Reilly asking whether Needle had urged other former clients of the Greene firm to raise the Section 6146 issue.

O'Reilly tried to show that Mrs. Shepherd had not authorized Needle's actions.

NEEDLE: Mrs. Shepherd, as you well know, suffered . . . permanent brain damage as a result of Kaiser's negligence. She does not articulate things particularly well, but she understands what's going on. She participated in the meeting . . . where we discussed . . . the applicability of MICRA and . . . when we should apprise your firm of our knowledge of it . . . .

O'REILLY: You never had a guardian ad litem or conservator appointed for Mrs. Shepherd, did you? . . .

NEEDLE: Mrs. Shepherd trusted me as a family friend as an attorney to do what was in her best interests. And I brought her to what I thought was one of the best and most successful medical malpractice firms in town, if not the state. And I, too, relied on the understanding of whom Greene, O'Reilly was and trusted that firm to take appropriate steps.

Needle conceded having "misled your firm" about how he learned of MICRA. "I was under no obligation to state to you everything." He might have heard about it in a medical malpractice litigation course taught by Tom Gerardi the year he graduated from law school (1977). He also admitted knowing some personal injury lawyers, belonging to the Los Angeles Trial Lawyers Association, and getting their newsletter. But "I hadn't thought of" MICRA. When the referee agreed with Gochis that this seemed irrelevant, O'Reilly insisted it tended to show that Needle's "ignorance of MICRA wasn't as he professes it to have been," which "relates to the credibility of this witness with regard to raising this whole thing" and "the legitimacy of the dispute with so many years in litigation." Needle conceded never objecting to the fact that the $400,000 general damages also exceeded MICRA's $250,000 limit. At the State Bar fee arbitration, Greene claimed Section 6146 was unconstitutional; after the Supreme Court upheld it in *Roa*, Greene argued that the Shepherds had waived it and the fee agreement was voidable rather than void. Needle had sought sanctions against Greene for frivolously appealing dismissal of the breach of contract lawsuit, but the Court of Appeal declined to impose them since *Waters v. Bourhis* was not filed until after the notice of appeal.[36]

36. It was decided December 5, 1985.

Greene testified that the primary reason the retainer did not mention Section 6146 was

> we did not handle that many medical malpractice cases . . . . [W]e would use this particular agreement on all of the cases that we took in, whether they were med mals or otherwise, in light of the fact that the kind of cases we took were substantial . . . .

GOCHIS: Mr. Greene, in 1982, were you aware of the provisions of Business and Professions Code 6147, which requires that there be a mention of 6146 in a retainer agreement?

GREENE: No, I don't believe that was required . . . . [N]ot if it was waived . . . that was the exact thing I was confronted with when they waived it there in July of 1982.

GOCHIS: Did you not consider it, Mr. Greene, to be sound policy and practice to have a most important issue, that is, waiver, written down and part of the retainer agreement?

GREENE: Not when I trusted my clients . . ..

GOCHIS: When did you tell them [about MICRA]?

GREENE: The day they came into my office . . . in July of 1982 . . . . I told them that this was a very difficult case, that we were going to have a hard time finding medical witnesses, which we did; and that there was at issue in the state the medical malpractice law that the legal profession in this city and in this state was not believing that that law was valid and in fact that it was a patent violation of the equal-protection clause of the state and federal constitution. It had been declared so by Judge Schifferman in Superior Court and Judge Rafaedi [*sic*—Rafeedie] in federal court, and there had been a disrecord of the appeal opinion to the effect it was unconstitutional in the courts in the probate area . . . . And I told them very directly that I did not intend to take this case, with the years of litigation, expense and costs and risk, if they were going to insist on a 10 percent attorneys fee beyond $200,000 on this case . . . . They insisted that I take the case . . . . Mr. Shepherd, being the one who handled and did all of the talking, said "We want you to handle this. We will waive this provision if you will do this." . . . I took the case under that assumption and I worked it up on that assumption and I lived up to my end of the bargain.

Asked again why he had no written waiver, Greene replied, "I ordinarily don't have to protect myself from people that are going to try to sandbag me." "I don't believe the law was in effect" at that time because "it was not being followed by the courts" or "the State Bar of California . . . the trial bar . . . and judges in this state." He did not think *Roa* required him to repay the excess. Asked why he did not put the disputed funds in a trust account, Greene said, "I had absolutely nothing to do with the placement . . . of the funds. In our office, no partner, in light of . . . the size and scope and number of cases, has anything whatsoever to do with whether the monies go to this account, that account or whichever account. Mr. Cholko, hired specifically from the Superior Court as the second in command of the court, had total control of all those decisions." "None of us in our office, with the operation that we have going, with the number of cases, including 850 asbestos clients alone, know where explicit [*sic*—specific] funds per client are." He did not instruct Cholko to put the money in a trust account after Needle complained, "because I never believed there was a dispute. I thought I was being sandbagged and being set up . . . by some people that were trying to get a better deal on fees."

> I was very explicit with them, they weren't going to get away with that . . . . [T]hey knew that any time . . . that we spoke by phone or in conference . . . we had discussed explicitly . . . that they had waived this, they demanded I get out of a jury trial in Ventura and hold up six lawyers, a jury and a judge so that I could come down and do this or else they would make a complaint to the State Bar on that. That was what Dick Shepherd told me so what was I supposed to do? . . .
>
> I have had clients before that . . . try to renegotiate an attorney's fee situation after they have originally signed the agreement. And then . . . they have rethought the thing out, after they have seen that I am not going to bend on it . . . they come back and live up to their end of the contract. I thought they were going to do that.
>
> Instead they came in at the last minute on this very day after approving [the fees] a few days before, when they were with Mr. Cholko, and on the day that I spoke to Mr. Shepherd when the case was settled for 650 and give them every single dime down to a nickel how much they were going to get, including a 40 percent fee, and Mr. Shepherd thanked me profusely for it and said, "Thank you, you have done a good job." . . . And I was angry . . . . [Needle and Richard] said "We're claiming now, today, the first time to you that MICRA applies." And I said "I don't agree with you." I said "I think you are going to rethink this, because I am not about to go back on our agreement, and I'm not going to have you go back on the agreement . . . . [Y]ou are going to see that what you got was the best deal available." I was proud of the job we had done . . ..

B. Greene's Defense

Opening the defense case, Caffray denounced the charges as "very, very incorrectly brought."

> [N]early the entire legal community regarded [MICRA] as unenforceable, unsettled and unconstitutional. The judicial and legal community was not following this law . . . . [T]here is a serious question under the circumstances considering the status of the law as to whether there was even a legitimate dispute.

When Gochis objected to Caffray asking Greene whether courts were applying the law, Caffray retorted: "was it known to be constitutional then and the answer is it was not."

Judge Jack E. Goertzen (just elevated from the Superior Court to the Court of Appeal) testified: "I do not know during that period of time of any of the judges who were in fact enforcing the provisions of MICRA." "Judge Schifferman . . . wrote a memorandum opinion at the time expressing specifically a finding of unconstitutionality of the limitation on general damages, and this was the general prevailing view." The BAJI committee was "waiting to see what the appellate courts might do." Los Angeles County Superior Court had "four or five settlement courts, and settlements were just going down every day without any MICRA problems being raised. Obviously not by the plaintiff but not defense either." Greene was an "outstanding member of the bar:" trial lawyer of the year, a member of the rare circle who "had made recoveries in seven figures," president of both the California and Los Angeles Trial Lawyers Associations.

Thomas Girardi taught medico-legal law at Loyola.

> I would say that the MICRA bill was probably the singular [*sic*—single] most important topic that was discussed during the semester. There were at least two full sessions . . . and then in all the other sessions we would use anthologies [*sic*—analogies] as to how MICRA would affect that particular aspect of the case . . .. [F]rom 1975 . . . when it was being discussed up in Sacramento up until the last time I taught the class, MICRA provisions accounted for approximately one-third of the exam . . .. We of course knew, that's in quotes, that it was unconstitutional because I was in negotiations up in Sacramento when the MDs initially went on strike. I was the liaison to the governor's office . . .. Jerry [Brown] was in the special session and said, okay, fine, he wanted to go ahead and sign it and I said, Jerry, this is devastating . . . to all the victims around . . . . And he . . . already had opinions from people that he trusted that it was unconstitutional anyway. He said it will put the MDs back to work, it is unconstitutional . . .. That prophecy was fulfilled. All the trial courts found it to be unconstitutional. . . . Schifferman . . . is considered really one of the brightest trial judges . . .. [H]e had been considered for the appeal court on numerous occasions and [is] a very conservative man . . .. When he came out with that opinion, all the trial judges that I know of absolutely knew that MICRA was unconstitutional . . ..

Girardi's retainer agreements between 1982 and 1984 mentioned Section 6146 and had clients explicitly waive it; but he had no cases large enough for MICRA to apply. He conceded, very reluctantly, that MICRA had been declared constitutional. "[T]he four guys loused this whole thing." "[I]n all honesty . . . the truth of the matter was that if someone did violate those provisions—I mean this from the bottom of my heart—it was not like violating a rule of the State Bar on accounting for monies to a client." "Logic compels all of us to know it was absurd." "If anyone in the world thinks this is a fair situation or a just situation or a constitutional situation, I will eat my hat."

GOCHIS: Prior to the time that these cases . . . said it was constitutional . . . 6146 . . . is the law of the state, correct?

GIRARDI: Well, we thought it to be an improper law of the state, yes.

GOCHIS: You hoped it would be found improper?

GIRARDI: Didn't hope, knew it, were morally certain of it . . . . [T]here is nothing confusing. It is plainly written, anyone can understand exactly what it says and it's total baloney. It's not right.

Court of Appeal Judge Eugene McCloskey had sat on the Supreme Court pro tem when it decided *Roa* in February 1985. "The opinion of most judges was that it was going to be held unconstitutional." The referee sustained Gochis's objection, observing: "regardless of what the judges sitting at the time thought . . . any statute that is passed by the legislature is presumed to be constitutional until it is found to be otherwise." But McCloskey testified that "the insurance companies were paying these sums in excess of the MICRA limit which is a good indication of what they seemed to think about the constitutionality." Schifferman's decision[37] "confirmed the opinion of all the judges I knew on the Superior Court in the Central District . . . ." On cross-examination, McCloskey said Greene told him "that he was really set up by the Shepherds and by a lawyer named Needle . . . ." When McCloskey saw that the retainer did not mention Section 6146, he told Greene: "You are like most attorneys. You get smart after the fact. Too many attorneys . . . get along talking and they get a little careless."

The referee sustained Gochis's objection to the defense offer of Frank Zolin, who had been Cholko's superordinate at the Superior Court. "[T]he issue is whether Mr. Greene . . . had set up a proper trust fund and put these funds in that trust fund . . . not whether or not that duty was delegated to a nonlawyer." Caffray retorted that "lawyers don't handle trust funds . . . a lawyer of Mr. Greene's particular involvement here couldn't go around and balance the books . . . ." The Referee also rejected testimony by John J. Collins, Kaiser's representative in the arbitration. When Caffray said, "this is to show the kind of job that Mr. Greene did," Gochis replied: "That he got an excellent result nobody is disputing . . . ."

Superior Court Judge Frank Baffa testified that judges were awarding 25 percent in minors' cases even when that exceeded MICRA. "Frankly we thought it was unconstitutional." On cross-examination, he said that "the retainer agreements I encountered during that particular period of time had no reflection on MICRA." He was unaware that this violated Section 6147. "[I]f the fee was, let's say, a third or 40 percent, in some instances 50 percent, I would ask them if that was acceptable to them and they would say yes." "I didn't feel it was my obligation"

37. Respondent's Exhibit B.

to tell plaintiffs about MICRA. "I looked at what was accomplished. In my mind you are not going to get any recovery at all unless you have a good lawyer to effect it for you. Without the lawyer, you get nothing, and frankly I happen to like lawyers and I like to protect them with their fees."

Charles O'Reilly testified that the firm grew rapidly because of the asbestos litigation. In 1980–81, they were negotiating block settlements for 850 victims against 20 to 25 defendants. "[I]t was creating a quagmire, bookkeeping nightmare, and potential trust problems beyond belief and beyond manageability, almost." They hired an outside law firm, a CPA, and Cholko. Gerald Agnew, the managing partner, "was the one that interfaced with the accounting and office management . . . because the rest of us, and particularly Mr. Greene, were in trial constantly." "[W]e were fortunate enough by the June of 1984 we had not had . . . one complaint by a client, one incident or dispute involving a client's money or trust account activities . . .." But that month, Agnew "left rather suddenly." "There was now this gap of about two months of a managing partner . . .." "At about the same time, they had to move offices. Although the firm's practice had been that "the attorney that worked on the case and knew the person . . . would usually be there at the accounting," the pressure of asbestos work made that impossible. "[B]y 1984 Mr. Cholko and his staff handled the accounting . . . ." "[I]f there was any question as to how it should be handled . . . it would come then from Cholko to the managing partner and then [be] brought to the partners' attention . . .." The Shepherds' case "was not brought to any of the partners' attention." O'Reilly testified that "it did not appear that there was a genuine dispute by Mrs. Shepherd, but Mr. Shepherd and Needle were fabricating this . . . to precipitate an inevitable reaction by Mr. Greene . . .." After the October 2, 1984, letter, the firm heard nothing from the State Bar for two years.

Greene began his direct testimony with a brief autobiography. He was a cab driver's son, had worked his way through high school, college, and law school, served in the JAG Corps, and practiced tort defense for two years before switching sides, eventually becoming a diplomate (the highest level) of the American Board of Trial Advocates. Needle "had inquired in specific about the expected attorney's fees and his referral arrangement," when he contacted Greene's firm. One reason for not putting a waiver in the retainer agreement was that Ken Collins "knew Joshua Needle and had a connection with him at law school. I had a verification from Collins that this is the kind of person—at least to me ostensibly would be a reliable type of person." He found Needle "extremely affable . . . appreciative that I would take the case. He said that he had no big referral fees before, he was looking forward to one in this case."

Although the firm had taken other medical malpractice cases, "we were very concerned . . . in light of court congestion time, amount of time needed to work the case up, expected costs, and . . . MICRA, that was in great and hot dispute . . .." After talking to Judith Shepherd, Greene "immediately assessed the fact that this was going to be a difficult, difficult case relative to proximate cause and to basically establishing a violation of a standard of care . . .." "I also told them that . . . it was going to be extremely difficult to get real good medical experts . . . very expensive . . . would take months . . .." There "was no assurance whatsoever of any success." Richard and Needle "both wanted me to come out and tell him what the case was worth, when he was going to get the money, what could be expected in terms of the amount of money." Mr. Shepherd "had recently sustained a severe heart attack and . . . high blood pressure condition and had to leave his business . . .." But Greene concluded "it would be almost impossible to make up a significant case of economic loss," and "since the Kaiser facility was providing all medical—there would be no medical loss . . .."

At that first meeting "Mr. Shepherd asked to have a private conference with Mr. Needle . . . about the attorney's fee issue because he thought that 40 percent was too high." But Greene explained to the Referee that "our competitors, Tom Girardi, Dave Harney, Ned Good . . . that's what they were charging and we had to be competitive with them." He told the Shepherds

> there was a law called MICRA that set limits on attorney's fees, it was unrealistic, it was impossible to live with, that any firm of substance taking cases at that time could not live with those particular fees, and that the prevailing authority . . . [was] that it would be held to be unconstitutional and had been held to be unconstitutional, and that the courts were not observing it . . .. Therefore I said to them . . . there is no way I can take it unless you waive MICRA. They said we want you to have this case, Mr. Greene. We have heard of your reputation, of your success rate, and we will waive MICRA.

In March 1984, Greene started trying a complex case in Ventura, representing four gas explosion victims against six defendants. Because he would have a time conflict with the medical malpractice arbitration within four or five weeks, he called Mr. Shepherd, who "was, to say the least, not the easiest person to deal with," and suggested his partner, Gerald Agnew, who "had received the trial lawyer of the year award from the Los Angeles trial lawyers in the preceding year." Mr. Shepherd "told me that under no uncertain terms would they agree with that, that they had . . . demanded that I handle this case, and part of the whole deal was the fact that they would waive this MICRA provision . . . and if they didn't get that, then they were going to make a complaint to the State Bar of California." He therefore persuaded the defense lawyers and judge in the Ventura case to give him a week. He obtained an expert opinion for $3,000 from a "top neurosurgeon," who suggested he contact a leading expert in subarachnoid hemorrhage, who agreed to testify for $1,500 up front. Greene also secured an emergency room (ER) doctor and nurse. But the week of the arbitration, the first two changed their minds, leaving Greene "with no one to basically handle the key issue of proximate cause."[38] After trying two or three other neurosurgeons,

38. This was a loss of chance case, requiring the plaintiff to demonstrate that delayed diagnosis lowered the probability of a good outcome.

he found one to testify. But at the end of his case, "the defense is refusing to offer a dime," and the neutral arbitrator said "he did not like the plaintiff's case."

The medical malpractice defendants put on Dr. Bill O'Rierdon [*sic*], who had testified for Greene on another ER case. "[W]ith that transcript I took his pants off . . . and he turned around and basically admitted everything I wanted him to admit." At that point Kaiser's arbitrator told Coulter (Kaiser's lawyer) he would find for Mrs. Shepherd. "Immediately after," Coulter called Greene and said "he wanted to talk to me privately about settlement." After negotiating for an hour or two, Coulter said his maximum was $650,000. Greene informed the Shepherds. Mr. Shepherd "told me that this was very interesting" but wanted to consult Needle and asked about the bottom line, after costs and attorney's fees. Greene got those numbers from Cholko and gave them to Mr. Shepherd. "Dick Shepherd then agreed that the sum would be acceptable . . . based upon the agreed contract of 40 percent and the anticipated costs of approximately $30,000 . . . and he wanted to know when was the money going to come in . . . ." When Greene accepted the settlement the Shepherds "thanked me profusely."

After Greene returned to the Ventura trial he got "a telephone call, from the office to the effect that suddenly on the day the money is coming in, Mr. Needles and/or Dick Shepherd are now claiming that the MICRA provisions on the attorney's fees are going to have to be observed." "Judy Shepherd came in and sat there and said absolutely nothing to me about any complaint about the fees and in fact wouldn't even look me in the eye when I confronted Needle and her husband . . .." Decisions about putting money received into trust accounts "had been delegated before this. I don't want anyone to think that it was only on this case that this was delegated."

Asked by Gochis if there was a fee dispute, Greene said, "maybe we are talking about words, but I really felt that this was the kind of a situation that I had seen before where I was trying to be maneuvered by a client to pay a lesser attorney's fee . . .." Pressed further, Greene insisted "it depends on whether you talk semantics between the word 'dispute' or 'disagreement'" but conceded that the Shepherds contested his fee. He did not instruct Cholko to segregate the disputed funds. "I just assumed he would do what he would have to do, what the regular procedures would have to be." He knew *Roa* dealt with attorney's fees, "but the big thing was it did not deal with the waiver issue." "[W]hen we were told that . . . our rights were extinguished by the appeals process, we made [the refund] immediately."

Cross-examined by O'Reilly, Richard denied having told Needle to send the letter the morning of the disbursement. In fact, he had been in the hospital with a heart condition July 4–7. But he agreed that when Greene told him on June 5 about Kaiser's $650,000 offer, he had already decided to raise Section 6146. "I didn't know it was going to bring about anger from Mr. Greene. I felt that Mr. Greene would do what was the right thing to do and perhaps not be angry . . .. I felt that he would be a gentleman about it . . .." He "absolutely" denied Greene had said he would net about $370,000. "Mr. Greene had informed me not to ask him about money matters at the first meeting." He had not told Greene about Section 6146 when he first heard about it from Rose because "I was not sure until June 5th that it pertained to our case." He did not immediately decide with Needle what to do "because I was going to Detroit [the next day], and figured we would discuss it when I came back." He returned June 23–24. He had not postponed telling Greene until after the arbitration because he only learned of the applicability of the section on June 5. He said nothing about the attorney's fee when he met Cholko on July 2 or 3, although he had decided to assert Section 6146.

On redirect, Greene reiterated that when Richard asked for the "breakdown" of the $650,000 offer he estimated the costs. "In 20-some years of representing plaintiffs, I have never had a case where the plaintiff did not know what the breakdown was going to be and how much they were going to get prior to making the decision to settle the case."

Lily Barry worked for the State Bar disciplinary process for seventeen years, ultimately becoming chief disciplinary counsel and then chief trial counsel; for the last five years, she had defended attorneys in disciplinary proceedings. If a lawyer delegated trust account management, "there will not be an omission or a failure or a breach by that attorney personally of that rule." She knew of no cases in firms with 22 to 23 lawyers in which "partners have been held in connection with some activities in dealing with trust funds of . . . an administrator properly selected." "[I]f an error happens . . . that cannot be imputed to the attorney for purposes of imposing discipline," . . . although "he may still be civilly liable." Nevertheless, a lawyer "has a duty to make sure that everything is done right and he cannot negligently delegate that responsibility to someone else." She agreed that "disputed funds must not be withdrawn."

Needle explained why his July 5 letter mentioned "any . . . purported waiver." "I was trying to make clear that . . . [Greene] didn't even ask for a waiver in his written retainer agreement. Now, subsequently I have learned you can't waive it even with a written retainer agreement, but I didn't know that at the time." "I anticipated that anybody would try to say that" the Shepherds had waived Section 6146. He had discussed earlier drafts of the letter with Richard. "The reason it didn't get sent to your office until Monday was because . . . I hadn't been able to reach Mr. and Mrs. Shepherd to discuss it with them." Needle had described the July 9, 1984, meeting at the July 30, 1987, deposition. Greene said, "that I was a son-of-a-bitch, that I had stabbed him in the back."

> When [Greene] handed me the check, I wrote a disclaimer on the back, saying that we were not accepting this in full settlement; that there was a dispute . . . I confirmed the contents of my letter saying that if he refused to follow the law, that we would pursue the matter, that we would not waive any rights under the law and I did those things that I thought necessary to protect those

> clients and those interests by writing and having Mr. Greene sign and initial the disclaimer on the accounting.[39] . . . [T]hat was the first I had seen the actual accounting . . . I had no way prior to that of having factored it into the MICRA formula, and so I told him that the disputed amounts should be placed in an interest-bearing trust account for my client's benefit because, in my opinion, it was their money, not your firm's.

Needle now testified, "During that meeting, Mr. Greene specifically said he was not going to pay me any referral fee." He had responded: "But Browne, you have sent me a signed letter. We have a contract."

O'Reilly concluded with an offer of proof (rejected) that Needle "had over a dozen discussions, conversations with Ms. Gochis" and "had from the beginning provided basically the Bar as almost an assistant prosecutor with all these different documents and pushed this thing all the way up through the prosecution today." Before closing argument, Caffray objected to the "great deal of unwarranted, inappropriate media coverage in this case," referring to a newspaper article headlined "Trial Lawyer Chief's Fee Dispute Will Go to Bar." When the referee refused to read it, Caffray said, "I am not suggesting that you read it. I think maybe my purpose has been achieved by adding this to the record . . . ."

Gochis argued that the "fundamental problem" with Greene's position "is that he does not have to abide by the . . . statutes which were in effect at the time that he acted." "It is specious to say that if I don't think there is a dispute, there is no dispute . . .." Greene "admits that he was told that there was a claim." "Mr. Greene should have said to Mr. Cholko, who, by the way, was in the room at some part of the meeting on July 9th, 'I don't agree that there's a problem here. I think these people are trying to shaft me . . . and I think we better put this money in a trust account and keep it there until it's resolved.'"

> [Q]uite a few prominent people came here and said that everybody knew that 6146 was going to be declared unconstitutional . . . . Everybody was wrong. When Mr. Greene entered into his contract with the Shepherds, 6146 was the law. Now, are we really going to say that if . . . the legal community does not like a law they don't have to buy it? . . . [A] lawyer cannot pick and choose what law he will follow and he cannot say it's unconstitutional, therefore I will not follow it . . . . You don't like a law? Great. You challenge it. Mr. Greene didn't have any particular challenges going in the courts. He simply wasn't following the law.

The retainer "reflects no . . . waiver." Greene's firm was "a major law office," and "the most important aspect of his contract, as he seems to have understood it, was the waiver." Yet, "that is the one thing which is not in the contract."

39. But Greene testified that he had not seen that disclaimer at the deposition; when he saw it during this hearing, he denied it was his handwriting.

Needle "admitted that he may have heard about 6146 when he was in law school. But he went to Mr. Greene because he didn't do medical malpractice cases and did not know about them. Mr. Greene was the one that had the obligation to say what had to be done and . . . have a contract that was appropriate and legal." Greene "did not give the money" to the Shepherds even after the Supreme Court repeatedly upheld MICRA.

Caffray argued that the retainer "was perfectly legal, valid, acceptable. The standard of the profession, nobody could raise one drop of complaint about it, but for the MICRA bill . . .."

> [A]ny of the constitutional attacks on any of the parts of MICRA would certainly have an overtone on the other parts, because the MICRA bill was all the same. It was designed to protect doctors and single them out as special folks in medical malpractice litigation. And it was designed to figure out every way they could to protect doctors . . . worst of all, or equally bad, to probe in and interfere with contracts, with the agreements between injured people trying to get competent lawyers to represent them.

There was "massive confusion" about MICRA's provisions, which "were the subject of generalized view as being unconstitutional by even the most conservative of juries [*sic*—'jurists']. The judges were not enforcing them . . .."

> Needle brought the Shepherds to Greene. They were his clients. He reviewed the contract and said go ahead and sign it . . .. [R]arely do I have clients come into hire me, but they bring their own lawyer along to review the deal. So things were different and special here. So Mr. Needle was not only their lawyer, he was hired. He was paid. He got a percentage of this . . .. [I]t's a funny thing the way it works out, Joshua Needle was the one that raised the fuss about this MICRA business. Ah. The contract isn't real, the very contract he had approved . . . he was going to get $51,000 if it went through.

Needle "made a big deal" of the fact that Mr. Shepherd cut Needle's contingent fees from 33 to 40 percent down to 20 percent. "So he is a martyr now. Poor soul." "[W]hen the money is paid, he gets exactly what he would have gotten in the first place." Needle might have forgotten what he learned in law school about Section 6146, but "he is a lawyer . . . . he was getting paid for representing these people . . . ." "Maybe the real guy that ought to be sitting here is Joshua Needle. . . . [I]t's no excuse for him to say, ah, MICRA is not my specialty." "[T]his contract was just as valid as can be. There was a waiver. We all know that." "[B]ut for this law that's on the books, this contract would be just as valid as can be. The law . . . was being challenged so severely that judges weren't even following it. Now, you know, the fabric of the law is uncertain. That's what we learn in law school . . . . [T]hings do ultimately get decided by our Supreme Court. But here, this was not decided." Caffray concluded:

> [T]he profession of law in California is far too valuable . . . that's why we have the clear and convincing rule . . . . His credentials are the result of going to law

> school, of practicing, of experiencing, of doing pro bono work, of being out there in the forefront, of trying lawsuits . . . . [H]is credentials is a massive thing and it's too worthy to have even a little piece torn off by such a proceeding as this.

O'Reilly argued that the Referee had heard "ad nauseum [*sic*] that Mr. Needle, Mr. Shepherd set this up to wait until the last minute." They were already "in an adversarial relationship with Mr. Greene" and knew they would "precipitate an angry reaction by Mr. Greene," who "had every right to be furious when he got that letter." O'Reilly denied Greene had initialed the note appended to the accounting, which allegedly created the dispute. The evidence "shows quite clearly they basically played Mr. Greene along . . .." "They all of a sudden later come up with this document saying you initialed it, there was a dispute now we are not only going to sue you legally and go after you civilly, but we are going to cooperate and precipitate a basic State Bar proceeding on you for doing this." "[O]f crucial significance, the client, Mrs. Shepherd, is not here as a witness." "Mr. Greene was totally entitled to rely on Mr. Cholko." "They claim Mr. Greene essentially should know every little dime and every one of those trust fund accounts for 850 asbestos clients."

The Shepherds raised no objection to Greene's fee when they signed the $650,000 draft. Richard Shepherd and Joshua Needle "wait[ed] silently for two years" until Greene had repaid the excess fee with interest.

> Then Mr. Needle, Mr. Shepherd and the State Bar all come down on Mr. Greene . . . now they have him here, a man of his reputation, contributions, skill, depth and character and embarrass him by accusing him of being a cheat and taking a client's money and not caring about a client's interest when that had been primarily what he devoted his practice to ever since I have known him in 1972.

Gochis said Mrs. Shepherd had not testified "because of a speech impediment."

C. Outcome of the Guilt Phase

Ruling immediately from the bench, the referee rejected the charge that Greene had failed to maintain the disputed amount in the trust account. "I don't think that the Bar requires that a lawyer in a situation such as the Respondent is in has to personally maintain the account . . .." Greene's firm's "provisions" were "probably above the standards in the profession."

> [A]t least a million dollars, if not more, would be available at that firm at all times so that no client's money was in jeopardy at any time. I think this is quite a different situation from the sole practitioner who, when he takes the money out of his trust account, pays it to the grocer . . ..
>
> With respect to the accusation of charging or collecting an illegal fee, . . .
>
> the State Bar should have taken into consideration the atmosphere in the legal profession as it existed in 1982 with respect to MICRA. Judge Schifferman had

> given the only written opinion on the matter and that held that it was unconstitutional, on a different issue, but nevertheless the tenor of all the lawyers and the judges at that time . . . was that it was unconstitutional . . . . the contract that was entered into was a proper contract under the circumstances.

He found that Greene advised the Shepherds and Needle he could not take the case if his fee were limited by MICRA. "As Lincoln said, all a lawyer has to sell is his time and I think he has to sell that time prudently and sell that time where it's going to do the most for him as well as for his law firm and for his clients." "Mr. Shepherd may not have understood what was going on and may well have gone over his head but I have no question Mr. Needle knew what was going on and knew what was happening and Mr. Needle, of course, had a fiduciary interest in it."

The referee's May 20, 1988, decision basically tracked his oral opinion. "Judges, lawyers and the malpractice insurance industry were ignoring MICRA, and were handling health care malpractice cases and fees as if the Act did not exist." "[B]y virtue of Respondent's extraordinary skill and effort, the case was settled for $650,000.00 ($400,000.00 over the non-economic limits of MICRA). The clients signed the draft in that sum without complaint . . . ." "During the pendency of the last appeal [in the two contract actions], the California Supreme Court, by a four to three decision, declared MICRA to be constitutional. Respondent thereupon refunded to the Shepherds all fees collected in excess of the MICRA formula plus interest." The referee found that "the dispute was as to the validity of the retainer contract and not specifically a fee dispute. If the contract was legal, the fee was proper, if it was found to be illegal, the fee had to be recomputed. That was done immediately upon the issue being decided by the Court of Appeals."

The State Bar sought review on May 27 on the ground that the findings of fact were not supported by the evidence. Its August 10 brief argued that the firm's reserves and size were irrelevant to the lawyer's obligation to escrow disputed funds. "A dispute is a dispute." Needle's July 9 letter "unequivocally put Respondent on notice of a claim." The illegal fee question was "one of first impression" and "concededly, a difficult one." But, "while it may be a mitigating factor that Browne Greene was one of a multitude disregarding a duly enacted statute in effect, it is no defense to a finding of culpability." Given the controversy over MICRA, "if waiver was the condition upon which Respondent took the case and the basis of his fee, perhaps the indispensable part of this written contract was a written waiver." Otherwise, "all a lawyer need do when a client challenges a plainly worded, objectively interpreted written retainer agreement, visibly in violation of a crucial statute, is to claim oral waiver. The statute could, thereby, be emasculated." "When Respondent solicited waiver, 6146 was extant law . . . . waiver . . . was an attempt to circumvent a law he (and the legal community) did not like." "*Any* good faith question of waiver . . . was foreclosed by *Roa* and *Waters*."

> It is one thing to make a challenge in the courts; it is another to act unilaterally on the unconfirmed belief that a statute, in effect, is invalid . . .. If this kind of circumvention on the part of a lawyer is ratified by a Bar, his brethren have no practical incentive to abide by laws if they do not like them or think they might be unconstitutional.

Greene replied on August 22, emphasizing Needle's role in the alleged waiver. "This 'dispute' over the fee was no dispute and was not legitimate." "[I]t would be an injustice to try to discipline the Respondent for failing to deposit funds that were the subject of a non-legitimate dispute."

Following oral argument by Gochis and Caffray, the Review Department decided on September 29.[40] It found that on July 9, 1984, Greene "believed in good faith that the provisions of . . . section 6146 were unconstitutional and that the statutory fee limitations had been lawfully waived by Mr. and Mrs. Shepherd." At the time, belief in its unconstitutionality "was widely held among members of the superior court bench and bar in Los Angeles County and that view was supported by the published opinion of a respected Los Angeles superior court judge; but there were at that time no appellate court decisions holding that section 6146 was unconstitutional or that its provisions could be waived." After the Shepherds won their fee arbitration in December 1984, Greene sued for his fees in February 1985, and the Shepherds sued to confirm the arbitration award in April. He lost and appealed both cases. That year one Court of Appeal upheld Section 6146[41] and another ruled it could not be waived.[42] In April 1986, a Court of Appeal rejected Greene's contract action.[43] Thereafter, "Respondent lacked any basis for a good faith belief that section 6146 was unconstitutional or that the Shepherds had lawfully waived its provisions." Nevertheless, he retained the excess fee (over $100,000) and pursued his appeal of the arbitration award on the ground that their action to confirm it was untimely. He lost that appeal in September.[44] The Supreme Court denied review on December 17, 1986. "The second appeal did not involve any matter that was a defense to Respondent's holding an unlawful fee." He paid the disputed amount plus interest on December 24, 1986.

The Review Department narrowly decided (6–5, two others disqualifying themselves) that Greene had held the funds in violation of Section 6146 from July 9, 1984, to December 24, 1986. But "resolving all possible doubts in favor of the Respondent, his good faith belief in [its] unconstitutionality . . . and in a lawful waiver," it found culpability only after the April 1986 Court of Appeal decision, although one of the majority would have found culpability from July 9, 1984.

---

40. Filed October 13.
41. Roa v. Lodi Medical Group, Inc., 37 Cal.3d 920 (1985).
42. Waters v. Bourhis, 40 Cal.3d 424 (1985).
43. Second Appellate District, No. B015650.
44. Shepherd v. Greene, 185 Cal.App.3d 989 (1986).

"No matter how strongly the bench and bar in Los Angeles County felt about Section 6146, that statute was a presumptively valid enactment . . . and in fact its constitutionality was upheld." If Greene's good faith were a defense to his violation of the trust fund requirements, "the Rule will become a dead letter. Presumably, every attorney engaged in a dispute with a client over attorney fees holds a good faith belief in his entitlement to the fees." The rule's function is "prophylactic." It "is an important promise by the Bar to the public, assuring that lawyers are not free to act unilaterally to take their claimed fees from their clients by force of their possession and professional skills." Greene commented that "the ultimate decider of this matter is the Supreme Court. I will fight this all the way and I will be vindicated."[45] On December 13, Caffrey unsuccessfully sought a continuance to appeal to the Supreme Court, which ultimately denied the petition.[46] Caffrey was "absolutely confident" of ultimate success; the prosecution was "a complete outrage."

D. The Penalty Phase

At the December 19, 1988, hearing on discipline, U.S. District Judge Dickran Tevrizian (Central District of California, who had also been a state court judge and practiced medical malpractice defense) testified that Greene, whom he had known since 1975, "has devoted a lot of time towards the victims in civil wrongs as a lobbyist" and "to streamline the courts," "clean up political contributions," "have judicial salaries increased," "get more judges in for the civil calendars that are congested," get "support staff for trial judges in the state courts." Because "there has been a finding of culpability," Gochis objected to Caffray asking whether Greene was "capable of having . . . the state of mind of willfully doing anything inamicable [*sic*—'inimical'] to a client's best interests." But the referee called this "a matter of character." Caffray objected to Gochis asking if Tevrizian knew "what Mr. Greene was found culpable of doing," insisting "this is still an issue that is far from decided." But the referee overruled him. Tevrizian did not believe Greene had done anything wrong.

Caffray again denied that "culpability has been found." The referee also was "particularly disturbed by a reference that is made several times throughout here that 'the Respondent . . . refused to retain the disputed sum in the trust account. I found in no instance where he refused to retain it in a trust account." The referee admitted he "never had an opportunity to read" the transcript, "but I really don't care to read it" since he had his own notes. Gochis took an exception "to this discussion of the evidence." The referee retorted that appellate courts "can do whatever they want. . . . but when I read something that is not, in fact, something that was related in the testimony . . . then I'm disturbed." "I'm certain that the

45. Philip Carrizos, *State Bar Panel Deeply Divided Over Greene Disciplinary Actin*, LADJ 2 (10.27.88).

46. Tom Dresslar, *Browne Greene Loses Round*, LADJ 24 (3.23.89); Green v. State Bar, S006789.

transcript does not state in any place that he refused . . . ." On December 13, the referee had agreed with Caffray that the Review Department had found Greene culpable only for failing to put the disputed funds in a trust account, not for violating MICRA. Gochis replied: "I not only disagree, I say, again, the statement of paragraph 15 of the decision of the Review Department says it specifically."

Orville A. Armstrong, California State Bar president in 1986–87 when Greene was president of the California Trial Lawyers Association, offered the usual generic character evidence. Thomas V. Girardi declared, "it would be impossible for [Greene] to willfully do anything to harm a client." (Caffray kept referring to "the charges," the "NTSC," and the "points the State Bar seeks to make as against Mr. Greene," despite Gochis's objections that the Review Department had found him culpable.) On cross, Girardi "truly" felt Greene "did not violate any responsibilities at that time." John J. Collins, Kaiser's arbitrator in the Shepherd case and State Bar Court judge for twelve years, declared Greene incapable of willful misconduct. He "absolutely" disagreed with the Review Department's conclusions. "I have held that view since I first got involved with the State Bar Court. I have publicly and in many transcripts expressed my opinion as to the quality of work that goes on at that level." He "wish[ed] there were a lesser level" than private reproval. "[T]here is too much airing of allegedly dirty laundry in the media that just causes me to suspect the whole thing."

Caffray returned to his theme:

> I say culpability has not been determined . . . . As I read those words, they say . . . "we find no culpability." . . . [A]t the end it says something and it used the term "culpability," which is totally inconsistent with the findings.

GOCHIS: [objected]

REFEREE: Ms. Gochis, I think he at least has a right to say what he is saying without interruption . . . .

CAFFRAY: If we really look at the cases they cite and we look at the flow of the statements they make, we will see they really . . . found no culpability. And the very end they make the statement "culpability having been found," which is inconsistent.

> Before the next witness testified, Caffray asked for "an absolute gag order," an order that the State Bar and no member of the State Bar will discuss this matter with the press. The last time around—

REFEREE: Aren't these matters confidential?

GOCHIS: No, sir, these are not confidential. They are public matters . . . .

REFEREE: Do I have the authority to do that?

CAFFRAY: Yes, I think you do . . . .

REFEREE: Do you agree?

GOCHIS: No, sir. First of all, I don't talk to the press anyway . . . .[B]ut the fact is these are public matters and I can't control what goes to the press.

CAFFRAY: If you have . . . some kind of private, say reproval or admonition and then it is in the press, the whole . . . heart of the process is undercut.

When Judge Baffa testified that Greene "would not do anything that would hurt his client in any way," Gochis insisted, "he did do something willful, at least as far as the Review Department is concerned."

CAFFRAY: Wait a minute. That's objected to . . . counsel is stating her conclusions . . . .

REFEREE: I think you should say that the Review Department has found culpability, rather than he did something willful . . . .[T]he issue of wilfullness [*sic*] . . . is not something that is before this court . . . .

Greene testified in mitigation about his pro bono activities concerning court congestion, no-fault, the Dram Shop Act, products liability, and MICRA. He was "in charge of raising sums of money for political campaigns, which was extremely instrumental in backing our ability to be effective in Sacramento against various interests that were trying to do away with the system" of joint and several liability and automobile insurance. He claimed to have been unaware of the Court of Appeal's dismissal of his contract case because it happened "two months before election day, June 3, 1986, when Prop 51 went to the electorate. And I was working full-time plus on the fund raising effort that ended up with us raising about $6,000,000 . . .." Between June and November 1986, "I was working on the campaign concerning . . . the independence of the judiciary," which was threatened by death-penalty advocates, who succeeded in defeating the retention elections of Supreme Court Justices Rose Bird, Malcolm Lucas,[47] and Cruz Reynoso. A month after the 1986 election, Greene became president of the California Trial Lawyers Association.

> That was a full-time endeavor in Sacramento for the next year when the MICRA battle was on and Senate Bill (SB) 241 and the tort reform issue . . . six months after the prior victory on 51, a coalition of 156 groups got . . . together known as P.I.C.R.A . . . . insurance companies, manufacturers, doctors, hospitals, cities, counties, governments, chambers of commerce. It was about everyone except the Nazi Party . . . one very, very ominous group.
>
> And they are proposing to change the system of law that we have had concerning torts that would have literally done away with the system as we have it . . . . [E]verything from product liability to the remainder of medical malpractice through punitive damage reform, cities and counties reform and so forth.
>
> My first task as president was to break up that coalition and . . . see that those issues were never put up on a ballot and we could win if they did.
>
> So what we planned to do was to fund-raise . . . but above all negotiate politically . . . with the cities and the counties and the governmental entities and

47. Actually, it was Joseph Grodin; Lucas replaced Bird as Chief Justice.

> thereafter with the manufacturers and . . . the doctors and the hospitals . . . to break up the coalition. . . . And that led to S.B. 241, which was the reform agreement on September the 11th, 1987, in Sacramento . . . the Governor blessed it and saved all of that debacle. . . . And the insurance industry is the opposition which was much easier for us to handle, which led to the victory that took place against Proposition[s] 106, 104, 101.

Over Gochis's objection, Greene testified he did not "willfully refuse to deposit sums concerning the Shepherd case in any trust account."

GOCHIS: This goes to the culpability phase, which has been decided.

CAFFRAY: No, it hasn't . . . [T]his is a brand new issue, which the Review Department injected . . . .

GOCHIS: Mr. Caffray is attempting to retry the culpability phase of the case . . . .

REFEREE: That is something that was never mentioned at the . . . other hearing . . . and I also seem to recall . . . that he paid it back with interest. Yes. I'll let him proceed on it.

GOCHIS: . . . [T]he Review Department obviously had the record in front of them so these things were discussed at the time of the hearing . . . .

REFEREE: We don't know what happened after June or when he first learned of this, but we are going to learn that . . . .

GREENE: I had nothing to do with the appeal. . . . I don't do appeals. . . . [A]nd number two . . . I had nothing to do whatsoever with the funds, where they went in the firm, whether they were in account 100 or account 1003. . . . We have never been accused of larceny or embezzlement or anything such as this.

As a Washington, D.C., cab driver, Greene's father "used to take lawyers and judges to the courts, particularly the United States Supreme Court. And when he would come home, he used to tell me about going to that court and about his particular view of educated people." Because Greene's father had only a third-grade education and "did not have the appearances [*sic*] of grammatical speech and such . . . he treasured people who did." Through a bible class, his father knew some judges and lawyers "very, very closely" and "treasured their relationships. And he introduced me to them when I was a boy. And I always looked up to them, because he did." No other family member "had an education of sorts."

Among Greene's professional associations,

> there is a special one known as the Inner Circle of Advocates, which you have to be asked to join. And it's known euphemistically as the heavy of the millionaires' club of America. To be able to get in that group, you had to have at least a $1,000,000 verdict. . . . [I]t has to have notoriety in terms of the challenge and the result. It cannot be a punitive damage verdict. . . . [A]nd you have to also have proven to have done pro bono work in your particular state.

He was inducted at the age of 42, becoming the youngest of the ninety-eight American members: "it's quite a group to belong to."

He was "proud of the way I represented" the Shepherds, "irrespective of what a review panel by a six-to-five vote thinks on one particular issue."

> I can stand before my maker, and I can have my own conscience on how I dealt with them . . . .I can look at Judy Shepherd just like I did when they came in my office on that day, when this issue was first raised, when I was blindsided by Needle and company, and I can look at Judy and say, "Judy, did I ever do anything at all that you didn't want me to do?" And she looked at me and said, "No." . . . [A]nd Judy Shepherd to this date hasn't been before this hearing officer to say whether she feels anything was done wrong.

The referee denied Gochis's motion to strike.

When Greene finished, Caffray renewed his attack on the Review Department.

> I think the Review Department's findings are wholly inconsistent.

GOCHIS: [Objected] The decision is here. It is a fact. We have to work with it. You have to decide what the discipline is going to be . . . .

REFEREE: [Overruled the objection]

CAFFRAY: Your Honor, what I simply have to say is that we have the findings that culminate with the statement "culpability has been found" and yet they have certain recitals of fact, six instances of which at least, that you pointed out, are recitals not of fact.

The statement in there that Mr. Greene refused to do something, which is not supported by the evidence. They're in other words, reaching out and going way beyond their mission and their authority.

Number two, they cite a number of cases . . . and the fact is that as recently as December 2 [1988], down came an opinion in which the Court of Appeal . . . [the referee overruled Gochis's objection that Caffray was arguing culpability] the court says . . . "it has not yet been determined conclusively whether a client may effectively waive the contingent fee limit." . . .

REFEREE: Well, I can't see where that is germane to this particular issue . . . .

[The case actually dealt with the procedural question of whether a lawyer sued by a client for a fee exceeding Section 6146 could cross-claim against former associates for failing to obtain a waiver, not with whether the waiver was effective.[48]]

CAFFRAY: We have a recommended finding by Your Honor. We have the Review Department. They take these findings, and they move them around, and then they come out with . . . their own findings . . . .I'm saying

---

48. Hal. W. Williams v. David Drexler and Gerald Ryckman, Court of Appeal, 2nd District, December 2, 1988, Respondent's Exhibit G.

they haven't cited the case correctly . . . . [There were] six instances where they say "refused" . . . implying some state of mind on his part. . . . he sure can't be willful if the folks waived it.

GOCHIS: [Objected]

REFEREE: I think you are going way beyond the purview of this court . . . . [I]f you are making an appeal, as you indicated . . . to the Supreme Court, I think that [the recent case] would be very valuable with respect to that.

But when Caffray persisted, the referee overruled Gochis's objection. Caffray argued that the Review Department agreed that, in 1984, Greene "had a good faith belief that it couldn't be an illegal fee." But in 1986, "that case came down, unpublished opinion entitled Greene versus Shepherd, boom . . . . He no longer could have a good faith point of view. And they inject something brand new . . . 'at that point in time he willfully failed to put this money in the trust account.' . . . [H]e's explained to you today why he couldn't willfully have done that." Gochis renewed her objection, and now the referee sustained it.

Judge Goertzen testified again that he would be "absolutely shocked and dismayed and completely surprised if [Greene] handled any client in an improper manner," but admitted he did not know what the Review Department found Greene had done.

Gochis said "that Mr. Greene is a skilled attorney is not at issue . . . ." Standard 2.7 recommends six months actual suspension for collecting an illegal fee. Standard 2.2 recommends three months actual suspension for failing to deposit disputed funds in a trust account. Neither recommendation was affected by mitigation. The State Bar sought only 90 days actual suspension.

REFEREE: If those are the minimums with respect to the matter that we have here today, I'm shocked that there are so many attorneys practicing law in this State . . . .

CAFFRAY: The task that you have today is complicated by the findings of the Review Department, which are quite convoluted and . . . self-defeating . . . recognizing the weakness and frailty of the findings of the Review Department and the fact that they essentially charge Mr. Greene with something brand new . . . you are entitled to say there should be no discipline here.

It is most probable that whatever happens here, it will go back to the Review Department. Therefore, I urged, strongly, that you award no discipline [and at most private reproval]. . . . [T]he ultimate losers are going to be the State Bar and all its members and the consumers if Mr. Greene is not reasonably treated here. . . . [The Review Department] say he willfully failed to deposit this in a trust account, and there is nothing but evidence to the contrary.

As the referee went through the alternative dispositions, Gochis mentioned admonition, which she opposed. Admitting he had never heard of it, he continued:

> [W]hat happened here at most was probably an indiscretion . . . by the . . . office manager . . . of the law firm, which I understood . . . was 20 or more

> attorneys . . . negligence, but certainly never willful misconduct. But I feel that I have no choice . . . now that they have overruled my determination in this matter, even though on grounds that I think there is no justification for in the record, although I have not read the transcript, but I think my notes are sufficiently complete that—at least the tenor of what was said would be in my notes. But I feel I have no choice.
>
> I once before released him with no admonition. . . . Now, I feel that I am obligated to take some steps. And admonition being the minimum that is available, admonition is what it shall be. And I do it with a great deal of reluctance, because I feel that the practice that was followed here is no different than the practice I have observed . . . .in a large firm . . . .

Gochis said the referee had to prepare a written decision. He was reluctant to do so and asked for a form

CAFFRAY: If Your Honor please, I want to, one, thank you very much for your wisdom; number two, I would like to deal with a matter that is very, very serious, and that is matter of no newspaper publicity.

REFEREE: . . . [I]f I felt I had the authority to make such an order, I would. But you can't make an order that's not enforceable . . . .

CAFFRAY: May I ask that you do this, if Your Honor please.

REFEREE: I'll make a recommendation that there be no publicity given to this matter.

GOCHIS: Once again, this is a public matter . . . .

CAFFRAY: Let me tell you, there was not only publicity, but there was publicity of a most demeaning sort.

GOCHIS: [Objected that Caffray was impugning her; he denied this]

REFEREE: Everything I have received from the State Bar has said "private and confidential." And here is one that says "public matter" on it. And I would think until these matters are totally concluded that they would remain private and confidential.

GOCHIS: Sir, rule 225 . . . does make them public. The State Bar publishes releases, and it is free to do so in a public matter.

CAFFRAY: If Your Honor please, the publicity can be defeating.

REFEREE: I agree. But I'm powerless to make an unenforceable order . . . .

CAFFRAY: When the Review Department came down with their decision, the first time I heard of this was when a newspaper reporter from the Los Angeles Times called me; thereafter . . . I called the State Bar . . . .I was told that they could not tell me anything. . . . During the conversation I was told, "Oh, the Los Angeles Times reporter is calling back." They'll have to talk to me later . . . .

GOCHIS: [Objected that Caffray was testifying; overruled]

CAFFRAY: And so here then came down an article in the *Los Angeles Times* which mischaracterized . . . therefore, I'm asking . . . maybe it's unprecedent [*sic*]—but that you direct that Ms. Gochis—

REFEREE: Ms. Gochis has said she doesn't speak to the press . . . .

CAFFRAY: I know she wouldn't, and I think she is fine.

GOCHIS: I could, but I do not.

CAFFRAY: . . . [T]hat she convey the message to . . . the public relations arm of the State Bar, telling them that we believe it will be inamicable [*sic*—"inimical"] to the best interests of the Respondent, of all members of the State Bar . . . if they . . . release any information about this proceeding which is not yet final to the press.

GOCHIS: . . . [A]nybody can come in here and watch this hearing and go out and talk to anybody they want to. This is a public hearing. Pleadings in this matter are public . . . .

REFEREE: I think an admonition would be less than private reproval . . . and I would think a private reproval would be kept private . . . .

CAFFRAY: . . . [I]t is clear that under the definition . . . that Ms. Gochis was kind enough and very honorable to show you, that admonition is technically not classified as discipline. Therefore, I trust . . . that the State Bar . . . would not state that Mr. Greene has been disciplined.

The referee said he could not do that.

The referee decided on January 19, 1989. He had "made findings of fact and concluded there was no cause for discipline." The Review Department reversed, "with Findings of Fact not supported by the evidence." The mitigating evidence was Greene's "exemplary character . . . his devotion to the legal profession, and his high standard of professional competence, conduct and ethics." He had

> unselfishly devoted substantial time and effort to the betterment of his profession and our system of justice. He has been honored by his peers with awards, citations, and election to offices of highly respected and honored legal societies and associations. Because it is mandated by the action of the Review Department, this Referee, with great reluctance, recommends to the Supreme Court that Respondent be admonished . . . for the conduct found by the Review Department to be in violation of the Rules of Professional Conduct and the Business and Professions Code.

The Notice of Admonition stated that the "proceeding does not involve a serious offense; no pecuniary loss has been suffered as the result of respondent's conduct; and, this does not involve a matter which (probably) is a Client Security Fund matter."

The State Bar sought review on February 14. Following a June 22 hearing, the Review Department decided August 8.[49] It found no aggravating circumstances and mitigation in Greene's practice without discipline since 1966, candor and cooperation in these proceedings, "reputation for honesty and integrity," and the fact that he "consistently and for many years has engaged in exceptional and important service to the public, the courts, and the legal profession." Since his failure to deposit the disputed funds in a trust account "did not occur until an adverse appellate opinion was rendered almost two years after the dispute arose," it rejected Standard 2.2's recommendation of a three months actual suspension. But it recommended greater discipline than that proposed by the hearing panel, which improperly believed "that Respondent was not in fact culpable of any violation . . . ." Admonition "is precluded under Rule 415." The violations were "serious offenses, involving a large sum of money and the public policy of the State as well as the interests of Respondent's clients, the Shepherds." It recommended public reproval and that he pass the MPRE. This was imposed on January 26, 1990. In 2009, Green was listed as one of the top ten lawyers in Southern California.[50]

E. Understanding Defiance

Disciplined lawyers resemble white-collar criminals in many ways. Ordinary crimes are a "whodunit:" The question is whether the state can prove that the accused committed behavior that is clearly criminal. In lawyer disciplinary proceedings, by contrast, the question is whether behavior the accused clearly committed was unethical. Greene—unrepentant to the end—insisted there had never been a fee dispute, Needle was to blame for concocting one, the Shepherds had waived Section 6146, it was unconstitutional, and he had delegated responsibility for finances to Cholko.

The evidence of the fee dispute was overwhelming. On the morning of July 9, 1984, Needle hand-delivered to Greene's office a letter asserting the Shepherds' claim to the excess fee and demanding that Greene either pay it that day or escrow it while the Shepherds appealed to the bar's fee dispute panel or the courts. This provoked a furious phone call from Greene, who threatened not to pay Needle's referral fee. At the disbursement meeting later that day, Needle and Richard Shepherd reiterated their claim, writing on the back of the settlement check: "endorsement of this check does not constitute a waiver of disputed attorneys fees ($153,350) nor, consequently, an acknowledgment that all funds have been received in this case." The disbursement itself included a note initialed by the Shepherds and Greene: "$153,350.00 in dispute subject to negotiation/litigation." Richard wrote Greene on July 23, reasserting a claim to the excess fee, challenging the expense accounting, demanding return of all documents and

49. The vote was 10–2; one judge disqualified himself, and one was absent.

50. Southern California Super Lawyers 2009, at 40. So was Greene's partner, Bruce A. Broillet.

photographs, and threatening both a lawsuit and an ethical grievance. Greene was so angry he refused to return the papers, telling the Shepherds to collect them from his secretary. When Needle also wrote on July 26, Greene's August 7 reply contested Needle's arguments. The Shepherds must have filed a grievance soon thereafter, because the State Bar wrote Greene about it on October 2, and he replied on October 25. The fee dispute panel upheld the Shepherds' claim on December 27. Greene refused to comply, suing the Shepherds for breach of contract on February 1, 1985. The Shepherds sued to confirm the arbitration award on June 4. Greene lost both actions after multiple appeals, finally satisfying the judgment on June 30, 1987, nearly three years after the dispute began.

Despite all this, he maintained: "I never believed there was a dispute. I thought I was being sandbagged and being set up . . . by some people that were trying to get a better deal on fees." He was "trying to be maneuvered by a client to pay a lesser attorney's fee." Whether there was a "dispute" or just a "disagreement" was a matter of "semantics." There was no dispute because he expected the Shepherds to back down! Needle and Richard "privately agreed to create a fee dispute," deliberately provoking him by raising Section 6146 for the first time on the day of the disbursement. As late as the Review Department hearing, Greene continued to deny there had ever been any dispute. Judith—the only one who could have had a legitimate dispute—expressed nothing but gratitude. (This argument took real chutzpah from the lawyer who had won a $650,000 judgment for her severe disability.) The transparency of these rationalizations suggests how strongly Greene needed to maintain his righteousness.

Greene sought to strengthen his position by blaming Needle, whose behavior was morally ambiguous at best. Needle accepted the Shepherds as clients because they were family friends, even though he did not practice personal injury law. He pocketed 20 percent of Greene's fee just for referring the Shepherds, eager for his first big referral fee. (Needle had been admitted to the bar less than five years at the time and was practicing alone. He chose Greene's firm because he knew an associate there, even though Greene claimed his firm rarely did medical malpractice.) Needle assured Richard that Greene's 40-percent contingent fee was appropriate (although this maximized his own fee at the Shepherds' expense). Needle also had an interest in not asserting the Section 6146 fee limit. He claimed ignorance of the section, even though he had taken medico-legal law from Girardi, who testified that MICRA figured prominently in the course. When Richard got a copy of Section 6146 from Jay Rose and showed it to Needle soon after May 10, 1984, the lawyer promised to research its applicability. But Needle had not done so when Richard raised it again on June 1 or when he did so for the third time on June 2 or 3, after Greene said settlement was imminent. When Richard visited Needle's office on June 5, the lawyer insisted Section 6146 was inapplicable, only to reverse himself after consulting another lawyer in the suite. Once Needle was forced to concede the applicability of Section 6146, he had an obligation to the Shepherds to assert it to Greene. (Whether or not his failure to do so earlier was unethical, it might have been malpractice.) Needle promptly gave the Shepherds that part of his referral fee generated by Greene's excessive fee. When the Shepherds retained Needle to recover the excess from Greene, Needle proposed a graduated contingent fee of 20/33/40 percent, depending on when the case ended, but his grateful clients insisted on paying him the 40 percent Greene had demanded. As a result, Needle stood to earn *40 percent* of Greene's fee rather than the 20 percent Greene had originally offered. And then Needle again referred the case to another lawyer. Although Caffray exaggerated in declaring that Needle should have been the one disciplined, there were several disturbing conflicts of interest in his representation of the Shepherds. None of these, however, excused Greene's unethical behavior.

Greene's fallback position was that at his first meeting with the Shepherds, he had agreed to handle the case himself in exchange for their waiving Section 6146. This seems unlikely (despite Needle's reference to any "purported waiver" in his July 9, 1984, letter). Greene would have had to explain the section to the Shepherds, which was contrary to his self-interest and inconsistent with Richard's insistence that he first learned about the section two years later from Jay Rose. Furthermore, waiver was unnecessary if, as Greene believed (and claims to have told the Shepherds at that first meeting), the section was unconstitutional. It is even harder to understand why Greene, who had practiced more than 20 years by 1982, would have omitted the waiver from the written retainer, especially since he claimed to have discussed it with the Shepherds at the time. Greene's explanations for this omission are unconvincing: his associate Ken Collins said Needle was reliable (which sounds more like an assurance that Needle would keep mum about Section 6146 out of self-interest); Greene did not handle many medical malpractice cases (but the firm's website lists it as one of his practice areas); he trusted his clients (but this is about him betraying *their* trust). Greene persisted in arguing waiver even after the California Supreme Court ruled in 1985 that clients could not waive Section 6146.

The most ethically troubling argument is Greene's continued insistence that Section 6146 was unconstitutional. He claimed that the law was not "in effect" if courts were not following it. He cited case law selectively, emphasizing Schifferman's declaration of unconstitutionality (although that only addressed the damages cap and was overturned on appeal) while dismissing *American Bank's* finding of constitutionality (because it only upheld the periodic payment section). Girardi, one of Greene's principal witnesses, was even more emphatic. Governor Brown himself believed MICRA was unconstitutional, signing it only to end the doctors' strike. *Roa* was decided by "four guys [who] loused this whole thing." MICRA was "absurd," "total baloney. It's not right." When Gochis asked if Girardi "hoped it would be found improper," he retorted: "Didn't hope, knew it, were morally certain of it." Greene maintained his position even after *Roa* upheld Section 6146. So did his lawyer, Caffray, arguing that a statute whose constitutionality has been challenged is unconstitutional until proven constitutional—just the opposite of the law.

Greene's last resort was to disclaim responsibility for escrowing disputed fees. The firm had hired Cholko from the Superior Court to take over accounting. With 850 asbestos clients alone, no lawyer could keep track of the flow of funds. Caffray affirmed that Greene was too busy and important to attend to anything as trivial as escrowing client money. O'Reilly blamed his partner's failure to do so on the abrupt departure of the firm's managing partner and the move to new offices. Greene claimed not to have understood that the State Bar's 1986 letter asking if he had placed the disputed funds in a trust account *required* him to do so. But none of this is relevant. Once the Shepherds disputed Greene's fee—as they unequivocally did on July 9, 1984, and reiterated in the weeks that followed—he had a personal obligation to escrow the disputed amount, a duty that could not be delegated.

How can lawyers—who devote their careers to making others obey the law—behave as though it does not apply to them? That is the core of this case and its most disturbing element. Was this a byproduct of Greene's extraordinary professional success: a cab-driver's son, the only educated member of the family, who rose to become "trial lawyer of the year," "diplomate" of the American Board of Trial Lawyers, and president of the Los Angeles and the California trial lawyers associations? He was proud to be one of the youngest lawyers admitted to the Inner Circle of Advocates, "euphemistically" (he means the opposite— "notoriously") known as "the heavy of the millionaires' club of America." Caffray praised Greene's "credentials" as "a massive thing . . . too worthy to have even a little piece torn off by a proceeding such as this." Greene seemed to feel that what he achieved for the Shepherds—turning a *defense* expert's testimony to their advantage after his own experts pulled out—justified his fee. He "had to be competitive" with big shots like David Harney, Ned Good, and Thomas Girardi by charging as much as them. (Competition is supposed to do the opposite—drive down prices; but when quality is hard to evaluate, price perversely becomes its signal.) Greene brought out the big guns during the penalty phase: Judge Tevrizian and former California State Bar President Orville Armstrong. He could not separate self-interest from public interest, characterizing his efforts on behalf of the California Trial Lawyers Association as pro bono activity.

Greene's conviction that he was above the law seems to have been shared, and may have been encouraged, by the judges before whom he appeared and the referee who heard the disciplinary case. Judge Baffa, who approved the Shepherds' settlement, did not know that Section 6147 required lawyers to mention Section 6146 in their fee agreements. He had no interest in those agreements and felt no obligation to educate plaintiffs about the law. Instead, he "looked at what was accomplished." "Without the lawyer, you get nothing, and frankly I happen to like lawyers and I like to protect them with their fees." The referee paraphrased Lincoln: "all a lawyer has to sell is his time and I think he has to sell that time prudently and sell that time where it's going to do the most for him as well as for his law firm and for his clients." The referee rejected Gochis's argument that

Greene had refused to escrow the disputed amount but would not read the transcript, relying instead on his notes. "I feel that the practice that was followed here is no different than the practice I have observed . . . in a large law firm." He was contemptuous of the Review Department—appellate judges "can do whatever they want" and had overruled him "on grounds that I think there is no justification for in the record," "with findings of fact not supported by the evidence." He disregarded its ruling that Greene had violated MICRA, letting the respondent relitigate *mens rea* during the penalty phase. Caffray encouraged this, disparaging the "weakness and frailty" of the Review Department's "recitals of fact, six instances of which at least, that you pointed out, are recitals of not fact." The referee resented (and ignored) the minimum penalties, which he claimed would eliminate most lawyers in the state. He sought to protect Greene's privacy—"I would think until these matters are totally concluded that they would remain private and confidential"—despite Gochis's repeated reminders that the proceedings were public. And he did not know he had to write a decision, asking Gochis for a form. He concluded that this was "not a serious offense," imposing only an admonition (which the law did not authorize). Even the Review Department was sympathetic, finding guilt by a vote of only 6–5, with two judges abstaining (presumably because they knew and would have voted for Greene). Greene remained proud of what he had achieved for the Shepherds, "irrespective of what a review panel by a six-to-five vote thinks on one particular issue." "I feel that the practice that was followed here is no different than the practice I have observed . . . in a large law firm." Encouraged by the judge who approved the settlement, other elite personal injury lawyers, the referee who heard the disciplinary proceeding, and five out of the eleven voting Review Department members (with tacit support from two more), Greene felt entitled to substitute his views for those of the California legislature and Supreme Court.

IV. "THE FOREMOST MEDICAL MALPRACTICE LAWYER IN THE COUNTRY, IF NOT THE WORLD"

A. The Koskoff Case

1. Culpability Brendan Koskoff was born with severe disabilities on July 11, 1974. On May 23, 1980, his parents, Richard and Martha, met a lawyer, David M. Harney, for two or three hours to discuss suing for medical malpractice. Although their claim was barred by the statute of limitations, that was tolled by reason of Brendan's minority. Judith testified that Harney said: "in the case of a minor, the judge decides the amount of the fee, but generally it is 25 percent."[51] The printed retainer declared "that as sole compensation for services rendered by said attorneys, the client will pay them 25% [handwritten] percent of any money or property

51. All testimony is taken from the disciplinary hearing.

paid . . . ." Handwriting at the end added: "David M. Harney will be personally responsible for supervising and handling this matter."[52] Harney filed suit on July 19, 1980, but the Koskoffs had no further contact with him until the day of trial. During the intervening twenty-eight months, his associate, Jim Pagliuso, took depositions, wrote letters, and arranged appointments. The case settled for $1 million on the day of trial, October 4, 1982, before Judge Baffa (who had also approved the Shepherd settlement).

> [M]ost of the talk in terms of the settlement, all of it actually, went on inside the courtroom, and Richard and I were in the hall outside of the courtroom . . . . [Harney] came out and advised us that a settlement had been offered. It was his best advice that we take the settlement rather than go to trial . . . . [A]t that particular time we said that the fees were acceptable.

The hearing before Judge Baffa was very brief.[53]

COURT: And the fee arrangement is acceptable to you also? [Both agreed.] Are you satisfied with his efforts on your behalf?

RICHARD KOSKOFF: Very much so.

COURT: I would say so. He did a good job.

HARNEY: Actually, Mr. Pagliuso, I think, should be given the credit. He has done all the work.

On October 29 Baffa approved the settlement and Harney's $250,000 fee.

In March 1985, the day after the Supreme Court upheld MICRA's limit on non-economic damages,[54] a jury awarded a Harney client $5.2 million for removing his healthy left kidney instead of his cancerous right one. Perhaps influenced by the Supreme Court decision, however, the jury gave the plaintiff only $101,000 for medical expenses and nothing for lost income (after the defense argued he had "sold" his insurance business to his son, losing nothing); the $5.1 million for pain and suffering would be reduced to $250,000. Harney called the award "terribly low" and said "We are going to go to the U.S. Supreme Court with this."[55]

On April 4, 1985—two and a half years after retaining Harney—the Koskoffs wrote him protesting his fee on the ground that Section 6146

> nullifies such contractual arrangements for contingency fees in cases such as Brendan's. Consequently, is Brendan not entitled to a repayment . . . ?[56] As Brendan's guardians, it is our fiduciary responsibility to guarantee that he

---

52. State Bar Exhibit 2.

53. State Bar Exhibit 5.

54. Fein v. Permanente Medical Group, 38 Cal.3d 137, 211 Cal.Rptr. 368, 695 P.2d 665 (2.28.85).

55. Dorothy Townsend, *Jury Gives Victim $5.2 million after Bungled Surgery,* Los Angeles Times B1 (Mar. 2, 1985).

56. Under that section, the fee would have been $141,667.

> receive all money to which he is entitled. . . . Knowing your genuine interest in Brendan, we contact you, asking what arrangements might be made to handle the above situation in a responsible and just manner.[57]

Martha said that on March 1, 1985, her mother "had seen an article in the *Los Angeles Times* about a law called MICRA.[58] . . . I subsequently read the article . . . . I didn't think that the law would apply to us, but I called Richard [from whom she was divorced] to ask him what he thought." Her father, a retired doctor, had never mentioned MICRA. Harney replied a week later: "It is my recollection that the fee in question in Brendan's case was awarded by the court for the services we rendered and the result we accomplished. We do not consider the award of fees by the court to be a 'contingency fee.'"[59] Harney's lawyer in the disciplinary proceeding, Gert K. Hirschberg, who was of counsel to Harney's firm, unsuccessfully sought to exclude both letters as "efforts on the part of the Kosksoffs to get a refund from Mr. Harney's office. Having failed, they filed suit and they have been using the State Bar as a collection agency." (By this time, the Shepherds had challenged Greene's fee and won its refund in an arbitration by the State Bar, which also had asked if Greene had escrowed the disputed amount. Harney, who claimed to be at the apex of the small group of elite Los Angeles personal injury lawyers to which Greene also belonged, would have known this.)

After Brandon's death, his estate sued Harney in 1986.[60] Both Koskoffs signed declarations in July and August 1988 that Harney had never mentioned Section 6146. At a September 14 hearing on their summary judgment motion (by which time the Review Department had affirmed Greene's penalty), Superior Court Judge Stephen M. Lachs accepted Harney's claim that he had discussed MICRA with them.[61]

COURT: Mr. Harney puts a lot of weight on the fact that Judge Baffa finally set a fee. But the actual agreement between Mr. Harney and the plaintiffs was an agreement in which he does not get paid unless there is a recovery. And I think that any lawyer would understand that as a contingent fee agreement.

THERESA IACOPINO (HARNEY'S LAWYER): . . . [T]here was an agreement for representation. There was no agreement as to the amount of recovery that Mr. Harney would receive . . . .

COURT: I think it is clear from the agreement and from the deposition that Mr. Harney's sole recovery would come about as a result of money or

57. State Bar Exhibit 3.

58. The Supreme Court had decided *Roa* on February 7.

59. State Bar Exhibit 4.

60. State Bar Exhibit 1.

61. Respondent's Exhibit 9.

property paid. . . . And for me that type of an agreement is a contingent fee agreement.

IACOPINO: Judge Baffa states in his declaration, "Said award of attorney fees was in no way made pursuant to Business and Professions Code Section 6146 which has to do with contingent fee agreement. Said award was made on the basis of the result accomplished and legal services rendered and costs advanced by said law firm . . . ."

COURT: I conclude that as a matter of law the agreement between Mr. Harney and the plaintiffs was a contingent fee agreement . . . I find that 6146 applies to this situation . . . .[M]y reading of the case is that [Judge Baffa] could not order that more be paid.

Iacopino noted that *Roa* was decided after the Koskoffs' settlement.

COURT: . . . I am not suggesting that Judge Baffa or Mr. Harney knew when this case was concluded that *Roa* would be decided the way *Roa* was . . . .[T]his says nothing about Judge Baffa. I practiced in front of Judge Baffa years ago. All judges should be like Judge Baffa.

The judge found that Harney had received an excess of $93,768.06. Although the Koskoffs had sought punitive damages, their lawyer, Barry Mullen, said they would accept the difference plus interest.

COURT: To say that . . . Mr. Harney recovered an amount in excess of what I am saying he should have has nothing to do with his integrity as an attorney. It has to do with an interpretation in 1982 of a statute that did not get fully interpreted until 1985 . . . . [Harney] has been an attorney in this community for a long time and well respected. . . . And I would assume that particularly in light of his derivation, if that is the word, you might say this got his Irish up.

The judge granted the plaintiff summary judgment for $103,333.33. Harney petitioned for a writ of mandate or prohibition in the Court of Appeal on September 27,[62] which summarily denied it two days later. He filed a similar petition in the Supreme Court on October 28.[63]

The OTC filed a NTSC on March 10, 1988 charging violations of BPC Sections 6068(a), 6103, and 6106 and RPC Sections 2-107 and 7-105. Harney answered on March 24, denying everything: the NTSC did not charge misconduct, it was barred by laches, there was no written contingency fee agreement, and he had no duty to advise clients of Section 6146. At the time of these events, "there was great consternation, controversy and dispute in the legal community of California as to the constitutionality of Section 6146 . . . [which] had come to rest in the California Supreme Court by a narrow 4 to 3 opinion." The "institution of this particular disciplinary proceeding is for the sole purpose of effectuating a civil

62. State Bar Exhibit 16.

63. State Bar Exhibit 14.

recovery, [and] constitutes an abuse of process." At the mandatory settlement conference in July or August, the State Bar counsel suggested the parties stipulate to abide by the outcome of the Greene case, still pending in the Review Department. Harney sought a continuance because he was on vacation in Ireland and had a heavy trial schedule; he rejected all requests for admissions and refused to answer any of the 30 interrogatories.

At the first hearing before Referee Leon S. Paule (a practitioner) on December 14. Hirschberg began: "the gentleman on my right . . . is the foremost medical malpractice lawyer in the country, if not in the world. Respected by the entire bench, the judiciary and the State Bar of California." MICRA "was known as the anti-David Harney statute. The evidence will show he was that famous." "[T]hroughout the time that the Harney firm represented the Koskoffs, there was a general perception that MICRA was unconstitutional." If so, "there is no basis for a disciplinary finding because he wouldn't have had the proper mens rea . . . ." Baffa's approval of the fee was *res judicata*. The fee was not unconscionable; even an unconscionable fee was not ground for discipline. Richard Koskoff had graduated from a good law school. The $1 million settlement (the insurance policy limit) gave each parent $125,000 (in anticipation of their wrongful death claim), in addition to Brandon's $500,000. Since there were three claimants, "the lawyer threshold of MICRA should apply" to each. The Harney firm had a high overhead.[64] Section 6146 was waivable. State Bar counsel Djinna M. Gochis interrupted this opening with repeated objections, most of which were overruled. Moving to dismiss, Hirschberg boasted: "I was on the Board of Governors of the State Bar and . . . I will testify as a witness at the time." After Gochis objected "to this entire tirade," the Referee denied the motion. When Gochis moved to put a case in the record, Hirschberg expostulated:

> Well, I was deprived of putting my last point on the record and I would like that permission.

GOCHIS: Your last point would have to do with your being a member of the Board of Directors.

HIRSCHBERG: Ms. Gochis, as you will find out, has a habit of interrupting in these proceedings.

REFEREE: Very well, and before Ms. Gochis proceeds, why don't you finish your point.

HIRSCHBERG: My point was simply this, that when I was on the Board of Governors—

GOCHIS: Precisely my problem

Hirschberg: Oh, come on.

GOCHIS: Sir, I can't.

---

64. Later Hirschberg argued that Harney's overhead should be considered a cost item, making his net fee compliant with §6146.

HIRSCHBERG: The Board of Governors enacted a policy for the Office of Trial Counsel . . . .

GOCHIS: Sir, I have to object to his testimony.

HIRSCHBERG: . . . [N]ot to proceed with any MICRA violations until the constitutionality had been established.

GOCHIS: I am going to make a motion to strike . . . .

REFEREE: That motion is granted.

Hirschberg moved to exclude Martha Koskoff's testimony on the ground that she did not appear at the deposition. "I received a very vicious telephone call from Ms. Koskoff's attorney who told my secretary that he would punch me in the nose." After argument about whether Martha had refused to testify or Mallen (her lawyer in the action to recover excess fees) had had a scheduling problem,[65] Hirschberg called Mallen "an unmitigated vicious liar who should be . . . disciplined himself." The referee sustained Gochis's objections to most of this and let Martha testify (as above). On cross-examination, she agreed that Harney had told them his fee would be approved by the court but denied he had set it at 25 percent "to soothe the fears of you and your husband that Mr. Harney may ask for more." When the referee discouraged Hirschberg from "asking questions that will bring forth inconsequential answers," the lawyer insisted he was "entitled to cross-examine her as to whether or not she was accurate in her recollection" that she had never heard of MICRA, "because as I remember it, MICRA was on television every night, in the newspapers." The referee retorted that he "never saw them. I never heard of it until this case." Asked if he had "any more constructive cross-examination," Hirschberg said, "Judge Baffa took a liking to these people. He said you should have more children." When the referee said he was,

65. On October 25, Hirschberg had drafted a subpoena for Martha to be deposed on December 1, notifying Gochis the same day and adding: "I do not believe that I need to extend any courtesy to Mr. Malen [*sic*]. He is not the attorney of record in this matter." Gochis replied on October 31: "As I told you, I understand Mrs. Koskoff is not in Los Angeles until the middle of November." The process server made three attempts to serve her before succeeding on November 30. The next day Hirschberg's secretary wrote him a note that Mallen had left a "screaming haughty message: 'I will be out of the country tomorrow . . . . My client, Martha Koskoff, will not be at the deposition since she was only given a twenty-four hours' notice . . . . Any more funny business and I will take him to court to sock him in the face. Will be back next week, on the 6th, or he can call me today, before 1 p.m.'" Respondent's Exhibit A. Mallen faxed Hirschberg the same day, observing that this was the first time Martha had been served even though she had been home all the previous week. "Naturally, I am sure you are aware that Mrs. Koskoff has a mentally retarded and physically handicapped child to care for and cannot simply drop everything without prior notice . . . am at a loss to explain why you would wait nine months to depose her, and then attempt to set her deposition on one day's notice." He was leaving for Mexico for a week. "You are welcome to contact me next week about rescheduling Mrs. Koskoff's deposition." State Bar Exhibit 1.

"not interested in your testimony," Hirschberg replied that he wanted to bring "out the fact that Judge Baffa spent a great deal of time. It is inconceivable that a Superior Court judge did not know."

Richard Koskoff testified that at the settlement conference Harney had said his fee was 25 percent; "I asked him on that whether he was willing to waive . . . he said he would waive the costs" of $14,000. "I did not know that there was a statutory fee limitation . . . ." His work in the Los Angeles city attorney's office concerned weights and measures and health and safety; although he did some tort defense, he did not handle medical malpractice. He subsequently consulted Harney about leaving criminal law, which he had practiced from 1976 to 1982. The referee stopped Hirschberg from showing that Richard was angry because Harney did not offer him a job. "We are wasting too much time and as far as I am concerned, we haven't really gotten to the basic issue before me." Hirschberg retorted: "that is because [Gochis] has no case." Richard said that when Harney refused to refund the excess fee. "I lost some respect." "I couldn't believe that Harney, since we had trusted him, had deceived us and I thought it applied to our case."

Harney testified that he learned at his first meeting with the Koskoffs that Richard was a lawyer and Martha a doctor's daughter.

> I said the case would not fall under Business and Professions Code 6146 because it's not on a contingent fee basis and no application was made to the court for approval of a contingent fee, and it would be the award from the court, and that the usual policy of 25 percent.

What he signed was not "called a 'retainer' because we're not retained financially." It was a "percentage agreement which coincided with the probate policy manual." Quoting *Black's Law Dictionary,* he denied it was a contingent fee.

HARNEY: [I]t doesn't relate to some casual fortuitous event. This was going to be an especially carefully prepared matter, and I would not take the case, if I thought the outcome was so uncertain and so fortuitous and casual. I don't practice law that way. Never have and never will.

GOCHIS: Your 25 percent was contingent upon getting a settlement or recovery by trial; that is correct?

HARNEY: Not contingent upon. The court, if as and when there were a successful recovery, would determine the fee and customarily the court in my years of practice has without exception awarded at least 25 percent and sometimes more . . . .I told the Koskoffs that in the event there would be no recovery, they would not have to repay me any costs or reimburse me for any of my time, overhead or energy.

"[I]t was a percent limit and a percent limit is not a contingent fee." Although he would get nothing if they lost, "it is like a real estate broker gets his commission." He admitted that in the petition for rehearing *Roa,* he had submitted a declaration that his "law practice is based strictly upon contingency agreements with plaintiffs. Some of which are subject to court approval if there is a minor or incompetent."

"[C]ertainly if they were intended at that time to claim that 6146 applied, they waived it . . . . the codes say you can waive any contract." (Harney made this argument three years after the California Supreme Court held that Section 6146 could not be waived.[66]) Asked how you could waive something that does not apply, Harney said "by fiat." "I cannot go through the mind of everybody in the world who signs a waiver. There are thousands and millions signed every day." Asked why the retainer did not mention Section 6146, Harney said "we have got shelves and shelves full of codes in books. I think we have 10,000 books in the office. Not one is mentioned."

> [T]he day they enacted MICRA, waiver was all over the place . . . .a Superior Court judge ruled that waiver was proper . . . .there is a writ [*sic*— "right"] of contract in the United States, and if somebody wants a certain attorney, and the only way he can get that attorney is to waive that restriction, then that person has the right to contract with that lawyer under a waiver . . .. I cannot see any public policy if there is just one client.

That Section 6147 made an agreement voidable for violating Section 6146 "means it's waivable." Judge Feiner had held that in *Fineberg*, and it was still the "general consensus of the Los Angeles judicial community." "[E]ver since I went to law school over 40 years ago, I was taught that under California law, the civil code, one may waive contractual and other rights. I have done a lot of research on this subject and the rule is that if a statute does not expressly prohibit waiver, the civil code does apply to it."

"[T]here is no contract in this case" because "a contract requires both sides to sign it," and the Koskoffs had not done so. The "only purpose of this piece of paper was to put a lid or a cap on the amount that the probate court could award . . . there is no agreement whatsoever with any parents. There is a piece of paper that applied only to the child, Brendan." He dismissed the Koskoffs' successful contract action: "the Superior Court judge in one department says that Judge Baffa eight years earlier was wrong. I do not know how that can ever happen . . . how one superior court judge can overrule another." It was impossible to contract with a minor: "all cases of minors were handled . . . through the probate court and we accepted whatever the award was . . . ." Section 6146 applied to fee agreements for representing minors only "if you got prior approval of a contract. But I did not know how you can do that and I have never gotten one in 39 years."

He told the Koskoffs Section 6146 "only applied to contingency fee agreements and this was not a contingency fee agreement," and the statute "was probably unconstitutional."

66. *Waters, supra.*

GOCHIS: Now, in 1980 was 6146 of the Business and Professions Code the law?

HIRSCHBERG: Just a minute—

HARNEY: It's unconstitutional.

GOCHIS: Who said it was unconstitutional?

HARNEY: A lot of people did.

HIRSCHBERG: [objected that Harney is] not an expert in constitutionality . . . and whether or not it was the law at that time, there is great uncertainty . . . I think the question whether it was a law is an unfair question and not within his expertise . . . .[W]as it the law at that time?

HARNEY: It depends whose perception. The Governor signed the bill that it was unconstitutional . . . to get the doctors and their wives off his back . . . now, what the effect of signing an unconstitutional law is, I believe it rendered it a null and void act.

GOCHIS: Had any court declared 6146 unconstitutional?

HARNEY: Many courts had declared similar laws unconstitutional.

GOCHIS: Had 6146 been declared unconstitutional . . . [in] 1980?

HARNEY: At the trial court level?

GOCHIS: Any level.

HARNEY: I'm not sure.

Harney testified that he had been

> [P]art of a group consisting of three justices on the Supreme Court out of seven, who said that the 6146 was unconstitutional. Many legal scholars, including Professor Tribe, and I would say the vast majority of the bar and judiciary in California thought it was unconstitutional. When, by a lot of dictum, the majority said that it was constitutional under the limited facts of that case, the Supreme Court having previously ruled that MICRA was unconstitutional, I became extremely interested in the matter of filing . . . the petition for rehearing and acting as an amicus curiae therein . . . . I still personally believe and I will testify under oath that that statute is unconstitutional.

Asked why MICRA was enacted, Harney was contemptuous:

> [T]he Supreme Court said in the American Bank that there was no basis for it . . . .I know what the self-serving people who put up 109 million dollars to get that legislation passed had to say about it.

He "absolutely" had not intended to violate the law in 1982. "I don't violate and never have violated any laws." Having talked to Justices Mosk and Bird since then, he still believed Section 6146 was unconstitutional. (They had *dissented* from the decision finding it constitutional.)

He did not secure a written waiver because Section 6146 "wasn't applicable." The agreement says, "'on behalf of Brendan.' Brendan, obviously, was a minor so anything, under the Probate Code, dealing with settlement or resolution of a minor's case would have to be approved by the Superior Court." He refused to say whether he still used the agreement "on the grounds it invades my attorney/client privilege with existing clients, and I don't think that's anybody's business at this point." Hirschberg twice objected to Gochis asking if Harney would behave the same way today, but when Hirschberg asked if Harney's views had changed, his client said: "Actually, they've been reinforced by a court of appeals decision" (which held that the Probate Court could award *less* than the Section 6146 limit, not *more*). When the Referee again overruled Hirschberg's objection to Gochis's question whether Harney had ever complied with Section 6146, Harney refused to answer, asserting "a duty to . . . claim the privilege of my clients." When Gochis explained she was not asking about any individual client, Harney maintained, "I have never in my life disregarded 6146 . . . I believe I have always complied with it . . . . I have dedicated myself to that." But he could not say how often he had applied Section 6146 since 1985.

The settlement conferences did not address Section 6146 "in view of our original discussion. I didn't think it was necessary, and I'm sure Mr. Koskoff and his wife didn't think so either."

> I did the master-minding and Mr. Pagliuso probably did a lot of the physical work, such as . . . any court appearances that were unrelated to settlement, in connection with answering interrogatories and . . . setting up and attending depositions. But I personally directly and constantly supervised everything that was going on.

He doubted Judge Baffa had seen the fee agreement: "it's not customary in a minor or an incompetent case because they're going to apply whatever they feel is proper at the discretion of the court." They had an agreement because the Koskoffs "wanted an absolute maximum on it . . . which was the 25 percent from the [probate] policy manual, and I exceeded [*sic*—"acceded"] to their choice." He knew that Probate Code Section 3302 rendered a fee agreement void unless approved by the court, but "nobody asked that the court determine that it was void . . . because Mr. Koskoff is the one who wanted the 25 percent in writing."

GOCHIS: Did it occur to you that if Judge Baffa saw the agreement, he might mention 6146 . . . ?

HARNEY: Judge Baffa is an intelligent person and knows what the probate policy manual is and was aware of it and approved and ordered the fee to be paid as it was.

HIRSCHBERG: [called the question objectionable, highly improper] and while I'm making this objection, you have interrupted at least five times.

GOCHIS: Counsel, make an objection. There are proper objections that you're entitled to make. Don't argue the case and don't interrupt me.

HIRSCHBERG: The truth is that the interruptions have been yours.

GOCHIS: This is my field right now, and I'm asking the question, you'll get your opportunity . . . . In order to determine whether or not the fee arrangement was agreeable to the Koskoffs, would not the judge have needed the fee agreement? [Hirschberg's objection was overruled.]

HARNEY: The Koskoffs got more than they asked for, and they asked to limit the percent to 25 percent, and came out to less than that . . . .

GOCHIS: Do you recall a time when [the Koskoffs] did mention 6146 to you?

HARNEY: I believe they made a complaint to the State Bar around that time, and they were saying something about 6146. And the Bar looked into it and the Bar . . . tossed it out . . .. [The Koskoffs] claim that somehow or other, by some stretch of their imagination, [6146] applied, and they hired some lawyer by the name of Max Factor [III], who gave me the same litany . . . .[T]hey had some goofy argument that it applied in this situation . . ..

GOCHIS: [What did the Koskoffs say?]

HARNEY: They wanted some money . . ..

GOCHIS: Did the Koskoffs tell you you collected a fee in excess of that provided by 6146?

HARNEY: That's the essence of their claim . . . I said something to the effect that they were all wet and that it was a goofy idea . . ..

It would have been "silly" to talk to the Koskoffs about "holding any amount in excess of the provision of 6146 separately, pending the resolution of the controversy with the courts." "I don't spend my time on silly conversations."

GOCHIS: Did you know what *Roa v. Lodi* was about?

HARNEY: I sure do. It was some weird application by the majority of Austro-Hungarian common law . . . .[I]t's very difficult, if not impossible, to understand the majority opinion . . . .

GOCHIS: The majority opinion is that the provisions of 6146 are constitutional; is that not correct?

HARNEY: With one type of application. Certain things were not argued in that case and not presented in the . . . four to three opinion, written by one Otto Kaus . . ..I believe Max and I had breakfast together, and I think that I told him the original American Bank case held the law to be unconstitutional, and then Justice Manuel passed away, and they reconstituted the Supreme Court, and on American Bank No. 2, the judgment of the trial court was affirmed, and

Justice Kaus was claiming somehow or another, even though he was affirming the judgment of the trial court that the law was constitutional, but it was all dictum, and then he used the dictum therefore in the *Roa* case to bolster up his argument that some aspect of 6146 was constitutional.

GOCHIS: The *Roa v. Lodi* case upheld the constitutionality of 6146, did it not?

HARNEY: A little bit . . .. [I]n the limited circumstances of that particular case, it did—very limitedly—without a lot of the legal arguments that are mentioned therein.

GOCHIS: Did it stand for the proposition that even where a client specifically wants to give more than provided by 6146, he cannot do so?

HARNEY: In the limited circumstances of that case involving a minor, it was to that effect . . . . [T]he attorney did virtually no work, and didn't take any depositions, and the trial court thought he was trying to overcharge.

GOCHIS: But *Roa* applied to a minor's compromise, basically, so the judge presumably in that particular case had to approved [*sic*] according to 6146?

HARNEY: No. No. No. The trial court had the discretion to award a fee, and he can choose any formula he wants.

GOCHIS: But *Roa* stands for the proposition that it must be in accordance with 6146?

HARNEY: That's not the way I read it.

GOCHIS: When Mr. and Mrs. Koskoff and/or Mr. Factor told you about *Roa v. Lodi*, did you offer to give the money back that you had already taken for your fees?

HARNEY: I didn't take any money. I resent that. I didn't take anything.[67]

GOCHIS: That you had collected for your fees?

HARNEY: It was a court order that I complied with, pure and simple. I didn't take anything.

GOCHIS: Do you need some time to relax? I don't want to have you be distressed.

HARNEY: I am distressed but . . ..

Later Harney claimed he would have been in contempt had he not complied with Baffa's "order."

67. At another point Harney proclaimed: "I do not take things from minors. I am awarded."

Gochis: Do you think you were under a duty to disclose the provision of 6146 at the time of your taking the case?

Harney: I don't think so.

GOCHIS: Why not?

HARNEY: Well, ma'am, there are literally thousands and thousands of code sections that somebody could claim may or may not be applicable to a given situation and, if I had to explain every code section to everybody who comes in, I'd only see one potential client in a lifetime. In the case of Mr. Koskoff it was discussed.

GOCHIS: Why in that particular case? . . .

Harney: I have told you . . . I've testified that it came up in the conversation with Mr. Koskoff, a lawyer, and it was in the context of Mr. Koskoff being a lawyer that 6146 came up, and it was explicated, as I already testified repeatedly.

Koskoff had brought up MICRA: "He had been out shopping. I forget how many other attorneys they had seen. He made it very apparent that he was a lawyer, knowledgeable." "I do not know of a lawyer who did not know about [Section 6146], whether he was in the criminal field, the civil field, or whatever . . ..." At the first meeting with the Koskoffs, "I called it the Keene bill or 'ABXX' or AB Double Cross." Asked why he had not put this allegation in his answer, Harney claimed not to remember his answer: "This thing has been going on, you know, for two and a half years. It has been extremely disruptive to my life and practice."

GOCHIS: Did you not think Judge Baffa's order would be affected by what the Koskoffs knew?

Harney: Wouldn't affect me. And I don't' think it would affect any sane judge . . .. [O]f course, if the State Bar is going to take the word from a lawyer who says he doesn't know about 6146 . . . which was well known to everyone in the legal community . . . then so be it.

When Richard applied for a job at Harney's firm, "he told me how bright and brilliant and well-read he was."

Harney had recently discussed the case with Judge Baffa, "because I thought the charges that were brought against me were absolutely insane." "I asked Judge Baffa what his understanding was . . . and he said 'I made an award and you're entitled to more. But I made the award as I did and approved the settlement and ordered it to be carried out.'" They had agreed that "6146 was referring to a contingency fee agreement, it had nothing to do with this case, since there was no contingency fee in this case." Harney maintained that a reasonable fee would have been "anything up to 50 percent," if neither the Probate Code nor Section 6146 applied. He concluded his direct testimony by agreeing he had not returned any money to the Koskoffs, "and I have no intention of ever doing so," reiterating this at the end of redirect:

GOCHIS: Despite all the case law that has come down since and despite *Roa* and despite *Waters* and despite Shepherd and Greene, you do not feel that you owe these people money?

HARNEY: Absolutely not. Never will.

GOCHIS: And if a court orders you to pay it back, will you pay it back? . . .

Harney: It will have to be the Supreme Court. Incidentally, I have never been held in contempt in my life.

Don C. Brown had been admitted in 1955 and practiced in Riverside since 1960, specializing in medical malpractice defense. In letters preparing for the hearing, Hirschberg recapitulated what Brown had told him. It "felt good to be on the other side" in disciplinary proceedings. "To say that MICRA has been counterproductive is an understatement." It had "passed constitutional muster by the smallest of margins. Even that has not been finally determined, at least to my satisfaction." "Throughout this entire period of time, there was a general feeling that MICRA was unconstitutional." "I see no way by which the State Bar can prevail." There was "no need" to explain MICRA to Richard Koskoff, "a seasoned attorney himself. (Seasoned enough to know to hire the Harney firm)." Hirschberg sought Brown's testimony that Harney "is most honorable, a leader in the legal community, and . . . was justified in ignoring MICRA."

Brown testified that the plaintiffs' bar "almost universally," "very clearly felt [MICRA] was unconstitutional," although "we, of course, understood that it was, in fact, constitutional." But "most judges" and "most attorneys" expected "it was going to be declared unconstitutional." Although he conceded on cross that it had never been declared unconstitutional, heinsisted, "it was not being followed by any of the courts that I am aware of." "[S]ince the *Roa* decision," however, "trial courts in approving minors' compromises have, in general, been following the guidelines of attorneys' fees set forth in MICRA."

Judge Dickran Tevrizian (who had testified for Greene) said that before 1985, the legal community generally ignored Section 6146, which was "presumed to be unconstitutional because of the way the MICRA legislation was enacted . . . very rapidly because . . . insurance companies were refusing to write insurance at rates the doctors could afford . . . .." The 25 percent fee Judge Baffa approved "is the standard fee." Harney was "probably one of the finest examples of a practicing attorney that has ever been produced in the state of California, if not nationwide." On cross, Tevrizian volunteered that an attorney like Richard Koskoff "is charged with knowing all provisions of the law," even when he was a client. There was "a great deal of confusion during this period" about whether Section 6146 applied to minors. Superior Court Judge Robert Schifferman and U.S. District Court Judge Edward Rafeedie had held other MICRA provisions unconstitutional. "[T]o this day I still think it's unconstitutional." "Technically," it was "passed and signed by Governor Brown into law. But there was a real serious question," whether such "special interest legislation, protecting only a medical profession, was a denial of equal protection . . . ." If a "client decides to choose the particular attorney because of that particular attorney's stature in a legal community, the client is free to waive the provisions of that statute." If the client is an attorney, "I do not know whether or not you really have to go through . . . what is called detailed explanation and waiver . . . ."

Judge Baffa testified that before the Koskoff case he awarded 50 percent to a firm that had obtained a "very good settlement," after winning an appeal to the California Supreme Court. At the time, he had expressed concern about MICRA, and Judge Steven Stauthers replied, "Don't worry about it. I don't think it's constitutional. Do what you think is fair." Those parents had accepted the 50 percent fee. The Koskoff case "stands out in my mind" because "I talked to the couple, nice-looking kids."

> I said, "[N]o, you are going to have additional children?" And the wife said, "No, this is a full-time job with this child." And I said, "Look, I have got four kids. They drive me crazy, but I don't know which one I would give away. Have some additional children."
>
> And they said "No, absolutely not." . . . I suppose the Italian and Jewish culture is the same: family, kids . . . . I really wanted them to have the choice of having a child . . .. I think they got divorced further down the line. It actually broke the marriage up. I understand that her father was a doctor, recommended the doctor who delivered the baby and he loused up the delivery . . ..

The defendant doctor's personal lawyer had told Baffa: "[M]y client would make a shitty witness. I don't want him on the witness stand. I think the case is worth a million and a half." But the hospital's lawyer "had it all worked out at $750,000." Baffa confronted him: "Look, we are dealing with Harney on this. If you are going to settle it, give me a million dollars . . .." Asked about the settlement, Baffa told Richard "I think it is very good. Mr. Harney has done a hell of a job for you actually because [the hospital's lawyer] had set it at $750,000 and he was hard to get off of that." Harney and Baffa had been friends for 30 years, socializing four or five times a year. Richard replied: "Well, if you feel that way, then that's good enough for me." Richard "would have much more background than the average . . . litigant, being a lawyer." Richard's cousin, a public defender, said Richard and he were "delighted with the settlement." "They talked with lawyers." "[W]ithout the lawyer, they wouldn't get anything. And I happen to like lawyers. I like to protect their fees. I like to see them get paid . . .. all the civil judges, Djinna [Gochis], would have been doing it." At the time, Baffa was not applying Section 6146: "I didn't think it was constitutional." He was unaware that Probate Code Section 3302 required him to see any fee agreement and would not have asked for the retainer even had he known the statute. "I really didn't care about contracts." (Hirschberg concurred, referring to the "purported" agreement and then substituting "relationship" for "agreement.") Baffa said judges "felt we could do what we felt was fair, Djinna." "See, historically, Djinna, at that time we were giving 25 percent on minors."

Leo Gelfand, a doctor who had become a plaintiffs' medical malpractice lawyer in 1957, testified "on the part of the plaintiff bar" that "no one believed that such a bill was or could be constitutional . . . and such doubts were fairly widespread on the bench and even some of the defense lawyers . . .." Harney was "without exception the absolute foremost malpractice lawyer in this area." The hospital's lawyers "wouldn't pay policy limits unless the lawyer appearing before them had a very well prepared and well thought out case . . .." Baffa, a judge "experienced in handling medical malpractice cases," was "primarily representing a minor . . .."

> [The] Koskoffs had nothing coming to them by David M. Harney. First of all, they had shopped this case before they came to the Harney offices . . . they knew what other offices were charging. . . . And they must have known about the Keene bill and MICRA.

He did not inform his own clients about Section 6146 and would not say whether he complied with it: "[T]he answer to that question is not as simple" as the question implied. He also refused to say whether he had contingent fee arrangements with minor clients: "I learned in the last few days that I am not certain completely as to what a contingency agreement is." He would just ask the judge to approve the settlement: "[T]hat to me was adequate."

John K. Trotter, who represented medical malpractice plaintiffs and defendants and had been a trial and an appellate judge, shared the "very widely held perception" that MICRA was unconstitutional. Harney "certainly" committed "no ethical or legal violation of any type or kind." Every "minor's compromise that was approved violated . . . what we felt was an improper piece of legislation." Harney was "held in the highest esteem by everybody that knows him" and "is without question one of the best lawyers . . . I have ever met." As a judge, he never applied Section 6146 to cases involving minors; "in a med mal case, which . . . are without question the most difficult cases to win . . . I would be most happy to give that lawyer the maximum fee, which is 25 percent."

Florence T. Pekard had practiced for 15 years before becoming a Superior Court judge handling minors' claims. In two cases in which liability was very tenuous, she had not followed Section 6146 "because I did not think that MICRA was going to be found constitutional." She did not know it applied to minors. She did not ask attorneys if they had discussed Section 6146 with their clients or believe they had a duty to do so.

Jack Tenner had practiced for 35 years, mostly plaintiffs personal injury law; eight years earlier he had been appointed to the bench, where he chaired the settlement committee. The legal and judicial community believed Section 6146 "could not logically or constitutionally be sustained. How could you set a fee for [a] certain kind of lawyers doing [a] certain kind of work," like medical malpractice, but not for lawyers handling other personal injuries? The settlement committees he participated in or chaired "never gave any thought at all that it would be held constitutional . . .. I never knew of a defendant attorney who ever suggested that it be considered in the approval of a settlement." Baffa's conduct "was perfectly proper." Tenner did not think Harney "did anything wrong." If other "members practice[d] in the manner in which Mr. Harney practices law, we would enjoy a much finer reputation . . . ." "I think the Koskoffs ought to give him a bonus for getting them a quarter of a million dollars. The money should belong to the kid." On cross-examination, however, he characterized "an agreement which provides for 25 percent of any recovery" as "a contingency fee agreement."

James Pagliuso explained in his deposition that he had obtained the medical records, prepared for and took or attended all the depositions, and participated in settlement conferences, although Harney suggested, "what dollar figure we wanted."[68] He did not remember talking to the Koskoffs about Section 6146. Although he believed they had signed and returned the fee agreement, he could not "ever recall having been before a judge on a minor's case where the judge . . . gave the slightest hint that he cared what the fee agreement was," either before MICRA or after. He had risen from law clerk to partner in Harney's firm before leaving in November 1987. The firm modified its retainers in response to MICRA: first saying "something about as [*sic*] the law was at the time the case was resolved" (anticipating it would be found unconstitutional) and then mentioning Section 6146 and requiring waiver as a condition of representation. He evaded answering whether it was a contingency fee because "you have to go to court to get it approved." Asked "why bother" having any agreement, he said it ensured "better client control . . . it probably prevents people from moving all over the place" from one attorney to another. When Gochis objected that Hirschberg "is testifying and the question is compound," the latter burst out: "I had not finished my question. If that lady cannot stop interrupting me, I am unable to handle this case." But the referee sustained the objection. Gochis also objected to Hirschberg asking whether Section 6146 "was publicized" in 1980.

REFEREE:	Mr. Hirschberg, this is irrelevant . . ..I told you before we even started that hearing that I had never heard of it and I had never even heard of Mr. Harney and I had never heard of him on t.v.
HIRSCHBERG:	Sir, I do not want to get personal. Your life is your life.
REFEREE:	Well, I was active in the legal field at the time.
HIRSCHBERG:	I do not know and I am not entitled to and I do not intend to ask you whether you had been in the City Attorney's office, whether you worked for a civil attorney by the name of Mark Fink. I think it is exceedingly improper for you to interject your own personal history, because you . . . are putting me into a position where I have to attack you, which I do not want to do.

68. Respondent's Exhibit C.

REFEREE: I am giving the reason why I am sustaining Ms. Gochis's objection, because it was not widely known in the legal profession at that time [though he denied taking judicial notice of that].

HIRSCHBERG: Sir, the fact that it was not well known in the legal profession is an entirely improper statement made by you. You are interjecting your own experience into this case and you should now disqualify yourself from sitting any further on this case.

REFEREE: I will not disqualify myself because I am not prejudiced one way or another. It is just that I think any discussion about the publicity of 6146 is really not relevant to this hearing.

HIRSCHBERG: You are depriving me of being able to cross-examine you at this time . . ..

He persisted in that line of inquiry by reading from Pagliuso's deposition:

> I am sure Mr. Koskoff knew [Section 6146] existed . . . . if you were around here in 1975 and 1976 and thereafter and you ever read the *Daily Journal* once in your life, I think there is no way that you would not know that these provisions existed . . . . if you even watched the evening news in 1975, these things were on every night. They had doctors' wives picketing the capital, and this wasn't something that was written on the 25th page of "lawyers on the move" in the *Daily Journal.*

Pagliuso testified that Harney "would usually discuss" MICRA with clients, most of whom already knew about it, since "it was in the *Los Angeles Times* and on CBS and NBC and ABC every week." "I do not think" Koskoff "is being forthright" in claiming ignorance. Because doctors were striking, "if somebody was in labor, they would have to go to county" hospital.

Judge William J. Rea, who had defended medical malpractice cases before being appointed to the Superior Court and then the U.S. District Court, said California trial judges "felt that the provisions of this act were unconstitutional." In his thousands of settlement conferences, "I did not apply, nor did the judges I know apply, that limitation to the type of case you are talking about." Harney's behavior "was perfectly within the canons of ethics," and he "always enjoyed the greatest respect among his colleagues . . . of any medical malpractice plaintiff's attorney." But Rea agreed that Section 6146 applied to the Koskoff case.

Although the referee agreed with Gochis that more such testimony was cumulative, he overruled her objection "in view of the prestige of the prospective witness," Andrew Hauk, chief judge emeritus of the Central District of California, who had been appointed to the Superior Court in 1963 and the federal court three years later. When Hirschberg began his hypothetical about the case, Gochis objected that Hauk was not a medical malpractice specialist.

HAUK: Now, wait a minute. Where do you get that? How do you know that? What proof do you have that I know nothing about it?

REFEREE: Sir, with respect, there is no question being put to you at the moment.

HAUK: I know, but statements are being made that are ridiculous. To give an offer of proof of that sort, that I know nothing about it, my dear lady, don't be fooled.

HIRSCHBERG: May I continue my question, your honor? This is in her usual habit of interrupting in the middle of a question.

GOCHIS: I am going to make the following statement. I am entitled to interrupt if I think a question is objectionable. I am going to make my record; that is my job as a State Bar attorney and I'm going to continue to do it.

HAUK: The offer of proof is what I object to.

HIRSCHBERG: The job as a State Bar attorney is to be honorable and have good manners. She may be honorable, she sure ain't got manners.

REFEREE: I disagree with that, but I will overrule the objection . . ..

HAUK: . . . Dave Harney, who is an excellent malpractice practitioner with the highest degree of competence and respect of the legal fraternity in my view and the legal profession, as well as the bar, and the judges, acted with propriety and circumspection and in my opinion acted constitutionally. This is a lot of nonsense that you can't get a judge to approve a settlement agreement because of an act like that that was applied retroactively instead of prospectively to an agreement made back in days before there was such a MICRA. I think he's entitled to have their respect in my opinion, and . . . decision in his favor here at this State Bar proceeding. He, I think, quite rightly resisted any attempt to apply this thing retroactively to him and got Judge Baffa to go along with it, and if that sort of thing isn't protected by the Constitution, I do not know what is . . . . [I]n the crisis of judicial admonition [*sic*—"administration"] that the Los Angeles Superior Court has gone through . . . in the overloads and excess cases . . . they assign such a large number of judges to settlement conferences. . . . Of course you do not have a full blown trial at the settlement conferences, but if these Koskoffs, and I understand he's a lawyer . . . he is no booby, and he knew exactly what he was doing and he should be held to it. Now, if the child somehow was hurt by this settlement . . . it is the fault of the guardian . . ..

Gochis's cross-examination elicited only abuse: "I said that. I will say it again young lady. Don't push me." Judge Hauk also wrote a letter emphasizing that both Harney and he belonged to the Knighthood of the Equestrian Order.[69]

Jack E. Goertzen had no medical malpractice experience but had served on the Superior Court and Court of Appeal. Harney "is probably one of the

69. A Catholic chivalric order dating from the Crusades. Respondent's Exhibit E.

finest—one or two or three at most plaintiff's attorneys I have ever come in contact with." "There was a general feeling that at least as to the damages and probably . . . the fee limitations there would be a federal finding of unconstitutionality" because they did not apply to automobile accidents. But he conceded that Section 6146 applied to the Koskoff case. When Gochis asked Goertzen how this case differed from Greene's, Hirschberg interrupted: "We have recipients who are the parents who were not damaged at all stealing $250,000 from their kid."

Eugene McCloskey had handled medical malpractice cases for both sides before being appointed to the Superior Court in 1976 and the Court of Appeal in 1980. He dissented in the Supreme Court's *Roa* decision and still believed Section 6146 was unconstitutional. Harney displayed "the highest ethical standard of lawyers practicing in the State of California." Judges approved 25 percent in minors' cases because both they and defense lawyers thought Section 6146 was unconstitutional. An "order approving a settlement is a judgment . . . it is *res judicata* and not subject to attack."

McCLOSKEY: I don't think there is any basis for disciplining Mr. Harney . . . . Mr. Harney's reputation is that of an eminent, truthful lawyer of the highest integrity and I think this proceeding is a disgrace on the part of the State Bar and I think your [Gochis's] laughter at such things—

GOCHIS: Sir, that does not answer the question and I was not laughing about David Harney or his reputation . . . .I make a motion to strike the judge's answer as not responsive to the question.

McCLOSKEY: The coupling, your honor, of the laughter with the conduct of the State Bar disciplinary thing and this setting is, I think, offensive not only to me but the whole judiciary . . . and most of the members of the State Bar. I think it is a disgrace to waste the dues of the State Bar at the time when there are so many necessary prosecutions in the proceeding of this nature. I don't think [there is] anything funny about it.

GOCHIS: Sir, I am going to make a motion to strike . . ..

McCLOSKEY: I have never seen an attorney laugh at a witness before.

GOCHIS: I wasn't laughing at you, sir, I would never laugh at you.

REFEREE: [granted the motion to strike]

HIRSCHBERG: May it be noted that your latest ruling is over my very, very strenuous objection . . ..

McCLOSKEY: [sought clarification about what was being struck]

GOCHIS: I am going to also ask that the judge's comments at this last moment also . . . be stricken.

HIRSCHBERG: Were you trying to muddy up the record, Justice McCloskey?

GOCHIS: I am going to object to that question. It is not relevant.

Before the next witness testified, the referee observed that "the criticism by the previous witness was entirely unwarranted. Both counsel here have vigorously and diligently represented their respective clients and they have done so in a respectful and courteous manner acting at all times in the finest tradition of the legal profession."

Harney's last witness was John S. Malone, who had worked for the State Bar from 1952 to 1978, as its highest officer for the last eight years, and now taught professional responsibility at U.C. Hastings. Harney had been "obeying a lawful order of the court." His "reputation as a bright aggressive trial lawyer . . . is beyond reproach." In 1980–82, the State Bar prosecuted only willful breaches of its rules. Malone evaded answering whether it had been proper to file the disciplinary charge, but on cross, he said he "would have difficulty finding probable cause to issue a notice to show cause." On redirect, he reiterated that "compliance with the lawful court order" was not "a willful breach of the rules of professional conduct" but conceded on recross that a lawyer's failure to mention Section 6146 to a judge "would be a factor that might lead to my changing my mind."

Harney represented himself when Gochis called Fred Hiestand, who had been a consultant to the legislature and Governor during MICRA's passage and remained involved after its enactment.[70] When Gochis asked Hiestand what cases Section 6146 affected in 1980, Harney objected "on the ground that Section 6146 speaks for itself. It requires a contingent fee contract. This witness cannot overrule the legislature even though he helped draft the measure." When Gochis tried to present the Koskoff case hypothetically, Harney objected "on the ground there is absolutely no evidence of any agreement. The document that is in evidence is signed only by David M. Harney. . . . With a minor you cannot have any kind of a contract without court approval." The referee overruled the objection. After Hiestand testified that "6146 applied in any case of medical malpractice . . . where the fees of the attorney were based upon the recovery to the client, whether that client be a minor or an adult," the referee overruled Harney's motion to strike. After the referee overruled Harney's objection to Gochis asking "if there was a contingency fee agreement, what, if any obligation . . . did Mr. Harney have in 1980," Hiestand replied:

> [T]he obligation of an attorney representing the client in a medical malpractice matter [is] to disclose to them what the law was with respect to the attorney's fees that an attorney could obtain.

GOCHIS: Now, does your opinion change because a judge has to approve a settlement on the part of a minor?

> [The referee overruled Harney's objection.]

70. His resume was State Bar Exhibit 13.

HIESTAND: . . . [T]he only possible circumstances in which it might change if there is a minor is if the amount that would be given under the MICRA schedule turned out . . . to be more than the amount that was authorized by the Probate Code and the local court rules . . . .

GOCHIS: . . . Assume [Harney] goes by the feeling that [Section 6146] is not constitutional, secures a waiver on the part of his client, what, if any, obligations did he have pursuant to that section.

[The referee overruled Harney's objection.]

HIESTAND: . . . [T]he attorney that is representing the client asking for the waiver should advise the client of their right to seek counsel to advise them about the waiveability of any of their rights. Because the attorney has a fiduciary responsibility to the client and once an attorney is asking a person, usually in this case people that are not on equal bargaining, you know, in most circumstances because they are distressed or they are not in the most normal rational sense of cognition . . . the attorney should take extra care. . . . Then I think until they get a declaration from the court saying that it can be waived, they should take the difference between what MICRA says and what they got in a waiver and place that in an independent trust account until a court conclusively determined for them that they can take that extra money.

HARNEY: I move to strike the answer under the circumstances of this case. Mr. Koskoff was a lawyer. Mrs. Koskoff was the daughter of a medical doctor and they sat on the case for six years before they ever went to a lawyer.

[The referee denied his motion.]

GOCHIS: Mr. Hiestand, would it make any difference to your opinion . . . if I told you that Richard Koskoff was a lawyer . . . ?

HIESTAND: In terms of protecting the interests of clients generally, no. If Mr. Koskoff was a medical malpractice lawyer . . . you would have a stronger argument. . . . But even though, because of the circumstances of the distress of the situation, it seems to me the only way you can assure that the client's rights are fully protected in that matter is to tell the client to get independent counsel . . . .

When Gochis asked Hiestand about the meaning of Section 6146, Harney objected: "I am the one on trial here, not this witness. How in the heck can he possibly indict me because of his expectations when he was a lobbyist for the bill." Hirschberg chimed in: "Are we going to have any fairness?" Harney concurred: "this is supposed to be a proceeding that has due process. If I am going to be charged after 40 years of law practice with a violation of state law because of his expectations or interpretations, there is no due process." After initially upholding the objection, the referee allowed the question.

HIESTAND: In drafting legislation, it is well known that if they want mandatory effect, you chose words such as "shall." If you want discretionary effect to it, you use "may." When drafting that section, it is my recollection that we made it clearly mandatory. Because early versions of the bill . . . contain language regarding possible waiver. But those versions were struck in the legislative process . . . . I filed an amicus brief in the Third District Court of Appeal and in the Supreme Court on behalf of a bipartisan group of legislative offices and members of both houses of the legislature. . . . .The legislators who had enacted it felt that—even some of them who didn't like it—

Harney: I would object to what some legislators felt as hearsay as conclusionary [*sic*] and to let that type of evidence come in to this proceeding is totally unfair and a denial of equal protection and due process.

[The referee overruled his objection.]

GOCHIS: Given the existence of *Roa*, what, if any obligation do you think that an attorney had after it was decided with regard to section 6146 . . . .

HARNEY: I object to that. I am accused of some conduct in 1980. *Roa* was not decided until 1985 . . . . I would like to have some due process rights here . . . .

[The referee overruled his objection.]

HARNEY: May I have the basis of that please . . . .

REFEREE: You are being charged with the statements in the NTSC.

HARNEY: It has nothing to do with . . . any other time after 1980 . . . .

GOCHIS: As you may remember even Mr. Gert Hirschberg has been asking his own witnesses about *Roa* versus *Lodi*.

HARNEY: I don't care what Mr. Gert Hirschberg has been doing . . . .

[The referee persisted in overruling the objection.]

HIESTAND: . . . [T]he obligation would be to inform the client that . . . even if the parents had voluntarily wanted to give the lawyer a greater amount of money . . . they would not be permitted to do so under the law . . . .

HARNEY: I move to strike . . . if he can overrule the Supreme Court then, I think, your honor, then I should be excused from further participation in these proceedings because I am not getting any due process whatsoever. . . . There has never been any case, any rule in the history of the State of California that David M. Harney was required after *Roa* to go back to any client and say now because of *Roa*, I am going to rebate a part of the fee. . . . To have Mr. Hiestand, who is totally connected with the organization that promoted and sponsored and kept up all of the efforts to keep these repressive measures in effect to come in here to testify against me . . . is just absolutely not fair.

REFEREE: . . . [T]he final interpretation of [Roa] will rest with me.

HARNEY: You do not need him to do that. You can read.

REFEREE: That's true, but I would like to get his opinion.

HARNEY: Can you get it privately because we do not need it in a public record. This is my life, my reputation in this case. I do not want his opinion in my record.

After the referee overruled Harney's objection, Hiestand testified that "statutes are presumed constitutional" and Section 6146 was never invalidated. In response to the Koskoffs' 1985 letter, Harney "should have either refunded the difference or offered to arbitrate the matter pursuant to the . . . local bar rules."

On cross-examination, Hiestand said he had worked for the legislature on MICRA from 1973 to 1977 and then for California Tort Reform, less than 15 percent of whose budget came from insurers.

HARNEY: You are supposed to be a very brilliant lawyer . . . .[Y]ou have been called that by your clients who were the sponsors of MICRA and the continuation thereof. . . . You do not know if the figure expended for the lobbying of MICRA was 109 million dollars? . . . [T]he proponents of MICRA among other things mobilized doctors' wives, had them leave their mink coats at home and go up to the Governor's office in Sacramento and camp out in the Governor's office, correct?

In response to Gochis's objection, Harney said his question was intended to expose "bias."

HARNEY: I mean, he is obviously the man behind the State Bar proceeding against David M. Harney. Some group of insurance companies who are out to get David M. Harney. This is a vendetta and I am entitled to bring this out.

[The referee overruled the objection.]

HIESTAND: The doctors' wives did demonstrate in the Governor's office, yes.

HARNEY: Many came from Beverly Hills, correct?

HIESTAND: We took no poll as to where they came from, but it would not surprise me that there were some from Beverly Hills.

They quibbled about whether there were hundreds or less than a hundred.

HARNEY: Incidentally, at the time that Governor Brown . . . signed MICRA in 1975, there was a marginal note there made by his Secretary of Consumer Affairs that the section was unconstitutional.

Hiestand answered yes; after Gochis successfully moved to strike, Harney asked it again.

REFEREE: What is the relevance to the charges against you?

HARNEY: The person happened to be Chief Justice Rose Bird. In 1975 [she] put the note . . . that law was unconstitutional . . . and in 1988, 13 years later, I am being prosecuted by the State Bar for violating that which was held to be unconstitutional in 1975 . . . .

HIESTAND: . . . It was her opinion, yes, that she felt it was unconstitutional. It was the opinion that was in her dissent in all of the MICRA cases . . . .

HARNEY: Isn't it also true that the Governor, who signed the MICRA bill . . . said that the law was unconstitutional? He was only signing it to get the doctors and their wives off of his back . . . .

HIESTAND: I never heard him say any such thing and I had many conversations with him about its constitutionality . . . .

HARNEY: How much are you being paid to be here?

HIESTAND: I was paid for my time by the State Bar, and I believe that came to about $1500.

Harney argued that when MICRA was amended to increase attorneys' fees in 1987, "everybody . . . said that the whole purpose of 6146 by those who lobbied for it, who got it passed, was to keep the good lawyers out of the big cases." Hiestand attributed the amendment to an "overall compromise." When Gochis objected to this line of questioning, Harney explained that

> the original law was perceived to be totally unconstitutional, because it was intended for one and only one purpose, and that was to force lawyers who were not competent to take medical malpractice cases and settle them out cheaply . . . 24 witnesses have all testified that everybody in the legal and judicial community thought this was unconstitutional. It was a very aberrational thing that the Supreme Court in 1975 [*sic*—1985] in a four to three decision authored by a certain justice, said it was constitutional.

The referee thought that Hiestand's participation in negotiating the 1987 amendment "would show partiality to attorneys rather than bias" against them.

Harney: The question now before the house is whether or not the increase in fees were [sic] due to the fact that there had been a tremendous outrage about the restriction of fees that kept confident lawyers out of the plaintiff's field in medical malpractice cases.

HIESTAND: . . . [A] strong segment of the bar felt that was a factor, but there were many other factors that went into that compromise legislation . . ..

HARNEY: How were you contacted in this case? How did you happen to show up here from Sacramento? Was there an ad in the paper for you? . . . [D]id [Gochis] tell you that David M. Harney was involved? . . .

HIESTAND: Well, after we discussed it as a sort of hypothetical, at the end of the matter, she said, "now I am going to tell you the name of the person who was involved." . . . I told her that I knew you. I respected you. I thought you were wrong in this instance . . ..

Harney asked about waiver.

HIESTAND: I did not think a waiver was something that was allowed for in the legislation . . . because this was an issue that came up and was debated . . . that since it was a public policy type of measure, that it was not waiveable. It was like a minimum wage or worker's compensation benefits . . ..

HARNEY: What do you think the evidence in this case is? Namely, the child and his parents received a net of $750,000 out of a $1 million policy . . . . [A]nd you're critical of me for handling that case?

After the referee sustained the objection Harney repeated the question.

HIESTAND: The law . . . seemed to me very clear on what 6146 regulates . . .. I was quite surprised when I read Judge Baffa's deposition. It seemed to me that they routinely ignored Section 6146 . . ..

HARNEY: [listed all the people who testified in his behalf] Does that change your opinion in the slightest? . . . Do you pretend to be some kind of a judicial authority? . . . Have you reported Judge Baffa to the Commission on Judicial Qualifications because of his violation of the law?

Gochis's objection was sustained. When Harney tried to get Hiestand to agree that an hourly fee could be contingent, Gochis's objection was sustained.

HARNEY: I thought that they were trying to disbar me because I illegally contracted for a contingent fee. I suppose I could have had these people agree to pay me $500 an hour which would have exceeded $250,000. . . . Now were you aware of the fact that this father, lawyer, and mother, daughter of a doctor, shopped this case around Los Angeles? . . . [W]ouldn't you assume that one of those shopees would have said something about 6146? [Objection] Do you know whether or not it was any kind of practice in 1980 for lawyers in the medical malpractice field to advise prospective clients about the provisions of Business and Professions Code Section 6146?

HIESTAND: Different lawyers were undertaking different approaches with it. Some were asking for waivers, some were saying they wouldn't do it because of 6146. Some were saying that they would have an agreement and if 6146 was later found to be unconstitutional, then they could get paid pursuant to their agreement.

HARNEY: In American Bank number one, all of MICRA was found to be unconstitutional . . . because there was no foundation ever established that there was, in fact, a crisis situation.

HIESTAND: There was a feeling that the rationale of that opinion . . . would apply to the other provisions of MICRA, even though I don't think he did say in his opinion that the whole act was unconstitutional.

HARNEY: Actually in American Bank number two . . . the trial court was again affirmed . . ..

HIESTAND: They affirmed the holding of the decision of the trial court but they reversed the reasoning of the first opinion and found [MICRA] did withstand constitutional scrutiny.

HARNEY: Well, you know, you cannot reverse reasoning, you can only reverse the lower court . . .. I am testing this witness as to his legal knowledge on cross and I think it is apparent that he doesn't understand the appellate process . . .. Isn't it true that in American Bank number two, the Supreme Court affirmed the order of the trial court denying the application of periodic payments under the Keene bill?

HIESTAND: Yes, that is correct. At that point the plaintiff had died. They said nothing would be served by periodic payments . . ..

HARNEY: Do you recall that there were some four United States Supreme Court Justices who wanted to take over [*Roa*]?

HIESTAND: Yeah, but if you don't have five, you don't have anything . . ..

HARNEY: Do you know who is behind the filing of the complaint against me in this proceeding?

HIESTAND: I assumed it was your former clients.

HARNEY: Do not assume.

Harney's motion to strike Hiestand's direct testimony was denied.

Thomas A. Girardi (who also testified for Greene) practiced and taught medical malpractice law and was "a close confidante of Governor Brown's."

> [T]he physicians were on strike. The special session of Governor Brown felt it was necessary to do something about the fact that Travelers [Insurance Co.] had dramatically raised their rates and there were negotiations that were taking place in an attempt to get the physicians to go back to work . . . . [O]n the one hand, the Keene bill was so anti-consumer that it was not in the Brown protocol of bills that they wanted passed . . . . On the other hand, as a matter of expediency, Brown had these physicians that were meeting 20 at a time in his chambers. . . . [Brown] formed the opinion, as related to me, that "the bill is unconstitutional anyway so let's sign it even though it is against the things that I think are appropriate . . . and get the physicians back to work." . . . [T]hereafter at every fundraising event he would be questioned as to why he would sign such a bill and he made no bones about it; that obviously some bill that comes down on the heads of a seriously injured malpractice victim and singles him out to bear the brunt of being unable to receive compensation has no way to pass constitutional muster . . . . [T]here was not one insurance company to my knowledge, there is not one trial judge or appellate judge, there is not one medical malpractice defense lawyer, and there was not one medical malpractice plaintiff's lawyer that felt that the bill was constitutional . . . .[T]he insurance companies . . . refused to lower their rates after MICRA came in because they publicly acknowledged that it probably would not pass the constitutional

> muster . . .. [T]he first opinion I saw was from Judge Schifferman, who quite frankly is considered by all attorneys as one of the brightest judges on the bench. He is a constitutional scholar. He is a man of great depth of thought. He . . . not only held that the bill was unconstitutional . . . but that opinion . . . was then sent out . . . to all of the Superior Court judges . . .. The judges in Torrance to a person . . . all were of the view that the bill was unconstitutional and communicated that in various settlement conferences with lawyers. The federal court also soon came down with a decision that the bill was unconstitutional.

Travelers "had to pay some $350 million for misrepresenting what would happen if they got MICRA passed." Harney's handling of the case "was totally appropriate." He was "one of, if not the finest . . . trial lawyer, but is also considered among the bar to be the most ethical lawyer who practices." "[T]here is no way that MICRA could have applied to this case." Girardi did not know why Harney would speak to the Koskoffs about Section 6146 "for a 1974 cause of action." When Gochis said Harney had not raised this defense, Girardi retorted: "Well, then maybe he is not as good of a lawyer as I thought he was." When Gochis said Girardi was talking about the damage cap rather than fee limits, the witness sidestepped: "I think the whole MICRA section is a rape and pillage by the insurance companies of badly injured people." "The law didn't go into effect . . .. No one upheld it. They finally on a four to three decision of the court the rulings were changed. Then we were all told we were wrong."

Henry W. Shatford practiced for twenty-seven years before serving another ten on the bench. When Gochis objected to his calling her "young lady," noting "I am also a counsel of the State Bar," Shatford retorted: "I am also a judge who is called here as a witness." "[A]ll the judges that I talked to thought that was unconstitutional." "I was aghast when it was sustained. I still am." It was "very clear" that this "is not a contingency fee contract." Harney's $1 million settlement was "almost unbelievable;" the average practitioner would have gotten $50,000 or $100,000. Shatford had "no idea" how a court could disregard Judge Baffa's order: "I would throw a motion like that out of my court in a New York minute." Asked by Harney whether Judge Lachs "has any special jurisdiction to overrule and reverse Judge Baffa," Shatford exclaimed: "I have never heard of such a thing in my forty-two years in the law business."

Anthony Murray, a medical malpractice specialist and former State Bar president, testified that "the overwhelming majority of lawyers and judges believed that the law was unconstitutional." Harney committed no "impropriety." When Hirschberg tried to introduce Harney's book, the referee declared it irrelevant to culpability. Hirschberg replied that it "has something to do with whether or not he rendered reasonable services." Harney had just advised him "there was testimony by Judge Baffa that because of his reputation he got the million dollars." When the referee admitted the book, Harney asked to substitute another copy because this one was dedicated to his wife. He read the inscription: "January 25, 1974, to my beloved wife, Evelyn, the inspiration for it all. Love, Dave."

Gochis recalled Martha Koskoff, over Hirschberg's objection that she had not responded to the subpoena for her deposition. Koskoff laid the foundation to introduce *another* retainer, identical to the one signed by Harney but also containing signatures of her and her husband.[71] This had been filed by Harney's associate Thomas Kallay in the Superior Court writ of mandate petition seeking review of the contract claim. Harney objected: "it's obvious to me that sometime at or about the time of the filing of the civil action, six years after the settlement of the matter, those signatures were added." Overruling the objection, the referee asked when she had signed it.

MRS. KOSKOFF: We signed it in Mr. Harney's office when he produced the second document I have [with his signature but not theirs]. I have never seen them since except the day of the trial. And this is not the exact document that I have. This is different—this comes from a different original, because there is a mistake here in the word "personally," and my document doesn't have that. This is a second original. So obviously what happened was that Mr. Harney made two originals, he kept one, and he gave me one.

HARNEY: [moved to strike] And if you allow this in, I mean, it's real denial of due process . . . .[T]his lady [Gochis], if she keeps interrupting, is denying me due process . . . .[T]hese people filed a civil action against me. They have produced now a document which they have added their signatures to. There is no question about it . . . . [A transcript] will show that this woman last week testified under oath that she never signed the agreement, never . . . .

HIRSCHBERG: There has been a rather cantankerous attorney representing . . . the Koskoffs. He served upon us discovery motions time after time after time. He served upon us motions for summary judgment. Your honor, in connection with these motions, he filed alleged exhibits. The document that she is trying to get in right now was copied by our office as having come from her attorney . . . .

Harney began cross-examination.

GOCHIS: Could I ask Mr. Harney not to stand so close to the witness, thereby intimidating her?

HARNEY: Are you intimidated? Are you?

MRS. KOSKOFF: I would prefer that you stood farther away, but I am not intimidated.

HARNEY: Thank you. May I stand where I am?

REFEREE: I would prefer you stand in front of the witness, Mr. Harney.

---

71. State Bar Exhibit 15.

HARNEY: And have this [exhibit] over my head? How do you want me to handle this, I mean, seriously.

Mrs. Koskoff insisted that "prior to 1985 I've seen this agreement . . . once in my life . . . in May 1980." But she could not recall signing it then or be certain that someone had not "transposed" her name. Asked by the Referee whether she would have complained to the State Bar if Harney had negotiated a refund of his fees, she said yes, "because I feel what Mr. Harney did was unethical, it was unlawful, and it speaks to a larger question . . . ."

Hirschberg stepped out of his role as counsel to testify that in 1980–83 he had been on the State Bar Board of Governors (BoG or the Board) Committee on Adjudication and Discipline, which was

> actually the governing board over the State Bar Court and the Office of Trial Counsel. And the issue came up whether trial counsel, Ms. Lily Barry's office, should file MICRA violations, because there were lots of MICRA violations: the 90-day provision, the attorney's fees provisions, and I remember specifically that we . . . instructed Lily Barry and the OTC to put all alleged MICRA violations on the back burner and not proceed with them . . . until the constitutionality had been established.

The State Bar itself found a MICRA section unconstitutional and dismissed a disciplinary complaint against Gary Paul for violating it.[72]

Hirschberg had "searched specifically for a retainer agreement . . . signed by the Koskoffs, and I found none." Mallen, their lawyer,

> papers our office with motions . . . . [and] is the type of man who attacks you personally and threatens you with violence . . . . [A]ttached to these many, many papers which he serves . . . were exhibits. And I am almost positive that one of the exhibits was the purported agreement which you put into evidence this morning . . . . [A]nd what Mr. Kallay . . . did, I think, is he Xeroxed one of the appendixes to one of these motions when he filed the writ of mandate in the Superior Court.

When Gochis said the only agreement Mallen attached to his summary judgment motion was unsigned, Hirschberg told her to check "the many discovery

---

72. Matter of Paul, L.A. No. 2957 (July 13, 1979), Respondent's Exhibit J. Paul had refused to file the 90-day notice of intent upon the defendant doctors as required by Code of Civil Procedure §§364-65, solely for the purpose of challenging its constitutionality. The action caused no damage. The State Bar also sought such review. The Disciplinary Board found the disputed sections unconstitutional.

> Section 365 was an apparent political attempt by the Legislature to appease the medical profession by punishing lawyers who were blamed by the doctors as the cause of the medical malpractice "crisis." There is no rational basis for disciplining lawyers to please doctors. Section 365 also violates the Equal Protection Clauses of the United States and California Constitutions.
>
> The Board concluded that Paul's violation did not constitute moral turpitude.

motions he made." Asked by Harney about his reputation, Hirschberg replied: "Well, it may be self-serving hearsay, but I think you are the greatest." He had not planned to testify until Gochis recalled Martha Koskoff.

Ellis J. Horvitz, who had taken "a very active role in defending the validity of the statute" on behalf of the Truckers Insurance Association and the California Hospital Association, said that until *American Bank II*, "there was a very substantial body of opinion, both bench and bar, that MICRA was unconstitutional," which persisted until *Roa*. After he agreed that one of the open questions was how Section 6146 applied to multiple plaintiffs, Gochis offered to prove that Harney never amended the retainer to make the Koskoffs his clients.

HIRSCHBERG: Counsel is confusing clients with plaintiffs. The older Koskoffs were not plaintiffs in the lawsuit; they sure in the world were clients of the office; and they sure as heck were recipients of $125,000 each, which they didn't deserve . . . .

After argument about whether a written retainer was required, Harney declared himself "really appalled" by Gochis's "bald statements" and "misrepresentations." She successfully moved to strike. Horvitz agreed that Section 6146 applied to the hypothetical facts of this case but added that "the defense and health care community were having a great deal of trouble getting the trial judges around the state to apply MICRA." Harney withdrew a question in response to Gochis's objection but sneered: "I wish this attorney would learn how to make a proper legal objection. And I haven't heard one yet. She makes speeches."

Hirschberg led Harney, the next to last witness, through his lengthy list of accomplishments: dean, board member, and president of the International Academy of Trial Lawyers, "probably the most prestigious group of trial lawyers in the world. It's limited in its members to 500 U.S. trial lawyers;" president of the Los Angeles chapter of the American Board of Trial Attorneys (ABOTA); and described as "a top trial lawyer in Los Angeles County" in *The Trial Lawyers*. Hirschberg called Harney "one of the great trial lawyers of our time," who had invested more than 1,000 hours in the Koskoff case. He sought to introduce the Paul disciplinary case because "we have his perception of unconstitutionality. That's the most relevant thing in this lawsuit." This effort ended in acrimony.

HIRSCHBERG: I can't think, Mr. Referee, of anything more relevant than this man testifying that he knew that there was a finding of unconstitutionality by the State Bar Court, the very tribunal that is trying to crucify him today.

GOCHIS: . . . [I]f his position is that the only reason he didn't discuss 6146 with his clients is because the State Bar wouldn't get him, then that's an interesting thought, but it's not relevant to the issues of this hearing.

HARNEY: Your honor . . . she made a false statement.

REFEREE: But you are a witness at the moment, Mr. Harney.

HARNEY: Well, it just shows malice on her part and the part of the State Bar.

HIRSCHBERG: She is dead wrong. We know that.

Bernard S. Jefferson, who had practiced for 25 years and been a judge for almost 30, said "a large number of judges and lawyers felt that that statute was unconstitutional." Harney behaved as a "competent and honest lawyer," exhibiting "the highest ideals of our profession." His fee "is a modest one under the circumstances." "[S]ince I consider the statute unconstitutional, I would say it would have no application," although he conceded that in 1980 "there had been no decision saying it was unconstitutional." It would have been "my responsibility, as a trial judge, if I felt that a statute is unconstitutional, to make the first decision." It made no difference "that Judge Baffa did not discuss Section 6146 anywhere in his decision" because "there is no necessity for a trial judge to indicate why he is doing something." Jefferson was "sure [Baffa] was aware of the statute" and "thought it was unconstitutional." But "I don't think he owes a duty to say to the lawyer's client, 'well, now look, you should know that there is this section that has limitations.'" And if the lawyer "feels the statute is unconstitutional, I don't think he has an obligation to discuss that with the client."

JEFFERSON: The client agrees that . . . this is a legitimate fee and raises no objection to it . . . .

GOCHIS: Your Honor, how can a client make an informed decision about what fees are fair to him or her if he is not told about the law that affects that fee? . . .

JEFFERSON: . . . [I]n the tort field, I think most people realize that they are going to have to pay on a contingent fee . . . the client can say, "well, no, I think it's too high" and go shopping and go elsewhere.

GOCHIS: I don't know that you answered my question . . . . [I]f there is a statute on the books . . . that said that there is a limitation to what you can collect, are you not, as an attorney, under an obligation to inform your clients of it?

JEFFERSON: No, I don't think so, if you feel that statute is unconstitutional.

The State Bar's opening brief on culpability, filed January 20, 1989, said Harney could have challenged the constitutionality of Section 6146 before Judge Baffa, but "it was simply ignored." Harney's claim to have been following a court order "hides behind Judge Baffa and evades responsibility." Judge Jefferson's assertion that a lawyer has no "obligation to inform a client of a statute affecting their relationship if the lawyer thinks it is unconstitutional . . . borders on the absurd. It certainly may justify the public's low opinion of lawyers." On February 6, the OTC moved to reopen in light of a Court of Appeal decision against Harney,[73] holding Section 6146 not waivable and declaring:

---

73. Fineberg v. Harney & Moore, 207 Cal.App.3d 1049, 255 Cal.Rptr.299 (2nd Dist. 1989).

> Implicit in the testimony of both David Harney and his expert is their assumption either that no lawyer would undertake representation of medical malpractice plaintiffs under the statutory fee limitation, or that lawyers engaged in that practice would lower the standard of responsibility afforded medical malpractice clients because of the fee limitation. The first of these assumptions is purely speculative; the second assumes a willingness on the part of medical malpractice lawyers, as a group, to violate their duty to their clients. We reject both assumptions . . ..

Hirschberg began his brief by noting that "the author . . . is not a stranger to the State Bar Court."

> [T]here has not been a more flagrant and outrageous crucifixion of a respectable member of the Bar community. From the mere fact that Mr. Hiestand, chief lobbyist and counsel for the CMA disclosed . . . this case is a vendetta brought by the CMA, the so called Tort Insurance Reform Group and others to harass Mr. Harney. . . . The purpose was to knock out Mr. Harney and the few other outstanding medical malpractice lawyers in order to effectuate the sinister purposes of MICRA . . .. [T]here was selectivity in choosing Mr. Harney . . . . State Bar counsel's blatant accusation of stupidity leveled at the testimony of Justice Jefferson is unfortunate, and just another indication that her hyperbole in seeking to repress the true reason why this is a sham proceeding which should have never been brought in view of the court order, waiver, and lack of willfulness. Justice Jefferson is perhaps the most respected jurist in California. He sports a Phi Beta Kappa key around his vest, managed to go to Harvard at a time when Harvard was not exactly open to students of his race, had a distinguished career on the Superior Court and Court of Appeal, and authored probably the most noteworthy treatise on evidence which can be found on the bookshelves of the Bar and the Judiciary. He is now a professor and president of a distinguished law school.

MICRA's "effectiveness" "had not been established until *Roa* came around in 1985." "It attacks credulity to say that Mr. Koskoff did not know of the provisions of MICRA and therefore did not waive them. Further, Richard Koskoff owed a triple fiduciary duty to the youngster from whom he stole $125,000." The Koskoffs' civil action seeking to recover the excess fee from Harney "makes the rigorous assistance in this State Bar proceeding suspect." The "testimony and behavior pattern of the Koskoffs were not exemplary. They were not straightfoward. They were greedy, and in the case of Richard Koskoff, his conduct did not rise to the level which is expected of an attorney and father." The State Bar allegation that many of Harney's witnesses "were mostly unfamiliar with the facts is a bold-faced [*sic*] falsehood for the making of which, State Bar counsel should be severely chastised." "[O]ut of greed," the Koskoffs "each collected $125,000 in anticipation of a future wrongful death, which never happened." If Harney were disciplined it would be "for receiving a fee pursuant to a lawful and final court order. What absurdity." The *Fineberg* decision had no effect on Harney's defense of waiver. "This is a disciplinary matter, not a civil suit."

Gochis declined to "address any vituperative [*sic*] aimed at the State Bar or its examiner." What Harney did when the Koskoffs asked about Section 6146 after *Roa* "is the proper subject of inquiry."

2. Penalty After notifying both sides that he had found liability, the referee began a mitigation hearing in April 1989. Hirschberg submitted ninety-one letters, called Harney the victim of "trumped-up charges" in a proceeding that "borders on the frivolous," and repeated all his allegations.[74] In addition to the usual character testimonials (one by California Attorney General John K. Van de Kamp),[75] many witnesses followed Hirschberg in relitigating guilt. Judge Manuel Real denounced the "unfounded charges." Reid Bridges found it "hard to accept that even the most preternaturally biased examiner could doubt [Harney's] honesty, integrity and devotion to his clients." G. Dana Hobart hoped the investigation was "not because our dues have been raised and you have a surplus of funds." Charges based on a MICRA violation were "simply an outrage." Stephen A. Kolodny agreed that "the investment of State Bar time in matters such as this" was "a misuse of the system and a terrible waste of valuable resources."

Hirschberg's mitigation brief again boasted of his "familiar[ity] with the State Bar disciplinary process." The culpability finding "was entirely erroneous." Any violation was "technical in nature, thus calling for no discipline." The Referee should "take judicial notice" that before *Roa* "fees varied between 40 and 50 percent." Since a court had approved the fees, the penalty should be an admonition. Harney showed his disdain for the proceeding by not appearing at the hearing. Hirschberg was even more contemptuous.

Hirschberg: I am now walking out of here because I think you have completely misunderstood everything in this particular case. I am taking my chances in the Review Department.

I don't know if you have ever tried a lawsuit in your life or not. We did check on you. You don't have an office. You are not listed in *Parker's Directory*. I think you have completely misunderstood this case. With that I am going out.

REFEREE: For the record, I do have the exhibits, two copies that you sent me.

GOCHIS: Before counsel walks out, I'm not sure whether counsel is offering any of this documentation into evidence. Again, if he is, it is really unnecessary since it's already in evidence.

---

74. Respondent's Exhibit F.

75. Respondent's Exhibit K.

As to the appropriateness of his arguing this case while walking out the door, I would submit this brief should not be allowed into the record since Mr. Gert Hirschberg insists on walking out and essentially is withdrawing as counsel of this situation.

HIRSCHBERG: As usual she is wrong. A brief is a brief. It is not evidence. I have filed it with you. It contains my allegations. It contains our position. If you don't consider it you won't be any different than the way you acted throughout these proceedings. We have evidence before you. We had the most outstanding people in California and the legal profession. You paid no attention to them whatsoever. If you pay no attention to this particular brief I cannot help it. I will have to take my chances before the Review Department, or if necessary before the Supreme Court of California.

GOCHIS: I have to reiterate, the method by which Mr. Gert Hirschberg is arguing his case is inappropriate to these proceedings and I would again point that out for the record.

HIRSCHBERG: Miss Gochis thinks by repeating herself she can make a point. Madam reporter, I would like a copy of today's transcript.

REFEREE: The record will show that Mr. Gert Hirschberg has left the hearing room. The hearing will proceed in his absence. Miss Gochis, do you have anything you wish to say in mitigation.

GOCHIS: I have nothing in aggravation, per se. I do, however, have some argument with regard to case law and with regard to the effects of respondent's contempt in these proceedings and its effect on any discipline that might be appropriate in this case.

The referee put in evidence the Supreme Court's January 4 denial of a writ of mandate to review the Koskoffs' successful contract action against Harney[76] and took judicial notice of the Court of Appeal judgment in Fineberg v. Harney.

Gochis argued about penalty.

> The respondent took unilateral action to circumvent a statute which was not complicated, certainly plain and which was applicable to the Koskoff case.
>
> ... The respondent has chosen for whatever reason to present no mitigation. He is expressing an opinion with regard to the State Bar proceedings ....
>
> This action is aggravation. His contemptuous attitude toward these proceedings, toward his need to mitigate is lack of appreciate [*sic*] or insight into the wrongfulness of what he has done, is aggravation.

---

76. State Bar Exhibit 17.

> We have a man here who is an exceedingly good attorney, who is famous, with a good reputation and is a prime attorney in the medical malpractice area. It is submitted that he has offered as a defense of culpability his reputation and his primacy in medical malpractice as a shield to discipline.
>
> Given his fame . . . his clients had . . . a right to expect better of him, they who relied on his talent . . . a petitioner's stubborn refusal to acknowledge the impropriety of his actions make [*sic*] it difficult to feel confident that he will conform his conduct to the required high professional standards in the future . . . .We have an attorney who . . . is stubbornly saying it's okay for what I did . . . .

She divided the ninety-one letters into three categories: those that did "not express any knowledge of what happened in this particular case," those that "very honestly" expressed "limited knowledge," and those that "indicate that the person has been told something." Those in the first two deserved no weight, and those in the third merited little because they "argumentatively provided the facts of the case and . . . leave the State Bar without any ability to cross-examine as to the knowledge or understanding of the witness." Arguing that Standard 2.7 required a minimum of six months suspension for willfully entering an agreement to charge or collect an unconscionable fee, harming Brendan Koskoff, she sought two years suspension stayed, and three months actual. Harney should repay his unlawful fee, submit future retainer agreements to the OTC for review, certify compliance with Section 6146 in any future medical malpractice matter, and bring any fee agreements involving minors to the judge's attention.

The referee began his decision by noting that Hirschberg had "immediately exited the hearing room" in the penalty phase. Harney's fee was contingent because it "was clearly based upon the eventual outcome of the case." Harney's amicus brief in *Roa* declared that his "law practice is based strictly upon contingent fee agreements . . . some of which are subject to court approval, if there is a minor or incompetent."[77] His own exhibit in this case affirmed that he "works on a contingent fee basis."

> An impressive cadre of Judges (4 Superior Court, 4 Circuit Courts of Appeal, 3 Federal, 2 temporary members of the California Supreme Court), and prominent attorneys (2 past State Bar Presidents and one former State Bar vice-President) all testified that during the period from 1975 . . . to 1985 [when *Roa* found it constitutional] . . . the general perception among those members of the legal community involved in medical malpractice litigation and the judiciary, was that Section 6146 was unconstitutional.

Harney submitted letters to that effect from judges on eighteen Superior Courts, four California Courts of Appeal, one U.S. Court of Appeal, and one Municipal Court, as well as dozens "from equally eminent individuals." Even after

77. State Bar Exhibit 8.

Roa, some Superior Court judges willfully disregarded Section 6146 because they still believed it unconstitutional, "thus violating the legal principle of *res judicata*," and they disseminated those views "by discussions among themselves, at luncheons and other gatherings attended by members of the legal community."

> Because the Respondent and other trial attorneys specializing in medical malpractice litigation are constantly exposed to the proclivities of these judges, their own relations with their clients are governed by the known views of the judges before whom they appear . . . .[T]he fault lies . . . also with those judges who persist in ignoring the statute and openly encourage attorneys to ignore it, despite the fact that it is a valid, enforceable statute.
>
> Some responsibility also rests upon those members of the Board of Governors of the State Bar who decided, shortly after 1975, that State Bar Court disciplinary cases involving violations of Section 6146 . . . should be "placed on the back burner" and not enforced.

Finding no moral turpitude, the referee recommended two years suspension, stayed, and probation on condition that Harney repay the excess fee plus interest and submit a compliant retainer to the OTC and Probate Court judge in minors' cases. The OTC recommendation that Harney pass the PRE was "an unnecessary affront to the numerous prominent and well-respected judges and attorneys who testified in his behalf or who wrote letters testifying to his integrity."

3. Review In his review brief Harney expressed even greater contempt for the referee.

> The purported findings and the recommendations of the Hearing Panel are an outrage. Words cannot more adequately express what took place than the conclusion of our closing brief . . . ["What an absurdity."] In four full days of heated hearings, compounded by innumerable judicial errors with respect to the admissibility of evidence, the State Bar brought in just two complaining witnesses and a non-percipient Dave Harney hater, attorney Herb Hiestand.

Since Hiestand was not an ethics expert, his "testimony must go out in toto." The "mere bringing of this matter was a political ploy, engineered by the CMA . . . ." Why were Harney's partners not charged?

> Why did the Bar spend thousands of dollars in obtaining a finding of discipline on exceedingly flimsy grounds when there are so many sleaze balls who go unpunished? With all the attorneys who charge unconscionable fees. . . . With all the conflict of interest cases around, with all the trust fund violations, with all the cappings . . . ? It is apparent that respondent, being perhaps the foremost malpractice lawyer in the country, was being selectively chosen (after Browne Greene) for a State Bar prosecution.

The Koskoffs "are tortiously chargeable with abuse of process." The requirement that Harney disclose future retainer agreements "seriously undermines and interferes with the attorney-client privilege, is unusually and unreasonably demeaning, and interferes with the client's right of privacy and violates the attorney-client relationship."

The Review Department found a contingent fee contract governed by Section 6146, even though the Koskoffs had not signed it. Although the State Bar had not proven that Harney "affirmatively misled his clients or the court" about the statute, Harney had not proven he informed the court or the Koskoffs about Section 6146 (or they knew about it). Although his fee was otherwise "fair and reasonable," it exceeded the limit even if Section 6146 applied to each claim individually. Until *Roa*, "a respected body of lawyers and judges held the good faith opinion" that Section 6146 "was unconstitutional and respondent honestly held that opinion himself." That "some Superior Court judges . . . still are wilfully [*sic*] ignoring section 6146" was mitigating. "Respondent has an otherwise well-deserved reputation for excellence." The Review Department found no moral turpitude. Ten judges voted for culpability and issued a public reprimand with the sole condition that Harney pass the PRE. One found a violation ofMICRA but would have remanded to the Referee to decide whether it was "*wilful* [*sic*]." One voted to dismiss, and two recused themselves.

Harney petitioned the Supreme Court for review in January 1990. The State Bar appeared to have closed this matter in 1986, only filing the NTSC two years later when the Koskoffs sued for the excess fee. Harney's reputation was "highly relevant" to culpability because it went to whether his violation of MICRA was "wilful [*sic*] and, equally important, it affects the weight to be afforded to his presumption of innocence." Harney questioned the "authorship" of the Referee's opinion, since Paule "stated ignorance of the entire 'MICRA' issue." The "legislature's omission of any reference to Section 6146" when it enacted Probate Code Section 3302, six years later, "evidences its intent that, in minor's [*sic*] cases, probate code Section 3302 *supersedes* Section 6146 (if Section 6146 ever did apply) . . . ." The "lack of a remedy . . . when application of Section 6146 results in a confiscatory fee, renders Section 6146 unconstitutional on its face" and "particularly" as applied in this case. The "so-called 'crisis' . . . underlying MICRA, cannot, fifteen years later, constitutionally permit Section 6146 to be used as a basis to impose discipline and punishment against Harney." The public reproval and PRE requirement "are designed only to cause [Harney] personal embarrassment."

> Recent history suggests that the membership . . . opposes any attempt by the State Bar to infuse itself into a *political* controversy such as this one, which caters to a "special interest" insurance industry/medical/hospital group. (Footnote: Can there be any question that the State Bar is engaging in purely political activity when it seeks a lobbyist for the CMA, Fred Hiestand, to testify against Harney?) The State Bar's actions in this case only tend to diminish the respect attorneys have for the State Bar.

Harney had "earned sufficient respect for his integrity that if this court tells him that he was wrong in his conduct, that Harney will not so conduct himself in the future."

Several months later he supplemented this petition. After arguing legalistically that the Review Department decision was "nothing other than 'minutes,'" he declared that the case turned on "a question of principle;" could a lawyer "be disciplined for collecting a fee which has been awarded by the Superior Court?" Who should "take the blame"? "[I]n a less than perfect world, honest men and women err and courts make mistakes but their errors and mistakes do not make them miscreants to be censured publicly." The State Bar had made an error after Harney filed this petition: "Such careless and even cavalier procedures are themselves open to censure." The reprimand was "indefensible" for an act of "overzealousness," which others had also committed. The State Bar responded that *Roa* painted "in graphic and florid details petitioner's improper conduct." Unlike the attorney in that case, Harney "chose to remain silent about MICRA and any agreement he had with the Koskoffs." "[A]lmost one full year before he settled the Koskoff matter, petitioner had changed his retainer agreements to reflect the provisions of MICRA. He had also included a provision requiring that clients waive MICRA . . . ." Harney could have shown his "good faith" by "advising the court and obtaining a ruling with respect to MICRA." The Supreme Court declined to review. Harney called the outcome "outrageous" because "a judge determined and awarded the fee. I'm getting reproved for not telling a lawyer what the law is when I did tell him and he knew." "I suppose emotionally it hurts, but I doubt that any friend or client will care."[78]

B. The *Paulis v. Harney* Case

While the Koskoff case was proceeding, the State Bar brought two more petitions against Harney in 1988 and 1990. Gochis and Hirschberg faced off again when these were consolidated in January 1991.[79] The OTC charged Harney with collecting a fee exceeding the Section 6146 limit, failing to inform Loretta Paulis about Sections 6146–47 or prepare a written retainer, misleading her into believing the court would set the fee, and failing to tell the court any of this. Loretta and her son William met Harney on December 30, 1986, and retained him the following February to sue Drs. Stanley Rouche and Johann Gritsch and St. Bernardine's Medical Center on behalf of Wendy Paulis, Loretta's adult daughter, who had been rendered permanently comatose by elective back surgery.[80] (By this time, the California Supreme Court had decided *Roa* and *Waters*, the Koskoffs had sued Harney for exceeding Section 6146, and the Court of Appeal had affirmed the Shepherds' excess fee claim against Greene.) The malpractice action was filed in March, and Loretta was appointed Wendy's conservator the next month. Harney settled the case for $3.45 million in July 1988 (by which time

78. Philip Carrizosa, *Reproval of Harney to Stand,* LADJ 9 (6.29.90).

79. The first seems to have been abandoned; the OTC pretrial statement and request for findings of fact and conclusions of law, Case No. 90-O-14277 (filed 5.1.91).

80. The OTC declared these facts undisputed.

the Review Department had affirmed Greene's culpability). Harney's office prepared the petition for compromise seeking a fee of $846,250 (25 percent), which Judge Turner approved that month. Although the judge knew about Section 6146, the probate policy manual limits were lower than MICRA's in most of the cases he handled. The OTC sought a year's suspension, stayed, and repayment of the excess fee ($257,000). Harney replied that Section 6146 was inapplicable and Judge Turner's approval was *res judicata;* and he accused the State Bar of selective prosecution.

Once again boasting he was "not a stranger to the State Bar Court," Hirschberg began his trial brief by denouncing "the most flagrant show of prosecutorial misconduct to hit the State Bar Court in its short history." Because Harney was "regarded as one of this nation's ten top trial lawyers, and as the top medical malpractice lawyer in the country," he "has naturally incurred the wrath of the California Medical Association, the California Hospital Association, and the Association for California Tort Reform . . . a powerful lobby of insurance carriers . . . ." The "State Bar at the urging of the medical and insurance lobby filed a disciplinary proceeding" against Harney in the Koskoff case.

Paulis hired C. Patrick Milligan to sue Harney for the excess fee. In his July 1990 deposition in that action, Harney explained the fee arrangement.[81]

> I didn't really propose anything. I was asked if there would be a fee that would be needed in advance, and I said that there would be no fee agreement whatsoever. The fee, if, as and when there would be a fee, would be determined by the Superior Court in San Bernardino County. I said that if there was no successful result, there would be no request for any fee. If there was a successful result, then the Court would determine what the fee would be.

Asked when the Section 6146 fee limitation had been enacted, Harney countered: "I'm not aware that they've ever been enacted. If you're talking about a contingent fee agreement alleged limitation, unconstitutional as it is, it was 1975." He had been "an opponent of the so-called bought-up legislation ever since it was talked about." Asked if he had spent money to oppose it, he retorted: "I didn't pay any member of the legislation [*sic*], as the proponents paid something like $109 million to get their legislation passed." He never discussed Section 6146 with Loretta "since it was not applicable." Only "idiots" thought it applied. "I have, I think, 8,000 law books in the office, and I didn't go through all the law books with her." He did not see how the section "is going to protect anybody, including Wendy Paulis." His fee was "far less than that allowed by the Superior Court rules." Each time Milligan, asked if the case settled for $3.45 million, Harney replied that the "payout figure" was $19 million; he was entitled to a third, whereas "the so-called fee allowed by the judge was something like

81. State Bar Exhibit 9.

four percent." He had not told Paulis about fee limitations because "there were no limitations . . . as to this case at that time nor now." When Milligan noted that "a high attorney's fee would work to your advantage and a low attorney's fee would work to the advantage of Wendy Paulis," Harney bristled: "[D]on't you ask me questions about did I take advantage of somebody. By you suing me, you are taking advantage of me . . . ask an intelligible question." Harney did not remember telling anyone in the family about Section 6146, but "one of the members of the Paulis family said . . . the mother was directly contacted by Curt Jure [a former paralegal in Harney's firm], suggesting that . . . Loretta go to Mr. Milligan and sue Mr. Harney for an alleged overcharge." Harney ridiculed Milligan for asking whether he had told Judge Turner that he was requesting a fee more than a quarter of a million dollars higher than that authorized by Section 6146: "I don't recall discussing the Veterans Administration fee limitations or Workers' Compensation fee limitations. . . . I don't think I pulled the book off the shelf [containing Section 6146], along with all of the other thousands of books in the law library." He admitted trying to avoid the Section 6146 limitation by securing client waivers.

> In the case of a consenting competent adult . . . I thought then and I still think that that [*sic*] is proper for such a waiver to be accomplished. . . . I thought at the time of enactment and today that the law is unconstitutional . . . in spite of a four to three decision . . . to the contrary, in which case . . . some four justices of the United States Supreme Court voted to grant certiorari.

Asked if Loretta had participated in calculating his fee, Harney insisted she "completely, totally, and absolutely agreed with the content of the petition as typed and presented and signed. Gleefully. Gleefully . . . . She was so happy about what I had done." He admitted receiving the fee but insisted, "I did not collect it. I didn't, you know, hire a collection agency or anything like that." He had been sued for exceeding Section 6146 in two other cases: "a premises liability case where the person is trying to claim that since the premises were defective in a professional building that somehow or another MICRA applied" and "a Tarasoff type of case." Even if a court held that Section 6146 applied, he would not owe Loretta a refund. "I don't see how the Court can hold it," and in any case Section 6147 "says that if there is noncompliance with 6146, then the attorney is entitled to reasonable value of services," which would be a third of the $3.45 million judgment and "maybe" of the $19 million "payout."

> I heard that none of you gentlemen [in the San Bernardino bar] would handle this case and they had to go out of county and got me to, I think, attain a tremendous result. And then I get sued. Wonderful. Ingratitude.

After every local lawyer rejected the case because "there was absolutely no evidence of malpractice," Harney spent $90,000 to prove liability. He had encouraged Loretta to secure the appointment of a conservator, who alone was his client.

He obtained "a tremendous settlement" after several days of trial. Since then Loretta had died, prompting "a bitter dispute in the Paulis family" over who should be Wendy's guardian, which "may be motivated by the siblings' desire to obtain administrator's fees, encouraged by the attorney for the siblings."

Harney would offer "the percipient testimony of not one, but two experienced [State Bar] Trial Counsel . . . [who] were clearly sub silenti agents of the [California] Medical Association and insurance industry and/or acting in a capacity as collecting agents on behalf of . . . the Koskoffs and the Paulis family."

> Is the State Bar a collection agency? Were State Bar funds expanded [*sic*] in taking nearly two dozen depositions, by two experienced attorneys of the Office of Trial Counsel for an offense which the State Bar itself deemed not worthy of even a 30 day suspension? Does there surface a political motivation?

Paul Caruso, "who has no equals in the area of trial lawyers representing entertainment and sports figures," and was himself subjected to disciplinary charges (later dismissed), would testify that "the State Bar selects prominent, high-profile figures, in its effort to win legislative acceptance for other ulterior motives." Joseph Alioto, "a leading anti-trust lawyer in San Francisco and the former colorful Mayor," would testify that the purpose of his own disciplinary case was "not to punish miscreant attorneys, but to get high profile attention in the legislature and in the media." Assembly Speaker Willie Brown would testify that his "charges too were dropped for the same reasons." The former chief trial counsel, present assistant chief trial counsel, and trial attorney all "stonewalled" when Harney asked about selective prosecution. Harney had been "selected as a respondent from a galaxy of California attorneys simply for exercising his First Amendment rights, to wit challenging the constitutionality and wisdom of MICRA." He would "settle for nothing less than a complete vindication." Hirschberg declared that "nearly all facts are disputed," listed eighteen witnesses, and estimated that trial would take four weeks. He submitted most of the Koskoff hearing transcript.

The OTC brief said that even though Harney "believes section 6146 to be disastrous legislation," he was "bound to obey the law. In order to justify his knowing and deceitful non-compliance, Respondent has dumped before this court an array of straw men and a flood of red herrings in a vain attempt to avoid responsibility . . . ." His failure to apprise his client and the court of Section 6146 showed his lack of "a good faith belief of entitlement to the fee which he collected." His understanding with Loretta was "a quintessential fee agreement" and his present denial "disingenuous at best." His invocation of *res judicata* was "further proof" of "an ongoing pattern of deceit." Indeed, his argument that Loretta and Judge Turner approved the fee "totally prostitute the doctrine." All of this constituted moral turpitude.

State Bar Court Judge Christopher W. Smith conducted nine days of hearings in November and December 1992. Hirschberg's brief said Milligan was "the attorney . . . culpable of misconduct" through his "extortionary [*sic*] threat to make a complaint to the State Bar if respondent did not immediately pay money to Milligan." Hirschberg sought to reopen the hearing in order to introduce a clipping (attached) about "Milligan and Judge Turner in a different, equally controversial matter."[82] Hirschberg also accused Deputy Trial Counsel Ronald E. Magnuson (who replaced Gochis) of "falsely" maintaining that no California court had defined contingent fee and asked "whether the State Bar is even-handed enough to do to Mr. Magnusson [*sic*] what it has done to respondent."[83] The State Bar had failed to prove that either Dr. Rouche or Saint Bernardine's Hospital were "*licensed* health care professionals," a precondition of Section 6146's applicability. Although Harney's complaint in the medical malpractice action had alleged licensure, it was not in evidence, and "the unlicensed practice of medicine is not uncommon." The basis for calculating the Section 6146 fee limit was Wendy's estimated lifetime payout, which had now grown to $21.7 million. Harney did not violate Section 6147 because there was no contingency fee to reduce to writing. Under that section, the client could avoid the (nonexistent) contingency fee agreement and pay a reasonable fee.

> How could the State Bar assert that respondent's fee was excessive? Respondent took a case that no other attorney in San Bernardino would touch. The medical records were . . . "totally white washed" . . . [R]espondent testified that his in-house and outside costs exceeded $100,000. Then, in a case where there was no settlement offer . . . respondent commenced the trial and, after several days of trial, persuaded the doctors and hospital to settle . . . .

The "most egregious and offensive allegation" was that Harney "misled Judge Turner." It was "downright irresponsible for the State Bar to raise this allegation as a triable issue." Harney had "spent forty years establishing and maintaining his reputation as a top-level trial attorney." The State Bar had "abused its immunity" by making that "cavalier and inflammatory accusation," which revealed "actual malice." It wanted to "silence" him by prosecuting "ludicrous cases" and "will continue to prosecute him on one trumped up charge after another, until the State Bar is assured that respondent is silenced once and for all." "Procedural irregularities have abounded in this case," "The State Bar refused to comply with discovery" and attempted to "dodge its own irresponsible and contemptible misconduct." The court "took extraordinary amounts of time to make decisions on motions" and disregarded "an abundance of evidence supporting respondent's contention that

82. Tommy Li, *Victim says justice wasn't done,* San Bernardino Sun (11.15.92). Respondent's Exhibit J (attached as Respondent's Exhibit K). Delores S. Jones alleged that Milligan had settled her $81,000 claim before Judge Turner for $25,000. "I truly believe that my judge was bought off, my attorney was bought off." "There was a stigma that everybody who lived in that area was on welfare."

83. State Bar Exhibit 1.

section 6146 is unconstitutional." Harney's continuing challenge to "every possible provision of MICRA" is "clearly political speech." When "respondent has been unsuccessful in his challenges . . . [he] has abided by the Courts' judgments . . . ."

Magnuson replied that

> out of a miasma of inaccurate characterizations, shrewd misdirection, calculated disorganization, personal invective, creative omission, intemperate exaggeration, tedious repetition, vituperative labeling and inventive hyperbole, Respondent has conjured a specter from which he argues that the State Bar has failed to meet its burden of proof.

Harney's "phantom argument" of discriminatory prosecution failed to show that other Section 6146 violators were not being prosecuted. His contention that his fee was not contingent would render Section 6146 "meaningless" with respect to infants and persons of unsound mind. His claim that the fee should be based on lifetime payout "is founded upon the unsupported assumption that periodic payments . . . were ordered," which Harney himself had testified was not so. In 1985, the California Supreme Court held that an attorney who settled a medical malpractice claim joined with another claim "must specifically advise the client of the pros and cons of alternative litigation strategies, including potential attorney's fees, and obtain the client's consent . . . ."[84]

In May, Judge Smith reprimanded Hirschberg for "unfounded, disrespectful statements and accusations against this Court" and found Harney guilty of violating Section 6146, charging an illegal or unconscionable fee, and failing to pay funds to which the client was entitled.[85] Harney declared that Smith's "extraordinary and unjustified act" of taking judicial notice that the medical malpractice defendants were licensed showed "bias, clear and simple." Judge Smith dismissed these "impassioned allegations" as "preposterous and unfounded." Hirschberg retorted that the judicial notice contained "particularly objectionable" statements and created an "appearance of impropriety" since the court had denied Harney's motion to disqualify Smith for cause and rejected Harney's allegations of selective prosecution. Judge Smith dismissed all these contentions. Harney's decision to "lie behind the log" about licensure was not the "brilliant and effective trial strategy" he shamelessly proclaimed but "trial by ambush," prohibited by Rule 1222.

Hirschberg's brief on discipline relitigated every issue concerning culpability. The court had "tentatively, albeit erroneously, found that respondent violated section 6146." A "law which makes illegal the receipt of a reasonable fee for hard work performed, and excellent results obtained, is itself illegal." The court could only hold a violation of Section 6146 morally wrong if it found, "as did a politically-pressured legislature, that doctors' medical malpractice premiums are more

84. Waters v. Bourhis, 40 Cal.3d 438 (1985).
85. Former RPC Rules 2-107(A) and 4-100(B)(4).

important than catastrophically-injured medical malpractice victims' right to full compensation for their injuries." Wendy Paulis had not been harmed because she "has been in a coma at all relevant times and is not even aware of these proceedings." Harney would repay whatever a court finally ordered. The $257,000 excess might seem like "a great deal of money" to "most people, particularly civil servants" (like Smith), but it is "not so large" for Wendy, "who, at $18,000 per month, has enough money to pay for her medical care for the rest of her life." Harney's firm "frequently invests more than said sum [$257,000] in costs on a case."

Hirschberg lauded Harney for challenging "many powerful economic and political interests." He had been "instrumental" in taking the Chevrolet Corvair off the market in the 1960s and doing the same to the Ford Pinto in the 1970s.

> While cynics at the State Bar may say that respondent was well-paid for his legal services in cases he has handled, the fact is that if respondent were interested in maximizing his fees, he would not seek to have unsafe products removed from the market.

He "has turned into an art form the ability to uncover negligence, even in the face of 'doctored' medical records, and to convey the horror to the jury of the patient's permanent, past and future suffering." Harney planned to call Hirschberg to testify about his "reputation, his honesty and good faith, his public service and pro bono activities." One "form of pro bono or charitable work" was Harney's refusal to charge clients he rejected for medical records, "which usually cost several hundred dollars." Because violation of Section 6146 was at most *malum prohibitum*, civil liability was the only appropriate remedy. An "admonition" would be sufficient because the two offenses together warranted only the public reproval already imposed on Harney in the Koskoff case.

Magnuson's very short reply brief noted that Standard 2.7 recommended a six-month actual suspension, regardless of mitigating circumstances (which were absent). Harney had recently been publicly reprimanded for similar misconduct and refused to refund the Paulis fee even after the Koskoff discipline became final. Nevertheless, the OTC felt bound by its original recommendation: a stayed one-year suspension, restitution of the fee, completion of the Bar Ethics School, and passage of the MPRE. Harney again skipped the penalty hearing.

Judge Smith dismissed the charges that Harney had violated both a court order and his duty to "support the Constitution and laws of the United States, and of this state."[86] The OTC should have amended the NTSC when it orally withdrew these "fatally defective allegations," which were "unfair to respondents and a waste of judicial resources." He also dismissed charges of violations, postdating the rules, and rebuked the OTC for failing to number exhibits. But otherwise, he ruled against Harney. He rejected the claim that the attorney who had

86. BPC §§6068(a) and 6103.

sought Loretta's appointment as Wendy's conservator played a significant role in the settlement; Harney had prepared the petition for compromise and was Loretta's only lawyer. When Milligan sought a refund of the excess fee, Harney maintained he had not received a contingent fee but rather "the reasonable value of our services."[87] Milligan consulted San Bernardino Superior Court Judge Kramer about whether it would be proper to ask Judge Turner about the fee and was urged to do so and copy all documents to the San Bernardino police department and district attorney. Milligan then sent copies and a complaint to the State Bar at the suggestion of Detective Gary Salazar. Judge Smith found that "no one with the State Bar has ever solicited [Milligan] to file a complaint against respondent." Milligan also sued Harney for the excess.[88] After Loretta died in April 1989 or 1990, the San Bernardino Superior Court appointed her sister, Joy Mahaffey, as Wendy's conservator. When the other siblings objected, the court made Public Guardian Melody Scott conservator of the estate, leaving Joy conservator of the person. Scott urged Milligan to pursue vigorously the civil action for the excess fee, which was scheduled for trial in a month.

Judge Smith found that Judge Turner's 25 percent fee award was not "based on or equal to the reasonable value of respondent's services." Indeed, Judge Turner "never heard any evidence on the numerous factors that are considered when setting . . . a reasonable fee." Judge Turner had not considered Section 6146 because "the Paulis medical malpractice suit was the first case he ever handled in which San Bernardino County's general limits were not below the MICRA limits." The Supreme Court had decided in *Roa* that the Section 6146 limits "are, to a large extent, for the benefit of the injured plaintiffs;" the Court of Appeal had decided in *Hathaway* that "courts do not have the power to award attorney's fees in excess of the section 6146 limits."[89] The Court of Appeal held in a case involving Harney that Section 6146 was not waivable.[90] Judge Smith ruled that a contingent fee in the context of Section 6146 was "any fee agreement in which the payment of the attorney's fee is conditioned upon a recovery," whether it was a percentage of recovery or determined by the court. He rejected Harney's *res judicata* argument because "the Superior Court did not have the power to award fees in excess of the MICRA limits" and the State Bar had not been a party. Harney's claim that the "true recovery" was $21.7 million "is frivolous and calls into question his professed good faith." A 1989 Court of Appeal found "virtual unanimity" among "experienced practitioners and courts" that "the manner of calculating attorneys fees . . . is to determine the present value of a stream of

87. State Bar Exhibit 2.

88. Paulis v. Harney, San Bernardino Superior Court Case 250,683, State Bar Exhibit 9.

89. Hathaway v. Baldwin Park Community Hospital, 186 Cal.App.3d 1247 (2d Dist.1986).

90. Fineberg v. Harney & Moore, 207 Cal.App.3d 1049, 1055-56 (1989).

future payments."[91] Harney's claim that his law firm, not he, received the fee was "meritless." Although an unwritten fee agreement was voidable, Wendy's estate had never sought to void it. Selective prosecution was not a defense in cases involving attorney fee agreements, and Harney had neither asserted it in a pretrial motion nor proved it.

Nevertheless, Judge Smith found that Harney "honestly, albeit erroneously, believed that section 6146 was not applicable to attorney's fees in the medical malpractice suit" and therefore lacked the *mens rea* necessary to violate the rules requiring attorneys to respect courts and not mislead a judge or judicial officer.[92] Harney's failure to return the excess fee violated the RPC.[93] But the judge found that this did not constitute moral turpitude and refused to consider it because of Harney's belief that Section 6146 did not apply. Harney had significantly harmed his client, although "the extent of significant harm . . . is reduced in light of the $3,450,000 recovery respondent obtained for his client." Because the fee contract antedated the public reproval in Koskoff, that case was not an aggravating circumstance. Harney's "numerous years of dedicated practice without any prior record of discipline," "candid and cooperative" behavior in this proceeding, and many witnesses who "testified as to the extraordinary good character of respondent" were "*very* strong mitigating circumstances." The OTC invocation of standard 2.7 was "frivolous" because it applied only to unreasonable, not illegal, fees. Judge Smith recommended a two-year suspension, stayed, 30 days actual suspension, restitution of $466,100 plus 10 percent interest, and completion of the State Bar Ethics School.

Less than three weeks later Harney moved for a hearing de novo or to introduce new evidence, and the State Bar moved for reconsideration. On July 28 the presiding judge had reassigned all proceedings to Judge David S. Wesley, effective August 1. The court granted a hearing on Harney's motion and ordered its clerk to testify whether Smith's decision had in fact been filed July 31 (when it was dated). After a hearing, Judge Wesley denied both parties' motions, provoking each to appeal to the Review Department. Harney moved to strike the State Bar's motion. The State Bar moved to strike portions of the declaration by Harney's new lawyer, Michael Friedman. The Review Department denied both motions and granted Harney three continuances to file his opening appellate brief.

The State Bar urged the court to "affirm, if not increase, the discipline," arguing that the 30-day suspension was too lenient because Judge Smith had failed to take account of Harney's willful violation of Rule 4-100 and prior discipline. Friedman's brief, three times as long, began by noting that Wendy Paulis "was brilliantly served and will enjoy the considerable comforts brought about by David M. Harney's skill and experience until the day she dies." She had already

91. Schneider v. Kaiser Foundation Hospitals, 215 Cal.App.3d 1311, 1318 (1989).

92. BPC §6068(b) and (d) and RPC Rule 7-105(1).

93. Former RPC Rule 4-100(B)(4).

"recovered $2,525,601" from "the settlement which Mr. Harney negotiated for her" and would, "if she lives a normal life expectancy . . . recover $21.7 million." Judge Smith had held that "the fee in this case has to be calculated in terms of the *cost* of the single-premium annuity . . . without the slightest reference to what the client will *recover*. . . . A more extraordinary (and erroneous) interpretation of the word 'recovered' cannot be imagined." The court had "blight[ed] a legal career of 46 years . . . on the arcane economic theory that the value of a judgment composed of future payments is the cost of the annuity bought to fund those payments." The Court of Appeal embraced that theory only in the *Schneider* case (decided more than a year after the *Paulis* award) and "ignored over forty years of California appellate decisions." The holding was "judicial legislation." "The imposition of discipline based on a decision which not only did not exist when the predicate event occurred but also purported to effect a change in the law is patently unlawful and unconstitutional." Furthermore, "there is simply no provision in the law which gives the slightest guidance on what the discount rate is or how it is to be determined for the purpose of calculating fees generated by a 'present value' judgment." " . . . [T]here was nothing 'contingent' about the fee when it was collected." The "statutory" fee simply had been "incorrectly calculated." "This was an error of law with which the Superior Court is as much chargeable as the attorney who submitted the request . . . legal error is not the necessary equivalent of a disciplinable offense. If it were, most lawyers would have to be disbarred." If the court was determined to apply Section 6146, the fee limits should not be those in effect when Harney was retained, but the higher ones applicable when the fee was collected, reducing the excess to $266,850. "The only conclusion possible" from Judge Smith's dismissal of some charges "is that this prosecution should never have been initiated." "Pressing obviously unmeritorious charges was part of the pattern of prosecutorial misconduct in this case." The proceedings had been "frequently overzealous, sometimes disingenuous but always groundless." The State Bar disciplinary process "should not have been made to serve the private ends of private individuals with murky motives."

> The unfairness and vindictiveness of these charges and prosecutions is only matched by their speciousness. . . . A lawyer who is repeatedly faced with specious and frivolous charges is very plainly prejudiced. . . . If an attorney filed as many patently frivolous cases as frivolous charges have been brought against Mr. Harney, he or she would be subject to discipline. Prosecution of crimes, as well as professional misconduct, involves the exercise of discretion. When that discretion has been abused, the prosecution spawned by the abuse should be disavowed and terminated . . . . The punishment, it is said, should fit the crime. But if there is no crime and there is punishment, the punishment itself is the crime. . . . [U]nder any civilized standard of law and ethics, no offense was committed.

The State Bar brief conclusively showed that periodic payment was neither sought nor ordered in Paulis. *Schneider* "merely published what was known and understood by experienced practitioners with virtual unanimity: that the present value of the stream of future payments . . . is the cost of the annuity" because the discount rate is "at best speculative." Harney himself "must have calculated [the discount rate] into the settlement figure." Even if the court used the present value figure proposed by Harney's expert ($4.2. to 4.5 million), his fee exceeded the Section 6146 limit. The State Bar Court "has previously held that it cannot declare a statute unconstitutional" but can only recommend that the Supreme Court do so in the course of reviewing punishment. Harney's argument that Section 6146 did not apply to court-ordered fees "would result in minors or incompetents being given less protection than everyone else," which "would undermine the purpose . . . [of] both . . . section 6146 and the scheme of laws regarding protecting minors and incompetents." "[W]hether or not the Wendy Paulis case was difficult, or the family had difficulty obtaining counsel, or how many depositions were taken, or if the settlement was an exceptional result, is not relevant to this matter." The brief concluded that Harney "tries to evade his responsibility by technicalities and distorted interpretations of the law" and "shows no remorse for his misconduct."

Harney's reply brief reiterated that because "to this day no one can say with any degree of certainty what the amount of the judgment was . . . it is impossible to hold" that he charged an illegal fee. He was "entitled to rely on the correctness of the Superior Court order" and refuse to return the excess. " . . . [H]ow can discipline be imposed for failing to return monies when no one can say what the amount is which should have been returned?" He "should not be suspended from practice for having failed to be clairvoyant." He filed a further brief six weeks later, declaring that the State Bar's measure of the value of the recovery "has no statutory support whatever, much less support in any sense even coincidentally resembling common sense." "It is astounding that the State Bar proposes to discipline a lawyer on the basis of a phrase invented by the State Bar for the purposes of this case"—"settlement value"—"a totally obscure concept." The State Bar contention that Harney must have adopted a discount rate in deciding what settlement to accept "is total nonsense." The State Bar's "unfair conduct" now extended to its brief, "which so frequently makes up 'law' and 'rules' without a shred of validity or authority."

The Review Department ruled on April 4, 1995.[94] Judge Stovitz began by declaring:

> The heart of this case is not, as respondent would suggest, a principled disagreement over the validity or interpretation of the statutory limits. . . . This case is about far more than an attorney simply collecting more fees than state

94. Matter of Harney, 3 Calif. State Bar Ct. Rptr. 266 (1995).

> law allowed. Rather, it reveals how an unsophisticated client, in this case an incompetent adult whose mother obtained respondent's services, can be taken advantage of by an attorney who fails to reveal material information in favoring his own interest over the client's interests in receiving all the recovery she is entitled by law to receive. This record and other appellate decisions arising out of respondent's conduct show that respondent has not gained any insight into his duty to protect his client's entitlement to her full share of the recovery. . . . Rather, because of respondent's intransigence, this client and at least three others have been forced to sue him in separate actions to establish his duty to follow state law. . . . Had the concealment been found to be intentional, disbarment would not have been inappropriate for the amount of money his client was misled to pay as a fee.

By the time Harney accepted the case, "the constitutionality of the attorney fee limits of MICRA had been settled for over a year." His failure to mention them to either Loretta Paulis or Judge Turner was "not reasonable" and "misled both the court and his client on a material matter" to the client's detriment and Harney's gain. Even if he believed he was acting properly, he was "grossly negligent" in withholding the information. His

> prior litigation experience and unquestioned, superior expertise regarding the application of MICRA and his knowledge of the disciplinary proceeding then pending in the State Bar Court challenging his fees in a court-ordered settlement of a medical malpractice case were sufficient notice to respondent that the limitations of section 6146 were relevant to his fee request in this case.

The 1985 *Roa* and 1986 *Hathaway* decisions made it unreasonable for him to claim in July 1988 that his fee did not fall under MICRA. "If he thought he had reasonable grounds to distinguish his situation from the ambit of the statute, he could have argued them to Judge Turner." He "clearly" collected a contingent fee. His invocation of res judicata was "frivolous and its reiteration at oral argument even suggests bad faith on his part. A nearly identical claim was rejected in a civil case in which respondent was a defendant."[95] Harney's "newfound claims" that the case settled for $21.7 million were "simply without merit." By "clearly and wilfully [*sic*]" defying Section 6146, he violated his duty to support the laws of California[96] and collected an illegal fee.[97] Failure to refund the excess constituted moral turpitude.

---

95. Schultz v. Harney, 33 Cal.Rptr.2d 276 (Court of Appeal, 2d Dist. 1994) (probate court's approval of Harney's fee not res judicata in action to recover fee exceeding §6146 limit).

96. BPC §6068(a).

97. RPC Rule 2-107.

> In light of his recognized expertise, his persistent claim that he was not obligated to discuss every law in every book in his extensive law library with his client and the judge regarding their possible application in the Paulis case is frivolous and betrays disdain for his client and the trial court. This case makes real the unlikely risk that the Supreme Court noted 10 years ago . . . that attorneys would act against client interests in disregarding the limits of MICRA. . . . We also conclude that respondent's persistent attempts, as late as oral argument before us, to portray himself as the victim of uncertain MICRA law is also aggravating as a demonstration of lack of candor in view of his superior knowledge of that legal subject . . . .

> The gravamen of this case is not simply respondent's collection of an illegal fee for his representation of Wendy. Rather, this case is about respondent's clear overreaching of his own client by concealing by recklessness or gross neglect from her representative and from the court a material fact and profiting handsomely as a result. . . . Given respondent's very expertise, a client would understandably look to him not only for the most diligent substantive representation but to protect the client's interests in ensuring that all of the recovery which was the client's share went to the client.

Although violations of Sections 6147–48 were not disciplinable, they might be aggravating. So was Harney's notice from the filing of formal charges in Koskoff that the State Bar considered his behavior ethically questionable. Other unreported cases of charging or collecting fees exceeding MICRA limits generally led to public reproval. One factor in determining discipline "is the extent to which the attorney has achieved appropriate insight into his misconduct." Although Harney had been sued four times for similar offenses and suffered two adverse appellate decisions, "he persists in defending his actions. We have grave concern that unless significant discipline is imposed, he will continue to ignore the law and his duties to his clients . . . ." As

> one of the most experienced practitioners in this field, whose career at the bar spanned 40 years, respondent had no excuse for allowing his intense dislike of MICRA to blind him to his obligations to client and court several years after the courts had resolved basic MICRA fee limit issues against respondent's position. Indeed, because of his stature as a professional, his conduct should have been an ethical model to others.

The Review Department recommended two years suspension stayed, six months actual (requiring Harney to notify all his clients), revision of his retainer, disclosure of MICRA limits to future clients and courts, and restitution of the excess with interest.

Harney's prompt request for reconsideration called the opinion "both unprecedented and apocalyptic" for holding that "an attorney may be punished not only for asserting a tenable position in good faith, but also that an attorney may be disciplined for complying with a court order." It would have "unpropitious effects" on Harney, his firm and clients, and the legal profession. He could not be punished for gross negligence because "the State Bar never charged Mr. Harney with failing to act competently." Indeed, there was no "triable question of fact" about gross negligence because of the uncontradicted evidence of his good-faith belief in the inapplicability of Section 6146. When he drafted the settlement "there was no authority whatsoever for the proposition that Business & Professions Code Section 6146 is applicable to a case such as Paulis." On the contrary, a Court of Appeal held on January 8, 1986, "that a fee award in a medical malpractice case was properly based on section 21.01-5 of the Los Angeles Superior Court Probate Policy Memorandum, rather than section 6146." That charges were "filed, and not proved, in Koskoff may not be used as a springboard to arrive at the conclusion that Mr. Harney should have known that the law required him to disclose the provisions of MICRA . . . ." His culpability in Paulis "rests heavily upon the proper definition of a 'contingency' fee, an issue which was not directly addressed in Koskoff." He distinguished *Roa* because "the parties acknowledged that they had previously contracted for a contingency fee." "If Judge Turner believed BPC Section 6146 may have been applicable, then he should have ordered a hearing." The proposed six months suspension "violates Mr. Harney's constitutional rights." "[T]he practice of law, by its very nature, requires an attorney to assert positions which are tenable when at all possible." He had also been denied due process by not receiving "notice of the contemplated discipline prior to its recommendation." The Review Department had "embarked on a dangerous and unchartered [*sic*] journey" and "violated Mr. Harney's right of access to the courts." Is "an attorney who asserts a tenable legal position required to disclose adverse authority when it is not directly on point?" Because Wendy's conservator had sued to recover the excess fee, the disciplinary proceeding was "double jeopardy," ignored the "finality" rule, and violated Harney's right to a jury trial. The court-ordered fee was not contingent because it "is not, in theory, dependent upon a favorable outcome for the client. Surely, Mr. Harney's noble statement to Loretta Paulis that he would not seek a court-awarded fee if there was no recovery does not make the fee a contingent one." BPC Section 6068, requiring attorneys to "support the law and constitution," was "unconstitutionally vague and ambiguous." Selective prosecution "based solely on an individual's notoriety" was just as "invidious" as discrimination based on race. Discipline "only serves to unfairly punish a lawyer who has been a credit to the legal profession for 47 years." He had had to decline being nominated Vice-Chair of the ABA Section of Tort and Insurance Practice because of this proceeding. In addition to relitigating every issue, he challenged Judge Smith's "jurisdiction" to render his decision after his term had expired, accused him of "misconduct" for allowing the State Bar to reopen its case, contested the "constitutionality of the State Bar Court" and the "propriety of the publication of the Review Department's Opinion," and asked how he could pay restitution while suspended.

The State Bar derided this motion as "the proverbial throwing everything *including* the kitchen sink at the matter hoping something somehow sticks." "[G]iven Respondent's continued claims, including that MICRA is unconstitutional . . . Respondent's conduct appears to be intentional . . . ." He "is not being disciplined for asserting a position" but "for his actions." His "argument is like saying that, because I believe the tax laws are unconstitutional, the government cannot prosecute me for failing to pay my taxes." Harney's double jeopardy argument was "frivolous," and his claim that this proceeding violated the finality rule had "no basis.'" His demand for a jury trial was "absurd," and his contention that the fee was not contingent was "meritless." The court had already rejected his "frivolous" argument that there was no statutory basis to determine the value of recovery. His continued citation and reliance on the unpublished (and hence privileged) decision in *Hidalgo v. Superior Court* should be considered aggravating. The

> Request for Reconsideration shows that Respondent continues to be unwilling to conform his conduct to the law and demonstrates that the discipline recommended may not be sufficient to force Respondent to conform to the conduct expected of an attorney in this state. Further, Respondent shows no remorse . . . .

To justify his claim of disproportionate punishment he misstated the actual recommendation in *Hidalgo* and failed to reveal that the case was under review. The State Bar moved to strike his seven volumes of appendices.

Harney requested leave to reply but, without waiting, appended a reply that began:

> The State Bar fails to come to terms with the fact that Mr. Harney has been punished for asserting a legal position at a time when the position found support in both published authority and the minds of many judges, legal scholars, and reputable lawyers.

It reiterated that Section 6146 "does not state . . . that it is applicable to court-ordered fees." He persisted in citing *Hidalgo*. That "the mere filing of charges . . . put Mr. Harney on notice that certain conduct was prohibited ignores fundamental principles of due process." The OTC prepared and tried the case, "never once presenting Mr. Harney with the charge that he was . . . grossly negligent in the *Paulis* matter." "If a felon convicted of robbery in the Superior Court would find himself convicted of murder by the Court of Appeal, the murder conviction would not stand for long." "Rudimentary fairness" required a rehearing. The Review Department denied his motion and the Supreme Court denied review.

Harney still declared his belief that "for every wrong, there is a remedy. I am supposed to be that remedy." Now, however, he rejected 99 out of a 100 cases because of the damage caps.[98] He was disciplined a third time in 1998 for overcharging clients a total of nearly $90,000 in two cases in violation of Section 6146 and suspended for three years (stayed) and ordered to make restitution and take the Multistate Professional Responsibility Exam.[99] He died on November 11, 1998, at 74, while undergoing surgery.[100]

C. "A Stubborn Streak"[101]

As both the California Supreme Court and the Review Department observed, law encounters difficulties in regulating lawyers, who spend their entire professional careers treating it as a means, not an end. J.P. Morgan allegedly declared: "I don't know as I want a lawyer to tell me what I cannot do. I hire him to tell me how to do what I want to do."[102] Most lawyers are glad to oblige, growing ever more cynical about law in the process. Lawyers have resisted other efforts to restrict their fees.[103] David Harney was far from the only lawyer who sought to evade BPC Section 6146 (a point he repeatedly made in his defense, as though massive resistance—like that of Southern segregationists resisting *Brown v. Board of Education*—made his actions less egregious rather than more). But Harney certainly was one of the more inventive and persistent in both seeking loopholes and justifying this to the State Bar. He denied the fee limitation was ever enacted. He brazenly declared: "I have never in my life disregarded 6146 . . . I believe I have always complied with it . . . I have dedicated myself to that." When, by "some stretch of their imagination," the Koskoffs first made the "goofy argument" that Section 6146 applied, the State Bar "tossed it out." Only "idiots" thought it applied to probate court cases. He would have been "crazy" to show Judge Baffa the fee agreement and had not mentioned Section 6146 because "I would have lied to Judge Baffa if I said any such thing. I am not a liar." (Was Harney unconsciously echoing Nixon's, "I'm not a crook"?)[104] Numerous lawyers and judges testified to the profession's widespread conviction of the section's invalidity. Judges systematically disregarded it (some out of ignorance, others believing it to be unconstitutional, though they did not so rule).

---

98. Peter H. King, *Hanging All the Lawyers,* Los Angeles Times, A3 (3.22.95).

99. Matter of Harney, California State Bar Court #20281.

100. Jason J. Song, *Plaintiffs Attorney David M. Harney, 74, Dies,* Los Angeles Daily Journal (11.16.98).

101. A characterization by John Collins, a younger personal injury lawyer, quoted in Harney's obituary. *David Harney, Known as 'Giant' of Medical Malpractice Law, Dies,* MetNews (11.16.98).

102. Quoted in Tarbell (1935). A similar quotation is attributed to Elihu Root: "The client never wants to be told he can't do what he wants to do; he wants to be told how to do it, and it is the lawyer's business to tell him how." *See* Swaine (1946-48: I/667).

103. Rosenthal (1974).

104. Carroll Kilpatrick, *Nixon Tells Editors, 'I'm not a Crook,'* Washington Post, A1 (11.18.73). President Nixon also said, "I have never obstructed justice."

Even defense lawyers, who had lobbied for the law, did not always invoke it. But most children quickly learn that others' misbehavior does not justify their own. Harney's duty was to his client, regardless of what others thought or did.

Harney dismissed Section 6146 as the law "which was held to be unconstitutional in 1975." Rose Bird, whom Governor Brown had appointed Secretary of Consumer Affairs (and later Chief Justice), told Brown so, and the Governor agreed (although Hiestand, who was close to Brown, denied that the Governor believed this and noted that he signed the bill).[105] "[W]hat the effect of signing an unconstitutional law is, I believe it rendered it a null and void act." Both a highly respected state court judge (Schifferman) and a federal court had held Section 6146 unconstitutional. Harney maintained that the first *American Bank* decision declared *all* of MICRA unconstitutional, but the ruling was necessarily limited to the periodic payment section. He blamed the second *American Bank* decision reversing this on a change in personnel, which was true but irrelevant. He noted that the latter decision affirmed the trial court, but it upheld the section's constitutionality. *Roa* was a 4–3 decision (but that is all it takes), "a very aberrational thing," "some weird application by the majority of Austro-Hungarian common law." "[I]t's very difficult, if not impossible, to understand the majority opinion," "authored by a certain justice," the "Austrian" Otto Kaus.[106] The case upheld Section 6146 "a little bit," in "limited circumstances," "very limitedly," only "with one type of application. Certain things were not argued in that case and not presented." But laws can no more be "a little bit" constitutional than women can be a little bit pregnant. Unlike Harney, the attorney in *Roa* "did virtually no work, and didn't take any depositions, and the trial court thought he was trying to overcharge." "[B]y a lot of dictum, the majority said that it was constitutional under the limited facts of that case." Yet, it had to be holding, not dictum. Harney "was part of a group consisting of three justices on the Supreme Court out of seven, who said that the 6146 was unconstitutional." Here, he equated himself with California Supreme Court Justices! Four U.S. Supreme Court Justices voted to review—but it takes five.

There were two basic problems with this line of argument. First, if Harney was so certain Section 6146 was unconstitutional, and he was one of the ten best trial lawyers in the country, why did he not challenge it? Gary Paul did, and the State Bar properly exonerated him of misconduct. Harney accused the State Bar of wanting "to silence respondent and . . . prevent him from challenging the applicability and constitutionality of section 6146." But he never tried to do so. Second, the California Supreme Court upheld Section 6146, and the U.S. Supreme Court declined to review. But Harney refused to concede, continuing to

---

105. Bird joined opinions finding unconstitutional both the periodic payment provision (twice) and the lawyers' fee cap.

106. Was there not-so-subtle anti-Semitism in Harney's repeated insults to Kaus and references to Beverly Hills doctors' wives in mink coats?

argue the section's unconstitutionality in Paulis after being disciplined for doing so in Koskoff. He even claimed that the increased availability of medical malpractice insurance (one of MICRA's stated objectives) retroactively invalidated the statute. This, however, is a legal impossibility.*

Harney conflated his contention that Section 6146 was unconstitutional with his criticism of it as bad policy. MICRA was "so-called bought-up legislation." It was "illegal" for the statute to outlaw "a reasonable fee for hard work performed, and excellent results obtained." Section 6146 was "totally unconstitutional because it was intended for one and only one purpose, and that was to force lawyers who were not competent to take medical malpractice cases and settle them out cheaply." Doctors and insurers spent $109 million to buy the legislature, which had favored their interests over those of "catastrophically injured medical malpractice victims." Doctors had gone on strike, and their wives had camped out in the governor's office. (As a proud member of the "million dollar" Inner Circle of Advocates, Harney was unlikely to win sympathy by sneering at his political opponents' wealth.) That same lobby of physicians and insurers had instigated these disciplinary complaints, whose real purpose was to eliminate Harney and other leading medical malpractice lawyers. The 1987 MICRA amendments raising the cap on lawyers' fees showed the "tremendous amount of outrage about the restriction that kept confident lawyers out of the plaintiffs' field in medical malpractice cases." I share Harney's view that MICRA was bad policy; but that is no excuse for flouting it.

Harney offered numerous other justifications for disregarding Section 6146. The fee was not contingent. "I would not take the case, if I thought the outcome was so uncertain and so fortuitous and casual. I don't practice law that way. Never have and never will." But then, *none* of his fees was contingent; and what else but the uncertain outcome justified taking so much of the damage award? His "noble" statement that he would not seek a fee if unsuccessful should not be turned against him. In fact, probate courts would not have awarded him anything for failure. There was "nothing 'contingent' about the fee when it was collected"—but that tautology applies to every contingent fee. He could have justified the same fee (or more) by charging an hourly rate—but no tort victim would or could pay that. The fee was awarded by the probate judge—but that did not make it any less contingent, and probate judges had no authority to disregard Section 6146. Finally, Harney's declaration accompanying Lawrence Tribe's amicus brief seeking reconsideration of *Roa* by the California Supreme Court stated that Harney's "law practice is based strictly upon contingency agreements with plaintiffs."

Harney claimed to have conditioned his representation on the Koskoffs waiving Section 6146. "The day they enacted MICRA, waiver was all over the place. Everybody in town talked about waiver." Asked how the Koskoffs could waive a law that did not apply, Harney replied "by fiat," adding the non sequitur: "I cannot go through the mind of everybody in the world who signs a waiver. There are thousands and millions signed every day." (Harney often seemed to forget he was addressing a referee, not a jury.) He stressed his clients' sophistication: Richard, a lawyer, and Martha, a doctor's daughter, had "shopped" the case to other lawyers: "[W]ouldn't you assume that one of those shopees would have said something about 6146?" (Not if they were as self-interested as Harney; in any case, they could not fulfill *his* obligations to clients.) The retainer included a handwritten addition that Harney "will be personally responsible for supervising and handling this matter." But it did not connect that promise to their alleged waiver of Section 6146. (The year before he settled the case, Harney added an explicit MICRA waiver to all his retainers.) Despite Harney's promise to be personally responsible, the Koskoffs insisted they had no further contact with him; and he confirmed that Pagliuso "has done all the work." It is not clear that the Koskoffs could have waived Brendan's rights even if waiver were allowed. Most important, Harney persisted in maintaining that the Paulis family had waived Section 6146 after the California Supreme Court held it was not waivable.[107] Hiestand correctly observed that a lawyer who asks clients to waive rights in his favor must inform them of those rights and urge them to consult independent counsel.

Harney also sought to evade Section 6146 by arguing that there was no "agreement," only a "relationship." At the same time, he maintained that the purpose of the "agreement" was to cap his fee at 25 percent. He claimed the Koskoffs had never signed the retainer, noting that their copy bore only his signature. The obvious explanation was that both sides signed copies and exchanged them without bothering to sign the one they received, which is why the Harney's copy—the one he filed in the contract action—did bear the Koskoffs' signatures.[108] (He actually argued that the State Bar Court's admission of a document *he* filed in the civil suit denied *him* due process.) Harney then accused the Koskoffs of adding their signatures later—a serious charge of evidence tampering, which he never even tried to substantiate and which was undercut by the fact that the document had always been in his possession. But even if these evidentiary arguments had been true, they were irrelevant: *Section 6146 applied with or without a written retainer.*

Having lost the arguments that Section 6146 was inapplicable, unconstitutional, and waived, Harney tried a new stratagem. He deliberately made *no* written fee agreement with the Paulis family and then contended that Section 6147 entitled him to recover in *quantum meruit* above the Section 6146 limit. But Section 6147 actually required lawyers to give clients a written fee agreement

107. Waters v. Bourhis, 40 Cal.3d 424, 220 Cal.Rptr. 666, 709 P.2d 469 (1985).

108. His associate, James Pagliuso, said that Harney "gave [the Koskoffs] the fee agreement. They were interviewing other lawyers, and the arrangement was that they were . . . to return the fee agreement to Mr. Harney if they wanted us to handle the case. I believe the fee agreement was returned."

and empowered them to void an oral agreement, something the Paulis family had not done.

Harney's legal last argument, in Paulis, was that the Section 6146 fee limit should be based not on the $3.45 million the defendants had paid but on the projected lifetime payout, which mysteriously rose from $19 million to $21.7 million. Arguing (without foundation) that he was accused of collecting an unreasonable fee, not an illegal one, he contended it was a mere 4 percent of the lifetime payout. When Judge Smith rejected this argument, following a recent a Court of Appeal ruling that reflected the unanimous opinion of tort practitioners, Harney assailed him for having "ignored over forty years of California appellate decisions." This again revealed Harney's constant conflation of what he thought the law should be with what it was. Harney argued there was no authoritative or legally mandated discount rate. But that would have been relevant only if the parties had agreed on a lifetime payout and asked the probate court to discount it to present value in order to apply the Section 6146 fee ceiling. Instead, the parties agreed on the settlement amount, which therefore could hardly be a "totally obscure concept," "invented by the State Bar for the purposes of this case." Nor was it "total nonsense" for the State Bar to find that Harney must have had a discount rate in mind when reaching a settlement. A fee based on lifetime payout could have exceeded the entire award; and lawyers, unlike victims, never accept periodic payment, which would make their fees contingent on the victim's lifespan.

Having exhausted his legal arguments, Harney turned to others. He won a "tremendous result" for his clients. "[T]he [Koskoff] child and his parents received a net of $750,000 out of a $1 million policy . . . and you're critical of me for handling that case?" Every other San Bernardino lawyer had rebuffed the Paulis family. Hirschberg introduced Harney's medical malpractice book to prove that "he rendered reasonable services" (which never was in question). Wendy Paulis "will enjoy the considerable comforts brought about by David M. Harney's skill and experience until the day she dies." (Since she will be comatose, she may not appreciate this.) Loretta Paulis had signed the fee agreement "Gleefully. Gleefully." For these clients to challenge his fee and complain to the State Bar showed base "ingratitude." Harney took victim blaming even further. The "greedy" Koskoffs, "who were not damaged at all," were "stealing $250,000 from their kid" in anticipation of his death, "which never happened." They "didn't deserve" the money. (But Brendan was brain damaged and died, and Harney himself drafted the settlement.) The Paulis family squabbled over the fees for administering Wendy's estate after Loretta's death (unseemly but common and anyhow irrelevant). It was Milligan who should be disciplined for suing Harney for an excessive fee (but Harney did not make a complaint to the State Bar, which would have rejected it as frivolous). It would have been "silly" to talk about depositing the disputed fee in a trust account. "I don't spend my time on silly conversations." The complainants were "tortiously chargeable with abuse of process."

Harney seemed most concerned about saving face. He clearly found the entire proceeding infra dig. He brought other big names—Joseph Alioto and Willie Brown—to testify that they, too, had been pilloried by the State Bar. He urged the State Bar Court to take account of his "reputation for excellence," which was relevant to *mens rea* (how?) and increased the presumption of innocence (why?). The prosecution had "blight[ed] a legal career of 46 years;" the Review Department had "unfairly punish[ed]" a "lawyer who has been a credit to the profession for 47 years." "I didn't take any money. I resent that." He twice pronounced: "I didn't take anything." Harney exaggerated his jeopardy: the OTC was "trying to disbar me because I illegally contracted for a contingent fee." Hirschberg twice accused the State Bar Court of the most "flagrant and outrageous crucifixion" of his client. The "discipline and punishment" were "designed" to cause "personal embarrassment." Harney refused to testify in mitigation, perhaps (accurately) seeing the penalty phase as a degradation ceremony; and Hirschberg rudely stalked out of the Koskoff penalty hearing. Harney demanded "respect for his integrity." No punishment was warranted; he would promptly comply with a ruling by the California Supreme Court that he follow Section 6146. He had committed no wrong; at most, he had made an "error of law," which many judges had affirmed. If legal errors were disciplinable offenses, "most lawyers would have to be disbarred." He should "not be suspended from practice for having failed to be clairvoyant." The State Bar was punishing him for "asserting a tenable position in good faith" and "complying with a court order." He did not want to be censured publicly and would "settle for nothing less than a complete vindication." He brooked no criticism. When Milligan stated the obvious—that a high fee worked to Harney's advantage and a low fee to Wendy's—Harney angrily denied "taking advantage" of Wendy and accused Milligan of "taking advantage" of him. He bristled at the accusation that he had misled Judge Turner. If "there is no crime and there is punishment, the punishment itself is the crime." He had committed no offense "under any civilized standard of law and ethics."

Harney saw the entire disciplinary proceeding as a "vendetta." Hirschberg called it "the most flagrant show of prosecutorial misconduct to hit the State Bar Court in its short history" and voiced outrage at the involvement of Hiestand, "obviously the man behind the State Bar proceeding against David M. Harney." The State Bar was "engaging in purely political activity when it seeks a lobbyist for the CMA . . . to testify against Harney." The respondent concurred: "To have Mr. Hiestand . . . testify against me . . . is just absolutely not fair." Although Hiestand was "supposed to be a very brilliant lawyer" and "pretend[ed] to be some kind of judicial authority," he actually "doesn't understand the appellate process." Harney upstaged his lawyer to cross-examine Hiestand and then abused that role to testify under the guise of making objections. Even when represented by Hirschberg, Harney often usurped the lawyer's role and raised his own objections. Like Caesar, he spoke of himself in the third person, complete with middle initial.

The OTC's mixed metaphor aptly captured Harney's defense strategy: "the proverbial throwing everything *including* the kitchen sink at the matter hoping something somehow sticks." A Probate Code amendment had implicitly repealed Section 6146. Referee Paule had not actually written the Koskoff opinion, and Referee Smith had filed the Paulis opinion after his term ended. Harney lacked the *mens rea* for culpability: Smith had found good faith in the Paulis case; although the Review Department found gross negligence, Harney had never been charged with that. "If a felon convicted of robbery in the Superior Court would find himself convicted of murder by the Court of Appeal, the murder conviction would not long stand." The OTC's failure to notify Harney of the proposed penalty denied him due process. He had a right to a jury trial. Suspension violated his constitutional rights. His former clients' contract actions rendered the disciplinary proceedings double jeopardy. The BPC mandate to support the laws and constitution of California was unconstitutionally vague. The State Bar Court itself was unconstitutional. Harney had no more obligation to inform judges or clients about Section 6146 than to tell them about Workers' Compensation or Veteran's Administration fee schedules or the myriad other laws in his firm's 8,000-book library. Why should he have to disclose authority "not directly on point?" "[T]here are literally thousands and thousands" of code sections. If he discussed each one, "I'd only see one potential client in a lifetime." He did not "collect" a fee because he had not hired a collection agency. The OTC had not proved that the defendants in the Paulis case were medically licensed; although Harney had alleged they were, this was not in evidence. That some charges had been dismissed showed that none should have been brought (even though others were upheld). The Review Department had ventured on a "dangerous and unchartered [*sic*—"uncharted"]" course and rendered an "apocalyptic" opinion. (Actually, it was Harney who was being apocalyptic.) The judgment would have "unpropitious" effects on him, his firm, and clients, and the entire legal profession. Harney was being denied "access to the courts." Some of his arguments were even more outrageous: Because tort damages forced manufacturers to take dangerous products off the market, he was motivated to sue by altruism, not profit (then why take a contingent fee?). Not charging for the medical records of potential clients he rejected was a form of pro bono practice. Wendy had not been harmed because the settlement's $18,000 a month for medical expenses was "enough money," and anyhow she was in a coma. The disputed $247,000 in fees might seem like a lot to poorly paid civil servants (like OTC lawyers and State Bar Court judges), but it wasn't really that much (to "millionaires club" members like Harney). How could he pay restitution while suspended? (What happened to those millions?)

Harney's fundamental ethical transgression was his denial that Section 6146 was law, even after the highest state and federal courts had upheld it. He was a recidivist, reenacting his defiance even while being disciplined for prior acts.[109] He continued to insist that "the trial court had the discretion to award a fee, and [the judge] can choose any formula he wants," denying that *Roa* held that "it must be in accordance with 6146." Asked if his views had changed, he remained adamant: "Actually, they've been reinforced by a court of appeals decision" (which held that the Probate Court could award *less* than the Section 6146 limit, not *more*). Disclosing whether he still used the unlawful fee agreement would violate lawyer–client confidentiality (a doctrine intended to protect the very clients he was accused of betraying). His moral arrogance, indeed solipsism, also pervaded the disciplinary proceeding. He still thought the charges "absolutely insane." Projecting his own failing onto his tormentor, Harney said the State Bar "frequently makes up 'law' and 'rules' without a shred of validity or authority." Hirschberg's brief called the culpability finding "entirely erroneous." Harney said in Paulis that the court had "tentatively, albeit erroneously," found guilt and accused Smith of relying on an "arcane economic theory": "A more extraordinary (and erroneous) interpretation of the word 'recovered' cannot be imagined." But Harney advanced these statements in the *mitigation* phase, not on appeal. Harney reiterated in Paulis the same arguments the State Bar Court had rejected in Koskoff: Section 6146 did not apply; the probate judge's approval of the settlement was *res judicata* (because the State Bar was Wendy Paulis's "alter ego"). He relitigated every issue, moved to reopen, offered new evidence and then introduced it without permission, and took every appeal. He openly defied the State Bar Court: even if it decided that Section 6146 applied he would not owe a refund because "I don't see how the Court can hold it." A Court of Appeal decision he disliked was "judicial legislation." To discipline him based on that change in the law would be "patently unlawful and unconstitutional." His insistence on fighting lost battles was further evidence that his paramount concern was saving face. "I don't violate and never have violated any laws." Asked if, "despite all the case law," you feel "you owe these people money," Harney proclaimed: "absolutely not. Never will." If any court ordered him to pay it back, "it will have to be the Supreme Court." He had "never been held in contempt in his life." After losing in the Review Department, he continued to maintain that he was being punished "on a novel theory" for taking a "tenable legal position" (repeated twice), which he "in good faith believes is inapplicable." The law was what he believed it

---

109. In August and September 1982 and again in January 1986, he obtained probate court orders for excessive fees to settle medical malpractice claims by Christopher Schultz; the excess totaled between $120,000 and $200,000. *See* Schultz v. Harney, *supra*.

should be.[110] All this belied his assurance that he always had abided by judicial decisions and always would.

Hirschberg displayed slavish loyalty to his client, on whom he fawned. MICRA "was known as the anti-David Harney statute. The evidence will show he was that famous." Hirschberg stepped out of role to testify for Harney, saying "Well, it may be self-serving hearsay, but I think you are the greatest."[111] Like Harney, he insisted that the constitutionality of Section 6146 "has not been finally determined, at least to my satisfaction." Hirschberg also referred to himself in the third person and emulated his hero's combativeness.[112] The Koskoffs' lawyer had been "cantankerous" in moving for summary judgment in the excess fee action (which they won). Repeatedly boasting that he was "not a stranger to the State Bar court," Hirschberg even attacked the referee. Paule should disqualify himself for admitting unfamiliarity with Section 6146; when the referee refused, Hirschberg accused him of "depriving me of being able to cross-examine you." He stormed out of the penalty phase because

> you have completely misunderstood everything in this particular case . . . . I don't know if you have ever tried a lawsuit in your life or not. We did a check on you. You don't have an office. You are not listed in *Parker's Directory*.

When Gochis urged Paul to reject respondent's brief in light of this contumelious behavior, Hirschberg exploded at the referee:

> If you don't consider it you won't be any different than the way you acted throughout these proceedings . . . .We had the most outstanding people in California and the legal profession. You paid no attention to them whatsoever.

Hirschberg was even more contemptuous of Gochis: "[S]he is dead wrong. We know that." "As usual, she is wrong." "Miss Gochis thinks by repeating herself she can make a point." He called her racist for accusing Judge Jefferson (an African-American) of "stupidity" (actually, she said his testimony was "absurd"). Jefferson was "the most respected jurist in California." Harney and his witnesses were equally condescending. He referred to Gochis as "lady," was "appalled" by her "misrepresentations" and "false statements," told her to "learn how to make a proper legal objection," and accused her of "malice" and making "speeches." She should be "severely chastised" for "a bold-faced falsehood." Judge Baffa consistently addressed Ms Gochis by her first name. Judge McCloskey accused her of laughing at him (but the referee struck his objection, saying she had acted in

---

110. Like Humpty Dumpty in *Alice in Wonderland*: "When I use a word, it means just what I choose it to mean—neither more nor less."

111. Harney revealed his opinion of Hirschberg by repeatedly taking over his own defense, declaring at one point that he did not care what Hirschberg said.

112. After Hirschberg alienated Judge Smith, Harney substituted Friedman, who was equally antagonistic to the referee.

a "respectful and courteous manner"). When Gochis protested against Judge Shatford repeatedly calling her "young lady" because she was "also a counsel of the State Bar," he retorted: "I am also a judge who is called here as a witness." Judge Hauk patronized Gochis as "my dear lady," called her statements "ridiculous," and warned, "[Y]oung lady. Don't push me." When she objected, Hirschberg attacked "her usual habit of interrupting in the middle of a question." When she replied that her "job as a State Bar attorney" was "to make my record," Hirschberg sneered: "[S]he sure ain't got manners."

Harney and Hirschberg aggressively attacked the OTC, calling the charges "trumped up," "frivolous," "cavalier and inflammatory," "false," "specious," "groundless," and "obviously unmeritorious." The State Bar had displayed "actual malice," been "downright irresponsible," and "abused its immunity." Its "actions in this case only tend to diminish the respect attorneys have for the State Bar." Harney and Hirschberg accused the OTC of a "pattern of prosecutorial misconduct," "unfairness and vindictiveness," and "frequently overzealous, sometimes disingenuous" behavior. They kept insisting that Harney was selectively prosecuted because he was "the foremost malpractice lawyer in the country," denouncing such bias as worse than racial discrimination. Although they sometimes maintained that the disciplinary proceeding had been "made to serve the private ends of private individuals with murky motives" (presumably the clients Harney had overcharged), they mostly claimed it had been brought at the behest of doctors and their insurers, threatening to offer "the percipient testimony of not one, but two experienced Trial Counsel" who "were clearly *sub silenti* agents of the Medical Association and insurance industry." But those witnesses never appeared. The Hearing Panel findings and recommendations were "an outrage." It committed "innumerable judicial errors." "Procedural irregularities have abounded in this case." The State Bar "attempts to dodge its own irresponsible and contemptible misconduct." Its "careless and even cavalier procedures are themselves open to censure."

Harney's witnesses were equally outraged. Judge Manuel Real denounced the "unfounded charges." Reid Bridges called Gochis the "most preternaturally biased examiner." G. Dana Hobart blamed the prosecution on "a surplus of funds" because "our dues have been raised." Stephen A. Kolodny denounced the "misuse of the system" and the "terrible waste of valuable resources." Eugene McCloskey said it was "a disgrace to waste the dues of the State Bar at the time when there are so many necessary prosecutions in the proceeding of this nature."

However effective Harney's histrionics may have been in swaying juries, they clearly backfired here.[113] The referee expressed his anger at Hirschberg for walking

113. When Gochis accused Harney of intimidating Martha Koskoff by standing too close when questioning her, the referee directed him to step back.

out of the penalty phase, noting that action at the beginning his judgment. (He also may have been angered by Harney's absence.) Hirschberg had indulged in "unfounded, disrespectful statements and accusations against this Court." Far from accepting Harney's argument that judicial disregard for Section 6146 justified his own behavior, the referee rebuked the judges and the State Bar Board of Governors for treating the statute as unconstitutional both before and after *Roa*. Judge Baffa may have typified the cozy relationship between lawyers and judges; he had been Harney's friend for 30 years; their families socialized four or five times a year. He disregarded the fee limit

> because I think we all felt that it just wasn't constitutional . . . without the lawyer, they wouldn't get anything. And I happen to like lawyers. I like to protect their fees. I like to see them get paid.

Although he "knew [Section 6146] was mandatory," "it wasn't to me, in the sense that I felt I could do what was fair." Both referees rejected virtually all of Harney's legal and factual arguments, and Paule found bad faith in the contention that the fee should be based on lifetime payout. Although Smith ended up strongly sympathetic to Harney, even finding his behavior during the proceeding "candid and cooperative," the Review Department decided that Harney was an incorrigible who refused to learn from experience. His self-interested betrayal of the trust of an "unsophisticated client," the mother of an incompetent adult, did not express "a principled disagreement over the validity or interpretation of the statutory limits." His claim of "expertise" made his clients even more dependent on him. His "new-found" argument that the settlement value was $21.7 million was "simply without merit." His "intransigence" and "frivolous" justifications, such as the claim that he was a "victim of uncertain MICRA law," showed "disdain for his client and the trial court." His continued defiance in four cases despite two adverse appellate decisions suggested he had not attained "appropriate insight" into his conduct. As in other disciplinary proceedings, the respondent's behavior in the State Bar Court was almost as important as the charges that had brought him before it in the first place.

4. PLAYING GAMES WITH SEGA

I. CONFLICT OF INTEREST

One of a lawyer's most fundamental ethical obligations is fidelity to clients. Conflict of interest rules seek to ensure this. A lawyer can only "enter into a business transaction with a client" if the terms are "fair and reasonable" and "fully disclosed and transmitted in writing . . . in a manner which should reasonably have been understood," the client is advised in writing "to seek the advice of an independent lawyer," and the client "consents in writing."[1] Lawyers are required to make written disclosure of any past or present "legal, business, financial, professional, or personal relationship" that might "be affected substantially" by representing the client.[2] The range of potential conflicts is very wide.[3]

After twenty-five years of practicing real estate and business litigation, mostly alone, Franklin Knight Lane II was retained by Jack Younesi, who introduced him to many other wealthy Iranian nationals.[4] Lane immediately loaned Younesi $5,000 and then made two other loans of $55,000 and $45,000, out of which Younesi paid Lane $17,200 in legal fees. The security for the last two was a house owned by Younesi's relatives, the Nehdars, and all of Younesi's personal property. Younesi also gave Lane a promisory note and confession of judgment, one hundred semiprecious stones, a power of attorney over all his stock and security accounts, and agreed to convey to Lane a half interest in property in Tehran, declaring that he had declined to consult another attorney first, as Lane had advised. After Younesi defaulted on the $5,000 loan (which was secured by a stock assignment), Lane demanded repayment of the outstanding $100,000, declared default three weeks later, and filed the confession of judgment in court. When he sued Younesi and the Nehdars for an equitable lien on the house, the Nehdars executed a second trust deed, with Lane as beneficiary and his shell corporation Providencia Ltd. as trustee. Lane arranged for two other clients to lend Younesi $15,000 each, secured by stock. When Younesi defaulted, Lane paid the clients. After Younesi was sued by three brokerage firms to which he had written bad checks, Lane persuaded him to stipulate to judgment in two. Younesi insisted he had a valid defense in the third. After Lane disagreed and

1. California Rules of Professional Conduct (RPC) Rule 3-300.

2. RPC Rule 3-310 (formerly Rule 5-102).

3. By far the best empirical study of how lawyers manage conflicts is Shapiro (2002). The best single case study is Regan (2004).

4. Matter of Lane, 2 Calif. State Bar Ct. Rptr. 735 (1994) (six months suspension, three years probation).

withdrew, Younesi represented himself but defaulted, incurring a $120,000 judgment. Lane sued Younesi and the Nehdars to foreclose on the house to recover the $120,000 Younesi owed him. After the Nehdars conveyed a deed in lieu of foreclosure, Lane leased the Younesis the house for $1,000 a month, applying whatever exceeded the cost of maintaining the property to Younesi's legal fees.

Lane also represented Younesi in a securities case and a personal injury case. Younesi assigned both to Lane, the former "to induce [him] to permit the undersigned and his family to remain as tenants" and the latter to pay attorney's fees and "other indebtedness." At Lane's repeated urging and after at least one eviction threat, Younesi filed a bankruptcy petition prepared by Lane (for $1,000), which noted a secured $60,000 debt to Lane for attorney's fees. Within a month of the filing (and without seeking bankruptcy court approval), Lane had the Younesis sign another lease, raising the monthly rent to $1,500 that year and $2,000 the next. Providencia filed an unlawful detainer action for nonpayment of rent, but Lane let the Younesis stay after they paid $3,000. Providencia later got a default judgment for unlawful detainer and a writ of possession but promised not to evict them until the end of a trial in which Laligo had sued the Younesis, Nehdars, Lane, and Providencia for conspiring fraudulently to convey Younesi's assets to shelter them from creditors. Nevertheless, Lane threatened eviction and demanded "a written waiver and relinquishment signed by [the Younesis] of any and all claims . . . including . . . any claim for any unethical conduct on my part." But the Younesis and Nehdars filed malpractice and other tort actions against Lane and Providencia and ethical complaints with the State Bar. A court set aside the house transfer, finding that the loans to Younesi were sham transactions without consideration and Lane had known the Younesis were clearly insolvent. When the Younesis vacated the defaults in the unlawful detainer action, Providencia brought another two days later, which was dismissed, and a third within a month, also dismissed. During trial of the Younesis' malpractice and tort claims, Lane offered to settle if Younesi persuaded the State Bar to drop the disciplinary investigation. A judge entered judgment N.O.V. for the Younesis against Lane in the tort action (although this was set aside on appeal because the motion was filed late). The Pasadena house was sold to satisfy the Laligo creditors.

Retained by Eleanor and Phillip Fairchild to update their estate plan, Anthony N. Fonte drafted a living trust, giving each trustee sole discretion to lend money to anyone and convincing them to name him rather than Phillip's daughter as successor trustee (claiming he could help with taxes and property management).[5] He did not give Eleanor time to read the document or advise her to seek independent counsel. After Phillip died, Fonte persuaded Eleanor to sell her residential land,

5. Matter of Fonte, 2 Calif. State Bar Ct. Rptr. 752 (1994) (60 days suspension, two years probation).

telling her not to worry about leaving money to Phillip's family (the trust's purpose) and suggesting that she secretly split any additional sale proceeds with him. After Eleanor paid another lawyer $7,000 to petition for Fonte's removal, he offered to resign if she released him from liability and withdrew her State Bar complaint.

Jan and Dan Curtis cared for Erwin and Marguerite Loeloff for nine months on the promise of inheriting their home, until a dispute ended this arrangement. Retained by the Curtises to explore a conservatorship of the Loeloffs, Fonte advised against it. Jan asked Fonte to intervene when Marguerite was hospitalized, but she refused to talk to him. At his suggestion (and with Jan's consent), Fonte returned to Marguerite's hospital room and offered to represent her in negotiating home care with the Curtises. When she agreed, Fonte had the Loeloffs grant him power of attorney and immediately made himself cosignatory on their bank account, transferring $5,000 to his client trust account and withdrawing $2,500 as attorney's fees. He drafted an agreement between the Curtises and himself (as agent for the Loeloffs), but Marguerite and Jan refused to sign it. He directed the bank to send him the Loeloffs' monthly statement and canceled checks and transferred a $26,000 savings account to a higher yielding term account in his name. He drafted a living trust, which they refused to sign. Finally, he told both parties to get separate counsel, withdrew from representing the Loeloffs, and refunded the remaining $2,500 from his trust account. After Marguerite's death, Jan's attorney demanded the funds Fonte had withdrawn from the Loeloffs' bank account. Fonte sent Jan his "final offer," claiming payment for 4.5 hours but offering to return $250 and waive additional fees if she agreed to settle all complaints and disputes.

After Paul D. Priamos represented MC in a divorce, she asked him to invest her property settlement in certificates of deposit so she could live on the interest.[6] While she was hospitalized for manic depression (as he knew she had been before), she gave him a general power of attorney. Between 1981 and 1988, he managed about $2.1 million, mishandling about half. He invested $500,000 in speculative ventures in which he had an undisclosed financial interest; many investments were not in her name; despite her repeated requests for an accounting, he provided only one handwritten summary of her assets; and he paid himself $450,000 in attorneys and management fees. He invested $27,000 in a company in which he was an officer and director (nearly 10 percent of its capital) and was unable to resell the shares. He created a partnership with her to invest in Tennessee walking horses, real estate, and other projects, dividing profits and losses equally but paying himself a "reasonable" hourly fee. Although the partnership agreement recited that MC "may not be stable enough to sign documents

6. Matter of Priamos, 3 Calif. State Bar Ct. Rptr. 824 (1998) (found to have misappropriated from another client; disbarred).

on her behalf," he did not advise her to consult independent counsel. He used $353,875 to buy thirteen horses, but neither the partnership nor MC was named on the title. He and his wife took sole title to the Tennessee horse farm in which he had invested $104,000 of MC's money, giving her an unsecured promissory note. When the Priamoses divorced three years later, the horse farm went to his ex-wife. He used $26,000 to buy undeveloped property in Molokai; although it sold for a profit, there was no accounting. He used $10,000 to buy property from his brother, putting the title in his and his wife's names. After reading in the newspaper that her property taxes were delinquent, MC questioned Priamos, who insisted her money was safely invested. Unsatisfied, she revoked the power of attorney and hired new counsel. When Priamos refused to turn over all assets, she sued to compel an accounting, dissolve the partnership, and recover damages. The lawsuit was stayed when Priamos declared bankruptcy, listing MC as an unsecured creditor for $1 million (a debt the bankruptcy court found nondischargeable). Her lawsuit exposed the fact that Priamos had paid himself $212,715 in management fees and $233,392 in legal fees. The only profit she ever realized was from the sale of one horse.

After developing a process to clean contaminated soil, Robert Ruppert joined with CERT Environmental Corp. (a Unocal subsidiary) to form Thermal Remediation Corp (TRC) to market it.[7] After CERT elected three Unocal employees to the TRC board and Ruppert chose himself, TRC hired him as president and chief operating officer (COO). Unocal lent TRC more than $4 million and contracted with it for soil remediation services potentially worth over $3.5 million. When the board discovered that Ruppert had engaged in financial impropriety and exceeded his spending authority, it reduced his spending authority from $25,000 to $100 a transaction. Because TRC made no profit and could not repay the loans, CERT tried to sell its 50 percent interest. Since it could not agree on terms with Ruppert or find another buyer, the CERT board decided to dissolve TRC, over Ruppert's opposition and directed him to comply.

Two months later, he notified all TRC vendors but simultaneously consulted James S. Davis, an insolvency and corporate law specialist, who advised that "Unocal was trying to dodge the $3,000,000 contract it had with TRC" and "the best way to stop Unocal . . . was to file a Chapter 11 bankruptcy petition." Without notifying the board, Ruppert hired Davis as a lawyer for TRC for a $20,000 retainer, giving him two personal checks: $5,000 (which Davis deposited) and $15,000 (which Davis held pending a forthcoming insurance settlement). Although Davis knew that TRC's Articles of Incorporation made Ruppert subordinate to the board, he filed the Chapter 11 petition without notifying board members, who were "hopelessly conflicted" because they were employees of

7. Matter of Davis, 4 Calif. State Bar Ct. Rptr. 576 (2003) (two years suspension, four years probation).

Unocal, which was both a creditor and a debtor of TRC. The day of this filing, at a scheduled and noticed meeting (which Ruppert skipped), the board suspended him as president, removed him as signatory on all TRC accounts, and revoked his authority to sign payroll checks. Two days later, Robert Kehr (a CERT lawyer) notified Davis of these actions, demanding that he stop representing TRC and adding that the board had "revoked any authority that [Ruppert] might otherwise have to represent . . . TRC" and that "any commitment [Ruppert] might otherwise have made on behalf of TRC to pay your fees . . . was in excess of his spending authority which was limited to $100 . . .." The next day, CERT's bankruptcy attorney repeated all this to Davis.

Davis replied to Kehr that he would enjoin "all unlawful interference with the reorganization effort" and threatened a RICO action against the three CERT directors, CERT, and Unocal, as well as a suit against both attorneys for wire and mail fraud. The same day Ruppert collected an $80,000 insurance check for TRC, endorsed it as "President TRC," and gave it to Davis, who deposited it in his client trust account. Once it cleared, Davis's office manager returned Ruppert's $15,000 check and sent a $50,000 check to Ruppert, who deposited it in a bankruptcy debtor-in-possession account. At a board meeting the next day, Ruppert and Davis did not tell the other directors about this transaction. A day later, Davis misrepresented to Kehr that Ruppert had individually paid his retainer. The board resolved to close the TRC office and ordered Ruppert to end all activity for TRC. Board chairman Dassler told Davis he was not authorized to act for TRC and directed him to withdraw, reiterating this five days later. Davis refused because of board members' conflict of interest.

Dassler demanded an accounting when he discovered what had happened to the insurance check five weeks later. Kehr made a similar request, asserting a Unocal lien on all TRC assets, including the insurance check, and asking Davis to return the balance in his client trust account. Davis refused. When Dassler wrote Davis's bank, Davis threatened to sue and ignored all of Dassler's subsequent efforts to trace the insurance proceeds, which Davis disguised in his billing statements. Knowing that Ruppert had left the state and could not be found, Davis told Dassler to ask Ruppert about the check. The bankruptcy court dismissed the petition and sanctioned Ruppert and Davis $2,500 each for filing it frivolously. Despite all this and TRC's dissolution by a Delaware court, Davis continued to bill the corporation for his legal services for two more years. In the disciplinary proceeding, he claimed he had simply encountered "battling factions" and made the best possible decision "on the front line."

Like other professionals—doctors, psychiatrists, priests—lawyers generally acquire immense authority over those they serve.[8] This is particularly true if the clients are elderly, mentally or emotionally unstable, or uneducated. For this

8. *See also* Matter of Conner, 5 Calif. State Bar Ct. Rptr. 93 (2008).

reason, it is essential that the lawyer perform a single, clearly defined, role, with undivided loyalty. As the principal case shows, role ambiguity and deceit can harm even a highly sophisticated corporation.

II. CONNING THE MARK

Brian Depew was admitted to the bar in November 1979 and Robert Crane a year later.[9] Crane joined the legal department of Sega Enterprises, Inc. (a Paramount subsidiary) in February 1982, with responsibility for developing business opportunities for non-arcade uses of video games by licensing spin-off products. (Before ownership of powerful PCs became widespread, virtually all video games were played in arcades.) In September 1983, Crane formed Universal Licensing, Inc., as sole proprietor. He convinced Sega to license Universal to manufacture and distribute floppy disks for *Zaxxon*, one of its most successful video games, for use on the Commodore C-64 home computer system, without disclosing that he was Universal, which could neither pay the license fees nor manufacture or distribute the disks. The contract provided for a $5,000 advance to Sega and a further guaranteed $5,000, against 6 percent royalties. After talking to Synapse Software, Inc., and Human Engineered Software Corp. (HES) and realizing *Zaxxon* was worth significantly more, he modified Sega's standard license to permit Universal to sublicense. Using the pseudonym "Steve Kness," Crane, as Universal, sublicensed *Zaxxon* to Synapse and told Sega that because Universal could not manufacture it he had "saved the deal" by finding a suitable sublicensee. On October 12, he wrote as Universal's "Steve Kness" to himself at Sega, memorializing Sega's approval of the sublicense. Crane then paid his friend Depew $1,000 to pose as Universal's general counsel in a meeting with Synapse, resulting in a sublicense for which Synapse paid a $50,000 advance against 16 percent royalties. On October 13, Crane arranged for Sega to sign the sublicense he had drafted. On behalf of Universal, Depew signed a sublicense omitting the financial terms, which Crane added to the agreement Synapse signed in November. Crane paid the $5,000 due Sega only after receiving $50,000 from Synapse in November, signing the cover letter "Steve Kness" and backdating it to September 30, when payment had been due. He hand-carried the check to Sega accounting to suggest, falsely, that it had been received during the ordinary course of business. He then helped Synapse obtain programming information from Sega.

In November, Crane met HES executives at Sega and learned they would have paid twice as much as Synapse. As a result, he asked Sega if he could include

9. These two paragraphs are taken from the notice to show cause (NTSC), Cases 80 O 14252 and 80 O 14253 (2.25.88). Although the disciplinary proceedings spell the name *DePew*, the State Bar spells it *Depew*.

Super Zaxxon in the *Zaxxon* sublicense, even though he knew the games were very similar and had prepared the copyright registration showing *Super Zaxxon* to be a derivative work. After Sega refused, Crane prepared an amendment to the Universal license on November 21, including *Super Zaxxon* on the basis of the similarity, signing his own name on behalf of Sega and "Steve Kness" on behalf of Universal. He learned in December that he would be laid off the next month for lack of work. Claiming to be Universal's licensing director, "Bruce Blumberg," he then tried to sublicense *Super Zaxxon* to HES in direct competition with Synapse's rights in *Zaxxon*. This resulted in an agreement after Crane left Sega, according to which HES would pay a $100,000 advance against 16 percent royalties; Crane signed for Universal as both Steve Kness and Bruce Blumberg. On his last day at Sega, Crane amended Universal's license to include *Carnival* and *Turbo* but never managed to sublicense those games.

After HES paid the initial $25,000 in mid February, it publicized its acquisition of *Super Zaxxon*. Writing as Universal's Bruce Blumberg, Crane falsely told Sega that its counsel had approved the *Super Zaxxon* sublicense and requested confirmation in writing. He told Sega attorney Bob Kupec (his former superior) that he (Crane) had approved it before leaving Sega. Kupec said Sega could not approve the *Super Zaxxon* sublicense if it conflicted with the *Zaxxon* sublicense. He later found no record of the HES-Universal sublicense. Crane hired Depew for $2,500 to act for Universal and badger Sega to approve the sublicense. Depew also told HES to ask Crane if he had approved the sublicense while still at Sega. Crane told HES that "Blumberg" had told him that Universal had acquired the *Super Zaxxon* rights under the license amendment.

Depew's 1988 answer to the NTSC denied everything and raised the defense of laches, since the State Bar had thoroughly investigated the matter in 1982–83.[10] Crane's answer claimed that for several months before, "he tried unsuccessfully to convince Sega management to develop the floppy disk market for *Zaxxon* and other video games owned by Sega for the home computer market, all for the benefit of Sega." The company told him "it was not interested in any further development of this market." He "formed Universal only after he was convinced that Sega had no intention of developing the floppy disk home computer market on its own and only after he had seen several of Sega's video games lose their popularity and marketability in the home computer market." He initially believed Universal was capable of manufacturing and marketing floppy disks, discovering only later it was not. He denied knowing the license was worth much more than Universal paid Sega and insisted that "the terms of the licensing agreement between Universal and Sega were fair to Sega." Nevertheless, he admitted culpability.

10. Depew Answer (Mar. 17, 1988).

At the disciplinary hearing before retired Superior Court Judge Harry T. Shafer, Depew's lawyer, Gert Hirschberg (who had had long experience at the OTC before leaving for private practice) was extremely aggressive toward OTC counsel Stephen J. Strauss.[11] (Shafer and Hirschberg were at least acquaintances and may have known each other as plaintiff's personal injury attorneys.) Making an offer of proof, Hirschberg gratuitously insulted Shafer by saying, "I'm trying to get [it] through your thin [*sic*] skull." Hirschberg demanded notes taken by Joshua S. Wattles (Paramount's deputy general counsel and senior vice president) of a meeting with Depew after Sega had learned of the deceit.

> The State Bar is supposed to be a fair organization. We're entitled to some due process here, and this guy [Strauss] is just hiding evidence. He is so bent and determined to get a conviction that he is concealing from me notes made by this witness.

After further colloquy about the notes (which had been disputed in discovery), Strauss exploded to the judge that "this man [Hirschberg] twists things . . . more than my wife or my three daughters." Hirschberg's March 28, 1989 trial brief was fiercely combative. Depew "is being put through the trauma of having to defend totally unfounded charges relating to an incident in his professional life where he was guilty, if anything, of poor judgment." Hirschberg could not "remember a more frivolous matter brought to trial. It is akin to a drunken driver making a U-turn on the Santa Monica freeway, and then suing oncoming traffic for injuries sustained." "The State Bar pleading is a model of uncertainty, vagueness and indefiniteness." The "conduct of the State Bar and its attorney were far from admirable."

The nastiness just escalated. When Strauss noted for the record that Depew was absent, Hirschberg accused him of "making a big issue out of nothing." (Depew arrived seven minutes late.) Strauss put on record Hirschberg's failure to file an answer to interrogatories or a response to the request for admissions (but he had given them to Strauss). Asked by the Referee if he objected to Strauss's copies of documents, Hirschberg conceded that "even [Strauss] wouldn't stoop to changing these things." But he accused Strauss of "the grossest type of misconduct" in appending Wattles's eight-page unsworn complaint to a motion for a continuance. "The person who should be charged with discipline in this matter is Mr. Strauss," whose justification just "makes the misconduct even more grievous." Strauss in turn objected to Hirschberg's characterization of his trial brief as "legitimate," since it had been served on him and the court just fifteen minutes before the hearing.

Hirschberg complained that Strauss

11. Unless otherwise noted, all the following is taken from the trial transcript of December 19, 1988, and March 28–31 and June 2, 1989.

> has accused me of being a drunk during [Depew's] deposition . . .. He has accused [Depew] of being a homosexual in this deposition. This guy has as much honor as a snake. I have caught him in a lie . . . . I am going to prove it because I just purchased the Grumman transcript for $230.

The referee cut him off and called a recess to let tempers cool.

But they didn't. When Strauss asked what Depew told Paramount about the San Francisco trip, Hirschberg interrupted.

HIRSCHBERG: May I just caution—

STRAUSS: He said Crane—

HIRSCHBERG: Please stop interrupting . . . .

STRAUSS: He is interrupting who, Mr . . . .

HIRSCHBERG: You interrupted me. How would you like a punch in the nose?

STRAUSS: Reporter, do you have that?

When the referee asked why Depew made representations to Kupec about the differences between *Zaxxon* and *Super Zaxxon*, Hirschberg interrupted again.

HIRSCHBERG: Crane was the expert in the field of copyrights.

REFEREE: [Depew] didn't know that.

STRAUSS: Objection. Why are we listening to Mr. Hirschberg on this point?

HIRSCHBERG: Can you tell him to stop interrupting me[?]

STRAUSS: There is no question pending to Mr. Hirschberg. He's not objecting. Why are we listening to him? Let's hear from the witness. Let's hear from Mr. Clare [Crane's lawyer].

HIRSCHBERG: Do you find him to be awfully offensive?

When Wattles testified that he had not reviewed notes of the meetings with Crane or Depew before being deposed, Hirschberg was incredulous.

HIRSCHBERG: What kind of nonsense are you giving us when you say that you did not review these notes?

WATTLES: I am not giving you any nonsense . . . .

HIRSCHBERG: I am leading to the fact that he is a liar.

Hirschberg sought (unsuccessfully) to show that Strauss had influenced Wattles's testimony, asking if the witness had been "told you might be called a snitch today?" and whether he intended his complaint "to be an opening statement by counsel?" Hirschberg was "still seething over the fact that this lawyer, Strauss, had the tenacity [*sic*—perhaps a malapropism combining temerity and audacity] to send you [the referee] a privileged and confidential statement of a witness attached to a motion for continuance without giving counsel . . . any idea . . .. That was misconduct . . . ." Strauss retorted, "At least I file my discovery. That's more than Mr. Hirschberg does." "I don't have to take this kind of personal abuse from Mr. Hirschberg when the record itself is clear." Hirschberg challenged Wattles's statement in the complaint about "vigorous negotiations over the phone" with Synapse's President, Igor Wolosenko, a "sophisticated and a tough bargainer," in which "Depew used his real name but Crane used the name 'Steve Kness.'" When Strauss objected that Hirschberg was "argumentative and badgering the witness," the latter retorted that Wattles "is getting more due process today, sir, than he gave Depew." When Strauss objected to the referee's characterization of Paramount's behavior, Strauss and Hirschberg kept interrupting each other, prompting the reporter to ask them to repeat.

REPORTER: I will put an off-the-record discussion then.

HIRSCHBERG: I don't think so. I think we should let the record indicate just how insolent Mr. Strauss can be.

REFEREE: That will go out.

STRAUSS: I want counsel's characterization of my behalf [*sic*— "behavior"] as insolent on the record at this point. Also his prior characterization of whatever it was that I said.

REFEREE: I will make the observation that it wasn't insolent . . . .

STRAUSS: I am simply trying to make a record [of a] continuing course of conduct by opposing counsel.

When Strauss objected to Hirschberg's offer of a May 11, 1984, letter not in evidence, the referee asked what Hirschberg was getting at.

HIRSCHBERG: If I could finish the question without this jerk interrupting all the time.

REFEREE: Just a moment. That remark will stay in the record only because it may give further emphasis as to what Mr. Strauss mentioned about conduct.

Hirschberg sought to depict Depew as Crane's dupe. Depew was now a partner in Engstroem, Lipscomb & Lack, the "a.v. litigation firm"[12] where he began practice in 1979. Crane had asked him to do "errand work," paying him "absolutely nothing": $1,000 to meet with Synapse and $2,500 for other tasks; he repaid all this to settle Sega's civil claim. Depew's only experience was tort litigation. "No one questions the lack of wisdom in stepping outside one's field. Fagan needed a young Oliver Twist, and Crane found him in Brian Depew."

His "right to negotiate [with Synapse] was in name only; it was nonexistent . . . because it was Crane's business and not Brian's."

> The evidence is almost uncontradicted: *Brian never knew that Sega did not know that Crane was Universal and Universal was Crane.* The testimony will show that Brian did inquire of Crane whether there was not something very, very unusual about an agent benefiting from his double dealings with a principal.

---

12. Martindale-Hubbell rating: legal ability and general recommendation both very high.

The HES sublicense was granted without the knowledge of Depew, whose "involvement was only as a part-time lawyer, whose function it was to sign letters, return phone calls, but not to enter into any negotiations, write checks, or take an entrepreneurial position." When the conflicting copyrights threatened to expose the whole scam, "Brian did the first bright thing in this scenario," by consulting a corporate litigator, Michael Sullivan. "Sullivan felt that Crane was up to his ears in trouble and that the criminal justice system might very well be involved. *No suspicion whatsoever was cast upon the conduct of Brian.* Sullivan's sage advice to Crane was to come clean, which Crane did. "The whole thing was an embarrassment to Sega, to Paramount, to its legal department, and to Wattles, who made the accusation to the State Bar." That explained the involvement of "high-powered counsel" from O'Melveny & Myers, and Wyman Bautzer. Only after the State Bar complaint was any "suspicion whatsoever cast upon Brian Depew, a pawn in this entire enterprise." His "crime was not lack of good faith, but lack of good sense." When the referee commented that it would have been a "good trick" if Depew's functions as Universal's president, secretary, and general counsel were merely "ministerial," Hirschberg insisted that Depew "was, in short, a dummy. That's why he is here today."

Crane's lawyer, David Clare, took the opposite tack. His client admitted misconduct in 1985 when first contacted by the State Bar. He had joined Sega just a year after being admitted, primarily to do non-legal marketing. He had violated his ethical obligations to Sega but was unsophisticated in the practice of law. It was

> undisputed that the opportunity that Mr. Crane went after as Universal was one which Sega had abandoned. One which . . . Crane had tried to interest Sega management into developing . . . an opportunity that would have gone to waste had not Mr. Crane stepped in . . ..

Asked "what is all that intended to prove," Clare said "it is not intended as a defense, it is intended as a mitigating circumstance." The referee replied: "you are in Lone Pine . . . just came out of Schatz's lovely bakery, had a full breakfast, got a hundred pound pack on your back and are looking at Mt Whitney."[13] Clare replied that when the copyright dispute between Synapse and HES erupted, Crane and Depew "believed they were still in the right and that they had a cause of action against Sega for not approving the sublicense, which demonstrates how far off base Mr. Crane's thinking was at the time." The referee observed,

13. The metaphor is intended to show that Clare had an uphill battle. Schatz's Bakery has branches in Bishop and Mammoth Lakes but not Lone Pine. The hike from the trailhead (above Lone Pine) to Whitney (at nearly 15,000 feet, the highest mountain in the continental United States) is 22 miles round trip, with an elevation gain of 6,100 feet. Nobody makes the climb with a 100-pound pack; backpackers continuing up the John Muir Trail would leave their equipment at Trailcrest before summiting.

however, that Crane's consultation of Sullivan "wasn't just mea culpa" but also reflected fear that the deceit would have "unraveled" because of HES's copyright complaint. Clare responded that Crane settled with Paramount by paying the $47,000 remaining in Universal's bank account and making monthly $250 payments for the last five years. The referee concluded that Crane's guilt "has been slammed dunked [*sic*]," and on mitigation "you got a long way to go . . . . from what I heard so far in the case, Mr. Crane embarked on a plan that was fraudulent, he continued it, that he entered into another plan with another company . . . and that when the bark of the pursuers was being heard by him, he went to the State Bar and confessed."

Crane testified that 80 percent of his work at Sega was licensing trademarks and copyrights for spinoff products, which required little legal knowledge. He created Universal Licensing between August and October 1983 to license Sega videogames for home computers. Wattles later testified that "the reason [Sega] had not gone into the floppy disk home computer game market was their belief that in comparison to the other market sectors that they were involved in and the amount of attention that they required and all the revenue that they generated that this was not a significant market sector for them."

Crane obtained a post office box and answering service for Universal but never held a corporate meeting. He sought the advice of Brian Depew, whom he had met as a law student when clerking at Engstroem, Lipscomb and Lack, where Depew was an associate. The two played tennis every six weeks. Crane had consulted Depew about the plan three times—by phone, after a tennis game, and at Paramount—before writing as Universal to seek a license from Sega. "I wanted to get his . . . legal thought on . . . the legality and integrity of this type of transaction" because "I wasn't comfortable with it." "I wanted to get the opinion of another attorney . . . .." "I respected [Depew] . . . as a bright person who was an attorney that I thought I could consult without having to engage another firm and pay legal fees." Crane showed Depew a license that another entrepreneur had obtained to produce *Frogger* (not a Sega product) for home computers for a $15,000 guarantee on 7 percent royalties.

> I asked would it be improper for me to submit to the company, without any influence of my own, a transaction of this nature. We talked about the corporate usurpation doctrine . . . for some times . . . . I came to the conclusion as long as I submitted it to the company without any recommendation or influence, that I wouldn't be violating the doctrine of corporate usurpation.

Wattles's notes of his May 13, 1984, meeting with Depew read: "The discussion of usurpation of corporate opportunity lasted one hour. Crane ended on the issue by asking Depew, 'You tell me if this is wrong.' Depew answered he didn't know . . . ." Hirschberg sought to shift all responsibility to Crane, claiming that Paramount's notes of that meeting said Crane "talked Depew into the idea." Crane now called that "totally inaccurate."

Depew remembered Crane's

> call at my home at around 10:00 o'clock in the evening, I was home in bed watching television with my wife, who is also an attorney . . .. [D]uring the course of this casual conversation, [Crane] had mentioned that he had gone out and purchased a video game from his employer and set up a company . . . he was going to sublicense the game . . . . that is when I introduced this concept of usurpation of corporate opportunity . . . . [Crane] had been involved in previous business dealings and would often come to me and brag about his business exploits . . . . I said, "It sounds to me like you are competing with your employer. I don't know if you can do that." I am the one that used the term usurpation of corporate opportunity. He didn't even know what the term meant and sounded like he had never heard it before. . . . [T]hat's when he went into this long explanation about how Sega had abandoned certain arcade games . . . he told me about one story of a farmer from the Midwest who out of his garage bought the licensing rights to an arcade game and turned around and sold it to somebody to manufacture and distribute and became wealthy overnight. He was infatuated with that idea . . .. My response to Mr. Crane was, "It is Sega's decision if they don't want to exploit a game . . . . I am not sure you can do what you are doing," and he said, "There is nothing wrong with what I am doing because I will be making them money . . .." After I explained my position to him, I very specifically said, "I have just exhausted the sum total of my knowledge of corporate law." . . . He said, "You don't know what you are talking about . . .. There can't be anything wrong with what I am doing if I am making them money . . .. Your analysis is flawed." . . . [T]hen I specifically said to him, "But you are going to be in a very strange position . . .. If there is a lawsuit, you are either going to be defending or prosecuting your case against your own employer." . . . He said, "Brian, you don't know what you are talking about. These deals are done every day. There has never been a lawsuit."

Crane had bragged about using his substantial inheritance from his father in 1980 to start a men's clothing business with his brother and participate in a property development syndication with Henry Winkler, a Paramount actor.

Depew remembered discussing the scheme again after playing tennis. "[I]t was a sophomoric discussion between two people on a purely gratuitous basis where he would say, 'I'm going to do this.' I said 'Well, I don't know if you can.'" The third meeting occurred at Paramount. "He was never offering to pay me for my time. He was never specifically indicating to me at this point he was going to retain my services." After another tennis game, Crane asked: "How would you like to be president of a company."

REFEREE: Why didn't you say no to his proposal?

DEPEW: Which proposal?

REFEREE: That you become secretary, that you become counsel to a firm that was going to be doing the very things that you, in your mind, found difficulty in grappling with.

DEPEW: First of all, he did not ask me to be counsel and president at the same time . . . . [Crane] said, "Look, it's absolutely nothing." . . . [T]his was a conversation with someone who I regarded as a close friend. It never occurred to me to suspect him of wrongdoing . . . . I never held myself out as president . . . . [M]y cards did not. They held me out as general counsel . . . . [S]igning incorporating documents is not creating detrimental reliance of a third party . . ..

Margaret Ann McGinnis, also a lawyer, married Depew in September or October 1983. (They separated in 1984 and divorced in 1988.) She had a general recollection of the phone call, in which Depew expressed concern "whether what Rob had done was appropriate for an employee to have done." "I heard enough that I was concerned as well." "I knew from what Brian was saying that he assumed that Rob's employer knew that Rob had purchased the property." The referee could not understand why there was any problem if Sega knew that Universal was Crane. McGinnis replied, "My sense of the conversation was that it wasn't in order to be convinced of the legality of anything but that Rob Crane was gloating over the fact that he had a property that was going to make him money." Crane was not seeking advice or asking Depew to get involved.

On September 13, 1983, Crane presented Michael Dulberg—Sega's "finance person," who "knew whether it was a fair transaction or not"—with Universal's offer to license *Zaxxon* and *Carnival* for a $10,000 advance against 7 percent royalties. Crane wrote that, "These properties aren't getting any more popular and this company [Universal] would like to consummate a license quickly in order to capture the Christmas market." "If you approve," Crane promised to "negotiate the best possible license agreement" and suggested Sega seek $15,000 and 10 percent. Instead, Universal reduced its offer to 6 percent because Sega would not license IBM rights. Crane never actually proposed the higher amount to Universal (i.e., himself). "In hindsight," he testified, "I wish I had consulted an attorney" at Sega. He had not asked Kupec, his superior, because each time Crane raised the possibility of licensing video games for home computers Kupec "would shrug it off."

On September 23, Crane wrote as Steven Kness on Universal letterhead to himself at Sega "to bring to the attention of the file that the [company's] name was changed" from Universal Marketing.[14] He used a pseudonym because of "discussions that I had with Mr. Depew previously about the usurpation of the corporate opportunity" but denied that he had hidden his identity because he knew he was doing something wrong. "I honest to God believed that after my discussion

14. Depew's Exhibit 45.

with Brian Depew . . . as long as I offered the transaction to the company separate from my recommendation . . . it wouldn't be usurpation of a corporate opportunity . . .." He did not call the State Bar's ethics hot line because he had not known about it.

The referee warned that the story wasn't playing in Peoria. Why hadn't Crane taken it "up with his boss, who he was going to work with . . . ?" Crane admitted that all his conversations with Depew concerned how "to keep myself out of the transaction." He told Depew that "Sega cannot find out that Crane is Universal . . . ." Had this emerged, "they wouldn't allow [the deal] because I wouldn't have the expertise." Crane "wanted to create the idea of a substantial entity" like Corn-Soft and Walt-Rich Marketing, two companies working out of garages and licensing Sega programs. The referee could not "fathom why you have to ask somebody else [i.e., Depew] as to what is propriety. On the face of it, it has a stench."

REFEREE: Am I to assume therefore, you wouldn't have done it if he hadn't encouraged you?

CRANE: No question about it . . . when we consulted Mr. Sullivan, as naive as I was, my mindset was that I had legal rights to pursue . . . my mouth opened in surprise. . . . I am remorseful and ashamed now that I am more mature . . . .

REFEREE: It is one thing to be remorseful and ashamed, it is another thing to dump on somebody . . . .

CRANE: . . . [Depew's] participation in going to San Francisco and continuing the transaction made me think it wasn't an improper transaction, because he is an attorney for which I am paying him fees and giving me this guidance . . . . [T]he transaction was legitimized by his involvement in not saying not to do it . . . . [H]ad he advised me of the things that Mr. Sullivan advised me later on . . . I wouldn't have pursued this endeavor. I am not that type of person.

Depew "was as ignorant as I was about the improprietiness [*sic*] of this type of transaction . . . it was an error in judgment . . . I am not trying to point a finger . . .." He "disagree[d]" with Depew's deposition that it was really Crane "who talked Mr. Depew into agreeing with the propriety of these actions." In his May 9, 1984, statement to Paramount, Crane said his "purpose was to bring Depew in to negotiate as an attorney on behalf of Universal." Depew had "agreed" but was "concerned." The notes conclude that Crane "talked Depew into the idea." Crane denied saying that, insisting that Depew "said based upon what I was showing him that it is proper." "I wasn't a rocket scientist. I wasn't a sophisticated person. I was naive and immature and inexperienced That is probably the reason . . .. I had no intention of defrauding or harming anyone." But he later admitted "I was a bigger schmuk than Brian."

Hirschberg called John C. Alva, since 1983 an investigator and administrator for the law firm of Louie Edelberg, where he claimed to have met Crane, who

> was attempting to have me make an investment in some type of corporate function which he was involved in at that time . . . Universal or Sega . . . he was in the business of not only representing them but of also forming various other corporations which he was able to do via the spinoff of business that came from Sega that Sega was no longer interested in.
>
> I . . . stated to him that from my personal experience in the business world that there was no corporation that would allow any product or potential client to be taken from their control or profits . . . he answered by advising me that . . . he had their complete and total authority to do this because they were no longer interested . . . . I told him that it was difficult for me to comprehend . . . that they would allow him to take a potential money maker regardless of how minute . . . I asked him if he had as part of his . . . contract with them, if he had the privilege of taking the spinoffs that they were no longer interested in. He told me exactly that this was the case.

At Crane's request, Alva arranged a meeting with Edelberg, to whom Crane made the same pitch.

> And Mr. Edelberg challenged him . . . "[W]ait a minute. You mean to tell me you are taking clients from Sega and Sega is allowing you to do this without some type of agreement?" And he said "Yes." And Lou said, "I can't believe that." The conversation was ended very abruptly. Mr. Crane and I left and went to my office there. And again, Mr. Crane advised me that Louie was giving him old fashioned ideas. That Mr. Crane had complete and total permission from Sega . . . that he had made a $5,000 purchase from one of the spinoffs and that he had . . . turned it into a $50,000 profit . . . . Mr. Edelberg was very upset having Mr. Crane in the office—he asked me not to have anything to do with Mr. Crane . . . . I told Mr. Crane that Mr. Edelberg wanted to call the California State Bar because of the fact that Mr. Edelberg felt it was very bad . . . Crane asked me if I could talk to Louie and stop him from doing that. And he said, "Does Mr. Edelberg have my card?" I said, "I am sure he does." He says, "Can you get the card? It's in his desk." I said I'd check. I walked into Mr. Edelberg's desk and removed the card from his desk and I destroyed it.

Cross-examined by Clare, Alva admitted that Depew's "face turned white" when Alva mentioned this incident at lunch three months before the disciplinary hearing. The night before this hearing, Clare had also talked with Walter Lack (Depew's senior partner).

> [T]he fact is in Mr. Edelberg's office on the second date, three or four days later, [Crane] returned and advised me and told me that he knew that by trying to pull the wool over my eyes that he really didn't have their permission and if there were any lawsuits involved—I told him it goes beyond lawsuits. I told him he was exposing himself to disciplinary proceedings . . . . I said, "not only

> that, but there is a fraud matter here. You could subject yourself to punitive damages rendered against you. He then told me, when have I ever known corporate counsels to get into lawsuits and end up in disciplinary proceedings? I took that into consideration. I said, "that's true." He said, "what they do is they sue one another." He said, "you don't go before the California State Bar, not for this type of thing."

Crane retorted that Alva was "an ambulance chaser" whose "occupation" was

> going out into the East Los Angeles portion . . . and investigating the various cases that he had brought to the firm for which he was paid by Engstroem, Lipscomb & Lack . . . . [I]n the two years that I was employed . . . the majority of Mr. Alva's income was derived from the cases that he would chase into the market, bring to the firm . . . .

Because Crane also spoke Spanish, "I spent a tremendous amount of time traveling with Mr. Alva, lunching with Mr. Alva, investigating in the field with Mr. Alva . . . ." Alva began working for the Engstroem firm in 1978; Depew joined it the next year; they knew each other "very well." Crane testified that "during the time I was there from '78 to'80, Mr. Alva was in the office at least three to four times a week." Crane denied Alva's entire story.

> I have never seen Mr. Alva since the day my father died, January 24, 1980. I have never heard of Mr. Edelman [*sic*]. I have never been to Mr. Edelman's office . . . . [T]he whole testimony that was represented by Mr. Alva was an out and out lie and consistent with the manner in which he conducted himself during the tenure in which I was a law clerk at that firm.

The referee was shocked.

REFEREE: I will have to look at this thing. Why would he make a statement like that? . . .

CRANE: That's the nature of his personality. He is a pawn to Walter Lack and the firm. That is where he derives his income from . . .

REFEREE: What would Alva gain by lying?

CRANE: He would gain the alliance and friendship of his colleague Brian [Depew] who would prosecute some of these cases.

Hirschberg claimed *Eddie* Edelberg would confirm that Crane had been in the office he shared with his brother Louie, but Eddie had been allowed to leave the hearing room, and Clare objected to him testifying by phone.

Writing as Steve Kness of Universal to himself at Sega on September 30, Crane lied that he was enclosing a $5,000 check for the license.[15] He testified that once he obtained the license

15. State Bar Exhibit 44.

> I called Soft-Cell, which was the major company in the industry that distributed these video game disks to the market place . . . and I asked how does one . . . get into the K-Marts and the like. They told me that it takes months to develop those types of relationships and contacts . . . . I looked in the magazine and tried to find a programmer that would be capable of converting the arcade version of the software to a video game disk software and I came upon a person in Texas or some state like that who advised me that it would cost me about a hundred thousand dollars up front fee . . . I tried to contact disk manufacturers to find out how one goes about obtaining the actual disk themselves and you have to go to Korea and buy huge volumes and spend a lot of money . . . . I determined . . . that I didn't have the capability to pursue this venture that I had sought out to do . . . . I found through a periodical that there were various companies that were successful in distributing and manufacturing these video game titles, so I called various companies, one happening to be Synapse and proposed a transaction . . ..

In that first conversation, he concealed his name and asked Synapse President Igor Wolosenko if he would be interested in *Zaxxon*. Wolosenko said he was and could sell 100,000 units, and he offered $50,000. Although Crane "was shocked," he immediately asked for $100,000. He responded to the referee's outrage: "I was trying to make money for the company as well. I was not benefiting myself on the sublicensing of this video game . . .." But he admitted that had he licensed *Zaxxon* to Synapse as a Sega employee, he would have earned only the salary he was also collecting. When Ken Grant at Synapse called him at Sega to confirm Universal's licensing rights, he nervously pretended to be Steve Kness, tried to disguise his voice, and lied that Universal "had acquired the *Zaxxon* rights long before they became hot."

The October 31 license stated that Universal would "manufacture, distribute and sell" *Zaxxon* cartridges and give Sega "samples of product's packaging, advertising, etc. for approval," as well as prototypes, although Crane knew Universal could do none of this. When he admitted Universal never tried to purchase licenses from other companies, Strauss attributed this to the fact that only at Sega could Crane create a paper trail misrepresenting that the initial licensing fee had been paid long before he actually could do so out of sublicensing fees. Crane returned to his theme:

> [I]t is such a stupid thing. I am not a rocket scientist. I don't think Brian was either. I engaged in a stupid transaction. It wasn't very smart . . .. I was a very unsophisticated individual and I didn't have the sophistication and the knowledge that I have now.

On October 12, Crane again wrote to himself as Kness, memorializing that Sega would prepare its standard sublicense to Synapse, which had the "experience and knowledge in the software area" to do the programming and packaging of *Zaxxon* in time for Christmas sales.[16] Although Crane admitted in his deposition that he "never affirmatively disclosed to [Sega] that Universal lacked the capacity to manufacture and distribute floppy disks," he now insisted he had "told Kupec that Universal lacked the capacity at the time of the Synapse contract." At his May 1984 Paramount interview, he claimed he had only learned the real value of the *Zaxxon* license from calls to Synapse and other manufacturers. Now he admitted not telling Sega when he "discovered that the rights to *Zaxxon* were valuable because there were a lot of these Commodore computers out there." Crane wrote to himself as Kness on October 13, enclosing a Synapse sublicense to be executed and returned.[17] The next day Depew wrote Synapse president Wolosenko enclosing "4 copies of duly executed sublicense agreement between Sega and Universal" and asking him to sign and return them with a $50,000 check by October 19. Crane wrote to himself as Kness on October 19, referring to Synapse as "the company [to] whom you have sublicensed *Zaxxon*."[18]

Crane claimed to have given Sega a reasonable opportunity to seek independent advice on the deal because "I submitted the agreement for the approval of Mr. Kupec who reviews all transactions before he signs them on behalf of the company."

STRAUSS: Wouldn't Mr. Kupec have relied upon you as an employee to bring him a fair deal?

CRANE: Yes.

STRAUSS: But you didn't tell Mr. Kupec that you were Universal, correct?

CRANE: Yes.

STRAUSS: Do think that was fair?

CRANE: Today, no.

Returning to his relationship with Depew, Crane repeated that, "I was a naïve unsophisticated individual."

REFEREE: Did you believe that Brian Depew was unsophisticated?

CRANE: No, I respected Brian. I thought he was very smart at what he did. . . .

REFEREE: Do you think Brian was savy [*sic*] and you were unsophisticated?

CRANE: Yeah, I thought Brian was savy [*sic*].

After they reached a tentative deal, Synapse wanted a personal meeting. Crane asked Depew to attend and printed up business cards describing him as general counsel. Depew was not just a messenger boy; he signed the Universal-Synapse sublicense as president.

---

16. State Bar Exhibit 39.
17. State Bar Exhibit 43.
18. State Bar Exhibit 41.

Depew met with Synapse, he maintained, only because Crane "had made arrangements for the two of us to meet separately with two potential customers." He denied Crane had no other business in San Francisco that day and just waited for Depew to finish. But Wattles remembered Depew saying that while he met with Synapse, Crane had gone to a restaurant. Depew testified: "I was specifically, expressly, and repeatedly told by Mr. Crane I had absolutely no negotiating authority." "Mr. Wolosenko was way over my head." "I told him I would take notes and I would take them back and consider them." Wattles's notes of the May 13 Paramount meeting read, "Depew showed Crane his notes of the meeting which consisted of handwritten interlineations or comments on the copy of the proposed Universal/Synapse license. Crane told Depew he had done well." Depew only learned what Crane paid Sega for *Zaxxon* at the April meeting with Sullivan. When Depew asked about the amount earlier, Crane replied, "You don't need to know that." "It struck me as unusual," Depew testified, but "I didn't know what to do." "When I agreed to be president to this company, I specifically asked Mr. Crane, 'What do I have to do? Is it going to require my time, and do I get paid?' and he said, 'You are not going to do anything. You're not going to get paid anything,' because the business wasn't doing anything."

As Universal's Kness, Crane wrote to himself at Sega on November 2 enclosing an executed sublicense agreement specifying $50,000 in royalties for the first time.[19] He filed the contract without showing it to Kupec. On December 9, he asked Kupec's permission to visit Synapse "to meet with the principals and review the program and packaging to ensure that they're on the right track." Kupec refused the next day.[20] On January 13, his last day at work, he wrote to "Kness," enclosing an amendment to the September 15 licensing agreement giving Universal additional rights to "Carnival" and "Turbo,"[21] which he called "very old titles that were just laying [*sic*] on the shelf that the company wasn't utilizing." But he dropped the idea when software manufacturers were uninterested.

On November 21, Crane wrote as Kness to himself at Sega "to confirm our telecon of today wherein Sega agreed to include the video game title 'Super Zaxxon' within the subject License agreement dated 9.15.83."[22] In the Paramount interview, he explained that having realized *Zaxxon's* value he thought he could make more money by including *Super Zaxxon*. He took a copy of the game when he was laid off on January 14 and first talked to HES about sublicensing it four days later. On February 3, he wrote as Universal's Bruce Blumberg to Jay Balakrishnan of HES:[23]

19. State Bar Exhibit 26.
20. State Bar Exhibit 34.
21. State Bar Exhibit 32.
22. State Bar Exhibit 36.
23. State Bar Exhibit 27.

> I enjoyed talking with you and discussing your company's licensing the "Super Zaxxon" video game.
>
> As promised, enclosed please find a video tape of the "Super Zaxxon" video game as well as three copies of our sublicense agreement for your review.

He asked for an executed copy within ten days. He altered the Sega sublicense to prohibit HES from further sublicensing *Super Zaxxon*, added an indemnification clause, precluded HES from putting Sega on the game title, and deleted Sega's copyright and trademark clause. HES required some changes, which he made before sending a revised sublicense on February 10.[24] On February 14, he executed a Universal-HES sublicense for Super Zaxxon,[25] signing as both Steve Kness and Bruce Blumberg because "I wanted the company to have an appearance that it had some size, substantialness to it." As Blumberg, Crane wrote himself at Sega on February 22.[26]

> In November we spoke and you agreed (as per our letter agreement of 11/21/83) to include the video game "Super Zaxxon" within the License granted us in September. I have just returned from my trip in the Orient and would like to refresh you where we left off regarding our sublicensing "Super Zaxxon." As we discussed in early January, we were in the process of negotiating a sub-license of this title and I am pleased to inform you that we have concluded our negotiations.

In fact, Crane had been laid off by Sega five weeks earlier, and the "trip in the Orient" was entirely fictitious. He received the first $25,000 payment from HES on execution and the second (of four) on approximately April 1, 1984.

III. GAME ENDED

HES became upset when Sega withheld permission to sublicense *Super Zaxxon*. On March 20, Balakrishnan called Depew and "Bruce Blumberg" (getting Universal's answering service). Depew was taken by surprise. Crane "kept me completely out of the loop of information about what he was doing." They had had no contact between the San Francisco trip and this phone call. "I thought it was a dead issue." But Crane's silence "wouldn't have been unusual." Depew responded by calling Crane, "I read him the riot act, and I said, 'What the hell is going on here? I'm getting calls from people about a game that I know nothing about.'" "Let me give you another example. After I had sent off the evolving sublicense agreement to Synapse, that whole transaction was consummated without my knowledge. Money had changed hands without my knowledge or involvement."

---

24. State Bar Exhibit 25.
25. State Bar Exhibit 64.
26. State Bar Exhibit 30.

Depew "set the fee at $5,000" for continuing to represent Universal. "I was upset with Mr. Crane. I didn't like the idea that he had completely failed to communicate to me this HES thing . . . and I had in my own mind wished that he would have said that $5,000 was too much and gone somewhere else . . .." The amount was "an advance against my time." "[T]his seemed like a relatively complex matter . . . ." "I had received a phone call out of the blue from someone up in the San Francisco area regarding a HES transaction . . . up until that phone conversation, I didn't even know HES existed." Wattles confirmed his deposition statement that Depew was "nervous about the representation" and felt "that the subject matter of the representation might not be altogether . . . kosher."

> In an attempt to dissuade Mr. Crane from obtaining [*sic*—"retaining"] him, [Depew] set a fee of $5,000 of [*sic*—"for"] what he felt at the time would be a single phone call and perhaps a letter to Sega. Mr. Depew knew that the purpose of his being retained was to permit Mr. Crane through artifice to make it appear Universal was a company controlled by individuals other than Crane. Mr. Crane was precluded from contacting Sega on behalf of Universal because they would discover his identity and that he was retaining Mr. Depew for the purposes of maintaining the concealment of that identity.

Crane said he orally agreed to pay Depew $5,000 for the services he had performed since the San Francisco trip in two installments:$2,500 at once and the rest later.

In response to Balakrishnan's call, Depew immediately telephoned Crane, who rushed to Depew's office and listened while Depew tried to persuade Kupec to change his mind. They drafted a follow-up letter, sent two days later, which Depew claimed was "my words, [Crane's] idea." Wattles's notes were consistent:

> Depew suggested that the 3.22.84 letter be sent to demonstrate that Universal legitimately owned Super Zaxxon rights. Depew at first took full credit for the letter but when questioned further about the suggestion in the letter that HES release the product using Universal's name instead of Sega's, Depew recalled that Crane had gone over the letter and had made that suggestion.

Depew claimed it would have been "physically impossible" for Crane to have overheard the conversation with Kupec because Depew had just telephoned Crane. Although the notes of the Paramount interview said Crane was present, "I misspoke myself."

STRAUSS: Do you recall telling the folks at Paramount [that] the telephone conversation between you and Kupec lasted approximately 15 to 20 minutes?

DEPEW: Uh huh.

STRAUSS: Do you recall telling him that Mr. Crane listened in and prompted you with answers when Kupec explained the difference in the game play between Zaxxon and Super Zaxxon? . . .

Depew: He prompted me in the letter . . . . [H]e would tell me what to say, and I would then put it into my own words.

Depew admitted saying "I reviewed the notes [of the May meeting] and I adopted them in sum and substance, but I was not going to adopt it verbatim . . . . [T]hey are, actually in looking at them, pretty accurate notes, but there are inaccuracies in there." He wrote the March 22 letter after having "exploded" at Crane "because I had the belief that he legitimately had title to this game, and my suspicion was that Sega wanted a better deal." Crane "knew what he was talking about, because I knew nothing about the arcade business or licensing or anything like that." "I wish I had" abandoned Crane then. "I have regretted that decision for the last five years."

On March 22, Kupec wrote Depew reaffirming his refusal to sublicense *Super Zaxxon* to HES because of its substantial similarity to *Zaxxon*.[27] Depew's March 22 letter (which crossed in the mail) summarized their March 20 phone conversation.[28] "Mr. Crane indicated that although the game was similar to Zaxxon, it had been separately copyrighted with the Copyright Office because of variations of game play and visual images." Sega had agreed by its November 21 letter (which Crane wrote to "Kness"), and Universal began sublicensing discussions "with Mr. Crane's assurances that he would consent to our sub-licensing Super Zaxxon . . .." When Universal next "spoke to Sega" in late December "and indicated we had some prospects . . . Mr. Crane again assured us that any sublicense agreement ultimately consummated by Universal would receive the approval and consent of Sega . . .." Universal proceeded to sublicense *Super Zaxxon* to HES. "By the time this agreement was consummated, Universal learned that Mr. Crane was no longer with Sega . . .. It is my understanding that notwithstanding the numerous assurances from Sega through its legal counsel, Mr. Crane, that Sega now chooses to substantially alter its position . . .."

Universal maintained the two games were different. "[T]his is substantiated to us by the fact that Mr. Crane has indicated to us that *Super Zaxxon* and *Zaxxon* are separately copyrighted . . . ." After watching both, Depew and Crane found "substantial differences," such as "the dragon and tunnel sequence." "[T]here is no doubt that Universal has the exclusive license to utilize Super Zaxxon as an independent property . . . ." He asked Sega to reconsider. "As your own records will no doubt reflect, Sega, through Robert Crane, has already provided such consent by means of representations made to Universal by Mr. Crane . . . ." Sega's refusal was "unwarranted, unreasonable and in breach of the terms of our contract with Sega." Sega's discussion with Synapse about the prejudice it might suffer if Universal sublicensed *Super Zaxxon* to HES was "an attempt to militate [*sic*—"motivate"?] their disfavor" and "perilously close to interference with our contractual

27. State Bar Exhibit 17.
28. Depew's Exhibit 18.

relationship." If Synapse complained about the *Super Zaxxon* sublicense "we will seek to hold Sega responsible for any and all damages . . . ." Kupec responded to Depew's March 22 letter but without enclosing "the copyright documents [Depew] requested," which "were the answer to the question as to whether or not they could withhold consent."

Crane testified that "at the time I thought I had a lawful right to the licenses that Universal had procured . . . then after further discussions with Sega, Brian and myself, we went to Mike Sullivan . . . not for the reason that we felt that impending doom, but to pursue our legal right because Mr. Sullivan was a business litigator and this just goes to show, again, how naïve and unsophisticated and unexperienced [*sic*] and stupid that I was . . . this seemed to indirectly ratify my position by his participation not in a conspiracy because Brian wasn't deriving any pecuniary benefit . . . ." Depew must have written the March 22 letter because "militate" was not in Crane's vocabulary (nor in Depew's, as the pretentious malapropism reveals). After they drafted the letter, Crane listened while Depew called Kupec, who would not approve the sublicense until others at Sega reviewed it. Depew gave Kupec Universal's answering service number.

Depew also talked to HES's lawyer Steve Hagen at Brobeck, Phleger & Harrison on March 20 and wrote him two days later, enclosing the contracts and correspondence and concluding, "Universal would be willing to allow HES to market Super Zaxxon under the name of Universal Licensing, Inc. so as to obviate any further need for written consent from Sega."[29] Hagen responded to Kupec the next day "to strongly protest Sega's actions, and to advise you that HES will not tolerate such unjustified interference."[30] HES had invested over $100,000 in developing and promoting *Super Zaxxon*. "We hereby demand that Sega immediately cease and desist from any interference with the Super Zaxxon sublicense between HES and Universal, and confirm in writing its earlier consent to this sublicense." Another Brobeck Phleger lawyer followed up on April 17 by sending Depew and Sega copies of the *Super Zaxxon* program, preparatory to distributing it by the end of the month; he looked forward "to meeting with Sega officers this week as planned to discuss 'Super Zaxxon.'"[31]

"[A]bout five or seven days later when [Depew] didn't get the documents" from Kupec, he told Crane, "[W]e have a serious impasse, it is a copyright issue. We are way beyond my expertise and my ability." He suggested contacting Sullivan, who told Depew when the three met at Hamburger Hamlet the next day: "Your friend is in trouble. Thank God you are not involved." Strauss read from Depew's deposition: "I never witnessed Mr. Crane using any pseudonyms, phony names ever."

---

29. Depew's Exhibit 19.
30. Depew's Exhibit 20.
31. Depew's Exhibit 28.

STRAUSS: As to the time when you went into Hamburger Hamlet, did you have any knowledge as to whether or not Kupec knew, or anyone at Paramount or anyone at Sega knew that Crane was Universal and Universal was Crane?

DEPEW: I had no knowledge. I had no occasion to know.

STRAUSS: At the Hamburger Hamlet meeting, did Crane advise anyone that he had used pseudonyms?

DEPEW: I think that is when I first learned that he used pseudonyms under the questioning of Sullivan.

But Crane insisted Depew had seen his signature as Steve Kness on a document before or after the San Francisco trip. Furthermore, Depew's March 22 letter to Kupec described Crane making arm's length deals with Universal. Strauss introduced a letter from Kenneth Kocourek (Depew's lawyer) to the State Bar special investigator on October 24, 1985.[32] "Mr. Depew first learned that Steve Kness and Bruce Blumberg were the pseudonyms of Mr. Crane at the time of his trip to Northern California on behalf of Universal. However, the significance of this fact did not register with him until some later time." Depew saw no contradiction "because you did not specify in your question using pseudonyms towards potential customers or the use of pseudonyms when communicating between Mr. Crane and his own employer Sega." Crane's "explanation to me was that he wanted to make Universal look bigger than it was like it had numerous employees." "I was not aware of any misrepresentation of facts made by Mr. Crane, so the fact that he was communicating through pseudonyms to me was innocuous." "I had no answer . . . when he said there can be no wrong if I am creating a profit . . . . he said, 'Look I got a lawyer in Century City.'"

Examined by the referee, Depew dismissed as "pure garbage" Crane's claim that he told Depew three times that Sega could not be allowed to discover his involvement and Kupec would never let him pursue the license openly. He denied that Crane originally asked for his help or that he said the scheme was "not improper." Cross-examined by Hirschberg, Depew called Crane a "con man." "[A]s I choked down dinner at Hamburger Hamlet hearing the full story . . . that's when I reached the conclusion that I had a friend that had not been completely truthful to me." He had stopped representing Crane only *after* talking to Sullivan because "I had an uncooperative client."

When the referee observed that you "retained your friendship," Depew objected:

> I felt betrayed, but I didn't feel as though he had, in a sense, given it to me in the way I'm getting it now today. Even then I didn't see what was going to

32. State Bar Exhibit 111.

happen to me now. I felt I had been betrayed, but not to the extent it was going to jeopardize my career and my future.

On cross-examination, Depew admitted that after the Paramount meeting the two men and their girlfriends had vacationed together in Banff, he invited Crane to a play he had produced, and Crane referred some cases to him. Clare introduced photographs of the four in Banff in March 1985, when they were still "best of friends."[33] In a February 18, 1987, letter, Depew thanked Crane for a referral.[34] Depew conceded that "the nature of the friendship had changed, but we had remained friends and in contact." Nevertheless, he "absolutely" felt victimized. "I told [Crane] I felt as though my friendship had been used." Crane testified that "as late as 1988 . . . I referred a case to Brian Depew for prosecution . . . I'm having a falling out now because there have been some discussions that aren't quite accurate."

Depew claimed to have believed Crane had told Sega he was Universal. "I just assumed he had." In the disciplinary hearing, there was a long argument about whether the license agreement Depew took to San Francisco contained Steve Kness's name. Confronted with his March 22 letter to Brobeck Phleger enclosing a November 21, 1983, letter from "Kness" to Crane with a notation that Crane received it, Depew had to admit, "as I sit here today, it obviously does" show that Crane had not disclosed his identity to Sega. But "back in March of 1984, no, it didn't." Hirschberg promised three witnesses "all of whom will testify that Crane told them . . . he had leveled with Sega." (But, like Eddie Edelberg, they never appeared.)

Depew tried to explain why he would raise the corporate opportunity usurpation doctrine if he believed Sega knew Crane was Universal. "Even if [Crane] had disclosed it, he's still acting in a dual capacity." "[T]hat is consistent with Mr. Crane's testimony yesterday that . . . when he asked me to be general counsel, [I] told him I would prefer that he brought his business in the firm. Now, if I thought that he obtained the game by artifice or device, I certainly wouldn't have wanted to bring his business into my firm." "[T]hat's when he told me that absolutely under no circumstances was he going to have Walter Lack tell him how to run his business." "I have only myself to blame . . . for not doing more research on usurpation of corporate opportunity." Crane had "posed the hypothetical . . . 'if I take $10 from you and go out and invest it and make $100 and give you back $50, how can you tell me you have been damaged?' . . . I simply was out of my league at that point in time." When the referee said "You should have told him to go to hell," Depew agreed: "I wish I had, sir. I wish I had."

Hirschberg called Michael R. Sullivan, who had previously been of counsel to the Lack firm for six months and a State Bar Court referee for eight to ten years, hearing about 30 matters, and had acted as an Office of Trial Counsel (OTC) examiner. He had been summoned to the Hamburger Hamlet meeting to advise

33. Depew's Exhibit AAA.
34. Depew's Exhibit AAAA.

on intellectual property issues, which were "a fight at the sublicense level over certain video game rights."

> The problem that our firm was ultimately engaged to assist in was to handle the situation as a consequence of certain rights having been improperly obtained by Rob Crane's company called Universal Licensing . . . we would have an extraordinarily difficult time defending a claim by the sublicensees. . . . I believe I used the term "containment" at that point to indicate my belief that the situation had ramifications far beyond the sublicense agreement . . . I did not hesitate to tell them that there was a potential criminal problem . . . and that I intended to associate Brian O'Neill . . . . Brian Depew was very peripheral to this discussion . . . the focus went almost exclusively, in my mind, to Rob's situation because he was Universal.

Indeed, Sullivan wrote Paramount's outside counsel on May 11 that "I am told by Rob Crane that [Depew] acted only in a ministerial capacity."[35]

When Sullivan told Crane to come clean "he immediately came back with his corporate opportunity doctrine. He said, '[Y]eah, but, yeah, but.' He was very defensive." "I said, you have the wrong body of law you are looking at here, Rob. It's not a question of corporate law. . . . You have this other body over here that deals with voidable transfers because of a lack of disclosure." "I think Rob appeared startled . . . he appeared stunned."

> I believe that the news I gave Rob Crane shocked him. . . . Sega having declined to pursue this opportunity, he didn't see what the problem was. I had to work with him hard at that point. All of a sudden the revelation hit him and he became emotional. . . . I gave him the advice that . . . in my judgment a good lawyer in this situation would . . . tell you to disgorge the profits, make a clean breast of it. And if you decide to follow that course you may hire us . . . . [A] day or two later he called and said, "Okay, I'm going to go with your program."

O'Neill, "one of the premier lawyers in the country in Rico[36] situations . . . concurred with me that the best course would be a complete disclosure . . . ." Sullivan called Sega. Their first meeting was with Kupec at Sega's offices.

> Brian O'Neill said, "I have some news for you, sir, which you may find shocking. . . . Rob Crane is Universal and Universal is prepared to restore to Sega all rights which it owns in the games . . . restore the licensing fee . . . ." And Kupec's reaction was dramatic. The man literally—his head snapped around. He was disbelieving.

35. Attachment to Depew's Exhibit 11.

36. Racketeer Influenced and Corporate Organizations (RICO) Act.

However, Wattles testified that Kupec first learned Crane was Universal at lunch at a chain restaurant in El Segundo with an attorney representing Crane (presumably Sullivan) on Friday, April 6. Kupec told Paramount the following weekend. As "damage control," O'Neill also asked whether the U.S. Attorney and Los Angeles District Attorney were interested in prosecuting (they were not). Depew was never mentioned.

At Paramount's initiative, Depew and Sullivan met Kupec and A. Robert Pisano (Paramount's outside lawyer at O'Melveny & Myers) at Paramount on Mother's Day (four days after Paramount had grilled Crane for four hours). Sullivan advised Depew, "'Maybe you ought to get a lawyer to go to this thing.' He said, 'What do I need a lawyer for? I am not under investigation here.' . . . I said, 'It's up to you, guy.'" O'Neill canceled at the last minute for family reasons. When the referee asked why they attended the meeting, Sullivan replied, "We wanted to go . . . because frankly, what I thought was going on is we were close to making a deal with Paramount . . . and Paramount . . . in their zeal to be complete, were simply completing their due diligence." Depew agreed that he had been "led to believe . . . that my reason for being at Paramount is they wanted to know what happened so they could improve their internal security." He now thought "con men" was a "very accurate characterization" of Paramount. That he consulted Walter Lack (the head of his firm) about then showed that "I felt very confident in what I was doing."

Sullivan talked to Depew "very frequently during the course of those months" but denied acting as his counsel or arranging the Paramount meeting. Crane, not Depew, was his client and O'Neill's. "Mr. Depew knew at that time I would attend as his friend for moral support but I was there for Crane." "O'Neill and I had discussed at that time [whether] there was a potential of a conflict in that Brian [Depew] was not asking for me to help him legally. As a matter of fact he didn't want any lawyers." Examined by Strauss, however, Depew said

> [I]t is difficult for me to pin down exactly what [Sullivan's] capacity was at the time of the hearing. He was a personal friend. He did give me advice. I did not specifically retain him. I did not pay him a fee, but he was there at partly my request. He may well have had an interest in protecting his client Mr. Crane. . . . He never gave me any advice during the statement itself.

During his deposition, however, Depew had said he considered Sullivan to be his lawyer, and "Mr. Sullivan . . . in fact had arranged the time and location and the purpose of the statement in meeting the people at Paramount . . . ." He now reiterated this on redirect. Sullivan explained to the Referee that

> O'Neill had worked out an arrangement with O'Melveny & Myers to the following effect that whatever Rob said during the interviews that we gave which were the condition to getting to settlement discussions that they not be admissible civilly. . . . Brian [Depew] said, would it be possible to get the same

> arrangement. . . . Brian O'Neill and I talked to Brian Depew about it and ultimately that arrangement was made at the Paramount meeting.

"Brian Depew is known to me as a very fine personal injury trial lawyer" but "does not have a great deal of law knowledge about business law frankly." Nevertheless, Depew was not "manipulative."

Sullivan conceded that Crane's decision not to disclose that he was Universal and "there was no true arm's-length negotiation between his then employer and his wholly owned company" was "an awful terrible decision . . . a totally incorrect decision." "Rob got into this [through] greed and stupidity." But he added: "Mr. Crane at the time he fully appreciated his situation was in my opinion totally candid . . . extraordinarily remorseful, repeated many, many times 'I can't believe I am so stupid.'" Once

> we were waiting to see Mr. O'Neill at his office on Ocean Avenue in Santa Monica and Rob was shaking physically. He was shuddering and he was on the verge of tears. And I walked him across Ocean Avenue to the park on the bluff and at that point he told me he felt he was coming apart mentally and that he didn't know what he was going to do. I would say that Mr. Crane at that point was hysterical. I formed the opinion he should not be left alone because I was afraid of what he might do. . . . Mr. Crane has always called me about once or twice a year [since 1984] and always in the same state. . . . He is extremely anxious, remorseful.

"I think that Rob was incredibly naïve, had no real world experience in business, frankly" and "is probably the most remorseful, sad person I have ever seen. I have never seen him manipulating."

Joshua S. Wattles, now Paramount's deputy general counsel and senior vice-president, had been a senior attorney in 1983. Paramount complained to the State Bar on October 1, 1984, after settling with Depew but not Crane. Wattles testified that Paramount paid HES $200,000 to withhold *Super Zaxxon* from the market while Synapse sought to market *Zaxxon;* Universal reimbursed Paramount for only $47,000. Lawyers' bills for O'Melveny & Myers and Wyman Bautzer exceeded $100,000. The referee allowed Wattles to testify that Paramount lost at least $253,000 but not how he felt about Crane's conduct. The referee rejected as "obnoxious" Clare's offer to show that Paramount made money from the Synapse licenses.

Walter Lack (the senior partner in Depew's firm) testified that Crane, who worked for him as a law clerk for nearly two years, referred a personal injury case in 1980–81, "in which we agreed to give him one-third of the fee at the conclusion of the case.[37] The case was tried by Mr. Depew. A verdict of $200,000

37. In 2009, Lack was listed as one of the top ten lawyers in Southern California. Southern California Super Lawyers 2009, at the age of 40.

was obtained." The defendants appealed. "We kept Mr. Crane apprised periodically of the status. He would call from time to time wanting to know when the case would settle." When it did in April 1986

> I called him at his office and told him that we were not going to pay him 100 percent of his one-third fee. And I explained why. I told him he had cost our firm and myself in particular untold hours of attorney time, embarrassment, grief; we had to call a partners meeting with Mr. Depew. And I said I think what is fair, given the amount of time I have had to devote to this . . . I would give him 50 percent of the fee which was about $11,700. He reacted very indignantly. He said it wasn't fair and it wasn't right. And I said that is my decision, Rob, you can take it or leave it. He then called one of my partners, Engstroem . . . he wanted a face-to-face meeting with me. I said I'm going to be in Manhattan Beach [near Crane's office] on Thursday night [May 15]. You can talk to me then. We met in the bar area. We immediately began discussing the situation and we went out into the patio area because we were getting a little bit heated in our discussion. I again reiterated my position. He told me that he had lost his inheritance. That things had gone—everything in his life had gone wrong. That he desperately needed the money. He didn't think it was fair what we were doing to him and he began crying. And he said, "Look, Brian did not have anything to do with this thing."

After Hirschberg interrupted his own witness—"Mr. Lack you are running off"—and then attacked Strauss for objecting, Lack continued:

> What [Crane] said was Mr. Depew had nothing whatsoever to do with setting the transaction up. All he did was write a couple of letters and that's why [Crane] agreed to reimburse Mr. Depew for the $3,500 Mr. Depew paid to the O'Melveny & Myers firm [for Sega].

Lack repeated Depew's story that he had urged Crane to retain the firm but was told "I don't want Walter Lack being involved in this." Lack declared: "I've always had a lot of warm feelings toward Rob, but Rob knows that I'm not going to go along with any nonsense." "Brian told me that he agreed to write a couple of letters for [Crane]. . . . I have seen them. And that was essentially the extent of it." Depew took a personal day to travel to San Francisco with Crane. "[W]e essentially vindicated [*sic*—"exonerated"] Mr. Depew of any wrongdoing." "[T]he reason why we gave [Crane] any money at all is we thought the matter was completely over and done with. . . . The State Bar proceeding did not come until much later." Crane had not joined Lack's firm after graduation partly because they did not want him but partly because "he wanted to go into corporate law." Furthermore, they needed someone immediately, and he did not pass the bar the first time. Crane disputed most of Lack's testimony. He never said Depew had nothing to do with this thing, or reimbursed Depew for repaying $3,500 to Paramount, or had been rejected by the firm, or failed the bar the first time. Lack would "color the truth" for "the same reason Mr. Alva would say all the things he did": Both do not "want to see any harm or damage sustained by Brian."

IV. EXPLAINING THE DECEPTION

Crane testified in mitigation.

> Before I respond I want you to understand that I am not trying to exculpate myself from liability. I admit and confess to the moral turpitude in which I engaged. As you know I testified that I am remorseful and ashamed and all the words that go along with it.

Crane's father died in his final law school semester, when he took legal ethics.

> During that whole period I was out of school and back home and destroyed. I had to leave Los Angeles and I didn't attend classes and I was administering the estate and it was a terrible situation. My mother had passed away when I was 12 and my father was 51 at the time.

Because he did not take the Multistate Professional Responsibility Examination (MPRE) before graduation, he had to do so after the bar exam.

> I did it under a crash course. . . . I am a terrific memorizer. I can tell you that I memorized my bar mitzvah course when I was 13. I can recite it to you word by word. . . . I have a semi-photographic memory. I memorized all the things and probably didn't pay enough attention to the principles as I should. Again I admit that what I did was wrong. . . . [I]t scares me that I could have done something like this. I deserve a strict punishment. I have been waiting for six years to finally receive the punishment because I deserve it because I did a terrible thing.

On an airplane, Crane ran into Pisano (the O'Melveny lawyer who had represented Paramount during these events and was now general counsel). "I approached him and apologized and I tried to beg forgiveness." Crane followed up with a handwritten letter (received April 9, 1987).[38] The encounter, he wrote Pisano,

> brought back memories of a period in my life I've tried to put behind. However, I enjoyed our conversation and hope that you sensed my remorse. As I explained, the monthly payments, although they are financially burdensome, are in a way comforting—my recognition of an act that was wrong and a way for me to pay. I'm sure you can understand that in comparison to the

38. Depew's Exhibit 62.

> shame I've experienced, the friends I've lost and the suffering I've endured over the last three years, the payments are but a small price I've paid.
>
> What I'm most concerned about is the fact that the State Bar has yet to take action on the complaint. . . . I'll need to apply to the Georgia Bar and I'm afraid that this problem may act as an obstacle in my being employed with Delta.
>
> There is not a day that goes by that I don't think about the trouble I've caused to so many people and I think over three years of suffering should be penalty enough to enable me to begin a new life. The experience has taught me a *great* lesson in life, one I'm thankful came at an early stage in my life—so that I may take the knowledge I've gained and live a life with the understanding of how important a license to practice law is—the fiduciary duty that is placed upon a lawyer—the trust, confidence, and ethics which are so important. With all this in mind, I've worked hard and done very well at Western [Airline], rising from a corporate attorney to a senior attorney and now beginning with Delta as a senior attorney.
>
> You mentioned that you would consider talking to someone, perhaps the State Bar, in helping me with my future plans. Again, I have no idea when they'll act upon the complaint, but I would greatly appreciate any assistance you may render in that regard. Just the writing of this letter has made me feel a little better in releasing some of the feelings I've repressed over the years. I've not wanted to share my shame with anyone and I think, during our short encounter, you understood why.

Crane now testified, "I didn't mean to scheme or hurt anybody." Sullivan "believed I had thought in my stupid naïve mind that I was doing the right thing. I didn't have the mens rea to commit the crime." It had been frustrating watching Sega "lose hundreds of millions of dollars for years and seeing management do nothing."

> I know I let down the legal community. I know there is a lot of discussion in society about the lawyers deviating from the course of right. I am ashamed that I cast more suspicion and taint upon the profession and I will forever live with that in my mind. . . . I know how important it is and what a privilege it is to have a license to practice law . . . anyone would have dreamed of to become an employee of Delta, one of the most revered companies to work for . . . and to have that taken away. . . . I have been a manic depressive for five years . . . we can't have any children. I can't even think about it because I am so afraid.

When Delta acquired Western, Crane moved to Atlanta in April 1987 and had to take the Georgia bar. "I was able to forestall the July bar exam by telling my superior that I was getting married in June . . . ." He disclosed the California complaint in his application for the February 1988 exam. When the bar refused to process it until the complaint was resolved, he told his boss.

> Delta had a policy that they couldn't allow that so they let me resign. It was a terrible time in my life. . . . . [T]here were three different occasions within four weeks where I was rushed to the hospital complaining of . . . a heart attack. . . . [M]y life was unraveling and I wasn't getting a hearing in California and I was going crazy. My wife and my marriage was falling apart. Sexually I don't have to tell you what that has been like. . . . I'm in a perpetual dormancy. . . . I know I deserve to pay the price. . . . I paid $18,000 in attorney fees to Sullivan. I am paying over $12,000 to my attorney here. . . . I have lost $16,000 [with the house] sitting dormant [for eight months] . . . [my wife] needs to be committed herself. . . . I have learned through therapy that the set of circumstances [in] which I was raised with my mother dying when I was 12 and my father had a heart attack that day when he was 37 and he had four more before he died; it was a terribly difficult environment. If for some reason my judgment may have been impaired—I don't again try to escape liability . . . throughout my whole life [with] my father all I can remember is him being in intensive care. He had five heart attacks and he was never well. And I was raised by a housekeeper pretty much. My mother had cancer when I was eight. . . . She was in the hospital from the time I was 8 to 12.

His present employer (in aircraft finance) did not know about these disciplinary proceedings.

Hirschberg closed by declaring Depew "a menace to nobody . . . anything more severe than a private reproval would be a great source of embarrassment and would constitute punishment because as you well know this is largely a defense firm and the claims people at the insurance carriers would look very unfavorably . . . ." Clare said Crane "admitted these charges from the time he received the complaint letter" and "has done whatever he could do to rectify the wrongdoing." Clare also noted the five-year delay in prosecuting. Strauss argued against mitigation. If "these two gentlemen didn't know what they were doing was wrong, doesn't that cause you concern? How could you hold out these two attorneys to the public's trust . . . ?" Crane should be disbarred and Depew suspended and given a lengthy probation. Over Strauss's objection Hirschberg insisted on responding "to the nonsense I have heard." Depew was "exceedingly negligent" but not "fraudulent."

V. WHAT'S THE SCORE?

The referee decided on August 23. "Basically Crane conceived an idea of sublicensing of games from SEGA to himself using a corporate façade known as Universal Lighting, Inc. [*sic*] and employing pseudonyms to conceal from SEGA his participation . . . ." Crane "has accepted culpability for conflict of interest and acting in derogation of the interest . . . of SEGA, and has substantially cooperated with the present inquiry." He "knowingly acquire [*sic*] pecuniary interests adverse to his employer and client," "sought to defraud and deceive SEGA," and "misrepresented to SEGA that UNIVERSAL did not have the ability to manufacture Zaxxon, but had found a sublicensee."

> Depew had expressed reservations to Crane about the concept of usurpation of corporate opportunity as being involved in the proposal by Crane about his subterfuge in concealment from SEGA of the inherent conflict of interest involved as well as the unfairness of SEGA. However, these expressions by Depew were more by way of "devil's advocacy" rather than an attempt to dissuade Crane. Depew's claimed assumption that Crane had the consent of SEGA to sublicense to UNIVERSAL and subsequent sublicense to SYNAPSE is not supported in any way and is entirely unrealistic and at least indicated gross negligence . . . .
>
> Crane engaged Depew (for a fee of $2,500) to make phone calls and to write letters to SEGA demanding approval of HES sublicense. Depew's arguments that his participation at that time . . . was solely as an attorney seeking to validate a copyright issue, while not conspiratorial, betray either a naivete (not accepted by the Hearing Officer) or is another manifestation of deeper involvement amounting to gross negligence.

The referee recommended that Crane be suspended for five years (three actual) and Depew for one (60 days actual).

Strauss moved for reconsideration. Depew's conduct was "willful and not merely grossly negligent." Crane committed twelve separate acts of moral turpitude and Depew at least three; Crane engaged in seven discrete business transactions. Strauss sought three months suspension, which would require Depew to notify his clients. "The Referee should not permit Mr. Depew to avoid said reporting requirement by lessening the period of actual suspension because of Mr. Depew's concern for his law firm." Clare reargued mitigation. Crane "should not be made to bear the permanent mark of Cain for misconduct committed at a very young age." Ever since the initial complaint in 1984, "Mr. Crane has suffered de facto discipline or punishment from the enormous stress from the lengthy pendency of this proceeding."

Hirschberg requested review, arguing that Depew "had no entrepreneurial position in Crane's scheme." He was "negligent, naïve, and immature but certainly not guilty of any moral turpitude whatsoever." Crane and he "are approximately the same age." (Actually, Depew was six years older.) "To effectuate this transaction [the license], Crane concealed from Sega the fact that he himself was the principal of Universal . . . ." (Hirschberg had argued earlier that Depew believed Sega knew.) Crane asked Depew to do unpaid "errant work" (a revealing Freudian typo). Depew was a tort lawyer. "No one questions the lack of wisdom in stepping outside one's field. Fagan needed a young Oliver Twist, and Crane found him in Brian Depew." "Brian's right to negotiate [with Synapse] was in name only; it was nonexistent." Crane overcame Depew's objections. "Having tasted the sweet smell of huge profits, Crane embarked upon an equally ambitious venture . . . the sale of Super Zaxxon . . . ." Depew's "involvement was only as a part-time lawyer, whose function it was to sign letters, return phone calls . . . ." Until the State Bar complaint, "there had been no suspicions cast upon Brian Depew, a pawn in this entire scenario."

Hirschberg again assailed the "misconduct of trial counsel, which infected the fairness of the trial and permitted the Referee to prejudge the case." "To submit unsworn documentary evidence to a trial Referee prior to the Hearing, and to conceal that fact can only be designed to unilaterally, ex parte, influence the Referee. That clearly was the purpose here, and the purpose was accomplished with remarkable success." "A 60-day actual suspension with its notoriety . . . could easily cause [Depew's] removal from the firm. . . . This type of cruel and unusual punishment is directly caused by the delay in this matter." "The incident itself and the resultant proceedings have had their saliatory [*sic*] effect." "It is even more illogical to assume that by causing Respondent to sit on his hands for 60 days he is going to emerge with wings in lieu of hands. . . . In fact, if 60 days of nonproductivity could transform one into an angel, perhaps we would all elect to be flying rather than making car payments." "The picture of respondent sitting alone and staring blankly at a wall in his home, while mentally flogging himself for a five year old act of negligent indiscretion, is both ludicrous and punitive . . . ." "[B]ut for the instant matter, respondent comes as close to being an angel as any mere self-supporting mortal can." "Depew was a mere dupe of his employer, Crane."

Strauss argued that Depew "testified falsely" that he believed Sega knew Crane was Universal. Crane's "claims of youthful inexperience are simply not supported by the evidence which conclusively shows Crane's dishonesty. If this were a case of youthful inexperience and not outright fraud, why the deception?" Depew "was a willing confederate and in that capacity served as an active co-conspirator who aided and abetted Crane." "According to respondent Depew, everyone is to blame but him." His "cavalier attitude toward his oath and duties as an attorney and toward the disciplinary process suggests that this court must honor his contemptuous challenge by disbarring him since no amount of actual suspension will suffice to protect the public when respondent claims he can learn nothing more from these proceedings." Both respondents should be disbarred. Hirschberg retorted that Strauss "has, clearly, lost all objectivity by now screaming for the execution of Brian Depew . . . ." Neither Depew nor he harbored "contempt for the proceedings. . . . It is the *examiner* and his *improprieties* that respondent's *counsel* holds [*sic*] in contempt." "The lady doth protest too much, me thinks [*sic*]."

The Review Department decided on August 3, 1990.[39] The case involved "an elaborate deception" of Sega by "one of its house counsel, aided by another

39. Matter of Crane and Depew, 1 Cal. State Bar Ct. Rptr. 139 (1990).

lawyer, for personal profit." Their consultation with Sullivan concerning copyright "dramatically changed the focus of their concern." "Apparently, until then neither Crane nor Depew realized the seriousness of their deception and the consequences that might ensue to their licenses to practice law." Addressing the "single most difficult issue raised by this proceeding," the Review Department found that "Depew must have been aware that Crane had concealed his connection with Universal from SEGA."

> By his own admission, Depew repeatedly discussed with Crane the propriety of Universal taking a corporate opportunity from SEGA which SEGA had turned down. It strains credulity that Crane and Depew would have repeatedly discussed this subject if Depew thought Crane had SEGA's informed consent. . . . We find irrefutable evidence that Depew must have known SEGA was ignorant of Crane's involvement in Universal in the March 22, 1984 letter which Crane and Depew jointly prepared. . . . This letter only makes sense if Depew thought Kupec was unaware of Crane's ownership and control of Universal.

The Review Department rejected Hirschberg's repeated charge that Strauss had sent the referee Wattles's State Bar complaint. "Crane's fraud does not rise to the level of a pattern of misconduct under Supreme Court precedent," but it was "surrounded by dishonesty and concealment." The State Bar Court could not estimate Sega's injury because there was no evidence about offsetting royalties. It declined to find that Depew lacked candor in testifying about his state of mind six years earlier but was convinced both parties believed at the time that their conduct was not wrong, which "might be attributed to their youth and inexperience." It "is undisputed that Crane dictated all of Depew's actions which were performed for Crane's benefit." But the court rejected the referee's finding that Depew was guilty of only gross negligence "in light of Depew's admission that he knew Synapse and HES were deceived by Crane's pseudonyms. Depew also had to know that SEGA was being tricked by Crane's pseudonyms and use of self-authorized sublicensing agreements." It found "highly questionable [Depew's] reconnection [*sic*— "recollection"] of the extent of his knowledge of wrongdoing at the time" and "evidence that to this day respondent does not fully appreciate the significance of his misbehavior." It reduced Crane's suspension to two years and Depew's to 45 days. Depew returned to practice 45 days later and is still with the Engstroem firm. Crane was reinstated in 1993 but has been inactive since 1995.

VI. NAÏVETÉ OR GREED?

Why did Crane hatch this scheme? He wanted to make money and had an inflated belief in his entrepreneurial skills, about which he bragged to Depew, who was his superior in age, experience, legal acumen, and status in the Engstroem firm. (The combination of boasting and claims of naïveté and inadequacy suggests a weak ego.) He had used an inheritance three years earlier to start a clothing business. His work at Sega, though legally unchallenging, taught him how to license its products. He presciently saw a lucrative business opportunity in marketing video games for home computers and was frustrated by his superiors' indifference. Garage inventors and start-up entrepreneurs were growing rich (greed was good in this age of Reagan). Crane did not approach any other game manufacturers because he knew no one would license him; only he could license himself.

Like all deceits, his became ever more elaborate and hard to sustain. He had to conceal his identity because Kupec would never license him: no business would let an employee moonlight as a potential competitor; and Kupec knew Crane lacked the know-how and resources to do what Universal proposed. Using his inheritance as start-up capital, therefore, Crane created a shell corporation, made Depew president, general counsel, and secretary, and rented a post office box and answering service—all to conceal his own identity. He filed fictitious tax returns. He misrepresented to Sega that Universal could reengineer *Zaxxon* for home computers and manufacture and market the disks. He pretended to advocate for Sega's interests by advising it to ask for more than Universal offered—but of course rejected this counteroffer as Universal's "Kness." He then dissimulated to Sega that he had "saved the deal" by persuading Universal to sublicense to Synapse once Universal "discovered" its incapacity. He hid his role in Universal from both Sega and Synapse by disguising his voice when talking to Wolosenko and paying Depew to represent Universal to Synapse in person. He lied to Sega that Universal had paid advance royalties in September (it could not) and then backdated the November check, depositing it surreptitiously. He hid Universal's inflated profits from both Sega and his good friend Depew (who might have asked for more money). He sought to explain them to Synapse (which had to see the contract figures) by misrepresenting that Universal had obtained the rights long before *Zaxxon* became a hot property. Realizing he had asked too little for *Zaxxon*, he amended the license to include *Super Zaxxon* in anticipation of being laid off by Sega. He sought no approval for this, knowing his superiors would balk at the copyright infringement. On his last day at Sega, he authorized a license for two other games and surreptitiously took *Super Zaxxon* with him. He deceived HES that Sega had licensed *Super Zaxxon* to Universal. As Universal's "Kness," he pretended to write to himself at Sega *after* being laid off, concealing this from HES. He argued to HES, Synapse, Sega, and Depew that *Super Zaxxon* did not infringe Synapse's rights in *Zaxxon*, although Crane had registered the former with the Copyright Office as a derivative work and included it in the *Zaxxon* license to Universal on the basis of similarity. He sought to anticipate the copyright problem by prohibiting HES from putting Sega's name on its game title and deleting Sega's copyright and trade mark in the sublicensing agreement. (But the elaborate ruse was doomed to exposure once Crane was no longer at Sega to intercept HES's communications.) He fabricated a fictitious "trip to the Orient" to exaggerate his sophistication in the computer game market. He created one pseudonym and then a second to give Universal "substance." He pocketed a second $25,000 from HES more than a week after the copyright infringement surfaced and tried desperately to save the deal by convincing HES that Universal had a valid license for *Super Zaxxon*.

How did Crane understand what he was doing? He had given Sega ample opportunity to pursue the home computer market. It was better off with his deals than without them. (Indeed, his lawyer made an offer of proof about Sega's earnings from the license, which the referee rejected as offensive.) He even claimed to be benefiting Sega, not himself. He had presented the deals without a recommendation, and his superiors had approved them. (But he urged Sega in writing to accept Universal's order because the Christmas season was approaching and "these properties aren't getting any more popular." And he "consulted" Dulberg, the financial officer, but not his own superior, Kupec, or the general counsel.) He turned Depew's *warning* about usurpation of corporate opportunity into a justification. He blamed Depew for not dissuading him—indeed, for convincing him of the scheme's legality by accepting three offices in Universal and negotiating with Synapse, HES, and Sega. But he told Paramount that Depew performed only ministerial functions. And he brushed off Depew's warnings (repeated by Alva and Edelberg), claiming greater sophistication in business practices.

After being exposed, Crane invoked youthful naïveté:

> I wasn't a rocket scientist. I wasn't a sophisticated person. I was naïve and immature and inexperienced . . . .
>
> I engaged in a stupid transaction. It wasn't very smart . . . .
>
> [H]ow naïve and unsophisticated and unexperienced [*sic*] and stupid that I was.

(Crane *was* naïve in agreeing to pay Sega $5,000 he did not have when he knew nothing about programming or distributing disks and soon learned they were beyond his ability.) By contrast, "I thought [Depew] was very smart at what he did . . . . I thought Brian was savy [*sic*]." Crane argued (bizarrely) that his persistence in the scheme after Sega refused to license HES demonstrated lack of *mens rea* (rather than greed or desperation). But as the prosecutor, referee, and Review Department responded, the elaborate deception belied Crane's protestations of innocence.

Crane pointed to his prompt full admission as evidence of contrition. (Sullivan seems to have persuaded Crane that this was the best damage control strategy. Although Sullivan testified to his client's remorse, Crane actually was more fearful of discipline.) "As you know I testified that I am remorseful and ashamed and all the words that go along with it" (phraseology that made the sentiments seem formulaic and perfunctory). But he concealed the disciplinary proceeding from

Delta as long as possible (and persisted in doing so from his next employer) and apologized to Pisano only when a chance encounter presented the opportunity to seek his intercession with the State Bar and save Crane's job at Delta. He persisted in maintaining his rectitude until the copyright dispute exploded the scam. The *Zaxxon* license was fair; he did not know it was worth more than the $5,000 Universal paid. (But Universal had already sublicensed it to Synapse for $50,000, all of which would have been Sega's but for Crane's deceit; Crane concealed this from Kupec and even asked Synapse for $100,000.) He had failed to take the MPRE before graduation because of his father's death and crammed for it by memorization. (But there was nothing subtle or arcane about his betrayal of Sega.)

Crane turned his entire autobiography into a mitigating narrative. His therapist attributed his misconduct as a lawyer to his troubled childhood: a mother who contracted cancer when he was eight and was in and out of hospital until she died four years later; a father who had a first heart attack at thirty-seven and then four others, dying at fifty-one; his own fears of heart attack, which hospitalized him three times. Crane argued he had suffered enough: the emotional stress and cost of the lengthy State Bar investigation, the loss of his dream job at Delta, manic depression, bad sex or none, a troubled marriage, his inability to have children, loss of income, reputation, and friends, and a squandered inheritance. The same self-pity emerged in his conversations with Sullivan, Lack, and Pisano.

Depew, by contrast, denied everything, demanding complete exoneration. Crane had called to brag, not to seek advice. Depew had just helped a friend, who treacherously sought to blame *him*. He had educated Crane about usurpation of corporate opportunity and warned against the scheme, only to have his advice disregarded. Depew never would have urged Crane to retain his firm had he believed the scheme was illegal. Crane was the mastermind and Depew a mere pawn (despite his three offices in Universal). He had not been appointed president and general counsel at the same time; his business card gave only the latter title. Crane even forged Depew's initials on documents. Depew was paid a nominal sum for the San Francisco trip. He knew nothing about computer games or business. (The two conspirators competed in naïveté.) He visited Synapse only because Crane had another meeting in San Francisco. He was a mere errand (or "errant") boy, without negotiating authority. He knew nothing of the deal with HES until it phoned him on March 20. He was unaware of Crane's use of pseudonyms before writing the March 22 letter, for which he was just Crane's scribe. He demanded $5,000 for continuing to represent Universal in order to discourage the retainer (but that also might have been hush money). He believed Sega knew Crane was Universal until they met with Sullivan at Hamburger Hamlet in April He felt betrayed by Crane, preserving the friendship only because he did not think their deception of Sega would lead to discipline. At the time, he thought Sega was greedily trying to extract more royalties for the licenses now that it knew their worth. Sullivan told him that only Crane was in trouble. Lack claimed that Crane exculpated Depew and testified that the firm had exonerated him; but Lack was obviously biased and the firm anxious about its own liability. Depew demonstrated his conviction of innocence by continuing to fight the copyright issue (even though he knew by then that Crane had obtained the licenses by deceit). Depew attended the meeting with Paramount because he thought it was interested only in tightening security. His refusal to hire counsel showed that he did not believe he was a suspect. Paramount executives were "con men" for failing to disclose he was under suspicion.

By seeking acquittal, Depew risked compounding his guilt. Some protestations of innocence were plausible (perhaps his urging Crane to retain the firm—although he may also have wanted to be a rainmaker). But others were contradictory or incredible. If he believed Crane had told Sega he was Universal, why warn about usurpation of corporate opportunity? He must have known of Crane's deception of Sega long before the Hamburger Hamlet meeting; indeed, he admitted knowing that Crane used pseudonyms but, implausibly, denied knowing why. (Hirschberg admitted that Depew knew of the pseudonyms as early as the San Francisco trip but claimed Depew did not know their purpose! From at least March 20 Depew was fully implicated in the scheme, contending that Crane had bound Sega in its contract with Universal when he knew Crane could not do so and even threatening to sue Sega for interference with contractual relations.) Depew's claim to have advised against the scheme was hypocritical given his extensive involvement. He knew Crane had no other San Francisco meeting. He engaged in the March 20 telephone cover-up and helped draft the March 22 letter. Although he now called Crane a "con man," they remained good friends long after these events. The $5,000 retainer he accepted in March might be hush money. Calling *Paramount* con men displayed real chutzpah. Alva's testimony and Eddie Edelberg's proffered corroboration showed that either they and Depew were committing perjury, or Crane was. The former is more likely. Having admitted guilt, Crane had little reason to lie; furthermore, he did not seem to need capital for his scheme. Alva was financially dependent on Depew's firm (though that does not explain Edelberg's involvement). Depew's ex-wife's testimony that Crane called only to brag was not very convincing. Although Sullivan represented Crane in the Paramount meeting, he was closely associated with Depew and the Engstroem firm.

Hirschberg advocated aggressively, knowing Depew could not be charged with his lawyer's excesses.[40] (Hirschberg may have felt greater license by reason of his prior association with the referee.) He dismissed the charges as "frivolous," gratuitously insulted Strauss (insolent, awfully offensive, liar, jerk), threatened to punch him in the nose during the disciplinary hearing, and accused him

40. He had been Depew's torts teacher and remained his friend. E-mail from Brian Depew to Richard Abel, Feb. 12, 2009.

of suppressing evidence (Wattles's notes) and of the "grossest type of misconduct" (sending Wattles's complaint to the referee), an allegation the Review Department found baseless. It was Strauss who should be disciplined, not Depew. Hirschberg was equally abusive toward Wattles, calling him a liar and a snitch and his testimony "nonsense." He insisted Depew was guilty of only youthful inexperience and gross negligence; he was a "dummy" who had ventured outside his narrow area of expertise (torts) and failed to conduct due diligence about Crane's activities. The State Bar should never have charged him. His low compensation confirmed that his responsibilities were purely ministerial. He was Oliver Twist in the hands of Fagan (proclaimed twice). To argue this, Hirschberg had to maintain that the respondents were about the same age, when Depew was six years older (a substantial difference at that life stage) and more experienced and successful. Hirschberg urged both the referee and the Review Department to consider the damage to the firm if the suspension required Depew to inform insurance clients. The referee's proposed 60-day suspension was "cruel and unusual punishment," from which Depew would learn nothing. Hirschberg's hyperbole seemed intended to appeal to a jury rather than to persuade: "but for the instant matter, respondent comes as close to being an angel as any mere self-supporting mortal can."

5. REACHING FOR THE BRASS RING

I. FRAUD

Lawyers are disciplined for a wide range of crimes.[1] Some are only tangentially related to their professional role: crimes of passion, drug offenses, drunk driving, tax evasion. But others cast doubt upon essential character traits on which clients rely.

After earning a B.A. from Pepperdine and a J.D. from Western State University College of Law, Frank S. Mitchell was admitted to the bar in 1982.[2] Six years later, he distributed a résumé declaring that he had enrolled in the University of Southern California (USC) LL.M. program and, by omitting the name of his law school, suggesting that it was also USC. He presented this résumé to Chase, Rotchford, Drucker, and Bogust and claimed the USC J.D. at the interview. After working for them for a year, he sent a résumé and cover letter to Cummins and White, again indicating a USC J.D. He also gave the résumé to an employment service, which prepared a new one that explicitly claimed a USC law degree. He offered this at an interview with Monteleone and McCrory, and did not correct the misrepresentation. During the State Bar investigation, he denied telling any law firm he had a USC law degree or intending to deceive anyone. After receiving no response to several hundred résumés listing Western State as his law school, he explained, an employment agency suggested he leave the law school blank. He wanted an interview, at which he planned to disclose the real facts.

Robert E. Wyrick, III was convicted of accepting two stolen truck tires and rims from a former client and recording the conversation of another client's son without consent.[3] On the basis of this and his admission of misusing the legal process in multiple cases, he was suspended for three-and-a-half years. While suspended, he applied to be a judicial arbitrator, claiming to be a member of the bar, and served on arbitration panels for seven months. He later denied knowing he had to be an *active* member. In 1984 (on probation after the end of his suspension), he was hired as an attorney in the Office of Administrative Law, after describing himself as self-employed since 1973 and a "Member, State Bar of California, Fact Finder, Arbitrator, Mediator, Conciliator and Labor Relations Consultant." During his seven months there, he applied to be a deputy attorney

1. Pinaire *et al.* (2006).

2. Matter of Mitchell, 1 Calif. St. Bar Court Rep. 332 (1991) (60 days suspension).

3. Matter of Wyrick, 2 Calif. St. Bar Court Rep. 83 (1992) (six months suspension, two years probation).

general in the California Department of Transportation, again representing himself to three interviewers as having practiced since 1973.

Kevin P. Kirwan was admitted in 1964 and went into partnership four years later with Charles Kamanski, who had clerked for Chief Justice Traynor and been managing partner of a Los Angeles tax firm.[4] A tax shelter they created in Arizona fruit orchards was ruined by a freak hailstorm, losing about $600,000 for a client, Peter Werrlein, who blamed Kirwan for the loss. When investors bribed Werrlein (a Bell City Councilmember) and Bell City Manager John Pitts to obtain approval for a card casino, Kirwan agreed to hold a 51 percent interest in the casino for Werrlein and Pitts (who were legally barred from doing so), in exchange for being relieved of the $600,000 "debt." Kirwan also was paid $150,000 (after taxes) to manage the casino. He committed perjury when applying for the casino license by failing to disclose the Bell officials' secret role. He also committed perjury in a Superior Court lawsuit by declaring that Pitts had no interest in the casino and claimed a fictitious sale of his own interest on his federal income tax. He lied to the FBI and then agreed with others to testify falsely if prosecuted. But in mid-1984, he repudiated all these lies, cooperated with the FBI, pleaded to lesser offenses, and resigned from the bar in 1988. His 1991 reinstatement petition was denied, but the Review Department reversed and remanded. The rehearing revealed that he had since been involved in an unsuccessful project to open a card casino in Oxnard, claiming to be a member of the bar and concealing his prior alcoholism and severe depression. This time, he was fronting for someone barred from operating the casino following a conviction for lewd and lascivious conduct with a minor.

Fifteen years after being admitted, Sandra Sue Sawyer met Robert Burlingame, who introduced investors to pig farm operators.[5] She gave him a financial statement and part of her 1982–1984 federal income tax forms (which she had never filed) to submit to a bank that was considering investing in a Texas feeder hog farm and a Kansas grain storage facility. A year later, she submitted the same forms for successful investments in a turkey farm and a hog feeding business in Nebraska. For the turkey farm, she also provided the forms to a skeptical FirsTier Bank, which made the loan after she met the bank officials and submitted a current statement showing a net worth of $12 million. The turkey farm failed, and she defaulted on the loan. When Burlingame told the bank that the returns had never been filed, it informed the FBI, and Sawyer pleaded to a misdemeanor.

In 1991, Czarine Hope James, a 55-year-old naturalized U.S. citizen from Jamaica with a high school diploma and a $6 per hour job, sought a short-term investment of her $68,000 life savings before buying a condominium. Bruce B. Kittrell (who had been admitted to the bar twenty-four years earlier) owned Bolden Group and Bolden Realty, which serviced real estate buyers who could

4. Matter of Kirwan, 2 Calif. St. Bar Court Rep. 692 (1994) (reinstatement denied).

5. Matter of Sawyer, 3 Calif. St. Bar Court Rep. 765 (1997) (18 months suspension, three years probation).

not qualify for conventional bank loans (i.e., subprime mortgages).[6] Presenting himself as a lawyer (without mentioning his ownership of Bolden Realty), he offered James an investment in a dance studio, which already had three mortgages totaling nearly $1.5 million, a $100,000 annual debt service on the first two, and income of just $70,000. Despite this, Kittrell earned at least $244,000 for managing the property between 1991 and 1993. When he listed it for $1.95 million in 1990, he received just one offer (for less than $1 million); and attempts to refinance it failed in 1990 and 1991. In March 1990, he issued a $450,000 third trust deed to service the first two; when that came due, he extended it to March 1993 and increased it to $550,000. He needed James's $68,000 to finance the $100,000 difference. A month before he met her, the holder of the first trust deed filed a notice of default. Kittrell assured James she would earn 14 percent interest, her principal would be repaid in three or four months, and she could not lose money. Within a week of their first meeting, James wrote a check to Bolden Realty. He failed to disclose that she was investing in a third trust deed whose amount was $550,000 rather than $450,000, or correct her misperception that repayment was to be in March 1992 rather than 1993. When she asked about repayment, he assured her it would be in April or May 1992. Relying on this, James thrice went into escrow to purchase a residence, losing her deposit each time when Kitrrell did not return her investment ($2,300 for escrow fees and storage of her personal property). James sued Kittrell for fraud, winning $217,235 compensatory and $61,000 punitive damages. Although Evan Borges represented James pro bono in that lawsuit, she paid about $10,000 in costs. Telling Borges he would not pay James, Kittrell declared bankruptcy, transferring an Arizona ranch worth $700,000 to his wife. Before the bankruptcy, Kittrell also owned an estate appraised at $2.9 million and an airplane worth $125,000. He claimed he had paid James $18,200 and had offered her another $17,400 but denied owing her anything since she had recovered more than her original investment from him and the Client Security Fund.

In each of these cases the lawyers misrepresented or concealed important facts about their backgrounds, activities, or finances. Because clients (as well as employers, adversaries, and fora) rely on the veracity of lawyers, such deceit can have profound consequences, as the following case demonstrates.

II. PRELUDE

Ernest Lee Brazil drove himself hard. After graduating from Ohio State University in 1965, he volunteered for the Navy, serving served two years in Vietnam during

6. Matter of Kittrell, 4 Calif. State Bar Ct. Rptr. 195 (2000), 4 Calif. State Bar Ct. Rptr. 615 (2003) (three years suspension, five years probation). The first decision relied on collateral estoppel of a civil judgment for fraud; the second tried the case *de novo*.

which he flew 213 combat missions, before leaving active duty in 1971. He graduated from Harvard Law School and passed the California bar in 1974, turning down a job with McCutcheon, Doyle (where he had been a summer associate) for one with Heller, Ehrman, where he was a litigation associate for three years.[7] Then he spent two years as a transactional attorney at Itel Corporation (a diversified transportation and logistics company), attributing his August 1979 departure to its financial difficulties.

There was disagreement about why he left his next position at Fox and Carskadon (the largest real estate company in northern California) after a year and a half. William Stark, who had been chief counsel, said he notified Brazil of "some problems" in mid-1981. Brazil

> was writing an extensive novel about his Vietnam experiences, using our display writer, word processing machine and his secretary to do it. He also was having an affair with one of the partners' secretaries, and there were rumors, although I did not know about it at that time, of him practicing law out of our offices.

When they discussed this at a lunch between August and October 1981, Stark told Brazil the book

> was totally out of line, it was using company assets inappropriately. With respect to the secretary, I warned that it was none of my business after hours but, in his position, it could not become notorious, it had to be discrete [*sic*]. And with the third, I told him I didn't have anything . . . but the rumors were flying and I did not want that going on because of the potential liability and implication that Fox was involved in the practice of law.

After this conversation

> the only problem that continued . . . was the practice of law or outside business activities. There was frequent phone calls that were not on Fox business . . . getting some ferryboat set up here in the Bay.

"But then there were also other management-related problems" with superiors and subordinates. For several months, Brazil had disregarded a letter demanding that Fox cease using another company's logo. He also threatened a senior vice president, ordered legal publications without authorization during a period of cost cutting, failed to process subordinates' requests for compensation reviews, and claimed to have organized fictitious meetings. Although Brazil "was a great guy, fun to be around, could tell a good story," Stark was concerned about honesty: "there were just too many things that didn't tie together."

Laying the foundation for cross-examination in the disciplinary hearing, Brazil's lawyer, Gary L. Fontana (of Thelen, Marrin), offered to prove that "Mr. Stark just

7. Stipulation of Facts (Jan. 3, 1992).

simply could not stand to have anybody around who threatened him, and so went through general counsel with some regularity." Still, "we've got 45 minutes, so we might as well indulge our curiosity." State Bar Court (SBC) Hearing Judge Jennifer Gee was not amused. In response to Fontana's questions, Stark confirmed Brazil's affair, flagrant use of company time to write the book, and persistence in practicing law after being reprimanded. His was the only letterhead that did not mention Fox and Carskadon: "bond paper with Ernest L. Brazil, and then after it the address and so forth, probably Attorney at Law . . . it looked like stationery that a sole practitioner would have." At the suggestion of the chief operating officer (COO), Stark asked for phone records:

> The rumor and allegation at the time was that he was calling his Navy buddies to obtain information for the book . . . . there were some to Columbus, Ohio, which was where his family was . . . some others to other cities, Washington, D.C. primarily . . . .

Confronted at the lunch, Brazil "looked at his plate . . . his only comment was something to the effect, gosh I'm sorry . . . ." Although Stark occasionally called his own family, Brazil regularly called his Navy buddies. Stark conceded that the secretary with whom Brazil had an affair previously had had one with her boss.

After Brazil left his next position at Bray (a financial company), because another got the general counsel job he sought, Governor Jerrold Brown named him Commissioner of Real Estate. Replaced by George Deukmeijian (Brown's successor) in 1983, Brazil launched Federal Pacific Corporation (FPC) with three colleagues to do mortgage banking. He claimed that he left when it was sold to a bank two years later. Testifying under subpoena, however, one of those colleagues, Ronald P. Isenberg, told a different story.

> [L]ess than two years later Mr. Brazil was terminated by the board of directors. . . . [T]he company was technically, and for all intents and purposes, bankrupt . . . management mistakes, poor market at the time, just an entire combination of things that led us to losing most of our initial capital. . . . [T]here were a level of advances that were not authorized. There were salary increases that were not authorized . . . over a period of time extending from shortly after the company's formation until shortly before [Brazil] left the company.

Between September 1, 1983, and March 12, 1985, Brazil received a cumulative salary advance of $92,807.28 (with interest).[8] He directed Isenberg to raise his monthly salary to $7,500 on September 15, 1984, and $8,500 a month later.[9] Isenberg complied because he "reported directly to Mr. Brazil, who was the president, chief executive officer (CEO), and chairman of the board."

8. State Bar Exhibit 52.
9. State Bar Exhibit 53.

Brazil signed his own advance checks after November 1984, when Isenberg refused, something he discovered only when the bank statements arrived. He conceded that his own salary increases during the period were not authorized by the board, but "I was worth it" and "my conditions for joining the company required a certain level of salary." Furthermore, they were authorized by his superior. In late 1984

> I was getting very uncomfortable with the future viability of the company . . . [and] some things that were going on, and I felt that the board as a whole needed to be made aware . . . . [T]he results culminated at the April 15, 1985 meeting in the termination of Mr. Brazil.

On April 26, 1985, Max Simpson, a director, demanded that Brazil make "immediate payment of all unauthorized advances and salary increases," $91,552.69 and $23,000 respectively.[10] Brazil repaid $2,040.79 on April 30 but made no further payments, and FPC sued.

Isenberg agreed on cross that he had never repaid his own salary advances but said he did repay other advances. He had not blown the whistle earlier because he was wearing two hats, as "an employee and subordinate" and "a member of the board of directors," and had "put my number one faith and confidence in Mr. Brazil to do the right thing." He "regarded Mr. Brazil as not only the guiding force behind this enterprise, in which I had sunk all of my assets, but he was also a very close and very dear personal friend." He did not think Brazil's behavior was right at the time, but "my job and my heart was supporting him in what he was attempting to accomplish here." Isenberg told the outside investors on the board that "the future of the company was not very promising. We had lost a tremendous amount of money. . . . Our seller servicer approvals were in jeopardy. Our bank lines of credit were in jeopardy." He conceded that the advances were not the problem.

Brazil testified that six to nine months after the founding of FPC

> Mr. Isenberg, who was the chief financial officer of the company, came into my office and said that our salary levels were totally inadequate for his needs and he presumed my needs, as well. And suggested that we give ourselves an increase. We discussed the matter at some length and concluded that she,[11] he and I owned about 75 percent of the . . . voting stock of the company at the time and controlled the board of directors, being three out of five, that we had authority to go ahead and increase the salary and present it to the board at some other time.

The advances were against bonuses; Brazil gave a promissory note for them. "I made every payment that was required under the note on a timely basis until

10. State Bar Exhibit 54.

11. An unnamed investor.

I was put into an involuntary bankruptcy in the latter part of 1988." He conceded on recross, however, that he had only executed the promissory note on June 12, 1986, to settle FPC's August 1985 lawsuit.[12]

III. INTERBANK MORTGAGE CORPORATION

In July 1985, Brazil helped organize and became president and 10 percent shareholder of InterBank Mortgage Corporation (IB). It became a "qualified" "seller/servicer" for both Fannie Mae (Federal National Mortgage Association) and Ginnie Mae (Government National Mortgage Association), which thereby agreed to purchase mortgages sight unseen. At its height, in the summer and fall of 1988, IB had 20 to 25 employees and was originating about $5 million in new mortgages a month. Toward the end of 1988, it had a $50 million mortgage servicing portfolio (for which it was paid a quarter to a half of a point).

A. Patrick Collins

The first transaction leading to the disciplinary proceeding involved Patrick Collins, a real estate developer for thirteen to fourteen years, who was building forty-four single-family homes in Merced to be rented under Department of Housing and Urban Development (HUD) Section 8 vouchers and who needed a take-out commitment for long-term financing in order to retire the construction loan. He knew that Brazil was a Harvard Law School graduate, former real estate commissioner, and partner of directors of the savings and loan that had lent the construction funds. On February 3, 1988, Brazil wrote Collins offering to lend $1,548,000 on the following terms: Individual investor owners, loan to value ratio of 75 percent, loans not to exceed $51,600 per unit, HUD Section 8 Voucher Program eligibility, appraisal, loan commitment fee, and occupancy.[13] Collins testified he had met all those requirements. He understood that funding would be triggered by the notice of completion and IB would provide the funds out of its own line of credit. On July 18, he sent Brazil a notice of completion with addresses of 30 of the homes.[14] Four days later, he provided copies of the $16,019.42 second mortgages his wife and he would provide for each house.[15] Thereafter, he phoned Brazil four or five times to ask why funding had not occurred. "[H]e would never return phone calls, but I successfully got through to him maybe three or four times." Correspondence "was all one-sided." Brazil told Collins, "they were having difficulty securing the funds . . . their letter of

12. State Bar Exhibit 65.

13. State Bar Exhibit 43 (Brazil's letter of Feb. 3, 1988, signed by Collins Mar. 16, 1988).

14. State Bar Exhibit 44.

15. State Bar Exhibit 45.

credit . . . had already been utilized and was not available." Collins sued Brazil (but was not allowed to testify about the consequences of the failure to fund). Brazil was "probably the worst businessman I've ever dealt with. And as to his credibility, he had very little."

On cross-examination, Collins maintained that "far in advance of completion" he had entered into escrow to sell 30 units to an institutional buyer. He never claimed he had 30 individual investors ready to buy. He was responsible for the habitability standards, Brazil for determining whether the loan to value ratio would meet Fannie Mae requirements. "[M]y understanding was that the appraisal category made direct reference to Mark Lawrence's [December 27, 1987] appraisal, which we all had in our hands." He remembered no conversations about Fannie Mae or Ginnie Mae. On redirect, he testified that purchase of the mortgages by those agencies was not part of his agreement with IB. He had given Brazil the names and creditworthiness of the institutional buyers. The only reference to Fannie Mae concerned habitability standards.

Brazil testified in rebuttal.

> [S]ometime during the month of July Mr. Collins sent a large package of documents to our office indicating that he was ready to begin in the process of closing the loans on these properties, and he delivered to my office the individual loan packages that he had prepared for the borrowers. He intended to have purchaser borrowers that he intended to sell the properties to. . . . [I]t quickly became apparent that there were some material, if not fatal, problems. . . . Mr. Collins had submitted applications for three purchaser borrowers . . . each having ten homes and ten loans . . . at least one, if not two . . . were not natural persons. . . . [W]hen this commitment was negotiated . . . back in the early part of 1988 I made it perfectly clear to Mr. Collins that these loans had to be made to individual purchasers in order for me to sell them. . . . [I]t's set forth on page 1 of commitments . . . Freddie Mac seller/servicer guidelines state specifically that they will not purchase loans wherein there is a borrower who has more than five mortgages . . . and Fannie Mae specifically says that they will not acquire any mortgage which is not made . . . to an individual natural person. . . . I told him . . . that under these conditions I couldn't take down these loans. . . . At one point he told me he was going to . . . make the purchasers agree not to acquire more than five of these units and that he would persuade his purchasers to take title as natural persons. . . .

Collins also offered to lend buyers $16,000 on each property, making them 100 percent financed, "which number one, Fannie May strictly forbids, and number two, in the industry would have made these loans totally unsalable to anybody." Nevertheless, Brazil "began to look around for other purchasers of these loans so that I could take them down for Mr. Collins. He was becoming increasingly frantic, calling about every day and basically driving me nuts."

Brazil talked to Peninsula Savings and Loan (Peninsula or Peninsula S&L), which he was about 30 days from acquiring, and made "a number of phone calls to other potential buyers on behalf of Mr. Collins and really got nowhere."

On recross, Hearing Examiner Julie W. Stainfield introduced Collins's July 25 letter to Brazil.[16]

> My Understanding of our phone conversation of July 20th is as follows. Your company will act as the direct lender on the first ten homes with the loans being made to Ted Mullennix. . . . I see no reason why loan documents are not prepared by InterBank by the week ending July 29th. Which individual will be processed next, Tom Titcomb or myself? Also I would expect the loan documents on these respective loans to be ready at short intervals of ten working days maximum. Please let me know for any reason if the schedule cannot be kept and the reasons why. . . . I remain very concerned that you work through my loan in as rapid a manner as can be done. My Maturity date on the construction loan is August 31st.

Brazil did not recall the letter but admitted the address was correct. Collins handwrote him again on July 29.[17]

> This letter is to confirm our telephone conversation of 7/27/88. It was agreed that your company would begin drawing loan documents for the first twenty homes on 8/1 with ten in Mr. Mullennix's name and ten in my name. The loan documents will be started on August 1st and completed by August 3rd and be in Merced by August 4th.

Brazil did not remember the letter or phone call. Collins handwrote again on August 11.[18]

> I would like to report what was told to me at our meeting today. Larry Winslow of Tracy Savings and Loan has asked to be kept apprised as the loans with him are now past due.
>
> You have reviewed Mark Lawrence's appraisal and it seems in order and well prepared. The Savings and Loan that you are working with is Peninsula Savings and Loan. Their appraiser has reviewed the appraisal and seems satisfied. Tomorrow, 8/12/88, the Peninsula appraiser will go to Merced to visit the property. On Monday, 8/15/88, you will receive financial information on Mr. Al Dicks, who is the TNT Equity Group's investor. Mr. Dicks will be on the title for purposes of the loan and the tax credit. As soon as you receive the information you will begin processing the loan documents on all of the units

16. State Bar Exhibit 58.
17. State Bar Exhibit 59.
18. State Bar Exhibit 60.

> for $52,000 per unit. If I have left anything out or misstated anything please correct me.

Brazil recalled the letter but not the meeting. He did not write back but "probably" responded orally "to dispute whatever he put in this letter. It was not my understanding at any time that I was going to process ten loans for the people he's talking [about] here. I seem to recall that he had a tendency to write letters where he would try and create some kind of record which didn't have anything to do with the understanding between the parties."

Collins wrote Brazil again on August 18, "to go on record with you for some of the damages I am incurring and . . . will incur."[19] These included higher interest payments, the inability to close sales until Brazil's loans were in place, "a number of trips to your Company, my lender's, my attorney's office, and miscellaneous other destinations," an "extensive" phone record, and "a great deal of strain you have caused" with his contractor and Tracy Savings. If he lost the sales or the property the damage "would be close to $1,000,000 and could lead to my bankruptcy."

> I cannot urge you enough to assign this the very highest priority and use the same persistence that you have seen me use on you to get the job done. If this project is not brought to successful fruition it could be the kind of mark that could end either of our ambitious careers. I remain very willing to work with you and I urged you to continually communicate with myself and the Construction Lender on your progress. To date we have received very little communication.

Brazil did not remember this letter. Collins wrote again on August 23 "to recap our telephone conversation" that day.[20] He had no

> intention to litigate with InterBank Mortgage Corporation, Tracy Savings and Loan or anyone provided I am treated fairly and . . . my loans are funded. You asked that I not make direct contact with your lenders and I agreed not to as long as I was kept informed in writing. . . . I had made contact with Peninsula Savings and Loan because I had been kept in the dark. . . . Mr. Brazil, please do not let this sensitive situation deteriorate by not giving it your closest attention. And remember that no matter how hard you are working, unless both Tracy and I are kept informed we will assume based on what has happened to date that not much is being done.

Brazil thought he remembered this letter and had responded orally. On August 24, J. Carter Witt answered Collins's August 18 letter, explaining that he was a shareholder of both IB and Tracy but "not at all involved in the day to day

---

19. State Bar Exhibit 61.
20. State Bar Exhibit 62.

operation of either company." He had discussed the situation with Larry Winslow and Lee Brazil and hoped it would be resolved satisfactorily. "Lee advises that he has several sources (unknown to me) that he thinks will fund the takeout. I believe he will pursue this diligently." Brazil remembered seeing the letter and discussing the matter with Witt.

Collins faxed Brazil in desperation on September 8.

> Lee,
> Your communications are slipping, please respond to your latest assurance to put Mr. Rouda and yourself in touch with Mr. Titcomb regarding the purchase agreement. If it is not necessary let me know by Friday 9/9 at 12:00 noon or I will contact Mr. Rouda and have him talk with Mr. Titcomb and myself.
>
> Also your conversation with Titcomb and myself of Tuesday 9/6 put the date for loan documents on 9/9. What is the current status for the loan documents. Contact me at [two phone numbers].

Brazil remembered receiving this the same day; he did not write back but might have responded orally. Indeed, he did not recall *ever* writing Collins after the original February 3 loan takeout commitment.

Fontana objected to the admission of letters Brazil did not remember receiving, arguing that the State Bar should have laid a foundation when questioning Collins.

> I don't see any relevance to this stuff . . . the bar wants to paper the record, just keep adding more and more paper that doesn't in any fashion assist their case. . . . [I]t's entirely possible that Collins didn't send this stuff, but rather this is stuff that was laying around in his file that he and his lawyer exchanged about how to set up Brazil. . . . I'm still resisting what I believe is an effort to coerce me into stipulating to facts which I think are a) irrelevant, and b) that I have doubts about. As an attorney I don't like doing those things. Because if I don't this proceeding is going to drag on for yet another several weeks.

He stipulated to their mailing but not the contents. The judge asked Stainfield how this was relevant to whether Brazil obtained the loan from Ben Hom under false pretenses (the most serious complaint, discussed below). She replied that Collins rebutted two of Brazil's claims: that Fannie Mae requirements were part of the agreement and that he had raised other problems Collins failed to correct. Fontana called this "much ado about nothing. You cannot keep this record open forever. This man is entitled to get back to the practice of law sooner or later. And this is . . . like trial by water torture. And I suppose [if] you keep the proceeding open long enough the whole thing becomes irrelevant." The letters went beyond redirect and were hearsay and improper: "[T]here's no way that this can be fair to keep this going on. This trial will never end." But the judge let Stainfield recall Collins to testify about the letters' content.

Fontana said he was available that day but on trial for the next two weeks.

Fontana: I just think it's unfair. It's costing us a small fortune to have this go on. This is just wrong— . . .

STAINFIELD: I don't think it's proper for counsel to be arguing the fact that the length of this case is causing him financial problems. . . . .

FONTANA: I assumed that the rules of evidence were going to control. . . .

JUDGE: Well, Mr. Fontana, in stating a lot of the objections you had I kept the examination of Mr. Collins very narrow. And Ms. Stainfield is right. . . .

FONTANA: Well, Your Honor, if Mr. Collins is coming back may I ask that a subpoena be issued that he be directed to produce all . . . communications between himself and Mr. Brazil . . . every piece of paper in his possession or control that mentions InterBank Mortgage. . . . I'm just saying I [should] be permitted to have discovery of brother Collins and all of his records. . . . All, not just what he chooses to have Ms. Stainfield think that she wants to introduce.

The judge reminded Fontana that he "just indicated that we don't want this proceeding to be prolonged any more than necessary." And Stainfield represented that she "personally sat down with Mr. Collins and got all of his paperwork and I turned it over to counsel." But because that representation did not "ease [his] concern," Fontana withdrew his stipulation that the letters had been sent and protested, "there's no point in finishing Brazil until we finish Collins; you're allow[ing] them to reopen the redirect. . . ."

Recalled, Collins naturally confirmed all the letters and phone conversations. Before signing the February 3 loan commitment, he had told Brazil that "being a tax credit project, that most likely the purchasers would be either an institution or limited partnership or a wealthy individual; that almost for certain it would be one or just a few buyers at most." Brazil had explained the reference to individual investor owners by saying, "[Y]ou could go with . . . Fannie May [*sic*] loans, for smaller buyers, and as a backup if the institutional buyers didn't come through, or I was unable to sell it to one party or one of the potential buyers I mentioned . . . I'd have the option of being able to sell it to a number of smaller buyers." John S. Banas III (Brazil's other lawyer in the disciplinary proceeding, also from Thelen, Marrin) sought to show that Collins had never sent the letters, asking him to produce fax confirmation sheets. Stainfield objected, and the judge denied the request. Banas tried another tack, arguing that the destination number of some faxes was 478-1068, whereas Brazil's number was 578-1068. The judge responded that Brazil admitted receiving some of those faxes, and communications without fax numbers may have been mailed. In the end, she admitted all of them.

Banas offered evidence that Collins sold the units for $61,437.50 (making the $51,000 loan more than 75 percent of their value) and inflated the appraisal to $68,800 to solve this problem. The judge was unconvinced: "[W]e don't know what went into the considerations and why the property was sold for $61,437 per unit."

Collins reiterated that he sold the properties for "around $80,000 apiece," but had convinced the assessor's office "that the value of the tax credits gave the properties a higher value than normal and I talked them into assessing the properties at a replacement value . . . around $61,000 or $62,000." Only the first sale was recorded "to hold down the property taxes." The second sale of the remaining ten lots "would bring the individual purchase prices at $82,500."[21] The second deed of trust was an incentive to himself "as the local property manager to keep costs down" and did not affect the 75 percent loan to value ratio. There were no problems with either that ratio or Section 8 compliance.

In 1987, Brazil became a director of Saratoga Savings and Loan (Saratoga or Saratoga S&L) in Los Gatos. Late that year its chairman and sole shareholder, Jess Rodrigues, asked if Brazil wanted to buy it. They negotiated for six months, and Brazil raised the necessary $25 million in capital. But in June 1988, Rodrigues "became rather irate about one of the points in the closing documents which required him to indemnify the acquiring entity for certain litigation that had been filed against the S&L . . . and walked out of the closing. . . ." Several weeks later, the chairman and CEO of Peninsula S&L offered to sell it to Brazil. Negotiations extended through the end of the year, with Brazil responsible for much of the due diligence. (Judge Gee had never heard that term.)

(A May 19, 1991 *Newsday* article told a different story, not adduced in the disciplinary proceeding.[22] In 1988, Wallace L. Ford II met Brazil, who had been a year behind him at Harvard, and together they sought to buy Saratoga. Ford moved Eagle Ventures, a shell company he started in New York in 1986, to IB's offices. The two invested over $200,000 of their own money, but the deal fell through. Rodrigues said, "They just couldn't come up with any money with the exception of one person. Only one guy had any money in his bank account. They owe me forty to fifty thousand dollars worth of notes that I haven't been able to collect on." Eagle then tried to buy Peninsula for $4 million. On September 15, 1988, Eagle agreed to put down a good-faith deposit. A Wall Street broker lent $350,000 in exchange for promissory notes and an 8 percent interest. The next day, Brazil opened a business account at Peninsula with a $250,000 Eagle Ventures check drawn on Citibank. Before it cleared, however, Brazil instructed Citibank to transfer $253,300 for an unrelated IB expense. When Citibank refused, because it had already received the check made out to Peninsula, Brazil ordered it not to honor that check. When Peninsula asked why the check had bounced, Brazil blamed Citibank. Confronted by Ford, Brazil admitted misusing the money and agreed to return it. In a 1988 deposition, Ford said:

> I indicated to [Brazil] that in fact he had committed an illegal act. He thought it was the subject of interpretation. I said, "Well, you know, nevertheless, it is important for you to put that money back into the account immediately."

21. Respondent's Exhibit RR.

22. Michael Weber, *Development Chief's Bank Deals Failed,* NEWSDAY 7 (May 19, 1991).

Brazil repaid the $250,000 with a $500,000 check from Ben L. Hom (see the following section). Peninsula would not cash it, so Brazil deposited it through an IB account. When IB declared bankruptcy, Eagle lost the $250,000. Ford never sought to recover it. But in order to let Eagle keep trying to acquire Peninsula, Ford tried to conceal from Peninsula why Brazil left, while suggesting to Brazil that IB later could be incorporated into Eagle. This stratagem failed when the California Department of Savings & Loan rejected Ford's November 1988 application. Two years later, IB's attorney sued Brazil for $6.3 million.)

B. Ben L. Hom

In May 1988, Brazil met Ben L. Hom, sole proprietor of Acorn Corporation (Acorn), an investor whose name he already knew. Peter Behr (an economist Brazil had hired to prepare filings for the Saratoga purchase) introduced Hom as someone interested in becoming a director of the Saratoga S&L and investing a million dollars. Brazil said he had enough capital but promised to keep Hom informed. When the Saratoga deal fell through, Hom repeated his interest in helping to finance the Peninsula purchase. Again, Brazil said he had enough capital but assured Hom he would be "the first person I called" if Brazil needed more. Instead, he called Hom on September 9 about a bridge loan for the ten Merced mortgages (discussed above). At the time, Brazil had a $2 million line of credit at Meridian and $1.5 million line at Commercial Bank of San Jose, but neither was available. The conversation about the fifteen-day bridge loan was reduced to writing that day.[23] Since the mortgages were to be resold to Fannie Mae, the duration was "something in the neighborhood of a week, which is a normal transaction time with FM." The underlying mortgages would be the collateral. Six days later, they concluded a Loan and Security Agreement for the $516,000. Brazil agreed to provide promissory notes and recordable deeds of trust and "all documents required to perfect Acorn's security interest," while representing that he was licensed and in good standing with the California Department of Real Estate and held "good and marketable title to the Mortgage Loans."[24] On the same day, he executed an IB Promissory Note for $516,000[25] at an annual interest rate of 12.5 percent and a personal promissory note guaranteeing the loan,[26] initialed an "additional agreement,"[27] received and deposited Hom's $516,000 check, and gave Hom a check for his 2.5 percent commission. Hom explained that the handwritten "additional agreement" was "important to me for the extra collateral and extra protection, meaning that Mr. Brazil would perform." "What it means is that two notes and two deed of trust has minimum

23. State Bar Exhibit 2.
24. State Bar Exhibit 3.
25. State Bar Exhibit 4.
26. State Bar Exhibit 5.
27. State Bar Exhibit 6.

equity of half a million to $600,000." The additional agreement also obligated Brazil to give Hom a "signed copy of Fannie May [*sic*] document."

Brazil testified that Hom called again that evening: "he wanted me to provide a personal guarantee . . . in the form of an additional promissory note. . . . In addition he asked me to provide some additional security for the loans." Brazil was "glad to provide the personal guarantee" but "really didn't have anything to offer" by way of additional security. "Mr. Hom was very insistent; he said that . . . you've got to provide some kind of additional paperwork on this deal. . . . My understanding was that Mr. Hom wanted me to create some paper." Hom asked for a deed of trust on Brazil's personal residence. "He did not ask for an additional note, simply a deed of trust, which I provided." As further collateral, Brazil gave Hom security interests in 1120 Beach Park Boulevard and 1103 Decatur Street, Foster City; 38576 Mission Boulevard, Fremont; 5131 Desmond St., Oakland; 2901 Koyenberg Lane, Modesto; and 445 Leigh Ave., San Jose. But IB owned none of those properties. On each of these six documents, Brazil forged the signature and used the official seal of Vicki L. Ellefson, a notary public working in IB's escrow and funding department.[28]

The next morning, Brazil brought the "additional collateral in the form of a number of deeds of trust and corporate assignments of deeds of trust." "Mr. Hom did not ask me for any evidence of ownership, nor did he inquire about it." The "corporate assignments and deeds of trust had no value and . . . Mr. Hom knew they had no value." True, "these were documents that on the face of them were recordable documents," but "without a notary stamp they couldn't be recorded." That was why he forged Ellefson's signature and used her notary stamp. Fontana argued that "the forgery count was absolutely immaterial. Because if Ms. Ellison [*sic*] had been present all she would have done is notarized that that was his signature. . . ."

Instead of funding the Merced mortgages (which were to be part of Hom's collateral), Brazil wrote a check for $500,000 to pay down IB's credit line at Meridian National Bank because "it was a half million dollars in good funds, they had to be deposited." He claimed that the Merced transaction never closed because Collins could not sell the houses.

C. Municipal Bond Defeasance

Paul Esch, the former finance director of the City of Emeryville, proposed a partnership with Brazil to do municipal mortgage bond defeasance, estimating that there were $2.5 to $3 billion worth of outstanding bonds in California and even more in 15 to 20 other states. Municipalities issue mortgage bonds, using their tax-exempt status to obtain lower interest rates for the benefit of residents, and then sell the mortgages to repay the bonds. The spread between the amounts due

28. State Bar Exhibits 9, 12, 14, 16, 18, 20.

bondholders and the mortgage payments "generated a very substantial cash reserve," which the city could use "for any other municipal purpose." Defeasing the bonds capitalized that cash flow and "freed up the city's bond capacity . . . for other purposes." This was a "seminal" transaction, which had never been done before in California or perhaps anywhere in the United States. Brazil testified that his first project came to fruition in September 1988: between $37 and $38 million for San Pablo. "[B]ecause of some very subtle tax provisions, we were not able to borrow from an onshore domestic bank, we had to borrow from a foreign bank," the Bank of Australia. "When all the dust settled there was to be a pot of approximately $3.5 to $4 million of residual proceeds and my initial agreement with the City of San Pablo was that they were to receive no less than $2.5 million from the transaction. And InterBank Mortgage would receive the remaining portion" and service the $38 million mortgage pool. Merrill Lynch was to buy between $28 million and $29 million, and the rest would be sold at discounts to savings and loans and thrifts.

Between September 15 and 22, Brazil phoned Hom, seeking bridge financing for the San Pablo deal. It was "absolutely essential that this transaction be closed on or about the 22nd." Homestead Savings and Mission Thrift each had agreed in writing to buy $1.5 million of lesser quality mortgages but not by that date. He needed the $1.2 million Homestead could not provide. "The transaction as I described it to Mr. Hom was complex, and Mr. Hom felt . . . it necessary to be accompanied by his counsel." The next day, they met with Hom's lawyer, Peter K. Boyle, at a Chinese restaurant. "The money would be delivered . . . to counsel, and then paid over to . . . the City of San Pablo."

The San Pablo transaction closed the morning of September 22. Brazil had acquired sufficient funds to "repurchase all the bonds . . . and to produce a residual of approximately $1 million," which went to the city that morning. They agreed to "continue the closing for approximately one week, during which time I could get the rest of the parties to fund into the deal and wrap up the closing." "Peninsula declined to fund their entire amount until [certain] documents were properly delivered." Homestead failed to perform without any reason. And "Mission told me that the only problem that they had was with a wire transfer, and that the funds would be in in the next one or two business days."

At 8 P.M. that evening, Brazil went to Boyle's office to sign the papers Boyle had drafted and get Hom's $500,000 check. They had not yet discussed fees. "My only recollection . . . was that [Hom] told me that the money would probably be expensive." That evening, Brazil made "some comment . . . to Mr. Hom" that the fees "were rather enormous." He explained to the court why he had agreed to pay $500,000 in fees for a $1.2 million loan.

> [E]arlier that day in the closing we were short approximately $1 million. The City of San Pablo gave me one week in which to bring the additional moneys to the table or . . . the actual finance director . . . told me he'd unwind the deal.

So at that point in the evening, it really didn't matter what kind of a fee Mr. Hom was charging.

This second loan and security agreement for an additional $1.2 million for 45 days to finance the bond defeasance obligated IB to pay Hom 10 percent annually, plus fees of $400,000.[29] Security consisted of guarantees by IB and Brazil, deeds of trust on two of the above-mentioned properties, and an interest in $2.2 million of the unsold loans. Brazil again promised to execute all notes, security agreements, and other documents to perfect those interests. The same day the parties signed a Brokerage Fee Agreement obligating IB to pay an additional $100,000 fee.[30] Brazil again used the $500,000 Hom gave him that day to pay down IB's credit line at Meridian National Bank rather than purchase the mortgages.

On September 26, the parties entered into a supplemental agreement giving Acorn a right to a 20 percent equity interest in all future IB bulk mortgage loan purchases from a municipality.[31] The next day, the parties made a second supplemental agreement reciting that "it now appears" that Homestead Savings was interested in purchasing the Merced mortgages "today or tomorrow" and agreeing that the proceeds would go directly to repaying Acorn.[32] (In fact, Homestead had offered to purchase the 30 mortgages from IB for $1,586,317 on September 16 and for $1,645,557.09 on September 27.)[33] On September 30, the parties concluded a third supplemental agreement, specifying that a substantial proportion of financing for the San Pablo transaction would be provided by Commercial Bank of San Francisco, money to which Acorn again would have first claim.[34] The same day, they signed a Final Agreement: Because "Acorn and Hom have recently felt an increased risk in the transaction," the parties agreed that Acorn's minimum return would be $500,000, before payments to anyone else, by October 3, out of escrow funds due IB, including those from Merrill Lynch ($435,000 holdback, $145,000 purchase of servicing), Peninsula Savings ($40,000 purchase of servicing), Bank of America ($51,000 holdback), Homestead Savings ($115,000 excess profit), and City of San Pablo ($257,000 holdback on sale to Peninsula Savings).[35] On October 3, Brazil wrote Hom a check for $500,694.44 on IB's Security Pacific National Bank account, which was returned for insufficient funds. On October 12, Brazil executed assignments to Acorn of any amounts due from the above entities.[36]

---

29. State Bar Exhibits 22, 23.
30. State Bar Exhibit 23.
31. State Bar Exhibit 25.
32. State Bar Exhibit 26.
33. Respondent's Exhibits S and T.
34. State Bar Exhibit 27.
35. State Bar Exhibit 28.
36. State Bar Exhibits 29–32.

Brazil still believed that either Homestead would buy the mortgages or he could find another buyer. "Mr. Hom and/or Mr. Boyle called me daily from the date of the 22nd of September to follow the progress of the bond defeasance closing . . . basically each time I saw them they had an agreement that they wanted me to sign." He explained why he had offered Hom an equity interest:

> At this point in time, the 26th of September, the . . . San Pablo transaction was not coming together as anticipated. InterBank owed Mr. Hom a million bucks and still had additional funds to raise and just about anything Mr. Hom wanted at this point in time I agreed to do it.

He expected the transaction to yield more than $1 million in profit, which would pay Hom's fees.

Boyle drafted all the supplemental agreements, which Brazil claimed he did not fully comprehend. For instance, the second supplemental agreement recited, "it now appears that Homestead Savings may be interested in purchasing all or a substantial portion of the unsold mortgages." In fact, Homestead had made that commitment several weeks earlier. The third supplemental agreement recited that "all funds obtained by or through a bank . . . shall be deemed to be treated as funds loaned by Acorn Corp to InterBank Mortgage." Brazil never understood that clause or asked what it meant. "The house was caving in from all directions and it just really didn't matter. The document didn't make any sense, but at this point nothing else was making a lot of sense, so if it made them happy, I signed it." The September 30 final agreement guaranteed Acorn and Hom a minimum return of $500,000, which Brazil described as "the two $200,000 fees set forth in the loan and security agreement and the separate $400,000 [*sic*—'$100,000'] fee that was set forth in the document captioned brokerage agreement." Brazil now interpreted language in the final agreement that "Hom shall be repaid the moneys that they have invested as capital" to mean "they were beginning to characterize the whole transaction as an investment," for which "the $500,000" was "a return."

Brazil explained why he never repaid Hom the $1,016,000. "There were two sources of repayment:" the loans Homestead promised to buy but did not (despite Brazil's "extensive efforts") and the "residuals" in the Final Agreement, which "were all swept into the company's bankruptcy" (see below). Fontana sought to show that the first loan "was usurious and unlawful." Over Stainfield's objection, Brazil testified that the interest rate was "approximately 59.9 percent." During voir dire about usury, he conceded, "there are a number of exceptions. And most . . . institutional or business lenders will fall into one of those exemptions. . . ." Nevertheless, he insisted that the first loan was usurious and the interest rate on the second "approximately 323 percent." But though he maintained that "I hadn't done the calculation" at the time of signing, he "knew that the rate was quite high. . . ."

Although IB was "a financially viable institution," it spent between $250,000 and $300,000 on the failed attempt to acquire Saratoga, and another $150,000 on the equally unsuccessful Peninsula purchase. "The demands on my personal time with respect to both of these acquisitions were very great:" negotiating with the owners, counsel and accountants on both sides, the Federal Home Loan Bank Board, Federal Savings and Loan Insurance Corporation, California Department of Savings and Loans, his economist and investors, and other lenders. He was "also involved in the due diligence:" "a review of the entire loan portfolios of all the institutions . . . the quality of their investments, the relationships of those institutions with respect to their regulatory agencies, their administration and operation" of both deposits and loans, any financial obligations, and litigation. The San Pablo transaction cost an additional $200,000, and "the time involved was simply enormous. It was by far the most complicated transaction I have ever been involved in and probably ever will be involved in." He had to deal with the "multitude of parties all represented by counsel. There were the formalities to be observed in dealing with the city, itself. There were appearances before the city's governing board . . . and there were no roadmaps of the transaction because one had never been done before." All this had a "negative" effect on IB's financial situation. Successful closure

> would have enabled InterBank to recover its expenses and regain a sound financial footing. . . . Mr. Esch and I had had conversations with several cities in southern California and the Bay Area as follow-on deals, and they were simply waiting for the successful conclusion of the San Pablo transaction prior to beginning their own defeasance transactions with IB as the underwriter. . . . [I]n the latter stages of the bond transaction, the latter part of September, the company's financial picture was becoming increasingly bleak.

He began to lay off employees.

Timothy W. Kremers was chairman, president, and CEO of Commercial Bank of San Francisco (Commercial) during the relevant period. Hom wanted to borrow money to lend IB, but Kremers testified that the $1.1 million to $1.2 million "was beyond our legal lending capacity." Instead, he tried to have Commercial buy the loan. On September 30, he told the Bank of America in Brazil's presence that "we were willing to go to a million dollars." Commercial paid that to Bank of America (B oA), as escrow agent for IB, earning a $30,000 fee and intending to sell the loan to Homestead.[37] At Brazil's request, Commercial did not immediately record the assignment "because Homestead was going to buy them. . . . And since B of A was holding them in escrow, we were protected." When Commercial attempted to record its interest on October 18, "we found that a Mr. Alcheck had

37. State Bar Exhibit 49.

already recorded an assignment the previous day." "B of A had released all of our documents to, under the verbal instructions of Mr. Brazil, Mr. Alcheck. We had no loans. B of A could not make us whole." Both B of A and Brazil assured Commercial that Brazil would make them whole. Commercial finally met Brazil again on October 19 or 20, with Hom and Boyle. "Mr. Brazil said that I shouldn't worry, that he'd take care of everything." But he never did. About a year later, Commercial settled with Alcheck, the City of San Pablo, and the trustee in bankruptcy for $750,000. Kremers called Brazil "dishonest. He attempted or successfully committed fraud, costing the bank attorneys fees and a loss of almost a million dollars." Fontana argued that Commercial bought the loan at a heavily discounted price, since Homestead's commitment letter promised to pay $1,645,557.09. Kremers responded that had Homestead performed, "we would have made thirty thousand dollars plus the earnings from the interest on the loans during the time that we held them." He conceded that had he perfected the security interest in the mortgages Commercial would have lost nothing.

D. Collapse

Acorn filed an involuntary bankruptcy petition against Brazil and IB in late November or early December 1988.[38] After a San Francisco district attorney's (DA's) investigator visited Brazil in November 1988, he learned from his attorney, Robert Carey, that the DA was considering criminal charges. But Carey reached an understanding that they would be dropped if Brazil repaid Hom. He began trying to do so during the Christmas holidays, studying defeasance transactions and determining which municipalities had outstanding mortgage bonds. He formed Equifund for this purpose in February 1989, first as chief operating officer, then as vice president. On February 28, he and Equifund Vice President Gus Chiamos (a former IB employee) contacted Financial Products and Services Corporation (FP&S) to execute the functions IB had performed in the abortive San Pablo defeasance; Brazil and Chiamos each were going to get 25 percent of the profits.[39] Of the 25 to 30 municipalities they contacted in March and April, five or six "gave very favorable responses. . . . we were on the verge of a successful completion with the City of Paramount . . . the City of Azusa, Simi Valley and several others when the charges were brought against me. . . ."[40] Fees for the City of Paramount deal were $263,173 plus "a substantial amount of revenues from the sale of the underlying mortgage servicing"; those from Azusa were $310,471. Alexandra J. Balitsky, an Equifund loan processor, testified that at the height of

38. In re Ernest Lee Brazil, Case No. 3-88-04131 WTC (U.S. Bankruptcy Court, N.D. Calif); In re Inter Bank Mortgage Corporation, Case No. 3-88-03667 WLK (U.S. Bankruptcy Court, N.D. Calif).

39. Respondent's Exhibit W.

40. Respondents Exhibit AA (initial letter from P. Andrew Resendez, FP & S, to City Manager, City of Fairfield, June 30, 1989, proposing bond defeasance).

the defeasance project she worked until 10 or 11 at night because Brazil was a "workaholic," a "perfectionist." He cooperated with the police in a sting operation that netted people who had defrauded First American (a real estate financier). But when the charges against Brazil were publicized, "the phone calls stopped . . . everything was frozen from there on up."

On June 27, the *San Francisco Chronicle* reported that "a San Francisco judge yesterday issued an arrest warrant for the former state real estate commissioner on charges that he failed to repay a financial backer more than one million dollars in business loans." Brazil immediately telephoned FP&S Vice President Andrew Resendez. The next day, Resendez faxed his superiors that "our proposals are on the verge of being voted upon. . . . However, disclosures in this article may cause problems unless we move to address them. Because of Brazil's legal problems I am urging both he [*sic*] and Gus Chiamos that Lee should step back from current prospects effective today."[41] Brazil would write all prospects explaining that Equifund's work was "mainly finished and further work is more effciently [*sic*] handled under [FP&S's] auspices and using our resources." On June 30, FP&S instructed fifteen municipalities to deal with it in the future, rather than Equifund.[42] Carey kept Hom informed of these efforts once or twice a week. Brazil testified: "We continued our efforts after the publication of the charges with the understanding with FP&S that Mr. Chiamos and I would become silent partners . . . neither signing any documents or correspondence or actually meeting with any of the city officials because of the publicity." FP&S general counsel notified Brazil on September 11 "of our decision to terminate our present brokerage agreement . . . because of the news of recent legal proceedings brought against you. . . ."[43] Brazil accepted this on September 25 but continued to work for FP&S "on a behind-the-scenes basis," never tellng Hom. The charges "and the attendant publicity eventually caused the termination of my agreement with Financial Services and Products Corp. [*sic*] and that, in essence, ended any opportunity that I might have had. . . ." "I was gone, ceased to exist." "This effort spanned the greater part of 1989, and I've probably expended a good thousand hours of effort to try to bring these deals into fruition."

To settle lawsuits by Hom and Acorn,[44] Brazil promised on November 27 to make full repayment in exchange for Hom's promise to appear at the sentencing hearing, "emphatically state that Hom is fully satisfied that Brazil is making satisfactory restitution," and "recommend . . . in the strongest possible terms that Brazil not be sentenced to serve any time. . . ."[45] Brazil agreed that the

---

41. Respondent's Exhibit BB.

42. Respondent's Exhibit AA1-5.

43. Respondent's Exhibit CC.

44. Acorn Corporation, v. InterBank Mortgage Corporation, San Mateo County Superior Court Civil Cases No. 334627 and 335624.

45. State Bar Exhibit 35.

$1,016,000 debt would be nondischargeable; he would owe simple interest of 12 percent from September 29, 1988, make annual payments of $200,000 beginning January 1, 1990, and assign Hom two-thirds of the first $100,000 and 80 percent of the excess of any contractual obligations and joint venture real estate financing transactions. Brazil did not fulfill the agreement. He never had any contractual obligations or real estate joint ventures. On May 30, 1990, Hom won a non-dischargeable judgment in his civil action against Brazil for $1,016,000.[46] It was never satisfied.

On December 11, 1989, Brazil was arraigned on two counts of theft for stealing more than $100,000 from Acorn Corporation and Ben Hom, and one count of forging Vicki L. Ellefson's name with intent to defraud them.[47] He pleaded not guilty. On the Pretrial Information Sheet, the assistant DA proposed a deal "(1) if on sentence date victim in person agrees to lesser sentence—or (2) if there is substantial restitution made and victim appears not to object in good faith." On February 6, 1990 Brazil changed his plea to *nolo contendere*. On March 14, he was suspended from the Bar pending final disposition. On April 3, he was sentenced to three years on the first count and two each on the second and third (two-thirds stayed), for a total of fifty-two months. This was suspended, and Brazil was placed on probation on condition that he make restitution of $300 to the victim, pay a $2,000 fine, and do 2,000 hours of community service.[48]

IV. DISCIPLINARY PROCEEDING

A. The Hearing

On January 22, 1991, Brazil was ordered to show cause why he should not be disbarred. After four unsuccessful settlement conferences, the case was set for trial. Because the offenses involved moral turpitude, Hearing Examiner Stainfield maintained that only strong mitigating circumstances could justify suspension. While not contesting the facts, Brazil argued that he had acted as a mortgage banker, not a lawyer, and sought less than five years suspension.

The hearing began on January 6, 1992.[49] Hom testified that he was owner and president of Realty Executive and had been president and chair of United Savings Bank in San Francisco from 1974 to 1986, when it was sold to Hibernia Bank. That year, when Hom founded Acorn (consisting of himself and a secretary), Peter Behr, an official at the Federal Home Loan Bank of San Francisco

46. State Bar Exhibit 36.

47. People v. Brazil, San Francisco District Attorney, Case No. 1175011.

48. State Bar Exhibit 1; *Ex-State Official Gets Suspended Sentence,* SAN FRANCISCO CHRONICLE B14 (Apr. 4, 1990).

49. Additional hearings occurred on January 7–9, February 13, 14, 11, 13, and March 3 and 16. The record was 1535 pages long.

(which governed USB), introduced him to Brazil (whom Hom knew as a lawyer and former California Real Estate Commissioner). Hom never got the Fannie Mae documents he requested or the notes corresponding to the deeds of trust. He waited to record the latter until Brazil failed to repay the money on the due date (September 29) "because we acted in good faith that the money was to be paid in the short time and also rely on the judgment that he is in good character and probably asked us not to record it since it was such a . . . short term loan." He conceded that the initial loan agreement said nothing about financing Merced mortgages. Outside Hom's hearing, Fontana argued that Hom's "primary security for the $500,000 was the . . . Merced loans . . . Mr. Hom's belated request to post the additional security was a subterfuge at best" since "he never bothered to record them." "[A] deed of trust without the underlying promissory note is useless as security. . . ." But the Judge still felt Brazil had offered property he did not own as additional collateral: "that means the result was totally fraudulent." When Hom returned to court he said his lawyer, Boyle, had recorded the deeds of trust at his request. Banas asked when.

HOM: Dumb question requires a good answer, because your client did not pay.

BANAS: And when was that, Mr. Hom?

HOM: Way after its due time.

He conceded that Boyle had told him "the security instrument was not good instrument." Asked what Boyle had said, Hom retorted: "that your client is not a good client." "[T]he $400,000 that you speak of to be paid to Acorn . . . was never been paid." The "broker's fee or other fee, was to be paid later, not taken off of the 1.2 million." Acorn wrote IB a check for $500,000 on Golden Coin Savings & Loan on September 22.[50] Hom had arranged for more than another million to be loaned to Brazil by Commercial Bank of San Francisco.

Fontana had Hom read the indecipherable September 15 handwritten note.[51]

(1) 2 Notes and deed of trust in the total amount of equity $500,000 to $600,000. [initialed and dated by Brazil and Hom]

(2) Sign copy of FNMA [Fannie Mae] Documents. Execute copy of Documents by FNMA and Lee Brazil [which Hom pronounced Liebesilk] [initialed and dated by both]

Above 2 Documents will be sign & delivered to Mr. B L Hom by 3pm 9/15/88 [initialed and dated by both]

Brazil never delivered the notes and deeds of trust or the Fannie Mae documents. Hom claimed he could record a deed of trust without a promissory note

50. State Bar Exhibit 24.

51. State Bar Exhibit 6.

but could not explain how. He acknowledged receiving the 2.25 percent fee for the first $516,000 loan.

Boyle testified that he had practiced banking law for more than 30 years. Hom introduced him to Brazil (and a woman described as Brazil's fiancée) at a Chinese restaurant in August or September 1988, when they briefly discussed the San Pablo transaction.[52] "I had represented United Bank on a number of matters over the years, and knew [Hom] pretty well. And I think he expected that I would serve as his counsel in any dealings on this matter. . . ." Boyle did not draft the September 15 documents. "I don't think I had much involvement in this transaction." "I'd had I don't think any prior experience directly with Fannie Ma[e] [*sic*] and I called them to get some information on their procedures in handling transactions of this type." He did not remember if there was any collateral because "the expectation was that this loan was going to be repaid within two or three or four days." Although he prepared the documents for the second loan, "when Mr. Hom and Mr. Brazil came to me they had pretty much worked out the arrangements of the relationship between them and they just told me what to put on paper." "[T]here was some confusion at the time . . . whether or not the notes for which the deeds of trust were security were also to be part of the collateral. And I don't know how that confusion ever arose in the first place, because the deed of trust, itself, isn't much value as collateral without a note." The two Foster City properties "were both single family residences. One is one that [Brazil] had just recently moved out of, and the other was one he said he'd owned for several years, and was using as a rental property." The equity was "substantial in terms of $100,000 or more each." Boyle attempted to record all the documents by mailing them to the respective county recorders in late September or early October. "[Y]ou don't need to present a note in the recorder's office to record it. The recorder will accept the deed of trust without a note."

The second loan obligated IB to pay Hom two fees of $200,000 and a third of $100,000, plus 10 percent annual interest on the $1 million for 45 to 60 days.

> Mr. Hom called me and said that none of the deeds of trust were any good. . . . And then he gave me the name of some title officers to call. . . . And I found out that the interest that Mr. Brazil claimed to have in the Foster City properties and InterBank claimed to have in the other two deeds of trust didn't exist.

As additional collateral IB was to give Acorn its interest in $2.2 million of the $4.7 million in unsold mortgages, but it never did.[53] Boyle and Percy Duran

---

52. Brazil had separated from his wife, Rosemarie, the previous January. She was hospitalized for a nervous breakdown for two and a half months that spring; Brazil saw or telephoned her every day. The "fiancée" must be the good new relationship that Kaye describes existing in 1990 (*infra*).

53. On October 13, Boyle wrote Homestead, enclosing the assignment to Acorn of any money due IB. State Bar Exhibit 46. Homestead replied on October 20 that because "several

drove to San Pablo to examine the properties, which "looked reasonably well maintained and cared for."

In his opening statement for the defense, Fontana acknowledged that the "events" to which Brazil pleaded nolo "were not . . . the kind of conduct that any of us would want to countenance." But though he was guilty of "bad judgment," "none of that activity had anything to do with the action by Mr. Brazil in the course of the practice of law."

> Mr. Hom lost $1 million in these transactions for reasons having absolutely nothing to do with that forged notary signature. Mr. Hom went into these transactions with his eyes open expecting to make a lot of money. His own documentation shows that he would have made a rate of return on his investments in the order of 300 or 400 percent in a matter of weeks. Mr. Hom thereafter chose to use Mr. Brazil's misuse of that notary stamp as a basis for filing a criminal complaint that ultimately resulted in those nolo pleas. . . . I hope the court will come to the same conclusion . . . that he never intended—

STAINFIELD: Objection, Your Honor.

FONTANA: What's going on with you?

STAINFIELD: That statement is improper.

FONTANA: Ms. Stainfield, I've kind of been patient because I realize that you are very much excited about this case, but the fact of the matter is Mr. Brazil's intent is very specifically relevant to this proceeding as an act of mitigation. In fact, if I have to read you the bar rules, I will. . . .

STAINFIELD: Your Honor, first of all, I object to Mr. Fontana's characterization of my personal involvement. . . . Number two, obviously Mr. Fontana is not aware of the law that Mr. Brazil's conviction . . . is conclusive evidence of his guilt. . . .

JUDGE: [allowed Stainfield to file her brief on that point] But I'm looking into the facts and circumstances . . . especially since we're talking about a nolo plea and not a conviction after a full jury trial. . . .

Fontana insisted that "good faith" and "lack of harm" were relevant.[54] "Mr. Hom is not some little old lady in tennis shoes. Mr. Hom is not some unsophisticated person. Mr. Hom got into this transaction expecting to make himself even richer than he already is. . . ." Brazil was suffering "financial pressures" and "personal and emotional trauma." "I believe in my heart this is a good person. I have known him myself for 17 years." When Stainfield objected to this, the judge

---

of the contingencies set forth in the letter of intent between Homestead Savings and InterBank Mortgage Corporation (dated September 27, 1988) were never satisfied," Homestead would "not be entering into any contract with InterBank Mortgage Corporation for the purchase of conventional first lien single family mortgages. . . ." State Bar Exhibit 47.

54. Bar Rules 1.2(e)(2) and (3).

warned Fontana against testifying. Before Brazil testified, Stainfield filed the state's trial brief on the conclusiveness for this proceeding of all elements of his criminal convictions.

Brazil said he pleaded *nolo contendere* "on the advice of counsel" because "it was felt that the charge related to forgery was almost an open and shut case . . . although I didn't necessarily intend to defraud Mr. Hom." Stainfield objected that Brazil's response "is a clear attempt to relitigate his innocence in the underlying criminal conviction." Fontana retorted:

> [T]his is about the fifth time Ms. Stainfield has interrupted an answer to make this same argument. . . . It's been overruled repeatedly. . . . I do object to her doing it in the middle of the witness's answers. . . . I have established to my satisfaction that every case that she cites either doesn't stand for the proposition or was decided long before the transitional rules . . . [which] specifically direct this court to consider the good faith of Mr. Brazil . . . the lack of harm to Mr. Hom. . . .

In response to the judge's question, Stainfield reiterated that a *nolo contendere* plea was considered a conviction for the purpose of subsequent cases, but Fontana insisted mitigation opened the question of good faith. Brazil explained that he pleaded rather than testifying about intent because "the chances of conviction" for forgery were "pretty high" and he feared that a guilty verdict on that count might lead the jury to convict him of the two grand theft charges, to which "I felt I had a very good defense." Brazil left IB the first week of November 1988. Hom filed for involuntary bankruptcy against IB and Brazil that month. Brazil had made partial restitution to Hom and performed 700 of his 2,000 hours of community service at the Veterans Center in Burlingame, counseling Vietnam veterans on legal problems and referring some to peninsula law firms on a no-fee, reduced fee, or contingency basis. But for the suspension, he would be able to provide "a great deal of assistance to these veterans" himself.

Direct examination concluded with Brazil laying the foundation to introduce eleven letters he had submitted to the probation department and judge at sentencing. Richard J. Guggenhime, a Heller, Ehrman partner, wrote that Brazil's "reputation of truth and honesty and his gentle character was [*sic*] excellent."[55] He would "always" consider Brazil a friend and declared "categorically" that his "demeanor, integrity and honesty in the social setting . . . has [*sic*] always been exemplary." Nicole A. Crittenden, a partner in Jackson, Tufts, Cole & Black, wrote at length about other qualities, including Brazil's "tremendous energy," but said nothing about his integrity.[56] Charles H. Clifford, another Heller, Ehrman lawyer, wrote that Brazil "was very concerned about advancing

---

55. Respondent's Exhibit A (Feb. 22, 1990).
56. Respondent's Exhibit B (Mar. 2, 1990).

professionally and doing a first-rate job for his client" and "working long hours."[57] "His current trouble is certainly out of character of what I expect of Ernest Lee Brazil and [I] can only hope that it is aberrational." Dr. Phillippe Lehot, a consultant engineer and computer scientist, could "not help feeling that this Lee Brazil is a fundamentally honest person" and "a hard working individual."[58] Lehot was "absolutely and totally convinced that [Brazil] will never repeat" the "mistakes" and "beg[ged] the court to exercise charitable clemency." Dr. Julie A. Quakenbush, an internist, viewed Brazil as "among my closest friends."[59] His ability to "go through an extremely lengthy and painful rehabilitation from a knee injury . . . without complaint, and with a smile on his face . . . truly attests to strength of character and will." They had discussed his "refreshing" "attitudes on law and justice. . . . In short, he is an honest man." If she ever needed a lawyer, "I would certainly require my legal counsel to have the morals and sincerity of Lee Brazil." "I trust him without limit." "I do not believe that it would be possible for Lee to allow anything like this to happen again." Tony Quintero, a lawyer and real estate investor, saw parallels in their "life experiences."[60] "[I]n striving for economic success, [Brazil] found himself unable to accept one of the inevitable facets of his life, failure. Facing the failure of his business enterprise, he made errors of judgment which have cost him dearly." Quintero found his "true character . . . honest and decent" and "would not hesitate to hire Lee Brazil in any capacity." Kenneth J. Oden flew over 125 combat missions with Brazil, who had been best man at his wedding.[61] For "almost a quarter century . . . I've always known him to be a man of honesty and integrity."

Brazil testified that he separated from his wife, Rosemarie Yule, in January 1988 as "the result of accumulative pressures that had arisen" during their ten-year marriage. "Years of marital therapy and individual therapy seemed not to be working. My involvement in the business of IB was draining my own ability to function well in a personal relationship." This "was an extraordinarily traumatic event in Rosemarie's life and my own." She had a nervous breakdown in February and was hospitalized for two and a half months, which he blamed on the separation. "She was intensely suicidal at the time." He visited her daily in hospital, and visited or talked to her daily after she was discharged. He was responsible for $20,000 in hospital bills and more than half the cost of her visits to a psychiatrist three to four times a week after release. Her daughter, Allison, had left her Colorado boarding school in December 1987; she refused to return or attend public high school, and Brazil could not get her into another private school. He attributed her behavior partly to the separation. "Although Allison was my

57. Respondent's Exhibit C (Feb. 28, 1990).
58. Respondent's Exhibit D (Feb. 27, 1990).
59. Respondent's Exhibit E (Feb. 27, 1990).
60. Respondent's Exhibit F (Mar. 5, 1990).
61. Respondent's Exhibit G (Feb. 28, 1990).

step-daughter . . . she was in fact the only child that I have had, and I felt very close to her."

Rosemarie wrote for the sentencing hearing that Brazil "has always been a man of high moral standards."[62]

> As an officer of a Mortgage Banking Company, he had trained the Operations Staff to be dedicated to quality, high conforming standards of Government and quasi-governmental regulating bodies. Proper documentation, quality loans and serving his borrowers were always of priority to him. Frailty is one thing, but one must take into consideration his strong and dedicated moral work ethic.

She testified in the disciplinary proceeding that she had been born in Shanghai, emigrated to the United States at nineteen, and graduated from Berkeley in 1967. She met Brazil in 1975 and married him in 1977. From late 1983 or early 1984 to January 1988, she was IB's vice president of sales. After they separated, she had a "nervous breakdown" and "was hospitalized for a few months." Her teenage daughter had to go live with relatives. "So, it seemed like at that time my professional life and my home life had all come crashing down. . . ." Brazil visited or called every day, "very often say[ing] that he felt very guilty about how things had led up to the point where I required that type of help."

> I wanted a little bit of his time; I wanted a little bit of his understanding. I wanted to know what was going on. . . . We're not just talking about . . . work, a job, a company. This was my life. I had every right to. . . . So, yes . . . I did talk and I did request time for all those normal human wants and needs. But I was denied. He was always involved in something, dealing with either a problem or with InterBank.

At the time he "had deteriorated so much from stress that I mean I couldn't believe it. It was a different person . . . it didn't seem very human because he was under extreme, extreme pressure, stress. . . ."

She filed for divorce in September 1988 and then left the country; the divorce became final in March 1989. They had maintained contact since, "even though it's been very difficult, extremely stressful." She described him as

> a workaholic. Always believed in doing his best and always believed in doing more than what was expected of him . . . he worked very very long hours, left early early in the morning and didn't come home till really late. As a matter of fact our entire family schedule had to have been changed because of these long hours. . . .

62. Respondent's Exhibit H (Feb. 28, 1990).

As Real Estate Commissioner, Brazil commuted from Foster City to Sacramento.[63] He continued to work "very long" hours at IB. "He felt very responsible for all the employees at InterBank . . . because there were people's lives that depended on the welfare. . . ." She did not believe he was guilty of forgery. Asked by Stainfield if "success was important to him," Yule responded, "No, no. Doing a good job was important to him." He was not paying spousal support.

Douglas H. Latimer, Rosemarie's first husband and Allison's father, wrote that Brazil's "human qualities" were "truly exceptional."[64] He played "a key parental role—one that was at least equal to my own, and probably greater." Brazil paid for Allison's private school when Latimer could not. "There is no question in my mind that the fact that Allison has emerged from her difficulties and become a self-sufficient person with a stable life and job is due in very large part to the emotional and other support that Lee gave her from beginning to end." Latimer had "also found Lee to be an exceptionally warm, intelligent, balanced, loyal and moral person in every other aspect of his life."

Brazil's younger brother, Harold, called himself the "black sheep" of the family, in contrast with "Ernie," the good brother, "a good student . . . an alter [*sic*] boy at church."[65] After their parents' divorce

> Ernie was forced into a surrogate father role, often counseling and disciplining me. In addition, he served as a confidante and a partner to our mother.
>
> Ernie helped guide us through those dark early days of our youth. We were a poor, single-parent family living in the midst of urban blight. . . . Ernie hated "the ghetto." he [*sic*] dedicated his life to getting as far away from it as he could. . . .
>
> Ernie always knew that he "could make it." In my mind, he did "make it," and he inspired me and others to do the same, despite our relatively humble beginnings. . . .
>
> I would like the Court to understand Ernie as an individual . . . the key to this case is not theft, nor the motivation of theft . . . [but] understand Ernie's role as an inspirational leader to his family and community.
>
> This role made it impossible for him to accept failure. When confronted with failure under the facts of this case, he saw he was left with only one alternative: to succeed.

63. Mapquest estimated that the 220-mile roundtrip would take nearly four hours.
64. Respondent's Exhibit I (Feb. 28, 1990).
65. Respondent's Exhibit J (Mar. 13, 1990).

> Ernie had been the perfect kid. he [*sic*] was highly intelligent, made good grades and was active in the church. Everyone liked him, and as he grew up, he demonstrated an exemplary lifestyle.

Harold had been inspired by his brother to attend college, join the Navy, and go to law school.

> Unfortunately, Ernie's life of success and the concomitant admiration by others came with a large price tag. It required him to perpetuate the inspirational symbol of success that he had become.
>
> Monetary considerations for Ernie were irrelevant. What was at issue for him was whether, in his own mind, he would let me, mom, and others down—whether he would let his inspirational image be shattered by falling flat on his face—by not putting together this deal. . . .
>
> I believe that had Ernie been able to break through the mantle of inspirational leader, he could have sought help from me or others with experience in such matters. He simply wasn't able to ask us or to seek help because it would be contrary to his successful image. . . .
>
> In waiving the preliminary hearing and entering his plea of *nolo contenderes* [*sic*], he sought to save the City and County of San Francisco some time and some money with regard to this matter. . . . I understand the complaining witness will indicate that Ernie is doing all that he can to make restitution. I have no doubt but that he will continue to do so.
>
> [He] recognizes his failure in judgment. . . .

Doris E. Duren, Brazil's mother, wrote that he had "always shown the virtues and attributes any mother would be proud of. As a very young person Lee was ambitious, disciplined and hard working."[66]

> Lee has not always had a father figure to guide and instruct him but that lack just seemed to intensify his [desire to] achieve and be able to give something back to the world and the family that guided and helped him.
>
> Lee is a very compassionate and loving person, always willing to help when it was needed and to share with others.
>
> My son is a product of Catholic schools where he excelled scholastically and was highly thought of by the teachers and nuns at St. Joseph's Academy. At a very young age Lee became an alter [*sic*] boy at St. Josephs' [*sic*] Cathedral here in Columbus. He would walk close to a mile in the early morning hours to assist the Priest's [*sic*] at Mass, offtimes [*sic*] in snow, rain and freezing weather.

---

66. Respondent's Exhibit K (Feb. 13, 1990).

> Lee has shown his love and devotion to me in many, many ways and has helped and guided his younger brother through the years.

Stephen D. Warren, who had known Brazil since they were "Alter [*sic*] Servers" in elementary school, "found Lee to be a person whose honor and integrity go unquestioned."[67] He had "complete trust and confidence in Lee's judgment." Edward F. Yule, Brazil's former brother-in-law, had "observed Lee to be a hard working manager whenever I visited his offices. It was obvious to me that he is dedicated to his work and to his staff."[68] George G. Weickhardt, a former Heller, Ehrman lawyer, also knew Brazil in other capacities.[69] "In my professional contacts with Mr. Brazil, he always exhibited high integrity, and great talent as a lawyer and businessman. Mr. Brazil was also a particularly hard working individual."

Miles N. Moore, founder and managing partner of a telecommunications distribution and service company, wrote that Lee

> has been a warm, engaging and truthfully sensitive individual, whose honesty and integrity has never had reason to be questioned. His consistent humility and cautious wisdom have had a dramatic and positive impact on the shaping of this man.
>
> Professionally, Lee has been energetic, inquisitive, and very conservative in his evaluation of any business plan or concept we have ever discussed. . . . [H]e was strongly adamant, also, in his advice against shortcuts and get-rich schemes.[70]

Moore also testified as a character witness that he had overlapped with Brazil at Itel, was his neighbor, and had sought advice on a business plan from late 1987 through the end of 1988. "[T]here are very few people in this world that I would trust with the security of my family as it related to providing them with judgment, support, and Lee Brazil is that individual." He had never seen Brazil "particularly stressed out . . . the most consistent thing about him is his stability." Although they were not neighbors after January 1988, he consulted Brazil on the business plan in September 1988.

Dr. Robert Kaye, a psychiatrist, first met Brazil for marital counseling in 1984 and saw him 150 to 200 times through August 1988. He wrote in his February 23, 1990, sentencing letter that "there has never been any evidence of sociopathy, antisocial behavior or criminal activity." "He is not the type of person to engage in premeditated illegal activity. It is possible that he acted on impulse or with poor judgement [*sic*], but not with criminal intent." He testified:

> The kind of stress that Mr. Brazil was experiencing in his marriage were [*sic*] related to very, very severe problems that his wife had and including verbal

67. Respondent's Exhibit M (Feb. 28, 1990).
68. Respondent's Exhibit N (Feb. 26, 1990).
69. Respondent's Exhibit U (Feb. 22, 1990).
70. Respondent's Exhibit L (Feb. 26, 1990).

> abuse, accusations of abandonment, telephone harassment while he was at work, paranoid episodes in which she would accuse people that he was working with of trying to take advantage of him, pressuring him to fire people who were working with him and therefore splitting his loyalty to her versus an employee, and then an actual decompensation in which [s]he began to lose weight, became suicidal, and had to be hospitalized. In addition to that, in the spring of 1988 after she got out of the hospital, her mother developed terminal cancer and she was putting a tremendous amount of pressure on Lee to respond to that, and then in the . . . early summer of 1988, a friend . . . who she had met in the hospital committed suicide and he was pulled into that tragedy also. . . . He tried first to understand Rosemary's [*sic*] position although it would shift and become incomprehensible at times. . . . I think he tried every psychological technique that he could muster up to try to calm her down. . . . Her anger was extremely intense at times. . . . If she became irate about something, she would literally go on for days and nights not letting him sleep, berating him, doing damage to his self esteem. . . . [After separation] it escalated. She tried to get him back by accusing him of abandonment . . . of being selfish. That would alternate with demands on him to take care of her and presenting herself as . . . a helpless victim . . . if he didn't take care of her, that she would possibly end her life.

The duration and intensity of such stress "causes one to have aberrant behavior . . . a distraction from all forms of functioning . . . a dysfunctional state in which a person could use shortcuts . . . could even abandon their value system." It would be "extremely inconsistent . . . that he would in a premeditated way think of harming another person." "He's the opposite type of person in all ways and perhaps to his detriment, to the extreme he tends to take on responsibility. . . ."

Kaye next saw Brazil in February 1990.

> He came to tell me about the charges against him . . . how horrible he felt about what he [had] done. . . . He was terribly remorseful. . . . He even had some suicidal thoughts himself. . . . He thought he might be disbarred. . . . He would lose his opportunity to ever fulfill a lifelong dream which was to be in politics. He felt his life was pretty much . . . over at times. There was no evidence I could see that he was feeling like a victim. He was not trying to blame anybody else. . . . [Acts like those he had committed were] probably less likely to occur than even before because he's had therapy and has a much better understanding of what happened to him and how not to get into a situation like that again. He is in a relationship with a woman who is a much healthier person which means that he is choosing better. He has learned new coping skills and all through the therapy was being made aware of the tendency to take care of too much and to try to rescue things that couldn't be rescued. . . .

Under cross-examination, Kaye conceded clinicians could not predict specific behavior, like stealing. "So, all I can say is that stress can cause a person to step outside of their value system . . . to have poor judgment. . . ." But he added: "[W]ith all that I know about him . . . he could not steal money. . . ." In 1990, "he told me that it was extremely difficult for him to experience any kind of failure. . . . He had a Catholic upbringing and he had two failed marriages in the past." "[H]e didn't have the strength to continue to go on . . . the stress was very, very intense. . . . he was asking questions of himself . . . [W]hy did I do these things? Where did I go wrong? How have I slipped? And this I remember from the notes: Was I just greedy in reaching for the brass ring? Do I have some basic character flaw?" Kaye had not seen Brazil between August 1988 and February 1990 "because he was successfully separating from his wife and . . . was in a new relationship with a very supportive person. . . ."

Resuming direct testimony, Brazil repeated his earlier deposition that he formed IB because "I wanted to manage, or perhaps run the company without any day-to-day input from other executives. . . ." He had told Hom, "there were a number of such municipal revenue bonds in existence in the state of California and that if this were successful we would have many opportunities to follow on with similar transactions." That was why the September 26 first supplemental agreement gave Hom an equity interest. He conceded that the September 22 loan agreement's representation that IB had a contractual relationship with all eventual end purchasers was false but insisted this was merely a recital. He also admitted the falsity of the September 27 second supplemental agreement's recital that Homestead might be interested in purchasing all the unsold mortgages.

Brazil acknowledged that a periodic paydown of IB's $2 million line of credit from Meridian was due on September 15. He never told Hom he had used the $516,000 for this purpose or that the Merced deal had fallen through. Over the fifteen-day period of the first loan, he remembered many conversations about the Merced deal, in which he told Hom, "[T]hey were still in the process. I anticipated closing these loans any day. . . ." On September 24, he conveyed 1103 Decatur Street, Foster City, to a third party, who recorded it on September 29; but he never informed Hom, to whom he had given a security interest in the same property on September 15. He never told Hom that he used the second $500,000 to pay down Meridian. He did not recall subsequently telling Hom the money had been used for the bond defeasance. He never informed anyone at IB about the first loan. He agreed that the $500,000 he received from the second loan "doesn't seem to relate in any clear fashion that I understood that day or today" to the September 22 loan agreement. "I assumed that there would be another $700,000 delivered pursuant to that agreement." "I was not in a position to negotiate the document. It was presented to me along with a check, here, sign it. I was in desperate straits at that time to try and pull a raft of transactions together. . . ." When he entered both agreements he "believed that the fees indicated . . . were nonvalid and not enforceable. . . ." Asked why he had not consulted *Black's Law Dictionary* on the meaning of unclear terms, Brazil angrily told Stainfield to "be responsive."

> I was at that time trying to close a $38 million deal on a bond. I was trying to close the purchase of an S&L for another four and a half million bucks. I was trying to operate a business which was funding about $4.5 to $5 million a month of new loans every month. I was trying to keep the lines of credit from which and with which I would continue to make those loans and keep IB in business in a functioning state. And I obviously was doing too much. And if I hadn't made errors along the way, you and I wouldn't be sitting here right now.

Fontana asked for a short break because Stainfield's questions were "particularly offensive to Mr. Brazil." He criticized her "demeanor" and "the suggestion that Mr. Brazil has the ability to pay Mr. Hom a multimillionaire $200,000 a year when he has been driven from his profession." Since Brazil did not want the break, Fontana requested it for himself. Brazil testified that on April 4, 1990, he paid Hom $50,000 (which he had borrowed) but nothing more.[71] He owed another $100,000 in legal fees, secured by a lien on his brother's house. He was presently earning only $3,000 to 4,000 a month. Fontana interjected:

FONTANA: Your Honor, is this a debtor's examination now? Is Ms. Stainfield proposing to try to assist Mr. Hom in collecting his pound of flesh . . . I don't want this record used by giving over to Mr. Hom and allow him and his attorneys to hound Mr. Brazil any more than he's already been hounded. . . . [Fontana demanded that any examination be confidential or sealed.] I just don't want [the proceeding] to be used as a vehicle for Mr. Hom to cause any more grief to Mr. Brazil and his family than he's already done.

STAINFIELD: Your Honor, I—I very strongly object about grief. This man has stolen a million dollars from Mr. Hom—

FONTANA: That's the most outrageous statement I have heard from the most . . .

STAINFIELD: I—I—I'm sorry.

FONTANA: . . . misinformed individual.

STAINFIELD: Your Honor, but I—I—I've sat here during the course of this week listening to these attacks on poor Mr. Brazil, those representations of poor Mr. Brazil and the evil Mr. Hom, and all I'm asking is that the court advise Mr. Fontana that it is improper to argue his case.

After the court denied Fontana's request to seal the record, Brazil conceded he had neither arranged to pay Hom nor discussed doing so. He had no property. Asked if he recognized any moral obligation to repay Hom, Brazil said:

> Yes, I do. Pardon me, strike that. I recognize an obligation to make Mr. Hom whole, not repay him. Because I was not paid by him. That's a very important

71. State Bar Exhibit 37.

distinction in my mind. I have always felt an enormous obligation to make Mr. Hom whole. I did my level best before my conviction to make Mr. Hom whole. And I worked many many hundreds of hours after my conviction in an attempt to bring through to fruition a couple of transactions which had the potential of making him whole. And I would like nothing better than to make him whole. But repay him is not the correct term, because I was not paid by him. And I have never received one red cent from him.

Asked whether the service was excessive, Brazil said that "at the time of the sentencing no one had ever heard of 2000 hours of community service being a part of a sentence . . . at the time the sentence was arranged I thought it was a bit much." But he was "remorseful to the bottom of my very being," and since it "may prove to be beneficial to the community . . . I do it gladly." Catherine S. Johnson, who started the new Veterans Center of San Mateo County, testified that Brazil worked more than the eight hours a week required by his contract and sought additional training in order to offer paraprofessional counseling.

Fontana objected to questions about Brazil's pro bono service. "[I]f it is a condition for continued employment as a member of the Bar of the State of California to do pro bono work, there are lots of people out there that the State Bar better go out and talk to." The issue was "pretty collateral." Stainfield's inquiry about present pro bono service "is the most bizarre question I've heard yet" because Brazil was suspended. Fontana directed Stainfield to refer to the deposition "if there is going to be an intelligent question." When Stainfield got Brazil to acknowledge that his deposition had dated Rosemarie's hospitalization as October 1988, not six months earlier, Fontana called it "the most preposterous cross-examination on the most trivial point." He threatened to introduce thousands of pages documenting Brazil's efforts to put together other bond defeasance deals to "establish without any doubt the nature of the efforts that have gone into trying to deal with who [*sic*] Mr. Hom has done."

STAINFIELD: I'm sorry counsel, the efforts to deal with . . .

FONTANA: What Mr. Hom has done.

STAINFIELD: Mr. Hom has done?

JUDGE: You mean Mr. Brazil.

FONTANA: No, I mean Mr. Hom. Mr. Hom is the one who has gotten Mr. Brazil into this position, your honor. . . . [N]ot surprisingly in light of the fact that Mr. Hom has now gotten him convicted of three felonies, that it was not very easy to get public entities to allow Mr. Brazil to do these transactions. So having reaped the whirlwind Mr. Hom now gets the benefit from it.

JUDGE: Mr. Fontana, I'm going to have to ask you to refrain from editorial comments and expressing your opinion of Mr. Hom.

Brazil testified that his use of the first loan to repay Meridian was consistent with his obligation to Collins because the line of credit "would be used to fund those loans at some point when the loans were ready to go." He made a similar argument about the second loan: "I had used a significant, substantial amount of our line . . . in working through payments related to the San Pablo transaction. . . . It was simply a cash management situation." "[A]t the time that those funds were transferred the arrangement with Homestead was, in my own mind, finalized and those funds were coming into San Pablo." But on re-cross he conceded that the credit line "had an annual provision requiring it to be cleaned down once a year before it was renewed. . . . at this particular time, the loan was completely used." Asked if Meridian "didn't want to fund those [Merced] loans as they did not meet their requirements and were not appropriate for your credit line," Brazil recanted that claim: "I've had time to think about that testimony . . . and I correct it now." He also changed his testimony about the validity of Hom's loans:

> I don't believe that Acorn is or was a licensee of the Department of Real Estate nor do I believe it had any other exemption available to it at the time. So, if it did not . . . then the interest rate and the fee in combination would have exceeded the interest rate that he could have [been] paid at the time without being usurious. . . . I calculated the APR at about 40 percent or thereabouts. So, at the time I think the maximum interest rate that you could have charged at that time . . . would have been somewhere in the 11 percent area.

Fontana testified on behalf of his client, who had been his junior associate at Heller, Ehrman. Fontana represented IB in the Saratoga and Peninsula acquisition attempts and the Pleasant Hill and San Pablo bond defeasances. He helped Brazil retain Bob Carey in the criminal case and wrote a letter for sentencing.

> I thought he had reasons to feel bitter. I have seen him . . . overcome that and get his life together. The strength that it has taken . . . only increases my admiration for him . . . for having survived what I think has to be one of the darkest chapters in almost anybody's life that I'm familiar with, at least as a practicing attorney.

He told Boyle and Kelly (Hom's other lawyer) "it was pointless for them to try to throw the company into bankruptcy because . . . any shortfall . . . would be dischargeable" since Hom could not prove fraud. The first loan was "an unsecured promissory note." The second "ultimately is described . . . in his own documents, as being an investment. . . ." That "plus the element of coercion that's shown by the various interest rates that are in the first payment and the [in]credible fees associated with the second . . . would have made a very difficult uphill fight for Mr. Hom to persuade a bankruptcy judge that he was anything other than an investor who had lost some money in a business transaction." But Hom's lawyers "had talked to the DA and . . . maybe he would do something to prevent that." It "was unpardonable" to make nondischargeability a condition of letting Brazil plead nolo. (This argument was stricken.)

> [O]n one level, Mr. Hom is out of pocket, or his company is out of pocket a million dollars, or thereabouts. But at the same time, he has already received $50,000 from Mr. Brazil. He has, no doubt, taken a tax deduction on his returns, which is worth in the order of three or four hundred thousand dollars. He's received in excess of $116,000 in the bankruptcy. . . . And I believe he stands to receive as much as an additional $250,000 when the bankruptcy is closed later this year.

The bankruptcy documents showed that Acorn got $169,348 as a first payout.[72] Fontana testified that Brazil's suspension "would only hurt Mr. Hom. The only way that Mr. Brazil is ever going to be able to pay, or repay the balance of the money . . . is if he can earn enough to do that. . . . he surely would be far more able to pay Mr. Hom if he could resume the practice of law." Fontana argued that Brazil had not been practicing law at IB but acknowledged that "he was involved in reviewing documents that were being drafted by people at our firm, he was involved in having negotiated some of the documents . . . without our involvement." Although he had heard that Brazil was asked to resign from Fox and Carskadon in 1980 "as a result of improper use of company time for personal projects and being inattentive to his job responsibilities" and was terminated by FPC in 1985 "for improperly authorizing himself a salary increase and an advancement of corporate funds," neither allegation affected his opinion of his client. He did not believe the first charge; Brazil had told him that Stark (the source) "did not like Brazil . . . [and] that the reasons for leaving the company had to do with . . . an offer to become commissioner of real estate." The second issue arose while "they were dissolving the company," and "they agreed to repay those earlier advances." In any case, if disbarment turned "on somebody at one point in time having been dissatisfied with their performance, there would be very, very few people, probably including myself, practicing law in this state." He first claimed not to have heard that the Department of Real Estate revoked Brazil's license in September 1989 because of fraudulent actions antedating those involved in this case. Then he repeated Brazil's account that it "had been the result of a default, not as a result of any litigated case," because "Mr. Carey's plan had been that with the criminal case outstanding it was not in Lee's interest to be testifying generally on any subject. . . ." Finally he offered another explanation for the complicated events leading up to the license revocation. He had heard that Brazil was indicted in August 1991 for unlawfully transporting

72. Respondent's Exhibit JJ.

stolen securities, but the U.S. Attorney's failure to take further action showed the indictment was "plainly in error."

Stainfield offered a great deal of rebuttal evidence, to all of which Brazil's lawyers objected. Fontana expressed concern "about the protracted nature of the proceedings" (having earlier explained that his firm was acting pro bono).

FONTANA: The State Bar is now combing the state looking for people to try to come in here and protract this proceeding....

JUDGE: Mr. Fontana, please refrain from making editorial comments.

Stainfield introduced the Department of Real Estate July 1988 disciplinary proceeding against Brazil, Rosemarie, and IB, including the cease and desist order, record, and September 1989 license revocation for fraud and dishonest dealing.[73] Because this dealt with conduct that antedated the events involved in this disciplinary case, Stainfield offered it to rebut Kaye's claim that Brazil's behavior was aberrational. Fontana argued that it could have been introduced in the case in chief and anyhow "wouldn't be admissible in the courts of this state . . . to prove anything." "[I]t is utterly improper for the State Bar [to] effectively—and I will use the word advisedly—sandbag us by now trying to throw this stuff in the record." It had nothing to do with the practice of law. "It's a blatant attempt to just fish around and see how much dirt she can dream up and drag it in here." It was "so wrong" to use the default judgment's "hearsay on top of hearsay:" "there's no due process safeguards to any of this material." When the judge seemed inclined to admit only the decision, Fontana renewed his objection, declaring that the procedure "stinks." The judge took the issue it under advisement.

B. Briefs[74]

Stainfield filed her fifty page post-trial brief on March 23, 1992. The case concerned "an attorney who stole in excess of one million dollars and, in connection with this theft, forged the signature of an employee on several security instruments and thereafter fraudulently tendered these instruments as purported collateral for the above-referenced funds." It "embodies the overwhelming necessity for the remedy of disbarment. . . ." Brazil may have

> *intentionally* drafted an Agreement by which his corporation would receive over half a million dollars knowing that . . . the finance terms stated therein would quite possibly never be valid and legally enforceable by Hom should InterBank not comply with the terms upon repayment of the loan. . . . The end result is therefore that in exchange for over half a million dollars provided to Respondent in a very short period of time purportedly to fund a series of mortgage loans, the bargained-for security that Hom at any time received for his loan was clearly fraudulent.

73. State Bar Exhibit 55.

74. The emphasis in all quotations from briefs on both sides was in the original.

In his November 1991 deposition, Brazil said the "major reason" the Merced transaction had fallen through was "the developer was having trouble with his Section 8" leasing. But neither that nor any other problem made Collins ineligible. The

> documentary evidence before the Court clearly supports both Collins'[s] version of the events and the conclusion that the Respondent, acting on behalf of InterBank, failed to come through with the agreed-upon funding for the development, and in all probability fabricated various alleged problems when it became necessary to suit his needs. . . . Hom testified that Respondent specifically indicated prior to the execution of Agreement #1 that the Merced loans had *already* been sold to FNMA, and that the proceeds from the resale would be used to repay the loan pursuant to the terms of the agreement. When Hom questioned Respondent regarding the status of the Merced transaction after September 15, 1988, Respondent stated that it had gone through. . . . It is abundantly clear that Respondent's method of operation . . . was and continues to be to represent as true whatever Respondent feels was or is necessary to achieve his desired end regardless of the consequences to others.

The second supplemental agreement to the second loan provided that Hom would be repaid "out of the escrow for the closing of the purchase by Homestead Savings," although Brazil "was merely engaged in negotiations with Homestead regarding their purchase from InterBank of various mortgage loans, and . . . InterBank, until September 27, 1988, did not have any kind of a binding commitment from Homestead."

Stainfield argued that mitigation "can properly be established only in connection with the respondent's attempts after the fact to make the victim of his/her crime whole or to in some other way to [*sic*] accept full responsibility for the criminal actions committed." Brazil's convictions for felony grand theft and forgery both required proof of specific intent. Bar Standard 3.2 prescribed disbarment for a crime of moral turpitude unless there were "the most compelling mitigating circumstances." The absence of other discipline was undercut by the fact that he had not practiced law for eight of the fourteen years since admission. Dr. Kaye's testimony had limited value because he "stopped treating Respondent in August 1988 (prior to the misconduct which resulted in his convictions)." Although Brazil agreed to make restitution in order to obtain Hom's support for a light sentence, he "made absolutely no attempt to voluntarily make restitution of any kind to Hom prior to the initiation of the criminal investigation against him by the San Francisco District Attorney's Office." He tried to arrange other bond defeasance deals "because he believed that an arrangement had been worked out with the district attorney whereby criminal charges would not be filed if he were to make full restitution or to engage in good faith efforts to make restitution to Hom." Aggravating circumstances included "the apparent planning and sophistication" of the offenses, "significant harm" to the victim, Brazil's "demonstrated indifference toward rectification or atonement," and his lack of candor during the disciplinary proceedings. He "misrepresented to the Court the circumstances of his leaving a prior place of employment," which in turn rebutted Dr. Kaye's "dubious testimony" that Brazil's conduct was "aberrational."

Brazil filed a twenty-seven-page brief two days later. The mitigating circumstances included: the absence of any prior discipline, "which is consistent with his record as a decorated officer of the Vietnam War . . . and as a servant of the State of California in the Department of Real Estate;" "the absence of any premeditated design to defraud and his honesty of intention throughout his dealings with Acorn Corporation"; "the lack of harm to Mr. Hom, evidenced not only by the fact that Mr. Hom required Mr. Brazil to consent to extraordinarily usurious and burdensome terms at the eleventh hours of both transactions, but also by the fact that Mr. Hom stands in a better financial position today than when he did at the time of Mr. Brazil's and InterBank's involuntary bankruptcies"; "the existence of severe situational stress"; "the absence of any evidence that Mr. Brazil has been anything but totally cooperative and candid . . . during the disciplinary proceedings"; his "*reputation for integrity, conscientiousness and caring*"; his "sense of remorse and recognition of his wrongdoing, and his immediate and spontaneous attempts to make Mr. Hom whole"; and his "*rehabilitative actions.*"

"Considering Mr. Hom's role" in negotiating both loans, "it is not surprising that Mr. Hom failed to remember much of anything that occurred." Brazil understood Hom's demand for "more collateral in the form of additional deeds of trust" as a request that Brazil "create some paper." "[T]here is no other feasible interpretation of Mr. Hom's last demand. As a sophisticated real estate investor in San Francisco . . . Mr. Hom was fully aware that the deeds of trust were worthless as security without an underlying promissory note. . . ." "Additionally, Mr. Hom's strong-arm negotiation tactics, as also evidenced by his demand for an increased interest rate at the time of execution, gives this Court an indication of which party was really the bad faith actor in this transaction." Brazil's forgeries were "done with the good faith belief that InterBank would honor its obligations to Acorn . . . thereby making the created collateral unnecessary." "Furthermore . . . Mr. Brazil's act of signing his secretary's name did not cause a different result. . . ." IB's use of both loans to pay down its credit line "is a non-issue. There was no contractual obligation in either the Merced Loan or the San Pablo Investment to use these monies in a particular manner." Paying down the credit line "gave [Brazil] ready access to that amount from the bank when and if InterBank needed it to consummate the intended transactions." "Mr. Hom was charging InterBank an annual percentage interest rate of 323%, when the usurious interest rate set by law at that time was anything in excess of 11%!" "[I]t is Mr. Hom's good faith which is seriously in question," not that of Brazil, who merely failed to display "good business sense" because of his "severe situational stress."

Hom was in a better financial position now than he had been after forcing IB into bankruptcy. "[B]y filing criminal charges for grand theft against Mr. Brazil, pursuant to facts which should have resulted in a civil action, Mr. Hom was able to transmute a dischargeable debt under the bankruptcy into a non-dischargeable debt owed personally by Mr. Brazil." Hom "used his overwhelming bargaining power—this time in the form of Mr. Brazil's potential incarceration as a result of the charges brought by Mr. Hom—to coerce Mr. Brazil into executing a document wherein Mr. Brazil is obligated . . . to pay Mr. Hom $1,016,000 as a non-dischargeable debt." "Mr. Hom has neither had a million dollars stolen from him, nor has he been the victim of a premeditated design to defraud him."

Stainfield filed a twenty-three-page rebuttal brief on March 30. Brazil's attempt to show lack of intent should be either disregarded or considered aggravation. "[T]he only urgency with regard to Respondent's obtaining Hom's loan related to Respondent's need to immediately honor InterBank's obligation to pay down their depleted corporate line of credit . . . which result[ed] in no benefit whatsoever to either Hom or Collins. . . ." Documentary evidence fully supported Collins's claim that he was always ready to perform.

> With respect to the alleged incorrect fax number, State Bar Exhibit 27(A), admitted into the record at *Respondent's* insistence (as part of his unceasing and inappropriate attempts to prove that Hom was indeed the "bad faith actor" in this matter), further establishes the pervasive nature of Respondent's blatant misrepresentation throughout this proceeding.

Collins had used IB's correct fax number.

> Respondent's testimony that this was never a number belonging to InterBank (and his presentation of Respondent's Exhibit OO in support of his testimony) was dishonest, and should be properly viewed by this Court as entirely consistent with the dishonest, fraudulent mindset exhibited by Respondent both in 1988 and throughout this proceeding. The only *credible* evidence before the Court verifies that at the time Respondent approached Hom regarding a purported loan for the Merced transaction, Respondent had absolutely no intention of using Hom's money . . . to perform under his agreement with Collins.

Because Acorn was Hom, he had no interest in "creat[ing] some paper" trail for others. The promissory notes were part of the collateral required by the first and the additional agreements. Brazil's assertion that his forgeries had no consequences was "nonsensical." Respondent's "testimony is not credible, and . . . the resulting inexcusable misrepresentations made under oath to this Court amount to clear evidence in aggravation. . . ." The claim that Hom suffered no harm "is absurd." "The fact that Hom may have received some money from InterBank's bankruptcy is not relevant to a determination of whether or not Hom was harmed as a direct result of Respondent's actions." "Respondent's continued self-portrayal as the actual victim in both the criminal and the instant State Bar proceeding is further evidence that he neither accepts responsibility for his actions nor exhibits the necessary rehabilitative demeanor justifying discipline short of disbarment."

His character witnesses "reveal a curious gap in Respondent's professional past that has been filled in only by anti-character witnesses presented by the State Bar. Curiously, no witnesses came forth to testify or to write letters regarding Respondent's reputation and alleged good character during his tenure at the Itel or Brae [*sic*] Corporations, Fox & Carskadon, the Department of Real Estate, Federal Pacific Corporation . . . or at InterBank, a period consisting of over ten years immediately prior to and during his criminal misconduct." "[P]ositive work initiated by Respondent only as a result of a court order is entitled to very little weight, if any, by the Court." "Respondent's focus throughout this proceeding on his work with the Viet Nam veterans, in light of his overall lack of perspective as to the crimes that he committed, can only be viewed as an attempt to 'sell' his commitment to the vets in exchange for and to avoid disbarment in the *same way* that Respondent 'sold' his having entered into a civil restitution agreement with Hom and his having consulted with and purportedly exhibited appropriate qualities to Dr. Kaye . . . in order to avoid prison." "[T]he 'substantial debt' that Respondent has incurred to date has been in fighting both his criminal and the instant disciplinary proceeding . . . rather than accepting the full consequences of his actions and using his energies to atone for his actions and move on." "Respondent has made absolutely no attempt to work out with Hom any kind of a workable restitution schedule with which he could comply within his present earnings and abilities in support of a possible finding in mitigation herein."

Brazil responded with twenty pages the same day. Neither the business transactions nor the criminal charges and conviction "had anything to do with the practice of law." The hearing examiner was guilty of "wildly-misplaced rhetoric."

> Aside from its "pound of flesh" rhetoric, and its miscitation of legal precedent . . . the most troubling aspect of the Examiners' Post-Trial Brief is the fact that counsel plainly does not understand commercial finance and mortgage banking transactions . . . nor the specific details of the particular transactions in which Mr. Brazil and Mr. Hom were involved.

Brazil continued to insist on his right to present evidence of good faith. "Examiners would have this court deny Respondent this fundamental due process right by effectively putting a muzzle on Respondent and only allow that evidence into the record which is convenient for Examiners."

C. Judgment

Judge Gee issued her fifty-two-page opinion on November 30, 1992. She viewed Brazil's fourteen years without discipline as a mitigating factor, rejecting the State Bar's argument that he was not practicing law for ten of them. She found Hom "uncooperative" and was troubled by his "refusal" to explain the discrepancies between his testimony and the loan documents. The judge was persuaded by Dr. Kaye that Brazil's "extreme emotional difficulties," which he no longer experienced, had been "directly responsible for his criminal acts." He had also been dealing with "tremendous financial pressures." His conduct "appears to have been acts of desperation brought on by a loss of judgment caused by severe stress," as "exemplified by" his "willingness to sign agreements he did not fully understand and that contained statements that he felt were inaccurate, as well as his agreement to commit InterBank to paying fees and interest rates which he felt were excessive and usurious." In performing his probation conditions, Brazil "worked more hours than were required and voluntarily attended Veterans Center staff meetings without claiming credit for the extra hours." Ms. Johnson found him "dependable and compassionate." Brazil had "made an extraordinary demonstration of his good character as attested to by a wide range of references in the legal and general communities who are aware of the full extent of Respondent's misconduct. . . ." Stark's negative portrayal of Brazil's behavior at Fox & Carskadon was contradicted by the company's fall 1981 newsletter. Judge Gee was "firmly convinced" Brazil should not be disbarred. His conduct was "an instance of aberrant anti-social behavior . . . an act of desperation brought on by the incredible psychological stress Respondent was experiencing at the time because of his marital problems, the imminent collapse of his business and all the events that surrounded it."

> Respondent's conduct was not interwoven into his practice of law, and more importantly, it did not extend over a lengthy period of time. This conduct took place within a period of less than 30 days. Disbarment would serve to deprive the public of a very competent, concerned, compassionate attorney who is not likely to ever engage in such conduct again.

She recommended five years suspension stayed, three-and-a-half actual, and five years probation.

D. Appeal

The OTC sought review on December 31, 1992, alleging erroneous rulings on admissibility of evidence, findings unsupported by the record, and inadequate discipline. The Deputy Trial Counsel's opening brief, filed April 26, 1993, sought disbarment. Brazil "engaged in a highly sophisticated criminal operation specifically directed at acquiring substantial amounts of money through the use of misrepresentations and abuses of trust and authority." He "remains completely lacking in any insight whatsoever into the magnitude of his misdeeds" and "has engaged in substantial misrepresentations concerning his misdeeds during the instant proceedings." "Respondent has failed to demonstrate through expert testimony the requisite nexus between his particular emotional difficulties and the specific acts of misconduct which resulted in his conviction" and to show that "he no longer suffers from the emotional difficulties that he contends caused his criminal actions or that he will not react similarly to recurring emotional difficulties. . . ." "No *expert* testimony was presented regarding the nature of the stress that Respondent was under after the last session with Dr. Kaye in August 1988, and whether it was 'directly responsible' for the acts in question." "[P]ositive work initiated by Respondent only as a result of a court order is entitled to very little weight, if any, by the Court." "Most of the witnesses and/or letters presented by Respondent had little or no information concerning the criminal misconduct by Respondent. . . ."

Although the Hearing Department was "not persuaded that Mr. Isenberg's testimony warrants great weight . . . given Mr. Isenberg's rather 'fortuitous' assumption of Respondent's duties, and ultimately, his title, immediately after the ouster that Mr. Isenberg initiated," there was an "extraordinary similarity between Respondent's cavalier treatment of corporate finances while at F.P.C. and his handling of corporate funds as well as funds loaned to InterBank several years later." Brazil had said in his deposition, "Four partners are too many partners for a small company. Just too many chefs in the kitchen. . . . I was the third partner to leave, just kind of a general dissolution. . . ." At the hearing he testified that he left when FPC was sold to a bank. Isenberg rebutted both explanations. Judge Gee struck Stark's testimony as "not proper rebuttal and irrelevant" and inconsistent with the newsletter; but Stark learned of Brazil's actions *after* the newsletter appeared. The brief reargued the admissibility of the Real Estate Department findings that, between February 1986 and August 1987, Brazil had not deposited advance fees and trust funds into a trust account, commingled more than $158,000 with IB corporate funds, failed to provide written accountings to borrowers, and engaged in fraudulent acts in a mortgage by concealing collateral liens on the property and misrepresenting its status.

Brazil's forty-six-page brief, filed July 14, 1993, defended the Hearing Department's "carefully reasoned 52 page decision," an "extraordinarily thorough and accurate analysis of the evidentiary record. . . ." He accused the hearing examiners of "mischaracterization of the evidentiary record," "editorial hyperbole," "manipulating small portions of the voluminous Trial Record, taking testimony out of context and consistently misrepresenting the nature of the evidence presented at trial." "[T]here is not [*sic*] document that refers to the [second] payment as a loan." The examiners' claim that Brazil failed to present expert testimony that he would not again react to emotional difficulties with criminal behavior was "astounding." "The Examiners seem neither to have listened at the hearing nor to have paid much attention to the Trial Record in arguing to the contrary." They

> present a novel theory about human nature . . . that, if an individual is experiencing trauma in his life but fails to tell friends or the general populous [*sic*] about it while the trauma is occurring, then the trauma must not really exist. This is ludicrous.

The examiners indulged in "pure fantasy" by making the "derisive and cynical" claim that Brazil had tried to sell his commitment to the veterans to avoid prison, "which scheme, according to Examiners, also apparently included staging his marital problems and his wife's suicidal condition, for Dr. Kaye's benefit!" The examiners' "complete failure to present any witness from the San Francisco legal community who would speak poorly of Respondent or his capabilities" was "noteworthy."

Judge Gee had properly found that Isenberg, Kremers, and Stark had "little credibility" because of their "direct self-interest in whatever testimony they provided at trial." She concluded that Kremers's "entire transaction was, at best, suspicious . . . including the fact that a financial institution such as Commercial bank [*sic*] would be entitled to receive a $600,000 profit on a $1,000,000 two-week transaction . . . much less that it would forego such profits . . . solely 'based on an *oral* agreement with an individual [Mr. Hom] who was not a party to the transaction.'" Hom's injury "has been substantially mitigated" by Brazil's $50,000 payment, the $169,348 first disbursement in bankruptcy, and now a second distribution of $727,989, for a total of $947,337—"full payment of the $516,000 loan . . . and a return of more than 86 percent of the $500,000 that Acorn 'invested.'" The brief commented that

> Mr. Hom has attained a certain notoriety in the news media recently for being fired from his post as San Francisco Redevelopment Agency Commissioner for "official misconduct," including alleged abuses of his public office in connection with the influence to solicitation of political contributions and attempts to obtain profitable contracts for personal friends.

Brazil concluded by asking to be relieved of paying the costs of the investigation "on the grounds of hardship and in consideration of his cooperation" and the mitigation evidence.

On August 2, the OTC moved to strike this brief and admonish both Brazil and his counsel. The mention of Hom's firing "is an obvious insinuation [*sic*] to a matter which is not properly part of the record" and "a blatant attempt by Respondent to conspire to distract this Court's attention away from the seriousness of his own criminal activities. . . ." Brazil responded on August 9. "Respondent's counsel (who are appearing in this matter on a 'pro bono' basis) were unaware of the requirement" of restricting their brief to the record. The motion brazenly appended the two articles the brief had improperly mentioned, "simply to clarify Mr. Hom's identity for the benefit of the Court."[75] Brazil did not "'assert' that

---

75. Phillip Matier and Andrew Ross, *Jordan Orders Redevelopment Chief to Quit*, SAN FRANCISCO CHRONICLE 1 (Apr. 21, 1993); Marc Sandalow, *Jordan Dismisses Hom After He Refuses to Quit*, SAN FRANCISCO CHRONICLE 1 (June 9, 1993). Hom was accused of soliciting political contributions to Mayor Frank Jordan from two developers with business before the Redevelopment Agency and seeking to influence staff decisions concerning property contracts and banking deposits. Jordan had appointed Hom eight months earlier. Agency staff had recently informed the City Attorney of Hom's other possible

Mr. Hom's wealth, his political connections or his activities as an official of the San Francisco Redevelopment Agency had direct relevance to this case."

> The OTC does not seem to dispute the fact that "Mr. Hom has attained certain notoriety in the news media." . . . Frankly, we thought that was a fairly benign reference to Mr. Hom's activities and the charges against him. Our only purpose was to assist the Court and answer the obvious question, "is the person who testified as the 'victim' in this case, the same Ben Hom who has received so much attention in the press recently?"

E. Review Department Judgment

The Review Department decided on February 7, 1994.[76] "Without dispute, the record shows that in September 1988 . . . [Brazil] misapplied over $1 million which had been given to his company by an investor for loans for specific transactions," using it instead to "reduce the debt of his business. He also forged the signature and notary seal of a notary public on six documents and gave the investor five documents purporting to show that he or his company had an interest in property when no such interest then existed." The only security in which Brazil actually had an interest he conveyed to another on September 24, without telling Hom, who lost over $1 million. "Only recently, due to bankruptcy court distribution of InterBank assets, did Hom recover most of his loss, nearly $900,000. Respondent still owes Hom slightly over $50,000." The convictions "necessarily" found specific intent. The magnitude of the crimes was "enormous."

> Knowing that Hom wanted as much security and formality as possible for the two loans, respondent defrauded Hom by giving him five security interests purporting to be those of InterBank or respondent when respondent knew that neither had any security interest in the subject properties. . . . Although respondent acted outside the practice of law, the crimes he committed were related to the very types of matters in which attorneys frequently act. . . .

The Review Department concluded that Brazil "did not make a showing of extraordinary demonstration of good character." "[N]ot all witnesses appeared familiar with the magnitude of his crimes, nor with all of the specific crimes themselves." While accepting Judge Gee's credibility determinations, the Review Department concluded that Brazil's emotional stress did not justify reduced discipline. It rejected Judge Gee's exclusion of the license revocation, which was

---

misconduct: steering Agency parking lot concessions to a friend, pressuring staff to give a friend a contract to develop condominiums, and asking the Agency to deposit money in a bank owned by a friend. Hom, who had previously served on the Human Rights Commission and the San Francisco Housing Authority, hired a lawyer and public relations firm and refused to resign. He organized several hundred Chinese-American supporters to rally at City Hall and accused Jordan's wife of using the mayor's bodyguards for personal purposes. When Jordan fired him seven weeks later, Hom threatened to sue.

76. Matter of Brazil, 2 Calif. State Bar Ct. Rptr. 679 (1994).

clearly relevant to whether his conduct was aberrational, but it did not rely on that action. The Review Department attached "no importance whatever to Hom's status or conduct as a city commissioner."

> Respondent's offenses were extremely grave and multiple examples of felonious and fraudulent misconduct, likely to impugn notoriously the confidence of the public in the legal profession. Moreover, respondent's experience in sophisticated law practice, public office and private business should have served him better to dissuade him from committing the felonies to which he pled no contest.

It ordered disbarment.

F. Coda

On February 22, 1994, Brazil moved for reconsideration. It was never "easy" to accuse opposing counsel "of deliberately misleading" the court or to say its decision "is wrong." But "the OTC has deliberately misled the court by falsely asserting that the character witnesses were not fully aware of the seriousness of the criminal charges against Mr. Brazil." He urged the Review Department "to recognize the grave disservice that has been done to the Court and to the search for truth by the misstatements and over-zealous tactics that have been employed by counsel for the OTC." "The decision erroneously suggests that Respondent achieved personal benefit." "The Court's statement that Respondent 'used the money to reduce the debt of his business' . . . is inaccurate. Mr. Brazil did not 'own' InterBank." "Using the money to draw down InterBank's line of credit, meant that the $516,000 and the $500,000 would 'earn' interest during the interval between Hom's payment and the date when the Merced loans or the San Pablo transaction could close." The court failed to give adequate weight to the trial department's credibility determinations. "Most of another full day of trial was spent hearing testimony from the victim,' Mr. Ben Hom. . . ." Brazil had been "amply punished by our criminal justice system for the forgery and fraud which he committed." The OTC responded that Brazil's assertions "that 'he acted *properly* and '*commercially reasonable*' [*sic*] in directing the funds as he did only serve to emphasize the fact that he continues to lack any insight whatsoever into the magnitude of his crimes. . . ." The Review Department denied reconsideration on March 9, 1994. The Supreme Court denied review on September 8.

Hom ran for San Francisco mayor in 1995; after a dismal primary showing, he spent more than $300,000 to help Willie Brown defeat Frank Jordan (who had appointed Hom to the Redevelopment Agency and then fired him). In 1999, soon after being appointed by Brown to the San Francisco Public Utilities Commission, Hom voted to negotiate a city lease for a building he partly owned and was forced to resign.[77] But in 2003, Brown nominated him to the San Francisco Port Commission.[78]

77. *Time to dump Hom,* San Francisco Gate A22 (Apr. 22, 2003).
78. *Reject Ben Hom,* SFBG.com (Feb. 26, 2003).

In October 1997. Brazil and his Equifund partner Robert Fitzpatrick were investigated by the San Mateo district attorney's office for allegedly embezzling about $3.4 million from Andrew and Elaine Morrow, in part to repay Hom. Equifund invested client money in second mortgages on depressed properties. In the affidavit to obtain a search warrant, the DA's office alleged that the two had sold properties in which the Morrows had a security interest without their knowledge, forging deeds of trust and checks payable to them.[79] Brazil and Fitzpatrick were arrested in February 1998.[80] According to the DA, they had begun by properly making loans of client money, but when the real estate market declined, they told investors that homeowners needed more time to repay the loans, or foreclosures were delayed. In fact, they sold the properties, using part of the proceeds to repay investors but spending the rest. Facing more than ten years if convicted on all 30 felony counts, the two pleaded *nolo contendere* to three counts of grand theft in October 2000 (although their public defenders claimed they had a legitimate defense). In February 2001, they were sentenced to sixteen months and ordered to repay at least half of the $3 million they stole.[81]

In 1995, the Supreme Court declined to reappoint five of the eight incumbent State Bar Court trial judges to a second six-year term: Presiding Judge Lise Pearlman and Judges Jennifer Gee, Alan Goldhammer, Ellen Peck, and JoAnne Robbins.[82] Gee said, "Judge Pearlman was the center of a lot of controversy, so it doesn't surprise me." Jerome Fishkin, a former State Bar prosecutor and now defense lawyer, who practiced extensively before Goldhammer and Gee, said, "three of the judges were viewed by prosecutors as too weak on discipline. The prosecutor's office did not want Goldhammer, Peck or Robbins on the bench. Gee is the surprise. Gee was well regarded by both prosecutors and defenders."

V. ENDS JUSTIFYING MEANS?

A. Brazil's Behavior

Brazil's complex transactions were difficult to understand—even by the participants in this drama. Fontana accused Stainfield of incomprehension. Judge Gee had never heard the phrase "due diligence." Hom deferred to his lawyer.

---

79. Benjamin Pimentel, *Convicted Swindler Investigated in Property Scam,* San Francisco Chronicle A15 (Oct. 25, 1997); *Denial in Case Of Alleged Embezzling,* San Francisco Chronicle A14 (Oct. 28, 1997).

80. Benjamin Pimentel, *Ex-Real Estate Official Jailed In Fraud Case,* San Francisco Chronicle A18 (Feb. 12, 1998).

81. Matthew B. Stannard, *Real Estate Fraud Brings Prison Term,* San Francisco Chronicle A13 (Feb. 3, 2001).

82. Michael Gebhardt, *Housecleaning at State Bar Court,* American Lawyer (July 7, 1995).

Even Brazil claimed not to comprehend some of the agreements he signed. Brazil and Fontana deliberately confused and obfuscated. The record is incomplete, disorganized, and unreliable. For all these reasons, I will begin by explicating what Brazil did. He appears to have acted in good faith in making the February 1988 take-out commitment to give Collins long-term financing to retire the construction loan for the 30 Merced homes, expecting to sell the mortgages to Fannie Mae. Mortgage lending and servicing was IB's principal activity at the time, and Brazil was a "qualified" "seller/servicer," from whom Fannie Mae would buy mortgages sight unseen. Brazil told Collins in July that Fannie Mae would not buy the loans (although this transaction does not seem to have been a requirement of IB's loan) but promised to approach savings and loans, starting with those he was trying to acquire. Collins's letters confirm his expectation that Peninsula would buy the loans. Indeed, when Brazil ignored these letters and phone calls, Collins contacted Peninsula directly. By September 8, when Brazil sought to borrow $516,000 from Hom for the first ten homes (after ignoring Collins's increasingly urgent entreaties that Brazil honor his contract), it had been clear for two months that Fannie Mae would not buy the mortgages. Nevertheless, Brazil represented to Hom that it would and promised Hom the Fannie Mae documentation. He reiterated this in the September 15 handwritten note and continued to maintain that the homes were security for Hom's loan and he had good title to the mortgages, although Brazil no longer intended to lend Collins the money and hence never acquired a security interest in the properties. Instead, he used the money to pay down his Meridian line of credit, due the day of Hom's first loan. Although Brazil claimed this would let him fund the Merced mortgages, he never used it for that purpose, even though the houses were completed (fulfilling Collins's contractual obligations) and Collins was desperate for money. Indeed, Brazil conceded that Meridian said the Merced deal was unsuitable for his line of credit. He knew Collins's deadline for repaying his construction loan was August 31 but did not seek a loan from Hom for the first ten homes until September 8.

Brazil gave the disciplinary proceeding multiple specious reasons for not funding the mortgages: Fannie Mae ineligibility, inability to sell the homes, lack of owner occupancy and individual owners, a maximum of ten units per owner, loan to value ratio, and appraisal. He admitted he had raised some of these objections as early as July and Collins had met most of them; had they been real obstacles, the deal would have fallen through long before September. Collins's letters show he had told Brazil there would be three individual buyers of ten houses each (not the Fannie Mae maximum of five); the August 11 letter named the third buyer and provided credit details. Individual owners were inconsistent with making the houses available as Section 8 rentals, explicitly mentioned in the February 1988 agreement. Although Brazil claimed that Collins's $16,000 second mortgages made the houses 100 percent financed and hence unattractive to any lender, he continued to seek one. Brazil told Collins he could not fund the mortgages because his Meridian credit line was exhausted, then that he had paid down the credit line so it could fund the Merced mortgages, and finally that Meridian had told him the Merced deal was unsuitable for his credit line. Brazil was simultaneously stalling Collins with these pretexts and telling Hom he had bought Collins's mortgages.

In fact, Brazil seems to have lost interest in the Merced deal, which would earn IB only $5,000 plus short-term interest (and possible loan servicing fees). He had bigger game in his sights: acquiring an S&L and, especially, the San Pablo bond defeasance, for which he needed money immediately. Brazil strung Collins along for months, both to evade liability for breach of contract and to hold out the security interest in the Merced homes (which he never acquired) in order to borrow from others like Hom. (Because Brazil was acting without telling anyone at IB, he must have been angered and perhaps concerned when Collins informed an IB shareholder, which may have evoked unhappy memories of Isenberg complaining to FPC's outside shareholder-directors about Brazil's self-dealing.) The $1,548,000 he was obligated to lend Collins far exceeded the $1,016,000 he got from Hom, all of which (and more) Brazil needed for the bond defeasance. Brazil made numerous other misrepresentations to Hom. He claimed to be licensed and in good standing with the California Department of Real Estate, which had issued a cease and desist order against him two months earlier. The additional security Brazil furnished at Hom's insistence—the marital home and a rental property—was fraudulent; indeed, nine days after allegedly giving Hom a security interest in them, Brazil conveyed one parcel to another without telling Hom. Despite providing this additional security in order to obtain the loan, Brazil argued that the only real collateral was the Merced properties (in which he had no interest). He persuaded Hom not to register title to the other collateral because the loan was short term and his own credit was good; but his real concern was that any registration attempt would expose the fraud. Brazil argued that his failure to provide promissory notes on the collateral showed it was never intended as security, but he had promised to provide the notes. Brazil never told Hom he had decided not to fund the Merced mortgages and used Hom's money for other purposes. The capstone of all these misrepresentations was the forged signatures and notary seals on the deeds of trust—essential to close the deal the next day and get Hom's check (to preserve the Meridian line of credit). Although even Brazil found this hard to spin, his lawyer made two arguments: had the secretary been in the office, she would have notarized the documents; and the additional collateral was unnecessary (because the deeds were not good security without the promissory note and the only security was the Merced loans).

Brazil made fewer misrepresentations to get the second loan, since his real purpose was to fund the bond defeasance. But he did lie in the September 22 agreement that IB had contractual relationships with all the ultimate loan purchasers. He deluded himself that Homestead's commitment "was, in my own mind, finalized." And again, he used the $500,000 to pay down his Meridian line of credit rather than buy some of the mortgage bonds. (That Hom expected him to do the latter is shown by the fact that his lawyer, Boyle, drove to San Pablo to inspect the houses and reported back.) Fontana offered other arguments. It was not a loan but an investment. (Brazil's Review Department brief shamelessly declared "there is not [*sic*] document that refers to the payment as a loan," even though the September 22 contract was entitled, Loan and Security Agreement.) This, however, was inconsistent with Fontana's argument that both loans were usurious and none of the commercial transaction exceptions applied. Brazil maintained (implausibly) that he had not bothered to calculate the interest rate. Since he clearly had, the usury allegation could only mean he never intended to repay the loan. (That the bankrupt IB repaid most of Hom's principal shows that the loans were not usurious.)

Brazil sought mitigation on the ground that his behavior was brief and aberrational. Several character witnesses testified to this (clearly coached by Fontana). And Judge Gee bought it: "[T]his conduct took place within a period of less than 30 days." That strategy let the OTC offer evidence of other similar misconduct. There was plenty, if much was improperly excluded at trial. At Fox and Carskaden, as early as 1980, Brazil acted as though the rules did not apply to him: using company time and resources to write a book; practicing law privately out of a company office; using stationary that did not even identify the company; ordering legal publications at a time of financial stringency; claiming to have organized fictitious meetings; and openly conducting an affair with a superior's secretary. He also seems to have dropped the ball on important matters—a trade name infringement claim against the company, subordinates' requests for compensation reviews—perhaps because he was juggling too many of them (as he did again eight years later). Brazil retorted that his accuser (Stark) felt threatened by him and that he had not been fired but quit because he was frustrated at being blocked from becoming general counsel. At FPC, five years later, he was terminated for taking unauthorized salary advances and increases. Brazil claimed both that authorization was unnecessary (because he controlled the board) and that his accuser (Isenberg) also accepted salary advances and increases (approved by Brazil). He again denied being fired but gave inconsistent reasons for leaving: There were too many partners (he being the third of four to leave), and FPC was sold to a bank. He claimed to have repaid the advances but made the promise only to settle the lawsuit against him and fulfilled it only until his 1988 bankruptcy (prefiguring the way he settled Hom's claims). Over the next two years (1986–1987) Brazil engaged in the actions that led the Real Estate Board to issue its July 1988 cease and desist order; specifically, he concealed liens on collateral for loan transactions (just as he did on the security he gave Hom) and deposited client trust funds in IB's corporate accounts (again treating other people's money as his own).

Contemporaneously with Hom's loans, Brazil engaged in several other dubious transactions. On September 15, 1988, Shear lent IB $350,000 to buy Peninsula.

After that deal fell through, it is unclear what happened to the money following IB's bankruptcy. The next day, Brazil deposited a $250,000 Citibank check from Eagle Ventures (his coventure with Ford) in Peninsula (presumably as part of the acquisition). But before it cleared, he instructed Citibank to transfer $253,000 to IB for an unrelated purpose. When Citibank refused because Peninsula had already presented the check for payment, Brazil ordered Citibank not to honor it—and then blamed the bank when it bounced. Brazil used $250,000 from Hom to repay Peninsula; but when they (understandably) would not accept his check, he put the money through IB, where it was lost in the bankruptcy. Eagle Ventures never recovered its $250,000. During this period, Hom sought to lend IB another $1 million to complete the bond defeasance (his only hope of recovering the $1 million he had already lent it) by borrowing the money from Commercial Bank. Claiming it was beyond their lending capacity (but perhaps actually being unwilling to lend to IB), Commercial Bank sought to buy the San Pablo mortgages to sell to Homestead. Commercial gave the $1 million to Bank of America as escrow agent, again persuaded by Brazil not to perfect its security interest through registration because the loan term was so short. But when Brazil assigned the same mortgages to Alcheck, Commercial Bank lost its $1 million.

In the aftermath of the collapse, Brazil escaped imprisonment for forgery and grand theft by agreeing to pay Hom $200,000 a year and assign him contractual and joint real estate obligations. (Unlike street crime, white collar crime often can be transformed into a tort and remedied by restitution.) At the time he made these promises, however, he knew the bond defeasance deals were dead (because of the publicity given his criminal charges), and he had no contractual or real estate obligations to assign (just as the collateral he gave Hom for the original loans was fictitious or impaired). And Brazil never told Hom that the Equifund brokerage agreement had been suspended. He boasted that he had "probably expended a good thousand hours of effort to try to bring these [bond defeasance] deals into fruition," arguing that his workaholism should exempt him from punishment.

Brazil was indicted in 1991 for transporting stolen securities (although the prosecution apparently was dropped). In 2000, he pleaded *nolo contendere* to embezzling $3.4 million from an elderly couple by forging deeds of trust and checks concerning mortgages they had bought through him. (Brazil apparently was still trying to repay Hom in order to avoid going to prison for the earlier conviction.) Although this occurred after the disciplinary process concluded, it continued a course of misconduct that had begun at least 20 years earlier.

B. Brazil's Legal Arguments

Fontana was a no-holds-barred, take-no-prisoners, scorched-earth litigator. He constantly attacked Hom and Stainfield, aggressively seeking to discredit all the State Bar witnesses. He (not Brazil) got so upset during the hearing that he called for a recess. Despite being Brazil's lawyer, he also testified for him.

Much of that testimony was incredible: the first loan was an unsecured promissory note (despite the numerous recitals of security and transfers of deeds of trust); the second was an investment (despite being titled "loan"). Because the loans were dischargeable in bankruptcy (since Brazil had committed no fraud), it was "unpardonable" for Hom to file a criminal complaint to pressure Brazil to agree to nondischargeability. Fontana seemed unable to follow the judge's direction to present evidence, not argue. He claimed his client had not been practicing law, even though Brazil had negotiated and drafted complex legal documents for IB. (Had a non-lawyer done this, it would have been unauthorized practice.) And the argument may also have been inconsistent with the July 1988 cease and desist order; since Brazil could no longer practice real estate, he must have been practicing law. Some of Fontana's allegations and arguments failed the laugh test. For instance, Hom was better off financially by the time of the disciplinary hearing than he had been when he forced Brazil and IB into bankruptcy; he was uninjured because he could take Brazil's bad debt as a tax deduction. Collins's written communications to Brazil were fabricated because they did not bear the correct fax number (they did). Treating the criminal conviction as *collateral estoppel* with respect to Brazil's *mens rea* would deny him due process.

Fontana clearly lacked sufficient distance from his client. Brazil had begun his career in California as Fontana's associate at Heller, Ehrman. Fontana represented Brazil in the abortive S&L acquisitions and the failed San Pablo bond defeasance. He directed Brazil to a criminal lawyer and wrote a sentencing letter. He took the disciplinary defense pro bono (but complained about what it cost him) and testified for Brazil, first improperly in the guise of argument and then as a character witness, "I believe in my heart this is a good person. I've known him myself for 17 years."

Fontana's most outrageous tactic was to portray *Brazil* as the victim, primarily of Hom but also of Collins and the State Bar. He harped on "what Mr. Hom has done," repeating the phrase twice more after being challenged by both Stainfield and the judge. He minimized Hom's injury while emphasizing his financial sophistication and unscrupulousness. He insisted that "Mr. Hom has now gotten [Brazil] convicted of three felonies" when it was Brazil who got himself convicted. Hom had "hounded" Brazil and "driven [him] from his profession." Brazil had been "amply punished" (although he had served no jail time and made almost no restitution). Fontana kept repeating that Hom's usurious interest rates demonstrated an "element of coercion"; Brazil accepted out of desperation. Fontana objected to Hom changing the first loan's points from 2 percent to 2.25 percent (but Brazil could have rejected the change). Fontana charged Hom with seeking to make a lot of money from these deals (not exactly an offense in business). Fontana harped on the fact that Hom was a "multimillionaire" (as though that made his $1 million loss less serious). He argued that a short suspension (rather than disbarment) would serve Hom's interest since Brazil could repay the debt only by resuming law practice (inconsistent with Fontana's argument that Brazil had not been practicing law). Fontana's Review Department brief revealed Hom's firing from the Redevelopment Agency, and then this highly experienced litigator disingenuously claimed ignorance of the State Bar's procedural rules. Those rules, which were the same as any legal process, require that evidence be introduced during trial, not argued *ab initio* on appeal). Yet, Fontana protested he was only trying "to assist the Court and answer the obvious question, 'is the person who testified as the "victim" in this case, the same Ben Hom who has received so much attention in the press recently?'" As late as the motion for reconsideration, Fontana kept putting any reference to Hom as "victim" in scare quotes. Hom certainly engaged in unsavory behavior, but he was bound by the ethical norms of business, not law.

Sometimes Fontana was carried away with his own eloquence (and perhaps overidentification with his client). "[I]t is Mr. Hom's good faith which is seriously in question, not Mr. Brazil's." Fontana condemned the disciplinary hearing for letting Hom and his attorneys "hound Mr. Brazil any more than he's already been hounded," using it as a "vehicle . . . to cause any more grief to Mr. Brazil and his family than he's already done." Was "Ms. Stainfield proposing to try to assist Mr. Hom in collecting his pound of flesh?" (The allusion, repeated later, conflated the Chinese-American money lender with the Jewish Shylock.) Fontana accused Stainfield of withholding evidence in Collins's file and subjecting Brazil to "trial by water torture" by deliberately protracting the proceedings in order to delay reinstatement. When Stainfield noted that Brazil "has stolen a million dollars from Mr. Hom" (the charge to which Brazil had pleaded *nolo contendere*), Fontana erupted, calling that "the most outrageous statement I have heard from the most . . . misinformed individual." When both Stainfield and the judge corrected Fontana's accusation about what "Mr. Hom has done," suggesting the lawyer meant Brazil, Fontana was unrepentant.

> Mr. Hom is the one who has gotten Mr. Brazil into this position . . . not surprisingly in light of the fact that Mr. Hom has now gotten him convicted of three felonies, that it was not very easy to get public entities to allow Mr. Brazil to do these transactions. So having reaped the whirlwind Mr. Hom now gets the benefit from it.

If we untangle the muddled metaphors, it is clear that Fontana blamed *Hom* for Brazil's failure to repay the debt.

Fontana tried similar tactics against Collins. He accused Collins (with the complicity of his lawyer and the OTC) of fabricating his one-sided correspondence with Brazil. (It was one-sided because Brazil never answered.) He tried to show (with some success) that Collins had engaged in questionable practices to minimize the assessed value of the Merced properties for tax purposes (which also would have cured the value to loan ratio problem). But of course this had nothing to do with Brazil's contractual obligations to lend the developer money.

In arguing for mitigation, Brazil claimed he had fully cooperated with the State Bar investigation and accepted responsibility for his actions. The opposite was true. He contested every charge (even though his felony convictions were conclusive on his guilt). His lawyer sought to exclude every piece of evidence, keeping out the behavior that led to suspension of Brazil's real estate license on the ground that the proceeding also involved Rosemarie Yule and IB. Fontana attacked every State Bar witness—Hom for cupidity, Isenberg for complicity, Stark for self-interest, and Collins for confusion. Brazil minimized the wrongfulness of his forgery on the irrelevant (and false) ground that it had not caused Hom to lose $1 million. He claimed that the additional (fraudulent) security was just intended to create paper (especially since the deeds of trust were unaccompanied by promissory notes) but could not explain whom Hom sought to impress since he effectively was Acorn. As Mary McCarthy said of Lillian Hellman, "every word" Brazil uttered "was a lie, including the 'ands' and the 'thes.'"[83] Brazil misrepresented why he had left both Fox and Carskadon and FPC, and why he had deposited Hom's loans in Meridian (not to earn interest but because otherwise he would have lost this indispensable line of credit). Brazil constantly denied responsibility. He rationalized pleading *nolo contendere* to forgery and grand theft and defaulting in his real estate license suspension as merely strategic decisions, claiming he had a good defense to grand theft and arguing that neither outcome was an adjudication of misconduct. (His public defender made the same claim about Brazil's 2000 *nolo contendere* plea to three counts of grand larceny.) To use the license revocation default judgment in the State Bar proceeding would deny him due process. Harold Brazil claimed his brother had pleaded just to save the government money! Even though the criminal conviction necessarily found specific intent, Fontana persisted in trying to prove Brazil's good faith. Fontana and others consistently characterized Brazil's ethical misconduct as just "bad judgment." Brazil himself said he was simply "doing too much," inevitably committing "errors along the way." He claimed to have obtained no personal benefit from Hom's loans because he owned only 10 percent of IB (although he ran it unilaterally). He had no obligation to "repay" Hom "because I was not paid by him." He had done his "level best" to make Hom whole even though "I have never received one red cent from him." He thought two thousand hours of community service was "a bit much" (although the alternative was prison). He treated promises to repay money as actual repayment. Each action Brazil cited as evidence of his willingness to take responsibility and make amends he performed only under legal compulsion: repayment of the salary advances (after a civil judgment), community service (to avoid jail following a criminal conviction), repayment of Hom (in exchange for the banker's indispensable

83. Spoken on Dick Cavett. William Wright, *Why Lillian Hellman Remains Fascinating*, New York Times (November 3, 1996).

support of Brazil's plea to avoid jail), repayment of only half of the $3.4 million he had obtained by fraud from an elderly couple (part of the criminal sentence). What Brazil represented as remorse actually was just anxiety about consequences. In fact, Brazil never fully repaid FPC, Hom, or the elderly couple. And Hom eventually recovered most of his principal from the IB bankruptcy distribution, not Brazil.

Brazil's other arguments in mitigation further undermined his claim to accept responsibility. He cited the emotional distress of his deteriorating marriage. Dr. Kaye strongly corroborated Brazil's account of marital difficulties during the three years of therapy (150 to 200 visits in 1985 and 1987). This experience may have been intensified by his parents' divorce when he was a child (especially since the family was Catholic) and the failure of his own earlier marriages. But there are many unanswered questions about the relationship. Although Brazil claimed to have worked for years to preserve the marriage, he admitted an affair with a superior's secretary at Fox and Carskadon in 1981 (four years after he married Rosemarie). If the marriage was so stormy, how could Rosemarie work as IB vice president of sales for the four years before their January 1988 separation? That separation presumably reduced Brazil's stress (he seems to have moved out of the marital home), although her suicide threats and nervous breakdown clearly affected him, and he remained in daily contact during her ten-week hospitalization. How did her July 1988 real estate license suspension affect Rosemarie? That seems to have been her sole source of income, and Brazil paid no spousal support (hard to reconcile with his claims of solicitude). That she filed for divorce in September suggests that she had accepted the end of the marriage. Furthermore, Brazil terminated therapy the previous month. He seems to have sold the marital home in September (after giving Hom a security interest in it), perhaps because Rosemarie left the country for an extended period about that time. Most telling is Boyle's casual reference to encountering Brazil with his "fiancée" at the September restaurant meeting with Hom. Kaye testified that when Brazil resumed therapy in 1990, he was in a much better relationship. All this suggests that Brazil's *emotional* stress had significantly decreased by September 1988, when his misconduct occurred. And even his therapist could suggest only a tenuous connection between such stress and criminal behavior. (Furthermore, Brazil repeated the behavior in the 1990s, years after the end of his marriage.)

Brazil also emphasized his enormous financial pressures. These were real. IB had to pay its 25 to 30 employees. It was servicing $50 million in mortgages and lending another $5 million a month. Brazil had agreed to lend Collins $1.5 million—money he did not have. Both his lines of credit were exhausted or unavailable; he needed $2 million to pay down his Meridian line of credit immediately or risk losing it—which would have been fatal to IB. He had just received a cease and desist order from the Department of Real Estate. Both efforts to buy savings and loans—which would have given IB access to substantial new funds—

failed at the last moment, after Brazil had raised substantial capital and incurred major expense. (Although Brazil claimed the Saratoga deal had collapsed when investors insisted on indemnity for outstanding legal liability, owner Jess Rodriguez said the problem was that investors would not come forward. Perhaps the precariousness of Brazil and IB were already known; the Real Estate Department had issued its cease and desist order against them in July.) And the San Pablo bond defeasance—the largest and most complex transaction of Brazil's career, which promised an enormously profitable new line of business—hinged on raising additional capital. Even for a workaholic like Brazil, the stress must have been almost unbearable. But it is unclear why this should mitigate given that all the pressures were self-inflicted, driven by Brazil's desire to deploy his considerable financial and legal talent in order to make money.

C. Brazil's Motivations

If this Brazil's financial plight does not justify, it may explain. By September 1988, Brazil was *desperate* to raise money. He was operating something akin to a Ponzi scheme, borrowing from the next credulous lender to repay the last (who had become anxious about his money), and using the same capital or property for multiple purposes. Brazil's last resort seems to have been Hom, a gambler willing to take high risks in the hope of high returns. Brazil needed the first $516,000 to preserve IB's line of credit with Meridian—and was prepared to forge his notary's signature and seal and commit fraud by offering as security property he did not own or sold soon thereafter. Although Brazil maintained that IB had gone to the Bank of Australia for most of the $38 million needed for the bond defeasance because of "very subtle tax provisions," Brazil and IB may no longer have been creditworthy to San Francisco lenders. At the September 22 partial closing, Brazil still needed more money because Peninsula wanted more documents, Mission was waiting for a wire transfer, and Homestead was backing out of its $1.2 million commitment. Brazil had "approximately one week" to raise the rest. He so urgently needed Hom's next $1,200,000 to keep the bond defeasance alive (the only way of forestalling IB's bankruptcy) that he entered an agreement without discussing the fees in advance, then promised to pay $400,000 in fees to get the first $500,000, and ultimately signed three supplemental agreements during the subsequent week committing IB to pay another $100,000 (in addition to the 10 percent annual interest) and giving Hom a 20 percent equity interest in order to get the remaining $700,000. (The supplemental agreement's recitals that Acorn would get an equity interest and that all funds loaned to IB would be treated as loaned by Acorn may have been intended to anticipate the argument that Acorn had charged a usurious interest rate.) Brazil committed additional fraud to get Commercial Bank to advance another $1 million because Hom required this in the third supplemental agreement. Brazil was prepared to sacrifice all the profits from this transaction both to save IB from bankruptcy and to gain the first mover advantage in what he hoped would be many other profitable bond defeasances.

If Brazil's immediate motivation was the urgent need for money, how did he get himself into that predicament? One possibility is simple greed—the same cupidity that Fontana (and Brazil) kept indignantly imputing to Hom. The desire to make money—and lots of it—presumably is what brought Brazil and Hom together. The bond defeasance transaction IB was pioneering offered the prospect of deals worth billions and profits of tens or hundreds of millions—a quantum leap for Brazil. Even if we credit Brazil's mother's and brother's protestations that he was uninterested in money for its own sake (and I remain skeptical), money was the index of success in Brazil's financial world.

Every character witness called Brazil an overachiever. They emphasized his workaholism, discipline, ambition, drive, will, need to succeed, attention to detail, and responsibility. His self-discipline—as an altar boy, surrogate for his missing father, student, in the military, and at work—testifies to a highly developed superego. His ex-wife complained that he constantly neglected her for his work, even when she was having a nervous breakdown after he ended the marriage. Harold Brazil saw his older brother as the good son, who assumed the paternal role after their father abandoned the family. His mother told a Horatio Alger story of Ernest making the long walk to church early every morning regardless of the weather. He was determined to get out of the "ghetto," to "make it." Kaye, his therapist, confirmed that Brazil needed to be respected, idealized, by his mother and brother, wife and step-daughter, employees, clients, colleagues, even his ex-wife's ex-husband. When the defeasance fell through (because of the criminal charges), Brazil said, "I was gone, ceased to exist." He *was* his achievements.

Brazil chafed at all authority and restraint. He repeatedly left positions because he insisted on complete independence, refusing to answer to anyone, taking credit for every achievement. He used his position at Fox and Carskadon to write a novel and practice law privately. He left Bray when he was passed over for general counsel. He took unauthorized advances and salary increases at FPC. He claimed to have left because the four partners were "too many chefs in the kitchen." He founded IB because he "wanted to run the company without any day-to-day input from other executives." He consulted no one about his loans. He misappropriated a subordinate's signature and notary seal. His only regret seems to have been his disappointed political aspirations. Those who insisted on his integrity seemed to confuse that with his loyalty to intimates, friends, clients—a trait that could have justified his unfairness to strangers (like Hom). Brazil's original sin was hubris and his conviction that his superior talents and almost superhuman efforts entitled him to use every available means to grab the brass ring.

6. SERVING TWO MASTERS

I. COMMUNICATION WITH A REPRESENTED PARTY

The Rules of Professional Conduct unambiguously state that "while representing a client, a member shall not communicate directly or indirectly about the subject of the representation with a party the member knows to be represented by another lawyer in the matter, unless the member has the consent of the other lawyer."[1] The reasons are obvious. Lack of expertise is the very reason clients retain lawyers. Because of the rule's clarity and obvious rationale, there are few examples of its violation.

Darryl Geyer, a young man who had left school in tenth grade, confessed to setting several fires, one of which badly damaged a San Francisco apartment house in June 1996, killing one person and injuring others.[2] A month after Kenneth Quigley was appointed to represent Geyer, several tenants retained Joshua M. Dale to sue the landlord for personal injuries, alleging negligent maintenance of the premises. Dale, who had been admitted less than two years earlier, specialized in driving under the influence (DUI) cases and was inexperienced in civil litigation. Facing a summary judgment motion, he asked to interview Geyer, but Quigley refused. Disregarding this, Dale waited in the Hall of Justice corridor, exchanged nods with Geyer on at least three occasions, and once said something like, "[W]e are going to have to talk someday." After four days of trial, Geyer pleaded guilty to six counts of arson. Separately, a judge convicted him of second-degree murder; but Geyer retained the right to appeal on the ground of an illegal confession. Before sentencing, Dale used the attorney's entrance to the San Francisco County Jail to meet Geyer face-to-face (rather than through the glass partition in the public reception area) and asked for a statement for the civil action. Geyer said he had to speak with Quigley but later wrote Dale that he had been unable to do so and "will be unable to respond to questions in regards to [the apartment house]. I'm sure that you understand." Nevertheless, Dale persisted, visiting Geyer five more times before sentencing, using the attorney's entrance to obtain face-to-face interaction and discussing Geyer's hopes, current events, and the difficulties of prison life in order to persuade him to testify. Geyer told Quigley he wanted to replace him but failed to do so.

1. California Rules of Professional Conduct Rule 2-100.

2. Matter of Dale, 4 Cal. State Bar Ct. Rptr. 798 (2005) (four months suspension, two years probation). Emphasis in original.

After being sentenced to 20 years to life (with the possibility of parole after 14 years), Geyer prepared a notice of appeal in propria persona. Visiting him in San Quentin before this was filed, Dale persuaded Geyer to sign an agreement to tell "the truth about the fire" for purposes of the civil action in return for Dale assisting Geyer's parole applications and urging the building tenants to testify on his behalf. Geyer agreed because he had lost faith in Quigley and could not afford other counsel, but he insisted on adding, "I have been assured by Joshua M. Dale, Esq., that this document cannot and will not be used or effect [*sic*] my appeal of my conviction in the San Francisco Superior court matter." When Dale filed a motion in the civil action containing Geyer's account of starting the fire (to support the allegation of landlord negligence), Quigley furiously demanded that Dale withdraw it. The next day, Dale wrote Geyer that, "Kenneth Quigley is trying to get my law license for talking to you even though you'd fired him, and he wasn't even your attorney after sentencing. . . . I again think that your telling the truth is the best thing you could have done." The district attorney (DA) had assured Dale that if Geyer overturned the homicide conviction, he would only serve eight years; Dale urged Geyer to "do your best to make your first parole hearing count." Dale wrote Geyer at least three more times to persuade him to testify in the civil action, including this:

> *Your declaration saved the tenants' case.* Thank you. Your letter of apology is spectacular, and the tenant [*sic*] will, and some have already, forgive [*sic*] you for the disruption to their lives. You have much to be proud of and I look forward to visiting soon. . . . [Y]ou are a special person on earth. . . .

He told Geyer he had "prepared some research on your parole hearing already, and included it with this letter." Two days after a lawyer was appointed as Geyer's appellate counsel of record, Dale warned, "I'd really be careful with any promises if they've seen you. They are the ones that got you convicted, remember?" He also enclosed

> some things like before. I've talked with several of the people at your new location. There are many things that you may do there. . . . I'll be able to do more down the road if you begin to send me promising things about you.

Three days later, Dale filed a motion asking the civil court to order Geyer's production at trial; he did not notify Geyer's lawyer, and no one represented Geyer at the hearing. A few days after the motion was granted, Dale settled the civil case for $400,000. He gave Geyer no further assistance. Geyer lost his appeal (although his declaration for Dale played no role).

In the case that follows, the communications with a represented accused were from the prosecutor (who could not be disciplined in California because he only belonged to the Arizona bar) and the lawyer for a co-accused.

II. REPRESENTING CO-CONSPIRATORS CHARGED WITH DRUG POSSESSION

A. Dramatis Personae

José Orlando Lopez was arrested on September 26, 1989. Two months later he, Antonio Hernandez Escobedo and Alfred Tarango Olivas were indicated by Assistant United States (U.S.) Attorney John Lyons before Judge Fern M. Smith in the Northern District of California for distributing 50 kilos of cocaine and two kilos of heroin. Lopez initially retained James Allen Twitty, who sought bail for all three. Then Lopez replaced Twitty with Barry Tarlow, and Olivas (who played a minor role thereafter) retained Harold Rosenthal, leaving Twitty with Escobedo.

Tarlow, who practiced with four associates in Los Angeles, was a formidable litigator. He had graduated from Boston University Law School in 1964 (ten years before Twitty qualified), first in his class, and was a senior law review editor. After about a year as an assistant U.S. attorney in California, he established his defense practice there in 1966 and was a California State Bar certified criminal law specialist from 1975. He had been president of California Attorneys for Criminal Justice (1977–78) and vice-chair of the ABA Criminal Justice Section and had been named one of the "ten best winning trial lawyers" by the *National Law Journal*, one of the eight best criminal defense lawyers in Los Angeles by the *Los Angeles Times*, one of California's Most Respected Lawyers by *California Lawyer*, and Criminal Defense Lawyer of the Year by the Century City Bar Association (1992). He was listed in Naifeh & Smith, *The Best Lawyers in America* (1983–2005) and selected as a "Super Lawyer" in 2005–08. He was on the board of the National Association of Criminal Defense Lawyers (NACDL) (1979–90), served as co-chair of its "Committee to Free the Innocent Imprisoned," and received the NACDL Lifetime Achievement award in 1992. He was on the board of the Southern California American Civil Liberties Union (ACLU) (1997–2006). In 1989, the California State Bar Board of Governors commended him for "outstanding contributions to the delivery of pro bono legal services." He was made a Fellow of the International Academy of Trial Lawyers in 1998. Colleagues and adversaries called him a "fighter scholar," the "ultimate advocate," and "the tiger," whose "reputation as a contentious advocate in the courtroom is unmatched."[3]

Before Tarlow entered the case, Twitty tried to negotiate pleas for Lopez and Escobedo, but Lyons was bound by the federal sentencing guidelines, which set a ten-year minimum with few exceptions. Lyons made it clear he would only consider a plea by both defendants, but Tarlow believed Lopez had a viable entrapment defense and broke off negotiations. He and Lyons fought

---

3. http://wikibin.org/articles/barry-tarlow.html

over discovery: Tarlow called Lyons grudging and noncompliant; Lyons accused Tarlow of aggressively filing unnecessary motions. Because Twitty visited the Pleasanton prison (where the defendants were held) more often than Tarlow, the latter authorized him to meet Lopez. In March and April 1990, Escobedo and Lopez jointly telephoned Twitty to discuss plea negotiations. Without informing Tarlow, Twitty went to the prison to discuss this with them. Both defendants asked him to arrange a meeting with Lyons. Lopez also asked Twitty not to tell Tarlow. Twitty had several more phone conversations with Lopez about this, visited the prison again to discuss it, and then explained the situation to Lyons, who approached Judge Smith, who assigned Magistrate Claudia Wilken to conduct a voir dire of Lopez.

B. The Thornburgh Memorandum

In doing this, Lyons was relying on a memorandum from U.S. Attorney General Richard Thornburgh, issued June 9, 1989,[4] deploring that American Bar Association (ABA) Prosecutorial Rule 7-104(A)(1) had been used "to prohibit communications by law enforcement personnel with the target of a criminal investigation, whether or not a constitutional right to counsel has attached." The rule had created a backdoor to a "right to counsel at the investigative stage," which the Constitution did not guarantee, and it threatened to impose "a substantial burden on the law enforcement process." The memo addressed situations in which an individual or organization was paying for the representation of others.

> It is clear that when an individual believes that his lawyer is representing not his own interests but the interests of a third party, and that announcing to his lawyer that he has made contact with government investigators could have dire consequences, the individual should not be channeled through the lawyer. . . . Sometimes, direct communications serve to benefit the client and to vindicate his rights.

Thornburgh declared that "the Department will resist on Supremacy Clause grounds, local attempts to curb legitimate federal enforcement techniques." An April 1980 Office of Legal Counsel memo had declared that "the extent to which the Department requires its attorneys to conform their conduct to judicial and bar association interpretations of DR 7-104 is solely a question of policy." On August 10, 1980, the Federal Bureau of Investigation (FBI) instructed all special agents that they could communicate with a represented defendant without the

---

4. State Bar Exhibit 10. Memorandum To: All Justice Department Litigators. From: Dick Thornburgh, AG. Subject: Communication with Persons Represented by Counsel. *See* Matz (1991). Thornburgh was reacting to a Second Circuit decision applying the ABA rule to prosecutors. U.S. v. Hammad, 858 F.2d 834 (2d Cir. 1988), cert. denied, 111 S.Ct. 192 (1990).

presence of counsel when the defendant initiated the contact and the agent informed the defendant of the right to separate counsel. Deputy Attorney General Schmults extended this to Department of Justice (DOJ) lawyers two years later.[5] Deputy Attorney General Burns wrote the D.C. Bar that in cases of conflict between federal duties and state ethical requirements, "the Supremacy Clause forbids the states from regulating the attorney's conduct."

Thornburgh instructed employees that prosecutors could encourage defendants, who wanted to avoid confronting their attorneys, to consult other counsel or seek to have such counsel appointed "as in the Organized Crime context." Prosecutors also could ask attorneys to disqualify themselves or move for disqualification in cases of "real and apparent" conflict of interest. "In sum, it is the Department's position that contact with a represented individual in the course of authorized law enforcement activity does not violate DR 7-104." Thornburgh proposed to codify the following:

> [A]n attorney employed by the Department, and any individual acting at the direction of that attorney, is authorized to contact or communicate with any individual in the course of an investigation or prosecution unless the contact or communication is prohibited by the Constitution, statute, Executive Order, or applicable federal regulation.

The memorandum infuriated many. One lawyer called it "a declaration of war on the defense bar."[6] A Special Committee of the Conference of Chief Justices asserted that "the Supremacy Clause cannot be used to justify pre-empting a state ethics rule by means of a regulation adopted by the Department."[7] At its next meeting, the ABA called the memo "a unilateral assumption of authority to render self-interested interpretations of ethical standards, and an unwarranted and unfounded use of executive power to create unequal classes of both litigants and lawyers."[8] The ABA president testified in opposition before a House subcommittee.[9] The Criminal Law Committee of the Association of the Bar of the

---

5. 30(4) U.S. ATTORNEY'S BULLETIN 73 (1982).

6. Tom Watson, *AG Decrees Prosecutors May Bypass Counsel; Move Is Assault on Ethics Codes, Defense Bar Claims,* LEGAL TIMES 1 (Sept. 25, 1989); *see also* William Glaberson, *Thornburgh Policy Leads to a Sharp Ethics Battle,* NEW YORK TIMES B4 (Mar. 1, 1991). *See generally* Bowman (1996); Mashburn (1995); Delker (1995); Gershman (1992: 446–48).

7. Special Committee of the Conference of Chief Justices, Comment on Proposed Regulation Governing Contacts by Department of Justice Attorneys with Represented Persons 13 (Mar. 31, 1994).

8. ABA HOUSE OF DELEGATES, REPORT NO. 301 (approved 2.13–14.90).

9. *Exercise of Federal Prosecutorial Authority in a Changing Legal Environment: Hearings before the Subcommittee on Government Information, Justice and Agriculture of the House Committee on Government Operations,* 101st Cong., 2d Sess. (1990) (Prepared Statement of William W. Taylor III).

City of New York concurred.[10] But Thornburgh accused "the defense bar, with ABA sponsorship" of "attempting to use rules of professional conduct to stymie criminal investigation and prosecution." He found it "curious and inappropriate that the ABA, in which the interests of the defense bar are well-represented, should be in the business of making rules for the government's conduct of criminal prosecutions," which "is the business of Congress and the courts."[11] In November, a House of Representatives subcommittee recommended changes in Thornburgh's proposal.[12] Yet in spring 1991, he justified the memo by telling about a drug "mule" who wanted to cooperate with the government but would not fire the attorney hired by the drug trafficker for fear of retaliation.[13]

C. Voir Dire of Lopez

On May 21, 1990, Wilken interviewed Lopez alone for thirty-five minutes.[14] Lopez said he had approached the government through Twitty, "my appeal attorney . . . the one doing my appeal . . . for bail," although he also identified Tarlow as his attorney.[15] Telling Lopez that Tarlow was "obligated to represent your best interests, and not anyone else's, even if someone else might be paying his bill," Wilken asked why he had not wanted Tarlow to be present. Lopez replied, "[I]t was just . . . to see if they wanted to work out a plea or not . . . and then I would go from there." Asked again, Lopez reiterated, "I wanted to see what I could do by myself. . . ." Wilken persisted, "If Mr. Barry Tarlow is being paid for by someone else, and the fact is that you can't afford to hire an attorney who you feel would represent your interests, then the court would appoint an attorney to represent you." But Lopez rejected her supposition, saying "[T]here is no attorney that I can depend on." All lawyers were "just out . . . to rip you off." When Wilken speculated that Lopez wanted to ask Lyons questions "without your lawyer knowing that you're doing this," Lopez retorted:, "[H]e'll know. Once I do it, he'll know." Lopez just did not want the "big expense—be out of my pocket just . . . to ask two questions." When Wilken suggested that Tarlow participate by phone, Lopez admitted, "I hadn't thought of that. . . ." But he rebuffed her offer to

10. Association of the Bar of the City of New York, Criminal Law Committee, *Regulating the Conduct of United States Department of Justice Employees Who Communicate With Persons Represented by Counsel.*

11. Joint Press Release of Attorney General Dick Thornburgh and Representatives of the National District Attorneys Association and the National Association of Attorneys General with attached releases (Aug. 6, 1990).

12. Don J. DeBenedictis, *Justice Ethics Policy Hit,* 77 ABAJ 20 (August 1991).

13. Thornburgh (1991). After Twitty's case had concluded, federal courts upheld their right to compel federal prosecutors to conform to ethical rules. Whitehouse v. United States District Court of Rhode Island, 53 F.3d 1249 (1st Cir. 1995). *See* Tarlow (1998).

14. State Bar Exhibit 1.

15. Tarlow confirmed that he made Lopez's bail application and probably his appeal of its denial.

arrange it when he said, "I would rather just ask [Lyons] the two questions myself." If so, Wilken persisted, why use Twitty? Lopez's reply was non-responsive, "[A]t this moment I don't trust nobody. That's why I wanted to . . . find out for myself." Wilken warned that the sentencing guidelines were so complicated Lopez would have difficulty knowing if he were being offered a good deal and again suggested a public defender.

Lopez's insistence that he wanted to "just talk to them myself, if they are willing to—" provoked Wilken to interrupt: "[T]hey won't tell you that until you tell them enough that they'll know that they want you . . . and if you do that, you're going to incriminate yourself and what you say will be used against you." But she could not overcome Lopez's confidence:

> I'm not going to say anything. . . . I was going to ask [Lyons] a couple of questions . . . either he tells me: "Yes, I do," then I'll find an attorney; and, if he says: "No, I don't," then, you know, I'll just go to trial. . . . [I]t's something I want to find out for myself. I don't want to depend on somebody in between. . . .

When Wilken suggested Lopez talk to Lyons *with* Tarlow, the accused resisted: "[Y]ou guys look at it from one point of view; we look at it from our point of view . . . it isn't just a—a game. . . ." He refused to disclose what he would ask the prosecutor, insisting, "[T]hat's up to me. . . ." Asked if he trusted the government, Lopez repeated, "I don't trust nobody." When Wilken observed, "[Y]ou're going to be speaking with the government without anyone to protect you," he insisted "[T]hat's the chances I got to take." Wilken persisted, "[Y]ou can have a lawyer to represent you." But this just made Lopez impatient, "I don't trust no lawyers . . . can't you understand? I don't trust no damn lawyers." That included the prosecution. "I'm not going to talk to them. . . . I'm taking my chance on asking two questions. And if that's what's going to do me in, then that's what's going to do me in." Wilken tried once more by stating, "[T]hey aren't going to know what sort of deal they can . . . offer you unless you tell them" something. Lopez claimed to understand this and said he appreciated her advice but insisted he was just going to ask two questions.

Lopez: I'm not dumb, or stupid, you know.

Wilken: You're also not a lawyer, and you don't know the details—

Lopez: . . . I've heard a lot of people . . . get lawyers, and you know what? Without nothing, nothing against them, they end up being . . . messed around real bad.

Wilken: And how many people do you know who represented themselves who have done better than that?

Lopez: I've heard of a few . . . that have done better. But . . . I have not heard of anybody that's done any better with lawyers . . . it's kind of sickening of just thinking of lawyers for this, and lawyers for that.

Wilken again offered a public defender, warning that Twitty would be seeking a better deal for his client, Escobedo. But Lopez repeated that "[Y]ou guys . . . are looking at one side." He had "seen what a public defender can do. . . ." Wilken bristled, declaring that she was "not one of 'you guys'" and had "no interest in the case." Her only role was to advise Lopez of his rights and the dangers of self-representation, "so that if that's what you decide to do, and later it turns out badly for you, there will be a record that will show that you were warned. . . ." Lopez claimed that public defenders "work with the government at all times." Wilken disagreed; public defenders were "very, very good attorneys . . . and they will do the best they can for what you want to do." But Lopez maintained he just wanted answers to two questions. If he decided to negotiate a deal, his family would help him hire a lawyer. He wasn't

> going to go in there and . . . give them this . . . no, no, no, no, no. I'm only going in there just to ask two simple questions . . . and I want to do it myself. . . . it's not about cooperating. . . . I've had two sets of lawyers already . . . and when this time came to . . . plea[d] . . . everybody gives me . . . different stories.

Although Lyons believed Lopez would cooperate, "I know the games they play and everything." Asked if he wanted protection in prison, Lopez was emphatic: "[N]o, no, no, no. I don't want no protection . . . . there's no problem" in Pleasanton.

After further warnings, Wilken had Lopez sign a formal waiver:

> Defendant Lopez understands that he is free to utilize Mr. Barry Tarlow in connection with his communications with the government, and in fact has been encouraged to do so, but states he does not wish to have Mr. Barry Tarlow present or have any knowledge of such communications. Defendant Lopez states that he believes Mr. Barry Tarlow does not represent his best interests in such circumstances.

Lopez said it was "just for today." Wilken agreed but added, "[I]f you go on from today, then I don't know what you'll do."

She then told Lyons that Lopez just wanted "to ask the government two questions . . . . [H]e says he doesn't wish to say anything to the government; he doesn't . . . wish to cooperate. . . ." After hearing the answers, "he may then wish to talk to Mr. Barry Tarlow, or may wish to . . . retain another attorney, or may wish to end the matter and go back to Pleasanton." Warned by Wilken not give away any information, Lopez assured her he would not. She cautioned Lyons, "[A]fter he's asked you the two questions and received the answers, we don't have, at least on the record, a waiver of counsel for any further discussions." Before those could occur, Lopez would have to appear before her again or talk to Tarlow or retain another lawyer. Lyons assured Wilken he did not intend to use anything Lopez said to him "on a more wide-ranging discussion."

"Perhaps Mr. Lopez wanted to make a kind of what we call an off-the-record proffer, or a free talk . . . whatever is said on that particular day is never used again for any purpose whatsoever," not even "to conduct further investigation which might then turn up further information." But Escobedo, if present, could use whatever Lopez said. Because Lopez was unsure what he would do after hearing Lyons's answers, the prosecutor proposed to "schedule another time with the court . . . this may be all a little elaborate and extended, but we want to make sure we preserve the defendant's rights."

Lopez asked two questions. First, how could [he] get out of prison *now*? And second, what was the government's best offer? He subsequently talked to Twitty and sought a second meeting with Lyons. Wilken conducted a voir dire of Lopez again on May 30.[16] Lyons said that at the first meeting, he had laid out the "options" available to Lopez "under various hypothetical scenarios." Lopez replied that he wanted to think about them. After Lyons left the voir dire, Wilken repeated that Lopez would "be entitled to have a lawyer, if you so wished it, to assist you in cooperating with the government, if that is what you wanted to do. . . ." Lopez said if he decided to cooperate he would "notify Mr. Barry Tarlow . . . but at this stage, I have not cooperated nor have I intended—I ask brief questions." He brushed off Wilken's repeated warnings: "[I]t was agreed . . . that everything that was discussed was completely off the record." Wilken remembered Lyons's earlier representations differently. The prosecutor had "said that he could make such an agreement with you if you decided to speak with him. I don't know whether he made that agreement with you or not. That is one example of why it's useful to have a lawyer representing you in these things." She recalled Lyons, who confirmed Lopez's recollection of "my agreement, and I repeated that agreement when he did come down to the office . . . and the same rules of the game would apply to this conference today."

D. Judge Patel Deals with the Damage

In August, Lyons inadvertently disclosed these meetings to Olivas's lawyer, Rosenthal. He contacted Twitty, who first denied meeting Lyons and then told Rosenthal not to "mess up the deal" by alerting Tarlow. But Rosenthal did tell Tarlow, who immediately obtained Judge Smith's permission to withdraw on August 15.[17] The court appointed William L. Osterhoudt, who moved to dismiss the indictment because of these meetings. Judge Smith denied bail to Lopez and

16. State Bar Exhibit 2.

17. Judge Smith stated:

> All I know is that Mr. Tarlow thinks it's best for him to withdraw. The government seems to think under the circumstances it's best. Mr. Lopez agrees that for whatever the reason there has now been a breach of the relationship. And so without in any way casting any discredit at all upon Mr. Tarlow because there is no reason to, I will grant the motion for him to withdraw.

Escobedo on November 8 but released Olivas. She recused herself from hearing Osterhoudt's motion, which was assigned to Judge Marilyn Hall Patel.

Osterhoudt filed a declaration by Tarlow[18] in support of the motion, asserting that Lopez was responsible for paying his fee and Tarlow knew no one else involved in the alleged illegal activities. Lyons had told Judge Smith there was "not a hint by anybody that [Tarlow had] done anything wrong [or] inappropriate." He had not conditioned representation of Lopez on non-cooperation, which would have been "improper." Rather, he had told Lopez what he told every client:

> Under our agreement, if an offer of cooperation was presented by the AUSA, I would convey that offer to Mr. Lopez for his consideration. I would not, however, be personally involved in the continuing negotiations with the government, since this conduct is personally morally and ethically offensive to me. Since Mr. Lopez had retained me to vigorously defend and try the case, another attorney would be willing and better able to arrange his informant activities [charging only $2-3,000, much less than Tarlow] . . . . I believe in aggressively defending the interests of my clients within the bounds of propriety. I have not adopted the "Go Along and Get Along" approach . . . [and] never sought admission to nor been invited to join the "Old Boys Club" of defense lawyers and prosecutors . . . . I attempt not to personalize this battle with prosecutors. Nevertheless, I have found that personal and ego problems do develop at times because of my adversarial style. . . . Therefore, even apart from my own ethical and moral position . . . I do not believe my participation in finalizing informant arrangements is generally in the best interest of a client. An independent lawyer who has a closer and friendly rather than adversarial relationship with the prosecutor's office, should be able to negotiate a better informer deal than I would be able to work out . . . . If negotiations proved unsuccessful, I would resume my representation of Mr. Lopez and would try the case unless matters had occurred during the negotiations that compromised my ability to defend him. I regarded the latter possibility as remote, since in ordinary plea discussions it is the defendant's attorney who does the negotiation and makes the representations upon which they are based. I would and have counseled against a defendant talking directly with the prosecutor in the negotiations phases . . . . Mr. Lopez understood our agreement and knew that he was not "losing" me as an attorney by merely expressing interest in pursuing negotiations with the government.[19]

Joint Excerpt of Record, filed Dec. 3, 1991 in the government's appeal from dismissal of the indictment.

18. State Bar Exhibit 11.

19. Tarlow said he would no more represent a snitch than he would "Nazis or an Argentine general said to be responsible for 10,000 'disappearances.'" Gail D. Cox, *Fighting*

Lyons had been "outraged when we filed a detailed formal discovery motion rather than possibly accepting the scraps of discovery he magnanimously felt he would voluntarily dole out." He was "extremely upset" by Tarlow's motions criticizing his failure to fulfill his agreement to produce materials. Twitty had "no express, implied, or apparent authority, or permission to discuss informant activities with Mr. Lopez," who had said "he was pressured by Mr. Twitty and Mr. Escobedo to talk with Mr. Lyons." The prosecutor "wanted a package deal" and "the cooperation of both defendants," which would make "a better deal available for Mr. Escobedo." Lopez reported that "Lyons, on more than one occasion, urged him to fire me as a lawyer." Lyons and Twitty had agreed never to tell Tarlow of the negotiations so that "when the case was tried I would be the only one in the courtroom who was unaware of the details of what had been discussed . . . concerning [Lopez's] knowledge and relationship to drug trafficking activities." "It was this deceit and secrecy, as well as the compromising or undermining of his defense by the disclosure at the meeting, not the fact of the negotiations, that doomed our attorney-client relationship" by interfering with Tarlow's "ability to present the defense that [Lopez] was framed and entrapped. . . ."

Judge Patel heard Lopez's motion to dismiss on November 19, 1990.[20] Twitty sought to close the hearing because (as he repeated twice) "there is I believe a substantial danger to Mr. Lopez and Mr. Escobedo." He also sought to assert *Lopez*'s attorney-client privilege, but Osterhoudt replied that everyone agreed Twitty had never represented Lopez. And when Twitty admitted that Escobedo was present at some of his conversations with Lopez, Judge Patel thought this stripped Lopez of any privilege, and Tarlow's absence created "an extraordinarily [*sic*] position of conflict."

Twitty testified that he had been approached by a brother on behalf of Escobedo, who introduced him to Lopez. The two accused initially agreed that Twitty would be Lopez's lawyer and asked him to obtain "new counsel" for the others. Twitty referred Olivas to Rosenthal. But when the lawyer proposed for Escobedo was unavailable, Twitty suggested Tarlow, who "said he was going to represent Mr. Lopez," so Twitty took Escobedo.[21] "It's a difficult and unusual situation, but it is one which all of the lawyers in the case and all of the defendants in the case knew and understood." After Twitty had talked with Lopez and Escobedo about negotiating, he "told them that they should consider carefully what they were doing and how they were doing it."

---

and Flaunting It: The Criminal Defense Bar's Best Defense Is Barry Tarlow—Just Ask Him, National Law Journal 29 (Apr. 19, 1993).

20. State Bar Exhibit 3. A stipulated corrected transcript, filed March 7, 1991, was State Bar Exhibit 4.

21. Elsewhere, Lopez said he got Tarlow's name from another inmate.

Twitty asked the court to read his declaration in camera because Osterhoudt's motion to dismiss contained

> certain statements . . . which suggested that one or both of these clients had done things, which if found out by certain people would put one or both of them in danger. . . . [It] should have been filed under seal . . . anybody who suggests that they have participated in a cocaine deal or program as large as the government claims in this instance . . . and that they may under some circumstances cooperate in some fashion, that they are placed in some sort of danger. . . . When you add to that that . . . Tarlow has made statements to local newspapers and is writing things in columns to the national defense lawyers' magazine . . . [it] would place them in danger.

Judge Patel responded that "enough proceedings have been conducted in camera at this point." Had "it not been for [Twitty's] conduct, this whole . . . problem wouldn't have been set in motion." Nevertheless, she read his declaration and filed it under seal.

When Patel again raised possible conflicts between the defendants, Twitty insisted that "all of the things have been discussed with both of the men and each of them know and understand [*sic*] the potential conflict and each of them has waived it" before the magistrate. Patel rejected Twitty's claim of Lopez's attorney-client privilege: "it's essentially not something that was authorized by Mr. Tarlow and was done behind his back." Twitty responded that "Mr. Lopez asked to speak to me . . . for the purpose of seeking a second opinion. . . ." "He said he wanted me to be his lawyer, but I told him I could not. . . ." Lopez also requested that Twitty not tell Tarlow any of this.

Asked if Lopez had safety concerns, Osterhoudt said his client felt "this matter is widely known at this point, and doesn't feel that it needs to be kept secret." Patel asked Alan Ellis (representing the National Association of Criminal Defense Lawyers) if Tarlow was entitled to refuse to represent clients who negotiate with the government, but Osterhoudt denied this was Tarlow's approach. Many defense counsel feel that having "litigated a hard case," they "are not the best people to negotiate a deal with the government." Tarlow's position was that if "you feel it's in your best interest, I am not going to discourage you. . . ." If negotiations failed and "you haven't compromised your case . . . I will try it for you. . . ."

Osterhoudt called Lyons, whose declaration listed two names the defendants had given him in their first (May 30) meeting. Osterhoudt quoted ABA Standard 3-4.1(B): "It is unprofessional conduct for a prosecutor to engage in plea discussions directly with an accused who is represented by counsel except with counsel's approval."[22] Lyons was unfamiliar with both that and a standard requiring

22. ABA Standards Relating to the Administration of Criminal Justice. Prosecution and Defense Function.

verbatim transcripts of meetings with an unrepresented defendant. He was also dismissive of them:

> The standards are not ethical rules and haven't been adopted by this district court; and second, where they are inconsistent with my duties as a federal prosecutor, the Supreme case [*sic*—"Supremacy Clause"] falls [*sic*] and the other prevails.

Lyons invoked

> the statute that authorizes the Department of Justice and the U.S. Attorney's Office to investigate and prosecute criminal matters. . . . [I]n my judgment when a defendant comes forward and says that he's going to give me a means to complete further prosecution, then in my judgment I am authorized by law to pursue that communication.

He talked to Lopez for "the completion of the prosecution or furthering of investigation, both of which are authorized by law." That "made it impossible to have Tarlow there in Lopez's view."

But Lyons maintained that he "didn't need a reason" to talk to Lopez. He had relied on the Thornburgh memorandum.

> It is not necessary that the lawyer be paid by somebody else, but the concern is that the defendant client will talk and somehow the contact with the government may get back to somebody they are afraid of through the lawyer and may have some reason which may or may not be disclosed to the government prosecutor about why they have a concern.

It was "important" that Lopez had initiated the contact. Lyons was initially approached by Twitty. "I asked about having Mr. Tarlow there and Mr. Twitty told me that his client didn't want—not his client—Mr. Lopez didn't want Mr. Tarlow there." Twitty told Lyons that "Lopez felt . . . Tarlow didn't represent his best interest in this particular context." "I thought I knew" why, "based on my understanding they have these kind [*sic*] of situations . . . plus specific facts I knew about this case.

> I knew there was a man whose identity I knew who had threaten [*sic*] the family both of Mr. Escobedo and Mr. Lopez who we believed to be the source of the cocaine that was sold to the undercover agent by Mr. Escobedo and Mr. Lopez. . . . [T]hey were afraid that somehow if Mr. Tarlow was involved in these discussions that this man might learn of it and their names and themselves might be in danger.

When pressed about the connection between the threat and Tarlow, however, Lyons conceded, "I knew nothing about Tarlow and what intention he may have with this." "I don't know the reason I didn't ask" Twitty. "I think I didn't ask him because I thought I knew the answer." Lyons "didn't know if Mr. Tarlow was being paid" by the traffickers or, if not, whether "it was still legitimate for Mr. Lopez to have a concern that word might get back to these associates by somehow involving Mr. Tarlow." Asked why the magistrate "seem[ed] to imply that someone else is paying the fees for Mr. Lopez," Lyons said he had not talked with the magistrate but had told Judge Smith "that the common context in the approaches normally made was . . . situations in which the defense lawyer is somehow connected to somebody else and that the defendant is concerned about word getting back." But he conceded that in their first meeting Twitty "indicated . . . that in fact I should not make that assumption and that the money provided for Mr. Lopez's representation was not provided by the source of the cocaine or some other third party. . . . Mr. Lopez was sitting right there . . . he didn't deny that that was the case."

Because Twitty had told Lyons that Tarlow would not participate in plea negotiations, the prosecutor had the "impression" that "if I involved Tarlow in these discussions, [Lopez] would lose Tarlow as a lawyer." Although he denied having been "annoyed" with Tarlow, Lyons admitted: "I was annoyed by the fact that he had filed discovery motions after being given open discovery. . . ." He never told Twitty or Lopez it would be "easier to make a deal if Tarlow were not in the case." Although he had "told Mr. Lopez that if he didn't want Tarlow there . . . he ought to have someone else there and fire Tarlow," Lopez "indicated that he didn't want to fire Mr. Tarlow." Lopez was very emotional, close to tears, when he asked the two questions: "[I]f there was a way that he could get out and be closer to his children," since his wife was seeking custody; and "in event of cooperation . . . how could the safety and security of his family be taken care of." Lyons denied that Lopez's waiver "applied only to asking a couple of questions" because "if the answer . . . were favorable . . . he may want to have further instructions [*sic*—'discussions']." "[T]he magistrate indicated to me that Mr. Lopez might want to discuss things further . . . right then in that same meeting." But Lyons conceded that the magistrate had told him to return if a further waiver were necessary.

Lyons said Twitty "indicated to me that Mr. Lopez had come to trust him and that he felt more comfortable if Mr. Twitty was there." He agreed with Judge Patel that he knew of no "circumstances where this waiver isn't put on the record." It should have been "part of the proceedings in front of the magistrate and . . . of the written waiver that was signed by Mr. Lopez." During the prosecutor's meeting with Lopez and Escobedo, Twitty gave advice "intended for both individuals . . . basically [trying] to reinterpret some things I was saying in regard to the sentencing guidelines." Although Lopez had said he did not want to inform, Lyons still "was interested in his cooperation." When Lyons insisted the defendants demonstrate good faith by providing useful information at the second meeting, he got the name and alias of one drug trafficker (which Twitty and Tarlow had revealed during discovery) and promises of two others. He claimed he had done "nothing" with this information and did not remember telling Twitty he had verified some of the facts. Lyons sent Twitty a potential plea agreement with Escobedo and described what he would offer if Lopez got another lawyer. Both defendants rejected it.

When the hearing continued, Lyons testified that had Twitty "simply said 'my guy wants to plead; no cooperation; but he doesn't want Mr. Tarlow to know about it,' I would have rejected that approach."[23] Instead, Twitty had indicated that both "wanted to cooperate and provide information." Lyons was interested in concluding this case and "finding out about the source of supply for this particular case, as well as about any other narcotics crimes that were going on. . . ." Noting that the magistrate had told Lyons that Lopez did not want to cooperate, Patel asked: "Didn't that suggest to you that maybe this wasn't going to be in furtherance of any of these objectives?" Lyons insisted that by telling Wilken that "nothing [Lopez] said was going to be used," he had "basically disabused" her "of that misimpression." He understood from her that Lopez "might want to continue the discussion" if he found the prosecutor's answers satisfactory. Lopez had rejected Lyons's offer of a lawyer because he was confident "he could handle it himself." Lyons did not ask Lopez if Tarlow was being paid by others because that would be "inculpatory," and Lyons "thought I knew the reason why [Lopez] didn't want Mr. Tarlow there."

> I was familiar with the general situation in which these approaches had been made to people in the Department of Justice in the situation in which a third party, a source of cocaine, Mr. Big in the organization . . . had either hired the lawyer . . . or somehow had some idea about what was going on with the litigation . . . and the usual concern expressed by the defendant in that situation is that if I change lawyers . . . or my lawyer is there, that this will signal somehow . . . that I am talking to the government and this will create a danger for me. Then I had information . . . that in fact Mr. Lopez and Mr. Escobedo both had been threatened by an individual. Their families had been contacted by an individual, who we believe to be a source of the cocaine, and indicated to the members of his family that if they ever cooperated or helped the government in any way, that they would be in danger.

But he admitted having no evidence that Tarlow's fee had been paid by another or that anyone other than the drug source was involved in making this threat.

Patel observed that this case fell into none of the problematic categories: organized crime, corporate crime, or conflict of interest. Even if it had, the assistant U.S. attorney's proper course would have been to ask the lawyers to disqualify themselves or move to disqualify them. But Lyons said he had not done so, claiming that his conduct was appropriate unless the defendant had not initiated contact, and there was "no danger to the defendant at all;" or there was

23. State Bar Exhibit 5 (Dec. 13, 1990).

"no legitimate and rational reason why the defendant's lawyer cannot be informed or cannot be replaced."

In response to Lyons's invocation of the Supremacy Clause and the ethical rule's authorized-by-law exception, Patel noted that the Northern District had incorporated California ethical rules (as other districts had done with the ABA rules)[24] and asked, "Are you suggesting that somehow those rules are not binding on prosecutors?"

LYONS: There may be instances in which the judicial branch of the government has set down rules that conflict with the statutory duties of the executive branch of the government. And in those instances it would seem that the ethical rules . . . do not apply that there is a separation of powers situation there.

COURT: What about your position as an officer of the court?

LYONS: My position as an officer of the court is, of course, to conduct myself in the most highly professional manner I can, and that is what I believe I have done.

COURT: . . . [Y]ou believe that this [Thornburgh] memo gives members of the Department of Justice who are members of the bar some authorization to conduct themselves differently . . . even if the local rules should conflict with some federal statute, somehow there is some overriding basis for departing from the rules of conduct adopted by the District Court[?]

Lyons responded with a hypothetical in which a local court rule requiring disclosure of evidence conflicted with a federal statute.

COURT: Is there a specific statute here that says that you have a right to talk to the defendant under these certifications [*sic*—"circumstances"]?

LYONS: I don't deny that you could probably distinguish away every analogy that I might come up with. What I am trying to do, basically, is answer your questions by saying there are instances in which this local court might do something that is in conflict with a federal statute—

COURT: What I am trying to find out is what is the federal statute here. . . .

LYONS: The federal statute that empowers the employees of the Department of Justice to prosecute and investigate violations of the criminal law.

---

24. That eliminated the state-federal conflict. Two District of Columbia federal judges made short shrift of the Supremacy Clause argument. One declared that "a policy memorandum issued by the head of an executive agency simply is not the equivalent of federal law." U.S. v. Ferrara, 847 F.Supp. 964, 969 (D.D.C. 1993). The other said the law "obviously does not establish a memorandum issued by the Attorney General as supreme over rules issued by a federal court." U.S. v. Adonis, 744 F.Supp. 336, 347 n.50 (D.D.C. 1990).

Patel noted that a week earlier, the U.S. Supreme Court had declared that the "very precious" right to counsel should "be scrupulously adhered to."[25] That, Lyons replied, was why he had gone to Judge Smith. "[W]hat is the point," Patel countered, if "the memo gives you this right"? Lyons agreed it was not necessary, adding that the Supreme Court "would probably agree that there was a knowing and voluntary waiver of the right to counsel."

At the end of Lyons's testimony, Osterhoudt argued that Lopez had been "vulnerable to an approach" because he was "deeply concerned about his children." He had no "intention of dislodging his attorney" but "was given to understand that Mr. Tarlow did not make the prosecutor comfortable, and . . . it would be much easier to address questions to [Lyons] without Mr. Tarlow." The drug traffickers Lopez had named for Lyons were inculpatory, given Tarlow's intention of arguing entrapment. It was "fanciful" to suppose Tarlow would try the case after these discussions, which he would inevitably discover since he had demanded "all the statements made by the defendant." Tarlow withdrew because "the government might have been able . . . to infer defense strategy from the information that was given and from the circumstances under which it was given."

Because Lyons had initiated the magistrate's voir dire, Patel indicated that, at this stage, she did not feel "prosecutorial misconduct" justified dismissal. "[A]t most it would require suppression of any inculpatory statements." Were Patel trying the case, she might sever the defendants and ask the U.S. attorney to appoint another prosecutor. She also would "probably do a very lengthy voir dire of Mr. Escobedo and raise some serious questions about conflict of interest and even go ahead and disqualify" Twitty. All this "speaks to . . . the dangerousness of this process. . . ." "Look at the length of time, the proceedings that have gone on before the magistrate, before Judge Smith, and now myself, to undo what was done because of following this Department of Justice policy."

Osterhoudt urged the court "to look carefully . . . past" Lyons's "basic decency as a human being" and make "a strong statement" that "this policy is very, very dangerous." "The sheer arrogance of the government's claim of power to override . . . disciplinary rules designed for all lawyers . . . must call for a strong response. . . ." "[N]o other remedy" except dismissal "is really available." The government's conduct "made it certain . . . that [Lopez] couldn't have a lawyer of his choice." This was "partly by design, because I don't think Mr. Lyons was comfortable with Mr. Tarlow . . . the vigorous, aggressive, probably annoying defense lawyer. . . ."

Lyons warned that Patel's decision would have an "impact" on disciplinary proceedings that had been instituted against Twitty in California and himself in Arizona. "Tarlow only says that he doesn't know any Mr. Big" and "was paid by Lopez. Now where Lopez got the money, and how he was able to get the

25. Minnick v. Mississippi, 498 U.S. 146 (Dec. 3, 1990).

money, and whether he got it from Mr. Big, or whatever he told Mr. Tarlow, remains to be seen. . . ." Osterhoudt countered that "Mr. Twitty violated a number of rules . . . and I think Mr. Lyons acquiesced in that. . . ."

When the hearing continued,[26] Osterhoudt claimed that Twitty (inexplicably absent) would testify that Lyons "was much more comfortable with Mr. Tarlow off the case . . . and that he saw that as an end product of this activity." Lyons retorted that Osterhoudt's "proffer is absolutely not true . . . [I]t would take a Machiavellian and subtle mind, far beyond what I actually have, to contemplate that. . . ."

Lopez finally testified. He had first hired John Myers but switched to Twitty after a couple of bail hearings.

> At that point [Twitty represented] mainly Escobedo and then he made a couple of appearances for me, just like Rosenthal does for Escobedo and Olivas[27] now. . . . Mr. Twitty was trying to get this lawyer from Milwaukee, but that never came to light. So I finally, through somebody at Pleasanton, they gave me the name of Tarlow, so I contacted Tarlow. . . . Mr. Twitty was not pleased when he realized that Tarlow was going to represent me . . . [he] said he didn't care who Tarlow represented as long as Twitty was in charge of the whole case. . . .

Twitty told Lopez and Escobedo "we should really talk to Mr. Lyons. There was an offer . . . ten years and up to probation." Lopez's children were "going through very hard problems with their mother," from whom he was separated; his oldest son had been put in foster care and then released to his mother. "[T]here was plenty of evidence that my children were being abused badly. . . ." "I was . . . like in a desperate situation to try anything for the children . . . and when [Twitty] told me there was maybe a possibility of bail or something . . . I jumped at that."

He met Lyons without Tarlow "mainly because of . . . the extra expense and the understanding," according to Twitty, that "it would be easier . . . to deal without Mr. Tarlow being present." Twitty said:

> [I]f we have to get Mr. Tarlow off . . . [Twitty] would be able to represent both Escobedo and myself and don't worry about having to pay the extra fee. . . . like I told Mrs. Wilken, my only thing was the extra expense. And then Twitty just said that it was not necessary for Tarlow to be here. And that . . . it would probably be easier to . . . work something out because Tarlow was . . . hard . . . he'd be real strong and aggressive on my behalf . . . . even though I did sign [the waiver] . . . in the back of my mind what I remember was . . . you can keep Mr. Tarlow like nothing happened and he can defend your case

---

26. State Bar Exhibit 6 (2.4.91). John T. Phillipsborn testified for the National Association of Criminal Defense Lawyers, which had filed a brief.

27. "Twitty" in the original.

and you will not . . . be giving up any rights because nothing will be held against you.

He had told Tarlow "at all times that . . . I wanted him as my lawyer."

Lopez's only concern was to get out on bail to be with his children.

I wasn't just going to go in there and cooperate . . . . [but] it was almost like they . . . led up to a second meeting . . . where they had to get something out of me before they could definitely tell me yes or no about it. . . . [A]t the first meeting they were trying to get things out of me, and I just wouldn't budge. . . .

At the second meeting, Lyons "told me that . . . I had to trust him and give him something of significance . . . before they could really tell me anything of whether I could go on bail or not. . . ." There was "pressure from Mr. Escobedo and Mr. Twitty" to provide "significant, substantial information concerning the transaction itself. . . ." Twitty said:

[Y]ou have got to give [Lyons] something of significance before he . . . tried to cooperate. You know what Mr. Rosenthal thinks of him. He thinks very highly of him . . . and then Mr. Escobedo mentioned in Spanish . . . you have got to give him something for the kids. . . . That's why I started. . . .

Lopez gave Lyons several names, including Alberto (and his two aliases), Carlos (whose alias was known to Alfonso, the informant), Jose Sanchez (whose name already was in the police report), and a woman who "was of very significant importance" because she had been the girlfriend of the two "who gave me the drugs . . . who was responsible for . . . the whole transaction." Escobedo talked less. "[H]e more or less would confirm certain things." Lopez was "pretty nervous."

Mr. Twitty must have thought that I was going to give some names that were mentioned in our defense strategy between Tarlow and Twitty. So when I mentioned the name Alberto, Twitty jumped in and said, "Wait a minute. You can't give that name. That is part of our defense, entrapment defense." And then that's when . . . he kept on . . . saying how . . . he felt our defense involved Alberto and . . . Carlos involving Alfonso, the informant.

Lopez had been angry "all along" that "these other two persons were not arrested, because I felt . . . Alberto and Carlos and the informant had used me . . . to cover up those two other persons that were on parole. . . ."

"[W]hen Twitty tried . . . to advise me about something" at the first meeting, "Mr. Lyons told him . . . you can't give him no advice . . . he's on his own." "[B]ut then when [Twitty] came up with the name Alberto . . . everything went along. . . ." Lopez told Lyons that to be an effective informant he needed to be out on bail, not just make phone calls, because "people had changed their phone numbers." He also wanted to "be with my kids." "[P]robably after two weeks they [the drug suppliers] would approach me for . . . the funds . . . that's the way I would start it . . . because it would be too dangerous for me to do anything like that." But the deal Lyons offered was "completely different than what I had [been] made to understood . . . originally with the prior lawyers we had been told . . . ten and ten, and now it was outrageous, fifteen and up." "I would follow the same guidelines without doing nothing as where I helped. . . ."

Lyons began his cross-examination by calling Lopez Escobedo. After Lyons got nowhere asking Lopez what *others* had said, Patel rebuked the assistant U.S. attorney, saying "[A]sking [Lopez] to recall what you testified to is not a very fruitful way to conduct an examination." Lopez said Myers (his original lawyer) had told them the government would offer him ten years, Escobedo eight, and Olivas three to five. He got Tarlow's name from an inmate named Walker, "I remember him telling me there was a book for me to read on trial lawyers . . . seemed like the guy knew pretty much himself. . . ." Tarlow never conditioned representation on Lopez not cooperating with the government. "[T]he only thing he asked me is . . . why did I want to hire him for. Was it to go to trial? Was it to try and work out a deal with the government? . . . I told him at the time I just wanted to fight the charges. . . ." "[T]he agreement was just that . . . he would represent me in my best interests . . . nothing that I decided to do would make him . . . step down. . . ." After Myers was replaced in February or March 1990, Twitty "told us there was a ten-year offer if we pleaded guilty." "[T]hat's when Escobedo approached Twitty . . . to contact [Lyons] and see if the offer was still available." "[T]he way I understood it was that it had to be a joint thing." Twitty "said he had learned it from [Lyons]." When Lyons denied having discussed an offer with Twitty, Lopez disagreed emphatically, "Oh, no, no, no. When Mr. Twitty first came into the case . . . he himself said that the government had approached him . . . that if we plead guilty, there was a ten-year thing on the table." Twitty, "asked you if the offer was still there. And then you said with cooperation . . . that possibility of up to probation. . . ."

Lyons expressed skepticism about such an offer "for two people charged with fifty kilos of cocaine and two kilos of heroin"; but Lopez insisted it had been made and "the government also had indicated that it had to be a package deal" of at least Escobedo and him. Escobedo "more or less was kind of pushy. So I said, yea, if we have to do something for the kids at the time, yes." "[A]ny parent that was going through what I was going through . . . would do . . . anything on this planet . . . for their children's safety. . . ." Lopez's "mind wasn't so hundred percent there . . . until one of us parents goes through a situation like that with the kids, then you know if your mind is there or if it's not there." Twitty told Lopez, "it would be a lot easier if Tarlow wasn't involved." "I wanted Tarlow to be involved, but they said . . . it was unnecessary." Lopez rejected Wilken's advice to get another lawyer "because if part of the deal was something to get me another lawyer . . . they could say . . . now you have to get rid of Tarlow." Lopez denied that Lyons had urged him to have a lawyer, "[Y]ou said, well, it's better if you get rid of Tarlow so we can work out a deal and get this thing over." Lopez conceded that Lyons might have said once "that the only reason to get rid of Tarlow was that you needed to have a lawyer there," but Lyons had raised the issue more than three times, once telling Lopez, "[I]t would be easier to get Tarlow out of the way so we can finish this deal and get it over with."

Lopez conceded that Twitty may have reported Lyons saying after the first meeting that they could not be released. But Twitty also told Lopez that "until the government got . . . something pertaining to the source . . . [Lyons] couldn't give us no direction." He insisted that Lyons held out the hope of release. Before the second meeting "Mr. Twitty had told me that it was better that . . . Tarlow not be there, and then [Lyons] more or less corroborated that. . . ." Lopez feared that having another attorney "may signal that . . . there was a conflict of interest with Mr. Tarlow and I didn't want nothing like that because I wanted Mr. Tarlow for my . . . lawyer if we went to trial. . . ." "[O]nce I knew there was nothing that could be done, then I would tell Mr. Tarlow everything." "No matter what happened, Mr. Tarlow will find out."

Shown Lyons's notes from the second meeting, Lopez identified the two names he had given. "[T]he first name is the one that supposedly threatened my family, which was totally false. It was my . . . ex-wife that was making a big propaganda about that name." When Lyons insisted she had reported threats, Lopez said "I don't know nothing about it." "She wanted protection and she would cooperate. But . . . probably against me. . . ." Lyons and Lopez argued about which names he had given and whether they were aliases or already in police reports.

> [A]t first I was very reluctant and I was trying to give as little as possible . . . but once I got going . . . just anything I could remember, was writing it out because I was so nervous.

They were planning to allege entrapment by "Alfonso, which is the informant, [who] was trying to protect the other two guys to set me up." Lopez also remembered admitting at the second meeting "more or less how the crime happened . . . how the drugs got in my possession. . . ." After it, he got a written offer. Twitty "told me . . . if we decided [to accept] that he would do both of them. . . ."

When Patel's hearing resumed, Twitty said Escobedo's brother first contacted him in October 1989 because the defendants were unhappy with their lawyers.[28] Twitty suggested that all three be represented by him and a Milwaukee lawyer, but the latter was unavailable. Twitty was Lopez's counsel of record for about two months and discussed strategy with both him and Escobedo. When Tarlow

---

28. State Bar Exhibit 7 (3.4.91); *see also* Steve Albert, *Justice Dept. Policy on Talks Faces Test*, THE RECORDER 1 (Mar. 5, 1991).

entered the case, the two lawyers agreed to re-allocate the clients.[29] "I have known Barry for many years and think the world of him as a lawyer." But Twitty agreed that Lyons "thought the case would be more difficult because of Mr. Tarlow," whom Lyons knew from appearances in the Arizona federal court. Lyons thought Tarlow "was a bit more abrasive than [*sic*—"and"] combative than he felt necessary . . . it would mean more work and the case would be more difficult. . . ." "I don't think he liked Mr. Tarlow. But there are lots of people who don't like Mr. Tarlow." Although Lyons never said, "he would be happy to see Mr. Tarlow off the case," Tarlow's participation changed everything. "Mr. Tarlow took the position of lead counsel essentially with the idea that you could not and should not trust anything that the government had to say about the case period." Twitty "usually" got discovery from Lyons "without having to file a motion or cause some major problem." But Tarlow told Twitty that he filed discovery motions before asking Lyons for the material, until "Judge Smith ordered the two of them to get together and talk about it. . . ."

Five or six weeks before the first meeting with Lyons, Escobedo called to say Lopez and he were thinking of pleading for shorter sentences. Twitty insisted on discussing this in person and spent several hours doing so. Both defendants "were really worried about their children, especially Mr. Lopez," whose ex-wife was making it difficult for him to talk to them. Having children the same age, Twitty was sympathetic. Lopez, who had been in jail six to eight months by then and had been denied bail by the Ninth Circuit, was concerned "he might not see the children until . . . they were grown." Twitty urged him to consult his "very talented counsel," but Lopez

> said he couldn't talk to Mr. Tarlow about it and was not going to . . . Tarlow had told him that if he had any idea about pleading guilty to any of the charges . . . he . . . would not represent him.

Although Twitty denied Tarlow had ever said this, both defendants insisted he had. Lopez wanted to "make an evaluation of Mr. Lyons's credibility." Asked if Lopez could trust Lyons, Twitty said he did not know, although "Rosenthal thought the world of him." Twitty warned, "this was a major change in everything . . . a giant step into the enemy camp. . . ."

One or both defendants called, "somewhat aggrevated [*sic*] and agitated that I had not set the meeting up yet." The next time Twitty visited Pleasanton, Lopez "told me that if I didn't let Lyons know that he wanted to talk to him, that he was going to call him collect from a pay phone. . . ." When Twitty communicated the defendants' request, the prosecutor immediately asked about Tarlow. Twitty explained Lopez did not want Tarlow involved or informed. Lyons said he needed the court's permission and "was trying to find time with Judge Smith when she

29. Tarlow insists there was no "allocation" of the clients; only Lopez ever approached him.

could hear it." He finally heard from her chambers that "she was not interested in having this appear before her since she was the trial judge and she would get a magistrate . . . to take care of it."

When Lopez asked at the first meeting what he could get for cooperating, Lyons said the deals "ranged all the way down to probation" for information "of major significance." Questioned about pretrial release, Lyons "did not accept the idea, but he did not rule it out. He suggested that there was at least a possibility of that." Lyons also said, "that if Mr. Lopez were to reach the conclusion that he wanted to plead guilty, and to assist the government . . . he would have to replace Mr. Tarlow as his lawyer. . . ." Lopez "understood that" but "wanted to be sure . . . Mr. Lyons understood that the only reason he was there was because he was afraid that something might happen to his children while he was away if he had to serve some time." When Lyons asked if Lopez was keeping Tarlow in the dark "because somebody else was paying the fee or because he was afraid that something might be communicated," Lopez said no; and Twitty "joined in that as emphatically as possible." In response to Patel, Twitty could not say "any stronger" that Lopez did not fear that, if Tarlow learned of the talks, it "somehow might get back to someone else in an organization who would do him harm." Twitty told Lyons both before and after the first meeting and again at the second, "that so far as I knew, no body [*sic*] that I supposedly worked for or with was paying any of [Lopez's] fees. . . ."

After several more phone conversations with Twitty, Lopez said he wanted to talk to Lyons again. Twitty warned that "all government prosecutors . . . have a standard policy of you show me yours and I may show you mine." At the second meeting, Lyons played bad cop. (He told a reporter, "It was the prospect of developing new prosecutions that was the primary factor.") He did not think Lopez was "genuine and serious" or "really wanted to do anything." Lopez was "not providing any information" and "was wasting his time." Lyons "had to go to all this trouble getting the marshals out to bring the guys in again." The proposal to gather information after being released "absolutely would not work." The accused had to "tell him the source of the stuff" and "make a case on that person." "[I]f that proved workable . . . maybe there could be . . . future release and doing some further work to the government's benefit. . . ." After asking about government help in gaining custody of his children, the witness protection program, and his sentence, Lopez gave two names to Lyons, who wrote them down, seeming to recognize them, and said he would get back to the accused (but never did). Neither defendant told Lyons anything that might compromise their cases. When Rosenthal said he had heard from Lyons that Lopez and Escobedo were going to plead, Twitty denied there was any agreement. Soon after the second meeting, Lopez said that his mistrust of Lyons had been confirmed by the prosecutor's disclosure to Rosenthal.

Cross-examined by Osterhoudt, Twitty said because Lyons had not been "totally cooperative" about discovery, Tarlow insisted on making a record of "what Mr. Lyons had done or had not done in response to each and every request." "[F]rustrated" and "aggravate[ed]" that Tarlow "didn't believe the government was being honest," Lyons told Judge Smith he had, "tried to talk to Tarlow" but had gotten nowhere. Lyons felt "the case would go along more readily and smoothly without Tarlow's presence." And "right after the first real hearing on the discovery situation, when it got a little hot in the courtroom," Twitty told both accused "that the case could be resolved better without Tarlow in it." Lyons clearly insisted on a package deal for both. The first time he talked to Lyons on Lopez's behalf, Twitty declared that "all the government's claims about dangers to the Lopez family are simply unfounded." Twitty believed Lopez's claim that Tarlow would withdraw if Lopez negotiated. Lopez never expressed concern about expense; Twitty even offered to have a friend represent Lopez without charge, but Lopez "said he didn't want it and didn't need it." Twitty claimed to have Tarlow's authority "to do anything at all necessary for the general defense and working out of the case"; but under pressure from Osterhoudt and Patel, Twity admitted that "Mr. Tarlow did not tell me that I had authority to negotiate anything with the government on behalf of Mr. Lopez." He maintained that Lopez approached him "to secure a second opinion." When Osterhoudt objected that Twitty "actually contacted the government," the lawyer said that he had "honor[ed]" Lopez's "request" because they had "become friends" and "I was the first guy they talked to about" the "problem with their families."

> I don't think that Mr. Tarlow or any other lawyer owns the client privilege. I think that belongs to Mr. Lopez in this instance. And I think that Mr. Lopez . . . can talk to Mr. Lyons about it . . . I don't think that I, as a lawyer . . . have the right to stop him from doing that . . . . he can talk to God about it if he wants.

When Lyons "pressed" the defendants for information at the second meeting and "they were unsure as to whether they could . . . trust him," Twitty did not advise either how to answer Lyons's questions.

When Patel's hearing resumed without Twitty, Lopez said under cross-examination by Lyons that he had been paying Tarlow by the hour.[30] Lyons argued that "another issue in this hearing is whether or not somebody else paid Mr. Lopez's fee"; but Patel ruled this "not appropriate" because Lyons had testified that he "never had any reason to believe someone else was paying [Tarlow's] fee" beyond a "suspicion" or an "assumption." She advised Lyons, "I don't know why in this case you're clinging to the Thornburgh memo. I would cut myself off from that as quickly as possible if I were you." Insisting that "to this day I have no evidence one way or the other," Lyons tried unsuccessfully to ask the same question three more times but only elicited Lopez's (accurate) recollection that

30. State Bar Exhibit 9 (3.18.91); *see also* Steve Albert, *Patel Puts Justice Dept. on Trial*, The Recorder 1 (Mar. 20, 1991).

he had expressed his concern about expense to Wilken, "[I]f there was somebody else paying the expense I wouldn't be worried about it."

Twitty (who arrived late because of flight delays) now denied telling Lopez it would be easier to deal with the government without Tarlow, who was aggressive, or that Lyons had said that; and he insisted Lopez never expressed concern about expense.

LYONS: Did Lopez tell you that he did not want Tarlow present at or told about the meeting and that he was fearful for his own personal safety and that of his family if too many people knew?

TWITTY: Yes, he not only told me that at Pleasanton several times, he also told me and you that at the first meeting in your offices.

But Twitty did not "believe that's the reason [Lopez] did not want Tarlow there." Rather, Lopez feared losing Tarlow at trial. Twitty reiterated that Lopez wanted to be released on bail (secured by the property of friends and family) and wear an electronic bracelet or be monitored by an agent while doing "some investigative work for the government" and helping it "make one or more cases against people that he suggested may be significant." Lopez's concerns about his children were "significantly stronger and much more vivid" than Escobedo's.

Twitty denied having "jumped up" at the second meeting or having said "anything to anybody about 'giving those names' or . . . 'revealing defense strategy'" because the two names had not "revealed anything." "[I]f anybody pressured Lopez to tell anything or provide anything it was" Lyons, who had said

> you were tired of spending all this time with these two guys and bringing them out from Pleasanton and taking up all the time, they provided you nothing . . . except to tell you that they'd like to get out on bail and go do some work in Southern California that you were not interested in that and unless they provided you something concrete now at this meeting everything was off.

Lyons suggested they make a "simple easy case" against the drug source before being considered for release. "[I]f they did the first part and did something super terrific in connection with Southern California, then something else would be done." Lyons was "aggravated" at "having wasted so much of [his] time with them . . . unless they did something of substance it was over." Lyons asked if Lopez understood that if he pleaded he might "have to get himself another lawyer and that would necessitate firing Mr. Tarlow." Questioned by Osterhoudt, Twitty denied telling the defendants, "[T]he case could be resolved better without Tarlow in it." But he acknowledged that Tarlow had complained about him to the State Bar and had written at least two columns about the case "in a fashion that was not particularly complimentary. . . ." When Rosenthal said he had heard about the meetings from Lyons, Twitty "sort of denied I even talked to Lyons . . . in order to do what I believe Mr. Lopez wanted done." In a second conversation, he "told Mr. Rosenthal not to tell Tarlow because . . . he would mess up the deal."

When Rosenthal disregarded this, "I told Rosenthal I didn't think he should have done it," but "I didn't get mad." In response to Patel, Twitty agreed that Lopez's concerns about his children related entirely to his ex-wife's behavior. Before summations, Twitty asked Escobedo if he wanted another lawyer. Patel said she would have the chief public defender advise him.

Osterhoudt called the Thornburgh memorandum "a recipe for disaster." Under Lyons's interpretation, "any AUSA who feels that it would further his or her investigation or their prosecutorial responsibilities is free to override these ethical rules to talk to people who are represented by counsel without counsel's knowledge or presence." There was no authority "for the kind of partial waiver of counsel" Wilken had elicited. The way "those proceedings began as two questions and ended with the imparting of significant information . . . at the insistence of the government" demonstrated the necessity for counsel. When Patel objected that Lopez had given no incriminatory information, Osterhoudt pointed to the drug source, the names, and Lopez's claim that Twitty objected that this disclosed defense strategy. The ABA standards required a verbatim transcript "precisely so this kind of dispute can be avoided." Lopez's "waiver" did not satisfy *Faretta v. California*.[31] "[E]ven more clear, I think, is the ethical violation which . . . we all agreed here cannot be waived. . . ." Lopez was misled that Tarlow's participation in the meeting with Lyons would have been too expensive and his presence would "dash any hope" of Lopez seeing his children. The "government thought here's a chance to get rid of Tarlow and deal this case out and had Mr. Lyons not inadvertently tipped his hand to Harold Rosenthal it might never have come out." Lyons "would be in violation of discovery orders" by concealing Lopez's comments from Tarlow, who would have tried the case not knowing of the meeting. Osterhoudt urged dismissal because Lopez "has still been deprived of his chosen counsel." Even if there had been no prejudice, "it's not isolated . . . it's a policy of the Attorney General. . . ." The magistrate's hearing only worsened matters by implicating the court.

Lyons replied that even if Twitty had interjected, "don't tell him about Alberto . . . you'll give away our defense strategy" (which the lawyer denied), "it would require somebody a lot more creative than I am to be able to devise some kind of defense strategy out of that information. . . ." The government already knew one name and never checked the other. The defense had cited no authority empowering the court to punish the government. The magistrate's hearing showed the "purpose on the government's part to not take advantage of the defendant. . . ." Lopez had said, "[L]ook, I'm afraid to tell my lawyer about this because it might get back to somebody. But I want to cooperate with the government and I'm in fear of my life and I'm in fear of my family's safety, if my lawyer's told about this." The ABA rules were merely "advisory"; the DOJ had never

31. 422 U.S. 806 (1975).

adopted them and objected to some. A prosecutorial offer is not "considered by the prosecutor to be part of the negotiations." Osterhoudt had offered no authority for the proposition that "Mr. Lopez has a right to a chosen counsel." The ethical rule provides "essentially that the government is not supposed to talk to a represented defendant unless authorized by law. The Department of Justice has interpreted that exception to mean that when a defendant initiated the conversation . . . it is possible to speak to that defendant."

Judge Patel interrupted.

COURT: What is the authorized by law we're talking about.

LYONS: . . . [A]uthorized by law includes the prosecution pursuing its investigative prosecutive [*sic*] function . . . in order to fulfill my job under the statutes that enable the Department of Justice. . . .

COURT: So that doesn't just drive a little hole into that rule, that drives essentially an enormous truck through it. It guts it.

LYONS: I don't agree.

COURT: What's left? . . . [A]nything you can do to effect or conclude a prosecution is in furtherance of that duty and is therefore authorized by law, correct? . . . Suppose that the Attorney General changes his mind next week and decides to broaden the policy, is it still authorized by law?

LYONS: . . . to say because you disagree that the Department should have taken that policy . . . therefore, I, without any prior notice to the prosecutor or the Department of Justice, now decide that that . . . it's so unethical that we're going to let Mr. Lopez go . . . I think is way beyond what is either required . . . [or] what is really possible and proper for this court to do. . . .

COURT: You seem to be saying that the court cannot interpret those words "as authorized by law." That the Attorney General can, that you can, but the court cannot.

The court could do so prospectively, Lyons parried, "but it is wrong to punish the government . . . to say, you took a guess, you rolled the dice and it's your problem. . . ." When Patel called the government's interpretation "very, very questionable," Lyons retorted that that was just "the court's view." Asked for a case supporting his position, Lyons said there was none because "it was up to those of us who must conduct ourselves every day under these rules and regulations to make a judgment"; and he questioned whether the government "should be punished" for acting in good faith.

Patel's comment was scathing.

> That good faith has cost the taxpayers an awful lot of money already . . . do you realize . . . how many courts around this country . . . will be taking up their times in ancillary proceedings . . . because it is apparently going to be left up to the particular prosecutor to interpret that . . . memo . . . [?] It's interesting that we're celebrating the 200th birthday of the Bill of Rights. . . . I know why

> all of those rights were so jealously guarded and included in the Bill of Rights. And it was not to protect the right of a prosecutor as authorized by law, but it was to protect individuals from an overreaching government, who can decide in a moment's notice when, unless restrained, it can interpret the particular provision differently and bring the whole weight of its force down upon an individual . . . . [W]hat this policy clearly speaks to is the kind of deviltry that it's going to create in the courts . . . . [I]f you're going to take the theory of the Attorney General logically, then every U.S. Attorney performs executive functions as a member of the executive branch of the government. And indeed you may find that none of you are subject to any of the rules of canons of ethics, of rules of the court and professional rules of conduct adopted by the federal courts.

Lyons objected that Patel assumed "lack of discretion . . . good will . . . good faith" and failed to acknowledge that "the object of the prosecutors to accomplish justice." She replied:

> The consequences are apparent even in this situation. . . . We have now a proceeding in which we may have one or two . . . less attorneys than we had before and changes of counsel. We have defendants who are in custody for much longer periods of time . . . proceedings that have taken extraordinary amount of time and the magistrate and the court all to satisfy some notion of the Justice Department that it can carve out this one exception. . . . We're all, as lawyers, bound by rules of conduct . . . it may well be that when the Justice Department has enacted a department-wide policy, that it is indeed the Justice Department that must suffer the consequences of that policy. And in order to send a message that it is not complying with the law, that its prosecutors are being asked to violate rules of conduct that are a part of the rules of the District Court in which all other attorneys have to abide.

Judge Patel rendered judgment on May 24, 1991.[32] She noted the "rapidly growing concern regarding the ethical conduct of lawyers." Complaints against federal prosecutors were rising partly because of the "evolving efforts by the Department [of Justice] to limit the rights of suspects and defendants," as in the Thornburgh memo. Patel deplored that the Attorney General purported to exempt federal prosecutors from "one of the most widely-accepted and time-honored ethical rules" at a time of increasing "prosecutorial misconduct and the ineffectiveness or non-existence of sanctions designed to prevent such misdeeds."

Although neither Lopez nor Twitty was "entirely credible," she found that Lyons had made it clear to the defendants he wanted a package deal. When Tarlow decided Lopez had a viable defense, however, negotiations ceased and

---

32. U.S. v. Lopez, 765 F.Supp. 1433 (N.D. Calif. 1991). Reported in the Los Angeles Daily Journal 1 (May 28, 1991).

litigation became "more combative." Twitty told Lopez "it was not necessary" for Tarlow to be present at meetings with Lyons and allegedly said, "Lyons believed it would be easier to reach a plea agreement if Tarlow were not present." Lopez maintained that both Twitty and Lyons told him that meeting with the government without Tarlow's knowledge would not jeopardize the lawyer–client relationship.

Patel dismissed as "completely devoid of merit" all of Lyons's arguments. The first was based on separation of powers. The second hinged on the exemption of all the meetings from Rule 2-100 on the ground that they were pre-indictment contacts. The third emphasized that Lopez had initiated the contact. Finally, Lyons noted that the waiver was elicited by the magistrate. The Thornburgh memo had "profound flaws." Even a "cursory examination" showed it was unsupported by authority, since none of its citations dealt with a post-indictment represented defendant. "This, of course, is not surprising in light of the tortured logic of the Attorney General's policy." Under the department's view, "it is not clear that there would be *any* conduct the prosecutor could not undertake, as long as it was pursuant to his or her responsibility to investigate and prosecute crimes." Code of Professional Responsibility Rule 2-100, first codified in 1908 and still in force in every state, recognized "the inherent danger in a [represented] layperson conducting negotiations with an opposing lawyer and the likelihood that such negotiations would destroy the confidence essential to the attorney-client relationship and hamper the subsequent performance of the represented party's counsel." The prohibition "is even more important in the criminal context."

Lyons's "brazen" characterization of this as a pre-indictment situation because Lopez was offering information on *other* cases "strain[ed] credulity" and was "entirely unpersuasive." Because Rule 2-100 served to preserve an attorney's effectiveness, a defendant could not waive it. The magistrate was operating "under the mistaken assumption that Lopez's attorney . . . was being paid by a third party." But Lyons had no evidence of this and had been told by Twitty it was untrue. The "preposterous" invocation of separation of powers was "patently without foundation." In another recent case, "the Department, apparently finding it to its advantage, took the position that local rules are federal laws and therefore supreme." The memo was "an arrogation of power essential to the functioning of the courts, and as such itself violates the separation of powers doctrine."

It was "no exaggeration" to say that the government "cost the defendant his lawyer," but there was no Sixth Amendment violation because Osterhoudt would provide "outstanding representation." Although dismissal was "an extreme remedy which should be used infrequently," it was appropriate here, both to vindicate defendants' rights and "to preserve judicial integrity and/or to deter illegal or improper conduct." The government's misconduct was "egregious and flagrant," an "intentional violation of the long-standing ethical prohibition."

Little else "could pose a greater threat to the integrity of judicial proceedings than a directive from the executive branch instructing its employees to disregard a rule duly adopted by the courts." The memo was "a frontal assault on the legitimate powers of the court."

Other remedies were inadequate. Suppression was inappropriate because the government was not seeking to use evidence against this defendant. Judge Patel rejected contempt or state disciplinary proceedings because Lyons was following the Attorney General's policy (but this did not apply to Twitty, whose behavior she was referring to the State Bar). Patel was "deeply skeptical" about the deterrent effect of a verbal admonition, since the Thornburgh memo had been "roundly and publicly condemned by legal ethics experts, the ABA, numerous state bars, and members of Congress" without effect. Indeed, Thornburgh had recently affirmed his intention to "stand by" prosecutors who violated Rule 2-100. "Moreover, recent history suggests that the Department of Justice is not at all conscientious about disciplining those department attorneys who engage in misconduct *without* the cover of official policy." Dismissal was the only effective deterrent.

> This court will not allow the Attorney General to make a mockery of the court's constitutionally-granted judicial powers. . . . The title U.S. Attorney does not give the prosecutor a "hunting license exempt from ethical constraints of advocacy." . . . If anything, government prosecutors owe a higher duty to the court and the criminal justice system.

Tarlow called Patel's ruling "wonderful." It "sends a message to Washington this Attorney General's office ought not to be able to ignore."[33] Twitty commented: "What am I supposed to do? I can't listen to what he says and tell his lawyer. It's either that or walk away from him . . . and I don't think *that's* fair to a guy who's locked up." Osterhoudt said Twitty should have asked the court to get Lopez representation. "But you can't be the go-between" with the prosecution. What had "swayed the judge was that they were going to keep doing it no matter what." Gerald H. Goldstein, a San Antonio lawyer and vice-president of the National Association of Criminal Defense Lawyers, was "surprised only at the seeming arrogance of the U.S. government. Here is a concept any schoolboy understands—if you have two teams on the field, both have to play by the same rules." Michael L. Bender, a Denver lawyer who was chair of the ABA's Criminal Justice Section, agreed that "the logic is obvious," but "not many judges have the internal fortitude to take on the government in this way." Following Patel's opinion, both organizations met with Justice Department officials to discuss the Thornburgh policy.[34]

---

33. Don J. DeBenedictis, *Justice Ethics Policy Hit*, 77 ABAJ 20 (August 1991).

34. Fred Strasser, *Thornburgh Exemption Is Rebuked*, National Law Journal 3 (June 10, 1991).

III. THE DISCIPLINARY HEARING

A. The Lopez Case

Even before Tarlow contacted the State Bar, it had received multiple complaints about Twitty. Three involved convictions for drunk driving on May 15, 1985; July 21, 1987; and September 8, 1989. In each instance, Twitty pleaded not guilty, secured repeated continuances, changed counsel (sometimes representing himself), moved to suppress urine tests, demanded a jury trial, and once provoked the issuance of a bench warrant and a motion for sanctions—before being convicted by a jury in the first case and pleading *nolo contendere* in the others.

Three other complaints were from dissatisfied clients. Gerald Bilton, who had retained Twitty in 1986 to defend a criminal case, could not get his file after replacing the lawyer in March 1988. Dr. Yacoub and R. Malakooti, who retained Twitty in a civil matter, could not recover the unearned portion of their $1,500 retainer when they replaced him in February 1988. Kathryn Kilroy, who paid Twitty a $25,000 retainer to dissolve her marriage, could not get back the remaining $15,000 when she replaced him in May 1987. (That three sets of clients fired him in three years is troubling.) Twitty also failed to cooperate with State Bar investigators. Tarlow complained about Twitty in August 1990, soon after learning of the secret meetings and withdrawing from the case. All these complaints were consolidated in March 1991 and set for trial in July.

In August, Twitty's lawyer, Christopher E. Rollin, asked Hearing Examiner Janice Oehrle to drop the non-cooperation count. Twitty objected that "the investigator who called him basically did not accept his story and was rude and abusive." Mrs. Kilroy had sought only a partial refund, and Twitty had repaid the $15,000 before she contacted the State Bar. Lopez "went before the U.S. magistrate who fully briefed him of his constitutional rights and asked if he still wished to go forward with the meeting" with Lyons. Rollin had "trouble equating driving under the influence with failure to support the Constitution of the United States." Twitty had just begun a 30-month program for drunk drivers.

Oehrle replied that State Bar examiners had made numerous phone calls and written eight letters about the three client complaints, but Twitty never responded. He "ignores clients and medical providers as well." "Mr. Twitty seems to feel that he can just pick and choose who [*sic*] he responds to in this business." Mrs. Kilroy had demanded back her entire retainer, but Twitty had returned only $10,000 before the complaint. Twitty's defense that he had once represented Lopez was irrelevant to his behavior after being replaced by Tarlow. Twitty could offer additional facts about the drunk driving convictions only to mitigate the sanction, not to contest guilt. Oehrle's initial offer was three years probation without the Lopez matter and four with it.

Twitty's other lawyer, R. Gerald Markle, objected that the Office of Trial Counsel (OTC) "has insisted upon a full and unqualified admission from Mr. Twitty at every turn." Even if he did not respond "timely and fully" to each inquiry, Twitty had not ignored "the disciplinary process from beginning to end." Markle also sought to relitigate the Kilroy refund and the "entire [Lopez] count," despite Patel's decision.

> All Mr. Twitty did was listen to what a former client, Mr. Lopez, told him he wanted to do, under circumstances in which Mr. Lopez's counsel (Tarlow) had not only told him were appropriate, but which were the subject of an approving court order. Furthermore, Mr. Lopez knew that Mr. Tarlow would (as OTC puts it) "terminate his representation of Lopez if he became aware of the meetings" and would also make the fact that Lopez was participating in such meetings known to the people in Lopez' "community." What on earth is wrong with Mr. Twitty speaking with Lopez and following his instructions under these circumstances? [A footnote questioned whether Tarlow had withdrawn from representation in Lopez's interest or his own.] It seems OTC is most interested in protecting Tarlow's interests, perhaps at Lopez' expense. [A footnote asked why "Tarlow had the unfettered discretion to 'immediately terminate his representation of Lopez' in light of the ethical and procedural requirements that withdrawal of counsel be by the client's consent or the court's permission."] In summary, Mr. Twitty's conduct in the Lopez/Escobedo case does not warrant disapproval, much less discipline.

Markle deplored that the OTC was "unfortunately . . . fixed in concrete" about the Kilroy deposit and again sought to delete evidentiary details of his client's September 1989 drunk driving arrest. "Although Mr. Twitty concedes an alcohol problem (for which he has been receiving . . . treatment), he is not a drug addict of the sort for which this 'standard' condition [providing a blood or urine sample within six hours of a request] was created."

At the voluntary status conference in December, Philip L. Johnson, the trial judge, felt Twitty was at least "an aider and abettor" of Lyons and at worst "a party to a conspiracy." When Lopez asked Twitty to arrange a meeting with Lyons, the lawyer could have refused to discuss the request, withdrawn from the case, or told Tarlow. Johnson found "some indication" that Twitty feared he would lose "part of the case if he didn't go along."

Oerhle added that Twitty could have told Tarlow "his client had a strategy he wanted to discuss. . . ." Once Twitty talked to Lyons "he crossed over the line," "set the thing up . . . made it possible for everything that happened. . . ." Twitty told Lopez he "could represent both of them . . . [and] save him some money." In voir dire, Lopez expressed the belief that "I'm still going to have . . . my attorney . . . no matter what I do here. . . ." "He had to have been told that by Mr. Twitty," who "planted . . . a couple of seeds . . . one with Mr. Lopez . . . another with Mr. Lyons." Lopez was "thinking, 'I'm saving money . . . I'm going to be able to ask these couple of questions . . . but still, I'm going to have Mr. Tarlow.'" Twitty "put into motion a process which, eventually led to a disastrous result of having a criminal defendant, who had engaged in a very heinous crime against the public, not only [in] this country, but possibly [in] the world, set free . . . to go out and do that again. . . ." He also did "two more egregious things": he tried "to conceal it from Mr. Tarlow" and "lied about it to Mr. Rosenthal." These acts showed "he knew it was wrong when he did it." Johnson replied that he would evaluate Twitty's conduct without regard to Patel's dismissal of the case, which he blamed more on Lyons.

Markle maintained that "the seed . . . for the prospective discussions with Mr. Lyons, came from Mr. Lopez, not Mr. Twitty," whose "initial reaction" was

> don't do it . . . you've got a capable lawyer . . . if you talk to Mr. Lyons and you give him information . . . that may serve to compromise Mr. Tarlow's ability to represent your interest. Talk to Barry about this. . . . if you're convinced that Barry will abandon your ship, in the event that you express an interest in talking with Mr. Lyons, then, fire Barry and get another lawyer.

Twitty was "placed in a quandary" when Lopez persisted. Lopez knew that the odds of acquittal "were not great, and that Tarlow found the only other option—cooperation—offensive. This situation was not "orchestrated by Mr. Twitty." "Jose Lopez knew exactly what cards were on the table." Twitty ultimately accepted Lopez's "pleas, and he agreed to tell Mr. Lyons that Mr. Lopez wanted to talk with him. That's really all that he did." Lyons "is responsible" for everything "from that point forward." Lopez

> talked to Jim Twitty, because he had talked to Jim Twitty throughout the case, and indeed there was a time when Jim Twitty was his lawyer . . . . [T]he reason Mr. Lopez was in the dilemma he was in, is because Barry Tarlow finds cooperating with the government, morally and ethically anathema to him. This is a case where Barry Tarlow should be sitting in the chair that Jim Twitty is sitting in . . . those defendant clients of his have one arm tied behind their back. . . .

Tarlow had "a duty to represent whatever client he undertakes. . . ." If he had "a disagreement with the concept of cooperation as a defense tactic, then he shouldn't be in the defense business."

> Of all the people involved here . . . Mr. Twitty is the least responsible. Mr. Twitty is the only lawyer in this case who tried to do, and did, what he thought was in the best interest of Mr. Lopez and the best interest of his client.

Telling Tarlow "would have been a violation of Mr. Twitty's duty of loyalty" because Lopez was "Mr. Twitty's former client." Twitty did not act "out of any self interest." To make him "the fall guy for this situation" would do "a disservice to all of the lawyers and all of the clients in California" by sending a message to the Tarlows and Lyonses "that what they're doing is perfectly fine." "Mr. Twitty would agree, that if he were able to do it over again, he would probably do things differently, more or less out of self interest." "[F]rom a policy standpoint,: however, Markle believed that it's better for society for Mr. Twitty to have done . . . what he did. . . ."

Although Johnson promised his decision in two weeks, he took nearly five months, by which time the parties had settled all the cases except Lopez. Johnson found no failure to support the constitution or laws[35] or moral turpitude, dishonesty or corruption;[36] but he did find communication with a represented party without the other lawyer's consent.[37] Markle sought review of whether the failure to return Mrs. Kilroy's retainer constituted moral turpitude, and the Review Department found none.

Three months after Johnson's decision, the OTC wrote Twitty, alleging that Escobedo had paid him a $150,000 retainer with the understanding that any unearned amount would be returned.[38] Escobedo (who was serving his ten-year sentence at Terminal Island and would not be released until at least 1997) now complained that Twitty's bail motion had been unprofessional and he had filed no other motions, simply joining those of the co-defendants. For a year, he stopped visiting Escobedo, who could not reach him by phone. In April 1991, Escobedo discharged Twitty, whom he accused of having

> attempted to persuade him into cooperating with the government and that a deal had been made, and his problems were over. Mr. Lopez advised you that he did not want to discuss the matter any further without his attorney being present with him. You attempted to convince Mr. Lopez to go ahead without his attorney. Mr. Lopez would not agree to do this. Mr. Escobedo did not feel that you were acting in his best interest by calling this special meeting without anyone's knowledge and by trying to convince Mr. Escobedo to cooperate with the U.S. Attorney who was his adversary. Mr. Escobedo further alleges that a hearing was held regarding government misconduct wherein you lied to Judge Patel about the meeting you held with Mr. Escobedo, Mr. Lopez and the U.S. Attorney. . . . . Thereafter Mr. Escobedo terminated your services. You told Mr. Escobedo you would visit him to give him an accounting and refund the unearned fees. You never rendered any accounting to Mr. Escobedo, never visited him, and have failed to return the unearned fees.

B. Additional Complaints

Three months later, Markle sent Oehrle a revised stipulation and mitigation statement. He also commented on the Escobedo complaint and one by Robert Zehm, another criminal defendant who accused Twitty of neglect and failing to return the unearned balance of a retainer. Markle was "disappointed" that the OTC had "elected to withhold" these complaints, even though he had represented Twitty for over a year. Its suggestion that Markle was concerned to get

35. Business & Professions Code (BPC) §6068(a).
36. BPC Rule 6-106 (since repealed).
37. BPC Rule 2-100(A).
38. State Bar Exhibit 1 (Aug. 31, 1992).

business was "as absurd as it is insulting." He accused the OTC of the very "ethical violation" for which it had successfully prosecuted Twitty: communicating with a represented party without notice to counsel. Oehrle, in turn, took "great offense at [Markle's] insinuation." Neither Twitty nor Markle had bothered to respond to the OTC's numerous letters. Markle should "have the courtesy" to address her when communicating with the OTC.

C. The Penalty Phase

Twitty submitted his declaration in mitigation a few days later. He had declined to pursue a collateral attack on Bilton's conviction because Bilton failed to produce the requisite newly discovered evidence. When successor counsel asked for the file, Twitty said Mrs. Bilton, a paralegal in the case, had the complete file. "In hindsight, I should have simple [*sic*] turned over my file." Twitty delivered the Yacoub file to successor counsel but failed to refund the $1,500 retainer. "Although I believe that I provided valuable services to Dr. Yacoub and the other doctors, I regret omitting to define the terms of my representation and, in particular, the fee agreement clearly." He agreed to return the $1,500. When Mrs. Kilroy asked for a refund he gave her two checks, one for $10,000 dated on delivery and the other for $15,000 postdated a month. She deposited the second after that date but "before I told her that sufficient funds were on deposit." He wrote a good check in October 1988. After representing Helen Foulds on contingency, he put the disputed $19,000 fee in his client trust account but failed to respond to her new counsel about the matter. Six months later, he sued her for breach of contract. "I believe that I am entitled to the fee claimed, particularly since I obtained a very favorable result for Ms. Foulds under problematic circumstances." The next day, he stipulated to Johnson's finding of a Rule 2-100(A) violation. A week later, Johnson recommended two years suspension, 30 days actual, and four years probation.

But two weeks after that, the OTC served Twitty with a notice to show cause (NTSC) on the two new counts.[39] Robert Zehm retained him on November 1, 1990, to file a Rule 35 petition challenging his criminal conviction, paying $5,000 in December and $15,000 in April 1991. Nevada local counsel missed the December 26 filing deadline by one day. Because this local counsel posed a possible conflict of interest, the federal court took eleven months to rule on Zehm's request to let Twitty and the local counsel substitute in. During this period, Zehm wrote Twitty repeatedly about the status of his case, eliciting inadequate responses. On October 2, 1991, the court allowed substitution and denied the Rule 35 petition as untimely but said Zehm could seek relief under 28 USC Section 2255. Zehm told Twitty he would do so *pro per* and asked for an accounting of fees and return of the unearned portion at least five times,

39. Case 92-O-10286 (Zehm); Case 92-O-15109 (Escobedo).

without response. When Zehm's *pro per* request was stricken on December 3 because he was still represented, he asked the court's help in removing Twitty. On April 13, 1992, the court ordered Twitty to withdraw or designate new counsel by June 2; he failed to do so until September 30. He also failed to respond to State Bar investigators in February and March 1992.

When Twitty moved to review Johnson's decision, the Review Department held that the stipulation bound the parties. Twitty denied the new charges and insisted both sides had reserved their rights to seek review. If this were denied, he would seek to try the entire case. The OTC supported him. The Review Department relented but warned it was "obligated to review the entire record" and might adopt "findings, conclusions and a decision or recommendation at variance with those of the hearing department."

D. The Ninth Circuit Modifies the Lopez Decision

The day before this latest ruling, the Ninth Circuit reversed Patel's dismissal.[40] By abandoning its reliance on the Thornburgh memorandum, the government had "spared us the need of reiterating the District Court's trenchant analysis of the inefficacy of the Attorney General's policy statement." Instead, the government argued that Rule 2-100 was not intended to apply to prosecutors during investigations, contact with Lopez was authorized by law, he was exercising his constitutional right to self-representation, and he had waived his rights under Rule 2-100.

The court held that Rule 2-100 applied to prosecutors from the moment of indictment. The magistrate's approval of the meeting was predicated on the "mistaken belief, fostered by Lyons," that Tarlow was being paid by a third party and Lopez feared he would pass information to those who would harm his family. Lopez could not waive Rule 2-100, which was "fundamentally concerned with the *duties* of attorneys, not the *rights* of parties." But though Lyons violated the rule, it was an abuse of discretion to dismiss the indictment because Osterhoudt was "very able" and Lopez not "substantially prejudiced."

Judge Betty D. Fletcher, concurring, was far more critical of all the lawyers. Tarlow was "not free to terminate his . . . representation of a client at will, or for mere personal considerations, or without the permission of the court."[41] "Moral repugnance" was not an adequate reason. Had there been "sufficient candor and trust" between lawyer and client, Lopez would not have felt "compelled to resort

---

40. U.S. v. Lopez, 4 F.3d 1455 (9th Cir. 1993) (District Judge Cecile F. Poole with District Judge Thomas G. Nelson).

41. This is incorrect. Tarlow informed Lopez at the outset that he would not conduct negotiations and would withdraw if Lopez decided to inform; and Judge Smith permitted Tarlow to withdraw. Freedman (1993). Tarlow (1995) defended his position. The U.S. Attorney's motion for a rehearing because of the majority's criticism of Lyons and Thornburgh was denied.

to clandestine meetings with the government." Twitty's conduct was "less than exemplary." Whatever "benign intentions" he may have had, "he ended up representing two defendants who had potentially conflicting interests." He "apparently advised both Lopez and Escobedo during the first meeting with the government, and may have pressured Lopez to provide information to the prosecutor during the second." Because Lyons insisted on a package deal, Escobedo "had an incentive to pressure Lopez to cop as well. Under these circumstances, Twitty was the wrong person to be acting on Lopez's behalf during plea discussions with the government." Lyons had "effectively misled" the magistrate who, in turn, failed to ask about Lopez's fee arrangement or whether he feared for his family's safety. "Contrary to the intent of the Sixth Amendment," Lopez "was left to face the 'prosecutorial forces of society' alone. . . ."

Osterhoudt called the opinion "a complete rejection of the government's claims" but was "disappointed that the court didn't sustain the dismissal" and planned to seek an *en banc* rehearing.[42] Lyons insisted he had never misled Wilken about Lopez's reasons for wanting to circumvent Tarlow. The court's decision was "contrary to what the record provides." U.S Attorney John Mendez also did "not accept the findings that Lyons misled the court or was reckless" and planned to ask the solicitor general to appeal because of Judge Nelson's criticism of both Lyons and Thornburgh. Tarlow moved to strike Fletcher's concurrence. "I just didn't walk out. The judge gave me permission to withdraw. You do not have to participate in conduct you find morally offensive."[43]

42. Rex Bossert, *Prosecutor Loses Battle on Ethics, But Case Revived,* LOS ANGELES DAILY JOURNAL 1 (Mar. 18, 1993). It was not granted.

43. Howard Mintz, *9th Circuit Attacks Feds for Talking to Suspects,* THE RECORDER 1 (Mar. 18, 1993); Monroe Freedman, *The Dilemmas of Double Lawyering,* THE RECORDER 10 (May 7, 1993). The Supreme Court did not hear the case; Fletcher's concurrence was not stricken. Another U.S Attorney subsequently failed to remove his similar New Mexico disciplinary proceeding to federal court, In re Doe, 801 F.Supp. 478 (D.N.M. 1992), and failed to enjoin the proceeding, U.S. v. Ferrara, 847 F.Supp. 964 (D.D.C. 1993), order aff'd, 54 F.3d 825 (D.C. Cir. 1995). The U.S. District Court in New Mexico rejected removal of another disciplinary proceeding for the same offense, In re Gorence, 810 F.Supp. 1234 (D.N.M. 1992). *See* Tarlow (1992; 1997). Clinton administration Attorney General Janet Reno significantly changed the Thornburgh policy after meeting with the ABA Litigation Section. Communications with Represented Persons, 59 Fed. Reg. 39,910 (Aug. 4, 1994), codified at 28 C.F.R. pt. 77. *See Compromise Sought with Defense Lawyers on Limits to Investigative Power,* DAILY REP. FOR EXECUTIVES 4 (Oct. 15, 1993). Courts subsequently applied state ethics rules to federal prosecutors. U.S. ex rel. O'Keefe v. McDonnell Douglas Corp., 132 F.3d 1252 (8th Cir. 1998); Matter of Howes, 123 N.M. 311, 940 P.2d. 159 (1997); *but see* U.S. v. Colorado Supreme Court, 988 F.Supp. 1268 (D. Colo. 1998), judgment aff'd, 189 F.3d 1281 (10th Cir. 1999). In October 1998, Congress passed the Citizens Protection Act, which explicitly subjected federal prosecutors to state ethical rules. It had been pushed by Rep. McDade, who was angry at the DOJ for unsuccessfully prosecuting him. The DOJ then persuaded Sen. Orrin Hatch (R-Utah) to sponsor SB 250, effectively repealing the

After a jury found Lopez guilty of all five counts in March 1995, Judge Patel sentenced him to 135 months, a three-level downward departure from the sentencing guidelines because the government's conduct "seriously affected" Lopez's opportunity for full and fair plea negotiations. The Court of Appeal affirmed in February 1997.[44]

E. The Review Department

In the Review Department, Twitty argued that he had "broad permission from Tarlow to communicate with Lopez for the purpose of preparing joint defenses. . . ."[45] Lopez sought a second opinion from Twitty, who alone "set aside considerations of self-interest in favor of the interests of justice." Tarlow and Lyons "each had their own agendas." Just as Lopez had feared, Tarlow withdrew when he learned of Lopez's cooperation. This was "consistent with [Tarlow's] practice generally," which "effectively deprive[s] his clients . . . of the full panoply of rights. . . ." Twitty's phone call to Lyons "reflected an effort to fill the void left by Tarlow's unprincipled representation. . . ." To have done what Johnson required "would have been to cast Lopez adrift. . . ." "If the subsequent communications between Lopez and Lyons violated Rule 2-100, then it is Lyons who is culpable of the violation . . . not Twitty."

The State Bar replied that Lopez testified that Twitty had told him Tarlow was unnecessary to the meeting with Lyons, and it would be "easier . . . to work something out" without Tarlow. Lopez also denied that Tarlow had ever threatened to withdraw if Lopez cooperated. Tarlow testified that he had assured Lopez he would resume representation if negotiations failed and had withdrawn because of the "deceit and secrecy," not the negotiations themselves. Lopez had consistently planned to tell Tarlow about the outcome of negotiations. Twitty could not offer a "second opinion" because he was "representing another client with adverse interests." It was Twitty, not Tarlow, who cast Lopez adrift. He "actively encouraged Lopez to participate in negotiations with the government without Tarlow," during which "Lopez was unrepresented and on his own while Respondent was off in the corner conferring with his own client." Twitty said he did not care that Lopez had hired Tarlow "as long as he [Twitty] was in charge of the whole case. His actions here reflect that he acted as if he were, indeed, in charge of the whole case."

In September 1993, the State Bar Court judge hearing the new charges, David S Wesley, granted Markle a continuance because of "the breakdown in communications between Twitty and his counsel," which began soon after Johnson

---

McDade Bill. Hatch's initiative was opposed by the American Corporate Counsel Association, the U.S. Chamber of Commerce, and the ABA. Tarlow (1999).

44. U.S. v. Lopez, 106 F.3d 309 (9th Cir. 1997).

45. Tarlow denied he had ever agreed on a joint defense. Telephone conversation, Jan. 26, 2009.

issued his May 1992 judgment. Oehrle also sought to reopen discovery to depose Escobedo (which another OTC lawyer had failed to do). Wesley granted both requests.

Allowed by the Review Department to file a supplemental brief, Twitty argued that the merely potential conflict of interest did not prevent him from offering Lopez a second opinion as an "independent lawyer." The ABA directed a lawyer to "decline to act for more than one of several co-defendants except in unusual situations," one of which was Tarlow's "self-imposed 'personal, moral and ethical' policy" and Lyons's reliance on the Thornburgh memo. After conducting the "careful investigation" urged by the ABA, Twitty "reasonably and correctly" concluded no conflict was likely to develop. Both defendants had "all the necessary information" and shared a "mutual desire to learn about the availability of a negotiated resolution through discussion with Lyons." The State Bar replied that Twity's second Rule 2-100 violation required another year of probation.

In his pretrial statement in the new cases, Twitty declared that Zehm had paid him $20,000 to file a post-conviction challenge to his three-year sentence for "a sophisticated narcotics trafficking scheme." Because Zehm also was being investigated for other drug crimes, they discussed cooperating in these to persuade the Nevada Assistant U.S. Attorney to recommend a more lenient sentence if they were successful in setting aside the original one. Twitty retained a Miami lawyer to work on the Federal Rule of Civil Procedure (FRCP) Rule 35 motion, paying him $5,000. They delayed the filing because success would just lead to reimposition of the mandatory sentence; but they ultimately sent it to local counsel, who missed the deadline. Twitty denied failing to communicate with Zehm and insisted he had earned his fee. Similarly, he claimed to have "performed all of the services necessary to Escobedo's defense," remained "in regular communication with Escobedo," and "fully earned" his fee. Wesley scheduled Escobedo's testimony but vacated that when the parties settled.

The Review Department issued its decision in January 1994 (before the parties had arrived at the final wording of their stipulation).[46] It agreed with Judge Patel that Twitty encouraged Lopez and Escobedo to negotiate with Lyons and advised both during the meeting. It rejected most of Twitty's factual arguments, especially his claim of authority to explore a deal for Lopez, since he assiduously sought to hide that from Tarlow, who had never threatened to withdraw if Lopez negotiated. Twitty's representation of Escobedo prevented him from offering Lopez an independent second opinion. The Review Department found several aggravating circumstances. The drunk driving convictions were supplemented by one for fighting in a public place. After improperly communicating with Lopez, Twitty lied about this to Rosenthal. In sentencing, the department focused on Twitty's "most serious misconduct . . . his improper communications with a

46. Matter of Twitty, 2 Cal. State Bar Ct. Rptr 664 (1994).

represented party," which both the U.S. District and Court of Appeal judges viewed as "very serious ethical breaches." By involving Lopez in secret plea negotiations, Twitty destroyed the "trust and confidence" necessary to the attorney–client relationship and may have compromised the entrapment defense. His misconduct was worse than that of Lyons, who followed the Attorney General's memo and approached the judge. The secret meetings wasted "considerable judicial time and effort" and lengthened the criminal case against Lopez by about three years. The Review Department relieved the parties of their stipulation and remanded the case to let them reach a new one or try the outstanding issues. Finding the proposed sanction inadequate, it instructed the hearing judge to recommend discipline in light of this opinion.

F. The Retrial

Wesley rejected the parties' stipulation in the two outstanding cases (which would have dismissed most of the charges) and added a 30-day suspension, stayed, and a year's probation. Twitty agreed to provide Zehm and Escobedo with an accounting of fees within 60 days and advise them of their right to arbitrate. Markle moved for permission to withdraw because Twitty had stopped communicating in spring 1993, resumed that fall as the trial date approached, then communicated less, and stopped entirely in March 1994. Wesley granted the motion. The OTC moved for sanctions against Twitty for failing to file his pretrial statement. Two days before the scheduled trial, the parties filed a joint stipulation about facts and culpability, which Wesley rejected. Twitty offered in mitigation that he had performed 7,000 hours of community service over the previous seven years, helped to reorganize and revitalize the local (Malibu) bar, of which he was secretary-treasurer, and had been dry since 1989. The parties recommended two years of suspension, 60 days actual, three years probation, and full accounting to Escobedo. The Supreme Court approved this (with slight modifications) in April 1995. The suspension began May 12.[47] Tarlow exulted (and exaggerated) that "California Supreme Court Dumps" "Jim ('Dump Truck') Twitty."[48] "[T]rue to form," Twitty "eagerly" "had inveigled Lopez into engaging in cooperation negotiations" in "flagrant disregard" of ethical rules and "deliberately concealed" this from Tarlow, "while making a litany of false claims to others that he was authorized. . . ." Tarlow hoped "the sanctions will help to discourage similar misconduct by other unscrupulous defense lawyers."

Twitty failed to comply with the Rule 955 order to notify clients, opposing counsel, and other parties of his suspension; he submitted the necessary affidavit of restitution to the Supreme Court in February 1996, eight months late. He was suspended again in May 1996 for failing to file quarterly reports, timely

47. "James Allen Twitty," *Los Angeles Daily Journal* 9 (June 26, 1995).
48. Tarlow (1996).

evidence of enrollment in a substance abuse program, and evidence of completion of an accounting course. Although the State Bar recommended disbarment (the usual penalty), the State Bar Court was moved by evidence that Twitty suffered from severe depression (because of his inability to practice law!) and extensive testimony about his good character, competence, and community service. It ordered a three-year suspension, stayed, three years of probation, and actual suspension from April 20, 1997 for one year and until he proved his rehabilitation.[49] Because Twitty then failed to comply with the conditions of his probation (filing reports late), it was revoked, and he was suspended for sixteen months, effective January 4, 1998, with credit for earlier involuntary inactive enrollment since May 13, 1996.[50] He was suspended again on July 21, 1997 for failure to pay Bar membership fees. In March 2002, he was declared administratively inactive for noncompliance with mandatory continuing legal education and has not been readmitted. Tarlow filed a complaint against Lyons with the Arizona State Bar, but Supreme Court rules make the outcome confidential.

IV. CONFLICT OF INTEREST IN CRIMINAL DEFENSE

Although the protagonists in this drama differ about details, the broad outlines of their actions are clear. The real ambiguity lies in their understandings and motivations. I will deal with the actors in turn, trying to explicate their accounts while acknowledging the inconsistencies, both internal and mutual.

Lopez seems to have initiated the chain of events. If Myers is correct about Lyons's initial offers, Lopez faced the longest sentence. Lopez also expressed the greatest anxiety about his children: His eldest son had been placed in care and then returned to his hostile ex-wife, who was obstructing Lopez's contact with the boy. (Lyons confirmed that Lopez was close to tears when they discussed this.) His desperation to get out of jail may have led him to exaggerate what Lyons did and could offer. Lopez himself said his mind "wasn't so one hundred percent there." It was implausible that in a drug deal this big (which eventually got him ten years) he would be released before trial (as bait for the drug source) and ultimately given probation and witness protection. He may also have been motivated by anger that Alberto, Carlos, and Alfonso (the informant) had used Escobedo and him as fall guys for two others on parole (who initially faced longer sentences). Indeed, Alfonso's actions were the basis for Lopez's entrapment defense.

Lopez gave multiple reasons for meeting Lyons without Tarlow. He seemed confused about which lawyers were loyal to which clients. At first Twitty had

49. 95-PM-1415. *James Alan Twitty*, Los Angeles Daily Journal 9 (May 5, 1997).
50. 95-N-16497.

represented both Escobedo and him. He called Twitty "my appeal attorney . . . the one doing my appeal . . . for bail." He said Rosenthal represented both Escobedo and Olivas. He claimed Twitty had told Escobedo and him to talk to Lyons, saying it would be easier without Tarlow, and had tried to advise him at the first meeting, until Lyons objected.

Lopez said he mistrusted all lawyers (an attitude tragically validated by the behavior of those involved in this case). But then why did he hire such a highly respected one and express so much concern about losing him; and why did he trust Twitty? Rightly believing Tarlow would not participate in negotiations, Lopez planned to hire another attorney to finalize the deal. He suspected public defenders of working for the government (a common cynicism among accused)[51] and rejected an appointed lawyer for fear this would become a pretext for denying him Tarlow. Since he was paying Tarlow by the hour, Lopez was concerned about the expense "out of my pocket" of prison visits to discuss negotiations and represent him in the meetings with Lyons. By using Twitty, Lopez was free riding on Escobedo's $150,000 retainer. Indeed, Lopez claimed that Twitty offered to represent him at no charge if he negotiated without Tarlow. Lopez did not originate the rumor that Tarlow was being paid by drug dealers, whom he would alert if Lopez negotiated with the government or fired him. He blamed his estranged ex-wife for starting the rumor that drug dealers threatened the children, in order seek both custody and government protection. Lopez rightly observed that he would not be worried about expense if drug dealers were paying Tarlow. He insisted he had planned to reveal the outcome of negotiations to Tarlow, who inevitably would learn about them since he had a discovery order for all contacts between Lopez and the government. But then why did Lopez tell Twitty, the magistrate, and Lyons he did not want Tarlow to know about the negotiations? Because he was afraid his lawyer would be angry and withdraw?

Lopez thought he could do better on his own and was only going to ask two questions. He was naïve about what would happen when he talked to Lyons, believing he could get answers without providing information. He disregarded the magistrate's warning that Twitty was seeking a better deal for Escobedo, his client. The formal waiver (which the magistrate seems to have written *before* the voir dire) erroneously stated that Lopez did not believe Tarlow represented his best interests and did not want his lawyer to know about the meeting. Lopez inconsistently maintained both that he did not want to cooperate with the prosecution and that he was eager to return to the community, contact the drug dealers, and help make the case against them. He started by saying nothing but soon found himself talking more and more freely, at the second meeting even describing how he got the drugs. He credulously credited Lyons's assurances that everything was off the record and nothing could be used against him. He said he had not yet

51. Casper (1993).

decided whether to cooperate, suggesting he did not appreciate the significance of giving Lyons information. He believed that secretly talking to Lyons would not deprive him of Tarlow's representation at trial. Lopez claimed that Lyons tried to get information out of him at the first meeting, even though the waiver of counsel was limited to Lyons answering two questions. He also said that Lyons (and perhaps Twitty) pushed him to furnish good information at the second meeting, where he did most of the talking.

Escobedo's role is less clear. Lopez described him as "kind of pushy." He may have suggested that Lopez talk to Lyons without Tarlow. Escobedo seems to have played on their shared love for their children. If Escobedo decided to do a deal, he had to involve Lopez, since Lyons had made it clear he would only consider them together. Escobedo's later disciplinary complaint against Twitty may have been opportunistic: once he was doing time he had nothing to lose in making it; and most prisoners feel a sense of injustice, which they vent at any available target (often their lawyers). Escobedo alleged that Twitty pressured both Lopez and him to plead and did nothing to defend him, leaving the burden on Tarlow. Both retainers created perverse incentives: Escobedo's $150,000 advance encouraged Twitty to minimize his effort; hourly fees (like those Lopez paid Tarlow) motivate lawyers to maximize their efforts (e.g., by trying cases).

The California State Bar had no control over Lyons, who was admitted in Arizona. But Osterhoudt's motion to dismiss necessarily exposed the prosecutor to judicial scrutiny. Ten years earlier, the Justice Department's Office of Legal Counsel had opined that non-lawyer conformity to disciplinary rules was "solely a question of policy." Two years after doing so, the Department extended that view to lawyers. Just before this case arose, Attorney General Thornburgh authorized prosecutors to deal directly with represented accused. Despite her outrage, Judge Patel had no way of countermanding the attorney general's directive, which complicated the legal (and ethical) evaluation of the conduct of Lyons, who was just following orders.

Lyons vividly showed how excessive zeal to convict induces prosecutors to violate ethical rules. He insisted on a package deal for Lopez and Escobedo and wanted them to name the drug source so he could clear up other crimes. Although he knew Lopez did not want to inform, he persisted in seeking cooperation. Before the first meeting, he assured Wilken he would not use anything Lopez said, disregarding the magistrate's instruction that he could only answer Lopez's two questions and not seek *any* information. He sought to "disabuse" the magistrate of her "misimpression" (although she was right). He insisted that the waiver allowed him to do more but then admitted the magistrate had said to return before going further. Lyons told Lopez before the second meeting that everything was off the record, obscuring the inevitable influence of the information on the course of the prosecution. Indeed, he warned Lopez that Escobedo (and Twitty) could use what they heard at the second meeting. He claimed to have forgotten telling Twitty that he had verified some of Lopez's facts. He played the bad cop at the second meeting, dressing down the defendants, demanding they name the drug source and cooperate in the prosecution, refusing to consider their release (while holding out that possibility in the future). Although Lyons heard Twitty deny that Tarlow was being paid by a third party (a statement in which Lopez silently acquiesced), the prosecutor extended the memo to other situations where the client feared the consequences if the lawyer learned about plea negotiations. Lyons disregarded Lopez's assertion that he intended to tell Tarlow, who inevitably would find out anyhow.

Lyons made several revealing misstatements. He referred to Lopez as Twitty's client, confused Lopez with Escobedo, and talked about Twitty and "my guy" as though Lopez was Twitty's client. He also said Twitty advised both defendants during the meeting. Lyons fell back on other rationalizations for his behavior. Lopez initiated the contact. Given his knowing and voluntary waiver of counsel, there was no need for the magistrate to conduct a voir dire of him. Lyons maintained that the information Lopez disclosed was worthless and did not compromise the defense. The prosecutor's conduct was appropriate unless there was "no danger to the defendant at all" or "no legitimate and rational reason why the defendant's lawyer cannot be informed or cannot be replaced." Lyons was so certain the drug source had threatened Lopez's family that he never discussed this with Twitty. Twitty told Lyons that Lopez said "Tarlow didn't represent his best interest in this particular situation." Although Lyons denied telling Lopez or Twitty that negotiations would be smoother without Tarlow, both remembered him saying it. When Osterhoudt accused Lyons of strategizing to get Tarlow to withdraw, the prosecutor insisted he was not clever enough for that.

Lyons embraced a preconception about what he kept calling the "general situation," disregarding inconsistent evidence. He "thought" he knew why Lopez was concerned "based on my understanding they have these kind [*sic*] of situations." He told Judge Smith that the drug source generally pays the lawyer, misinformation the judge seems to have passed on to the magistrate (who kept insinuating it to Lopez despite his refusal to concur). Lyons did not ask Lopez if Tarlow was being paid by another because the information would be "inculpatory." Although Lopez had said only that Tarlow refused to participate in negotiations, Lyons himself decided this meant Tarlow would withdraw if there were negotiations (indeed, that may have been Lyons's motive for participating). Even in front of Judge Patel, Lyons continued to maintain that Lopez may have gotten money for Tarlow from Mr. Big and told Tarlow that (though it is unclear why this would matter).[52]

Lyons was woefully ignorant of the ABA prosecutorial standards, which prohibit meeting a represented client without the lawyer's approval and require a

52. Tarlow denied knowing anything about how Lopez paid his fee.

verbatim transcript of any such meetings. He was unaware that the Northern District of California had adopted those standards, which he disparaged as "merely advisory." He maintained that a prosecutorial offer was not part of negotiations and his contacts with the defendants were "pre-indictment" because they pertained to possible future indictments for other crimes—arguments that did not pass the laugh test. He claimed that the supremacy clause trumped ethical standards that were "inconsistent with my duties as a federal prosecutor." (But the supremacy clause is irrelevant to *federal* courts.) He claimed that the "authorized by law" exception included his legal obligation to prosecute (and use Lopez's offer to complete this and other prosecutions)—an exception that would swallow the rule. He outraged Judge Patel by arguing that only the DOJ, not she, could interpret "authorized by law." He could not cite any case authorizing his conduct because it was up to him to "make a judgment." Government should not be penalized for acting in good faith. Challenged by Patel, he complained that she distinguished his (inapposite) analogies. He dismissed her criticisms as mere disagreement with DOJ "policy." He invoked separation of powers as a justification for ignoring ethical rules imposed by the judiciary. His duty as an officer of the court obligated him to behave in "the most highly professional manner I can"—but not to obey ethical rules.

Although Twitty's lawyer argued that Tarlow, not Twitty, should be before the State Bar, Tarlow violated no ethical rule. He claims to have told Lopez he would communicate any plea offer but not negotiate with the government because another lawyer could do so more cheaply (since it required less skill) and more effectively (given Tarlow's well-earned reputation for vigorous advocacy). Tarlow had assured Lopez that if negotiations failed he would still represent his client at trial. (But Lopez expressed anxiety about this, which Judge Fletcher attributed to the defendant's antecedent lack of trust in Tarlow.) Tarlow justified his withdrawal on the ground that the secret negotiations compromised his defense strategy and undermined the essential trust between lawyer and client. But it is also true that Tarlow's profound suspicion of prosecutors aggravated these consequences.

The behavior of the defendants, other lawyers, and judges helps to illuminate Twitty's conduct, my real concern. How did he behave toward Lopez, and why? At first he seems to have represented all three accused, ostensibly in bail applications but inevitably also in strategizing about their defense. There were potential conflicts even at that early stage, since the government could use bail to play defendants off against each other. But the experience may have led Twitty to feel he could continue representing Lopez even after he became Tarlow's client. Tarlow may have reinforced this belief by his reluctance to visit Lopez in jail and his consequent willingness to let Twitty keep strategizing with Lopez. But Tarlow's determination to try the case must have felt to Twitty like an interference. Twitty claimed to have Tarlow's authority "to do anything at all necessary for the general defense and working out of the case"; but under pressure from Osterhoudt and Patel, he admitted that "Mr. Tarlow did not tell me that I had authority to negotiate anything with the government on behalf of Mr. Lopez." Twitty offered to have a friend represent Lopez free of charge in the meetings with Lyons. When the defendants got Lyons's written offer, Twitty offered to represent Lopez in finalizing it. Markle even argued that Twitty had a duty to Lopez as a former client. Twitty argued that he could act for Lopez under an exception to the conflict of interest rules, disregarding the fact that Lopez was represented. He claimed that the conflict was only potential and the defendants both wanted to learn what the government would offer. But each did not want to disclose to the other what he would give in return or get (at the expense of the other).

Twitty offered contradictory and implausible accounts of how Lopez came to retain Tarlow. Twitty originally proposed that he and a Milwaukee friend represent all three defendants. But given the potential conflicts, Twitty should not have mentioned any lawyers to the others (much less his friends). Twitty claimed to have suggested Tarlow; but Lopez was adamant that he had gotten the name from a jailhouse lawyer, who had a book touting Tarlow's accomplishments.[53] Given Twitty's knowledge that Tarlow would vigorously defend the charges and refuse to negotiate, it seems unlikely that Twitty would recommend him. Although Twitty claimed that he and Tarlow divided up the clients, Tarlow maintains that Lopez called him cold.[54]

There was considerable evidence that Twitty wanted Lopez to get rid of Tarlow (despite Twitty's understandable denial). Twitty said Lyons found Tarlow abrasive. He himself said Tarlow believed "you could not and should trust anything that the government had to say about the case." Tarlow filed discovery motions, while Twitty successfully negotiated these matters with Lyons. As early as the first discovery dispute, Twitty said Lyons told him the case could be resolved more easily without Tarlow. Twitty seems to have repeated this to both defendants. Twitty said both Lopez and he believed negotiating would provoke Tarlow to withdraw. And Twitty said Lyons stated, and Lopez understood, that he would have to replace Tarlow if he pleaded guilty. Twitty claimed to have advised Lopez against negotiating; but he and Escobedo negotiated with Lyons and required Lopez's participation in order to succeed. Twitty emphasized to Lyons that Lopez did not want Tarlow to learn about the negotiations. When Lyons inadvertently disclosed them to Rosenthal, Twitty lied and then urged Rosenthal to keep the secret from Tarlow, who "would mess up the deal." (Twitty blamed both actions on Lopez.) Twitty insisted (unconvincingly) he was not angry at Tarlow, although

---

53. Tarlow denied that Twitty ever sent him any case. Telephone conversation (Jan 26, 2009).

54. He remembered because he got the call during the Thanksgiving weekend. Telephone conversation, June 2009.

Tarlow had written two uncomplimentary columns about him and complained to the State Bar.[55]

Twitty offered a number of rationalizations that were unpersuasive at best and sometimes frivolous. He claimed that Lopez initiated the contact with Lyons, threatening to call the prosecutor directly if Twitty declined to mediate. But there is evidence that Escobedo urged Lopez do to this, and that Twitty wanted Escobedo to plead and knew Lyons demanded a package deal. Even if Twitty was carrying out Lopez's request, that action still raised ethical concerns. Twitty claimed to be offering Lopez a second opinion. But even if Lopez sought one (for which there was no evidence), *Twitty* could not offer it while representing Escobedo. And he did much more than advise Lopez; he acted as his lawyer. Twitty claimed that Lopez talked to him because they were friends. He persisted in declaring that Lopez and his family were in danger. (If anyone was suspect of being paid by drug dealers it was Twitty, who received a $150,000 retainer from Escobedo and a $20,000 retainer from Zahm, another convicted drug dealer. Maybe that is why he explicitly told Lyons that nobody he supposedly worked for was paying Lopez's fees.) He reiterated that allegation before Judge Patel, seeking (unsuccessfully) to close the hearing and (successfully) to submit his declaration under seal. Markle reiterated the danger that Tarlow would transmit information about the plea negotiations to "the community." Twitty sought to assert Lopez's attorney-client privilege even though he was not Lopez's lawyer. At the same time, he admitted that Escobedo was present when Lopez spoke, which would eliminate any such privilege. Then he denied that Tarlow owned the lawyer-client privilege and asserted that Twitty could not stop Lopez from talking to anyone (both of which were irrelevant). Twitty maintained that he did not advise Lopez at the second meeting and also that Lopez gave nothing away. But Lopez insisted Twitty jumped up when he named Alberto, confirming the significance of that name to Lyons. And Lopez did give Lyons the name of the drug source.

Given the stakes in criminal prosecutions and the vulnerability of defendants, it is amply clear why neither prosecutors nor lawyers for other parties (co-defendants or civil plaintiffs) should be allowed to communicate with represented parties.

---

55. In March, Tarlow (1991) described *Lopez* as "the case where Assistant United States Attorney AUSA [*sic*] John Lyons and erstwhile defense lawyer James Twitty of Los Angeles joined in a conspiracy to interview the author's client during a pending criminal case and concealed the secret communications after the deal collapsed." "Jim 'DT' (Dump Truck) Twitty, attempted to maintain a low profile during the hearing. However, an objective analysis demonstrates that his machinations were at least as ethically or morally culpable as the conduct of Lyons."

7. CHAMPIONING THE "DEFENSELESS" AND "OPPRESSED," PROTECTING "WIDOWS AND CHILDREN"

I. RESPECT FOR THE JUDICIAL PROCESS

Lawyers play many essential roles in the administration of justice. One of the most sensitive is mediating between their clients' passions and the integrity of the judicial process. A lawyer must obey "an order of the court requiring him to do or forbear an act connected with or in the course of his profession," as well as the attorney's oath.[1] Lawyers may be tempted to violate these obligations by identifying too closely with clients and causes or becoming personally hostile to opposing counsel or the court.

Some defense lawyers cross the boundary between representing clients charged with past crimes and facilitating further crime. Robert Lahodny, son of the Coronado city manager, referred many clients to Phillip DeMassa and then persuaded the lawyer to invest in a Santa Barbara house, which Lahodny would renovate and, live in rent free and then share in the resale profit.[2] DeMassa, representing targets of a grand jury investigation into the Coronado Company for international drug dealing, claimed not to know at the time that Lahodny was a company "runner." After the indictment revealed this, Lahodny left for a long "vacation" in Mexico and Tahiti and returned under an alias, resuming the renovation and giving contractors large cash tips. After a driving under the influence (DUI) arrest, in which Lahodny gave another alias, he spent two days at the Santa Barbara house with DeMassa, who referred him to a lawyer, who pleaded Lahodny under the alias without ever meeting him. Lahodny ultimately surrendered to face the drug charges. Charged as a co-conspirator with the Coronado Company, DeMassa pleaded to harboring a fugitive and three currency offenses.

Some lawyers simply tamper with the judicial process. Waldo A. Brown paid a municipal court clerk to dismiss DUI charges on a plea to the lesser offense of reckless driving, without notifying the judge or prosecutor.[3] After Respondent A lost a personal injury case for a friend's permanently disabled eighteen-year-old son,

---

1. Business & Professions Code (BPC) §6103.

2. Matter of DeMassa, 1 Calif. State Bar Ct. Rptr. 737 (1991) (60-day suspension, one-year probation).

3. Matter of Brown, 2 Calif. State Bar Ct. Rptr. 309 (1993) (resigned with disciplinary charges pending).

the lawyer wrote all the jurors explaining the unavailability of Workers' Compensation, the employer's obligation to protect employee safety, and the inadequacy of the defendant's $50,000 settlement offer.[4] He also complimented three named jurors who voted for liability, and noted that his office had paid all the jurors' per diem and a third of their lunch expenses. Donald J. Loftus concealed from a doctor the fact that he planned to sue for malpractice, secretly recorded their conversation, and then lied about doing so.[5] After losing the case, he telephoned a juror at work, asked about the judge's decision to suspend deliberations for a day and, when the juror refused to provide an affidavit about this, threatened to tell the juror's employer. Representing the father in a child support dispute, Henry D. Fandey gave his client two books on how to change his identity, advised him on how to avoid leaving a paper trail, arranged to sell his California house, helped him move to El Paso, and found him a place there.[6] After Daisy Palella was sued for divorce in Texas, Daniel M. Chesnut sought to avoid that court's jurisdiction by falsely claiming he had personally served her husband in California.[7] Defending an unlawful detainer, John F. Farrell falsely claimed that another tenant of the landlord had been subpoenaed, substituted that name on another subpoena, and served it when the tenant voluntarily appeared in court.[8] Representing the temporary conservator of a defendant and cross-complainant in a personal injury action, Thomas J. Jeffers repeatedly sought continuances and failed to appear at hearings, responding evasively when the judge asked about the defendant's failure to communicate before ultimately admitting that the defendant was dead; Jeffers had also concealed the defendant's assets.[9] Representing himself and his mother in bitter property disputes with his ex-wife, Walter A. Varakin sued her and her lawyer for slander and infliction of emotional distress.[10] Over the course of ten years, he filed numerous frivolous motions and appeals, for which he was sanctioned fourteen times (more than $80,000). Courts found that he had mischaracterized the record, failed to support factual assertions, misrepresented legal authorities, "ignored the most elementary rules of appellate review and presented an incoherent mélange of half-formed arguments and hints of error," appealed on grounds that had already been rejected or never raised at trial, and "unnecessarily wasted the

---

4. Matter of Respondent A, 1 Calif. State Bar Ct. Rptr. 255 (1990) (acquitted).

5. Matter of Loftus, 5 Calif. State Bar Ct. Rptr. 80 (2007) (90-day suspension, 18 months probation).

6. Matter of Fandey, 2 Calif. State Bar Ct. Rptr. 767 (1994) (one year suspension, three years probation).

7. Matter of Chesnut, 4 Calif. State Bar Ct. Rptr. 166 (2000) (six months suspension, two years probation).

8. Matter of Farrell, 1 Calif. State Bar Ct. Rptr. 490 (1991) (six months suspension, three years probation).

9. Matter of Jeffers, 3 Calif State Bar Ct. Rptr. 211 (1994) (two years probation).

10. Matter of Varakin, 3 Calif. State Bar Ct. Rptr. 179 (1994) (disbarred).

time and resources of the parties and the court" in order to delay satisfying the judgment. He failed to report the judicial sanctions, even in response to State Bar (SB) questions, or to cooperate with its investigation.

Lawyers can become so invested in cases that they will not let their clients quit. Elodie McKee and Don Porco retained James C. Regan (under a contingency fee agreement authorizing $200 per hour for any appeal) to sue the City of Burbank and its employees for slander.[11] The individual defendants successfully moved to strike this as a strategic lawsuit against public participation (obtaining a $15,000 attorneys fee award); and the action against Burbank was dismissed. Four days before this, McKee and Porco each gave Regan a $250 check with "appeal" on the memo line. Within a month, however, McKee phoned to say that neither wanted to appeal. Regan immediately hung up, did so two more times that day, and filed the notice of appeal the next day without informing them because "I don't know that it's wise to put so many things in writing." Learning this a week later, Porco phoned Regan and said "I told him to get my name off of it. I didn't want that appeal." McKee filed a *pro per* substitution of attorney, but the court continued to recognize Regan as attorney of record, because he said McKee had failed to return the substitution of attorney form. Porco asked for his case file but never got it. After the trial court entered a $63,000 judgment against the three, Regan filed a supplemental notice of appeal for all of them. He never replied to their registered letter, declaring that he did not have their authority to appeal. They reasserted this six months later, moving to dismiss both Regan as their attorney and the appeal. Instead of replying, he filed an appeal brief on behalf of all three. After the court dismissed the clients' appeals, Regan moved to vacate that order, strike their motion, and reinstate the appeals, declaring that the mentally ill McKee "imagines that she is a lawyer" and the senile Porco "has no idea of what is happening [and] is under Ms. McKee's influence." "Neither Mr. Porco nor Ms. McKee *actually want* the appeal dismissed," and they "*specifically requested that counsel undertake these appeals.*" They filed a "letter of opposition" to Regan's motion. In response, Regan phoned Porco—his first communication in nine months—urging continuation of the appeal and warning Porco to have no more contact with McKee, who was not acting in his interest. Porco denied he was under anyone's influence. Both wrote Regan that they did not want to appeal and asked him to sign the substitution of attorney form. Instead of replying, he filed a declaration on behalf of all three, asking that the "Letter of Opposition" be stricken and declaring that "Mr. Porco has never requested that his appeal be dismissed." Regan claimed he had only recently learned about McKee's opposition to the appeal. Porco and McKee asked the court to honor its earlier dismissal of their appeals, which it did. McKee again

11. Matter of Regan, 4 Calif. State Bar Ct. Rptr. 844 (2005) (75-day suspension, two years probation) (emphasis in original).

wrote Regan that both had fired him and asked for signed substitution of attorney forms. Instead, Regan filed a motion reiterating that neither wanted their appeals dismissed and disparaging McKee's mental capacity. He repeatedly tried to collect fees for his legal work from Porco's insurer but failed to answer its request for a letter of representation.

The Round Valley Nation (RVN) retained Patrick J. Maloney, Jr., and his associate Thomas S. Virsik (who was 30 years younger) to advise about an effort to depose Round Valley Indian Tribes (RVIT) as the tribal government.[12] Although RVN overwhelmingly won an election it organized in April 2000, neither the Bureau of Indian Affairs (BIA) nor the U.S. Department of Interior's Office of Self-Government (OSG) recognized RVN. A bank refused Maloney's instruction to transfer the tribe's assets to RVN. After RVIT sued RVN leader Carlino Bettega for employment harassment, Maloney submitted a request for dismissal (RFD) on behalf of Janice Freeman, who purported to act *pro per* for RVIT. Maloney failed to notify Stephen Quesenberry of California Indian Legal Services, who had represented RVIT for nearly 30 years, or disclose to the court that Freeman and RVN were his clients. After the court refused to file the RFD, Virsik prepared another, which Maloney signed as attorney for RVIT, even though he was attorney of record for Bettega and knew Quesenberry represented RVIT. In support, he filed a declaration describing the "Constitutional election" as a conclusive victory for RVN and falsely stating that "no Tribal member (or anyone else) has to date challenged the election." The respondents also misrepresented that RVN had terminated Quesenberry and directed him to dismiss the lawsuit against Bettega. Maloney filed an opposition to RVIT's motion for sanctions because "the governing body has since dismissed the action." Virsik prepared a third RFD, describing the respondents as attorneys for "Round Valley Nation f/k/a Round Valley Indian Tribes" and a Notice of Change of Name of RVIT to RVN so the latter could dismiss the action. Quesenberry strongly resisted all these actions, which were taken "without any authorization of [RVIT], with full knowledge that [Maloney's] client [RVN] has no lawful authority to act on [RVIT's] behalf, and without informing the Court . . . that the United States government has reaffirmed that the duly authorized and governing body of the Tribes is the Tribal Council [of RVIT]."

The court *sua sponte* directed the clerk not to file either RFD and found that Maloney "is not the attorney for the plaintiff named in this action. Interim Tribal Council is not a party to this action." The same day the respondents filed a Supplemental Declaration in Support of Dismissal, attaching a letter "from an unidentified employee of BIA" stating that it "did not recognize the political faction known as the [RVN]," which Maloney claimed he had received only after

---

12. Matter of Maloney and Virsik, 4 Calif. State Bar Ct. Rptr. 774 (2005) (Maloney suspended for 90 days, Virsik 60; both given two years probation).

filing the original declaration. In fact, Maloney knew that the "unidentified employee" was the superintendent of the California BIA. Although he also knew the BIA rejected RVN's victory, he insisted that the effect of the "Constitutional election" was "to divorce the Tribes from the BIA and instead proceed under a self-governance program of the Department of the Interior." But he failed to disclose that the OSG Director had excluded RVN from the program because it did not meet the criteria and was not "the tribal governing body recognized by the" BIA. The court awarded $2,000 sanctions against the respondents for their "surreptitious attempt . . . to dismiss the action and perpetrate a fraud upon the court and opposing counsel." They filed an opposition to this, continuing to maintain that RVN had properly dismissed Quesenberry. Six months later, he reported their failure to pay sanctions to the court, which ordered them to show cause why further sanctions should not be imposed. Even at the disciplinary proceeding two years later, Maloney insisted "I don't know of any BIA disapproval of the constitution," and Virsik maintained the BIA had approved RVN's constitution because as "a matter of the administrative law standard, failing to act, they approved it."

James Cooke retained Carey B. Scott to bring Workers' Compensation and tort claims for severe injuries.[13] Allen Jones (business manager of Cooke's union) became concerned about Scott's performance, consulting Krissman, a lawyer at the Silver firm, which had hosted a dinner seminar Jones attended. Responding that neither Martindale-Hubbell nor O'Brien's Evaluator rated Scott, whom none of Krissman's partners knew, he offered to give Cooke a "second opinion." In an extended phone call, Krissman claimed he could do a better job than Scott, who had never handled a case that big, and arranged to meet Cooke. Cooke reported this to Scott but insisted he was "totally and completely satisfied" with the lawyer and had no intention of meeting Krissman or switching lawyers. Scott blew up at Jones the same day and unsuccessfully tried to reach Krissman. Before the meeting date Scott sued Krissman and the Silver firm for intentional interference with contract, disparagement, and defamation (the first lawsuit), arranging for the complaint to be served during the scheduled meeting (which was never held). Scott and his wife began socializing with the Cookes, including a trip to Hawaii and camping vacations; and Scott encouraged Cooke to observe Scott's other trials and participate in his own case. Scott settled Cooke's personal injury claim for $5.2 million, earning more than $1.6 million in contingent fees.

After the Silver firm won a nonsuit in Scott's case, Judge Ross *sua sponte* held a sanctions hearing and ordered Scott to pay the firm $218,299. Before that was reduced to a written order, Scott moved to disqualify Ross on the grounds that he knew several members of the Silver firm, one of whom (Stolpman) had helped

13. Matter of Scott, 4 Calif. State Bar Ct. Rptr. 446 (2002) (60-day suspension, two years probation).

him win appointment to the bench, and that his demeanor, comments, and questions during the trial and his rulings showed bias. After this was denied, Scott petitioned for a writ of mandamus and unsuccessfully appealed its denial to the California Supreme Court; unsuccessfully appealed the nonsuit, sanctions, and denial of a rehearing to the California Court of Appeal and California and U.S. Supreme Court; unsuccessfully sought another writ of mandate, claiming new evidence that Ross had telephoned the Silver firm six times close to the trial and had participated with firm members in the Los Angeles Trial Lawyers Association for fifteen years; and unsuccessfully appealed this to the California Supreme Court.

Scott then sued Ross, Krissman, Stolpman, and Robert Baker (defense counsel in the first lawsuit) for violation of his civil rights (the second lawsuit), reiterating his earlier allegations and adding that Ross had been Baker's friend, attended Baker's parties, and telephoned Baker's law office around the time of the trial. After granting Ross's motion for summary judgment, the court *sua sponte* dismissed the entire lawsuit for lack of subject matter jurisdiction. The same month (reiterating earlier allegations), Scott filed a third lawsuit to set aside the judgment and sanctions in the first lawsuit on the ground that the defendants had concealed material facts and procured the judgment by extrinsic fraud. The judge decided for all defendants: "I really sincerely feel that anyone who heard [the first lawsuit] . . . would have granted the non-suit." A week later, Scott sued Baker and Ross for civil rights violations and defamation and Baker for fraudulent billing (a fourth lawsuit), repeating the earlier allegations. Scott claimed that after retiring from the bench, Ross told several other judges, "I've got another lawsuit by C. Brent Scott," to which they replied, "Oh, my god, no. Him again." Ross responded, "Yeah, He'll never quit; same allegations." Scott claimed that Ross blamed him for the cost of defending himself before the Commission on Judicial Performance. The court granted the defendants' demurrers. Scott paid half of the sanctions before declaring bankruptcy.

Perhaps the most notorious controversy concerns Stephen Yagman, who moved to disqualify Chief Judge Manuel L. Real of the Central District of California in a *pro per* lawsuit Yagman brought against several insurance companies.[14] Judge William D. Keller (randomly assigned) denied the motion[15] and ordered Yagman to show cause why he should not be sanctioned for failing to disclose that another court had already rejected a similar motion. Finding that Yagman had violated Federal Rules of Civil Procedure (FRCP) Rule 11 and the court's inherent authority but concluding that his "professional history suggests that neither monetary sanctions nor suspension appear to be effective in deterring [his] pestiferous conduct," Keller recommended that the State Bar

14. This account is taken from Standing Committee on Discipline v. Yagman, 856 F. Supp. 1384 (C.D. Calif. 1994).

15. Yagman v. Republic Ins., 136 F.R.D. 652 (C.D. Cal. 1991).

discipline him.[16] Yagman responded that Judge Keller "has a penchant for sanctioning Jewish lawyers: me, David Kenner, and Hugh Manes. I take this to be evidence of anti-Semitism."[17]

Contemporaneously, Yagman submitted an entry to Prentice-Hall's *Almanac of the Federal Judiciary*, alleging that Keller mistreated two criminal defense and two civil rights lawyers, three of them Jewish.

> It is an understatement to characterize the judge as "the worst judge in the central district." It would be fairer to say that he is ignorant, dishonest, ill-tempered, and a bully, and probably is one of the worst judges in the United States. If television cameras ever were permitted in his courtroom, the other federal judges in the Country would be so embarrassed by this buffoon that they would run for cover. One might believe that some of the reason for this sub-standard human is the recent acrimonious divorce through which he recently went: but talking to attorneys who knew him years ago indicates that, if anything, he has mellowed. One other comment: his girlfriend is, or was, the newly-appointed U.S. Attorney in Los Angeles, Lourdes Baird, who, like the Judge, is a right wing fanatic.

The judge hearing the sanctions motion (not Keller) disbelieved Yagman's claim he had not intended that the entry be mailed and also found that he had sent Keller a copy anonymously. Yagman's firm bought a half-page *Los Angeles Daily Journal* advertisement asking to hear from any lawyer sanctioned or threatened by Keller. Yagman also wrote Keller, asking if there were "reasonable grounds to file an action against [him] for, inter alia, furnishing to the Daily Journal a copy" of his sanctions order. About the same time, Yagman told attorney Robert Steinberg, "there are certain judges I want to be in front of for my Civil rights cases who are favorable to my point of view. And I'd like to recuse out the ones who are extremely unfavorable." When Steinberg suggested this was unethical, Yagman retorted that he could "practice law the way he wants to."

Steinberg reported this to the Central District's Standing Committee on Discipline, and Keller formally complained to it. When Keller recused himself in another of Yagman's cases,[18] the lawyer called it "remarkable that Keller admits

---

16. Yagman v. Republic Ins., 137 F.R.D. 310 (C.D. Cal. 1991); Susan Seager, *Judge Sanctions Yagman, Refers Case to State Bar,* LADJ 1 (June 6, 1991) Two years later the Ninth Circuit affirmed Keller's denial of the motion to disqualify Judge Real but vacated the sanctions and remanded for assignment to another judge. In re Yagman, 796 F.2d 1165 (9th Cir. 1986). Judge Real challenged the reassignment, but Yagman successfully petitioned for writ of mandamus, Brown v. Baden, 815 F.2d. 575 (9th Cir. 1987), and the U.S. Supreme Court denied Judge Real's petition for certiorari, Real v. Yagman, 484 U.S. 963 (1987).

17. Susan Seager, *Judge Sanctions Yagman, Refers Case to State Bar,* Los Angeles Daily Journal 1 (June 6, 1991).

18. Marshall v. Gates, 812 F.Supp. 1050 (C.D. Calif. 1993).

his bias against me, and recuses himself, which is great for my client." The Standing Committee initiated a disciplinary proceeding, which Judge Real referred to Ninth Circuit Chief Judge Wallace, who assigned Circuit Judges Reed, King, and Conti, who referred it back to Judge Real, who appointed Judges Rafeedie, Davis, and Williams, who found a prior history of judge shopping. In 1981, Yagman "simultaneously filed five similar complaints in this district, and dismissed four of them within 73 minutes after they had been assigned to various judges." He admitted the violation, paid a fine, and performed pro bono service. After an adverse jury verdict in a civil rights case, Yagman filed a new action, charging the same defendants and now their lawyers with depriving his client of civil rights and engaging in racketeering, mail fraud, and obstruction of justice and alleging that Judge Hupp had "conspired with the defendants and with their legal counsel to obstruct justice in the federal courts. . . ." Although the dismissal was affirmed on appeal, Judge Hupp had since recused himself in every case involving Yagman.

When Reginald Ronell "Ron" Settles died in jail after being forcibly subdued by two police officers, Yagman represented them in suing the forensic pathologists for defamation. After Judge Real directed a verdict for the defendants and imposed $250,000 in sanctions, Yagman appealed, charging that Real displayed "patent hostility" to his clients and "exhibited a strong personal bias and prejudice against Stephen Yagman of unmistakable longstanding [*sic*], and a partiality for the defendants." He also alleged that Real had taken the case away from Judge Lydick six days before trial to prevent Yagman from testifying against the nomination of Real's colleague, Lucas, to the California Supreme Court. Real "consistently has been held in the lowest regard by virtually the entire community since he took the bench" and had "mental disorders." While rejecting these charges, the Ninth Circuit disqualified Real because "the massive sanction award and the numerous allegations of bias and overreaching have combined with this poor lawyering to reach an entirely unfortunate end result: the fragile appearance of justice has taken a beating."[19]

The Standing Committee ordered a two-year suspension.[20] Rather than acknowledging error, Yagman had "attacked the impartiality of both the Standing Committee and the members of this Panel," just as he "accused Judges Real, Hupp and Keller of bias, incompetence and/or lack of integrity." He had written in the *Los Angeles Times*:

> I am a Jew who believes a federal judge is an anti-Semite. And if friends of that judge who were appointed to the bench by the proven anti-Semite Nixon and the odious Reagan attempt to harm me based on trumped-up charges for holding my belief, I cannot let that deter me. I'm a realist who holds a correct

19. In re Yagman, 796 F.2d 1165, 1188 (9th Cir. 1986).
20. Standing Committee v. Yagman, 856 F.Supp. 1395 (C.D. Calif. 1994).

but unpopular opinion and who expects and who will bear the wrath of opponents whose righteousness is only surpassed by their lack of integrity.[21]

The Court of Appeal reversed, holding that Yagman's statements were opinions based on facts not proven false and hence protected by the First Amendment because they did not present a clear and present danger to the administration of justice.[22]

Lawyers are strongly motivated toward zealous advocacy by the fees they earn, the recognition they receive, identification with clients and causes, antipathies to adversaries, opposing counsel, and judges, and simple delight in practicing their craft. For litigation to produce justice, however, lawyers must play by the rules. The above cases reveal many of the ways lawyers violate those rules, by facilitating or covering up criminal behavior, attacking judges, corrupting the judicial process, improperly influencing juries, making frivolous arguments or repeating rejected arguments, concealing or misrepresenting the facts (such as that your client is dead!) or the law, disregarding procedures, persisting in representing an unwilling client, and refusing to accept defeat. The following case illustrates many of those temptations.

II. THE ALLEGED LEGAL MALPRACTICE IN REPRESENTING MARIA SEWARD

Maria Seward was badly injured on November 16, 1980, when the car in which she was a passenger was struck head-on while traveling in the proper lane.[23] She lost her spleen, could no longer have children, and suffered spinal and dental damage. Fresh empty beer bottles were found in the oncoming car, which had been seen swerving and passing on blind curves for several miles. It was driven by Thomas Peters, the successful motivational author of *In Search of Excellence,*

---

21. Exhibit A to Petitioner's Supplemental Trial Brief Re Sanctions.

22. Standing Committee v. Yagman, 55 F.3d 1430 (9th Cir. 1995). *See also* Matter of Anderson, 3 Calif State Bar Ct. Rptr. 775 (1997) (100 unprivileged derogatory statements about the Orange County Superior Court, but the OTC had not proved their falsity). Yagman was suspended for a year in 1998 for collecting an "illegal or unconscionable" fee. Thom Mrozek, *State Bar Rules Yagman Violated Conduct Rules,* LADJ 1 (July 17, 1995); Martin Berg, *Yagman Faces Bar Suspension For One Year,* LADJ 1 (Jan. 7, 1998). He was suspended again in 2007 following a conviction for tax evasion.

23. This narrative is taken from the respondent's offer of proof regarding witnesses disallowed by the State Bar Court (3.21.94) and Dee Ziegler, *Legal Malpractice Case: Settlement Confidentiality Challenged,* San Francisco Daily Journal (Nov. 11, 1988), Exhibit J of Answer to Notice to Show Cause (July 15, 1993); State Bar's Exhibit 4. Unless otherwise noted all information is taken from the transcripts of the legal malpractice trial or the disciplinary proceeding.

who had $3 million in liability insurance. Seward sued both her driver, Charles Higgins, and Peters; she was represented by John C. Elstead of The Law Office of Gerald Sterns, which was in turmoil at the time. On September 1, 1982, partner Thomas G. Smith wrote eponym Gerald "Jerry" Sterns, condemning Elstead's incompetence and jealousy. Smith also warned that "the biggest crisis we have is money," which the firm was spending "like a bunch of drunken sailors."[24] "[W]e will be out of business before too long." Now that they were engaged in the demanding Johns Manville asbestos litigation, money management was "an even more pressing problem." Smith called it a "farce" to pretend he was office manager because he "never had either total authority or responsibility." "[C]ountless dollars were wasted and not an insignificant amount stolen" under the previous manager, Clapper, who had told Sterns "he charged for roundtrip from the airport to his own home because that was the way it was done at the Walkup office. That was an outright lie."

> Adding a few hundred dollars of phony case costs for ICI [Investigative Consultants International] is not going to cure the problem. It is tacky, unethical and is causing concern among the lawyers. We would be in a hell of a fix if, for example, we get involved in litigation or arbitration over the fees in the Kelly Parks case with the Paden office if they start to question why we have a $500 fee for ICI on the cost statement.

Smith also accused Elstead of neglecting valuable clients. Another firm lawyer was "embarrassed" to be working on one of Elstead's cases "because it has been so poorly handled." Elstead "works a great many three- and four-hour days and lies about where he is going and why he is going to be there."

> In my view the whole office would be better off if John were not here. . . . You tried to control him by means that are demeaning to you, to the office and to the entire staff . . . it is like paying ransom to Idi Amin so he will not destroy the office. . . . John saying that Kitty [Catherine Singels, who was both Smith's wife and his secretary] is using her relationship with me to the detriment of the office is untrue.

Elstead had billed the Nairobi air crash clients for a $129 personal trip from Seattle to Boise. "If he had taken $120 from petty cash to spend on himself with no intention of repaying it you would have been outraged."

Sterns was aware of the problems. In response to Elstead's August 22 memo on "claimed personal cases," Sterns had replied, on August 30, that Elstead's

---

24. Respondent's Exhibit C. Damer obtained this memo from Smith's widow, Catherine Singels, who had been a secretary in Sterns Smith Elstead & Walker from September 1977 to 1982 and in the Law Offices of Gerald C. Sterns until 1985 and had typed the memo for Smith.

position was "in conflict with the long settled policies of this office."[25] Sterns had "reiterated many times" that "any fee or bonus an attorney receives on any bona fide personal referral depends on the circumstances and will be dealt with on a case by case basis."

> [T]o obtain a complete picture of the financial relationship between you and this office, after we receive[d] your claim of "personal" cases, we did some analysis of expense[s] on your cases and activities, and have come up with a number of items which tend to be offsetting, or at least require some further explanation. . . .

After discussing four other cases, he turned to Elstead's representation of Seward.

> Even if Seward is personal to you I would have some serious problems with paying you anything near 1/3rd of the fee or a bonus. The case was one of absolute liability and was filed in a county with a fairly current calendar, yet took 32 months to resolve. No 998 or similar tactic was employed in all this time which probably would have made a substantial difference in the defense approach. This case was not worked up adequately nor properly prepared and I question whether the realistic value of the case was obtained in settlement. It surprised me to hear you had settled it for $100,000 total as I understood you to say it was worth $150,000 at least, and probably much more.

He attached an October 8, 1981, memo in which Elstead had valued the case at $175,000 to $225,000, asked $195,000, and said "the carrier is anxious to settle." Instead, Elstead settled for $90,000 compensatory and $10,000 punitive damages on May 16, 1983.

III. THE MALPRACTICE CLAIM

In 1984, Seward retained Nicholas Raymond Damer to bring a malpractice action against the Sterns firm, its lawyers, and its insurer, Lawyers Mutual Insurance Company.[26] She offered to settle for $11.95 million. Elstead was represented by Robert Gebhardt of Bronson, Bronson & McKinnon. At the April 19, 1988, mandatory settlement conference the lawyers offered $150,000 and the insurers $50,000, contingent on sealing the settlement. Damer responded the next day.

> [M]y client did reject and continues to reject these proposals—however they might be modified or clarified—because the amounts offered are inadequate

25. Respondent's Exhibit D.

26. Seward had since married and taken the last name of her husband, John Sargent, but I will use the name in which the lawsuits were filed.

> under the circumstances, and because an integral condition (namely, confidentiality) is unacceptable regardless of the amounts. . . . I admire her highly principled stand in this matter, and I am sure that her remote ancestor, President Lincoln's Secretary of State, William Seward—a highly regarded lawyer during his time and career, would be quite proud of Maria at this moment. There is simply no reason why Maria and I should join in any pact whereby other persons harmed by the defendants, would be unable to gain information regarding the circumstances of Maria's case, directly from the source.

He cited a "60 Minutes" episode

> in which the State Bar's "Ethics Monitor" was quoted as recommending that the interests of society, in assuring honest, competent lawyering, would be best served if dissatisfied clients proceed *simultaneously* with private complaints to the State Bar *and publicly filed malpractice suits.* In other words, Maria Seward does not wish to engage in a conspiracy of silence for the benefit of the defendant attorneys. . . . [T]o the extent the potential for discovery, of the facts underlying her case, might motivate the attorney defendants to treat their clients better in the future, then Ms. Seward will have accomplished one of her major objectives in this litigation.

Damer wrote Seward the day after rejecting the offer, seeking her

> written authorization to file a class action suit, against Sterns and Elstead, to compel an accounting and a refund of all funds properly owed you even if your malpractice case should result in no recovery. . . . The pendency of this suit will greatly increase the pressure for a settlement. . . . I need your authorization *immediately, before* Sterns attorneys send you a refund in an attempt to moot your claims.

She signed and returned a statement authorizing "the filing of a class action suit of the sort mentioned above. I agree to serve as class representative."

Damer asked Judge Frank (who was trying the case) to compel the defendants to undertake good faith settlement negotiations under local rule 2.6E, without seeking a confidentiality agreement, which violated the public's right to know about legal malpractice as well as Business and Professions Code (BPC) Section 6068, requiring lawyers to report misconduct to the State Bar.[27] He cited a

27. Senate Bill 1498, subsequently signed into law, requires courts to report to the Bar any claims or judgments against an attorney for fraud, breach of fiduciary duty, misrepresentation, or gross negligence. It gave the Bar access to sealed malpractice files.

San Francisco Superior Court opinion ordering a legal malpractice settlement unsealed.[28] At the May 13 hearing, defense lawyers ridiculed his motion. "Frankly, plaintiff's attorney's eagerness to publicize his allegations and any settlement in this case ignores the best interests of the plaintiff, his client." Elstead's lawyer said the case Damer cited did not prevent parties from negotiating a settlement and not filing it with the court. An unpublished 1985 Court of Appeal decision criticized Damer for insulting and threatening the court.[29] The insurance company lawyer called Damer an "inexhaustible source of gibberish." Defense lawyers sought sanctions against him for making the motion. In support, Elstead's lawyer wrote:

> As any reasonable attorney would have understood, defendant's confidentiality requirement only would have barred plaintiff from publicizing the terms of any settlement. Defendants have never required as a condition to settlement [that] the court file be sealed or that plaintiff refrain from making a complaint to the State Bar.

On May 20, the court denied Damer's motion. Judge Frank's June 8 order declared that "the legal authority cited by plaintiff provides absolutely no support for the relief sought by her." Damerremained defiant, telling the *San Francisco Banner/Daily Journal* (*Daily Journal*).

> They could throw $3 million and she wouldn't take it under these conditions. Her attitude is that if Sterns and Elstead don't have anything to be ashamed of, then there is no need for confidentiality. If they do, then their clients have a right to know.

On July 2, Damer asked for a rehearing. But on July 14, Judge Hart ordered him to pay the defendants sanctions of nearly $5,000.

Damer wrote Seward on November 15, complaining about a *Daily Journal* article "very slanted in favor of Sterns, which might be expected."[30]

> My partner, Lance Stryker, suspects that Sterns may have prompted the article—but even if the newspaper initiated the idea of publishing the article . . . opposing counsel may have threatened a libel suit, to insure a "spin" in their favor.

"[W]e suspected that [reporter Dolores 'Dee' Ziegler] was simply a 'tool' of the opposition lawyers, who were attempting to get a copy of our Trial Brief and other 'confidential' and 'sensitive' material shortly before trial." "Sterns' behavior has been bizarre on other occasions." The article included defense "pot shots" at Damer and "background facts about Sterns which would appear to imply that he

28. GHD Associates Inc. v. Furth 796803.

29. Coastside Publishers and Printers v. Bauer, A025325.

30. Respondent's Exhibit J of Answer to Notice to Show Cause (July 15, 1993).

could do no wrong even if he tried." Still, "it may be read by persons who are in a position to influence the attention and importance given to the issues in the pending appeal."

On November 18, Seward replied that she was "disturbed that an individual or persons from the opposition were able to approach this reporter in such a way that a biased article was published." "I am growing weary of constant delaying and I wish to have this matter brought to a timely and appropriate conclusion."

> Throughout this whole ugly business, I have come to really appreciate, more and more, your awesome and prodigious skills, which are being utilized on my behalf and, perhaps, ultimately for many others who have been abused by some members of the San Francisco legal community. . . . John and I are both very grateful to you and your office for bringing to bear so much talent and experience.
>
> Keep on truckin'!!
>
> With warmest regards.

On November 28, Damer gave *Daily Journal* publisher Guy P. Everingham "written notice" of libelous statements and demanded corrections. He asked why Ziegler requested "a copy of my typically confidential trial brief the very week before the trial was scheduled to begin" and relied on defense lawyers' characterizations rather than checking with Damer or waiting for the transcript. Why did the article not mention "relatively recent, embarrassing and equally irrelevant items" about the defense lawyers?

Although the legal malpractice trial was due to begin at the end of January 1990, some 90 *in limine* motions delayed opening argument to February 21. The previous December, Damer had learned that the Sterns firm was representing most of the plaintiffs in a $50 million lawsuit in Contra Costa Superior Court arising out of an airplane crash into a Sun Valley shopping mall on December 23, 1985, killing seven, injuring 75, and causing property damage to 40. But Damer heard about overcharging by the Sterns firm in that case only on Monday, February 5, 1990, when the clerk of Judge Alfred Chiantelli (who was hearing Seward's case) brought to everyone's attention a television report of allegations about Sterns's billing abuse raised by two other firms representing plaintiffs in the Sun Valley case (Lazzarini & Frazier, and Nelson, Warnlof & Vencill). Damer later remembered hearing that the TV story

> apparently was devastating, showing the bloody bodies of the victims being dragged out of the Sun Valley Mall, and then the next thing on the screen would be a picture of Sterns' ten thousand dollar bill for a dinner at Star's Restaurant, which he was trying to charge to the clients. Then they would show more bloody bodies and then they showed the invoice for his trip to London on the Concorde, which he was trying to charge to clients.

Damer got an anonymous phone call soon afterwards, leading him in mid February to meet Catherine Singels and obtain Thomas Smith's damning memorandum to Sterns about Elstead (discussed above).[31]

Damer associated Gerson B. Mehlman, a Baltimore lawyer, to help in Seward's case. But Mehlman did not arrive on January 31, as promised. Because the trial was about to begin, Damer had been denied a continuance, and his partner was involved in other litigation concerning the Sterns firm,[32] Damer also associated Robert Denebeim at the suggestion of Denebeim's Redwood City landlord. Denebeim wrote Damer on February 2 to confirm the previous day's telephone conversation agreeing to be "associate counsel" for a "fixed fee of $15,000" and "assist you in a secondary capacity, and under your instruction."[33] Denebeim had explained this to Seward by phone. Researching the Sun Valley case in the Contra Costa clerk's office at Damer's direction, Denebeim reported finding objections[34]

> that Sterns didn't do the work for which he is seeking compensation . . . that he lost about $120,000 in interest while he was the custodian of settlement funds. They are demanding that he account for his time (which will be interesting since in our case we know that he does not keep time records).

Some $250,000 of Sterns's expenses were challenged on the ground that he was billing clients at four times what he was paying outsiders and billing for secretarial work, which would normally be part of overhead.

On February 23, Damer sent Gebhardt a "Confidential privileged settlement proposal" open to the end of the day: Lawyers Mutual would pay $1 million (the malpractice policy limit), and Elstead would agree to entry of a judgment against him for $3 million and "waive any rights under Judge Hart's [sanctions] rulings, and any demand for confidentiality." On March 6, while the trial was proceeding, the defendants offered $500,000. Damer testified that this proposal contained "certain bizarre provisions": the "jury would be under a perpetual gag order," and "all my files and copies of my files would be purchased." It "was immediately rejected as unacceptable to Ms. Seward." But the following day

> the jury was temporarily excused and Mr. Denebeim read into the record the settlement, which was essentially the same thing that had been proposed the day before, except the figure was now $750,000 and it was

---

31. Declaration of Catherine E. Singels, Custodian of Records of Thomas G. Smith, Respondent's Exhibit II.

32. Damer explained that this was *his* case concerning alleged embezzlement from the Alameda County employee pension fund, in which Gebhardt's firm represented one of the principal defendants. Stryker took over the trial because Damer feared that "Gebhardt, in collusion with Chiantelli, would arrange to have me arrested in front of the jurors. . . ." E-mail (Jan. 22, 2009).

33. Respondent's Exhibit FF.

34. Respondent's Exhibit GG.

> specifically provided that all my files and all copies of my files would be turned over to Robert Gebhardt as the designated agent for their perusal and destruction by the defendants.[35]

Damer immediately "attempted to withdraw as counsel, indicating that I could not ethically participate in such a settlement." His request was denied, even though Seward was being represented by Denebeim and Mehlman. Defendants' motion for a non-suit was unopposed, "thereby excusing the judge from any duty to report whatever he learned in the trial to the State Bar." After the judge entered the non-suit he recalled the jury, "basically threatened [them] with contempt proceedings if they ever discussed the case publicly," and discharged them. Gebhardt said on the record:

> [O]ne of the moving forces of this settlement is for the defendants hopefully to rid themselves as much as possible of any involvement with Mr. Damer and so the agreement—that he . . . not use directly or indirectly any information gained in this case in any other litigation.

But when Damer was told "I was to come back to court on a certain day, bring my files and turn them over to Gebhardt, I told the court, very respectfully, I would not do that. I was then taken into custody."

> I repeatedly asked for the right, under Rule 3-700, to keep a copy of my files and to not disclose any secret portions of my file which would reflect materials or information entrusted to me by informants to whom I had made promises of anonymity, with Maria Seward's knowledge and consent.

That day Damer telephoned the State Bar, asking them to send a representative to the next day's hearing "so as to be able to verify my complaints about [Chiantelli's], shall we say, 'unusual' behavior . . . because there was a scheme going on to destroy evidence."[36] He was directed to Jeanette Shipman, who had worked for the Sterns firm when it represented Seward and was a named

---

35. Damer elaborated in a January 20, 2009 e-mail to me. Denebeim had been suggested by Gerald Schneider, an attorney specializing in drunk driving, whom Damer planned to use as an expert witness. A few days after Damer hired Denebeim, he and Schneider "suddenly appeared, in the evening, at my office, saying they wanted to 'discuss' a 'proposal'" to "take over the case and be the lead trial attorneys for Seward. Indeed, they had even prepared a lengthy fee contract. . . ." When Damer refused, Schneider insisted he had to go to Hawaii to interview another expert witness, retired Judge Melvin Cohn. At the subsequent fee arbitration before Judge Lanam (see below), Schneider and Denebeim denied under oath ever seeking to take over the case. Damer produced their draft fee contract and a letter from Schneider stating that "one of the consequences" of his Hawaii meeting with Cohn "is that I may become chief trial counsel. . . ."

36. Damer wrote me that during the first three weeks of the trial he repeatedly asked the judge to remove the names of Sterns and Bridgman as *pro tem* judges on a sign the jurors passed every morning, "creating bias." "Only after I said I was going to the Presiding

defendant in her lawsuit. Refusing to discuss it with her, Damer then called the Los Angeles office and talked to William Davis. "He assured me an independent and special prosecutor would be immediately appointed, he would let me know if they could get someone up to the court the next day." Damer also contacted the Court of Appeal and the Commission on Judicial Performance. The same day, Damer gave Seward "three full large storage boxes of materials she had maintained as a 'parallel file' to mine."

On March 8, Damer appeared, represented by Cynthia M. Frazier (who also represented plaintiffs in the Sun Valley Mall case and had publicly accused Sterns of overbilling expenses). Chiantelli now granted Damer's motion to withdraw, substituting Denebeim.[37] They then had this colloquy:[38]

DAMER: Your Honor, I need a written order because I can't seek a writ on a transcript that isn't prepared.

COURT: I understand.

DAMER: Okay?

COURT: I understand.

DAMER: I ask for that, I beg for that in due process.

COURT: That is correct. And you will get one.

On Friday, March 9, when the hearing concluded, Chiantelli denied Frazier's request for a 30-day stay of his order so they could seek a writ before the documents were to be delivered on Monday, March 12. This provoked Sterns's lawyer, Glenn Allen.

ALLEN: [T]hey are going to take a writ or go to the Appeals Court to try to eliminate confidentiality in this matter. To me that makes a joke of this whole settlement. What was purchased was confidentiality. . . . The *quid pro quo* is gone.

COURT: Let me tell you this, you settled with Maria Seward, that is the end of the case. All right. Have a nice weekend.

DAMER: Your Honor, am I to . . . understand that I would be held in contempt if I don't turn these files over by . . . 9:00 A.M. Monday?

The clerk's minutes declared: "Records sealed by Order of the Court." That evening, at Gebhardt's request, Judge James B. Scott agreed to become custodian of the documents. On March 11, Chiantelli told him he was appointed and directed him to collect the documents from Damer on March 12.

Judge, to effect the removal, did Chiantelli finally take action in that regard." E-mail (Jan. 20, 2009).

37. Respondent's Exhibit B of Separate Statement detailing insufficiency of State Bar responses to Respondent's first set of interrogatories (Jan. 12, 1994).

38. Exhibit B, p.223, to Respondent's Trial Brief.

On Saturday, March 10, Seward left a message on Damer's answering machine:[39]

> I think there's something that you need to hear from my mouth, and so that's why I'm calling. First of all, I made a deal with the defendants and I want you to go along with it. I want you to turn over the files to Judge Scott, and I don't want you to do anything to violate the court orders . . . I don't want you to interfere with my position, and basically, I just want to get on with my life. I do not want to rehire you. . . . I agree that any of the sensitive material that's in your files shouldn't be given to Gebhardt, but I would like you to turn it over to Judge Scott. I hope this clears up any misconception that you have about me being coerced. I have not been coerced. I'm not hungry. I made this decision on my own. . . .

When Damer sought help in segregating the files over the weekend, Denebeim refused because he had not been paid enough and Mehlman "had abandoned him and gone off to Disneyland." If Chiantelli ordered a mistrial on Monday, Denebeim would have to conduct a jury trial, something he had never done. Judge Scott went to Damer's office on March 12 but was given just four of the twelve boxes, containing only Seward's medical records.

IV. DAMER'S ALLEGED DEFIANCE OF A COURT ORDER

On March 13, Frazier went to the bailiff for Contra Costa Superior Court Judge Richard Patsey, who was hearing the Sun Valley Mall case, and tried to file Smith's memo to Sterns about expense overcharges.[40] Frazier believed it had not been included in Chiantelli's confidentiality order since it had not been filed in Seward's case nor obtained through discovery.

> However, in the spirit of providing Mr. Sterns with an opportunity to review the matter prior to its public dissemination, while providing this court with the opportunity to review evidence appropriate to the case as required by my duty as an attorney, I requested that the matter be kept under seal.

The bailiff told her the judge refused to accept it under seal, which Patsey reiterated when Frazier telephoned him at 2 P.M. Damer said, "I reprimanded [Frazier] for taking that action without my knowledge, and told her there were other legitimate ways to get it before Judge Patsey without putting herself at risk."

---

39. Respondent's Exhibit OO.
40. Respondent's Exhibit BB.

On March 16, Damer hand-delivered a nine-page letter to Patsey, giving Sterns a copy and attaching under seal material from the sealed hearing.[41] He wrote "as a potential lienholder" in the Sun Valley cases, "as a friend of your court, as a citizen of our great state and nation, and as one who wishes to avoid the perpetration of a fraud." He understood that a "substantial portion" of the contested expenses in the Sun Valley cases concerned Investigative Consultants International (ICI) charges. The material under seal "demonstrates that the Sterns firm, since 1982, systematically, deliberately and persistently generated false invoices for charges from I.C.I.," which had business dealings with Sterns about which "every Sterns client—and your court—should have been fully and candidly informed long, long ago." ICI was the firm's tenant in San Francisco and also may have been in Hawaii and London. Sterns deducted all the ICI invoices from Seward's settlement, even though he could document less than a third of the $3,000. He billed Seward $42.50/hour for ICI but paid it only twelve to fourteen dollars. Sterns had charged Seward for

> knowingly false "Travel and Entertainment" expenses—including a steak dinner (allegedly related to a meeting with a claims adjuster . . . which never occurred) and a [$300] plane trip from Texas that had *nothing* to do with my client's case.

Sterns had "*personally* . . . attempted, with an amazing amount of overreaching, to suppress and destroy the evidence hereby being presented to you" and had "tried to *buy* my file so he could be in a position to 'shut me up' with threats to *sue* me for abuse of process."

Damer argued that the "evils" of "'secrecy' arrangements, including 'stipulated gag orders,' are readily apparent from the circumstances now before you." Sterns had been "successful in effectively 'bribing' my former client to obtain her complete silence." The papers "should *not* ever be 'sealed' again, no matter how much money Mr. Sterns agrees to give up. . . ." "It took *two court orders* to produce the August 30, 1983, memo; Sterns *never* revealed its existence and even *denied* its existence, under oath, *several times*. . . ." Damer sent Chiantelli a copy of this letter, requesting permission to let Patsey review the documents. "I do not believe that Judge Chiantelli can constitutionally or lawfully prevent me, as a private citizen who is not an attorney of record in his court, from communicating with you." If he spoke with Chiantelli, Patsey should

> PLEASE KEEP THIS IN MIND. Mr. Sterns—*a "pro tempore" member of the same bench*—was successful in persuading Judge Chiantelli to view me as some vindictive individual in pursuit of some irrational vendetta. . . .

41. Respondent's Exhibit H to Answer to NTSC (July 15, 1993).

Sterns had blocked Damer's change of venue motion on behalf of Seward,

> even though Mr. Sterns was (no doubt by *pure coincidence,* he will claim) "volunteered", by his firm, and elevated to the "Judge Pro-Tem" panel in the San Francisco venue . . . *shortly before the trial was to begin*; even though Mr. Sterns appeared again as a designated member of that panel *while the trial was still ongoing*; even though Sterns' first attorney in *Seward v. Sterns*—Richard Bridgman, a *critical witness* in the case—was likewise conveniently honored *on the eve of and throughout the first three weeks of trial*; and even though one of the jurors was a Deputy City Attorney for the City and County of San Francisco and another juror was the Official Court Clerk to Municipal Court Judge Phillip Moscone.

Chiantelli had denied Damer a two-day continuance while giving Sterns two years. On the "eve of the trial," Sterns "hired the law firm that employed, *as an attorney,* the *son* of the *very judge who would rule on the opposed motion to continue—all without disclosure to me.*" In the past three months, Chiantelli "took actions to place himself squarely on the side of joining with Mr. Sterns in an effort to suppress the evidence. . . ." It "seems that many judges almost *automatically* give the benefit of the doubt to Mr. Sterns, despite the clear requirement that every benefit of the doubt be given to Mr. Sterns' *clients, including* widows and orphans. . . ."

Damer "detest[ed] what Mr. Sterns has *done*" but did "*not* even *know* Mr. Sterns well enough to nurture some deep-seated antagonism toward him of a *personal* nature even were I foolish enough to harbor such self-destructive sentiments towards *anyone.*"

> Despite the attempts of Mr. Sterns, and his attorneys and numerous known and undisclosed allies, to poison judges' minds and to intimidate me from pursuing a client's specific interests and the public's general interest, I remain unwilling to passively observe the continued erosion of faith in the judicial system and the continued crumbling of the very foundations of the ideal of liberty under law.

On March 19, Judge Patsey returned Damer's papers unread and criticized him for scheduling a hearing on April 6 without asking the court.[42] Patsey would hear a motion only if "properly filed, served and calendared and if it does not contain private communications to the Court." Damer received this on March 22. Frazier had an April 3 hearing on a motion to Judge Patsey to reconsider his refusal to examine the Philip Stuto-ICI billings. Damer refiled his motion on March 23.[43] Because there was "no *written* order . . . sealing *any* records" in Seward's case he enclosed those records again, this time not under seal. Patsey allowed most of the Stuto-ICI charges, while rejecting $45,000 for meals and

---

42. Respondent's Exhibit SS.
43. Respondent's Exhibit UU.

travel claimed by Sterns.[44] Patsey denied Sterns's motions for sanctions against Damer and to strike his filing. On April 17, Damer sought a lien and leave to intervene, declaring that "Sterns believes that he lawfully purchased all of my files . . . *including evidence damaging to him*" to "prevent me . . . from recovering our fees, costs and expenses. . . ."

On March 19, Damer also wrote Chiantelli "implor[ing] him to reconsider his confidentiality order.[45] He hoped the judge would see how he "may appear to have assisted in betraying [Sterns's] clients" and have "the grace and humility to take remedial action." "For obvious reasons, I will not ever be coming before you in the future. . . . I have better things to do than be sent to jail." He was preparing a writ of prohibition "to prevent you from having me arrested or all my files seized." He refused to surrender the remaining files. "John Kennedy once said that mistakes emerge from errors only by our refusals to accept them as mere examples of our fallibility." The judge had been "ill used" by the defendants' lawyers.

> At an early point in the testimony, in a sidebar conference, you realized that perjury was surely occurring in your presence. . . . You looked at Mr. Gebhardt and Mr. Allen with a pained look on your face and exclaimed: "What are you guys trying to do to me?"

The same day Chiantelli filed his March 8 minute order that "the case file and all exhibits . . . [be] sealed." Damer filed a notice of appeal that day, indicating "that the enclosed documents are to be placed under seal per an existing court order."[46] The clerk refused to accept them on March 22 without a court order. Damer wrote the clerk the next day, petitioning for a writ of prohibition against being held in contempt, doing so this time without seal because "the involved clerk for Respondent Court recently reported that there *is* no *written* order sealing that court's files." He filed the petition in a sealed envelope with only the cover page stamped and returned. The petition was denied because he had not yet been held in contempt.

On March 30, Sterns filed a motion under seal to set aside the settlement and declare a mistrial,[47] complaining that Damer "outright accused the defendants [specifically Elstead] of stripping the Sterns' office file [of a report by chiropractor Michael Myers] to protect themselves." Those "false" and "prejudicial" accusations "contributed to the defendants' willingness to terminate the trial by settling the action." Opposing this on Seward's behalf, Denebeim argued that the defense did not settle because of Damer's alleged misconduct but rather "have always professed that misconduct was part of Damer's *modus operandi*" and "insisted

---

44. Respondent's Exhibit XX.
45. Respondent's Exhibit QQ.
46. Respondent's Exhibit I of Answer to NTSC (July 15, 1993).
47. Respondent's Exhibit PPP.

upon having recourse against him as part of the settlement."[48] They settled before Sterns testified because they doubted they "had received an adequate defense under their liability insurance policy" and therefore "didn't know what evidence Plaintiff would be presenting at trial."

> During the settlement negotiations, and the "voir dire" of Plaintiff . . . Defendants discovered the evidence that had previously been unavailable to them due to the sanctions against them that had precluded discovery, the bungled production of documents, and their inability to identify "the mole." After acquiring this information, the Defendants concluded that they had agreed to pay too much money for what they thought the case was worth.

Mehlman filed a declaration in support of Seward. The file sent by Elstead was a single one- to two-foot box, whereas Elstead had referred to a five-foot file in "boxes." The defendants also never sent the August 30, 1983 memorandum criticizing Elstead for settling too low and dividing the fees. But Mehlman agreed that file stripping had nothing to do with settlement.

> [T]he primary reason the case was settled was a desire on the part of both defendants and plaintiffs to end the litigation between them before Gerald Sterns took the stand and was cross examined on various misstatements he had made . . . and on various financial practices. . . .

Sterns's lawyer Glenn Allen had told Mehlman that "once Sterns took the stand 'and blood was let,' there would be no possibility of settlement." Although the insurer did not believe the case was worth "anything near what the plaintiff was demanding," they offered more to protect Sterns's reputation.

Sterns's reply agreed with much of this. Defendants were "flying blind" because they

> did not know what kind of documents might be shoved in front of them during trial because of the lack of discovery by the defense and the fact that the original *Seward v. Peters* file had been turned over to the plaintiff without a complete copy being retained. . . .

The settlement was far higher than the expected verdict "because of the harassment and obsessive pursuit of defendants by Damer. . . ." The first motion to set aside the settlement was provoked by "the hopeless specter of Damer's clearly unrelenting obsession with publicizing himself and his claims in this matter." The present motion dealt with "*Damer's fraud prior to the settlement.*"

---

48. Respondent's Exhibit PP: Plaintiff's Points and Authorities in Opposition (April 17, 1990).

On April 4, Chiantelli filed his "temporary and conditional" "Order Re: Settlement Agreement."[49] "Extraordinary circumstances" compelled "that the file of this matter be sealed from the public." The jurors, parties, and present and former lawyers were forbidden to discuss the case with anyone. Justice Scott would receive and secure Damer's files, while granting access to the State Bar and district attorney (DA). All others would have to seek Chiantelli's approval "after a noticed motion" and a "showing of good cause." Chiantelli would review the situation every three months; when he determined the files were no longer needed they would be shredded.

On April 27, Denebeim moved for entry of judgment and sanctions against the defendants, declaring that "it is difficult to imagine more frivilous [*sic*] motions than the two filed on behalf of defendants"[50] to set aside the settlement. At the time of the settlement, it was so "clear that attorney Damer intended to violate it" that defendants insisted on retaining recourse against him; yet now they moved to set aside the judgment on that ground. The second motion "was a bizarre concoction of spurious arguments . . . a clumsy attempt to mislead the court into believing that the Myers report was a *sine qua non* of their decision to settle." Sterns

> wants a forum to point the finger of blame anywhere but at himself. The list of scapegoats . . . can be expected to grow in proportion to the panic accompanying his sinking (or sunken) reputation.

He was feeling "buyer's remorse" about what he paid "after his wife attacked the settlement in open court."

> The Sterns defendants are hateful and vindictive towards Plaintiff. This is why they speculated that Plaintiff was behind the Mehlman "revelation" and suggested that he aided Damer's alleged misconduct.

They were seeking to avoid interest accruing at about $6,250 a month. If media publicity of the second motion "occurred as a result of their sending the moving papers to Damer, then they should be sanctioned for the same reason. . . ."

On March 28, the Coalition for the First Amendment, represented by Judith Epstein, challenged the sealing order on behalf of the *Daily Journal*.[51] On April 20, it published a lengthy front-page article about the case, including the settlement amount, having discovered from "documents recently filed in the state appeal court" that the "highly unusual, confidential settlement . . . indefinitely silences all parties and jurors in the case" and tolled the statute of limitations for

---

49. Respondent's Exhibit D in Separate Statement detailing insufficiency of State Bar's Responses to Respondent's First Set of Interrogatories (Jan 12, 1994).

50. Respondent's Exhibit PPP.

51. Respondent's Exhibits WW and MMM.

Sterns and Elstead to sue Damer for abuse of process or malicious prosecution.[52] On May 4, it published another front-page article on the excessive expenses claimed in the Contra Costa case.[53] Although the pilot had only $5 million in insurance, Sterns had secured a $10.6 million settlement for the 100 cases by convincing the airplane manufacturer and mall owner they were liable despite the National Transportation Safety Board finding that the pilot had been disoriented by fog. Sterns was the lead attorney on a steering committee representing 40 firms. In the course of a single year, he authorized payment of nearly $700,000 expenses to his firm and others. The original two protesting firms were joined by five more, representing nearly 20 clients seeking an accounting for items including $300 meals and a $2,290 trip to London on the Concorde.

The paper quoted Sterns, "We were flying blind during this whole thing." "Someone had to do" the administrative work. "We're not Price Waterhouse. We are a small plaintiffs' firm and we are doing the best we could." He would never again undertake this "enormous, almost backbreaking burden." "Bring in an MBA, a CPA, let the plaintiffs pay him a fee to do it. We're lawyers, not accountants." His bookkeeper and bookkeeper's assistant quit under the strain. One steering committee member said: "Maybe there was a shortcoming there, but we shouldn't be personally critical of Sterns for that. It is difficult to personally supervise a 40-person law firm and try a case at the same time." Another committee member called Sterns "a fine and capable lawyer but he could probably use some help in the accounting department." After a six-month battle over expenses, Sterns reduced his request by $85,000, and Judge Patsey rejected $29,740 of the remaining $678,273 claim. He awarded the two complaining firms $1,883 each in sanctions against Sterns. But finding that Sterns and Timothy Abel (another plaintiffs' lawyer) had had a "dramatic impact" on the cases, he awarded additional fees of $195,000 to Sterns and $40,000 to Abel. He also awarded the six steering committee members $750,000, of which Sterns would get $211,500 to $317,250. Patsey called Sterns "indispensable."

> [W]ithout the experience that he brought to the case, without his theories of liability, without his knowledge of the witnesses on behalf of the plaintiffs that supported those theories and without . . . the respect that the two largest defendants held in him [*sic*], the settlement[s], at least with Beech [Aircraft] and Taubman [the Sun Valley Mall owner] . . . would not have come about, or . . . would have been significantly less than they were.

---

52. Dee Ziegler, *Judge Orders Malpractice Files Shredded,* San Francisco Banner/Daily Journal 1 (Apr. 20, 1990).

53. Dee Ziegler, *Sun Valley Mall Crash Settlement Marred by Allegations of Financial Mismanagement,* San Francisco Banner/Daily Journal 1 (May 4, 1990).

On May 5, Epstein wrote Chiantelli at Damer's request asking him to issue a written minute order.[54] Chiantelli finally did so on June 19, although Damer was omitted from the service list and only got it months later from the *Daily Journal*.[55] Chiantelli ultimately returned all trial exhibits to the parties, vacated the gag order on the jurors, and unsealed everything except Damer's March 16 and 31 letters to him, Catherine Singels's declaration, the documents presented at the March 9 hearing, the transcript of the March 7–9 hearing, the settlement agreement, and the motions for an order to show cause and to set aside the settlement agreement and declare a mistrial.

On May 23, the defendants moved for an order to show cause why Damer should not be held in contempt. He responded:[56]

> Taking Defendants' approach to the extreme, it could be argued that Damer would be obligated to publish an apology to Defendants, or to genuflect before them in the Courthouse foyer, simply because they paid the plaintiff enough money to motivate her to formally request such conduct from Damer "as a condition of settlement."

He denied Denebeim's claim that he felt "bitter regret" over lost fees. He had told Seward that even had she been offered $2 million, "I still would probably not earn my normal top hourly rate, much less the rates charged by defendants' attorneys." He had also said "she was free to settle for any lesser sum." The "true vendettas" were by Elstead and Gebhardt. Elstead had sued Damer for libel in 1985 for criticizing Elstead's handling of Seward's case (but allowed the suit to lapse). "Gebhardt appears to be similarly embarrassed by having to settle a case for $750,000.00 when my client's initial demand, in 1985, was only $600,000.00." Damer accused Gebhardt's firm of "attempting to use these proceedings to embarrass me" at a time when Damer's firm was suing Gebhardt's client for mismanaging and embezzling the retirement funds of 1,100 Alameda County employees.

Damer's repeated requests for a transcript of the March 7–9 hearing were ignored until he moved to dismiss the contempt citation. On July 28, Judge Leighton Hatch ordered dismissal unless Damer got the transcripts and minute orders on August 8, two days before the contempt hearing.[57] The court clerk's minutes were brief.[58] On March 7, "the court ordered the record, clerks [*sic*] minutes and records, and all exhibits sealed prior to" the next day's hearing. On March 8, "the court heard Defendants' motion for order for return of documents to Defendants" and "took the motion under submission." Jeanette Shipman's

54. Respondent's Exhibit YYY.
55. Respondent's Exhibit DDD.
56. Exhibit B of Respondent's Trial Brief.
57. Respndent's Exhibit NNN.
58. Respondent's Exhibit JJJ.

lawyer obtained an order enjoining Damer from contacting her in any way. "The court additionally ordered all court records, exhibits, both marked and unmarked, and clerk's minutes and records sealed" and continued the matter to the next day "for further consideration of Defendants' motion for return of documents." The March 9 minutes declared, "Records sealed by Order of the Court." Page 2 was numbered the second of four pages, but there were no more.

At the August 10 contempt hearing, Gebhardt argued that Damer was aware of the court's orders but conceded, "I don't recall saying anything about a minute order." "The only written thing I know of is April 4th, Mr. Damer stated he got that in the mail." At a further hearing on November 21, 1991, Chiantelli admitted there was no minute order, "That's when we didn't have the clerk. Nothing was indicated on the matter because I thought there was. The clerk who was a temporary clerk would have put it down in the minutes, and it was discovered that it was not put in the minutes."

On August 29, Judge Hatch found Damer guilty on three grounds. They were failing to deliver the records to Judge Scott and violating the confidentiality agreement by filing the petition for mandate with exhibits and the notice of motion in the Sun Valley case. He fined Damer $1,000 on each count but stayed the order to let him seek extraordinary relief.[59] He also granted sanctions of $2,852.90 to Elstead.

State Bar Court Special Examiner Robert Hawley[60] wrote Damer on January 29, 1991, about his failure to report the contempt citation and sanctions to the State Bar. Damer replied, on March 13, that the reporting requirement was satisfied by Hawley's obvious knowledge of both.[61] Until Damer knew "the nature of any accusations or charges" "I am neither able to understand the rationale of your demands nor obliged to 'cooperate' with you." Damer would not reveal the files he was on record as having refused to give Judge Scott. He offered to duplicate his entire file at the State Bar's expense, after segregating "materials which I am required to withhold." He assailed Hawley for not acting against Sterns.

> As you dallied, you allowed these men to delay indefinitely, if not forever, any refunds to the thousands of clients against whom . . . were regularly assessed, in a "tacky" and "unethical" manner, "phone case costs" of $500.00 or more per client. . . . I expect your appointment has something to do with these Fabian ploys[62] since Landels, Ripley & Diamond [Hawley's firm] was the

---

59. The California Supreme Court denied review on March 28, 1991; the U.S. Supreme Court denied certiorari on October 7, 1991. Damer v. Superior Court, 502 U.S. 822 (1991).

60. A partner in Landels, Ripley & Diamond.

61. Respondent's Exhibit CCCC (Aug. 26, 1994).

62. Damer is referring to the strategy of the Roman dictator Quintus Fabius Maximus, nicknamed Cunctator (Delayer), who refused to engage his enemy directly, instead seeking to weaken him through a war of attrition.

> ultimate landlord to Sterns and ICI . . . where all three establishments shared adjoining suites. . . . Could it be that your firm not only made a profit from Sterns' practices, but also even knew all about them and could be properly made a "deep pocket" defendant in a suit for restitution?

Damer asked Hawley to disclose facts that could indicate a conflict of interest or "irrebuttable presumption against impartiality" and urged him to "immediately resign as a participant in this purported 'investigation'" in order "to save the State Bar . . . and our entire profession, any further unavoidable embarrassment."

> Please do not underestimate my resolve. Over two decades ago, after my graduation from law school, I volunteered for duty in a foreign war to which sons and daughters of ordinary American citizens were being sent in the place of "well connected" people like you and your partners. I simply am not going to sit by and see ordinary Americans victimized by an "old boy network" which nominally disqualifies the San Francisco State Bar office in this matter, but then appoints an "independent" man as "Special Examiner" who *just happens* to be *both* a former attorney in that San Francisco office *and* a junior partner in a firm financially intertied [*sic*] with the firm under "investigation," and who *just happens* to permit a *lawyer* under investigation [presumably Jeanette Shipman], one supposedly *totally disengaged* from any participation therein, to attend a closed court proceeding in which she was *not* involved as a party and where she *was* accompanied by a staff investigator from her own San Francisco State Bar office!

On February 7, 1991, Denebeim moved to unseal the records, which were "necessary" in Seward's legal malpractice lawsuit against Damer & Stryker, whose misconduct "must be exposed for the protection of the public at large."[63] Allen opposed this for Sterns. On May 1, Chiantelli released to the San Mateo Superior Court under seal the transcript of the March 7–9 hearing, Damer's March 8 memo opposing the settlement, Denebeim's points and authorities opposing the motion to set aside the settlement, Chiantelli's April 4 Order, the transcript of Judge Hatch's August 10 and 24 contempt proceedings, and Hatch's contempt order.

On March 13, Damer wrote Deputy District Attorney David Moon (with whom he had once worked). Although he accused Denebeim of seeking to destroy evidence and learn the identity of his informants, he focused on the Sterns firm.[64]

> *Millions* of dollars are at stake here, in the form of restitution owed Defendants' clients. Defendants, from 1980 to 1990, represented *thousands* of clients. If each was cheated of the sums stolen from my former client, about $5,000,000.00, including interest, is owed. . . . Obviously, it is possible

63. Respondent's Exhibit WWW.

64. Respondent's Exhibit A to Trial Brief (July 29, 1994).

> that Defendants—who are very savvy politically—have made significant contributions to one or more of [D.A.] Arlo Smith's campaigns. Therefore, I request that you not share this material or this letter with *anyone* there unless the matter is first cleared through a standard "conflict of interest" check. . . . Eventually, I may have to go to the United States Attorney, or to the press. My adversaries have "friends in high places" in both Republican and Democratic circles, and apparently have not been afraid to use their "connections." . . .
>
> The Defendants, having failed to have me jailed for the several hundred days claimed to be appropriate, are now sure to press for my ultimate disbarment. . . . [T]he former Deputy District Attorney, who presided as the trial judge, made it very clear that he would attempt to get the authorities after me should I persist in my unflinching refusal to be part of the "cover up."

Two weeks later, Moon asked for more information about the confidential Smith memoranda. Damer replied that the excess expenses might amount to $10 million over the previous decade and the under-settlements $10 million to $100 million. He warned Moon to be "very careful" about whom he consulted. Leo Murphy, a "very popular former" DA, now worked for Gebhardt's firm. Damer claimed the depositions and trial transcripts "irrefutably establish perjury." But on May 10, Moon reported that a superior told him to "decline further involvement of this office as not properly within our area of responsibility" and advised Damer to consider complaining to the State Bar and filing a civil action. Damer "repeatedly press[ed] the State Bar to prosecute" Sterns, but it did nothing.

On May 21, Denebeim sought $25,000 in sanctions against Damer for refusing to deliver the Seward files.[65]

> [D]uring the time that I was associate counsel with Damer, he put me in the position of being on a "need to know" basis with regard to documents and evidence he regarded as particularly sensitive. . . . Presently, Damer is threatening to disclose many intimate and private details of Maria Seward Sargent's personal life as part of his claim that she has breached a duty that she owes him and this caused him to have to do so much extra work that it is possible that she may receive only a tiny fraction of the interpleaded sums. . . . I have personally heard Damer claim that he was going to make "a career" out of suing Gerald Sterns and brag that he was going to make a big reputation for himself in the legal malpractice field using the case as his vehicle.

Damer objected to this as double jeopardy since he had already been sanctioned and held in civil and criminal contempt for the same act. Furthermore, why should he give his files to a court that had a track record of losing things? The *Daily Journal* had reported that the court had lost unsealed copies of the same

65. Respondent's Exhibit K of Answer to NTSC (July 15, 1993).

files and could not even find the transcript of Damer's last contempt hearing. Judge Hatch denied Denebeim's motion and left that order to be typed; but it, too, was lost.[66]

On October 22, 1991, the Court of Appeal dismissed all of Damer's appeals for lack of standing unless he delivered all the documents to Scott within fourteen days.[67] On April 10, 1992, Damer moved to transfer the appeals to "a new division whose impartiality could not reasonably be questioned." The Court of Appeal "seemingly intended to deprive Damer of the privacy of his work product, the inviolability of his informants' anonymity, and the evidence necessary to fulfill fiduciary duties to victims of the original Sterns defendants." The court knew that the State Bar and DA "have committed themselves to doing *nothing* to assist Sterns' victims." Seward had "blatantly violated her fiduciary duties, as a representative of a class, by settling under an arrangement which requires her to cooperate in suppressing and destroying evidence vital to interests of other class members."

On July 14, 1992, Damer wrote the State Bar in Los Angeles, objecting that Hawley had said the Bar had abandoned his grievance against Jeanette Shipman.[68] Immediately after obtaining summary judgment for herself as a defendant in *Seward v. Sterns*, on the ground that she was merely the firm's employee, Shipman filed two cases against it claiming $30,000 in fees, which were resolved by secret arbitration. While Seward appealed the summary judgment, the principal case reached settlement, one of whose terms was abandonment of the appeal, "the destruction of all evidence that might impugn Jeanette Shipman, and the sealing of all court records relating to the case." That included a "very damning piece of evidence," a September 1992 interoffice memo, which "suggests she is one of the 'other lawyers' aware of the firm's 'phony case cost' scheme used to embezzle client funds." After Damer complained about Shipman, she tried to disavow the settlement. Her lawyer "came to court brandishing the sword of a malicious prosecution suit as a weapon with which to discourage complaints against Jeanette Shipman." Damer wanted his complaint against Shipman reopened and pursued together with his March 1990 complaints against Sterns, Elstead, and others. He asked:

> [W]hy has the State Bar refused to take the totally tainted "special investigator" off of the case despite the clear conflicts of interest? And how did the State Bar come to hire and retain an attorney as an "Investigative Trial

---

66. Dolores Ziegler, *Paper Loss Turns Into Counsel's Gain,* SAN FRANCISCO DAILY JOURNAL (after May 30, 1991), Respondent's Exhibit P to Answer to Amended NTSC (Oct. 25, 1993).

67. State Bar's Exhibit A to Supplemental Trial Brief (8.11.94). The U.S. Supreme Court denied certiorari on October 5, 1991. Damer v. Superior Court, 506 U.S. 825 (1992).

68. Respondent's Exhibit F.

> Counsel" when records on file, in local courts, show that she made statements under oath that were absolutely untrue? . . . These events suggest that . . . the State Bar exists to protect the high and mighty attorneys and to make scapegoats out of small practitioners. 99.999% of all disciplined lawyers are sole practitioners who cannot afford to fight the State Bar system. To my knowledge, never has any big law firm—or any member of the "old boy network"—ever been successfully prosecuted by the State Bar.

Damer appended two newspaper accounts. In late 1990, the *Daily Journal* objected that, although most of the papers in *Seward v. Sterns* had been unsealed on April 27, four boxes of files were still sealed.[69] Even "the unsealing order apparently is sealed." When the *Daily Journal* tried to see the files a month later, "the clerk produces a few recent documents and tells you the rest of the file is missing."[70] Even Chiantelli told Ziegler that sealing was "something that should not be used indiscriminately or very often if at all. [I] do not want to advocate the sealing of court records, even though I did it." Sterns and Elstead said they had sought the sealing order to protect themselves against "Damer's demonstrated hatred for the defendants—together with claims he wishes to attract other clients of defendants for future legal malpractice cases." Damer retorted, "Personal malice does not motivate me to prosecute any litigation." The newspaper noted that Damer's "previous opposition to confidentiality agreements has landed him in hot water with the Superior Court." A bill sponsored by the Center for Public Interest Law granted the State Bar access to secret proceedings in January 1989. Judge Hatch sealed the contempt hearing against Damer, his order, and the *Daily Journal* memo opposing the sealing. The *Daily Journal* objected to the sealing of "transcripts of three days of settlement proceedings that reportedly erupted into brawls and hostilities. . . ."

> When the *Daily Journal* tried to cover these hearings, it was tossed out of the courtroom. We and the court were told it was in the best interests of plaintiff . . . to keep this information under the hat. Now that [Seward] is filing another legal malpractice suit—this one against Damer—she wants the file unsealed.

Denebeim claimed the files were necessary "to protect both the plaintiff and the public from Damer" and had even filed a copy of the *Daily Journal's* brief in favor of access. The paper asked, "Did the public not need protection in March?"

---

69. Dolores Ziegler, *Malpractice Case Escalates Into Battle of Wills*, SAN FRANCISCO DAILY JOURNAL (late 1990).

70. Dolores Ziegler, *The Court Report: Public's Need for Protection In the Eye of the Beholden*, SAN FRANCISCO DAILY JOURNAL 2 (Feb 25, 1992).

On January 14, 1992, Damer wrote Joseph W. Cotchett, who had represented Sun Valley victims.[71] Although Damer called his letter "more . . . a challenge than an accusation," he maintained that Cotchett had "assisted" Sterns in giving the "absolutely false impression" that Sterns's $125,000 overcharge in that case was only the result of "innocent [in]attention, acceptable ignorance, and understandable incompetence."

> The law profession is so without ethics, Mr. Cotchett, because powerful people like you, who are in positions of influence, permit this type of shenanigans to go on. . . . Yet even more outrageous is the fact that a wealthy, prestigious lawyer like you, who has made a fortune off of the sins of other professionals, turns his eyes away from his colleagues' misdeeds, yet thinks himself worthy, I am told, of hand-picking judges and seeking the office of Attorney General of the state of California.

"Rather than being a 'good old boy' on *Sterns*' behalf," he urged Cotchett to file an amicus brief for Damer. "[T]he issue being posed in this litigation, ultimately, is quite simple: how much secrecy can wealthy crooks buy?" Cotchett's "purported desire to 'clean up the legal profession,'" which he had voiced to a reporter in 1991,[72] apparently "does not extend to any lawyer who works with you in cases where your cooperative effort make [*sic*] you both a good deal of money. . . ." Damer concluded:

> Fortunately, there is still the "court of public opinion" which may have some objection to my perhaps impending imprisonment, as well as some questions why you—and other high-ranking men of the law—never did anything about this situation. Remember what Edmund Burke said would happen if "enough good men did nothing?"

The State Bar informed Damer in July 1992 that Hawley had been removed from the investigation. But when Hawley wrote him again on December 3, Damer complained that he had been "misled" and that Shipman also still worked for the State Bar, which "may explain why there has been a decision in her favor." In fact, Mark Fredkin replaced Hawley (who had become a full-time State Bar attorney, a fact Damer found "not particularly reassuring"). Damer assumed Denebeim had filed the complaint

> in the hope of discrediting me and stealing the fees my partner and I earned over a decade. Indeed, the hogwash in Hawley's draft "Notice to Show Cause" bears a striking resemblance to Denebeim's "First Amended Cross-Complaint" for malpractice.

---

71. Respondent's Exhibit CCCC (Aug. 26, 1994).

72. *Counsel Warns of "Ethics Gap" Yawning Wide to Entice Incautious Professionals, San Francisco Daily Journal* (Nov. 19, 1991).

V. THE DISCIPLINARY PROCEEDING

A. Culpability

The State Bar finally served the NTSC on Damer on May 3, 1993, charging him with taking positions detrimental to his client.[73] He promptly sought an extension of time to answer because of the "great, and even perhaps totally insurmountable difficulty in obtaining counsel." One defense specialist had declined because Damer had complained against two State Bar employees. The State Bar's decision to prosecute him after rejecting his own complaints against others "is the typical conduct employed by a governmental institution and its allies in the private sphere, to discredit and incapacitate any 'whistleblowers'. . . ." He offered a sealed envelope with the Chiantelli hearing record, which the State Bar Court refused to accept. He complained that Hawley (the previous investigator) had "attended nearly every court proceeding that the Defendants, in the underlying *Seward v. Sterns* case, had directly and indirectly brought against the Respondent." He was pursuing a claim against Hawley for violating his civil rights. He also objected that Fredkin refused to reveal "all of the elements of his own employment history" and "all of his social and financial connections with the interests of the Defendants." Damer had asked the State Bar's Complaint Audit and Review Department to investigate the dismissal of his complaint against Shipman. At the semi-annual public hearing of the State Bar Board of Governors (BoG or the Board) on December 5, 1991 (in which the only other "public" member was Damer's videographer), Damer had voiced his grievances and asked: "Has anything ever said in meetings like this ever led to any meaningful and permanent changes?" The present proceeding was his "last chance to conduct a public dialogue on the legitimacy of the type of 'secret settlement'" he had rejected.

> [A] proper ruling in this case, on my behalf, may precipitate a scandal of major proportions further impeaching the integrity of the State Bar as it is presently configured . . . the true purpose behind these disbarment proceedings is to force me to choose between continuing with my livelihood and surrendering the identity of informants and the evidence necessary to the large class of my adversaries' victims.

He asked the hearing judge, Alan Goldhammer, to disclose "any grounds for recusal or disqualification," insisting he meant "no personal offense" and did "not wish to take 'a shot at a king.'"

Although Damer's motion for more time was unopposed, Goldhammer denied it. "I believe many attorneys who represent Respondents before the State Bar Court would be delighted to achieve notoriety resulting from antagonism by the Office of Trials [*sic*—the OTC] . . . [which] would be attractive to

73. No. 90-O-15007. His conduct allegedly violated BPC §§ 6067, 6068(e), and 6103.

potential clients." There were no grounds for his recusal. Damer moved for reconsideration, appending a letter to him from Tom Low:

> Having given this a lot of thought . . . I nevertheless feel that insofar as you have named Robert Hawley as a defendant in a civil rights suit, I cannot represent you. I think you have raised many interesting issues and, perhaps more importantly, issues of great importance. Were it not for the fact that you named Mr. Hawley, I would be happy to represent you and perhaps change the legal profession.

Goldhammer was unmoved. Damer again requested reconsideration, citing the "'old adage' that if a lawyer represents himself, the quality of his representation may be fatefully, prejudicially, compromised" and seeking more time for discovery. At the March 8, 1990, hearing Damer's adversaries had said he "needs some mental help" and his "alleged infirmities" justified the secret settlement. He feared those same enemies might "finally effectuate [his] discrediting" and "resurrect such a preposterous rationale to have Respondent's 'ticket pulled,'" as they had threatened. Goldhammer also denied Damer's request for appointed counsel because the State Bar Court could not punish him. Goldhammer refused to extend the time for discovery since Damer had not proposed a plan; the judge warned that he could consider meritless dilatory motions to be aggravating circumstances. The same day, however, Damer moved to supplement his requests, having found a case allegedly granting a right to counsel in license revocations.[74] Goldhammer promptly rejected this, ruling that Damer had "completely miscited and misunderstood" the case.

The day after that Damer wrote Fredkin, reiterating his refusal to deliver the files to Scott because Gebhardt knew where they would be kept. "Remember that lawyers ruthless enough to steal from widows and orphans, and lawyers undergoing media scrutiny for their overcharges . . . are hardly lawyers to be trusted for their fidelity to decency." He also feared accidental destruction.

> [W]hatever copies my former partner, Lance Stryker, took with him at the end of 1990 [when the partnership dissolved] were nothing more than cinders after his home was vaporized in the October, 1991 Oakland Hills fire.

Denebeim had had "his greedy eyes on my earnings" ever since he first demanded $15,000 to accept the settlement on Seward's behalf. Denebeim had "set up" the settlement as a pretext to sue Damer for malpractice. Mehlman had told Stryker that Seward had agreed to give Denebeim half of whatever they kept from Damer. Since Damer was entitled to about $500,000, "Denebeim and Seward had major motives to concoct 'settlements' that would 'transfer' such sums to *them*." Damer concluded, "to the extent your 'case' against me depends

74. Borror v. Department of Investment, 15 Cal.App.3d 531, 91 Cal.Rptr. 525 (1971).

on Robert Denebeim's credibility, you may wish to reevaluate the wisdom of investing much more time."

Damer finally answered on July 15.[75] There had never been any settlement in Seward's case. She "did not agree to turn over to her *adversaries* her private correspondence with *Respondent.*" He had not "argued against" the "stated interests" of his client, who had said "she did not want her sensitive correspondence with Respondent to be accessible to Robert Gebhardt or any other agent of the Defendants." She lacked "full cognizance" of the settlement, asking him on March 7, "Can I find out what the terms of the [deal]—I don't know what we left on the table last night." The Court's April 4 Order was at variance with its March 9 "oral directives," omitting the requirement to notify Damer before shredding the files. By April 4 some defendants had moved for a mistrial; had it been granted, Seward would have lacked the evidence to recommence the action. She "was utterly without the right or power to sell or to sacrifice the class interests for her sole benefit. . . ." Damer attached the letter he had written Judge Patsey on March 16. He claimed "a right to maintain the privacy of his files *even against the wishes of his former client. . . .*" By "virtue of the adversarial positions" taken by Seward from March 7 onward, Damer "has at all times been privileged to assert his own rights to said client's 'disadvantage'" to protect himself from Seward's December 1990 malpractice lawsuit and let him file complaints against Chiantelli "and the State Bar's corrupt disciplinary practices." The State Bar Court was not competent to judge him "to the extent that [a] private Court may be unable to address constitutional issues and is funded by collecting money penalties. . . ." Denebeim was seeking "to misappropriate Respondent's fee" and "avoid repaying approximately $100,000.00 of costs" in violation of Rule 5-100 forbidding an attorney from initiating an administrative proceeding to gain advantage in a civil matter. The contempt citation lacked an "appropriate order to show cause" and denied Damer his right to a jury trial and to cross-examine witnesses. The contempt hearing judge "implied that he would not personally approve of said [sealing] orders or of the conduct of the trial judge," imposed only "token" penalties, declined to enforce them, and rejected a May 1991 motion for further sanctions. No appellate court "ever rendered an opinion *on the merits.*"

> Despite the fact that over 10,000 petitions for review are submitted annually, the most senior and a highly esteemed scholar on the California Supreme Court, Justice Stanley Mosk, voted to grant Respondent's petition.

The day Damer filed his answer, the fear he had expressed a week earlier came true. A fire gutted Judge Chiantelli's chambers.[76] A Fire Department investigator

---

75. Fifteen single-spaced pages and seventeen more of attachments.

76. Malcolm Glover and Jim Heron Zamora, *Fire Guts Judges' Offices in Hall of Justice*, San Francisco Examiner (7.15.93), Respondent's Exhibit P to Answer to Amended NTSC (Oct. 25, 1993).

sought to "spike" a rumor that a cigarette had caused it. The building banned smoking, and the investigator found no evidence of it in chambers. But the judge was a heavy smoker; and the newspaper reported that "investigators noted an ashtray full of butts on the bailiff's desk in Chiantelli's courtroom on Wednesday night, but it was missing on Thursday morning." The judge said no court files had been lost but otherwise declined comment. Damer sent this account to Fredkin on July 27, claiming that papers he had entrusted to Chiantelli were destroyed, including "correspondence with Seward wherein she committed to represent the interests of the class of Sterns' victims, and . . . proof of Sterns' and Elstead's perjury that they themselves produced. Do you need any further demonstration of the reasons why I could not entrust all copies of my files to others?"

At the first status conference on September 21, Goldhammer ordered the State Bar to charge Damer with violating BPC Section 6106 or drop the allegation of continuing to disobey a court order. After it dropped the charge Damer filed a new answer. Negotiations to settle Seward's case

> first occurred in clandestine meetings . . . [with] Denebeim and Mehlman, in a drinking establishment. . . . Respondent was deliberately and secretively excluded . . . despite his explicit rights under his fee agreement with Seward . . . and despite the fact that such activities, by Denebeim and Mehlman, were a blatant violation of Respondent's rights under his contracts with those lawyers. . . .

There never had been any settlement because the defendants had repudiated it by March 9, Chiantelli refused to enforce it, and the defendants moved for a mistrial. Chiantelli's oral order "need not be obeyed" and was not reduced to writing until April 4. Neither Judge Hatch nor the defendants had sought to have Damer jailed for contempt because that would "give Respondent standing to seek habeas corpus relief in the federal courts, which may lead to a ruling that the alleged March 9, 1990 orders would have been utterly void and a violation of Respondent's due process and constitutional rights."

> [N]o lawyer ought in good faith to obey the alleged orders or the alleged "instructions" of Seward, or to avoid challenging such "orders" or "instructions" in every way. Submission to said "orders" would subvert the RULES of professional conduct and the State Bar Act and would subordinated [*sic*] Respondent's obligations, as a lawyer and citizen, to his financial self interest.

At the next status conference, Goldhammer ruled that Damer could only make an offer of proof of his reasons for not obeying valid orders and expressed the tentative belief that "good faith" was not exculpatory and would be mitigating only if Damer had complied with the court orders. But Damer had "indicated that even if this Court were to find that [he] is continuing to violate a valid and final court order, [he] does not intend to obey the court order." Damer demanded that Fredkin tell him "exactly what portions of which alleged orders are involved" and objected that "the identities of my accusers can be hidden from me with 'privilege claims.'" Criticizing the inadequacy of the State Bar's answers to his first set of interrogatories, Damer declared that he had tried to withdraw as counsel "as soon as the unethical provisions of Sterns' settlement demands were recited" but "was compelled to remain in a locked courtroom while terms of a purported 'settlement' were recited in a 'Star Chamber' mode into a record he was forbidden ever to possess." He called the settlement and order "preposterous" six times. Either the order had expired in July 1990, when it was not reviewed every three months, as required, or it "was essentially a mere sham."

After two more unsuccessful settlement conferences, the State Bar filed its pretrial statement. Damer had "approached this matter with almost religious zeal." Although he had "cross-examined his own client relative to the settlement terms in an attempt to change her mind," Seward was "unequivocal in wanting to adopt the settlement." Damer continued to deny the legality of Chiantelli's order, even after exhausting appeals.

> It would create a complete breakdown of the legal system if lawyers, who have exhausted available appellate review could continue to refuse to obey orders because of their beliefs. . . .

Since good faith was not a defense the bar would call no witnesses. Its trial brief reiterated this, asking "are we going to disband our rule of law"?

Damer (now represented by Michele R. Wallace) filed his pretrial statement. He twice derided Chiantelli as more familiar with criminal practice than civil, accused him of being the "defendants' scribe," and called his order "bizarre" and "appalling." Damer could be found guilty only if "*no reasonable attorney could contend that the orders in question were invalid or unenforceable.*" Buying evidence was "*prohibited by Business & Professions Code §6129.*" BPC Section 6068(h) required him "never to reject, for any consideration personal to himself . . . the cause of the defenseless or the oppressed." He planned to call numerous witnesses, including Hawley (who "acted as [the defendants'] agent in diverting Respondent's complaints to the State Bar"), William Davis ("who arranged for Hawley's appointment in order to divert Respondent's charges into an 'investigation' of the Respondent"), and Judge Chiantelli ("whose violations of law led to the incineration of various documents (and which even threatened the lives of all persons incarcerated at 850 Bryant . . ."). He rejected bifurcation of guilt and penalty because "Respondent demands this persecution end, now." He later added as witnesses the State Bar Deputy General Counsel (who "stated that Respondent had a right to keep his files") and the settlement judge, Jennifer Gee (who "can testify as an expert in that a reasonable attorney could in good faith object and refuse to comply with the orders alleged by the State Bar"). But Goldhammer granted the OTC's objection to *all* these witnesses on the ground that Damer had filed his pretrial statement too late and limited the Respondent to his own testimony and documents he had filed.

Damer moved to dismiss on three grounds, namely, the charges failed to specify which orders he disobeyed; those orders were "facially invalid"; and he in good faith believed them "to be preposterous, appalling and invalid." He also filed an offer of proof with respect to the disallowed witnesses. This proceeding was "beginning to resemble the strange netherworld of the contempt hearings," in which "events would be manipulated to just *avoid* confronting Respondent's substantive challenges to alleged 'orders,'" and Damer "was also denied, by a judge, the opportunity to call any witnesses. . . ."

Damer used his offer of proof to advance numerous contentions. Francis Bassios

> a twenty-year veteran of the State Bar trial counsel's staff, stated, at a meeting of the Hellenic Law Society, that all attorneys had an "absolute right to keep a copy" of his or her files. . . . Bassios shut up as soon as he learned of Respondent's identity.

State Bar Monitor Robert Fellmeth called Chiantelli's actions "'irresponsible,' and implied Respondent's anti-confidentiality stance was commendable." Gerald Sterns would "admit his unlawful business practices" and "how he routinely settled cases 'cheap' in order to maintain cash flow when his improvident spending habits led to the imposition of federal and state tax liens on his assets. . . ." Sterns also "would purport to pay legitimate case costs with checks from his operating account, only to 'void' the checks after their amounts had been deducted from his clients' settlements." Richard Bridgman would testify about how "he attempted to intimidate, patronize, and even to physically threaten Respondent. . . ." Robert Gebhardt, whose home was threatened with foreclosure, "desperately needed to prove himself a 'rainmaker' with Lawyers Mutual and his firm . . . [which] had seen its lawyers and/or staff go to jail for embezzlement *more* than once in the last few years. . . ." But Gebhardt "is one of the 'untouchables' in terms of power and political influence; his father is a retired Federal Bureau of Investigation (FBI) executive and the Bronson firm has arranged more 'lateral promotions' for its members (judicial appointments to the superior court and federal benches) than any other single law firm in Northern California history. . . ." Fearing that Sterns's memo to Elstead "would be *sprung* on Elstead at trial," Gebhardt "decided at last to 'play it safe' and amend Elstead's discovery responses, cleverly 'hiding behind the flag' when Elstead said he had found the [smoking gun] memos—*having forgotten their existence*—under Navy commendations in his attic!" Glen Allen would testify "how his firm filed the first contested motion for a continuance in 1987, before Judge Perasso, without telling Respondent that Judge Perasso's son and namesake was a lawyer in Allen's office. . . ." Denebeim would admit "how *he and Seward* have sought to publicize what *they*—in March of 1990—PROMISED TO KEEP TOTALLY CONFIDENTIAL . . . [to] advance their pecuniary goals. . . ." Denebeim would reveal "his close financial and professional links" with Cotchett's firm, "which in turn is connected financially to the Special Examiner's law firm, in that Joseph Cotchett and Allen Ruby are the lead co-counsel in . . . the 'Technical Equities' litigation, in which more than $100,000,000.00 is at stake." Hawley would testify about "implicitly promising the State Bar proceedings would 'go easy' on Respondent . . . if Respondent would turn over what Hawley apparently believed were materials damaging to himself"; he also would testify about "his role in Fredkin's appointment" and "his relationships with Shipman." Chiantelli would testify about "whatever favorable arrangements may have occurred as to himself, personally, after the 1990 fiasco," "his relationships with the Olympic Club, a membership in which Gebhardt insinuated . . . would be a very pleasant diversion," and the judge's "role in this prosecution since Chiantelli, as a former Deputy District Attorney himself, has connections with the State Bar. . . ."

When the hearing began, however, Goldhammer reiterated that Damer could not offer witnesses because he filed his pretrial statement late, "[Y]ou have to make those in an orderly manner. . . . This trial was arranged for on a one day trial on the basis of both counsel's [*sic*] representation. . . . I have other matters. . . ." Damer sought relief "on the grounds that on the day that the pretrial statement was due, my mother-in-law died, I was taking care of four children, and I was in the middle of a jury trial." He offered a judge's condolence letter, which "moved me to tears because the last sentence said [of his mother-in-law], 'she loved nothing better than a good fight for a just cause, her advocacy on behalf of union members will be missed. . . .'" Goldhammer had to interrupt twice to make Damer stop. Fredkin said Damer had sought no relief at the time. Wallace again moved to dismiss. Comparing himself to a tax protester, Damer declared that "taking a philosophical position in the United States of America still isn't a criminal act yet." He insisted on knowing exactly what orders he violated. "I think at stake here is . . . the very primal fundamental protection of due process, the concept of a court of record . . . that everything that went on in March . . . was in a star chamber closed door proceeding. . . ." When Goldhammer said Fredkin could submit the transcript, Damer objected that it was still under seal. Goldhammer offered to admit it under seal.

DAMER: Your Honor, that would be absolutely unlawful. . . . . This is a public proceeding. . . .

WALLACE: If you seal the transcript, how are we going to discuss the issues that the transcript raises?. . . .

FREDKIN: The very term [*sic*] which is being objected to [i.e., sealing] . . . is now being used to protect Mr. Damer from going forward.

COURT: . . . .[T]hat's why I said . . . we can't have it both ways.

Fredkin waived opening statement because the contempt citation was collateral estoppel. Wallace sought to make hers *before* the prosecution case "because I think there are some real mistaken beliefs about what this case is going to be about." Goldhammer found both sides "a bit off track." He did not agree "that this is an open and shut case" simply because the trial judge found that Damer had violated a court order; but he also disagreed with "Damer's position that this court will go into, as a matter of fact, whether he was in good faith." Wallace denied there had "ever been any review by any court as to the validity of the orders."

After Goldhammer admitted the Chiantelli record under seal, Damer said Fredkin should have sought Chiantelli's permission. Damer claimed to be "extremely concerned . . . for Ms. Seward," fearing that Sterns and Lawyers Mutual would charge Fredkin and Denebeim with violating the secrecy agreement, thereby abrogating her right to the $750,000. Fredkin also offered the orders and contempt finding and the numbers of the transcript pages on which the prosecution would rely. The parties then squabbled about whether the transcripts were identical. When the State Bar rested, Wallace renewed the motion to dismiss. Goldhammer tentatively denied it, while conceding that he felt some confusion. If Damer presented a "legal basis for objecting to Judge Chiantelli's order," Goldhammer was inclined to dismiss the complaint. An example would be a "patently invalid" order directing an attorney to shoot the bailiff. And disagreeing with the State Bar, Goldhammer was inclined to address "the question of whether Mr. Damer had some public Attorney General like capacity to violate the court order."

Damer submitted seventy-eight exhibits and renewed his offer of proof regarding witnesses. Goldhammer declined to hear them, mentioning only the most outrageous proposal to call Judge Anthony Kline to testify about what he meant in an opinion. Before beginning, Damer warned "that I do tend to be long winded . . . we'll probably go all day explaining these events. But . . . I'll be happy to do it again for someone who is receptive to listen." He argued that "once an attorney representing a prospective class assumes a fiduciary duty . . . [that attorney] cannot simply sell out the members of that class for the benefit of the first client to come to them." Asked by Goldhammer for authority, Damer declined to offer citations because "you personally participated in some of the cases. . . . During your tenure at the legal aid clinic . . . you were involved in some of the very class actions in question."

On May 27, 1993, Damer wrote Fredkin that he assumed the State Bar was seeking disbarment, or a suspension conditioned on surrender of his files, which would be even more permanent since he would never comply.[77] He warned:

> All damages that I suffer, from still further loss of business, will, in my view, be actionable against some persons or institutions, if I am ultimately vindicated herein or in Federal court.

77. Respondent's Exhibit D to Trial Brief.

Goldhammer sealed the entire file and exhibits on April 1, 1994. On May 6, he denied Damer's motion to dismiss for failure to allege a disciplinable offense; and two weeks later, he denied a second motion to dismiss for vagueness. Damer's objection was "quite disingenuous inasmuch as he had no difficulty ascertaining to which orders of Judge Chiantelli he was referring when he stated he was refusing to comply with them." Confidentiality agreements were legal, and Chiantelli "had authority to weigh and determine whether class action concerns, for an undetermined class in an unfiled class action, outweighed the desire of Respondent's client . . . to arrive at a settlement. . . ."

When the hearing resumed on July 21, Wallace renewed the motion to dismiss, but Goldhammer told her to brief it. Damer began describing his extensive experience representing legal malpractice clients, starting from his very first case in 1973, but Goldhammer restricted him to the Seward transcript. Damer said Elstead testified he had never offered to represent Charles Higgins, the driver of Seward's car; but a letter from Elstead to Higgins (admitted at trial but since destroyed) proposed to do so and enclosed a fee contract and medical records release. Damer said:

> [A]t the conclusion of that session [in the trial of Seward's malpractice claim], which is not reflected in the transcript, Mr. Gebhardt was overheard saying, "they've got us, they've really got us." And shortly after that he approached us and indicated a half million dollars might be forthcoming, without any condition of confidentiality.

Goldhammer, however, refused "to re-weigh the entire case." Chiantelli's order would be invalid only if "there was absolutely no reason for the trial court to have acted the way it did." When Wallace tried to show Sterns's misconduct, Goldhammer cut her off. However, she did introduce evidence that Sterns's lawsuit in San Mateo Superior Court, interpleading the $750,000 his firm owed Seward, was scheduled for trial in January 1995. There were cross-complaints by Denebeim, Mehlman, and Seward against Damer for legal malpractice and by Damer against them and Sterns, Lawyers Mutual, and Hawley. Damer had "not been able to verify whether [the $750,000] is still there now, or whether some secret ex parte order . . . has caused all or any part of it to be disbursed."

Damer viewed Chiantelli's order "as a sham because he effectively denied me any appellate relief. . . . I felt that when I went to the Court of Appeals I must sound like a mad man, saying that these things actually happened in an American courtroom . . . the hostility directed by Judge Chiantelli showed me little doubt as to his motives. . . ." Damer quoted Daniel Webster and then Oliver Wendell Holmes's declaration that the "history of liberty is the history of procedure." But when Goldhammer objected that "we're going over all the old ground," Damer ended direct.

Under cross-examination, Damer said he never filed a class action on behalf of Sterns's former clients because "it would have allowed Sterns to conduct discovery." Damer remained defiant that the outstanding sanctions, fines, and costs "will not be paid. I will go to jail if an OTSC is brought to enforce their payment, and then I will seek a writ in the federal courts. . . ." He could not recall any demands by Denebeim that he turn over the files to Scott. But Fredkin produced a letter from Denebeim dated January 24, 1991, which read, "I demand that Nicholas Damer and/or Damer & Stryker, immediately transfer all files to the court appointed receiver, James Scott, as required by court order."[78] When Damer denied recognizing Denebeim's signature, Goldhammer warned that this "goes to Mr. Damer's credibility and to his posture before this court." Damer retorted that Denebeim's letter "doesn't give any definition as to what is material personal to Maria Seward that is not supposed to be turned over and it clearly misstates the scope of the court order." He denied that he wrote to Judge Patsey under seal because of the confidentiality order.

On redirect, Damer said another reason he had not yet filed the class action was that establishing overcharging in Seward's case first "would be collateral estoppel and *res judicata*" in such an action. Damer objected to a motion by Denebeim because "the same thing is happening here that happened in front of Judge Hatch. Denebeim gets to make his claims. I don't get to cross examine him." But Goldhammer cut him off, "I've heard that speech, enough." Damer's response to Denebeim (a motion for a writ of *supersedeas* and clarification of reconsideration)[79] provoked an exasperated Goldhammer to exclaim, "[I]t's just repetitive . . . we've had an awful lot of paper that's extraneous in this record already, and I would ask you not to lodge it." Unmoved, Damer insisted on doing so.

Goldhammer disregarded this to pursue his own agenda.

COURT: Did you go to Judge Chiantelli to try to get permission to write to Judge Patsey . . . ?

DAMER: No. I was informed that if I appeared before Judge Chiantelli, I would be summarily arrested. I was informed that by a confidential source. . . .

B. Argument

After Damer rested, Goldhammer offered his tentative opinion that "this is kind of blown a bit out of proportion." Writing to Patsey would not have been "a problem except [Damer] wrote . . . some fifty other attorneys" (in the Sun Valley Mall case). Damer quickly protested that he had not served them. Goldhammer continued, "a gag order is a special kind of order, because once it's disobeyed it's like popping a balloon . . . you can't blow it up again." An "oral order is a court order, it does not have to be . . . reduced as to writing. . . ." The case "boils down to a couple of fairly simple propositions." Damer could have told Chiantelli he had

78. State Bar Exhibit 6.

79. Respondent's Exhibit UUU.

an obligation to inform the Sun Valley judge and plaintiffs. If Chiantelli disagreed, he could have appealed. "But, he didn't do that . . . for reasons that I'm not . . . convinced . . . show he wasn't culpable of violating that court order." Nevertheless, Goldhammer asked Fredkin, "[W]hat's the State Bar's interest in an attorney who disobeys a single court order in the context of a complicated case, with a lot of very important concerns with regard to the public policy involved."

Goldhammer expected to find culpability but not "a terribly serious violation."

> [W]e want attorneys to be ardent advocates for positions and that means that they do take judges to the wire and opponents to the mat . . . [but Damer] was doing it deliberately . . . he was going to show [Chiantelli] he was wrong by disobeying the order, and that's not the way to do it. If you want to get into a spitting match with a judge, you'd better get another judge on your side to overrule the order.

At the same time, Damer's many attempts to do so after the fact were mitigating.

> I don't think that it's appropriate to say to an attorney, well, not only will the courts have the sanction authority over you and the contempt power over you but, God help you if you break the order, the Bar is going to take your license too. Show me a pattern of violating court orders, a pattern of belligerence, sure.

Still, Goldhammer was troubled by Damer's refusal to pay the sanctions. "I don't think it's appropriate for the Bar to have attorneys out there saying, well, you know, we don't have to obey orders, we can just flaunt [*sic*—"flout"] them. . . ." But he found the contempt order to turn over the files "over-broad" because "it duplicates what Judge Chiantelli had already ordered, and it's insulting. I don't think attorneys should be insulted by judges. This was a case that involved a lot of emotion all over the place." Goldhammer "really sort of admired the straight up . . . we disobeyed Judge Chiantelli's orders and we had a higher interest at stake," although he disagreed with that stance "because I think there were other avenues that could have been taken. . . ." But he disliked "this kind of whining . . . there wasn't an order, but if there was an order I did obey it, but if I didn't obey it then I did obey it in this sense and so forth and so on." He could "appreciate some of Judge Chiantelli's reactions. No judge likes to be bullied or papered. . . ." Judges want lawyers to "exercise some self-restraint. And maybe you need to look into that a little more." Damer's problem "from the get go, is that . . . there's nothing that's inherently wrong with a judge weighing the interests and coming out dead wrong." The potential for a class action by the Sterns's firm clients "was very dubious" because "everyone is damaged in an individual way." Instead, the State Bar should have done something about Sterns's behavior, which was "essentially a consumer fraud concern . . . it's sort of a deceptive practice to pretend that [investigators] are not in-house."

Goldhammer was pretty certain about culpability but not sanction. Once Damer had disobeyed the order "the major part of his disobedience was really over. . . ." Although the "papering and the magnifying of every little issue" was "a significant magnifying factor," "we want to be really careful of quarterbacking after the fact."

> [S]ome years later, I can say, gee, why didn't you go to Judge Chiantelli and just ask him or just appeal his order if he denied you? But, I can appreciate, in the heat of the moment, when your client has turned her back on you, and your colleagues have turned their backs on you, that one is not thinking as logically or as unemotionally. . . . That's part of the problem, you know, when we switch from being an attorney for a client and having our own interests involved. . . .

Since Goldhammer saw no reason to fear that Damer would repeat this behavior, the Bar did not have a lot at stake.

Wallace and Damer argued that the failure to file a timely pretrial statement should not preclude them from presenting evidence on penalty, but Goldhammer ruled that Damer could move to reopen the proceedings if a reviewing court decided to impose serious discipline, since he did not plan to do so. Goldhammer acknowledged that "the Court of Appeal should and would have overturned" the trial court's "over-broad" sealing order.

> But, there is no appellate ruling, and I think that this is the kind of an order that an attorney has to obey until he gets a ruling that permits him to disobey it . . . [O]therwise we just don't have an orderly system . . . some orders need to be followed even when you disagree with them.

When he expressed concern about "some of the bullying of this court," Wallace quickly offered an apology "because that was not either one of our intents." Goldhammer replied, "[I]f you're going to go to the federal court, go, don't threaten a judge"; and he advised them to "have a better sense of proportion. This just didn't require this kind of paper."

In his trial brief, Damer emphasized his self-restraint.

> Rather than storm out of the hearings before Judge Chiantelli and hold a press conference on the courthouse steps, with copies of the really "juicy" stuff for each media representative, *Respondent tried to work within the system.*

He repeated his many criticisms of Chiantelli's orders. "*Any*" finding of culpability

> will send a message to every malpractice insurer and embezzling insured lawyer, you are free . . . to compel unwilling attorneys—and their victimized clients, eager for monetary settlements, to cooperate in suppressing evidence of theft and misconduct and in forcing the disclosure of the identities of confidential informants who helped build those clients' cases.

He warned Goldhammer against "misus[ing] the sword of justice against any who would champion the cause of the 'defenseless and oppressed.'" He deplored this "Court's comments, in 1993, that Respondent may be suspended unless and until he breaches his vows of secrecy given to his informants. . . ." The State Bar had waited more than three years to charge him. By "merely insinuating these proceedings . . . the Bar caused exactly the type of devastating effects Respondent's various adversaries surely intended to inflict since March of 1990."

The State Bar's Supplemental Trial Brief said Damer's brief reminded it of "Don Quixote tilting at windmills." Damer had been retained "to represent the interest of one person, Maria Seward," who had been "put through a horrible experience which to this day has not ended for one reason, the continued assertion of moral superiority by the Respondent." Seward had

> received nothing but grief and more litigation because the vision of Respondent conflicts with what his client wants. His client is not the public, his client is not a consumer advocacy group, his client is not the State Bar, his client was Maria Seward and he completely ignored what she wanted.

Damer had an "absolute obligation" to follow her wishes and Chiantelli's orders.

> Respondent has consistently and repeatedly indicated that he is going to place himself in the position of legislator, judge and executive and will make his own law based on justice as he believes it should be meted out. This country has long ago determined that vigilante justice leads to the disintegration of law and order, not the propagation of it. . . .

The State Bar (hyperbolically) compared Damer's behavior to Nixon's in Watergate and repeated the defendants' charge that Damer "wanted to use information he obtained in the Seward matter to pursue Sterns in other actions, all to the benefit of Damer financially." As late as 1993, he continued to disclose the sealed information in unrelated litigation.

> Are we now going to endorse a system that as long as attorneys really have strong policy reasons behind their views, they do not need to follow court orders inconsistent with those beliefs?

The State Bar sought a public reprimand and suspension until Damer paid the $3,000 in penalties and gave his files to Judge Scott.

Damer renewed his request to reopen the case to present additional evidence and argument. Since violating his nondisclosure agreements was "not a possibility," the proposed penalty was more severe than disbarment, "from which at least readmission is some day possible." His defense was not "disproportionate" to the penalty, nor had he tried to "bully" Goldhammer. "Whether or not Judge Chiantelli or any other judge may *personally* disfavor Respondent or his 'style,'

Respondent is simply *correct.*" The "Special Examiner's claims of 'harm to Seward' border on the totally preposterous. . . ." Indeed, Seward and Denebeim "now look longingly to this court to give them weapons for their devious enterprises." The "greatest irony" is that Sterns "was a thief, plain and simple," whereas Goldhammer, "whose life's work started as an adviser to the impoverished and advocate for the oppressed is being requested to be an apologist for an embezzler and the executioner of the thief's adversary's career." He sought to offer "details of the various financial interrelationships involving Denebeim, Sterns, the Special Examiner's firm and others."

Goldhammer denied Damer's request and considered the case submitted for decision. But the same day Damer wrote an "Objection to format of special examiner's objection and respondent's request for clarification of scope and effect of 'sealing' and 'gag' orders issued by the State Bar." He wanted to provide "input to the investigation and confirmation process relating to the proposed appointment, as a Federal judge, of the managing partner of the firm known as Cotchett, Illston and Pitre," which was co-counseling in the Technical Equities Litigation with the firm of Fredkin, who had presented himself as a "seemingly disinterested volunteer." Furthermore, Cotchett's and Sterns's firms were "*actively involved in a joint venture*" in the US Air/PSA crash near San Luis Obispo. Sterns was "a master of media manipulation, who managed to have a beautiful female associate appear on the Channel 7 news the very evening of the disaster in question, soliciting potential clients."

> A fair conclusion . . . is that Sterns has been able to influence the selection of both the gentlemen who have served as "Special Examiner" in this case; and that Sterns and Denebeim have used their links to the Cotchett firm to in turn get the Fredkin firm involved in professionally disabling Respondent. . . .
>
> Such is the web woven with efforts to suppress the truth and do "favors" and make "accommodations" of the sort described—in the current hit movie "Clear and Present Danger"—as the "Potomac Two Step". . . .
>
> Potential misuse of this Court's orders present [sic] a "clear and present danger" in terms of chilling Respondent's free speech rights.

C. The Hearing Judge's Decision

Goldhammer rendered his decision on December 3, 1993, referring to all the parties by first name because of the sealing order. He summarized the events, noting that Chiantelli's sealing order allowed the State Bar access to the file. The transcript showed that "tempers were short on the part of all concerned" and Damer "understandabl[y]" felt "victimized under the time-pressured circumstances." The order to turn over his files to Judge Scott did not issue until April 4 and failed to assure Damer notice before they were destroyed, as Chiantelli had promised on March 9. Nevertheless, Goldhammer found many grounds to criticize Damer. He willfully violated Chiantelli's sealing order by contacting the approximately 70 Contra Costa litigants. Goldhammer was unimpressed by the "claimed illegality" of Sterns's firm. "It is customary for law firms to bill for in-house paralegals at rates higher than cost." Damer's filing of the petition for extraordinary relief was a "mistake of law," but he made no effort to publicize it. He had not willfully violated Chiantelli's April 4 turnover order, which was redundant, given the gag order. Disobedience did not merit suspension. But Damer's argument that he did not know which files to give Scott was "disingenuous." And he had no "legitimate concern" about the destruction of his files once he had given them to Scott, although he deserved notice before they were shown to others because of the danger that Sterns could gain access. Punishing Damer for refusing to pay sanctions would be duplicative. "This court, ordinarily, should not act as a collection agency even for other courts. . . ."

Once he had exhausted his appeal from Chiantelli's order, Damer could not challenge its validity.

> Orders . . . which, as here, seek to maintain the status quo in a sensitive or potentially damaging situation, must be accepted by attorneys as valid until set aside by a higher court because, otherwise, there would be a breakdown in law and order, and no rule of law. . . . once confidentiality is breached, it is essentially an irretrievable breach . . . One who violates a confidentiality order takes the ability to decide the privacy issue away from the court. . . . The gratuitous flagrance of Respondent's disobedience to Judge Chiantelli's orders is what arises [*sic*] to the level of misconduct.

On the other hand, Damer had eighteen years of "unblemished practice." His

> poor judgment took place in the midst of one of the most incredibly difficult situations an attorney might encounter. Respondent's case was covertly snatched away from him during trial by his co-counsel. . . . [He] had legitimate concern for the public policy not to have secret settlements shield wrongful actions, sincerely believed he had obligations above and beyond those to his own client, and had to act quickly in a heated and hostile situation while under enormous time pressure because of the need to confirm settlement or re-start the trial.

But his behavior in the disciplinary hearing

> was replete with obstructionist tactics that went well beyond what could be termed "hard-ball" litigation tactics. Particularly in the initial stages prior to being represented, Respondent repeatedly raised arguments of very dubious merit, all too often cloaked in excessive verbiage, disorganized, and almost incomprehensible . . . for Respondent to repeatedly raise the same issues in the same venue and case in the face of previous adverse rulings on those

issues accomplished nothing positive and was inappropriate. I attach too great an importance to an attorney's due process right to be heard to consider Respondent's behavior here, although it seemed to border on bullying, as aggravating.

Goldhammer did not find bad faith. There was little harm to Seward or the administration of justice because the defendants sought a mistrial before Damer disobeyed any order. Acting out of "an incorrect but well-intentioned belief . . . is not the stuff which warrants significant discipline." He recommended private reproval and passage of the MPRE.

D. Review

Damer requested review because any discipline, "however slight," conflicted "ominously" with the Rules of Professional Conduct, state and federal constitutions, an American Bar Association (ABA) formal opinion about costs and expenses, and legislative reforms prohibiting the suppression of evidence about attorney misconduct. He had given "the judiciary every fair chance to correct its errors" before taking "reasonable and ethically imperative" "last-minute actions necessary to try to prevent a gross injustice." The disciplinary proceeding was "the carrying out of a threat made implicitly by the involved judge, and *explicitly* by the settling parties, in March of 1990." Judge Chiantelli was "utterly ignorant of the relevant and governing law" and approved a "blatantly illegal settlement, which would have prohibited Respondent's former client from reporting 'Gerald's'[80] misconduct to the State Bar." Unless Damer were vindicated, "the only lawyers who ever seek to follow the written rules will be lawyers driven out of business and hounded with years of costly, all-consuming contempt and disciplinary proceedings." "[E]very judicial officer involved to date has adroitly avoided a thorough, substantial review of the ultimate legal issues. . . ." The Review Department had "a unique opportunity" to "give definitive guidance to lawyers and trial judges alike."

Fredkin agreed to Damer's request for a limited review without transcript if he would accept Goldhammer's factual findings. But Damer could not agree "to facts for which there is no evidence in the record." The illegality of Sterns's practices, "admitted" by his own partner, was "confirmed by the recent resignation of Associate Attorney General Webster Hubbell . . . for similar conduct and an even more recent resignation by a major partner of Latham and Watkins." The "religious zeal" with which Fredkin charged Damer was "shared by the Whitewater Special Prosecutor." Damer could not have asked Chiantelli to let him submit material to Patsey because Chiantelli was "ready, willing and able to insult, berate, intimidate and even jail Respondent if Respondent did not cooperate

80. Damer followed Goldhammer's practice of using first names; he is referring to Sterns.

with the suppression of evidence. . . ." On March 7, Chiantelli had declared: "[I]t is a civil contempt that I will put you in jail until I have enforced you to follow my civil order." Two days later, he had threatened "to put [Damer] in custody until he decides to follow my order." His "deliberate plan" was "to prevent Respondent from seeking any meaningful appellate remedy" by issuing an order at 5:30 P.M. on Friday and requiring compliance at 9 A.M. the following Monday. Damer concluded that he

> was *right* "on the law" in March of 1990, regardless of how many other judges at so many levels have avoided directly opining on these issues. This case should finally be streamlined so a focused published opinion can be generated which *condemns* Gerald's practices and precludes *any* settlement arrangements designed to conceal such "cash flow" remedies.

Presiding Judge Lise Pearlman denied Damer's request for summary review, since he challenged material findings of fact. Damer sought an extension of time to file his opening brief because he was representing himself in the malpractice case, a "professional 'life or death' contest" brought by Seward, represented by Denebeim—"the very parties who initiated this State Bar proceeding for the very purpose of gaining an advantage in the Superior Court suit." Denebeim had admitted in his December 1994 deposition that "it was . . . clearly my intention that the Bar would prosecute you and that your professional standing and reputation would be adversely affected as a result of the administrative review of your conduct. . . ."

Although Damer hoped the additional 60 days would let him write a "shorter and more concise" brief, he submitted 30 pages.

> [T]he explanation for Respondent's tenacity can be found in the ironic note in Shakespeare's *fearful* query, posed *confidently* by an assassin over his victim's body: "how many ages hence shall this our lofty scene be acted over, in states unborn and accents yet unknown?" . . . [T]he self-serving abuse of power will endure until, in James Madison's words, "men were angels."

Since there would be a long wait for "universal sanctification," those who wield power "could at least be motivated to *act* honorably by *fear of exposure.*" Damer repeated all his arguments. Chiantelli "apparently" had "promised personally to assist the defendants in controlling litigation." Damer listed Seward's many sins, concluding that "any pretense, to adopt . . . a Greta Garbo pose of 'I just want to be let [*sic*] alone!' is no more credible than if Madonna made such a statement." Corruption "can even visit the highest and most surprising places." "Popular entertainment portrays not only lawyers as corrupt, but judges as well," including "nearly the entire German judiciary," leading "to the most apocalyptic consequences in recorded history."

> The crusade against perceived misuse of power has *recently* employed the most tragic of tactics—bombs instead of arguments, lodged by those who

> believe their concerns are willfully ignored and that open, *peaceable* protests will only lead to further persecution.

He condemned the State Bar's "appalling and disgusting" prosecution, ending melodramatically:

> [C]hiseled both in the "MEMORY OF THE PEOPLE" and in the Lincoln Monument is the image of an ideal—the smart yet honest lawyer—as well as that man's last major utterance, concluding with a dedication to the *cause of widows and orphans.*

The Review Department should declare secret settlements unlawful "skullduggery," whose defiance was privileged. "A lawyer should never be disciplined who indisputably acted, as Judge Goldhammer correctly found . . . for 'principled' reasons 'primarily with the interests of others in mind.'"

The same day, Damer moved to submit papers just filed by Denebeim, as well as thirty-seven pages from Denebeim's December 1994 deposition.[81] In them, Denebeim conceded that under the settlement, "Judge Chiantelli would allow Gebhardt to either have access to or see these records that you did not want him to see." Damer asked rhetorically, What if he had "accused the judge of . . . exposing his genitalia to the jury?" Who would the Court of Appeal believe without a transcript? He charged Denebeim, Gebhardt, and Chiantelli with "conspir[ing] to keep a transcript from me so I could not show the Court of Appeals just how bizarre those proceedings were." Damer elicited Denebeim's admission that "I do want financially something out of this and I do want to see you stripped of your degree . . . but at the time this case was settled, I wanted you to go along with their settlement and collect all of your fee." In a recent statement, Denebeim described the period leading up to the March 1990 trial of Seward's claim against Sterns as

> a time of high anxiety and stress for Damer, who had a low opinion of his trial abilities and doubted his ability to try the case efficiently. He was concerned about the affect [*sic*] that his odd personality would have on a jury. He was afraid he was overmatched by opposing counsel. He doubted whether he could obtain a fair trial in a San Francisco court, and obsessed over conspiracy theories. . . . Throughout the trial Damer's behavior was unusual. He had wide mood swings. He would yell. He would act paranoid.

The State Bar's reply brief criticized Damer for attempting "to raise this matter to both literary and legal heights that are not justified by the facts or the law," as "is his custom."

81. Exhibit B to Respondent's Rule 306 motion for judicial notice and augmentation (June 16, 1995).

> Are we going to disband our rule of law and allow the losing side of any controversy to not follow the Court's Order because it contends, despite the result, that the Judge was wrong . . . ?

Its failure to prosecute Sterns "may demonstrate that others, perhaps more objectively placed, have determined that, in fact, there is even 'less than meets the eye'. . . ."

Damer's response began by accusing the State Bar of a "presumptuous, righteous pose—as if damnation were predestined for Respondent." He asserted his right to ask that it be stricken (for failing to cite the record by page number) and wondered "whether the State Bar's Special Examiner even *read* this Court's rules. . . ." "[M]ost shocking" was the Bar's disregard of ABA Model Rule 3.4, "which plainly allows a lawyer to commit civil disobedience if acting forthrightly. . . ." The finality the State Bar invoked might only reflect "an appellate tribunal's wish to avoid embarrassing a colleague." But exoneration of Damer would not inculpate Chiantelli because the judge "did not *author* his directives—*Gebhardt* did." Furthermore, Chiantelli had told Damer on March 7, "I think that you have nothing but concern for your client in this case, and that is not sarcastically said." Judges like Chiantelli "are *expected* to have thick skins and to tolerate criticism." Although Fredkin implied that Damer would be "edified and rehabilitated" by attending the State Bar Ethics School, it was he "who had to educate *Judge Chiantelli*, and the defendants . . . about the numerous ethical rules being violated. . . ." This prosecution "offends respect for the 'fundamental rule of ethics—that of common honesty'. . . ."

Damer saved his harshest words for Fredkin's suggestion that Sterns was "undeserving of prosecution."

> The Special Examiner should "get real" before his own credibility suffers irreparably; Sterns' insurer did not pay $750,000 to buy *rusted cap pistols*, but to get *smoking guns*. . . . [C]laiming Sterns' *non-prosecution* equates with his *veritable innocence* is perhaps the equivalent of arguing that the *non-renewal* of certain State Bar Judges' *nominations* "determines" their "objective" *unworthiness*,[82] or that "understandings" *never* arise, at levels where Sterns' advocates operate, in closed private rooms, putting greens of the Olympic Club, or other places safe from public scrutiny or the risk of discovery.

Damer argued that the State Bar should be sanctioned for its failure to cite the record by being compelled to reimburse him for its cost. "[T]his disregard of clear rules of procedure—*even after* a warning—is especially amazing given the 'rules are rules' dogma and cant of the prosecution. . . ." To allow Fredkin "*some special dispensation*" would "*deny Respondent due process and allow the Special*

82. Pearlman, Gee, and Goldhammer had just not been renominated, to the surprise of many observers.

Examiner to, in effect, violate the Rules of Professional Conduct." The "absurdity" of permitting "the prosecutor's word to be the equivalent of this Court's acts" resembled a *Mad Magazine* cartoon, which Damer attached.

Damer also sought possible grounds for recusing Review Department members, asking them to disclose "all facts which could lead any reasonable person to doubt any member's impartiality," including participation in any "secret settlement." He attached newspaper articles questioning the conduct of one of Judge Pearlman's partners.

> [T]he State Bar Court is being viewed as in turmoil as a result of some recent, in effect, "firings" of some well-respected Judges . . . [who] are perceived as having been under some form of covertly imposed political pressures generated by the Board of Governors—e.g., for being too *lenient* on Respondents. One cannot even rule out the possibility that Judge Goldhammer . . . has been punished for his "leniency" on *this* Respondent, whose sacrifice for, e.g., Gerald Sterns' and Jeannette Shipman's sake, was not deemed *complete* enough by the "powers that be."

Unless he were completely exonerated, Damer threatened, "this case is headed for the same quest for plenary review that Respondent sought—and was denied—with respect to Judge Chiantelli's appalling 'orders.'" The entertainment industry had not "failed to note the public's willingness to accept possibilities that widespread corruption permeates *every* aspect of the legal community." Tom Selleck had recently starred in a television show about "*corruption among judges involving the wealthy and powerful.*" He accused the special examiner of trying to "delay these proceedings until at least one member of the Review Department is removed by virtue of her term's expiration."

Fredkin replied that Damer had "typically" misconstrued his request and used it to raise "totally unrelated" matters. "Mr. Damer has always confused fact with argument and important findings with collateral issues." Fredkin had participated "on a pro bono basis" and advanced all the costs.

Damer immediately submitted a further reply without waiting for permission. The Bar's tactics were "PARTICULARLY PERNICIOUS" because they used the contempt judgment in this "FLAWED, BOOTSTRAPPED PROSECUTION." The contempt citation "was merely some ritualized sacrifice." "The State Bar cannot prove a whit of ANY truth. . . ." Its "feeble structure . . . fails, without a foundation of factual truth or fundamental fairness." Fredkin's "unsupported factual representations" bordered on "the arrogant, presumptuous and reckless." "THIS PROCEEDING MUST REND THE VICIOUS WEBS AND CIRCLES OF DECEIT IN WHICH THE SPECIAL EXAMINER MAY WELL HIMSELF BE UNWITTINGLY TRAPPED."

> Perhaps . . . if the Special Examiner is forced to actually *read and cite to* the documents . . . [he] will at last, in good faith, conclude that this proceeding is unworthy of his time and join Respondent in a request for a dismissal. . . .

He ridiculed Fredkin's "noble donation of his time to the worthy cause of going after the Respondent."

Fredkin had declined to prosecute Sterns because "the Sterns/Cotchett/Fredkin firm's [*sic*] links are *irrefutably provable*." "As Respondent's young children might say, 'What a coinkydink!!!'" A July 10, 1995, *California Lawyer* article showed "another multi-million dollar case where Cotchett's firm and the Ruby-Fredkin firm have been working together." "And to 'take the cake' for 'coinkydinks' please see the attached Court document showing Seward and Denebeim's new ally, their lawyer David Byers, who shows *an address in the Cotchett building itself*!!!" Damer analogized the *Bonfire of the Vanities* and financial misconduct by military officers to the way "the State Bar's 'old boy network' worked to 'cover up' Sterns' thefts." "It is *Respondent's* practice and income which dwindled to near oblivion . . . thus if any sympathy is due *anyone or anything*, such sentiments might be better directed to Respondent." Because Judge Pearlman was due to retire within weeks, "there may be a 'Freudian slip' in the Special Examiner's use of 'Dear Sirs'. . . ." "Based on an article just published by the Presiding Judge herself, it is reasonable to assume that the new member will be more 'acceptable' to the State Bar's ruling clique." Fredkin was "a very smart lawyer," who knew "the most acceptable meaning of the old Irish advice, 'Don't hire the lawyer who knows the law; hire the lawyer who knows the judge.'"

Damer quoted at length from Denebeim's December 1994 deposition about the March 1990 hearing.

DENEBEIM: . . . [T]he bailiff turned to me when you were making one of your long strenuous objections and said . . . I think the judge is just letting him go on and on so he will go crazy and attack somebody and then I can shoot him.

DAMER: Did you overhear the bailiff's physical threats to me?

DENEBEIM: No, but I know the bailiff didn't like you and I think the bailiff got in trouble on account of what happened. . . .

DAMER: The bailiff had already been in trouble before this ever happened for being violent as a sheriff's deputy. . . .

DENEBEIM: You were definitely very hostile towards everyone and there was . . . something like [a] read my lips kind of comment and you were definitely trying to incite the other and whip things up so that there was so much hostility and animosity that it would break the settlement down. . . . [I]t was directed at Mr. Sterns and in what I thought was a very unprofessional manner. And I believe the judge even said, "Mr. Damer, please . . . direct your remarks to me." . . . you were very sly about it, but you were definitely threatening the judge with the allegation that he was acting wrongfully in violation of the public trust. . . . You were very I would say clever in not bluntly telling him that he was going to get in trouble if you could have your way . . . it was clear . . .

> that you had contempt for what the judge was doing . . . that you felt that he was totally out of line as far as his responsibilities to Abraham Lincoln and the United States and George Washington and apple pie. . . . I have never seen with my own eyes anybody be as abrasive and take on a judge like you did on that day.

Before oral argument, Damer sought rulings on his three pending motions, invoking "the former Presiding Judge's and others' 1995 public comments on the circumstances behind her, Allen Goldhammer's and Jennifer Gee's 'firings' and 'non-rehirings'. . . ." Damer had "systematically been denied due process and intends to seek it in every available forum, state and federal. . . ." He wrote separately that "a recently decided case, in an eastern Federal Court of Appeals . . . may fully exonerate Mr. Damer." His new lawyer, Harold A. Justman, sent the court a letter to Damer from William F. Lanam, a retired Superior Court judge, who ultimately arbitrated *Seward v. Sterns.*

> I had considerable concern when I analyzed the effects of Judge Chiantelli's orders, directing . . . any lawyer to turn over all of his or her files, including "work product" to the opposition. It becomes an even more egregious matter when that lawyer is not even allowed to retain *any* copies of his or her files . . . and is specifically excluded from any form of personal release. . . . It was obvious during our hearing that many individuals, who were then involved in the underlying litigation, would have taken great pleasure in destroying you professionally and personally. To strip any attorney of any and all records . . . is to deny that attorney the right to defend himself. To then trust to others that these records will not be intentionally or accidentally destroyed or lost is asking too much. . . . [Chiantelli's order] may well be viewed as an abuse of discretion. . . . As a practicing attorney, I would be unwilling to obey such an order until any and all appellate relief had been exhausted. I do not . . . criticize Judge Chiantelli. He was dealing in a highly charged emotional situation and your approach during the climactic situations on March 7, 8, and 9 seemed to be neither subtle nor constructive in resolving the problems. It does appear that your demeanor may have contributed to angry or thoughtless reactions by others.

On March 7, 1996, Lanam awarded over 51 percent of the interpleaded funds to Damer, 42 percent to Seward, and 6 percent to Denebeim; but the Review Department excluded this from its record.[83]

Damer responded in writing to the five questions the Review Department asked at oral argument. He invoked "the American Bar Association's guidelines, which allow open refusals to obey orders as they are being issued." He argued

83. Appellant's request to advance disposition of cause pending before Review Department (Jan. 27, 97).

for the first time that he filed in Contra Costa Superior Court "*solely* as a 'private litigant" in an attempt to secure his fee. Discipline would be "a collateral legal consequence which would justify the filing of a writ of habeas corpus. . . ." Although the Review Department refused to admit the arbitration result, the fact "that Respondent's fee claims have been ultimately vindicated, six years later, cannot be ignored. . . ." A "lawyer is obligated to 'Just say no!' regardless of the resulting adverse effects on the client's settlement or finances." He compared Seward to a client seeking to renege on a medical lien. The Review Department should

> publicly declare that a lawyer's bold resistance, to efforts to shield attorney misconduct from exposure, *are absolutely valid, in "good faith," and ought to be encouraged*. . . . Just as a doctor cannot buy the silence of those he wilfully [*sic*] abused, so also a lawyer must be barred from purchasing similar suppressions. . . .

Fredkin repeated his previous arguments. "[O]ne of the most compelling" charges against Damer was the fact that the "substantial cash settlement" was "tied up for years because of bickering that was brought on only" by his conduct, in violation of his undivided loyalty to Seward.

Eight months later, Justman (Damer's lawyer) asked for a decision, sought judicial notice of cases decided since he had submitted his brief, and repeated the entire narrative in highly inflammatory language. "From the outset . . . Denebeim and the allies were intent on destroying Respondent's professional reputation and practice." Damer quoted California State Bar President Thomas Stolpman, "When we stand by and watch a colleague violate a lawyer's duties as an officer of the court, or we allow unethical behavior to occur without doing something about it, we implicitly accept that conduct." This statement, Damer claimed, "implicitly exonerates Respondent for his refusal to remain silent about Sterns." Damer had "placed his fee, his career, and his family's future at risk" in the face of "ill-advised trial judges, eager to end acrimonious malpractice suits." He concluded, "Most of the Review Department's workload involves the analysis of tawdry, self-serving misconduct. . . ." He, by contrast, was the rare respondent found to have acted in a "principled" way, "primarily with the interest of others in mind," who should be exonerated by reason of the "equities" and for "the betterment of the profession." Fredkin objected to Damer's "lengthy and erroneous citation of past fact . . . matters that have absolutely no bearing on the case" and "unrelated" "public pronouncements by others." Justman retorted that Fredkin's letter lacked "any factual or legal foundation" and was "plagued with both draftsmanship errors and absolutely inaccurate conclusory statements." "The Review Department and the trial department have made more than enough allowances for Mr. Fredkin's inattention and neglect. . . ." "One explanation" was "harassment of Respondent." Fredkin's tactics "smack of bad faith and bad form." To impose any discipline "would be to embarrassingly engage in institutional hypocrisy."

The Review Department decided two weeks later.[84] It asked the OTC to investigate Damer's charges against the Sterns firm.[85] When Damer left the March 6 settlement negotiations at 5:30 P.M. for a

> prior family commitment . . . he instructed his two subordinate co-counsel not to continue the discussions in his absence . . . in part, because he believed that [Seward] was under too much stress to rationally continue discussing settlement.

Disregarding this, they settled for $750,000 "with the superior court's 'approval.'" "Before dismissing the parties that night, the superior court told them that, if the settlement agreement was not finalized by 9:30 the next morning, testimony would promptly resume." The next day, Damer rejected the settlement, claiming that Seward "was too distraught from the pressures of trial and the discord among her three attorneys to be capable of giving her informed consent to any settlement at the time." Sterns said

> his original attorney in the malpractice case improperly turned over to respondent during discovery, a large amount of confidential firm information (financial and personal) that was private and privileged without objection, confidentiality agreement, or protective order. According to this partner's admissions before the superior court, one of the primary reasons that he agreed to settle the malpractice case and to force his insurance carrier to pay [Seward] such a large sum of money, was to buy his peace and get back all of those allegedly confidential records.

Because Chiantelli proposed to enter a nonsuit, the Sterns firm would not have to report the malpractice judgment to the State Bar. Seward was to direct her attorneys to transfer all their files to the Sterns firm "regardless of whether obtained through formal discovery or [Damer's] own investigation." Any claim against Damer was tolled until he breached the confidentiality agreement. He was prohibited from soliciting the Sterns firm's former, current, or future clients for claims against the firm and could not use any information he had gained while representing Seward in a lawsuit against the defendants. But the U.S. Supreme Court had held that attorneys have a "right to solicit business for pecuniary gain by sending truthful and non-deceptive letters to specific potential clients known to face particular legal problems."[86] Chiantelli repeatedly rejected Damer's requests to tape record the proceedings or obtain a transcript. Damer claimed to need his records for a *quantum meruit* claim for fees (against Seward

84. Matter of Respondent X, 3 Calif. State Bar Ct. Rptr 592 (1997).

85. Much of the following narrative is new, presumably drawn from the sealed transcript and settlement agreement. Because the Review Department affirmed the private reproval, it named none of the parties.

86. Citing Shapero v. Kentucky State Bar Ass'n, 486 U.S. 466 (1988).

and her new counsel) and to sue Sterns for abuse of civil process (a fraud suit that was about to be dismissed for failure to prosecute), but Chiantelli agreed to let Damer apply to Scott for access to his files for these purposes. When Damer sought to file his notice of appeal under seal, the clerk who had filed the sealing order eight days earlier denied there was any such order and refused to accept the pleadings. Because Damer did not receive the order until March 22, he claimed to believe it was suspended during the intervening six days, when he wrote Judge Patsey.

The Review Department had "no doubt that [Damer's] violation of the court order was wilful [*sic*]." Damer contended the order was unconstitutional. The judge hearing the contempt matter apparently relied on the "collateral bar rule" prohibiting a contemnor from challenging the validity of a court order when defending against the contempt. But that was not the law in California. When Damer was denied appellate review of Chiantelli's order "he exercised his right under California law to choose to violate the order." But Damer also waived personal appearance in the contempt proceeding and lost his appeals. The Review Department "properly defer[ed] to the collective judgment of the courts of record which heard the contempt proceeding. . . ." Although Damer had withdrawn from representing Seward, he still had a fiduciary duty "to act consistently with his client's settlement agreement at least to avoid revealing to others the amount of the settlement as well as the evidence. . . ."

The Review Department found mitigation in Damer's eighteen years without discipline, "principled approach to the basic settlement," and "sincere beliefs that he was acting in support of sound public policy." The violation was "unique," and he had "sought first to test by extraordinary writ the court order he violated." The Department affirmed the private reproval and eliminated the Multistate Professional Responsibility Examination (MPRE) requirement but ordered public disclosure of the proceedings.

Damer filed for reconsideration.

> The regrettable reality is that this Review Department is the *first* judicial body to move courageously, despite Sterns' considerable political "clout," and to take any decisive action to remedy wrongs Sterns did to his clients over at least one decade.

While "not unmindful of his risks involved in trying to appeal further," Damer was motivated by "potential benefits to the bar, the bench, and the public." The rules for review were "not yet blessed with clarity." In "the hope of promoting judicial economy" he would "not correct every discrepancy in the text of the OPINION." The Review Department had failed to note that Seward had sued Sterns's insurers and accused them of "destruction of evidence as a *regular business practice*" and of insisting on total silence by the insured's victims.

> Since the OPINION allows such practices to continue whenever Lawyers' Mutual's or other defense counsel or defendants can convince

underconfident or overworked trial judges to approve such "deals"—and even to issue orders for compliance with sweeping secrecy schemes—the OPINION makes bad public policy. . . .

The Review Department said Sterns had converted slightly more than $1,000 when he actually converted $3,000, a "felony-level crime," which "may yet merit disbarment." "What is 'wilful' [*sic*] must be viewed in context, and the 'doctrine of necessity' . . . is somewhat analogous here."

[B]y breaching her fee agreement, plotting to sue Respondent for malpractice and seeking to use his "principled" positions as an excuse for cheating him of just compensation, Seward necessarily had waived any entitlement to secrecy regarding the settlement figure.

To avoid the "temptation" to "argue major issues that were addressed and considered previously," Damer concluded with an analogy.

How many teenage girls continued to be sexually exploited while Mary R.'s attorney honored the stipulated "gag" and sealing orders? How many orphans received smaller settlements because Gerald Sterns was able to charge "phony" investigative costs freely? How long to [*sic*] decent lawyers wait "in good faith" as children are raped and robbed?

If Damer "ever asks that judicial notice be taken of the "widow's" Declaration," will he be "susceptible to seven more years of disciplinary threats?" Does he have "any real hope of persuading Judge Chiantelli to recant now?"

On April 14, the Review Department denied the motion for reconsideration. On December 23, the California Supreme Court denied Damer's petition for a writ of review. On May 18, 1998, the U.S. Supreme Court denied certiorari.[87] As of 2008, Damer remains an active member of the bar.[88]

VI. THE TEMPTATIONS OF THE CHAMPION

What explains Damer's behavior? He declared himself a passionate advocate for his client. In April 1988, he rejected Sterns's $200,000 offer because *Seward* refused to seal the record regardless of the amount. He claimed to be subordinating his own financial interest to his obligations as a lawyer and citizen.

---

87. Damer v. State Bar of California, 523 U.S. 1121 (1998).

88. Damer represented a client who brought a legal malpractice action against four large firms. The trial court granted summary judgment because the statute of limitations had run and awarded sanctions of nearly $15,000 against Damer and his client, finding that "what had been energetic advocacy became groundless pursuit of a meritless claim and firmness of resolve, truculence." The Court of Appeal upheld summary judgment but reversed the sanctions. Levin v. Graham & James, 37 Cal.App.4th 798 (1st Dist. 1995).

(His contingent fee created mixed incentives: On one hand, to settle with minimum effort; on the other, to maximize recovery, especially since the smoking gun memo raised the possibility of punitive damages.) At the same time, he persuaded Seward to authorize him to file a class action for overbilling Sterns's other clients in order to increase the pressure for settlement, making sure she did so before Sterns mooted her claim by paying it. Damer stood to earn a much higher fee in the class action (for which he had no other clients). As early as November 1988, Seward told Damer she was tired of fighting (about an accident that had occurred eight years earlier); and her March 1990 phone message unambiguously and emphatically embraced the settlement. But Damer claimed to know her interests better than she, ridiculing her desire to be left alone. When suing her for fees after she fired him, Damer threatened to reveal sensitive details about her life (his precise accusation against Sterns).[89] Instead of fulfilling his fiduciary duty to her, he accused her of violating an alleged obligation to Sterns's other victims.[90] But Damer never filed the class action. Indeed, without Seward (who had fired him) he had no client. And he ultimately abandoned his claim to have been championing her, maintaining instead that he had filed in Contra Costa personally, to recover the fee she owed him. Damer claimed her malpractice lawsuit relieved him of any fiduciary duty, but it was filed long after he breached his duty. And he fought to maximize his share of the $750,000 settlement from Sterns, ultimately pocketing 51 percent and leaving Seward just 43 percent.

One of Damer's motives seems to have been anger at Sterns. Even before the Sun Valley Mall case, Damer was contemplating other lawsuits against the Sterns firm for expense padding, as well as a disciplinary complaint. That case confirmed Damer's conviction that the firm systematically bilked clients. Damer may also have been jealous of the fame and fortune of Sterns, who led the Sun Valley class action committee, which sought $50 million and recovered more than $10 million, generating huge fees and bonuses to Sterns. Damer's competitiveness was visible in his boast that even a $2 million settlement of Seward's case would not generate his normal hourly rate, much less what defense counsel charged. Damer moved to intervene in the Sun Valley Mall case to seek a lien (presumably on money owed to Sterns, which Damer claimed as fees for Seward's settlement). Although Damer denied harboring personal animus against Sterns (or anyone!), he clearly had a long-standing feud with all the defendants and their lawyers in Seward's lawsuit. Elstead had sued him for defamation; in another case, Damer opposed Gebhardt, who represented a client accused of

89. Damer wrote me that when Seward declared during and after the March 1990 hearing that "she WOULD be suing me for malpractice. . .[a]ll 'confidentiality' obligations on my part, toward HER, thereby were terminated." E-mail (Jan. 22, 2009).

90. Damer wrote me: "as is firmly established, a lawyer's obligations to the overall 'system' can transcend, and override, the client's views of her personal 'interests.'" E-mail (Jan. 22, 2009).

mishandling the retirement funds of more than a thousand employees. Denebeim testified that Damer bragged he would make his name by suing Sterns for malpractice. Yet it is striking that Damer's own proposal in Seward's case was the $1 million liability insurance policy and a $3 million personal judgment against Elstead but nothing against the firm.

Damer's basic strategy—progressive escalation—was consistent with both cold calculation and excessive emotional engagement. (He quoted the adage that a lawyer should not represent himself—and then did just that.) As soon as Seward accepted the defendants' offer Damer complained to both the State Bar and the State Commission on Judicial Performance and later accused the State Bar of "corrupt disciplinary practices." He complained to a friend in the San Francisco District Attorney's office—and then threatened to go to the U.S. Attorney and the press when the DA declined to act. He sought to enlist Cotchett and then threatened to appeal to the "court of public opinion." He had been moved "to tears" when a judge said his recently deceased mother-in-law "loved nothing better than a good fight for a just cause."[91]

Damer's defiance of Chiantelli's sealing order was not an isolated event. Although he constantly invoked due process, accusing Chiantelli of operating a "star chamber," Damer refused to accept any limits on his own overzealous advocacy, disingenuously praising his self-restraint in not giving the press the "juicy" parts of the sealed record. He could not distinguish between important and unimportant rule violations (resisting paying for the transcript because Fredkin did not cite its page numbers). He (and his counsel, Wallace) sought to relitigate everything. Damer continued to raise extraneous objections to the contempt citation after exhausting his appeals (although he had a legitimate grievance at initially being denied a written order, tape recording, and hearing transcript). He objected that no appellate court had decided the merits (because he refused to comply with the order that he surrender his files). He dared judges to jail him for contempt so he could seek federal habeas corpus (even making the ridiculous claim that *any* discipline would let him do so). He defied the *res judicata* effect of final judgments. He renewed motions to dismiss after they were denied. He invoked the sympathy of the judge who had found him in contempt and Judge Mosk's sole dissent from the California Supreme Court's denial of review. He proposed to call a large number of wholly inappropriate witnesses—the State Bar deputy counsel, the settlement judge, and other judges—to testify about what they had meant in an opinion. He constantly indulged in overkill, submitting seventy-eight exhibits. He repeatedly sought extensions of time to file papers and then filed late when permission was denied. Barred from calling *any* witnesses as a result of his delays, he made an offer of proof of what they

91. Damer used the on-line name "NicLiberty." He wrote me that "if one primary purpose of a 'discipline' system is to 'teach' (going to the root meaning of 'discipline') I did not 'learn' anything; I would do the same again. . . ." E-mail (Jan. 15, 2009).

would have said and abused the argument over it to allege that Sterns would have admitted routinely settling cases low in order to increase the firm's cash flow because he was a spendthrift, who owed federal and state taxes. When the Review Department refused to admit the arbitrator's judgment in his dispute over Seward's settlement, Damer simply paraphrased it. When Damer claimed a right to court-appointed counsel in the disciplinary proceeding, Goldhammer warned that frivolous motions could be aggravating factors. Disregarding this, Damer supported his claim with a case that Goldhammer called "completely miscited and misunderstood." Damer also ignored sage advice from Goldhammer (a retired judge), "[I]f you want to get into a spitting match with a judge, you'd better get another judge on your side to overrule the order."

Damer claimed that he, alone, behaved idealistically. Some actions supported that claim, e.g., his adamant refusal to give the State Bar the files he would not surrender in response to Chiantelli's order. But his shifting positions and strange bedfellows often seemed more strategic than principled. He found himself allied with his adversary Sterns in opposing the settlement with his former client (Seward) represented by his former employee (Denebeim). He accused Seward and Denebeim of filing grievances against him as leverage in the malpractice suit Denebeim filed for Seward against him; but Damer himself filed a grievance against Sterns as leverage in his lawsuit challenging Sterns's excessive expenses. Damer wanted to be relieved from the sealing order (in Contra Costa Superior Court) but also wanted his fee paid out of Seward's settlement (which the San Francisco Superior Court made contingent on the sealing). He initially denounced the *Daily Journal*'s coverage of Seward's case but then joined forces with it in seeking to unseal the record because the *Journal* was not bound by the judicial order and had no financial interest in the settlement. When Fredkin wanted to use the sealed transcript in the disciplinary proceeding, Damer objected that it was still under seal. And when Goldhammer admitted it under seal, Damer (champion of the people's right to know) objected that disciplinary proceedings were public, claiming to fear that Sterns would use the disclosure to repudiate the settlement (which Damer had attacked). Of course, Damer was not the only inconsistent actor. After agreeing to the sealing of the record in San Francisco, Denebeim needed it unsealed in Seward's legal malpractice case against Damer in San Mateo. And Chiantelli gave the San Mateo court the very transcript he refused to let Damer submit in Contra Costa.

One constant throughout the proceedings was Damer's anger and the response it provoked. His only tactic was attack, which he deployed indiscriminately. He threatened to sue the *Daily Journal* for libel. He accused Chiantelli to his face of betraying Seward and mocked him for not being man enough to admit his errors, like John F.Kennedy. He scared Jeanette Shipman sufficiently for her lawyer to seek an order prohibiting contact with her. He asked the State Bar Complaint Audit and Review Department to review the rejection of his complaint against Shipman. When Hawley asked why Damer had not reported the contempt citations and sanctions, Damer said the question showed that the State Bar already knew about them (hardly responsive and irrelevant to Damer's statutory obligation to report). He attacked Hawley for not acting against Sterns (which was outside the special examiner's responsibility), blamed such inaction on the fact that Hawley's firm was Sterns's landlord, and demanded that Hawley recuse himself. Damer sued Hawley for violating his civil rights. (He even threatened to sue Hawley's firm on the ground that, as landlord, the firm was vicariously liable for legal malpractice by its tenants!) As soon as Hawley was replaced by Fredkin, Damer sought to disqualify him, as well. He asked, patronizingly, if Fredkin had ever read the State Bar Court rules, accused him of not reading the record, and called him "arrogant, presumptuous, reckless," entrapped in "vicious webs and circles of deceit." He threatened Fredkin, too, with personal liability for any losses Damer suffered from the disciplinary proceeding.

Damer refused to "cooperate" with the State Bar until he knew the charges. He demanded that it pay to duplicate his file. As the only outsider at the State Bar Board of Governors semiannual public meeting, he videotaped himself complaining about his treatment. He immediately sought to expose Goldhammer's bias (while claiming no disrespect). When writing Cotchett (another plaintiffs' lawyer in the Sun Valley Mall case), ostensibly seeking support, Damer could not refrain from calling him complicit with Sterns (while simultaneously denying doing so). He accused Chiantelli of conducting a "star chamber" and denounced the settlement and order as "preposterous" at least six times. He called Chiantelli "utterly ignorant" of the law (especially civil procedure), mocked him as the defendants' "scribe," and dismissed his orders as "invalid," "bizarre," and "appalling." The contempt citation was a mere "ritualized sacrifice," the disciplinary proceeding "appalling and disgusting," and the State Bar "presumptuous, righteous" in seeking Damer's "damnation" simply to avoid embarrassing Chiantelli.

Damer refused to pay for the transcript—a precondition for appealing to the Review Department. He challenged all the Review Department members for bias, attaching a newspaper article questioning the conduct of one of Pearlman's partners. He gratuitously offended her by dwelling on the fact that she, Gee, and Goldhammer had not been renominated, implying that this "firing" demonstrated their incompetence. Disregarding Goldhammer's sensible advice not to alienate judges, Damer repeatedly threatened to appeal. While sympathizing with Damer's plight before Judge Chiantelli, Goldhammer resented Damer engaging in the same kind of deliberately provocative behavior during the disciplinary proceeding, including bullying, threatening, and filing unnecessary motions and challenges. Others saw Damer in a similar light. Denebeim believed Damer was trying to stir up hostility before Chiantelli in order to destroy the settlement. Even Lanam, who awarded Damer 51 percent of the settlement, criticized him for being "neither subtle nor constructive" and contributing "to angry and thoughtless reactions by others."

The internal inconsistencies in Damer's multiple justifications for his behavior quickly became apparent. When he first sought to submit material to Patsey under seal he called himself both "a potential lienholder"[92] and a friend of the court and citizen who sought to prevent fraud. He declared that because Chiantelli had let him withdraw, the judge no longer had any power over him but then refused to appear before Chiantelli on the ground that the judge had summarily jailed him for contempt, putting him in jeopardy of further imprisonment. On March 23, Damer refiled the unsealed record before Patsey, claiming that a clerk had told him there was no sealing order. But on March 19, Chiantelli had filed his minute order sealing the file, and Damer had filed a notice of appeal declaring that the materials had been ordered sealed. Damer defied Chiantelli's order and then claimed ignorance of what he had been charged with defying. He denied that Denebeim demanded compliance with the turnover order. Confronted with Denebeim's letter showing he had done so, Damer claimed not to recognize Denebeim's signature! He invoked an (irrelevant) prohibition against buying evidence. He even denied there had ever been a settlement. He excused his defiance of Chiantelli's orders by claiming a good-faith belief that the judge was wrong, comparing himself to a tax protester and maintaining that he merely took a "philosophical position."

Even if his justifications were unconvincing, Damer did have some real grievances. Chiantelli sealed a lot of material he should not have, ordered Damer to surrender privileged material, and authorized the destruction of his files without notice. Damer could not obtain a writ of prohibition because he had not yet been held in contempt. He could not appeal without a record of the proceedings, which he had been forbidden to tape record. (Indeed, the contempt judge rightly declined to proceed unless Damer was given a transcript.) He was unable to appeal his contempt conviction because he refused to comply with the order to surrender his files. He claimed, legitimately, that had the settlement been set aside (as Sterns twice moved to do), Damer would need the papers he had been directed to surrender in order to retry the case.

Damer's behavior sometimes seemed paranoid: he "demanded" an end to "persecution" and displayed both a need for martyrdom and an inability to accept defeat. He was consumed by self-pity: "It is *Respondent's* practice and income which dwindled to near oblivion . . . thus if any sympathy is due *anyone or anything*, such sentiments might be better directed to Respondent." He repeated insults by others, although they clearly stung. Denebeim said Damer had a low opinion of his own trial ability, worried about how his "odd personality" would affect the jury, and feared he was outmatched by Sterns. Damer displayed "unusual behavior" and "mood swings"; he would "yell" and "act paranoid." The

92. Damer e-mailed me (Jan. 22, 2009) that he asserted a lien "in order to prevent Lawyers Mutual from paying Seward and Denebeim the $750,000 in a way that eliminated Sterns' and his insurer's exposure to my fee/cost claims. . . ."

bailiff said Chiantelli let Damer rant on and on "so he will go crazy and attack somebody and then I can shoot him." (Damer claimed the bailiff had been in trouble for violence before.)

Damer spun ever more complex conspiracy theories, concocting new ones to explain each defeat. He alleged corruption in the "highest and most surprising places." He was fighting an "old boys network"; adversaries used "connections" with "friends in high places." Political influence made Gebhardt "untouchable." To thank Chiantelli for his treatment of Damer, Gebhardt even got the judge nominated to the Olympic Club, where "understandings" were reached in closed private rooms and on putting greens. Damer qualified many accusations with the modifier "apparently," so they could not be falsified. He drew analogies to popular culture without acknowledging that these were fictitious: *Mad Magazine*, a television show about judicial corruption starring Tom Selleck, Tom Wolfe's *Bonfire of the Vanities*.

Damer initially viewed the *Daily Journal* as an enemy and Dee Ziegler as "simply a tool" of the defendants. He rationed Denebeim's information on a "need to know" basis (flaunting his own military service). He accused Denebeim of being closely connected with Cotchett's firm, which in turn was associated with Hawley's firm. He charged Elstead with concealing the Smith memorandum and then claiming to discover it under his Navy commendations (an attempt to "hide behind the flag"). Damer objected that Sterns was a judge pro tem on the San Francisco Superior Court, where Chiantelli sat; so was Richard Bridgman, Sterns's first lawyer and a witness in the case. On the eve of the trial, the Sterns firm hired a judge's son. Sterns's lawyer, Glen Allen, filed a motion before a judge whose son worked in Allen's office. Damer denounced the defendants' contempt motion as an attempt to make him "genuflect before them in the courthouse foyer" and have him jailed for several hundred days (a danger he claimed was still real). A "confidential source" warned him against reappearing before Chiantelli, a former assistant district attorney, who threatened to get the authorities after Damer and used his prosecutorial connections to initiate and control the disciplinary process. Chiantelli's "hostility" left Damer in "no doubt" about the judge's motives. When Chiantelli finally issued the written minute order months after rendering it orally, the clerk omitted Damer from the service list, so he only got it from the *Daily Journal* several months later. After Damer lost his appeals, he sought to transfer them to another court because of bias. Damer accused Denebeim and Mehlman of conspiring with Seward to settle with Sterns behind Damer's back (in a "drinking establishment") so they could sue him for legal malpractice.

He saw the entire disciplinary proceeding as a conspiracy by his "enemies" to have "his ticket pulled" (a sanction no one else took seriously) because he was a "whistleblower."[93] Any suspension would be tantamount to disbarment because he would never comply with the reinstatement condition that he surrender his papers to Judge Scott. After Damer objected that Special Examiner Jeanette Shipman had worked for the Sterns firm before she joined the San Francisco office of the State Bar, it appointed Hawley. Damer immediately challenged him as a former attorney in that office, who had let Shipman (while "under investigation" by the State Bar) attend a closed hearing on Damer, accompanied by a San Francisco State Bar investigator. He also noted that Hawley's firm rented space to Sterns's firm. Hawley "diverted" Damer's State Bar complaint against Sterns. Hawley offered leniency on condition that Damer surrender documents potentially damaging to Hawley, who had a prior relationship with Shipman and had arranged to be replaced by Fredkin. Damer blamed Fredkin for the State Bar's failure to prosecute Sterns (although this was outside Fredkin's control). Damer accused Fredkin of seeking to delay the disciplinary proceeding until Judge Pearlman's term expired. A State Bar attorney declared that lawyers had an absolute right to retain their legal papers but recanted on learning that Damer was in the audience. Damer complained to the San Francisco District Attorney's office, warning his friend there that the DA might have received campaign contributions from members of the Sterns firm. The DA declined to act. Damer later noted that a previous DA (Leo Murphy) now worked for the Gebhardt firm. Damer feared that the $750,000 settlement Sterns had impleaded had disappeared. Long after Goldhammer closed the liability phase, Damer kept making far-fetched collateral attacks on its fairness: the managing partner in Cotchett's firm had been nominated to a federal judgeship; that firm was connected with those of Fredkin and Sterns. Goldhammer had not been renominated to the State Bar Court because he was too lenient toward Damer.

Some of Damer's behavior seemed fueled by resentment of more successful lawyers. He was just an "ordinary citizen," who had volunteered to fight in Vietnam, while Hawley and other "well connected people" evaded military service. Gebhardt's firm had sent more members to the bench than any other in Northern California. In his initial letter to Cotchett (ostensibly seeking support), Damer could not refrain from maligning him as a "high ranking," "wealthy, prestigious lawyer . . . who has made a fortune off of the sins of other professionals" and "thinks himself worthy, I am told, of hand-picking judges and seeking the office of Attorney General of the state of California." Sterns and other lawyers were "wealthy crooks." Damer could not resist dwelling enviously on the fact that Cotchett and Fredkin were involved in a case worth $100 million.

93. He e-mailed me (Jan. 15, 2009): "the prosecution of myself was part of a plan to force me to go along with the cover-up of Sterns' various thefts from his clients, by threatening my livelihood, etc. The threat to get me disbarred, if I did not 'go along,' was first made ON THE RECORD in court in March 1990."

But Damer could have deployed the (overused) riposte: just because I'm paranoid doesn't mean people aren't out to get me. He refused to appear personally to challenge Chiantelli's orders on the ground that Chiantelli had summarily jailed him for contempt. In the transcript he had sealed, Chiantelli had threatened Damer with civil and criminal contempt and jail until he complied with the judge's orders. Judge Patsey's disallowance of some of Sterns's expenses in the Sun Valley Mall case strengthened Damer's charge that the firm systematically padded its expenses. It did seem an extraordinary coincidence that Damer's State Bar complaint against the Sterns firm was assigned to Jeanette Shipman, the firm's former employee. Damer's complaint that Hawley was biased did lead to his replacement by Fredkin. Several lawyers did decline to represent Damer before the State Bar Court, some citing his charges against State Bar employees. Damer's fear of losing control of papers he delivered to Judge Scott may have seemed excessive—until his law partner's house burned down with all his papers and a suspicious fire damaged Judge Chiantelli's chambers and some of Damer's papers (a week after Damer warned Fredkin of this possibility). There was strong evidence that Chiantelli had violated the no-smoking rule and the Fire Department had covered up. After David Moon expressed interest in Damer's charges against Sterns, his superiors told him it was outside their jurisdiction. In his December 1994 deposition, Denebeim admitted wanting to see Damer "stripped" of his "degree" (i.e., his bar membership) and conceded that Chiantelli's order would have allowed Gebhardt access to Damer's records. Judge Lanam, who arbitrated the division of the $750,000 award to Seward, criticized Chiantelli's orders (which Lanam would not have obeyed as a practitioner), confirmed that others were hostile toward Damer, and awarded him 51 percent of the disputed funds. And the Review Department directed the OTC to investigate Damer's allegations against Sterns—seven years after Damer had made them.

Damer's persecution complex fueled an insatiable need for vindication. He acknowledged being "long winded" and "happy" to spend "all day explaining these events . . . for someone who is receptive to listen."[94] He began his evidence in mitigation by tracing his legal career from the very beginning, to show he had always championed the underdog. Although he was never in jeopardy of more than a private reprimand if he admitted error, he refused to accept any discipline, "however slight," declaring defiantly: "Whether or not Judge Chiantelli or any other judge may *personally* disfavor Respondent or his 'style,' Respondent is simply *correct*." He had been "*right* 'on the law' in March of 1990, regardless of how many judges at so many levels have avoided opining on these issues." He claimed the approbation of notables: Judge Mosk had voted to review his contempt judgment (but was the only California Supreme Court judge to do so). In criticizing Chiantelli, State Bar Monitor Robert Fellmeth implicitly affirmed

94. Damer sent me four e-mails, totaling over 20 pages, criticizing this chapter.

Damer's conduct. A State Bar president had called on lawyers to report misconduct. A U.S. Court of Appeals decision justified his actions. Even after partial exoneration by the Review Department, he relitigated every issue, insisting on complete exculpation. He took credit for his restraint in not correcting "every discrepancy in the text of the opinion." The lawyers Damer associated with (Cynthia Frazier) or retained (Michele Wallace) shared his passion for justice; his last lawyer even had the perfect surname, *Justman*.

Damer consistently exaggerated both the stakes and his own nobility. The disciplinary proceeding violated the Model Rules of Professional Conduct, ABA opinions about expenses, legislation about attorneys suppressing evidence of their misconduct, and state and federal constitutions. If he were not vindicated, law-abiding lawyers would be "driven out of business and hounded with years of costly, all-consuming contempt and disciplinary proceedings." Frustrating the call for justice would foment violence. The State Bar called him a Don Quixote. Damer accentuated his written claims by using typeface (capitals, italics, underlining, boldface), hyperbole, quotations (often inapt), metaphors (both inappropriate and exaggerated), and poetic devices like alliteration ("particularly pernicious," the "feeble structure . . . fails, without a foundation of factual truth or fundamental fairness"). He linked Maria's determination to expose Sterns to her distinguished (but remote) ancestor, William Seward (Lincoln's Secretary of State). Damer compared himself to Lincoln, a "smart yet honest lawyer," whose final words concluded with "a dedication to the cause of *widows and orphans*." (Denebeim reported that Damer likened himself to Lincoln and Washington during the hearing before Chiantelli.) Damer claimed that he, not the State Bar, was the real protector of clients against Sterns's misconduct. He kept inflating the magnitude of Sterns's alleged misconduct from $5 million to $10 million in excess expenses and from $10 million to $100 million in undersettlements. Damer could not abandon the cause of "the defenseless or the oppressed." His "life's work started as an adviser to the impoverished and advocate for the oppressed. . . ." He identified *himself* with a judge's praise of his deceased mother-in-law, who "loved nothing better than a good fight for a just cause." To explain his own "tenacity," he invoked Shakespeare's assertion that this "lofty scene" would "be acted over, in states unborn and accents yet unknown" for "ages hence,"[95] as well as Madison's warning that "the self-serving abuse of power will endure until . . . 'men were angels.'"

Damer sustained his delusions of grandeur with irrelevant analogies. He urged Chiantelli to heed John F. Kennedy's words and admit error. He invoked the movie "Clear and Present Danger" to argue that Chiantelli's actions were a

95. Damer is quoting Cassius after the assassination of Caesar—a strange metaphor, unless Damer believed that Sterns's wrongdoing resembled the Roman emperor's tyranny.

clear and present danger to his own speech.[96] He mentioned the resignation of Associate Attorney General Webster Hubbell as a result of the Whitewater investigation, comparing his own "religious zeal" to that of special prosecutor Kenneth Starr. Damer parroted Nancy Reagan's call to "just say no" to drugs to explain why he had said no to Seward, whom he compared to a client trying to renege on a medical lien (which Seward had not done). He cited the rule that doctors could not buy silence from those they willfully abused (although parties settle contract breaches and tort claims all the time—even for intentional conduct). He invoked the "doctrine of necessity." At the very end he asked "how long to [*sic*] decent lawyers wait 'in good faith' as children are raped and robbed?"

Damer's hyperbole provoked the State Bar to exaggerate as well. Although it criticized him for trying "to raise this matter to both literary and legal heights that are not justified by the facts or the law," as "is his custom," it reciprocated by magnifying the danger of his "religious zeal," comparing his behavior with Nixon's in Watergate. Damer's "gratuitous flagrance" threatened "vigilante justice" and a "complete breakdown of the legal system." Such conduct would "disband our rule of law." He had made himself "legislator, judge and executive." Failure to punish him severely would "endorse a system" in which attorneys could simply act according to their own beliefs. But Damer was neither the knight on a white horse he imagined nor the satanic figure the State Bar feared but rather the unfortunate byproduct of an adversary process that encourages each side to launch a moral crusade by demonizing its opponent. If he was a Don Quixote, some of his windmills actually were dragons.

---

96. Although the film's title quotes Justice Holmes's test for speech unprotected by the First Amendment, it actually deals with an alleged threat by South American drug traffickers to the security of the United States.

8. MAKING REGULATION WORK

To paraphrase Tolstoy, good lawyers are all alike; every bad lawyer is bad in his own way.[1] Or consider Hemingway's putdown of his friend and rival. The central character in *The Snows of Kilimanjaro* remembers "poor Scott Fitzgerald and his romantic awe of [the rich] and how he started a story once that began, 'the very rich are different from you and me.' And how someone had said to Scott, 'yes, they have more money.'"[2] Tolstoy cautions against generalization; Hemingway warns it is likely to be banal. Criminologists agree. Criminals are not different from the rest of us, and white collar crime (of which ethical misconduct by lawyers is a subgenre) does not differ greatly from business as usual. Those accused or convicted often make the same complaint: everybody does it—I just happened to get caught.

That is why detailed case studies are at the heart of this book. It is essential to understand what these lawyers did and why they did it.[3] Only then can we look for commonalities across cases, develop hypotheses for quantitative testing, and suggest remedies that transcend unique circumstances. In order to expand the number of instances and see whether jurisdiction matters, I also will refer to the seven New York lawyers described in my earlier book, whose cases are briefly summarized here.

David Kreitzer, a solo practitioner, operated a tort settlement mill, handling well over a thousand claims a year with the help of newly qualified lawyer associates and paralegals. Inevitably, the office missed deadlines and made mistakes. When cash flow became a problem, Kreitzer participated in a scheme to kick back 10 percent of payout to insurance claims adjusters to expedite processing. Joseph Muto filed asylum petitions for undocumented Chinese immigrants on behalf of "travel agencies," which did everything but conduct immigration court hearings. He not only handled 400 cases a year himself but also had a flying phobia, making him miss appearances outside New York. As a result, his clients suffered deportation orders and had to hire other counsel to reopen their cases on the ground of inadequate representation. Lawrence Furtzaig overcame considerable disadvantage to become an equity partner in a highly respected real

1. Anna Karenina begins: "Happy families are all alike; every unhappy family is unhappy in its own way."

2. Fitzgerald's story is "The Rich Boy" (1926). The riposte actually had been made by critic Mary Colum to Hemingway, when the author boasted that "I am getting to know the rich." Eddy Dow, Letter to the Editor, New York Times (Nov. 13, 1988).

3. Support for the view that diverse behaviors warrant different responses can be found in Zacharias (2003b).

estate firm. Even billing 2,200 to 2,400 hours, however, he could not keep up with the demands of work, making up a $60,000 loss in one case out of his own pocket and forging documents to hide other mistakes. Benjamin M. Cardozo (a distant collateral relative of the judge) and Deyan Brashich fought successfully to get Babette Hecht several million dollars under her mother's will. But they only presented her with the particular solution that maximized their one-third contingent fee. Brashich went on to overbill Ljubica Callahan, a fellow Serbian immigrant, in her estate dispute. Philip Byler successfully transmuted his good friend James Morgan's Internal Revenue Service (IRS) claim for over $200,000 in back taxes into a $50,000 refund—and then pocketed it as his fee, refusing to escrow the money when Morgan objected. Arthur Wisehart represented Joan Lipin in claiming sexual discrimination and sexual harassment by the general manager of the American Red Cross (ARC) of Greater New York, even hiring her as a paralegal when an ARC blacklist prevented her from getting another job. After the ARC stonewalled all discovery requests for years, it left Lipin's complete file on a conference table during motion practice. She appropriated the four-inch file, which Wisehart used to demand a million dollar settlement. Wisehart relentlessly fought Judge Moskowitz's decision to dismiss the case with prejudice, even accusing the judge of mental incapacity, following her diagnosis and treatment for breast cancer.

This conclusion will explore the similarities and differences among the behaviors of these sixteen lawyers and others who appear in the chapter introductions.

I. THE CASES

A. Solicitation

Scapa and Brown hired Gumban (the ex-cop) and Buchanan to solicit automobile accident victims (paying them amounts partly contingent on the outcome and size of the ultimate settlement). California prohibits that behavior, and the U.S. Supreme Court has upheld such rules.[4] But what is wrong with solicitation? Tort law awards damages in order to compensate victims for their injuries and deter negligence. Despite endless propaganda by insurers and repeat-player defendants about the "tort litigation crisis," we have known for decades that only about one serious accident victim in ten recovers damages.[5] Many victims do not know their rights, how to claim, what it will cost, the likelihood of success, or what they might recover.[6] Defendants already enjoy huge advantages over plaintiffs: by delaying payment, they can force needy accident victims to settle for pennies on the dollar. The anti-solicitation rule aggravates this inequality by letting

4. Ohralik v. Ohio State Bar Association, 436 U.S. 447 (1978).
5. Abel (1987).
6. Felstiner *et al.* (1981).

defendants and their insurers aggressively negotiate releases (even in hospital rooms), while forbidding plaintiffs lawyers from approaching potential clients in person or even by telephone.[7] The prohibition is particularly hurtful to those lacking personal contacts with lawyers: the poor, elderly, racial minorities, immigrants, or non-English speakers. Scapa and Brown claimed they had chosen Gumban and Buchanan in order to increase access to justice by Filipinos. Regardless of whether or not that was their real motive, it may have been an effect. Although clients are the source of almost all ethical complaints, the only "client" who complained against Scapa and Brown was the State Bar lawyer they unfortunately solicited. Because law-abiding plaintiffs personal injury lawyers do not solicit, victims reliant on solicitation have a much narrower choice of legal representative. Furthermore, solicitation is a much more efficient way of informing victims of their rights than (constitutionally-protected) advertising,[8] which must be disseminated scattershot to an audience almost all of whom has no present need for a personal injury lawyer. The ban's perversity and hypocrisy are evidenced by the nearly century-long cycle of passive tolerance of ambulance-chasing, periodically punctuated by short-lived moral crusades against it.[9]

Regardless of the merits of allowing solicitation, Scapa and Brown and their employees engaged in many other objectionable practices[10] (partly because of the ban): referring clients to doctors in exchange for kickbacks; colluding with doctors to inflate special damages; having clients sign retainers without seeing lawyers; asserting liens for lawyers fees under *quantum meruit* without regard to effort expended; threatening to seek punitive damages for nonpayment of the lien; using the lien to block insurance company payments and car repairs; and covering up the solicitation by forcing clients to sign false disclaimers. Like other lawyers operating high volume practices,[11] Scapa and Brown delegated much of the work to non-lawyer subordinates without exercising adequate supervision. Indeed, they deliberately treated Gumban and Buchanan as independent contractors in order to create deniability about their actions and thereby claim moral irresponsibility. The cappers enjoyed the autonomy, even passing themselves off as lawyers. (Buchanan had begun law school, and Gumban aspired to become a lawyer.) Some of the lawyers described in the introduction to Chapter 2, "Cops Chasing Ambulances," went further, basically handing over their practices to non-lawyer "administrators" while collecting monopoly rents for doing little or nothing, simply by virtue of possessing a bar admission card. (That they could pay "administrators" $500 a case is some evidence of the size of these rents.) These scenarios evoke Uriah Heep's degradation of Mr. Wickfield in Dickens's

7. Florida Bar v. Went For It, Inc., 515 U.S. 618 (1995).

8. Bates v. State Bar of Arizona, 433 U.S. 350 (1977).

9. E.g., Reichstein (1964; 1965); Ward (1974).

10. In this they resembled Ohralik (1978), *supra*.

11. Engstrom (2009).

David Copperfield. But if lawyers can pay contingent referral fees to other lawyers,[12] why not let them pay laypersons, who can refer cases far more cheaply?

Two of the New York lawyers in my earlier book relied on referrals to operate volume practices. David Kreitzer got his personal injury clients from other lawyers (who either did no personal injury work or felt the cases were not worth their time).[13] Highly skilled litigators like Browne Greene and David Harney (discussed next) get most of the lucrative cases. What is left for lawyers like Kreitzer and Scapa and Brown (e.g., soft-tissue injuries) neither requires great legal skill nor justifies the investment of significant lawyer time. Kreitzer declared that his "philosophy" was "pretty much . . . somewhere down the line we should be able to get some sort of settlement . . . ."[14] As a result, the lawyers delegated much of the work to subordinates. But that inflates overheads, which in turn compel the firms to operate at high volume. Just as Scapa and Brown paid cappers to generate clients, so Kreitzer kicked back 10 percent of the damages to insurance adjusters to accelerate payment. A high volume of low-profit cases also meant poor service: little contact with lawyers, chronic delay, unanswered phone calls, even lost files and missed statutes of limitation. These one-shot clients could not inflict significant reputational damage on the lawyers, who had other sources of business. Indeed, both Scapa and Brown and Kreitzer sought to transform disciplinable misconduct into "mere" incompetence, i.e., to turn crime into tort, for which the appropriate remedy was compensation, not punishment.

The respondents rationalized that other personal injury lawyers also paid lay intermediaries to get cases and kicked back 10 percent to insurers. But most do not. Why did these three lawyers break the rules? The simplest explanation is usually the best: they saw a chance to make much more money and were willing to run the (small) risk of punishment, which they sought to minimize through cover-ups: paying the cappers for "investigation" and having clients sign disclaimers, disguising the 10 percent kickback as a fee for negotiation. With more than a thousand live cases, Kreitzer must have been doing very well. Scapa and Brown acknowledged aspiring to emulate the entrepreneurial success of Jacoby & Meyers. And the lawyers could see nothing wrong with what they were doing. Payments to cappers and insurers came out of the lawyers' fees. Tort victims were not hurt (except by neglect). The complaints that triggered investigations in both states came from insurance companies concerned about fraud.

Joseph Muto also got clients from lay intermediaries (a necessity for many immigration lawyers, who lack the networks, cultural familiarity, and language skills to attract and interact with clients).[15] But like some of the California personal injury lawyers discussed in the introduction to Chapter 2, "Cops Chasing

12. Parikh (2001; 2006–07).
13. Abel (2008: Chapter 2).
14. *Id.*, 96.
15. *Id.*, Chapter 3.

Ambulances," (and unlike Scapa and Brown, and Kreitzer), Muto was controlled by the "travel agencies," rather than vice versa. Unlike Scapa and Brown, and Kreitzer, Muto was a newcomer to this practice, but he was a quick study: by making per diem appearances for other immigration lawyers and imitating colleagues, he quickly learned the (illegal) ropes, adapting other lawyers' paperwork with little or no modification (just as Scapa and Brown borrowed the client "disclaimer" of solicitation). Like other volume practitioners, Muto was overworked, underprepared, and often unreachable. His clients, like those of Scapa and Brown and some of the other personal injury lawyers in the introduction to Chapter 2, were disproportionately drawn from poor, ethnic minority, immigrant communities.

What remedial measures do these behaviors suggest? First, as a torts teacher for 40 years, I have long believed that the costs of operating a fault-based system far outweigh the benefits, at least with respect to automobile accidents, where drivers are about equally likely to be victims or tortfeasors.[16] No-fault would compensate victims quickly and cheaply, while eliminating virtually all the problems discussed above. But the plaintiffs' bar has repeatedly blocked that reform. Similarly, comprehensive medical insurance would make accident victims less dependent on tort claims and render their repeat-player loss insurers (subrogated to the claims of insureds) more equal adversaries of liability insurers. (Indeed, the same insurer often would be on both sides.) Second, I have argued that lawyers should be allowed to solicit clients, subject only to the usual consumer protection rules against harassment, overreaching, and misrepresentation.[17] That would eliminate the State Bar Court hearing judge's sole rationale for punishing Scapa and Brown: the competitive advantage they obtained over law-abiding attorneys. The most recent U.S. Supreme Court opinion on the subject upheld Florida's limitation on lawyers writing to tort victims on the ground that the State Bar claimed this damaged the legal profession's reputation.[18] But the evidence of any causal nexus with this obviously anticompetitive rule is extremely suspect. Third, all the cases discussed above clearly demonstrate that the legal profession's restrictive practices, which construct arbitrary boundaries between lawyer and non-lawyer work, create irrationalities and inefficiencies. Much of what is protected by the lawyers' monopoly could be performed far

---

16. Abel (1990).

17. Abel (1987).

18. Florida Bar (1995), *supra*. Other states continue to seek to restrict truthful lawyer advertising. Karen Donovan, *Street Scene; Some Lawyers Ranked 'Super' Are Not the Least Bit Flattered,* NEW YORK TIMES C6 (Sept. 15, 2006) (New Jersey attacked "New Jersey Super Lawyers" magazine); Karen Donovan, *New York Law Firms Struggle With New Restrictions on Advertising,* NEW YORK TIMES C5 (Mar. 2, 2007); Dirk Johnson, *Look at This Ad, but Don't Get Any Ideas,* NEW YORK TIMES 4 p.14 (May 13, 2007) (Chicago banned billboard featuring sexy woman and man and advising, "Life's short. Get a divorce.").

more cheaply by non-lawyers, and arguably just as competently. Most other countries narrowly limit that monopoly to court appearances. There is very little technical legal work involved in processing automobile accident settlements. Indeed, the very insurers who complained about lawyers using laypersons to approach accident victims themselves use non-lawyer claims adjusters to secure releases.[19] Automobile clubs negotiated accident claims for their members until barred from doing so; union representatives long have helped members claim workers compensation. Recently, lay claims agents have represented all kinds of personal injury victims in the United Kingdom.[20] We would do much better to jettison rent-seeking professional self-regulation for the discipline of the market, and where it fails, the state.

But even if all those reforms were implemented (a political impossibility), I remain troubled by the willingness of these lawyers to flagrantly disregard the law and evade responsibility for doing so. I return to that concern below.

B. Fees

That lawyers practice to earn money—and the more the better—is neither surprising nor dishonorable. As the New York lawyer Benjamin M. Cardozo said in my earlier book about his efforts on behalf of the beneficiary of a multimillion dollar trust: "I don't work for nothing. Not with this kind of money involved."[21] The problems arise from *how* fees are determined. Market economies view supply and demand as the appropriate mechanism to set prices. But that assumes free competition. Lawyers struggled long and hard to professionalize precisely in order to restrict competition.[22] Indeed, one of the bar's first actions, once it gained the power, was to set minimum fees and discipline lawyers who undercut them. In the thirty-five years since the Supreme Court ruled that fee schedules violate antitrust laws,[23] there has been very little price competition. Even when lawyers quote hourly fees, they will not (and often cannot) specify in advance how many hours they will spend. House counsel for large corporations may force firms to engage in beauty contests and bid for projects; but individuals find it almost impossible to compare the fees of potential lawyers. Indeed, David Harney was openly resentful of a client who dared to "shop" her case.

Personal injury victims confront unique problems in controlling fees. First, they are unusually vulnerable and needy; one-shot litigants dependent on repeat-player lawyers. The clients of Greene and Harney had suffered medical catastrophes, rendering them permanently disabled. Almost no such victim could afford to pay hourly fees for the necessarily complex and lengthy representation.

19. Ross (1970).
20. Abel (2003: 230–33).
21. Abel (2008: 284).
22. I have made this argument in previous books. Abel (1988; 1989; 2003).
23. Goldfarb v. Virginia State Bar, 421 U.S. 773 (1975).

The contingent fee solves that dilemma. It also *purports* to align the economic interests of lawyers and clients.[24] The problem is that all lawyers charge virtually identical percentages, regardless of the risk of losing, and most accept only sure winners. The time they invest bears no relationship to the rewards they reap. Indeed, some lawyers charge "contingent" fees even if there is no contingency, e.g., no-fault payment of medical expenses or life insurance. For a client dissatisfied with the lawyer's performance, the costs of switching horses in midstream are high and include duplication of effort, loss of advantage in litigation, and the emotion invested in a "white knight." Although a client is legally entitled to discharge a lawyer at will, lawyers routinely refuse to surrender files, fail to sign substitution forms, and assert liens unjustified by the work done, billing the cost of generating a form each time it is merely copied.

The massive market failure problem created by professional self-regulation has largely been ignored. Lawyers widely flouted the New York law requiring them to register contingency fee agreements when settling cases.[25] California's Medical Injuries Compensation Reform Act (MICRA) is virtually the only example of meaningful fee regulation, perhaps because it was enacted in response not to the personal injury victims who paid the fees but to the overwhelming political pressure from the insurers, hospitals, and doctors they sued. Greene, Harney, much of the personal injury bar, and many other lawyers were outraged by the law. I fully share their criticisms. Rising medical malpractice premiums are attributable to a combination of medical errors and falling returns on insurers' investments.[26] There is no principled case for regulating lawyers fees in medical malpractice cases but not other tort claims. A constitutional challenge was entirely appropriate, even admirable. But the California Supreme Court rejected it, and the U.S. Supreme Court declined to review.

In light of that defeat, the respondents' actions are deeply troubling (especially those of Harney, who persisted even after the State Bar had found Greene guilty). They disregarded their obligation to inform clients about Section 6146 of MICRA, as well as its Section 6147 mandate to give clients a written retainer explaining the Section 6146 limits. They presented settlements to probate court without informing the judge of Section 6146. They asked clients to waive Section 6146 without urging them to get independent legal advice; and they continued that practice even after the California Supreme Court predictably declared that a statute intended to protect clients from lawyers could not be waived by clients at the lawyer's behest. Harney argued that his fee could not be contingent, either because he would never take a losing case (in which case his "contingent" fee was unjustified) or because the outcome was no longer uncertain once he had

24. *But see* Schwartz & Mitchell (1970).

25. Rosenthal (1974).

26. Tom Baker, *Liability = Responsibility*, New York Times (July 12, 20.09); Hunter *et al.* (2009).

won! Harney sought to claim in *quantum meruit* and then simply stopped writing fee agreements, both in defiance of the explicit language of Section 6147. The respondents argued that MICRA should be presumed unconstitutional, although *all* statutes are presumed constitutional until declared otherwise. They drew comfort from the fact that other lawyers and even some judges disregarded the law.[27] Most troubling of all, they continued to maintain the invalidity of MICRA after a final decision that it was constitutional. Emulating the Sun King, these eminent lawyers apparently believed *la loi, c'est moi,* meaning, *I* am the court of last resort; if I believe the law is bad, then it cannot be the law. Like Caesar, Harney referred to himself in the third person (exceeding even the Roman Emperor's egoism by using all three names). Both respondents (especially Harney) displayed contempt for the State Bar Court, treating its decision even to hear their cases as *lèse majesté.* When asked why he did not discuss Section 6146 with his clients, Harney sneered, "I don't spend my time on silly conversations."

How could *lawyers* do this? The paradoxical answer is: That is exactly what lawyers do. Law schools teach students to argue both sides of every case. Lawyers then spend their entire professional lives manipulating the law to their clients' advantage. In the process, lawyers necessarily develop an entirely instrumental, strongly positivist conception of law. They become Oliver Wendell Holmes's quintessential "bad men,"[28] strategizing how to avoid the law until the cost is raised too high. That is one reason why the law school professional responsibility course poses a unique pedagogic challenge.[29] It is the only occasion when law students, who have been rewarded everywhere else for their skill in sophistry, pilpul, must take the law seriously as an end not just a means, accepting their obligation to obey its spirit, not just its letter.

The prominence of these two personal injury lawyers—who had attained the pinnacle of the professional hierarchy—also may have shaped their behavior.[30] They saw themselves as indispensable champions of medical malpractice victims, describing who deserved their clients' gratitude by virtue of the unique skills they had acquired, the effort they invested, and the stunning victories they achieved. By invoking Section 6146 after the case was won, those clients (egged on

---

27. Both respondents claimed vindication in the fact that they lost by just one vote: MICRA in the California Supreme Court, Greene in the Review Department. But of course that is all it takes.

28. Holmes (1897).

29. Pipkin (1979).

30. Hubris may also explain the behavior of other recently disgraced prominent lawyers like Dickie Scruggs, *see* Richard Fausset, *Katrina lawyer charged with bribery,* LOS ANGELES TIMES (Nov. 29, 2007); Nelson D. Schwartz, *Court Intrigue for the King of Torts,* NEW YORK TIMES §3 p1 (Dec. 9, 2007), and William Lerach, *see* Michael Parrish, *Leading Class-Action Lawyer Is Sentenced to Two Years in Kickback Scheme,* NEW YORK TIMES (Feb 12, 2008).

by envious, lesser lawyers) had treacherously sprung a trap. Just as Scapa and Brown saw themselves as targets of an insurance industry vendetta, so Greene and Harney claimed persecution by insurers and medical care providers, deriding MICRA as the "anti-David Harney" act (intended to discourage him and other highly qualified lawyers from handling medical malpractice cases) and denouncing the State Bar for using an insurance industry lobbyist as a witness.

My two New York fee cases display some striking parallels. Cardozo and Brashich failed to inform Babette Hecht about the fee implications of alternative resolutions of a trust dispute or to tell the surrogate court what they had already been paid, when requesting additional fees.[31] Byler simply appropriated as his fee the entire Internal Revenue Service (IRS) refund he had obtained for James Morgan and then constructed an account of his hours and chose an hourly rate that coincidentally produced exactly that amount.[32] All four cases involved vulnerable clients: victims of catastrophic torts, an impoverished elderly woman dependent on a contested trust, and a taxpayer facing an IRS demand for hundreds of thousands of dollars. In each case, the lawyers had won what they viewed as an extraordinary windfall, namely, huge tort damages, the division of a multimillion dollar trust corpus, and the transformation of an enormous tax deficiency into a substantial refund. Claims that the fees were undeserved, advanced late in the day by ungrateful clients, who were provoked by grasping inferior lawyers, denied the entire edifice of professional self-esteem these lawyers had constructed. Each lawyer felt that this "found money" was *his* as much as his client's because the lawyer had wrested it from a formidable adversary by the exercise of great skill and effort.[33] Like Greene and Harney, Byler insisted there was no fee dispute because Morgan could have no legitimate complaint about the fee. But this sense of entitlement coexisted uncomfortably with the subterfuges all four lawyers used to hide their fees from scrutiny.

The commonality across subject matters is not accidental. Individuals who are not wealthy retain lawyers only on the rare occasions in which some aspect of their lives is capitalized: the capacity to work and enjoy is diminished by physical injury, a life's savings are inherited, the government claims taxes for several years, a lengthy marriage ends with divorce, an immigrant is threatened with deportation, or an accused is facing serious criminal charges. All the lawyers expected—and initially enjoyed—gratitude for their achievements. Its replacement by ingratitude—and in Byler's case bitter enmity—strengthened the lawyers' convictions that they deserved their fees. Accused of taking advantage of their clients, they retorted that the ungrateful clients were taking advantage of them.

---

31. Abel (2008: Chapter 5).

32. *Id.*, Chapter 6. For a fictionalized account of bill-padding, *see* STRACHER (1998).

33. Like Harney, Byler wrote about himself in the third person in his response to my account of his case. Abel (2008: 367–73).

But such emotional inversions by clients are the exception. In most cases, the pervasiveness, intensity, and persistence of gratitude make it unlikely that clients will enforce fee limits. This is particularly true during an ongoing lawyer-client relationship (as Stewart Macaulay generalized about contractual relationships decades ago).[34] Just as the clients of Greene and Harney waited to invoke Section 6146 until they had won, so Byler precipitated the fee dispute only after pocketing his client's tax refund. The clients of Cardozo and Brashich declined to seek fee refunds even after their cases ended; the only complainants were the surrogate and disaffected relatives. It was other lawyers who urged Greene's and Harney's clients to invoke MICRA, which underlines how essential it is for clients to get legal advice about fees independent of the lawyers who charge them. But Greene and Harney deeply resented the lawyers who advised their clients to assert the Section 6146 limit. Cardozo misrepresented to his client and her adult children that the surrogate would not hear their fee objections. And Byler was furious when his client, James Morgan, sought the advice and intercession of his brother, the noted legal ethics scholar, Thomas Morgan.

These diverse cases suggest a variety of solutions. First, tort is not the only, or necessarily the best, response to medical malpractice (just as it is not to automobile accidents). Sweden opted for no-fault compensation decades ago, with results that seem to please patients and doctors (if not lawyers).[35] Second, if we preserve tort (as seems politically compelled in the short run), the contingent fee is not the only mechanism for financing litigation, and may not be the best.[36] Greene, Harney, Cardozo, and Brashich all had contingent fees (and Byler felt entitled to take 100 percent of the refund). It is hard to justify these fees in terms of market principles. There are several other funding mechanisms, including legal aid (which covered personal injury in Britain until recently) and fee shifting and legal expense insurance (which now fund personal injury litigation there through conditional fees, which pay a premium for success but not a percent of damages).[37] Third, if we retain contingent fees, the legal profession should create mechanisms by which clients could get independent advice before signing retainers. Lawyers could be encouraged to compete in charging lower percentages. Fee agreements might be made public documents, exposing them to criticism. Ex post remedies can help (if they are less desirable): Many bar associations operate fee dispute mediation programs.[38] Britain has an elaborate process for costing the value of a lawyer's services (as American courts do on the

34. Macaulay (1963).

35. Rosenthal (1988).

36. Kritzer (1998) concludes that lawyers generally do better by charging contingent rather than hourly fees. For a study of clients' views about alternative funding methods, *see* Moorhead & Cumming (2009).

37. Abel (2003: Chapter 8).

38. *E.g.*, Lebovits (2009).

infrequently when statutes authorize fee shifting). None of these proposals, however, addresses the misplaced sense of entitlement displayed by these lawyers.

C. Conflicts of Interest

Corporate law firms have elaborate mechanisms for identifying and handling potential conflicts of interest among their clients who are large, numerous, and diverse.[39] For this reason, professional responsibility courses devote considerable attention to conflicts problems. But large firm lawyers rarely are disciplined, and the solo and small firm practitioners (who are disciplined) rarely are accused of conflicts of interest between clients. Some practices are unlikely to encounter inter-client conflicts: divorce, personal injury, housing. Perhaps for this reason, many practices simply disregard the issue.[40]

All lawyers, however, encounter another kind of conflict—between themselves and their clients. The claims of overcharging discussed above are one, unavoidable, example. Two cases in this book arose out of another instance, namely, the temptation of lawyers to betray clients. For Crane, the betrayal involved his employer Sega; for Twitty, it was his colleague's client Lopez. Whereas the typical conflict of interest problem is the possibility that a lawyer's loyalties may be divided between *clients*, here the problem is the *lawyer's* self interest, specifically, Crane's in earning royalties from sublicensing Sega's games for home computers and Twitty's in minimizing the effort needed to earn his $150,000 retainer from Escobedo by arranging a deal for co-accused Lopez.[41] Each lawyer convinced himself he was actually benefiting the client—:Crane got Sega royalties it otherwise would not have earned; Twitty was trying to get Lopez a deal Tarlow would not negotiate. In order to do this, each lawyer had to blind himself to his own interest. And though both lawyers claimed purity of motive, they indulged in secrecy and deceit. Crane involved his friend Depew, concocted shell corporations, backdated documents, created aliases, and impersonated voices. Twitty secretly approached the prosecutor, (Lyons), participated in the negotiations between Lyons and Lopez and Escobedo, and sought to conceal all this from Tarlow. Similarly, Dale (described in the introduction to Chapter 6, "Serving Two Masters") covertly sought to persuade a represented criminal defendant charged with arson and homicide to provide evidence for tenants suing the building owner, in exchange for help in securing lenient punishment and early parole. The deceptions emerged accidentally. Crane's activities came to light when a sublicensee questioned a game's copyright, Twitty's when Rosenthal told Tarlow. Both Twitty and Dale undermined the represented client's trust in his own lawyer. Several respondents blamed other lawyers. Crane claimed to

---

39. Shapiro (2002); Griffiths-Baker (2002).
40. Levin (2004–2005).
41. *See* Eldred (2009).

have heeded the more experienced Depew. Twitty implicated Lyons. Crane criticized Sega for ignoring the potential home computer market for its games. Twitty disparaged Tarlow for refusing to represent clients in negotiations. Crane was unusual (among my nine California lawyers) in fully admitting his misconduct and promptly disgorging the profits of his scheme (one of the seven New York lawyers also did so). But Crane then offered, in mitigation, an elaborate autobiography of childhood trauma, inexperience, and present suffering (economic, marital, emotional, and professional).

In each of these cases, the rules were clear and clearly violated. A lawyer should not have a pecuniary interest in a client's business. If the lawyer does, the interest should be fully disclosed and the client advised to seek independent counsel about the conflict. That would have precluded Crane's deceit. A lawyer must not deal with a represented party without the consent of that party's lawyer. That would have precluded Twitty's secret intervention. But since rules are not self-enforcing, it is important to consider why these lawyers violated them and what could be done to discourage noncompliance. Crane sought an easy road to riches. Had he done so as an entrepreneur, and succeeded, society would have applauded. Instead, he abused his insider position as house counsel. Requiring lawyers to disclose to their firms and employers all outside business interests would inhibit the abuse of inside information. Twitty wanted to plead his client Escobedo (an easy way to earn his $150,000 retainer); Lyons's insistence on a package deal and Tarlow's refusal to negotiate frustrated Twitty's goal. If Tarlow's derogatory reference to James "Dump Truck" Twitty is accurate, the latter's behavior was not unusual. Hence, part of the problem may be the perverse incentives of fees: hourly fees encourage lawyers to run up the meter; package fees motivate them to minimize effort. Public defenders do not suffer from these distortions, but secure salaried employment encourages shirking.[42] Whatever the justification for allowing prosecutors to meet privately with defendants whose representation is funded by a third party, there is no justification for the lawyer of a co-defendant doing so. Perhaps judges should routinely conductvoir dire of defendants to explore whether this is happening.

D. Fraud

Because the division of labor (of which lawyers are a prominent example) is founded on trust,[43] fraud represents a serious threat (clearly evidenced by the cases discussed in the introduction to Chapter 5, "Reaching for the Brass Ring"). Brazil's one unambiguous fraud was also his most trivial, namely, misusing his secretary's notary seal and forging her signature after business hours—despite the fact that she would have notarized the document the next day. But all his transac-

42. *See, e.g.*, McConville & Mirsky (1986–87).

43. I develop this claim in Abel (2008: Chapter 1).

tions with Collins and Hom were tainted by fraud, which also seems to have infused his previous employment and enterprises. Indeed, as was true of many of the other lawyers I studied, the behavior disciplined expressed a long-standing pattern. By 1988, Interbank Mortgage Corporation was juggling more transactions than it could fund, forcing Brazil (who effectively was the company, even though he owned only 10 percent) to seek money or security from one deal in order to finance the next, the same behavior that is found in check-kiting, embezzling, and Ponzi schemes. Had he been able to keep all the balls in the air, nobody might have been the wiser. But as soon as one brick in the edifice fell, the entire structure collapsed.

Brazil's motive was transparent: he *was* his financial achievements. (His mother and brother denied he was motivated by greed; and Brazil sought to deflect that accusation to Hom; but Brazil clearly saw money as the index of his success.) Failure meant annihilation to him, just as it had to the New York lawyer Lawrence Furtzaig, who actually contemplated suicide when it became clear his partners would discover how he had deceived them.[44] Indeed, none of the sixteen disciplined lawyers I studied was a slacker. On the contrary, they inverted Thorstein Veblen's *Theory of the Leisure Class,* displaying conspicuous production rather than consumption.[45] (Competition to bill the most hours is common among large firm associates.) Kreitzer, Muto, Furtzaig, Brashich, Byler, and Wisehart, whose behavior was discussed in my earlier book, were all workaholics. So too were Scapa and Brown, Greene and Harney, Crane and Depew, Twitty, and Damer, the attorneys considered herein. It is striking that the two most extreme examples—Brazil and Furtzaig—had been abandoned by their fathers as children and then assumed the paternal role in both their families of origin and families of procreation. Brazil supported his stepdaughter and continued to care for his wife even after they separated. Furtzaig supported his wife and triplets. Many of these lawyers invoked their hard work to justify the rewards they believed they deserved, as well as the corners they cut to capture those rewards. They made other arguments against punishment. Their own superegos had already judged them harshly. They advanced rationalization commonly offered by white collar criminals in their pleas for lenience: because they had climbed so high, they had fallen further. Like Crane, Brazil sought to transmute fraud into bad judgment. Just as Crane sought mitigation by disgorging the profits of his deceit (and Greene and Harney returned the excess fees, if under duress), so Brazil based a similar plea on promises of restitution to Hom (which he never fulfilled). A high proportion of the sixteen lawyers invoked personal obligations and tragedies: Kreitzer (cancer), Muto (the death of his mother and cousin, and his wife's disability), Furtzaig (the birth of triplets), Cardozo

44. For "more than a couple of years . . . I'd been staring at my window considering jumping out . . .." Abel (2008: 199).

45. Veblen (1925).

(old age), Brashich (caring for his disabled mother, grandmother, and seriously ill daughters), Scapa and Brown (distracted by a wedding), Crane (the childhood deaths of his mother and father), Brazil (his wife's mental breakdown and his stepdaughter's dropping out of school), and Damer (his mother-in-law's death). Like many others, Brazil claimed to feel remorse—but it was really just regret at being caught.

As in previous cases, the frauds Brazil committed were patently wrong—indeed, criminal. The problem is that if the threat of criminal punishment does not deter, professional discipline is unlikely to do so. These lawyers seemed unable to admit the possibility of being wrong. They were not unique in this, and perhaps not even extreme. Once people commit to a course of conduct they find it easy to lose perspective. The remedy, clearly, is to elicit the less interested judgments of others. But Brazil would not take advice or guidance; he had left several previous enterprises for that reason and created Interbank so he could run it himself. Furtzaig, the New York lawyer, felt unable to consult his senior partner because he could not bear to disappoint that surrogate father. Condemning his mother-in-law for medicating herself "to the point of zombieism, just completely non-functioning as a human being," he declared, "I hate to believe that I need help."[46] (The reactions of these two fatherless men were mirror images: Furtzaig sought a father substitute; Brazil became his own father, rejecting all others.) Both cases suggest that collective practice structures can be antidotes to poor individual judgment, especially if the collectivity is responsible for its members' misconduct.

E. Excessive Zeal

This, for me, is the most troubling category of lawyer misconduct.[47] Its victim is the legal system, not individuals. And the behavior is morally ambiguous: how to distinguish zeal from zealotry.[48] After all, we exhort lawyers to engage in "zealous advocacy," praising those who confront the worst odds and take the greatest risks, even when they fail. Clarence Darrow and William Kunstler were folk heroes. Damer and Yagman (in California), and Wisehart (in New York) were highly competent, dedicated lawyers. Whereas the fourteen other lawyers in my two books often acted selfishly, Damer was pursuing the interests of his client (and others) who had been overbilled by the Sterns firm, and Wisehart was using evidence (which he believed his adversary should have produced in discovery) to support a strong case for sexual harassment and discrimination. (The similarities between these lawyers' behaviors, despite the enormous differences in their

---

46. Abel (2008: 200).

47. Doctors exhibit analogous behavior. Laurie Tarkan, *Arrogant, Abusive and Disruptive—and a Doctor*, New York Times D1 (Dec. 2, 2008).

48. Zacharias (2009a) contrasts the "integrity ethics" that restrain zeal from the rules of the lawyer's role.

backgrounds and the subject matters of the underlying cases, strengthen my conviction that this is a behavioral syndrome.)[49] Whereas the other lawyers flouted, evaded, or distorted the law and then tried to cover up their misconduct, these two lawyers openly sought to enforce the law. Both had smoking gun documents. Damer's showed that that the Sterns firm routinely padded expenses, Wisehart's revealed that the ARC executive director was a serial sexual harasser. The boundary beyond which zeal becomes excessive is uncertain and inevitably colored by (often strong) feelings for and against the parties, their causes, and their lawyers. Champions of unpopular causes (like Stephen Yagman) protest against being targeted for judicial sanctions and bar discipline; and evidence often supports such charges.[50] The Ninth Circuit ultimately upheld his right to voice strong criticisms of judges. Stephen Keim, discussed in the introduction to Chapter 7, "Championing the 'Defenseless' and 'Oppressed,'" courageously exonerated his client, Dr. Mohamed Haneef, of suspicion in the terrorist bombings in London and Glasgow—only to suffer a disciplinary investigation as a result.

Law school teaches students to advance every possible argument, no matter how unpromising it may seem; issue-spotting exams reward such inventiveness. A lawyer who refrains from trying a tactic, however unlikely, may commit malpractice. But the fundamental justification for every legal system is to resolve disputes in which both parties are convinced they are right. That is possible only if lawyers follow the rules of the game. Even if (especially if) they disagree about everything else, lawyers must agree on procedure; those who cut procedural corners gain an unfair advantage and compromise the system's integrity and the legitimacy of its outcome. These lawyers refused to follow procedures. Damer disobeyed a judge's order sealing a settlement, Wisehart sought leverage for a settlement by using opposing counsel's papers, which his client (who was also his paralegal) took from a conference room table without permission.[51]

---

49. Damer had been an undergraduate and law student at University of San Francisco and always practiced alone or in a small firm; Wisehart had obtained a B.A., LL.B. and M.P.A. from Michigan and been an associate at Chadbourne Parke, house counsel to American Airlines, and general counsel for REA, before starting a two-person practice.

50. Garbus & Seligman (1976); Harvard Civil Rights-Civil Liberties Law Review (1970); New York University Law Review (1974); Moliterno (2005).

51. Harvard Law Professor Charles Nesson suffered a $675,000 judgment against his client, Joel Tenenbaum, for illegally downloading and sharing 30 songs without paying. He advanced a "fair use" defense against the advice of experts, who were proved right when the judge ruled against it. He urged Tenenbaum to admit his actions "because it's the truth," and Nesson wanted a principled victory. Tenenbaum felt Nesson did an "absolutely brilliant job." A blogger called Nesson "my new HERO." Nesson now insists the issues are "teed up beautifully for higher courts." Anyhow, "Law in the court of public opinion is what shapes law in the courts and the real world." John Schwartz, *Tilting at Internet Barrier, a Stalwart Is Upended,* New York Times A1 (Aug. 11, 2009).

Once lawyers commit such a transgression, they typically aggravate the offense, multiplying procedural objections, moving to recuse unsympathetic judges, taking every possible appeal, naming opposing counsel and judges as defendants in new lawsuits, and constructing elaborate conspiracy theories to explain away subsequent defeats. This is a paranoid style, which produces an account of the world that cannot be falsified because each inconsistent piece of evidence is fitted into the existing schema.[52] There was always some truth in these lawyers' accusations. For instance, Chiantelli's order did exceed his authority; after Damer refused to surrender his files for fear of their destruction there was a fire in Chiantelli's courtroom (apparently because he was violating the no-smoking rule); the selection of New York judges is deeply politicized (as Wisehart claimed). Moreover, sometimes the lawyers' tactics worked. Yagman got Judge Real disqualified in the Settles case, and Wisehart forced Judge Moskowitz to recuse herself.

These lawyers used a scattershot approach, seemingly unable to distinguish between important and unimportant issues, cogent and frivolous arguments. Constant hyperbole undermined their credibility. Their behavior transformed the initial sympathy of judges (Goldhammer for Damer, Moskowitz for Wisehart) into antipathy. Goldhammer warned Damer: not to "threaten a judge." Moskowitz took umbrage when Wisehart threatened to appeal her rulings. Some lawyers pursued the cause even after their client told them to stop. Examples are Damer, as well as Regan in the introduction to Chapter 7. Although these lawyers initially justified their conduct in terms of loyalty to client, they ended up disparaging the clients' capacity to make decisions. Some even misrepresented their clients' identity (Maloney and Virsik in the introduction to Chapter 7).

Why do some lawyers transgress procedural rules, especially unambiguous ones like those broken by Damer and Wisehart? Perhaps it is related to the nature of the case. The unpopularity and jeopardy of criminal defendants may encourage strong identification by their lawyers, whose loyalty has led them to put a perjurious witness on the stand,[53] refuse to disclose the whereabouts of a homicide victim to her grieving parents,[54] conceal the murder weapon,[55] or pass information from a jailed client in violation of court orders.[56] Lawyers for organized crime may be overzealous in order to get repeat business. Cause lawyers embrace the ends of their clients, which they see as transcending the individual case.[57]

52. Shapiro (1999: Chapter 3).

53. Green (2007); Asimow & Weisberg (2009).

54. Melinkoff (1973).

55. Commonwealth v. Stenhach, 356 Pa.Super. 5, 514 A.2d 114, appeal denied, 517 Pa. 589, 534 A.2d 769 (1987).

56. Julia Preston, *Lawyer in Terror Case Apologizes for Violating Special Prison Rules*, New York Times (Sept. 29, 2006).

57. Scheingold & Sarat (2004).

Are there character traits that predispose lawyers to excessive zeal? Whereas law school teaches students to tolerate ambiguity—uncertain facts, indeterminate law, and subjective values—these lawyers saw the world in black and white. For many lawyers, experience breeds cynicism about the possibility of attaining justice; but decades of practice just intensified these lawyers' outrage about injustice. They were right about everything, and everyone else was wrong (perhaps they had to think this because their conspiracy theories would collapse otherwise). They demonstrated their inerrancy by cataloguing others' mistakes.[58] Both Damer and Wisehart refused to confess error, although doing so probably would have let them escape any penalty. Damer compared himself to Washington, Lincoln, and Kennedy. Every fight was David against Goliath. These lawyers felt persecuted by opposing counsel and judges and betrayed by friends—and then provoked those responses, perhaps to confirm their world view. They courted martyrdom. Damer was briefly jailed for contempt and claimed to fear being jailed again if he ever ventured before Chiantelli. Wisehart defied Judge Moskowitz, saying, "If you are going to send me to The Tombs because I want to be heard, you go ahead and do it."[59] They constructed their outsider status and gloried in it. They said and seemed to believe that the legal system would collapse if they did not prevail. (The State Bar mirrored this apocalyptic view in the belief that the legal system would collapse if they were not disciplined.)

These lawyers expressed strong emotions towards clients, adversaries, opposing counsel, and judges. Psychotherapists spend years seeking insight into how feelings may distort their understanding of patients. Lawyers rarely exhibit such self-knowledge. Damer and Wisehart were strongly protective of their female clients (precisely, the countertransference psychotherapists are trained to recognize). They displayed many of the markers of a paranoid style, such as the inability to accept external authority, hyperconsciousness of rank, and acute sensitivity to rebuff.[60] Many lawyers develop a strong personal antipathy toward their opponents, such as the way Greene and Harney regarded doctors and their insurers, or the feelings of Cardozo and Brashich about the large firm lawyers representing their client's estranged brother. or Byler's fury at Thomas Morgan's intervention on behalf of his brother James.

58. Damer sent me twenty pages of e-mail in rebuttal, correcting every typo of an early draft of Chapter 7. Byler wrote a six-page page rebuttal in my earlier book, attacking my "mediocre dishonest professor's tale, told for the purpose of a cover up. . . ." Abel (2008: 367).

59. Abel (2008: 436). Richard Fine, a lawyer, chose three months of solitary confinement in an 8-foot by 13-foot cell for contempt rather than comply with a judge's order. Victoria Kim, *Lawyer takes a stand from his cell*, Los Angeles Times (June 7, 2009). Fine had been disbarred in February 2009 for behavior similar to, if more extreme than, that of Damer and Wisehart. Kenneth Ofgang, *Supreme Court Orders Disbarment of Attorney Richard I. Fine*, Metropolitan News-Enterprise 1 (Feb. 12, 2009).

60. Shapiro (1999: Chapter 3).

Damer and Wisehart took hostility to another level. Damer's anger at the Sterns firm seems to have antedated the Seward case and persisted long after it concluded. Wisehart also had clashed with Weil Gotshal before representing Joan Lipin; and Stephen Yagman's battles with judges lasted for decades. Damer and Wisehart seemed to resent the wealth and prestige of opposing counsel. Wisehart believed his Weil Gotshal adversaries were laughing at him. Damer claimed the bailiff had told Denebeim (who had betrayed him), "[T]he judge is just letting [Damer] go on and on so he will go crazy and attack somebody and then I can shoot him." Damer was "moved... to tears" by the eulogy a judge offered for his recently deceased mother-in-law—"she loved nothing better than a good fight for a just cause"—perhaps because he did, too.

Insofar as these behaviors express deeply ingrained character traits, little can be done to discourage them. The disciplinary process is unlikely to be an effective deterrent. Both Damer and Wisehart saw it as another element in a vast conspiracy, which just strengthened their determination to continue fighting. Are there structural remedies? One justification for the English divided profession, which required that clients first retain solicitors, who alone could brief barristers, was to create distance between litigants and those who advocate for them in court. The English Bar also followed the "cab rank rule," obligating barristers to take any case they were competent to handle. It was not uncommon for a barrister to prosecute in the morning and appear for the defense in a different case that afternoon. But now the Crown Prosecution Service has assumed that role, and professional and even lay clients have direct access to barristers. In any event, the cab rank rule always was more honored in the breach than the observance. In the United States, clients demand total fidelity, and some lawyers feel wedded to causes, not just clients.[61] Excessive zeal by a few lawyers may be a price worth paying for such loyalties.

II. COMMON CAUSES

I believe my twelve narratives confirm the need for caution in generalizing about unethical lawyers. The behaviors are fundamentally different. They do not express a common pathology. Ethical rules, however appropriate for *judging* conduct, are useless for understanding it. Nevertheless, my previous book identified behavioral traits shared by the seven New York lawyers, transcending the offense. The nine California lawyers offer a further opportunity to explore these generalizations (which ultimately have to be tested quantitatively).

61. Scheingold & Sarat (2004).

A. Protestations of Innocence

Virtually all these lawyers maintained their innocence to the very end: all but Furtzaig in New York and Crane in California. This tends to be true of white collar criminals generally, who (unlike ordinary criminals) do not see themselves as deviants or outlaws and claim (often accurately) that many others behave the same way. The disciplinary process merely intensified the lawyers' convictions of their own righteousness. Any remorse they voiced was either a hypocritical pretense to mitigate the penalty or an expression of regret at having been caught. They may be more cautious about being discovered in the future, but there was little evidence of rehabilitation. Indeed, Brazil persisted in committing similar frauds, for which he ultimately went to prison.

B. Experience

The behavior was not caused by inexperience. In New York, only Muto was new to the game (immigration), and even he had been admitted more than a decade earlier. In the Sega computer game licensing case (Chapter 4, "Playing Games with Sega"), Depew had been admitted four years and Crane three. Nevertheless, Depew cautioned Crane against "usurpation of corporate opportunity" (but then joined him in committing it). All the other lawyers (including those in the chapter introductions) had many years, often decades of experience. Ethical misconduct is *learned* behavior;[62] it is not the product of ignorance. Kreitzer learned from other personal injury lawyers (and crooked claims adjusters), Muto from other immigration lawyers (and "travel agencies"), Scapa and Brown from other ambulance chasers (from whom they borrowed the cover-up disclaimer), Greene and Harney from other lawyers and even judges, Crane from Depew, and Twitty from the prosecutor. Byler and Wisehart both asked colleagues for counsel—and got bad advice. Brazil had been the ultimate authority in his role as California Commissioner of Real Estate.

C. Rule Ambiguity

Nor was the behavior caused by rule ambiguity. Of course, there are ambiguous ethical rules: professional responsibility casebooks and legal scholars focus on them.[63] But the rules in these cases were clear, as I believe they are in most disciplinary proceedings (they certainly were in the hundreds I read in New York and California). The neglect committed by Kreitzer and Muto was extreme. Kreitzer's 10 percent scheme was clearly illegal, and he persisted after being charged! Similarly, Furtzeig's forgery of court papers and Brazil's misuse of his secretary's notary stamp were inexcusable. Cardozo and Brashsich had a clear obligation to present their client with the fee implications of alternative

62. Levin (2004–2005). On the importance of mentors, *see* Kay & Wallace (2009).
63. For an 800-year history of ethical rules, *see* Andrews (2004).

trust settlements. Byler could not simply appropriate the tax refund and clearly had to escrow it when Morgan protested. Wisehart had to give the Weil Gotshal papers to the judge to determine his right to use them. Scapa and Brown clearly broke the law against solicitation. Greene and Harney clearly violated MICRA. Crane could not disguise his identity from his employer when proposing a deal. Brazil could not deceive Hom when borrowing money. Twitty could not arrange for Lopez to negotiate with the prosecutor without asking Tarlow. Damer could not defy Chiantelli's order.

D. Greed

The behaviors reflect greed more than need. None of the lawyers suffered the kind of poverty we associate with street crime. None was a substance abuser. Brazil rightly feared his deals would fall through unless he raised more money, but he had initiated them. *All* the lawyers were pursuing money, some hoping for greater wealth than they had ever enjoyed. In New York, Kreitzer operated a settlement mill processing well over a thousand cases a year, Muto bragged of earning $4,000 a week from immigration cases, much of it for pro forma appearances. Furtzaig had become an equity partner in a boutique real estate firm. Cardozo and Brashich claimed a huge contingent fee for resolving a multimillion dollar trust dispute. Byler appropriated his client's entire $53,000 IRS refund as a fee. Wisehart stood to earn a contingent fee from substantial compensatory and possible punitive damages for sexual discrimination and harassment. In California, Scapa and Brown were emulating Jacoby & Meyers. Greene and Harney insisted on their usual fees in defiance of MICRA. Crane anticipated huge profits from licensing Sega's computer games for home use. Brazil believed that municipal bond defeasance could earn him millions. Twitty saw persuading Lopez to cop a plea as an easy way to earn his $150,000 retainer from Escobedo. Even Damer hoped to be lead attorney in a class action against Sterns for bill padding.

E. Psychic Rewards

Most lawyers are not just interested in money. They also want the psychic reward of helping clients and the gratitude that often follows. Tort lawyers obtain essential compensation for accident victims; Kreitzer bonded with at least some of his clients. Muto derived enormous satisfaction from fighting deportation proceedings and basked in the thanks he received from clients when walking through Chinatown with his daughter on Sundays. Furtzaig was concerned to please an extremely demanding senior partner (and father surrogate). Babette Hecht called Cardozo her "knight in shining armor." Ljubica Callahan was deeply dependent on Brashich, another Serbo-Croatian-speaking immigrant. James Morgan told Byler that it felt "like a divine gift to have a friend like you in this hour of need and I am very grateful for your help."[64] Wisehart not only took Joan Lipin's case

64. Abel (2008: 290).

for a contingent fee and invested untold hours in fighting Weil Gotshal over discovery but also hired her as a paralegal when the American Red Cross blacklist made her unemployable. Scapa and Brown claimed to be increasing access to justice for Filipino Americans. Greene and Harney vociferously maintained that clients with difficult cases should be grateful to have such extraordinary lawyers and believed those clients were—until lesser lawyers interfered. Crane felt Sega should be grateful he had earned royalties for the company that would not otherwise have been received (even though he had to employ deceit because of the company's inability to recognize a business opportunity). Brazil constantly harped on the effort he took to conclude Collins's loans and the usurious interest greedily demanded by Hom. Twitty insisted he had done Lopez a favor by arranging a negotiation with the prosecutor, in which Tarlow refused to participate. Maria Seward lavished praise on Damer (until she replaced him with Denebeim and accepted the defendants' offer).

> Throughout this whole ugly business, I have come to really appreciate, more and more, your awesome and prodigious skills, which are being utilized on my behalf and, perhaps, ultimately for many others who have been abused by some members of the San Francisco legal community . . .. John and I are both very grateful to you and your office for bringing to bear so much talent and experience.

F. Accounts

All these lawyers constructed accounts to justify or at least excuse their behavior.[65] Kreitzer, Muto, and Scapa and Brown declared they were increasing access to justice, and future clients would suffer if the lawyers were suspended or disbarred. Furtzaig believed (probably correctly) that his senior partner would not accept any explanations for the failure to evict tenants or collect rent—and (clearly erroneously) that this could be covered up indefinitely. Cardozo and Brashich convinced themselves they had negotiated the best—indeed, the only—resolution of the trust dispute. Byler justified a right to the entire tax refund by claiming an hourly rate he had not regularly charged and concocting a bill based on hours that deviated from his own "Red-book entries." Wisehart insisted that Weil Gotshal had left its papers on the conference table to entrap him—and also that he was legally entitled to appropriate them. Greene and Harney adamantly maintained that MICRA either did not apply or was unconstitutional. Crane contended he had fulfilled his fiduciary duty to Sega by presenting the licensing deal, even if he had concealed his identity. Brazil asserted that Collins had prevented the loans from being financed and greed had led Hom to make bad investments. And Damer persistently claimed to represent the class of Sterns's victims, even though he had no client. Several "neutralization devices" recurred in multiple cases.[66]

65. Scott & Lyman (1968). Hall & Holmes (2009) argue that lawyers have an elevated tendency toward and capacity for rationalization; *see also* Hall (2010).

66. Matza (1964).

These lawyers sought to commute crime to tort by transmuting ethical failing into technical incompetence or bad judgment and making or offering restitution. They blamed others, such as clients, lawyers with whom they had collaborated in the misconduct, opposing counsel, counsel of co-accused, subordinates, employers, and judges. They believed they were above the law in each of the following: Kreitzer in operating the ten percent scheme, Muto in failing to follow routine procedures, Furtzaig in forging legal documents, Cardozo in misrepresenting that the surrogate would not review his fee, Byler in appropriating the tax refund and then denying that Morgan's objection constituted a dispute, Wisehart in appropriating the Weil Gotshal papers and using them to demand a settlement, Scapa and Brown in buying cases from cappers, Greene and Harney in persistently flouting MICRA after it had been upheld, Crane in deceiving his employer, Brazil in appropriating his secretary's notary stamp and forging her signature, Twitty in secretly arranging Lopez's meeting with the prosecutor, and Damer in defying Chiantelli's order.

G. Habitude

The behavior was not aberrational. Lawyers in disciplinary proceedings often contend that they have suffered a momentary lapse in judgment (caused by financial embarrassment, marital discord or family problems, substance abuse, or some other extrinsic factor). On the contrary, most of the conduct in these twelve cases was chronic. Kreitzer had built up his settlement mill over many years. Muto consistently neglected all his clients. Furtzeig just dug himself deeper as he took on more work and covered up errors with greater deceit. After Brashich was charged with misconduct toward Babette Hecht, he behaved similarly toward Ljubica Callahan—and actually cited his earlier performance as a defense in the later proceeding. Byler had clashed with other clients over bills. Wisehart (like Yagman) had systematically sought to recuse unsympathetic judges. Scapa and Brown deliberately constructed their Bay Area satellite office on ambulance chasing. Greene and Harney evaded or defied MICRA in multiple cases. Crane sought to license to competitors games he knew were covered by the same copyright, continuing even after he was laid off by Sega. Brazil had clashed with previous employers and partners and then defrauded other clients after being disciplined. According to Tarlow, Twitty had "dumped" other clients. Damer's behavior in the disciplinary proceeding replicated the behavior he had exhibited in the case with Sterns. Character is destiny. Habits are hard to change. Once these lawyers committed to an action, they found it difficult to change course.[67]

67. Atul Gawande (2010) offers persuasive evidence that simple checklists can change habitual behavior by doctors.

III. CURES

In recapitulating the cases at the beginning of this chapter, I emphasized their differences and proposed responses specific to each category. The common causes I identified in the previous section—convictions of innocence and self-righteousness, extensive legal experience, violations of clear rules, the combination of greed and a desire to be helpful and appreciated, rationalizations, and perseveration—hardly encourage optimism about the possibility of changing behavior. One response would be resignation about an inevitable few bad apples in any barrel. I reject that. We do not know how many bad apples are inevitable—if any. And rot spreads. Lawyer misconduct sets a bad example, teaching others how to cut corners and encouraging them to believe they can do so with impunity. I will conclude, therefore, with some thoughts about reforms that might reduce ethical misconduct and how to achieve them.

Let me start with self-regulation, where I began this book.[68] Cases heard by the State Bar Court represent the tip of the proverbial iceberg, the apex of a typical litigation pyramid, whose base is the "dark figure" of actual misconduct.[69] We know that attrition occurs at each level. Some merely reflects false positives, acceptable behavior requiring no correction. But many missing cases signify underenforcement, most of which is attributable to the failure to bring misconduct to the attention of the State Bar. What could be done to increase the proportion of misconduct investigated? Almost all complaints come from clients, their friends and relatives, or the opposing party.[70] Could we encourage more clients to complain? Many already are strongly motivated to do so, including the personal injury victims neglected by Kreitzer, the Chinese immigrants neglected by Muto (especially because disciplinary complaints were a prerequisite to reopening their deportation orders), and the clients overcharged by Byler, Greene and Harney, and Twitty or defrauded by Brazil. (Even some of these clients were motivated or guided by lawyers.) Nevertheless, a great deal of lawyer misbehavior will never be exposed by clients. Furtzaig successfully hid his failures from clients for years, even paying $60,000 from his own pocket to do so. Babette Hecht continued to defend Cardozo even after being told of his misconduct; Ljubica Callahan declined to claim the money Brashich was ordered to pay her.

---

68. For yet another skeptical view of self-regulation, *see* Perlman (2003). For a convincing argument that tax lawyers have acted collectively to outlaw abusive shelters, *see* Rostain (2006b).

69. For a recent study of Canadian lawyer self-reports of their behavior, *see* Wilkinson *et al.* (2000); Mercer *et al.* (2005).

70. Between 75 and 80 percent of complaints to the Intake Unit in 1996, 1997, and 2000 came from the client or a close friend or relative and another 3 to 10 percent from the opposing party. State Bar of California (2001b: Attachment 8).

Joan Lipin, who appropriated the Weil Gotshal papers, was hardly going to encourage Wisehart to surrender the smoking gun that might win her case.

Although San Francisco automobile accident victims were surprised to be contacted by Gumban and Buchanan before accident reports were publicly available, most were happy to be told that a lawyer was interested in their cases. Even large corporations like Sega and Paramount might not have uncovered Crane's deceit if greed had not led him to sublicense what was effectively the same program to two competitors. Having asked Twitty to arrange a meeting with the prosecutor, Lopez was hardly going to complain. And Maria Seward had little interest in enforcing Judge Chiantelli's sealing order (although she may have worried that the settlement would be set aside). We can generalize from these cases that clients often are ignorant of the law, unable to observe the lawyer's behavior, and indifferent to or even complicit in ethical violations.

The study cited above also found that only 4 percent of complaints were filed by lawyers (about equally divided between opposing and successor counsel). That should not be surprising, given the "blue wall" covering up police misconduct, the reluctance of doctors to report malpractice by others,[71] or the conspiracy to conceal sexual abuse by priests.[72] My twelve cases confirmed lawyers' reticence and help to explain it. Lawyers who earned fees by referring personal injury cases to Kreitzer were not going to accuse him of neglect, nor were those who also gave insurance agents 10 percent kickbacks to accelerate settlement. Other immigration lawyers who depended on "travel agents" were not going to endanger that lucrative arrangement by accusing Muto of doing so. Opposing counsel who benefited from the incompetence of Kreitzer and Muto were not going to complain; but it is striking that even successor counsel, seeking to reopen deportations on the ground of Muto's inadequate representation, were reluctant to file the indispensable disciplinary complaints.[73] The lawyers fighting Cardozo and Brashich over Babette Hecht's trust were not privy to her fee

---

71. On the difficulty and reluctance of doctors to expose even unlicenced imposters, *see* Collins & Pinch (2005: chapter 2). A 1961 study found that only 30 percent of surgeons would be willing to testify against a surgeon who had removed the wrong kidney. *Medical Economics* (Aug. 28, 1961). Although the situation has improved in the last half century, a 2010 study found that about a third of physicians still did not agree with the professional commitment to report those who are significantly impaired or incompetent; and a third of those who knew an incompetent colleague did not report this. DesRoches et al., *Physicians' Perceptions, Preparedness for Reporting, and Experiences Related to Impaired and Incompetent Colleagues,* 304 *JAMA* 187 (2010).

72. A nurse who reported the misconduct of a doctor to the Texas Medical Board was criminally prosecuted for "misuse of official information," although the jury took less than an hour to acquit. She is now suing for damages for the prosecution and for being fired. Sack, *Nurse to Stand Trial for Reporting Doctor,* New York Times §1 p14 (Feb. 2, 2010); Sack, *Whistle-Blowing Nurse Is Acquitted in Texas,* New York Times (Feb. 12, 2010).

73. Abel (2008: 121).

arrangements. Lawyers who do not chase ambulances may suffer a disadvantage but rarely know what their illegal competitors are doing. All plaintiffs lawyers detested MICRA, if only some defied or evaded it; the mystery is why defense lawyers condoned violations of a law for which they had lobbied. Other lawyers would find it almost impossible to observe a lawyer defrauding his own employer (as Crane did Sega) or client (as Brazil did Collins and Hom). Twitty successfully conspired with Lyons to conceal the prosecutor's negotiations with Lopez from Tarlow; it was only when Lyons mistakenly told Rosenthal that the latter felt an obligation to inform Tarlow. Thus, although lawyers certainly know the ethical rules better than clients and perceive some behavior invisible to clients, there is much that even they do not see and a variety of reasons why they do not complain about what they do observe. Those reasons include indifference, complicity, material advantage, and a disinclination to encourage other lawyers to complain—perhaps about them.[74]

The relatively rare situations in which lawyers do file complaints are equally revealing. Furtzaig's firm reported him in order to limit its liability to clients. Byler had the misfortune to overcharge the brother of Thomas Morgan, a leading authority on legal ethics. Similarly, Gumban and Buchanan made the mistake of capping a State Bar lawyer. The Weil Gotshal lawyers were already furious at Wisehart and eager to take advantage of his ethical violation, thereby winning a case they probably would have lost on the merits. Lawyers sought to earn contingent fees by recovering the amounts Greene and Harney had charged in violation of MICRA. The Sterns firm had ample reason to seek revenge against Damer (whether or not they wanted to have "his ticket pulled"). All these lawyers complained for personal reasons—monetary, professional, emotional—not just out of civic responsibility.

The California study found that judges filed less than one percent of complaints.[75] Judge Baffa's explanation for why he uncritically approved Greene's fee in disregard of MICRA is telling:

> I looked at what was accomplished. In my mind you are not going to get any recovery at all unless you have a good lawyer to effect it for you. Without the lawyer, you get nothing, and frankly I happen to like lawyers and I like to protect them with their fees.

All judges once were lawyers. Before being elevated to the bench, most practiced with the very lawyers who committed misconduct, often for decades. Many judges continue to socialize with their former colleagues, who have appeared before them in the past and are likely to do so again in the future. But even if

---

74. For suggestions about how to encourage associates to blow the whistle, *see* Long (2009).

75. On the role of judges in promulgating ethical standards, *see* Zacharias & Green (2009b).

judges were less sympathetic to lawyers, they still would have missed much of the misconduct in my twelve cases—deceit by Furtzaig, Crane and Brazil, Byler's overcharging, and ambulance chasing by Scapa and Brown.

The unusual situations in which judges did complain help us to understand these exceptions. Immigration judges filed grievances against Muto out of solicitude for those they would have to deport because of his incompetence and anger that he had wasted their time and displayed insufficient deference.[76] Surrogate judges are responsible for protecting the interests of vulnerable clients like Babette Hecht and Ljubica Callahan. By telling Judge Moskowitz that a cancer diagnosis and treatment had rendered her mentally incompetent, Wisehart made her recuse herself but also provoked her to complain. Judge Patel was outraged by U.S. Attorney General Thornburgh's arrogance in asserting that Department of Justice attorneys could not be bound by ethical rules (even those adopted by federal courts)[77]—and at Twitty for suggesting that Lyons meet privately with Lopez. And Judge Chiantelli was angry enough at Damer's defiance to jail him for contempt.

Could we increase the proportion of misconduct reported to the State Bar? Clients might be given further incentives to complain. Other jurisdictions not only punish unethical lawyers but also make them compensate clients for inadequate professional services.[78] When I broached this idea to the Professional Discipline Committee of the New York City Bar, members peremptorily dismissed it with the argument that clients already file far too many unwarranted grievances. And resistance by lawyers has forced other jurisdictions to curtail the circumstances in which compensation is paid.[79] Lawyers could be compelled to carry malpractice insurance, making it more likely that damages would be paid (and hence that claims would be filed). Although virtually all other countries do this, the only American state to require insurance is Oregon. A 1988 survey of more than 12,000 California lawyers suggested that only 17 percent were insured.[80] Most state bar associations have even refused to mandate that lawyers tell clients whether they are insured. We saw California's struggle over that in Chapter 1, "The Politics of Self-Regulation." The Virginia State Bar Council voted

76. The federal government has considered giving immigration judges greater power to discipline lawyers who appear before them. Richard B. Schmitt, *Immigration lawyers' misconduct targeted in federal proposal,* Los Angeles Times (Aug. 23, 2008).

77. On the authority of federal courts to regulate lawyers, *see* Zacharias & Green (2003).

78. Canada, Australia, and the U.K. Paton (2008).

79. Haller (2009).

80. The survey sampled nearly 2,000 defense lawyers, nearly 3,000 plaintiffs lawyers, 3,400 lawyers with disciplinary complaints, and more than 4,000 random lawyers. Of the 89 percent who responded, only 17 percent (1801) reported their annual premium, suggesting that the rest were uninsured. Donna M. Hamlin and Craig Harkins, *Final Report: State Bar of California Questionaire [sic] on Professional Liability Insurance* (1988), in Fellmeth (1988a: Exhibit G).

down a reporting requirement 60–11 in 2008.[81] Any effort to encourage lawyers to report their colleagues raises concerns that such complaints will become strategic weapons in litigation and negotiation, as has happened with sanctions motions. Perhaps lawyers could be given incentives for turning themselves in, as the Treasury Department has done in its efforts to enforce Foreign Assets Control.[82] I find it hard to imagine judges reporting much more misconduct.[83]

Most reform proposals focus on the disciplinary process.[84] As I showed in Chapter 1, California has witnessed repeated cycles of exposé, reform campaign, incremental change, and reversion to routine.[85] In 1929, the year after it was created, the State Bar investigated an impressive 1,531 lawyers. But the numbers fell steadily over the next two decades, to less than a tenth of that number in 1948, despite the enormous growth of the legal profession (see Table 1). The State Bar closures forced by the legislature and Governor in the late 1980s and late 1990s also drastically cut the number of complaints (see Table 2). (Similar cycles can be seen in response to activities as diverse as nursing,[86] hospitals,[87] and yoga instruction[88]—and as I write, most urgently in financial markets.) The recurrent criticism is that too few complaints result in significant punishment.

---

81. 77 U.S. Law Week 2307 (Oct. 17, 2008).

82. 31 CFR Part 501 (8.8.08). I am grateful to Prof. Perry Bechky, University of Connecticut Law School, for this.

83. Greenbaum (2009).

84. *E.g.,* Cagle *et al.* (1999).

85. The classic work is Cohen (1972). For revisions, *see* Goode & Ben-Yehuda (1994); McRobbie & Thornton (1995); Hunt (1997); Ungar (2001); Hunt (1999); Garland (2008).

86. Charles Ornstein and Tracy Weber, *Nurses license renewal stiffened,* Los Angeles Times (Oct. 11, 2008); Charles Ornstein and Tracy Weber, *New rules for nurses,* Los Angeles Times (Oct. 24, 2008); Tracy Weber and Charles Ornstein, *Panel slow to act on nurses' crimes,* Los Angeles Times (Nov. 2, 2008); Charles Ornstein and Tracy Weber, *Health staff background checks lag,* Los Angeles Times (Dec. 30, 2008); Tracy Weber and Charles Ornstein, *Board takes no public action against some King/Drew nurses,* Los Angeles Times (July 12, 2009); Charles Ornstein, Tracy Weber and Maloy Moore, *When Caregivers Harm: Problem nurses stay on the job as patients suffer,* Los Angeles Times (July 12, 2009); Tracy Weber and Charles Ornstein, *Schwarzenegger sweeps out nursing board,* Los Angeles Times (July 14, 2009); Charles Ornstein and Tracy Weber, *California nursing board's executive officer resigns,* Los Angeles Times (July 15, 2009); Michael Rothfield, *New California nursing board members sworn in,* Los Angeles Times (July 16, 2009); Tracy Weber and Charles Ornstein, *Loose reins on nurses in drug abuse program,* Los Angeles Times (July 25, 2009); Michael Finnegan and Charles Ornstein, *Nursing board seeks to triple enforcement staff,* Los Angeles Times (July 28, 2009); Tracy Weber, Charles Ornstein and Rong-Gong Lin II, *Schwarzenegger vows to boost patient protections,* Los Angeles Times A1 (Aug. 13, 2009).

87. Alex Berenson, *Weak Oversight Lets Bad Hospitals Stay Open,* New York Times A1 (Dec. 8, 2008).

88. A.G. Sulzberger, *Yoga Faces Regulation, and Firmly Pushes Back,* New York Times A1 (July 11, 2009).

The remedy usually proposed is to shift regulatory responsibility from the profession to the state.[89]

Historical data confirm that lawyer discipline in California exhibits high levels of attrition, especially at the early stages of the process.[90] During the State Bar's first two decades, only a third to a tenth of investigations led to notices to show cause (NTSCs), whose numbers steadily declined from a high of 367 in 1928 to just 19 in 1948 (see Table 1). The Board of Governors dismissed a large proportion of NTSCs, and the Supreme Court consistently rejected the Board's recommendations to disbar lawyers. There were fewer than ten disbarments in 17 of the 21 years, averaging just six a year. In the last 30 years, complaints have stayed relatively constant, perhaps because Intake consistently classifies two to four times as many of the calls its receives as inquiries (see Table 2). A very high proportion of complaints are dismissed: from 1987 to 2008, dismissals outnumbered complaints 120,250 to 92,489.[91] Between 1987 and 1995, dismissals were two to five times as numerous as Statements of the Case (and 19 times as frequent in one aberrational year). During the last two decades, NTSCs fell within a fairly narrow range: 241–584 (see Table 4).[92] By contrast, other dispositions generally were twice as common (although the ratio declined from more than 3:1 in 1997 to about 1:1 in 2007). When one alternative disposition (admonitions) was eliminated, its place was taken by directional letters, which in turn gave way to warnings and resource letters. This is not necessarily a bad thing: Much lawyer misconduct is handled better by non-punitive remedies. Like NTSCs, State Bar Court filings fell within a fairly narrow range, rising from 527 its first year to 1,182 and then falling back to about 600 at the end of the period, averaging 748 (see Table 5). (In both instances, this constancy is probably attributable to institutional capacity.) Although annual disbarments fluctuated wildly from none to 89, they averaged 45 (compared with just 6 in the State Bar's first 20 years) and were greatly outnumbered by suspensions. Only a small fraction of cases filed led to those two serious penalties. At the same time, less than 10 percent of cases were dismissed, suggesting that the Office of Trial Counsel (OTC) prosecuted few false positives.

---

89. Paton (2008); Terry (2008) (regulation of lawyers as "service providers"). For a recent proposal to strengthen state regulation of corporate lawyers in the U.K., *see* Smedley (2009). Zacharias (2009a) argues that self-regulation is a "myth" because lawyers already are heavily regulated by the state.

90. HALT: An Organization of Americans for Legal Reform gave California a D+ in its 2006 Report Card on Lawyer Discipline and a D– for "Adequacy of Discipline Imposed," ranking it 45th out of 50 states.

91. Data are missing for three of those years.

92. Excluding a low of 174 in 1999 because of partial closure and a high of 603 in 1991 because of an earlier closure.

After reading 200 State Bar Court cases, I believed that penalties were sufficiently severe. Six of the seven New York lawyers I studied never returned to practice; although six of the nine California lawyers continued or resumed practice, they were not disciplined again.[93] American criminal justice seeks to compensate for its failure to apprehend most offenders by punishing a few severely, as exemplified by rigid sentencing guidelines, the Rockefeller drug laws, three-strike rules, and the death penalty. But there is no evidence that harsher punishments were necessary to deter these lawyers from recidivism or would have discouraged others from following their example. Although many lawyers sheepishly admit that the first things they read in professional journals are the disciplinary reports—the equivalent of gossip columns—there is no evidence that they draw the conclusion that these lawyers got away with murder. For most targets of complaints, the disciplinary process *is* the punishment.[94] They consider the financial cost, emotional stress, loss of self-esteem, and harm to professional reputation devastating.[95] (Shakespeare has Iago use the last consequence to inflame Othello's jealousy.)[96] Publicizing accusations might be an additional deterrent, but it would also increase the harm to innocent lawyers from false positives.[97] Every study of deterrence concludes that the certainty of punishment is far more effective than severity. We should direct our attention to increasing

---

93. I do not disagree with the view advanced by Robert Fellmeth that a relatively small number of lawyers—he estimated one to two thousand—are chronic offenders, responsible for a disproportionate share of client complaints. Fellmeth (1989b: 20).

94. Feeley (1979).

95. For an analysis of the potential influence of reputation on ethical behavior, *see* Zacharias (2008). Punishment for scientific misconduct, surprisingly, did not necessarily end careers. Redman & Merz (2008).

96. Good name in man and woman, dear my lord,
Is the immediate jewel of their souls.
Who steals my purse steals trash; 'tis something, nothing;
'Twas mine, 'tis his, and has been slave to thousands;
But he that filches from me my good name
Robs me of that which not enriches him,
And makes me poor indeed.
OTHELLO, Act 3, scene 3, lines 155-61.

97. In June 2008, the Internal Revenue Service announced that it would publish more frequent and extensive accounts of disciplinary actions against attorneys and other professionals. *OPR Announces Disciplinary Sanctions With New Format Describing Misconduct*, 105 DAILY TAX G-1 (June 2, 2008). I am grateful to Professor Dennis J. Ventry, U.C. Davis Law School, for this. For a prediction that disciplinary procedures will become more transparent, *see* Zacharias (2003a). A study of the Los Angeles County Sheriff's Department found that complaints against deputies, whether or not proven, strongly predict future misconduct. Winton, *System for Identifying Problematic Deputies Works Well, Report Says*, LOS ANGELES TIMES A3 (Sept. 9, 2009).

the proportion of misconduct subjected to regulatory scrutiny rather than inflicting exemplary punishments on a few highly visible miscreants.

A variety of other responses have been considered. Most involve state action.[98] Legal scholars devote a great deal of energy to refining ethical rules.[99] But there was little ambiguity about whether rules had been broken in my twelve cases (or in the dozens more in the chapter introductions in both books, or the several hundred decided over the course of a decade, which I read in each jurisdiction). There is a lot of truth in the folk wisdom many professional responsibility instructors offer students: if you have to ask whether it's ethical, it probably isn't. Legal educators call for more education (surprise!).[100] But there is no evidence that either the American Bar Association's requirement of education in professional responsibility starting in 1973 (in response to Watergate), or the Multistate Professional Responsibility Examination following soon thereafter, has made lawyers more ethical. Almost all the lawyers I studied were convicted of ethical misbehavior decades after graduating; it is hard to imagine what difference law school could have made. Most lawyers treat mandatory continuing legal education—especially in ethics—as a pointless obligation.[101] I saw no evidence that ignorance of the rules explained the misbehavior of the twelve lawyers I studied. Could entry barriers screen out future rule breakers?[102] The Gluecks' proposal in the 1950s to identify juvenile delinquents before they committed any crime effectively discredited that strategy.[103] Character and fitness committees have abused their authority by discriminating against ethnic minorities and other outsiders;[104] they have demonstrated no ability to exclude unethical lawyers.

If state action seems unpromising, what about the market? There is evidence that patient input improves the outcome of medical care.[105] Clients are the most effective monitors of at least some forms of lawyer misconduct, as well as competence.

---

98. For a discussion of the relative merits of regulation by courts, legislatures, and the market *see* Barton (2003).

99. For thoughtful studies by philosophers of the basis of ethical rules, see Luban (2007); Carle (2008); Markovits (2008).

100. E.g., Economides & Rogers (2009); Rhode (2009). Evans & Palermo (2005) find that education has "zero impact." Corbin (2005) finds that experienced practitioners adapt to their environment.

101. For a skeptical view of the ability of MCLE to inculcate "judgment," *see* Wendel (2009); for a more enthusiastic view, *see* Hellman (2010).

102. Barton (2001); Levine & Pearce (2009).

103. Glueck & Glueck (1950).

104. Auerbach (1976: 125-28); Rhode (1985: 499).

105. Karen Barrow, *Armed With Knowledge, Driven to Fight*, New York Times F5 (Sept 23, 2008); Denise Grady, *Shorter Radiation For Cancer of the Breast*, New York Times F1 (Sept. 23, 2008) (Dr. Anthony Zietman, Harvard Medical School: "Patients have to speak up"); cf Rosenthal (1974).

(Of course, clients can also encourage misbehavior, as Joan Lipin did Wisehart's.) Part of the reason why large firm lawyers rarely are disciplined is that their corporate clients keep them in line. The individual clients in my twelve cases found it difficult to do so, both because of their ignorance and vulnerability and because they were one-shot customers, lacking the economic clout of repeat-player corporate (and very wealthy individual) clients. Could this be changed? Medicare regulates quality as well as price, in part by refusing to pay for additional services needed to correct provider error.[106] Physicians are ahead of lawyers in advertising competitive prices.[107] Personal injury victims (like those of Kreitzer, Scapa and Brown, and Greene and Harney) could be collectivized through loss insurance, which would simultaneously make them whole and subrogate their (repeat-player) insurers to their claims.[108] Immigrants might join ethnic associations, which would retain lawyers (that actually is the origin of the earliest legal aid societies).[109] Unlike their nineteenth-century counterparts, however, many immigrants today are illegal (e.g., Muto's Chinese clients). And some of the clients in my twelve cases defy collectivization: sexual harassment victims (Lipin), trust beneficiaries (Hecht), taxpayers (Morgan), criminal accused (Lopez—except through organized crime), legal malpractice victims (Seward). Lawyers can be disciplined by third-party payers: franchise law firms, state legal aid, and legal expenses insurers. Hyatt Legal Services (a franchise operation) excludes lawyers with disciplinary complaints and requires members to carry $100,000 in malpractice insurance.[110] But there are very few disciplinary complaints against legal aid lawyers (despite many questions about their competence and zeal). And unlike clients in Germany (and England since the Courts and Legal Services Act 1999), few Americans have legal expenses insurance.[111]

Could we make the market work better by improving the information available to clients before they retain lawyers? The internet certainly facilitates this.[112]

---

106. Kevin Sack, *Medicare Won't Pay for Medical Errors*, New York Times (Oct. 1, 2008). The American Hospital Association and the Joint Commission are considering which of a new set of infection control guidelines they will use in accrediting hospitals. Kevin Sack, *Infection Control Guidelines Issued*, New York Times A15 (Oct. 9, 2008).

107. Lisa Girion, *Doctors' list puts a price on care*, Los Angeles Times A1 (May 28, 2007) (HealthCare Partners Medical Group, California's largest private practice, serving more than 500,000, put the price for 58 common procedures on its website).

108. But since we do not even effectively require *liability* insurance, it in hard to imagine mandating that everyone, including the poor, must carry loss insurance. Still, universal health care would be a step in the right direction.

109. Abel (1985).

110. http://www.legalplans.com/attorneys.html. I am grateful to Prof. Perry Bechky, University of Connecticut Law School, for bringing this to my attention.

111. This traditionally was a fringe benefit negotiated by unions; but the proportion of workers who belong has fallen to 12 percent.

112. Abel (2006–07).

I am confident that fewer clients would have retained Kreitzer or Muto had they known about the lawyers' neglect, or Scapa and Brown had they known about their ambulance chasing. Furtzaig's firm immediately fired him in order to protect its reputation. Ljubica Callahan might have had second thoughts about Brashich (despite the ethnic connection) had she known how he and Cardozo had treated Babette Hecht. Morgan might not have turned to Byler had he known about his good friend's earlier fee disputes with clients. Sega would never have hired Crane had they known his propensity for deceit. The clients of Greene and Harney might have insisted that they comply with Section 6146, even if that meant losing those lawyers as a result. Collins and Hom might have steered clear of Brazil had they known of his prior conduct. But information has limits. Zagat's, Craigslist, and Yelp have succeeded because consumers believe that the experience of their fellows offers useful insights into quality (if professionals have their doubts).[113] There are increasingly sophisticated efforts to measure the quality of health care.[114] But any meaningful index must control for inputs. That has been a strong objection to the use of test scores to measure teacher effort and efficacy.[115] Controlling inputs is even more difficult in evaluating legal services.[116] Clients must want and be able to use the information; too much is as useless as too little. Hecht refused to acknowledge Cardozo's betrayal. Lopez sought Twitty's intercession with the prosecutor. Lipin urged Wisehart to keep and use the purloined papers. Seward could discharge Damer but could not stop him from defying Chiantelli's order—purportedly in her name. And lawyers like Wisehart, Damer, and Yagman court a reputation for (over)zealous advocacy. But several current efforts suggest these obstacles can be overcome.[117] Avvo rates 1.3

113. Donald G. McNeil, Jr., *Eat and Tell,* New York Times D1 (Nov. 5, 2009); Steve Lohr, *The Crowd Is Wise (When It's Focused),* New York Times §3 p.4 (July 19, 2009).

114. Steve Sternberg and Jack Gillum, *"Double failure" at USA's hospitals,* USA Today (July 9, 2009); Centers for Medicare & Medicaid Services, New Ratings for America's Hospitals Now Available on Hospital Compare Web Site (July 9, 2009); www.hospitalcompare.hhhs.gov; Lisa Girion, *California hospitals graded on death rates,* Los Angeles Times (1.22.09); OSHPD Research Brief #1, *Mortality in California Hospitals, 2006* (Nov. 2008). For an argument that baseball statistics should be adapted to measure the performance of medical care providers, advanced by an odd trio, see Billy Beane, Newt Gingrich, and John Kerry, *How to Take American Health Care From Worst to First,* New York Times A31 (Oct. 24, 2008) (Beane is a former Major League player and currently general manager and minority owner of the Oakland Athletics). Paul O'Neill, Secretary of the Treasury from 2001 to 2002, advocates "a prompt, detailed and hard-headed study of every example of error, infection and other waste in five major medical centers." Paul O'Neill, *Health Care's Infectious Losses,* New York Times A19 (July 6, 2009).

115. Jennifer Medina, *Teachers to Be Measured Based on Students' Standardized Test Scores,* New York Times B3 (Oct. 2 2008).

116. Rosenthal (1976); Carlson (1976).

117. Ward (2010). But one disgruntled lawyer has sued Avvo; and the Florida Bar continues to prohibit client testimonials. *See also* Berenson (2001).

million lawyers, using publicly available information on years in practice, work history, professional recognition and prior discipline, as well as client reviews; its website receives 2 million visits a month. The Association of Corporate Counsel has posted 1,800 member evaluations of outside counsel. Martindale-Hubbell introduced client ratings in 2009.

Another reason why large firm lawyers are not disciplined is that their firms exert control.[118] (Of course, collectivities can foster or cover up misconduct as well as prevent it.[119]) Partners (liable for malpractice) would be unlikely to tolerate the behavior of Kreitzer, Muto, Brazil, or Twitty. Indeed, Furtzaig's firm promptly fired him. In his reply to my chapter, Muto praised the "ideal" "structure" of his non-lawyer job at the New York State Department of Human Rights.[120] Had Byler been a partner, rather than of counsel, he might have had to follow the firm's policies with respect to written retainers and escrowing client funds, especially after a fee dispute. But Cardozo and Brashich (while not partners) cooperated in overcharging Hecht; and Scapa and Brown collaborated in chasing ambulances. Both Greene and Harney were partners in highly respected firms. And if compelled to partner, I can imagine Wisehart, Damer, and Yagman seeking out other overzealous lawyers or compliant subordinates.

None of the proposals discussed in this chapter is a panacea. But the amount of lawyer misconduct might be reduced by all of them—encouraging more complaints by clients, lawyers, and judges; compensating inadequate professional service; mandating malpractice liability insurance; publicizing misconduct earlier and more widely; giving potential clients better information about the price and quality of legal services; limiting rules against solicitation to preventing fraud and overreaching; making lawyers fees transparent; involving third-party payers in controlling lawyer performance; and increasing the incentives for firms to do so. The problem is not knowing what to do. In April 1988, California State Bar Monitor Robert Fellmeth made the following recommendations.[121]

(1) Consortium on competence.
(2) Alcohol and substance abuse program.
(3) Malpractice insurance.
(4) Mandatory continuing education.
(5) Specialization/retesting.
(6) Client trust fund monitoring.
(7) Consumer trust fund.
(8) Written fee agreements.
(9) Client disclosure agreements.

---

118. Richmond (2007–08); Chambliss (2006; 2009).
119. Regan (2004); Rostain (2006a); Alfieri (2006).
120. Abel (2008: 191).
121. Fellmeth (1988a: 61).

It is profoundly discouraging to see how little had been done to implement his suggestions in the succeeding twenty-one years. The problem is lack of political will. As Chapter 1 showed, the State Bar acts—reluctantly—only when journalists expose a scandal and the government threatens to seize regulatory power or not approve State Bar dues. The clients subject to lawyer abuse are difficult if not impossible to organize for the same reason that the market leaves them vulnerable: they are dispersed, and their problems with lawyers are infrequent. Politicians occasionally are attracted to lawyer-bashing as a populist strategy but rarely stick with the issue long enough to ensure that reforms are effected and implemented. Innovative entrepreneurs might compete to offer individual clients cheap, competent, ethical services if regulators stopped obstructing them.[122]

122. Seron (1996); Van Hoy 1997). *See* Clementi (2004).

TABLES

TABLE 1 DISCIPLINE DURING THE STATE BAR'S FIRST TWO DECADES[1]

Year	1928	1929	1930	1931	1932	1933	1934	1935	1936	1937	1938
Investigations	1072	1531	960	750	490	394	444	626	247	160	287
NTSC	367	132	178	84	75	77	123	101	77	85	73
BoG dismissed	337	90	125	58	45	36	76	55	42	51	37
BoG private reproval	0	3	14	8	7	10	6	7	5	6	6
BoG public reproval	12	20	11	4	3	3	8	7	8	5	3
BoG recs suspension	7	7	15	10	13	17	20	19	14	11	12
BoG recs disbarment	11	12	13	4	7	11	13	13	8	12	15
SC dismissed	0	0	0	4	0	1	1	2	2	1	2
SC reproved	0	0	0	1	1	1	0	0	0	0	0
SC suspended	0	15	16	18	12	13	23	19	15	12	11
SC disbarred	0	14	8	5	3	8	9	9	14	10	5
Resignations	1	2	7	2	7	9	1	9	12	14	8

[1]Blaustein & Porter (1954: Table 23).

Year	1939	1942	1943	1944	1945	1946	1947	1948
Investigations	382	158	190	122	128	171	181	148
NTSC	86	37	51	27	26	30	48	19
BoG dismissed	54	7	26	12	7	21	33	10
BoG private reproval	7	2	6	1	4	3	0	1
BoG public reproval	5	4	2	3	5	2	5	1
BoG recs suspension	8	17	9	10	8	2	3	7
BoG recs disbarment	12	7	8	1	2	2	2	0
SC dismissed	1	1	0	1	1	1	0	1
SC reproved	0	0	0	1	0	0	0	0
SC suspended	11	12	10	9	8	5	4	7
SC disbarred	13	5	8	4	2	0	3	0
Resignations	6	6	4	2	3	0	0	2

TABLE 2 INTAKE[1]

Year	1977	1978	1979	1980	1981	1982	1983	1984	1985	
Complaints	5,238	5,321	5,875	6,357	6,946	7,779	8,094	8,329	7,981	
Year	1986	1987	1988	1989	1990	1991	1992	1993	1994	1995
Inquiries		11,081	17,462	19,767	20,143	20,754	21,741	20,625	17,534	15,957
Complaints	8,574	7,542	4,376	5,267	5,980	6,447	8,181	7,247	6,642	6,119
Dismissals[2]		8,831	3,356	4,350	4,318	4,451	5,165	4,638	4,426	5,134
Statement of Case		465	1,273	1,747	1,484	1,420	1,319	1,200	1,671	993
Ratio of Dismissals to SoC		19	2.6	2.5	2.9	3.1	3.9	3.9	2.6	5.2

[1] 1984–86 from California Auditor General (1988: Table B-3); 1987–88 from Gallagher (1993: Tables 1 and 2); 1988–89 from State Bar of California (1990b: 23); later figures from Annual Reports on the State Bar of California Discipline System.
[2] From 2003: Inquiries closed.

	1996	1997	1998	1999	2000	2001	2002	2003	2004
Inquiries	15,327	15,164	8,040	8,405	10,846	11,138	11,784	11,947	12,383
Complaints	6,048	5,811	1,876	2,055	4,033	3,929	4,176	2,969	3,770
Dismissals	3,308	3,438	2,861	2,355				10,609	10,477

	2005	2006	2007	2008
Inquiries	11,620	11,647	11,739	11,664
Complaints	3,196	3,151	3,010	2,802
Dismissals	9,962	11,079	10,647	10,845

TABLE 3 COMPLAINT ALLEGATIONS[1]

Year	1988	1989	1990	1991	1992	1993	1994	1995	1996
Performance	5,404	5,964	5,404	5,477	6,073	6,438	6,795	6,198	4,577
	43%	39%	39%	40%	36%	35%	35%	35%	35%
Handling of funds	1,726	2,748	2,988	2,892	3,608	3,305	2,557	2,153	1,838
	14%	18%	21%	21%	21%	18%	13%	12%	14%
Duties to clients	2,255	2,893	2,021	1,910	2,440	3,744	3,428	3,481	2,110
	18%	19%	14%	14%	14%	20%	18%	20%	16%
Personal behavior	1,586	1,560	1,479	1,244	1,954	1,874	2,493	1,935	1,356
	13%	10%	11%	9%	12%	10%	13%	11%	10%
Interference with justice	675	967	778	858	1,268	1,213	1,847	1,327	987
	5%	6%	6%	6%	8%	7%	10%	7%	8%
Fees	685	806	699	550	784	865	1,440	1,439	1,082
	5%	5%	5%	4%	5%	5%	7%	8%	8%
Duties to State Bar	49	284	335	492	455	544	479	719	870
	0.4%	2%	2%	4%	3%	3%	2%	4%	7%
Professional employment	173	131	282	271	300	390	388	529	332
	1%	1%	2%	2%	2%	2%	2%	3%	3%
Total	12,553	15,353	13,986	13,694	16,882	18,373	19,427	17,781	13,152

[1]From Annual Reports on the State Bar of California Discipline System.

Year	1997	1998	1999	2000	2001	2002	2003	2004	2005	2006	2007	2008
Performance	5,209	2,345	6,251	3,407	3,178	4,097	38%	35%	37%	34%	35%	34%
	38%	41%	34%	35%	34%	34%						
Handling of funds	1,626	763	2,781	1,205	1,155	1,559	8%	10%	11%	11%	12%	10%
	12%	13%	15%	12%	12%	13%						
Duties to clients	2,370	908	3,084	1,464	1,564	1,753	15%	16%	16%	15%	15%	15%
	17%	16%	17%	15%	17%	15%						
Personal behavior	1,290	557	1,845	996	1,062	1,529	14%	12%	10%	12%	10%	10%
	9%	10%	10%	10%	11%	13%						
Interference with justice	1,047	369	1,421	995	962	1,202	12%	9%	9%	11%	10%	11%
	8%	6%	8%	10%	10%	10%						
Fees	1,172	541	1,690	918	940	1,230	11%	12%	11%	11%	13%	14%
	9%	9%	9%	9%	10%	10%						
Duties to State Bar	832	242	1,185	575	438	511	0%	4%	5%	5%	4%	5%
	6%	4%	6%	6%	5%	4%						
Professional employment	213	57	202	108	85	170	1%	1%	1%	1%	1%	1%
	2%	1%	1%	1%	1%	1%						
Total	13,759	5,782	18,459	9,668	9,384	12,051						

TABLE 4 OTC DISPOSITIONS[1]

Year	1987	1988	1989	1990	1991	1992	1993	1994	1995	1996	1997
Admonition	69	118	54	60	119	89	42	58	2	1	
Directional letter							156	916	607	555	601
Agreement in lieu of discipline		2	11	50	125	94	117	162	110	103	138
Resignation with charges pending	50	68	81	92	96	108	103	84	101	93	115
Stipulated discipline	47	48	41	67	122	110	115	162	152	92	99
Warning letter			353	550	620	546	492	658	883	650	915
Notice to show cause	241	266	316	376	603	444	444	471	512	522	584
Resource letter											

Year	1998	1999	2000	2001	2002	2003	2004	2005	2006	2007	2008
Admonition											
Directional letter	206	6	0	0	0	172	0	0	0	0	0
Agreement in lieu of discipline	82	19	35	76	39	36	42	39	25	28	32
Resignation with charges pending	51	68	93	102	88	86	82	63	84	93	63
Stipulated discipline	44	36	221	137	146	154	217	168	136	99	115
Warning letter	423	21	0	0	69	1	331	286	232	131	247
Notice to show cause	248	174	383	309	402	298	405	347	369	319	369
Resource letter		413	401	117	98	19	16	30	23	9	35

[1] From Annual Reports on the State Bar of California Discipline System

TABLE 5 STATE BAR COURT PROCEEDINGS[1]

Year	1984	1985	1986	1987	1988	1989	1990	1991	1992
Disciplinary cases filed				527	622	707	691	1,182	938
Dismissal	31	56	37	58	36	38	72	111	93
Private reproval	48	59	19	23	20	28	41	80	100
Public reproval	23	33	35	29	31	46	40	34	71
Suspension	95	82	86	123	133	221		64	30
Disbarment	18	25	38	56	69	89	9	47	34
Resignation							26	89	157
Year	**1993**	**1994**	**1995**	**1996**	**1997**	**1998**	**1999**	**2000**	**2001**
Disciplinary cases filed	904	1,007	977	901	956	432	468	762	745
Dismissal	143	155	120	153	139	120	83	45	42
Private reproval	119	122	97	99	119	79	31	74	122
Public reproval	71	56	67	55	66	33	21	44	50
Suspension	52	52	53	45	54	34	44	50	378
Disbarment	40	36	40	26	26	1	9	0	59
Resignation	135	122	118	85	130	54	55	67	113

[1]1984–89 from Gallagher (Table 4) and State Bar of California (1990b: 28, 33); later figures from Annual Reports on the State Bar of California Discipline System. The figures for 1990–2000 indicate only interim suspensions; I have excluded those for failure to pass the PRE. Starting in 2005 there is a single statistic for all reprovals. Changes in categories make some numbers suspect.

Year	2002	2003	2004	2005	2006	2007	2008
Disciplinary cases filed	772	664	750	633	639	561	610
Dismissal	32	41	55	45	58	34	37
Private reproval	62	69	106	144	96	95	67
Public reproval	44	61	65				
Suspension	306	258	287	261	250	170	245
Disbarment	50	71	67	58	71	66	63
Resignation	77	80					

REFERENCES

Abel, Richard L. 1985. "Law Without Politics: Legal Aid under Advanced Capitalism," 32 *UCLA Law Review* 474.

_____. 1987. "The Real Tort Crisis—Too Few Claims," 48 *Ohio St. L.J.* 443.

_____. 1988. *The Legal Profession in England and Wales.* Oxford: Basil Blackwell (reprinted as *The Making of the English Legal Profession*, 1800–1988. Washington, D.C.: Beard Books, 2005).

_____. 1989. *American Lawyers.* New York: Oxford University Press.

_____. 1990. "A Critique of Torts," 37 *UCLA Law Review* 785.

_____. 2003. *English Lawyers between Market and State: The Politics of Professionalism.* Oxford: Oxford University Press.

_____. 2006–07. "How the Plaintiffs' Bar Bars Plaintiffs," 51 *New York Law School Law Review* 345.

_____. 2008. *Lawyers in the Dock: Learning from Attorney Disciplinary Proceedings.* New York: Oxford University Press.

Alfieri, Anthony V. 2006. "The Fall of Legal Ethics and the Rise of Risk Management," 94 *Georgetown Law Journal* 1909.

American Bar Association, Commission on Evaluation of Disciplinary Enforcement (McKay Commission).1992. *Lawyer Regulation for a New Century.* Chicago: ABA Center for Professional Responsibility.

American Bar Association, Commission on Evaluation of Professional Standards. 1981. *Model Rules of Professional Conduct (Proposed Final Draft).* Chicago: ABA.

American Bar Association, Special Committee on Evaluation of Disciplinary Enforcement (Clark Committee). 1970. *Problems and Recommendations in Disciplinary Enforcement.* Chicago: ABA.

American Bar Association, Standing Committee on Professional Discipline. 2001. *California: Report on the Lawyer Regulation System.* Chicago: ABA.

Amsterdam, Anthony G., and Jerome Bruner. 2000. *Minding the Law.* Cambridge, MA: Harvard University Press.

Andrews, Carol Rice. 2004. "Standards of Conduct for Lawyers: An 800-Year Evolution," 57 *SMU Law Review* 1385.

Arts, W., R. Batenburg, and P. Groenwegen. 2001. *Een kwestie van vertrouwen. Over veranderingen op de markt voor profesionele diensten in de organsatie van vrije beroepen.* Amsterdam: Amsterdam University Press.

Asimow, Michael, and Richard Weisberg, 2009. "When the Lawyer Knows the Client Is Guilty: Confessions in Legal Ethics, Popular Culture, and Literature," *18 Southern California Interdisciplinary Law Journal* 229.

Auerbach, Jerold J. 1976. *Unequal Justice: Lawyers and Social Change in Modern America.* New York: Oxford University Press.

Barton, Benjamin H. 2001. "Why Do We Regulate Lawyers?: An Economic Analysis of the Justifications for Entry and Conduct Regulation," 33 *Arizona Law Journal* 429.

_____. 2003. "An Institutional Analysis of Lawyer Regulation—Who Should Control Lawyer Regulation, Courts, Legislatures or the Market," 37 *Georgia Law Review* 1167.

Berenson, Steven K. 2001. "Is it Time for Lawyer Profiles?" 70 *Fordham L. Rev.* 645.

Blaustein, Albert P., and Charles O. Porter. 1954. *The American Lawyer: a Summary of the Survey of the Legal Profession*. Chicago: University of Chicago Press.

Bowman, Frank O. 1996. "A Bludgeon by Any Other Name: The Misuse of 'Ethical Rules' against Prosecutors to Control the Law of the State," 9 *Georgetown Journal of Legal Ethics* 665.

Brien, A. 1998. "Professional Ethics and the Culture of Trust," 17 *Journal of Business Ethics* 391.

Burt, Robert. 1980–81."Conflict and Trust Between Attorney and Client," 69 *Georgetown Law Journal* 1015.

Cagle, M. Christine, J. Michael Martinez, and William D. Richardson. 1999. "Privatizing Professional Licensing Boards: Self-Governance or Self-Interest?" 30 *Administration and Society* 734.

California Assembly, Subcommittee on the Administration of Justice. 1985. *Joint Interim Hearing on Attorney Discipline* (September 30).

California Auditor General (CAG). 1976. *Review of the State Bar of California*. Report 284.1 (August).

______. 1977a. *Opportunities to Improve Management of the State Bar of California*. Report 284.2 (January 18).

______. 1977b. *The State Bar's Implementation of Auditor General Recommendations*, Letter Report 296.1 (November 14).

______. 1977c. *Report to the Joint Legislative Audit Committee: A Management Review of Registration, Examination and Discipline*. Letter Report 296.2 (December 13).

______. 1988. *A Review of the State Bar of California's Processing of Complaints against Attorneys Accused of Misusing Client Trust Funds*. P-716. (June).

California Joint Legislative Audit Committee, Office of the Auditor General. 1975. *The Medical Malpractice Insurance Crisis in California*. Report 265.2.

California Legislative Analyst's Office. 1991. *A Review of the State Bar Court* (December 19).

California State Auditor. 2001. *State Bar of California: It Has Improved Its Disciplinary Process, Stewardship of Members' Fees, and Administrative Practices, but Its Cost Recovery and Controls Over Expenses Need Strengthening* 99-030 (April).

______. 2003. *State Bar of California: Although It Reasonably Sets and Manages Mandatory Fees, It Faces Potential Deficits in the Future and Needs to More Strictly Enforce Disciplinary Policies and Procedures* 02-030 (April).

______. 2005. *State Bar of California: It Should Continue Strengthening Its Monitoring of Disciplinary Case Processing and Assess the Financial Benefits of Its New Collection Enforcement Authority* 05-030 (April).

Carle, Susan. 2008."Structure and Integrity," 93 *Cornell Law Review* 1311.

Carlin, Jerome E. 1966. *Lawyers' Ethics: A Survey of the New York City Bar*. NY: Russell Sage Foundation.

Carlson, Rick J. 1976."Measuring the Quality of Legal Services: An Idea Whose Time Has Not Come," 11 *Law & Society Review* 287.

Carr-Saunders, A.M., and P.A. Wilson. 1933. *The Professions*. Oxford: Clarendon Press.

Casper, Jonathan D. 1993. "Did You Have a Lawyer When You Went to Court? No, I Had a Public Defender," in George F. Cole (ed.), *Criminal Justice: Law and Politics*. Belmont, Ca.: Wadsworth.

Chambliss, Elizabeth. 2006. "The Professionalization of Law Firm In-House Counsel," 84 *University of North Carolina Law Review* 1515.

______. 2009. "New Sources of Managerial Authority in Large Law Firms," 22 *Georgetown Journal of Legal Ethics*.

Clementi, Sir David. 2004. *Review of the Regulatory Framework for Legal Services in England and Wales: Final Report.*

Cohen, Stanley. 1972. *Folk Devils and Moral Panics: The Creation of the Mods and Rockers.* London: MacGibbon & Kee.

Collins, Harry and Trevor Pinch. 2005. *Dr. Golem: How to Think about Medicine.* Chicago: University of Chicago Press.

Collins, Mary, 1992. "Top Secret: Lawyers on Trial," *American Journalism Review* (Jan/Feb).

Commission to Examine Solo and Small Firm Practice. 2006. *Report.*

Corbin, Lillian, 2005. "How 'Firm' Are Lawyers' Perceptions of Professionalism?" 8 *Legal Ethics* 265.

Coyle Report. 1984.*Report of Subcommittee on Expediting the Disciplinary Process to the State Bar of California Board Committee on Adjudication & Discipline* (March 27).

Cressey, Donald R. 1953. *Other People's Money: A study in the social psychology of embezzlement.* Glencoe, Ill.: Free Press.

Delker, Neals-Erik William. 1995. "Comment: Ethics and the Federal Prosecutor: The Continuing Conflict over the Application of Model Rule 4.2 to Federal Attorneys," 44 *University of Kansas Law Review* 855.

Economides, Kim and Justine Rogers. 2009. *Preparatory ethics training for future solicitors.* London: Law Society.

Eldred, Tigran W. 2009. "The Psychology of Conflicts of Interest in Criminal Cases," 58 *University of Kansas Law Review* 43.

Engstrom, Nora Freeman. 2009. "Run-of-the-Mill Justice," 22 *Georgetown Journal of Legal Ethics* 1485.

Evans, Adrian and Josephine Palermo., 2005. "Zero Impact: Are Lawyers' Values Affected by Law School?" 8 *Legal Ethics* 240.

Fallers, Lloyd A. 1965. *Bantu Bureaucracy: A Century of Political Evolution Among the Soga of Uganda.* Chicago: University of Chicago Press.

Feeley, Malcolm. 1979.*The Process Is the Punishment: Handling Cases in a Lower Criminal Court.* New York: Russell Sage Foundation.

Fellmeth, Robert C. 1987a. "The Discipline System of the California State Bar: An Initial Report," 7(3) *California Regulatory Reporter* 1 (Summer) (abbreviated version of 1987b).

_____. 1987b. *A Report on the Performance of the Disciplinary System of the California State Bar.* Initial Report (June 1).

_____. 1987c. *First Progress Report of the State Bar Discipline Monitor* (November).

_____. 1988a. *Second Progress Report of the State Bar Discipline Monitor* (April 1).

_____. 1988b. *Third Progress Report of the State Bar Discipline Monitor* (September 1).

_____. 1989a. *Fourth Progress Report of the State Bar Discipline Monitor* (March 1).

_____. 1989b. *Fifth Progress Report of the State Bar Discipline Monitor* (September 1).

_____. 1990a. *Sixth Progress Report of the State Bar Discipline Monitor* (March 1).

_____. 1990b. *Seventh Progress Report of the State Bar Discipline Monitor* (September 1).

_____. 1991a. *Eighth Progress Report of the State Bar Discipline Monitor* (March 1).

_____. 1991b. *Final Report of the State Bar Discipline Monitor* (September 20).

Felstiner, William L.F., Richard L. Abel and Austin Sarat. 1981. "The Emergence and Transformation of Disputes: Naming, Blaming, Claiming . . .," 14 *Law & Society Review* 631.

Freedman, Monroe, 1993. "The Lawyer Who Hates SNITCHES," *Legal Times* (May 3).

Gallagher, William Thomas. 1993. "Controlling Professions: The 'Crisis' of Professional Self-Regulation in the California State Bar." Ph.D. dissertation, Jurisprudence and Social Policy, University of California, Berkeley.

Garbus, Martin and Joel Seligman. 1976. "Sanctions and Disbarment: They Sit in Judgment," in Ralph Nader and Mark Green (eds.), *Verdicts on Lawyers*. New York: Crowell.

Garland, David. 2008. "On the Concept of Moral Panic," 4 *Crime, Media, Culture* 9.

Gawande, Atul. 2010. *The Checklist Manifesto: How to Get Things Right*. N.Y.: Metropolitan Books.

Gershman, Bennett L. 1992. "The New Prosecutors," 53 *University of Pittsburg Law Review* 393.

Gilb, Corinne Lathrop. 1956. *Self-Regulating Professions and the Public Welfare: A Case Study of the California State Bar*. Ph.D. thesis, History of American Civilization, Radcliffe College.

Gillers, Stephen. 1993. *Report on Lawyer Discipline submitted to the Supreme Court of New Jersey*.

Glueck, Sheldon and Eleanor Glueck. 1950. *Unraveling Juvenile Delinquency*. Cambridge, Mass.: Harvard University Press.

Goode, Erich and Nachman Ben-Yehuda. 1994. "Moral Panics: Culture, Politics, and Social Construction," 20 *Annual Review of Sociology* 149.

Green, Bruce A. 2007. "Criminal Defense Lawyering at the Edge: A Look Back," 36 *Hofstra Law Review* 353.

Greenbaum, Arthur F. 2009. "Judicial Reporting of Lawyer Misconduct," 77 *UMKC Law Review* 537.

Griffiths-Baker, Janine. 2002. *Serving Two Masters: Conflicts of Interest in the Modern Law Firm*. Oxford: Hart Publishing.

Grossman, Steven A. 1976. "An Analysis of 1975 Legislation Relating to Medical Malpractice," in David G. Warren and Richard Merritt (eds.), *A Legislator's Guide to the Medical Malpractice Issue 3–11*. Washington, D.C.: Georgetown University Health Policy Center and National Conference of State Legislatures.

Hall, Kath. 2010. "Why Good Intentions Are Often Not Enough: The potential for ethical blindness in legal decision-making," in Reid Mortensen, Michael Robertson, Lillian Cobin, Francesca Bartlett, and Kieran Tranter (eds.). *Reaffirming Legal Ethics*. London: Routledge.

Hall, Kath and Vivien Holmes. 2009. "The Power of Rationalization to Influence Lawyers' Decisions to Act Unethically," 11 *Legal Ethics* 137.

Haller, Linda. 2009. "A Consumer Discipline Tribunal: Tribunal responses to consumer protection reforms." Presented to the Annual Conference of the Law and Society Association, Denver, May.

Halliday, Terrence C. 1987. *Beyond Monopoly: Lawyers, State Crises, and Professional Empowerment*. Chicago: University of Chicago Press.

Handler, Joel F. 1967. *The Lawyer and His Community*. Madison: University of Wisconsin Press.

Harvard Civil Rights—Civil Liberties Law Review. 1970. "Comment: Controlling Lawyers by Bar Associations and Courts," 35 *Harvard Civil Rights—Civil Liberties Law Review* 301.

Heinz, John P. and Edward O. Laumann. 1982. *Chicago Lawyers: The Social Structure of the Bar*. NY: Russell Sage Foundation and Chicago: ABA.

Hellman, Lawrence K. 2010. "Carnegie's Missing Step: Prescribing lawyer retraining," in Reid Mortensen, Michael Robertson, Lillian Cobin, Francesca Bartlett, and Kieran Tranter (eds.), *Reaffirming Legal Ethics*. London: Routledge.

Holmes, Oliver Wendell, Jr. 1897. "The Path of the Law," 10 *Harvard Law Review* 457.

Hunt, Alan, 1999. "The Purity Wars: Making sense of moral militancy," 3 *Theoretical Criminology* 409.

Hunt, Arnold. 1997. "'Moral Panic' and Moral Language in the Media," 48 *British Journal of Sociology* 629.

Hunter, J. Robert, Gillian Cassell-Stiga, and Joanne Doroshow. 2009. *True Risk: Medical Liability, Malpractice Insurance and Health Care*. New York: Americans for Insurance Reform.

Kay, Fiona M., John Hagan, and Patricia Parker. 2009. "Principals in Practice: The Importance of Mentorship in the Early Stages of Career Development," 31 *Law & Policy* 69.

Kay, Fiona M., and Jean E. Wallace. 2009. "Mentors as Social Capital: Gender, Mentors, and Career Rewards in Law Practice," 79 *Sociological Inquiry* 418.

Keene, Barry, 1976. "California's Medical Malpractice Crisis," in David G. Warren and Richard Merritt (eds.), *A Legislator's Guide to the Medical Malpractice Issue* 27–34. Washington, D.C.: Georgetown University Health Policy Center and National Conference of State Legislatures.

Kritzer, Herbert M. 1998. "The Wages of Risk: The Returns of Contingency Fee Legal Practice," 47 *DePaul Law Review* 267.

Kroeker, Mark A. 1985. *Investigative Process of State Bar of California: A Consulting Report to the State Bar Subcommittee on Expediting the Disciplinary Process* (June 20).

Lebovits, Gerald. 2009. "NYCLA's Fee-Dispute Program: Part 137," *New York County Lawyer* 4 (April).

Levin, Leslie C. 2004–05. "The Ethical World of Solo and Small Law Firm Practitioners," 41 *Houston Law Review* 309.

Levine, Samuel J., and Russell G. Pearce. 2009. "Rethinking the Legal Reform Agenda: Will Raising the Standards for Bar Admission Promote or Undermine Democracy, Human Rights, and Rule of Law?" 77 *Fordham Law Review* 1635.

Long, Alex B. 2009. "Whistleblowing Attorneys and Ethical Infrastructures," 68 *Maryland Law Review* 101.

Luban, David. 2007. *Legal Ethics and Human Dignity*. New York: Cambridge University Press.

Lui, Elwood. *1999a. Report of Special Master, 12.4.98–2.11.99. In re attorney discipline system; Requests of the Governor and the State Bar of California (s073756)* (filed February 16).

______. *1999b. Report of Special Master, 2.12–6.22.99* (filed June 24).

______. *1999c. Report of Special Master 6.23–9.24.99* (filed October 12).

______. *2000. Report of the Special Master, 9.25.99–3.28.00.*

Macaulay, Stewart. 1963. "Non-contractual Relations in Business: A Preliminary Study," 28 *American Sociological Review* 55.

Markovits, Daniel. 2008. *A Modern Legal Ethics: Adversary Advocacy in a Democratic Age*. Princeton, N.J.: Princeton University Press.

Mashburn, Amy. 1995. "A Clockwork Orange Approach to Legal Ethics: A Conflicts Perspective on the Regulation of Lawyers by Federal Courts," 8 *Georgetown Journal of Legal Ethics* 473.

Matz, A. Howard. 1991. "Lawyers on the Attack: Prosecutors' and Defense Lawyers' Effort to Curb the Other Side's Perceived Misconduct," 161 *PLI/Crim* 177.

Matza, David. 1964. *Delinquency and Drift*. New York: John Wiley & Sons.

McConville, Michael and Chester L. Mirsky. 1986–87. "Criminal Defense of the Poor in New York City," 15(4) *Review of Law & Social Change (Special Issue)*.

McRobbie, Angela, and Sarah L. Thornton. 1995."Rethinking 'Moral Panic' for Multi-Mediated Social Worlds," 46 *British Journal of Sociology* 559.

Mellinkoff, David. 1973. *The Conscience of a Lawyer*. St. Paul, Minn.: West Publ. Co.

Mercer, Peter, Margaret Ann Wilkinson, and Terra Strong. 1996. "The Practice of Ethical Precepts: Dissecting Decision-Making by Lawyers," 9 *Canadian Journal of Law and Jurisprudence* 141.

Mercer, Peter, Christa Walker, and Margaret Ann Wilkinson. 2005. "Testing Theory and Debunking Stereotypes: Lawyers' Views on the Practice of Law," 18 *Canadian Journal of Law and Jurisprudence* 165.

Moliterno, James. 2005. "Politically Motivated Bar Discipline," 83 *Washington University Law Quarterly* 725.

Moorhead, Richard and Rebecca Cumming. 2009. "Something for nothing? Employment Tribunal claimants' perspectives on legal funding." London: Employment Market Analysis and Research, Department for Business Innovation and Skills.

Parikh, Sara. 2001. *Professionalism and Its Discontents: A Study of Social Networks in the Plaintiffs' Personal Injury Bar*. Ph.D. dissertation, sociology, University of Illinois, Chicago.

_____. 2006–07. "How the Spider Catches the Fly: Referral Networks in the Plaintiffs' Personal Injury Bar," 51 *New York Law School Law Review* 243.

New York University Law Review. 1974. "Note: Attorney Discipline and the First Amendment," 49 *New York University Law Review* 922.

Parsons, Talcott. 1968. "Professions," 12 *International Encyclopedia of the Social Sciences* 536. New York: Macmillan.

Paterson, Alan. 2008. "Breach of Trust or Breach of Loyalty: How Best to Characterise Lawyer Deviance?" 11 *Legal Ethics* 115.

Paton, Paul D. 2008."Between a Rock and a Hard Place: The Future of Self-Regulation—Canada between the United States and the English/Australian Experience," 2008 *Professional Lawyer* 87.

Perlman, Andrew M. 2003. "Toward a Unified Theory of Professional Regulation," 55 *Florida Law Review* 977.

Phillips, Orie L., and Philbrick McCoy. 1952. *Conduct of Judges and Lawyers: A Study of Professional Ethics, Discipline, and Disbarment*. Los Angeles: Parker.

Pinaire, Brian K, Milton J. Heumann, and Jennifer Lerman. 2006."Barred from the Bar: The Process, Politics, and Policy Implications of Discipline for Attorney Felony Offenders," 13 *Virginia Journal of Social Policy and Law* 290.

Pipkin, Ronald M. 1979. "Law School Instruction in Professional Responsibility: A Curricular Paradox," 1979 *American Bar Foundation Research Journal* 247.

Powell, Michael J. 1986. "Professional Divestiture: The Cession of Responsibility for Lawyer Discipline," 1986 *American Bar Foundation Research Journal* 31.

Practising Law Institute. 1992. *The Attorney-Client Relationship After Kaye-Scholer* (Corporate Law and Practice Course Handbook Series Number 779). New York: PLI.

Redman, Barbara K., and Jon F. Merz. 2008. "Scientific Misconduct: Do the Punishments Fit the Crime?" 321 *Science* 775.

Regan, Milton C., Jr. 2004. *Eat What You Kill: The Fall of a Wall Street Lawyer*. Ann Arbor: University of Michigan Press.

Reichstein, Kenneth J. 1964. *The Professional Ethics of Lawyers: A Situational Approach to the Study of Deviation and Control*. Ph.D. dissertation, sociology, Northwestern University.

_____. 1965. "Ambulance Chasing: A Case Study of Deviation and Control within the Legal Profession," 13 *Social Problems* 3.

Rhode, Deborah L. 1985."Moral Character as a Professional Credential," 94 *Yale Law Journal* 491.

Richmond, Douglas R. 2007-08. "Professional Responsibilities of Law Firm Associates," 45 *Brandeis Law Journal* 199.

_____. 2009. "Legal Ethics in Legal Education," 16 *Clinical Law Review* 43.

Robinson, W.W. 1959. *Lawyers of Los Angeles: A History of the Los Angeles Bar Association and the Bar of Los Angeles County*. Los Angeles: Los Angeles Bar Association.

Rosenthal, Douglas E. 1974. *Lawyer and Client: Who's In Charge*. New York: Russell Sage Foundation.

_____. 1976."Evaluating the Competence of Lawyers," 11 *Law & Society Review* 257.

Rosenthal, Marilynn. 1988.*Dealing with Medical Malpractice: The British and Swedish Experience*. Durham, N.C.: Duke University Press.

Ross, H. Lawrence. 1970. *Settled Out of Court: The Social Process of Insurance Claims Adjustments*. Chicago: Aldine.

Rostain, Tanina. 2006a. "Partners and Power: The Role of Law Firm Organizational Factors in Attorney Misconduct," 19 *Georgetown Journal of Legal Ethics* 281.

_____. 2006b. "Sheltering Lawyers: The Organized Tax Bar and the Tax Shelter Industry," 23 *Yale Journal on Regulation* 77.

Royal Commission on Legal Services. 1979. *Final Report*. London: HMSO (Cmnd 7648).

Scheingold, Stuart A., and Austin Sarat. 2004. *Something to Believe In: Politics, Professionalism, and Cause Lawyering*. Stanford: Stanford University Press.

Schneyer, Theodore J. 1983. "The Incoherence of the Unified Bar Concept: Generalizing from the Wisconsin Case," 1983 *American Bar Foundation Research Journal* 1.

Schwartz, Murray L., and Theodore Mitchell. 1970. "An Economic Analysis of the Contingent Fee in Personal Injury Litigation," 22 *Stanford Law Review* 1125.

Scott, Marvin B. and Stanford M. Lyman. 1968. "Accounts," 33 *American Sociological Review* 46.

Seron, Carroll. 1996. *The Business of Practicing Law: The Work Lives of Solo and Small Firm Attorneys*. Philadelphia, PA: Temple University Press.

Shapiro, David. 1999. *Neurotic Styles*. New York: Basic Books.

Shapiro, Susan P. 2002. *Tangled Loyalties: Conflict of Interest in Legal Practice*. Ann Arbor: University of Michigan Press.

Smedley, Nick. 2009. *Review of the Regulation of Corporate Legal Work*. London: Law Society.

Smith, Bradley A. 1994. "The Limits of Compulsory Professionalism: How the Unified Bar Harms the Legal Profession," 22 *Florida State University Law Review* 36.

State Bar of California. 1990a.*Discipline System: The State Bar Court* (January).

_____. 1990b. *Lawyer Discipline in California: A progress report for 1988 and 1989.*

_____. 1995. *1994 Report on the State Bar of California Discipline System*. (April).

_____. 1996. *1995 Report on the State Bar of California Discipline System* (April).

_____. 1997. *1996 Report on the State Bar of California Discipline System* (April).

_____. 1999. *1998 Report on the State Bar of California Discipline System* (April).

_____. 2000. *1999 Report on the State Bar of California Discipline System* (April).

_____. 2001a. *2000 Report on the State Bar of California Discipline System* (April).

_____. 2001b. *Investigation and Prosecution of Disciplinary Complaints Against Attorneys in Solo Practice, Small Size Law Firms and Large Size Law Firms* (June).

_____. 2002. *2001 Report on the State Bar of California Discipline System* (March).

_____. 2003. *2002 Report on the State Bar of California Discipline System* (April).

_____. 2004. *2003 Report on the State Bar of California Discipline System* (April).

_____. 2005. *2004 Report on the State Bar of California Discipline System* (April).

_____. 2006. *2005 Report on the State Bar of California Discipline System* (April).

_____. 2007. *2006 Report on the State Bar of California Discipline System* (April).

_____. 2008. *2007 Report on the State Bar of California Discipline System* (April).

State Bar of California, Discipline Evaluation Committee (Alarcon Committee). 1994. *Report to Board of Governors* (August 27).

State Bar of California, State Bar Court. 1994.*Response of the State Bar Court to the Report of the Discipline Evaluation Committee* (November).

Stracher, Cameron. 1998. *Double Billing: A Young Lawyer's Tale of Greed, Sex, Lies, and the Pursuit of a Swivel Chair.* New York: William Morrow.

Swaine, Robert T. 1946–48. *The Cravath Firm and Its Predecessors* (2 vols.). New York: privately printed.

Tarbell, Ida M. 1925. *The Life of Elbert H. Gary: The Story of Steel.* New York: D. Appleton & Co.

Tarlow, Barry. 1991."RICO Report: Thornburg's *[sic]* Folly Update," 15 *The Champion* 42 (March).

_____. 1992. "RICO Report: Who Will Watch Justice's Watchdogs?" 16 *The Champion* 33 (September/October).

_____. 1995. "The Moral Conundrum of Representing the Rat," 19(7) *The Champion* 15 (August).

_____. 1996. "RICO Report: California Supreme Court Dumps Twitty," 20 *The Champion* 54 (April).

_____. 1997. "RICO Report: Ethics Rules Really Do Apply to AUSAs," 21 *The Champion* 53 (September/October).

_____. 1998. "RICO Report," 22 *The Champion* (May).

_____. 1999. "RICO Report," 23 *The Champion* (June).

Terry, Laurel S. 2008. "The Future Regulation of the Legal Profession: The Impact of Treating the Legal Profession as 'Service Providers," 2008 *Journal of the Professional Lawyer* 189.

Thornburgh, Richard. 1991. "Ethics and the Attorney General: The Attorney General Responds," 74 *Judicature* 290 (April–May).

Turrentine, Lowell. 1935. "May the Bar Set its Own House in Order?" 34 *Michigan Law Review* 200.

Ungar, Sheldon. 2001. "Moral Panic versus the Risk Society: The implications of the changing sites of social anxiety," 52 *British Journal of Sociology* 271.

Van Hoy, Jerry. 1997. *Franchise Law Firms and the Transformation of Personal Legal Services.* Westport, Ct.: Quorum Books.

Veblen, Thorstein. 1925. *The Theory of the Leisure Class: An Economic Study of Institutions.* London: George Allen & Unwin.

Wallace, Jean E., and Fiona M. Kay. 2008."The professionalism of practising law: A comparison across work contexts," 29 *Journal of Organizational Behavior* 1021.

Ward, Baxter. 1974. *Illegal Attorney Referral Activity in Los Angeles County* (Report to the Board of Supervisors).

Ward, Stephanie Francis. 2010. "Grade Anxiety," *ABA Journal* 49 (February).

Weber, David O. 1987. "'Still in Good Standing': The Crisis in Attorney Discipline," 73 *ABAJ* 58 (November).

Wendel, W. Bradley. 2009. "If Lifelong Learning is the Solution, What is the Problem?" Available at SSRN: http://ssrn.com/abstract=1361695.

Wilkinson, Margaret Ann, Christa Walker, and Peter Mercer. 2000. "Do Codes of Ethics Actually Shape Legal Practice?" 45 *McGill Law Journal* 645.

Wood, A.Y. 1926. "State Bar Organizations in California," in *Historical and Contemporary Review of the Bench and Bar of California*. San Francisco: Recorder Printing and Publishing Co..

Zacharias, Fred C. 2003a. "Reform or Professional Responsibility as Usual: Whither the Institutions of Regulation and Discipline?" 2003 *University of Illinois Law Review* 1505.

_____. 2003b. "The Purposes of Lawyer Discipline," 45 *William and Mary Law Review* 675.

_____. 2008. "Effects of Reputation on the Legal Profession," 65 *Washington and Lee Law Review* 173.

_____. 2009a. "The Myth of Self-Regulation," 93 *Minnesota Law Review* 1147.

_____. 2009b. "Integrity Ethics," 22 *Georgetown Journal of Legal Ethics* 541.

Zacharias, Fred C., and Bruce A. Green. 2003."Federal Court Authority to Regulate Lawyers: A Practice in Search of a Theory," 56 *Vanderbilt Law Review* 1303.

_____. 2009a. "The Duty to Avoid Wrongful Convictions: A Thought Experiment in the Regulation of Prosecutors," 89 *Boston University Law Review* 1.

_____. 2009b. "Rationalizing Judicial Regulation of Lawyers," 70 *Ohio State Law Journal* 73.

INDEX

A

ABA. *See* American Bar Association (ABA)
Accidents, 69, 73–74, 80–81, 84, 86, 90–91, 93, 96, 114, 121, 432
Affirmative action, 19
Alarcon, Judge Arthur, 37
Alcohol and substance abuse program, 33
Alleged legal malpractice
  in representing Maria Seward, 383–85
Alternative Discipline Program (ADP), 62
American Bank, 133, 160, 192, 216
American Bar Association (ABA), 1, 5, 14, 58–60, 330–32, 356, 364–65, 421, 440, 485, 488
  Prosecutorial Rule 7–104(A)(1), 330
  Standard 3–4.1(B), 338
American Board of Trial Attorneys (ABOTA), 192
American Civil Liberties Union (ACLU), 329
American Institute of Accountants, 5
American Red Cross (ARC), 444
Applicant Evaluation and Nomination Committee, 42
Associated Credit Bureaus of California, 5
Association for California Tort Reform, 46, 50
Attorney General Select Committee on Internal Procedures, 30
Attorney misconduct, 7, 12, 35, 54, 421, 491
Attorneys fees. *See* Fees
Auditor General, 8, 16, 26–27, 30, 479, 486

B

Baffa, Judge Frank, 140, 152, 163, 167–68, 171, 174, 176, 189, 193, 215, 225, 467
Bankruptcy, 125, 230, 271, 278, 282, 288, 304–5, 308–9, 313, 319–21, 325, 380
Bar associations, 64–65
Bar Ethics Committee, 62
Bates, 102
Behrmann, Michelle, 81–83
Board of Governors (BoG). *See* State Bar Board of Governors (BoG)
Bond defeasance, 283–88, 301, 303, 307, 318, 320, 325
Bragg, Lawrence, 68
Brazil, Ernest Lee, 271–326, 454–6, 461–65, 467–68, 482–83
  behavior, 316–20
  legal arguments, 320–25
  motivations, 325–26
Brosterhous, Raymond, 20
Brown Act, 50
Brown v. Board of Education, 215
Brown, Michael S., 70–119, 444–47, 451, 455–56, 461–64, 468, 481–83
Buchanan, Robert, 70, 78–80
Bureau of Indian Affairs (BIA), 378
Burrell, Judge Garland E., Jr., 47
Business and Professions Code (BPC)
  Section 6068, 386
  Section 6146, 127, 168

C

California Assembly, 22–24, 123, 126, 486
California Association of Collectors, 5
California Auditor General (CAG). *See* Auditor General
California Bankers Association, 5
California Bar Association Proceedings, 1–2
California District Attorneys Association and Kopp's bill, 44
California Judges Association, 44
California Land Title Association, 5
California Medical Association (CMA), 126, 194, 198–99, 201, 220
California Real Estate Association, 5
California State Automobile Association (CSAA), 72*n*15, 83
California State Bar Association, 2

California Supreme Court, 14, 20, 32, 66, 108, 119, 133, 148, 160, 165, 169, 176, 196–97, 215–18, 380, 449–50
California Trial Lawyers Association, 60, 87, 105, 128, 151–52, 161
California, discipline system in, 21, 28
Cappers, 3, 67–68, 70, 72, 76, 78, 80, 92, 94, 96–97, 99, 101, 106–8, 110–11, 113–19, 445–46
Carnival, 233, 240
Chiantelli, Judge Alfred, 388, 393, 408, 410, 413, 414, 415, 416, 417, 425, 427, 439, 466, 468
Chief Trial Counsel (CTC), 16, 23, 39, 144, 390
Client Relations Committees, 27
Client Security Fund (CSF), 12, 31–32, 50, 66
Client trust accounts, viii, 22, 26, 53, 62, 67, 121, 128, 229, 231, 361
Client's money, 10, 23, 141, 147
CMA. *See* California Medical Association (CMA)
Cohen, Alan Lee, 86–87
Cohn, Judge Melvin, 390*n*35
Collateral estoppel, 271, 321, 412, 415
Collins, Patrick, 275–82
Commission on Evaluation of Disciplinary Enforcement, 36
Commission on Judicial Nominees Evaluation, 51
Commission on the Future of the Legal Profession, 43
Committee on Adjudication and Discipline, 17
Committee on Admissions and Discipline (CAD), 23
Committee on Discipline, 15
Committee on Professional Responsibility and Competence, 61
Committee on Regulation, Admissions and Discipline, 61
Committee on Suppression of Soliciting Legal Business, 3
Common causes, unethical lawyers
- accounts, 463–64
- experience, 461
- greed, 462
- habitude, 464
- protestations of innocence, 461
- psychic reward, 462–63
- rule ambiguity, 461–62

Communication with represented party, 327–28
Complainants' Grievance Panel, 30, 35, 39
Conference of Bar Association Delegates, 9
Conference of Delegates, 2, 18–19, 48, 49, 60, 62, 65
Conflict of interest, 227–32
- in criminal defense, 367–73

Consumerism and legal profession, 11–19
Conti, Judge, 392
Contingent fees. *See* Fees
Contract, 46, 49, 75, 81, 85, 94–95, 111, 135, 138, 145–46, 148, 159, 169, 249–50, 317–19
- illegal, 129–30

Court of Appeal, 25, 56, 135, 139, 149, 154, 197, 207, 209, 211, 213, 364, 383, 403, 431
Coyle Commission, 24
Crane, Robert, 232–67, 453–56, 461–64, 466–68, 482
Crosby, Judge William, 128
CSF. *See* Client Security Fund (CSF)
CTC. *See* Chief Trial Counsel (CTC)
Cumis, 122
Cures, for lawyer misconduct, 465–76

D

Damer, Nicholas Raymond, 384–441, 455–60, 462–64, 467–68, 482–83
- alleged defiance of court order, 392–405
- argument, 415–19
- culpability, 406–15
- hearing judge's decision, 419–21
- review, 421–31

Deception, 257–59
Department of Justice (DOJ), 5, 64, 331, 339, 341–42, 352–54, 356, 363, 371
Depew, Brian, 232–67, 453–55, 461
Disbarment and suspension, 26, 63
Disciplinary hearing
- additional complaints, 360–61
- Lopez Case, 357–60

Ninth Circuit, Lopez decision modification, 362–64
penalty phase, 361–62
retrial, 366–67
Review Department, 364–66
Disciplinary process
professionalizing, 25–43
reducing cost of, 38
self-regulation, 43–59
Discipline Audit Panel, 39
Discipline Evaluation Committee (DEC), 37, 45, 48, 492
Discipline system, 28, 30, 33, 38, 40, 42, 45, 50–51, 54, 433, 483, 487
District attorney (DA), 397
DOJ. *See* Department of Justice (DOJ)
Dramatis personae, 329–30
Driving under the influence (DUI) cases, 327, 375
Drug court, 62
Duxbury, Marc A., 69–70

E

Early Neutral Evaluations (ENEs), 58
Education, and careers, 34
Equal Rights Amendment, 19
Ethical rules, 119, 332, 339, 342, 352–53, 363, 366, 369, 371, 460–61, 467–68, 472, 486
Ewsley, Judge David S., 42

F

Faretta v. California, 352
Federal Bureau of Investigation (FBI), 270, 330, 411
Federal Pacific Corporation (FPC), 273
Federal Rules of Civil Procedure (FRCP)
Rule 11, 380
Rule 35, 365
Federal Trade Commission (FTC), 17
Fee dispute, 98, 126, 128, 135, 143, 148, 158–59, 451–52, 474–75
Fees
attorney fees, 57, 97, 109, 125, 127–28, 132, 134, 137, 142–44, 150, 165, 182, 207–8, 228–29, 259
agreements, 15, 22, 112, 136, 161, 169, 171–72, 176, 178, 197, 201, 207–8, 215, 218–19, 361, 409
Browne Greene. *See* Browne Greene
contingent fees, 31, 88–89, 92, 108, 112, 114, 119, 121–23, 125, 163–64, 168, 174, 178, 204, 207, 213, 220–21, 449, 452, 462–63
court-ordered, 210, 213–14
illegal fees, 147, 155, 210–12
Koskoff case, 162–200
legal fees, 111, 227–28, 230, 238, 302
overcharging clients, 121–23
Paulis v. Harney case, 200–215
"Stubborn Streak, A," 215–25
Feiner, Judge, 169
Feinberg v. Harney, 169, 193, 195, 196
Fletcher, Judge Betty D., 362, 371, 373
Frank, Judge, 386–87
Fraud, 269–71, 315–16
appeal, 311–14
Brazil's behavior, 316–20
Brazil's legal arguments, 320–25
Brazil's motivations, 325–26
briefs, 306–10
hearing, 290–306
Interbank Mortgage Corporation. *See* Interbank Mortgage Corporation
judgment, 310–11
prelude, 271–75
Review Department judgment, 314–15
Frogger, 238

G

Gee, Judge, 281, 310–15, 316, 319
Genesis of the fee dispute, 126–38
Goertzen, Judge Jack E., 139, 155
Goldhammer, Judge, 423
Greene, R. Browne, 126–62, 164, 166, 175, 181, 188, 198, 200–201, 446, 448–52, 455, 459, 461–65, 467, 481–83
defense of, 139–47
genesis of the fee dispute, 126–38
guilt phase, outcome of, 147–50
penalty phase, 150–58
understanding defiance, 158–62
Gumban, Joseph, 70–78

H

Harney, David M., 65, 161–225, 446, 448–51, 451n33, 452, 455, 459, 461–65, 467, 481–83
Hart, Judge, 387, 389
Hatch, Judge Leighton, 399, 400, 403, 404, 409
Hathaway, 207, 211
Hauk, Judge, 180, 224
Hidalgo v. Superior Court, 214
Hom, Ben L., 282–83
Hupp, Judge, 382

I

Innocence, protestations of, 461
Insurance disclosure rule, 60–61
Insurance Disclosure Task Force, 60
Interbank Mortgage Corporation
  collapse, 288–90
  Collins, Patrick, 275–82
  Hom, Ben L., 282–83
  municipal bond defeasance, 283–88
Internal Revenue Service (IRS), 444, 451, 471
Investigative Consultants International (ICI), 393
IOLTA (Interest on Lawyers' Trust Accounts), 50
Itemization, 81–83, 98, 100

J

Jefferson, Judge, 193, 223
Jennifer, Judge, 273
Joint Legislative Audit Committee, 16, 50
Jones, Francis E., III, 68
Judicial process
  respect for, 375–83

K

Keller, William D., 380–81
King, Judge, 392
Kline, Judge Anthony, 413
Kopp's bill, 45
Kramer, Judge, 207
Kroff, Steven, 69

L

Lachs, Judge Stephen M., 164
Lanam, Judge, 439
Langhauser, Judge, 40, 175
Law Practice Management and Technology Section, 61
Lawyer civility code, 63–64
Lawyer discipline, 1, 13, 22, 53, 470, 488, 490, 493
Lawyer misconduct, viii, 456, 470, 472, 475, 488
Lawyer Protection Act, 40–41
Legal ethics, 6, 13, 31, 257, 467, 485, 487–90
Legal fees, 111, 227–28, 230, 238, 302. *See* Fees
Legal Services Trust Fund, 27
Life Underwriters Association, 5
Loan documents, 277, 279, 311
Loans, 227–28, 230, 270, 275–88, 292, 301–4, 306–8, 312–14, 316–19, 321, 324, 326, 463
Local Administrative Committee (LAC), 3
Lopez case, 357–60
  decision, modification by Ninth Circuit, 362–64
  Review Department, 364–66
Los Angeles City Council, 3
Los Angeles County Bar Association, 60
Los Angeles Special Local Administrative Committee (LAC), 3
Los Angeles Trial Lawyers Association, 105, 136, 380
Lui, Judge Elwood, 54, 58
Lydick, Judge, 386

M

Malpractice claim, 385–92
  argument, 415–19
  culpability, 406–15
  hearing judge's decision, 419–21
  review, 421–31
Malpractice in law, 13–14
Malpractice insurance bill
  State Bar's opposition to malpractice insurance bill, 65
Malpractice insurance, 31, 59–64
Malum in se, 104, 119

Malum prohibitum, 104, 119, 206
Mandatory Continuing Legal Education (MCLE), 31, 47, 50, 53, 55–56, 367, 472
McCloskey, Judge Eugene, 140, 223
McKay Commission, 39
MCLE. *See* Mandatory Continuing Legal Education (MCLE)
Medical Injuries Compensation Reform Act (MICRA), 121, 123–26, 449
  Browne Greene. *See* Browne Greene
  Koskoff case, 162–200
  overcharging clients, 121–23
  Paulis v. Harney case, 200–215
  "Stubborn Streak, A," 215–25
Medical malpractice nonpecuniary damage cap, 46, 47
Mens rea, 162, 166, 208, 220, 221, 258, 264, 321
Monopoly of lawyers
  limitations on, 64
Moscone, Judge Phillip, 394
Mosk, Judge, 433, 439
Moskowitz, Judge, 459, 468
Multistate Professional Responsibility Examination (MPRE), 257, 430
Municipal bond defeasance. *See* Bond defeasance

N

National Association of Criminal Defense Lawyers (NACDL), 329
Nelson, Bruce E., 67
Nelson, Judge, 363
Nolo contendere, 290, 294, 316, 320, 322, 323, 357
Non-lawyers, 32, 67, 71, 102, 104, 111, 119, 321, 445, 448
Notice to show cause (NTSC), 78, 232*n*9, 361

O

Obrien, Judge, 55
Office of Chief Trial Counsel (OCTC), 39, 59
Office of Intake, 39
Office of Investigations (OI), 18, 33, 35, 39, 116
Office of Self-Government (OSG), 378
Office of Trial Counsel (OTC), 17–18, 40, 62–63, 71–72, 107, 110–11, 128, 191, 200–201, 203, 206, 220–21, 224, 313–15, 357–58, 360–62, 470
Ohralik, 108
Overcharging clients, 121–23

P

Pacific Legal Foundation (PLF), 20, 34, 57
Paramount, 232, 234, 235–37, 239, 241, 246, 248, 251, 254–55, 256, 257, 264, 266
Parkinson's Law, 38
Patel, Judge Marilyn Hall, 335–56, 360, 365,369, 370–71, 468
Patsey, Judge Richard, 392, 394, 399, 408, 415, 430, 439
Paulis v. Harney, 200–215
Pearlman, Judge Lise A., 42, 109, 111–12, 422, 426
Perasso, Judge, 411
Politics and lawyers, 19–25
Professional self-regulation, 64–66. *See also* Self-regulation
Prohibition on solicitation, 67

Q

Quantum meruit claim, 95, 115, 123, 218, 429, 445, 450

R

Rafeedie, Judge Edward, 175
Rea, Judge William J., 179
Real, Judge Manuel, 195, 224, 380, 381*n*16, 382, 458
Reed, Judge, 382
Regulation, 443–44
  conflicts of interest, 453–54
  excessive zeal, 456–60
  fees, 448–53
  fraud, 454–56
  solicitation, 444–48
Repeaters Task Force, 33
Representing co-conspirators charged with drug possession
  dramatis personae, 329–30
  Judge Patel, 335–56

Representing co-conspirators charged with drug possession (*Cont.*)
Thornburgh Memorandum, 330–32
Voir dire of Lopez, 332–35
Res judicata, 166, 181, 198, 201, 203, 207, 222, 415, 433
Respect for judicial process, 375–83
Retail Merchants Credit Association, 5
Retainer agreements, 82, 88, 127, 132, 137, 140–41, 144, 148, 191, 197–98, 200
Review Department, 42, 56, 110–12, 149, 151–58, 162, 195–96, 199, 208, 212–15, 220–22, 261–62, 314–15, 364–66, 427–31, 434–35
Richardson Committee. *See* Attorney General Select Committee on Internal Procedures
RICO Report, 492
Roa v. Lodi Medical Group, 134–35
Ross, Judge, 379
Round Valley Indian Tribes (RVIT), 378
Round Valley Nation (RVN), 378–79
Rules of Professional Conduct (RPC), 10, 128
Rural lawyers, 64

S

San Diego County Bar Association, 49
San Francisco Bar Association, 2
San Francisco Examiner, 21, 28, 48–49, 51–52, 66, 408
San Francisco Police Department (SFPD), 70, 72–73, 80–81, 84, 90, 92, 117
Sandles, Janice, 84–86
Scapa, Robert B., 70–118, 444–47, 451, 455–56, 461–64, 468, 481–83
Schifferman, Judge Robert, 147, 161, 175
Schneider, 209–10
Schneider, Gerald, 390*n*35
Scott, Judge James B., 391, 392, 400, 418, 419–20, 421, 438, 439
SEGA
conflict of interest, 227–32
conning the mark, 232–47
deception explanation, 257–59
game ended, 247–57
naïveté/greed, 262–67
score, 259–62
Self-regulation
chronic contradictions of, 59–64
disciplinary process, 43–59
political engagement, perils of, 19–25
politics of, 1
professional, 64–66
professionalizing discipline, 25–43
rise of consumerism and, 11–19
Senate Bill (SB), 152
Senate Judiciary Committee, 22, 51
Seronio, Constance, 80–81
Settlement agreement, 180, 397, 399, 429
Settlement, secret, 406–7, 423, 425
Seward v. Peters, 396
Seward v. Sterns, 394, 403–4, 406, 427
Seward, Maria
alleged legal malpractice in representing, 383–85
SFPD. *See* San Francisco Police Department (SFPD)
Shafer, Judge Harry T., 234
Shatford, Judge, 224
Sine qua non, 397
Smith, Judge Christopher W., 203, 205–6, 207, 208, 209, 219
Smith, Judge Fern M., 329, 330, 335–36, 343, 348–49, 350, 370
Sole practitioners, State Bar discipline discriminated against, 41
Solicitation, 67–70
Behrmann, Michelle, 81–83
Buchanan, Robert, 78–80
cappers' modus operandi, 70–107
closing arguments and briefs, 105–7
Cohen, Alan Lee, 86–87
defending, 113–19
expert witnesses, 87–90
Gumban, Joseph, 72–78
Hearing and Review Department judgments, 107–13
legal argument, 94–95
mitigation and aggravation, 102–5
other clients, 90–92
respondents' testimony, 95–101
Sandles, Janice, 84–86
Seronio, Constance, 80–81
Tashiro, Kenneth, 83–84
State Bar (SB), 123, 377
State Bar Act, 2

State Bar Board of Governors (BoG), 4, 191, 406
State Bar Court (SBC), 14, 26, 273
State Bar of California discipline system, 479–80, 482, 491–92
State Bar of California, 3, 5, 14–15
  Client Security Fund and, 66
  Committee on Discipline, 15
  professionalizing disciplinary system, 25–43
State legislators, as lawyers, 65
Stauthers, Judge Steven, 176
Steedman, Donald, 71
Steele, Corey, 69
Stovitz, Judge, 210
Sua sponte, 378, 379, 380
Subcommittee on Expediting the Discipline Process, 17
Super Zaxxon, 233, 235, 246–50, 255, 261, 263–64
Supersedes, 199, 415
Supremacy clauses, 330–31, 339, 342, 371

T

Tarlow, Barry, 329–41, 343–52, 354–59, 362–73, 453–54, 462–64, 467
Tashiro, Kenneth, 83–84
Temptations of champion, 431–41
Tevrizian, Judge Dickran, 150,
The Dentists Insurance Company (TDIC), 122
Thermal Remediation Corp (TRC), 230
Thornburgh Memorandum, 330–32
Turbo, 233
Turner, Judge, 201–4, 207, 211, 213, 220
Twitty, James Allen, 329–30, 332–41, 343–52, 354–73, 453–55, 461–68, 482–83

V

Victims' Bill of Rights, 19
Voir dire of Lopez, 332–35
Volunteer Investigative Assistance Program, 27
Volunteer referees, elimination of, 32

W

Wallace, Judge, 382
Waters v. Bourhis, 136
Werchick, Arne, 87–90
Wesley, Judge David S., 208

Z

Zaxxon, 232–35, 240, 244–47, 249, 255, 263, 265